2020 Case Supplement

Constitutional Law
Third Edition

Constitutional Rights: Cases in Context,
Second Edition

Constitutional Structure: Cases in Context,
Second Edition

2020 Case Supplement

Constitutional Law: Cases in Context,
Third Edition

Constitutional Rights: Cases in Context,
Second Edition

Constitutional Structure: Cases in Context,
Second Edition

Randy E. Barnett
Carmack Waterhouse Professor of Legal Theory
Georgetown University Law Center

Josh Blackman
Professor of Law
South Texas College of Law Houston

Wolters Kluwer

Published by Wolters Kluwer in New York.

Wolters Kluwer Legal & Regulatory U.S. serves customers worldwide with CCH, Aspen Publishers, and Kluwer Law International products. (www.WKLegaledu.com)

To contact Customer Service, e-mail customer.service@wolterskluwer.com, call 1-800-234-1660, fax 1-800-901-9075, or mail correspondence to:

> Wolters Kluwer
> Attn: Order Department
> PO Box 990
> Frederick, MD 21705

Printed in the United States of America.

1 2 3 4 5 6 7 8 9 0

ISBN 978-1-5438-2027-0

About Wolters Kluwer Legal & Regulatory U.S.

Wolters Kluwer Legal & Regulatory U.S. delivers expert content and solutions in the areas of law, corporate compliance, health compliance, reimbursement, and legal education. Its practical solutions help customers successfully navigate the demands of a changing environment to drive their daily activities, enhance decision quality and inspire confident outcomes.

Serving customers worldwide, its legal and regulatory portfolio includes products under the Aspen Publishers, CCH Incorporated, Kluwer Law International, ftwilliam.com and MediRegs names. They are regarded as exceptional and trusted resources for general legal and practice-specific knowledge, compliance and risk management, dynamic workflow solutions, and expert commentary.

Contents

2020 Case Supplement

Constitutional Law: Cases in Context,
Third Edition

Constitutional Rights: Cases in Context,
Second Edition

Constitutional Structure: Cases in Context,
Second Edition

Chapter 1

The Founding

ASSIGNMENT 1

1. John Locke: On the State of Nature and the Origin and Purpose of Civil Society and Government

The Founders were very much influenced by such natural rights thinkers as John Locke, Hugo Grotius, Samuel von Pufendorf, and Emmerich de Vattel. Following are the fuller passages from which the excerpts appearing in the casebook were taken.

STUDY GUIDE:

- What do you suppose is the persistent appeal of "state of nature" theorizing?
- How does Locke's vision of the "state of nature" differ from that of Hobbes (as it appears in the casebook)?
- Can you imagine why these words of Locke would be considered so great a threat to the established authority in general and of the Crown in particular?
- What is Locke's argument for government?
- What does he say is lacking in the state of nature?
- What is his argument for majority rule?
- Can a majority form a government over a dissenting minority?
- Finally, notice how Locke identifies the separation of legislative, executive, and judicial powers.

JOHN LOCKE, SECOND TREATISE OF GOVERNMENT: AN ESSAY CONCERNING THE TRUE ORIGINAL, EXTENT AND END OF CIVIL GOVERNMENT, 1690

CHAPTER 2
Of the State of Nature

§4. To understand political power right, and derive it from its original, we must consider, what state all men are naturally in, and that is, a state of perfect freedom to order their actions, and dispose of their possessions and persons, as they think fit, within the bounds of the law of nature, without asking leave, or depending upon the will of any other man.

A state also of equality, wherein all the power and jurisdiction is reciprocal, no one having more than another; there being nothing more evident, than that creatures of the same species and rank, promiscuously born to all the same advantages of nature, and the use of the same faculties, should also be equal one amongst another without subordination or subjection, unless the lord and master of them all should, by any manifest declaration of his will, set one above another, and confer on him, by an evident and clear appointment, an undoubted right to dominion and sovereignty. . . .

§6. But though this be a state of liberty, yet it is not a state of licence: though man in that state have an uncontroulable liberty to dispose of his person or possessions, yet he has not liberty to destroy himself, or so much as any creature in his possession, but where some nobler use than its bare preservation calls for it. The state of nature has a law of nature to govern it, which obliges every one: and reason, which is that law, teaches all mankind, who will but consult it, that being all equal and independent, no one ought to harm another in his life, health, liberty, or possessions: for men being all the workmanship of one omnipotent, and infinitely wise maker; all the servants of one sovereign master, sent into the world by his order, and about his business; they are his property, whose workmanship they are, made to last during his, not one another's pleasure: and being furnished with like faculties, sharing all in one community of nature, there cannot be supposed any such subordination among us, that may authorize us to destroy one another, as if we were made for one another's uses, as the inferior ranks of creatures are for ours. Every one, as he is bound to preserve himself, and not to quit his station wilfully, so by the like reason, when his own preservation comes not in competition, ought he, as much as he can, to preserve the rest of mankind, and may not, unless it be to do justice on an offender, take away, or impair the life, or what tends to the preservation of the life, the liberty, health, limb, or goods of another.

§7. And that all men may be restrained from invading others' rights, and from doing hurt to one another, and the law of nature be observed, which willeth the peace and preservation of all mankind, the execution of the law of nature is, in that state, put into every man's hands, whereby every one has a right to punish the transgressors of that law to such a degree, as may hinder its violation: for the law of nature would, as all other laws that concern men in this world be in vain, if there were no body that in the state of nature had a power to execute that law, and thereby preserve the innocent and restrain offenders. And if any one in the state of nature may punish another for any evil he has done, every one may do so: for in that state of perfect equality, where naturally there is no superiority or jurisdiction of one over another, what any may do in prosecution of that law, every one must needs have a right to do.

§8. And thus, in the state of nature, one man comes by a power over another; but yet no absolute or arbitrary power, to use a criminal, when he has got him in his hands, according to the passionate heats, or boundless extravagancy of his own will; but only to retribute to him, so far as calm reason and conscience dictate, what is proportionate to his transgression, which is so much as may serve for reparation and restraint: for these two are the only reasons, why one man may lawfully do harm to another, which is that we call punishment. In transgressing the law of nature, the offender declares himself to live by another rule than that of reason and common equity, which is that measure God has set to the actions of men, for their mutual security; and so he becomes dangerous to mankind, the tye, which is to secure them from injury and violence, being slighted and broken by him. Which being a trespass against the whole species, and the peace and safety of it, provided for by the law of nature, every man upon this score, by the right he hath to preserve mankind in general, may restrain, or where it is necessary, destroy things noxious to them, and so may bring such evil on any one, who hath transgressed that law, as may make him repent the doing of it, and thereby deter him, and by his example others, from doing the like mischief. And in the case, and upon this ground, EVERY MAN HATH A RIGHT TO PUNISH THE OFFENDER, AND BE EXECUTIONER OF THE LAW OF NATURE. . . .

§11. From these two distinct rights, the one of punishing the crime for restraint, and preventing the like offence, which right of punishing is in every body; the other of taking reparation, which belongs only to the injured party, comes it to pass that the magistrate, who by being magistrate hath the common right of punishing put into his hands, can often, where the public good demands not the execution of the law, remit the punishment of criminal offences by his own authority, but yet cannot remit the satisfaction due to any private man for the damage he has received. That, he who has suffered the damage has a right to demand in his own name. . . .

§13. To this strange doctrine, viz. That in the state of nature every one has the executive power of the law of nature, I doubt not but it will be objected, that it is unreasonable for men to be judges in their own cases, that self-love will make men partial to themselves and their friends: and on the other side, that ill nature, passion and revenge will carry them too far in punishing others; and hence nothing but confusion and disorder will follow, and that therefore God hath certainly appointed government to restrain the partiality and violence of men. I easily grant, that civil government is the proper remedy for the inconveniencies of the state of nature, which must certainly be great, where men may be judges in their own case, since it is easy to be imagined, that he who was so unjust as to do his brother an injury, will scarce be so just as to condemn himself for it: but I shall desire those who make this objection, to remember, that absolute monarchs are but men; and if government is to be the remedy of those evils, which necessarily follow from men's being judges in their own cases, and the state of nature is therefore not to be endured, I desire to know what kind of government that is, and how much better it is than the state of nature, where one man, commanding a multitude, has the liberty to be judge in his own case, and may do to all his subjects whatever he pleases, without the least liberty to any one to question or controul those who execute his pleasure and in whatsoever he doth, whether led by reason, mistake or passion, must be submitted to. Much better it is in the state of nature, wherein men are not bound to submit to the unjust will of another. And if he that judges, judges amiss in his own, or any other case, he is answerable for it to the rest of mankind.

§14. It is often asked as a mighty objection, where are, or ever were there any men in such a state of nature? To which it may suffice as an answer at present, that since all princes and rulers of independent governments all through the world, are in a state of nature, it is plain the world never was, nor ever will be, without numbers of men in that state. I have named all governors of independent communities, whether they are, or are not, in league with others: for it is not every compact that puts an end to the state of nature between men, but only this one of agreeing together mutually to enter into one community, and make one body politic; other promises, and compacts, men may make one with another, and yet still be in the state of nature. The promises and bargains for truck, &c. between the two men in the desert island, mentioned by Garcilasso de la Vega, in his history of Peru; or between a Swiss and an Indian, in the woods of America, are binding to them, though they are perfectly in a state of nature, in reference to one another: for truth and keeping of faith belongs to men, as men, and not as members of society. . . .

CHAPTER 8
Of the Beginning of Political Societies

§95. Men being, as has been said, by nature, all free, equal, and independent, no one can be put out of this estate, and subjected to the political power of another, without his own consent. The only way whereby any one divests himself of his natural liberty, and puts on the bonds of civil society, is by agreeing with other men to join and unite into a community for their comfortable, safe, and peaceable living one amongst another, in a secure enjoyment of their properties, and a greater security against any, that are not of it. This any number of men may do, because it injures not the freedom of the rest; they are left as they were in the liberty of the state of nature. When any number of men have so consented to make one community or government, they are thereby presently incorporated, and make one body politic, wherein the majority have a right to act and conclude the rest.

§96. For when any number of men have, by the consent of every individual, made a community, they have thereby made that community one body, with a power to act as one body, which is only by the will and determination of the majority: for that which acts any community, being only the consent of the individuals of it, and it being necessary to that which is one body to move one way; it is necessary the body should move that way whither the greater force carries it, which is the consent of the majority: . . . and so every one is bound by that consent to be concluded by the majority. . . .

§97. And thus every man, by consenting with others to make one body politic under one government, puts himself under an obligation, to every one of that society, to submit to the determination of the majority, and to be concluded by it; or else this original compact, whereby he with others incorporates into one society, would signify nothing, and be no compact, if he be left free, and under no other ties than he was in before in the state of nature. . . .

§98. For if the consent of the majority shall not, in reason, be received as the act of the whole, and conclude every individual; nothing but the consent of every individual can make any thing to be the act of the whole: but such a consent is next to impossible ever to be had, if we consider the infirmities of health, and avocations of business, which in a number, though much less than that of a commonwealth, will necessarily keep many away from the public assembly. To which if we add the variety of opinions, and contrariety of interests, . . . [s]uch a constitution as this would make the mighty Leviathan of a shorter duration, than the feeblest creatures, and not let it outlast the day it was born. . . .

§99. Whosoever therefore out of a state of nature unite into a community, must be understood to give up all the power, necessary to the ends for which they unite into society, to the majority of the community, unless they expressly agreed in any number greater than the majority. And this is done by barely agreeing to unite into one political society, which is all the compact that is, or needs be, between the individuals, that enter into, or make up a commonwealth. And thus that, which begins and actually constitutes any political society, is nothing but the consent of any number of freemen capable of a majority to unite and incorporate into such a society. And this is that, and that only, which did, or could give beginning to any lawful government in the world. . . .

CHAPTER 9
Of the Ends of Political Society and Government

§123. If man in the state of nature be so free, as has been said; if he be absolute lord of his own person and possessions, equal to the greatest, and subject to no body, why will he part with his freedom? Why will he give up this empire, and subject himself to the dominion and controul of any other power? To which it is obvious to answer, that though in the state of nature he hath such a right, yet the enjoyment of it is very uncertain, and constantly exposed to the invasion of others: for all being kings as much as he, every man his equal, and the greater part no strict observers of equity and justice, the enjoyment of the property he has in this state is very unsafe, very unsecure. This makes him willing to quit a condition, which, however free, is full of fears and continual dangers: and it is not without reason, that he seeks out, and is willing to join in society with others, who are already united, or have a mind to unite, for the mutual preservation of their lives, liberties and estates, which I call by the general name, property.

§124. The great and chief end, therefore, of men's uniting into common-wealths, and putting themselves under government, is the preservation of their property. To which in the state of nature there are many things wanting.

First, There wants an established, settled, known law, received and allowed by common consent to be the standard of right and wrong, and the common measure to decide all controversies between them: for though the law of nature be plain and intelligible to all rational creatures; yet men being biassed by their interest, as well as ignorant for want of study of it, are not apt to allow of it as a law binding to them in the application of it to their particular cases.

§125. Secondly, In the state of nature there wants a known and indifferent judge, with authority to determine all differences according to the established law: for every one in that state being both judge and executioner of the law of nature, men being partial to themselves, passion and revenge is very apt to carry them too far, and with too much heat, in their own cases; as well as negligence, and unconcernedness, to make them too remiss in other men's.

§126. Thirdly, In the state of nature there often wants power to back and support the sentence when right, and to give it due execution, They who by any injustice offended, will seldom fail, where they are able, by force to make good their injustice; such resistance many times makes the punishment dangerous, and frequently destructive, to those who attempt it.

§127. Thus mankind, notwithstanding all the privileges of the state of nature, being but in an ill condition, while they remain in it, are quickly driven into society. Hence it comes to pass, that we seldom find any number of men live any time together in this state. The inconveniencies that they are therein exposed to, by the irregular and uncertain exercise of the power every man has of punishing the transgressions of others, make them take sanctuary under the established laws of government, and therein seek the preservation of their property. It is this makes them so willingly give up every one his single power of punishing, to be exercised by such alone, as shall be appointed to it amongst them; and by such rules as the community, or those authorized by them to that purpose, shall agree on. And in this we have the original right and rise of both the legislative and executive power, as well as of the governments and societies themselves.

§128. For in the state of nature, to omit the liberty he has of innocent delights, a man has two powers.

The first is to do whatsoever he thinks fit for the preservation of himself, and others within the permission of the law of nature: by which law, common to them all, he and all the rest of mankind are one community, make up one society, distinct from all other creatures. And were it not for the corruption and vitiousness of degenerate men, there would be no need of any other; no necessity that men should separate from this great and natural community, and by positive agreements combine into smaller and divided associations.

The other power a man has in the state of nature, is the power to punish the crimes committed against that law. Both these he gives up, when he joins in a private, if I may so call it, or particular politic society, and incorporates into any common wealth, separate from the rest of mankind.

§129. The first power, viz. of doing whatsoever he thought for the preservation of himself, and the rest of mankind, he gives up to be regulated by laws made by the society, so far forth as the preservation of himself, and the rest of that society shall require; which laws of the society in many things confine the liberty he had by the law of nature.

§130. Secondly, The power of punishing he wholly gives up, and engages his natural force, (which he might before employ in the execution of the law of nature, by his own single authority, as he thought fit) to assist the executive power of the society, as the law thereof shall require: for being now in a new state, wherein he is to enjoy many conveniencies, from the labour, assistance, and society of others in the same community, as well as protection from its whole strength; he is to part also with as much of his natural liberty, in providing for himself, as the good, prosperity, and safety of the society shall require; which is not only necessary, but just, since the other members of the society do the like.

§131. But though men, when they enter into society, give up the equality, liberty, and executive power they had in the state of nature, into the hands of the society, to be so far disposed of by the legislative, as the good of the society shall require; yet it being only with an intention in every one the better to preserve himself, his liberty and property; (for no rational creature can be supposed to change his condition with an intention to be worse) the power of the society, or legislative constituted by them, can never be supposed to extend farther, than the common good; but is obliged to secure every one's property, by providing against those three defects above mentioned, that made the state of nature so unsafe and uneasy. And so whoever has the legislative or supreme power of any commonwealth, is bound to govern by established standing laws, promulgated and known to the people, and not by extemporary decrees; by indifferent and upright judges, who are to decide controversies by those laws; and to employ the force of the community at home, only in the execution of such laws, or abroad to prevent or redress foreign injuries, and secure the community from inroads and invasion. And all this to be directed to no other end, but the peace, safety, and public good of the people.

2.   James Madison: On the Alleged Failure of the Articles of Confederation

STUDY GUIDE:

- When reading Madison's complaints about the Articles, you must keep in mind that a great many people either did not share these complaints, or thought that they could be cured by making changes to the Articles, rather than by replacing them altogether. For this reason, when the Constitution was proposed, it was also bitterly opposed.

- There is much of interest in this essay that presages the new Constitution, as well as future constitutional controversies. One is Madison's strong concern for commerce. Another is his belief that a constitution should be ratified by the people. Why was that deemed by him to be so important?

- What is Madison's proposed solution to the problem of faction?

Prior to the adoption of the Constitution, the United States was governed by the Articles of Confederation (which appear in the beginning of the casebook). During the post-Revolutionary period, many Americans became unhappy with the general state of the economy and with the behavior of state governments. In an essay prepared in advance of the Philadelphia Convention, Madison summarized what he and others perceived as the deficiencies or "vices" in the form of government defined by the Articles. That the Articles were deficient in these ways was one of the principal assumptions underlying the formulation and eventual adoption of the Constitution. The list he provided is a useful summary of these defenses.

Madison also addresses an important problem with then-prevalent political theory: how to explain the adoption of bad policies and widespread violations of rights by state governments that are "republican" in form and therefore accountable to "the People." At the time, state governments were largely run by a single popularly elected assembly, to which the executive and judiciary were subservient. Such governments were widely thought to be the proper alternative to rule by an aristocracy as the means of protecting the retained rights of the people. Yet, those who favored a new constitutional structure believed these republican governments to be pervasively violating the people's rights, which was simply not supposed to happen.

In this essay (summarized by bullet points in the casebook), Madison attempts to answer this question with an early version of the argument he later presents in *The Federalist, No. 10*: his theory of "faction" that explains how majoritarian rule can come to violate unjustly the rights of the people.

JAMES MADISON, VICES OF THE POLITICAL SYSTEM OF THE UNITED STATES, APRIL 1787: 1. *Failure of the States to comply with the Constitutional requisitions.* This evil has been so fully experienced both during the war and since the peace, results so naturally from the number and independent authority of the States and has been so uniformly exemplified in every similar Confederacy, that it may be considered as not less radically and permanently inherent in, than it is fatal to the object of, the present System.

2. *Encroachments by the States on the federal authority.* Examples of this are numerous and repetitions may be foreseen in almost every case where any favorite object of a State shall present a temptation. Among these examples are the wars and Treaties of Georgia with the Indians — The unlicensed compacts between Virginia and Maryland, and between Pena. & N. Jersey — the troops raised and to be kept up by Massts.

3. *Violations of the law of nations and of treaties.* From the number of Legislatures, the sphere of life from which most of their members are taken, and the circumstances under which their legislative business is carried on, irregularities of this kind must frequently happen. Accordingly not a year has passed without instances of them in some one or other of the States. The Treaty of

peace—the treaty with France—the treaty with Holland have each been violated. The causes of these irregularities must necessarily produce frequent violations of the law of nations in other respects.

As yet foreign powers have not been rigorous in animadverting on us. This moderation however cannot be mistaken for a permanent partiality to our faults, or a permanent security agst. those disputes with other nations, which being among the greatest of public calamities, it ought to be least in the power of any part of the Community to bring on the whole.

4. *Trespasses of the States on the rights of each other*. These are alarming symptoms, and may be daily apprehended as we are admonished by daily experience. See the law of Virginia restricting foreign vessels to certain ports—of Maryland in favor of vessels belonging to her own citizens—of N. York in favor of the same.

Paper money, instalments of debts, occlusion of Courts, making property a legal tender, may likewise be deemed aggressions on the rights of other States. As the Citizens of every State aggregately taken stand more or less in the relation of Creditors or debtors, to the Citizens of every other States, Acts of the debtor State in favor of debtors, affect the Creditor State, in the same manner, as they do its own citizens who are relatively creditors towards other citizens. This remark may be extended to foreign nations. If the exclusive regulation of the value and alloy of coin was properly delegated to the federal authority, the policy of it equally requires a controul on the States in the cases above mentioned. It must have been meant 1. to preserve uniformity in the circulating medium throughout the nation. 2. to prevent those frauds on the citizens of other States, and the subjects of foreign powers, which might disturb the tranquility at home, or involve the Union in foreign contests.

The practice of many States in restricting the commercial intercourse with other States, and putting their productions and manufactures on the same footing with those of foreign nations, though not contrary to the federal articles, is certainly adverse to the spirit of the Union, and tends to beget retaliating regulations, not less expensive & vexatious in themselves, than they are destructive of the general harmony.

5. *Want of concert in matters where common interest requires it*. This defect is strongly illustrated in the state of our commercial affairs. How much has the national dignity, interest, and revenue suffered from this cause? Instances of inferior moment are the want of uniformity in the laws concerning naturalization & literary property; of provision for national seminaries, for grants of incorporation for national purposes, for canals and other works of general utility, wch. may at present be defeated by the perverseness of particular States whose concurrence is necessary.

6. *Want of guaranty to the States of their Constitutions & laws against internal violence*. The confederation is silent on this point and therefore by the second article the hands of the federal authority are tied. According to Republican Theory, Right and power being both vested in the majority, are held to be synonimous. According to fact and experience a minority may in an appeal to force, be an overmatch for the majority. 1. If the minority happen to include all such as

possess the skill and habits of military life, & such as possess the great pecuniary resources, one third only may conquer the remaining two thirds. 2. One third of those who participate in the choice of the rulers, may be rendered a majority by the accession of those whose poverty excludes them from a right of suffrage, and who for obvious reasons will be more likely to join the standard of sedition than that of the established Government. 3. Where slavery exists the republican Theory becomes still more fallacious.

7. *Want of sanction to the laws, and of coercion in the Government of the Confederacy.* A sanction is essential to the idea of law, as coercion is to that of Government. The federal system being destitute of both, wants the great vital principles of a Political Cons[ti]tution. Under the form of such a Constitution, it is in fact nothing more than a treaty of amity of commerce and of alliance, between so many independent and Sovereign States. From what cause could so fatal an omission have happened in the articles of Confederation? from a mistaken confidence that the justice, the good faith, the honor, the sound policy, of the several legislative assemblies would render superfluous any appeal to the ordinary motives by which the laws secure the obedience of individuals: a confidence which does honor to the enthusiastic virtue of the compilers, as much as the inexperience of the crisis apologizes for their errors. The time which has since elapsed has had the double effect, of increasing the light, and tempering the warmth, with which the arduous work may be revised. It is no longer doubted that a unanimous and punctual obedience of 13 independent bodies, to the acts of the federal Government, ought not be calculated on. Even during the war, when external danger supplied in some degree the defect of legal & coercive sanctions, how imperfectly did the States fulfil their obligations to the Union? In time of peace, we see already what is to be expected. How indeed could it be otherwise? In the first place, Every general act of the Union must necessarily bear unequally hard on some particular member or members of it. Secondly the partiality of the members to their own interests and rights, a partiality which will be fostered by the Courtiers of popularity, will naturally exaggerate the inequality where it exists, and even suspect it where it has no existence. Thirdly a distrust of the voluntary compliance of each other may prevent the compliance of any, although it should be the latent disposition of all. Here are causes & pretexts which will never fail to render federal measures abortive. If the laws of the States, were merely recommendatory to their citizens, or if they were to be rejudged by County authorities, what security, what probability would exist, that they would be carried into execution? Is the security or probability greater in favor of the acts of Congs. which depending for their execution on the will of the state legislatures, wch. are tho' nominally authoritative, in fact recommendatory only.

8. *Want of ratification by the people of the articles of Confederation.* In some of the States the Confederation is recognized by, and forms a part of the constitution. In others however it has received no other sanction than that of the Legislative authority. From this defect two evils result: 1. Whenever a law of a State happens to be repugnant to an act of Congress, particularly when the latter is of posterior date to the former, it will be at least questionable whether the latter must not prevail; and as the question must be decided by the Tribunals of

the State, they will be most likely to lean on the side of the State. 2. As far as the Union of the States is to be regarded as a league of sovereign powers, and not as a political Constitution by virtue of which they are become one sovereign power, so far it seems to follow from the doctrine of compacts, that a breach of any of the articles of the confederation by any of the parties to it, absolves the other parties from their respective obligations, and gives them a right if they chuse to exert it, of dissolving the Union altogether.

9. *Multiplicity of laws in the several States.* . . . Among the evils . . . of our situation may well be ranked the multiplicity of laws from which no State is exempt. As far as laws are necessary, to mark with precision the duties of those who are to obey them, and to take from those who are to administer them a discretion, which might be abused, their number is the price of liberty. As far as the laws exceed this limit, they are a nuisance: a nuisance of the most pestilent kind. Try the Codes of the several States by this test, and what a luxuriancy of legislation do they present. The short period of independency has filled as many pages as the century which preceded it. Every year, almost every session, adds a new volume. This may be the effect in part, but it can only be in part, of the situation in which the revolution has placed us. A review of the several codes will shew that every necessary and useful part of the least voluminous of them might be compressed into one tenth of the compass, and at the same time be rendered tenfold as perspicuous.

10. *Mutability of the laws of the States.* . . . We daily see laws repealed or superseded, before any trial can have been made of their merits: and even before a knowledge of them can have reached the remoter districts within which they were to operate. In the regulations of trade this instability becomes a snare not only to our citizens but to foreigners also.

11. *Injustice of the laws of States.* If the multiplicity and mutability of laws prove a want of wisdom, their injustice betrays a defect still more alarming: more alarming not merely because it is a greater evil in itself, but because it brings more into question the fundamental principle of republican Government, that the majority who rule in such Governments, are the safest Guardians both of public Good and of private rights. To what causes is this evil to be ascribed?

These causes lie 1. in the Representative bodies. 2. in the people themselves.

1. Representative appointments are sought from 3 motives. 1. ambition 2. personal interest. 3. public good. Unhappily the two first are proved by experience to be most prevalent. Hence the candidates who feel them, particularly, the second, are most industrious, and most successful in pursuing their object: and forming often a majority in the legislative Councils, with interested views, contrary to the interest, and views, of their Constituents, join in a perfidious sacrifice of the latter to the former. A succeeding election it might be supposed, would displace the offenders, and repair the mischief. But how easily are base and selfish measures, masked by pretexts of public good and apparent expediency? How frequently will a repetition of the same arts and industry which succeeded in the first instance, again prevail on the unwary to misplace their confidence?

How frequently too will the honest but unenlightened representative be the dupe of a favorite leader, veiling his selfish views under the professions of public good, and varnishing his sophistical arguments with the glowing colours of popular eloquence?

2. A still more fatal if not more frequent cause lies among the people themselves. All civilized societies are divided into different interests and factions, as they happen to be creditors or debtors — Rich or poor — husbandmen, merchants or manufacturers — members of different religious sects — followers of different political leaders — inhabitants of different districts — owners of different kinds of property &c. &c. In republican Government the majority however composed, ultimately give the law. Whenever therefore an apparent interest or common passion unites a majority what is to restrain them from unjust violations of the rights and interests of the minority, or of individuals? Three motives only:

1. a prudent regard to their own good as involved in the general and permanent good of the Community. This consideration although of decisive weight in itself, is found by experience to be too often unheeded. It is too often forgotten, by nations as well as by individuals that honesty is the best policy.

2dly. respect for character. However strong this motive may be in individuals, it is considered as very insufficient to restrain them from injustice. In a multitude its efficacy is diminished in proportion to the number which is to share the praise or the blame. Besides, as it has reference to public opinion, which within a particular Society, is the opinion of the majority, the standard is fixed by those whose conduct is to be measured by it. The public opinion without the Society, will be little respected by the people at large of any Country. Individuals of extended views, and of national pride, may bring the public proceedings to this standard, but the example will never be followed by the multitude. Is it to be imagined that an ordinary citizen or even an assemblyman of R. Island in estimating the policy of paper money, ever considered or cared in what light the measure would be viewed in France or Holland; or even in Massts or Connect.? It was a sufficient temptation to both that it was for their interest: it was a sufficient sanction to the latter that it was popular in the State; to the former that it was so in the neighbourhood.

3dly. will Religion the only remaining motive be a sufficient restraint? It is not pretended to be such on men individually considered. Will its effect be greater on them considered in an aggregate view? quite the reverse. The conduct of every popular assembly acting on oath, the strongest of religious Ties, proves that individuals join without remorse in acts, against which their consciences would revolt if proposed to them under the like sanction, separately in their closets. When indeed Religion is kindled into enthusiasm, its force like that of other passions, is increased by the sympathy of a multitude. But enthusiasm is only a temporary state of religion, and while it lasts will hardly be seen with pleasure at the helm of Government. Besides as religion in its coolest state, is not infallible, it may become a motive to oppression as well as a restraint from injustice.

Place three individuals in a situation wherein the interest of each depends on the voice of the others, and give to two of them an interest opposed to the rights of the third? Will the latter be secure? The prudence of every man would shun the danger. The rules & forms of justice suppose & guard against it. Will two thousand in a like situation be less likely to encroach on the rights of one thousand? The contrary is witnessed by the notorious factions & oppressions which take place in corporate towns limited as the opportunities are, and in little republics when uncontrouled by apprehensions of external danger. If an enlargement of the sphere is found to lessen the insecurity of private rights, it is not because the impulse of a common interest or passion is less predominant in this case with the majority; but because a common interest or passion is less apt to be felt and the requisite combinations less easy to be formed by a great than by a small number. The Society becomes broken into a greater variety of interests, of pursuits, of passions, which check each other, whilst those who may feel a common sentiment have less opportunity of communication and concert. It may be inferred that the inconveniences of popular States contrary to the prevailing Theory, are in proportion not to the extent, but to the narrowness of their limits.

The great desideratum in Government is such a modification of the Sovereignty as will render it sufficiently neutral between the different interests and factions, to controul one part of the Society from invading the rights of another, and at the same time sufficiently controuled itself, from setting up an interest adverse to that of the whole Society. In absolute Monarchies, the prince is sufficiently, neutral towards his subjects, but frequently sacrifices their happiness to his ambition or his avarice. In small Republics, the sovereign will is sufficiently controuled from such a Sacrifice of the entire Society, but is not sufficiently neutral towards the parts composing it. As a limited Monarchy tempers the evils of an absolute one; so an extensive Republic meliorates the administration of a small Republic.

An auxiliary desideratum for the melioration of the Republican form is such a process of elections as will most certainly extract from the mass of the Society the purest and noblest characters which it contains; such as will at once feel most strongly the proper motives to pursue the end of their appointment, and be most capable to devise the proper means of attaining it.

Chapter 2

Foundational Cases on Constitutional Structure: The Marshall Court

No new cases or readings.

Chapter 3

Enumerated Powers

STUDY GUIDE:

- The next case is noteworthy, not for its majority opinion that is based on statutory interpretation, but for the concurring opinion by Justice Thomas in which he discusses the scope of the Indian Commerce Clause.
- Some scholars have contended that, because the first statute regulating "intercourse" with Indian tribes reflected a broader meaning of "commerce" than Justice Thomas attributed to the Interstate Commerce Clause, his interpretation of "commerce" is refuted.
- What follows is a brief point-counterpoint by Jack Balkin and Robert Natelson discussing the 1790 statute.

Adoptive Couple v. Baby Girl
133 S. Ct. 2552 (2013)

JUSTICE ALITO delivered the opinion of the Court.

This case is about a little girl (Baby Girl) who is classified as an Indian because she is 1.2% (3/256) Cherokee. Because Baby Girl is classified in this way, the South Carolina Supreme Court held that certain provisions of the federal Indian Child Welfare Act of 1978 required her to be taken, at the age of 27 months, from the only parents she had ever known and handed over to her biological father, who had attempted to relinquish his parental rights and who had no prior contact with the child. The provisions of the federal statute at issue here do not demand this result. Contrary to the State Supreme Court's ruling, we hold that 25 U.S.C. §1912(f)—which bars involuntary termination of a parent's rights in the absence of a heightened showing that serious harm to the Indian child is likely to result from the parent's "continued custody" of the child—does not apply when, as here, the relevant parent never had custody of the child. We further hold that §1912(d)—which conditions involuntary termination of parental rights with respect to an Indian child on a showing that remedial efforts have been made to prevent the "breakup of the Indian family"—is inapplicable when, as here, the parent abandoned the Indian child before birth and never had custody of the child. Finally, we clarify that §1915(a), which provides placement preferences for the adoption of Indian children, does not bar a non-Indian family like Adoptive Couple from adopting an Indian child when no other eligible candidates have sought to adopt the child. We accordingly reverse the South Carolina Supreme Court's judgment and remand for further proceedings . . . .

The Indian Child Welfare Act was enacted to help preserve the cultural identity and heritage of Indian tribes, but under the State Supreme Court's reading, the Act would put certain vulnerable children at a great disadvantage solely because an ancestor — even a remote one — was an Indian. As the State Supreme Court read §§1912(d) and (f), a biological Indian father could abandon his child *in utero* and refuse any support for the birth mother — perhaps contributing to the mother's decision to put the child up for adoption — and then could play his ICWA trump card at the eleventh hour to override the mother's decision and the child's best interests. If this were possible, many prospective adoptive parents would surely pause before adopting any child who might possibly qualify as an Indian under the ICWA. Such an interpretation would raise equal protection concerns, but the plain text of §§1912(f) and (d) makes clear that neither provision applies in the present context. Nor do §1915(a)'s rebuttable adoption preferences apply when no alternative party has formally sought to adopt the child. We therefore reverse the judgment of the South Carolina Supreme Court and remand the case for further proceedings not inconsistent with this opinion.

It is so ordered.

JUSTICE THOMAS, concurring.

I join the Court's opinion in full but write separately to explain why constitutional avoidance compels this outcome. Each party in this case has put forward a plausible interpretation of the relevant sections of the Indian Child Welfare Act (ICWA). However, the interpretations offered by respondent Birth Father and the United States raise significant constitutional problems as applied to this case. Because the Court's decision avoids those problems, I concur in its interpretation.

I

This case arises out of a contested state-court adoption proceeding. Adoption proceedings are adjudicated in state family courts across the country every day, and "domestic relations" is "an area that has long been regarded as a virtually exclusive province of the States." *Sosna v. Iowa* (1975). Indeed, "[t]he whole subject of the domestic relations of husband and wife, parent and child, belongs to the laws of the States and not to the laws of the United States." *In re Burrus* (1890). Nevertheless, when Adoptive Couple filed a petition in South Carolina Family Court to finalize their adoption of Baby Girl, Birth Father, who had relinquished his parental rights via a text message to Birth Mother, claimed a federal right under the ICWA to block the adoption and to obtain custody.

The ICWA establishes "federal standards that govern state-court child custody proceedings involving Indian children." The ICWA defines "Indian child" as "any unmarried person who is under age eighteen and is either (a) a member of an Indian tribe or (b) is eligible for membership in an Indian tribe and is the biological child of a member of an Indian tribe." As relevant, the ICWA defines "child custody proceeding," §1903(1), to include "adoptive placement," which means "the permanent placement of an Indian child for adoption, including any action resulting in a final decree of adoption," §1903(1)(iv), and "termination of parental rights," which means "any action resulting in the termination of the parent-child relationship," §1903(1)(ii).

The ICWA restricts a state court's ability to terminate the parental rights of an Indian parent in two relevant ways. Section 1912(f) prohibits a state court from involuntarily terminating parental rights "in the absence of a determination, supported by evidence beyond a reasonable doubt, including testimony of qualified expert witnesses, that the continued custody of the child by the parent or Indian custodian is likely to result in serious emotional or physical damage to the child." Section 1912(d) prohibits a state court from terminating parental rights until the court is satisfied "that active efforts have been made to provide remedial services and rehabilitative programs designed to prevent the breakup of the Indian family and that these efforts have proved unsuccessful." A third provision creates specific placement preferences for the adoption of Indian children, which favor placement with Indians over other adoptive families. §1915(a). Operating together, these requirements often lead to different outcomes than would result under state law. That is precisely what happened here. See *ante* ("It is undisputed that, had Baby Girl not been 3/256 Cherokee, Biological Father would have had no right to object to her adoption under South Carolina law").

The ICWA recognizes States' inherent "jurisdiction over Indian child custody proceedings," §1901(5), but asserts that federal regulation is necessary because States "have often failed to recognize the essential tribal relations of Indian people and the cultural and social standards prevailing in Indian communities and families." However, Congress may regulate areas of traditional state concern only if the Constitution grants it such power. Admt. 10 ("The powers not delegated to the United States by the Constitution, nor prohibited by it to the States, are reserved to the States respectively, or to the people"). The threshold question, then, is whether the Constitution grants Congress power to override state custody law whenever an Indian is involved.

II

The ICWA asserts that the Indian Commerce Clause, Art. I, §8, cl. 3, and "other constitutional authority" provides Congress with "plenary power over Indian affairs." §1901(1). The reference to "other constitutional authority" is not illuminating, and I am aware of no other enumerated power that could even arguably support Congress' intrusion into this area of traditional state authority. See Fletcher, The Supreme Court and Federal Indian Policy, 85 Neb. L.

Rev. 121, 137 (2006) ("As a matter of federal constitutional law, the Indian Commerce Clause grants Congress the only explicit constitutional authority to deal with Indian tribes"); Natelson, The Original Understanding of the Indian Commerce Clause, 85 Denver U. L. Rev. 201, 210 (2007) (hereinafter Natelson) (evaluating, and rejecting, other potential sources of authority supporting congressional power over Indians). The assertion of plenary authority must, therefore, stand or fall on Congress' power under the Indian Commerce Clause. Although this Court has said that the "central function of the Indian Commerce Clause is to provide Congress with plenary power to legislate in the field of Indian affairs," *Cotton Petroleum Corp. v. New Mexico* (1989), neither the text nor the original understanding of the Clause supports Congress' claim to such "plenary" power.

A

The Indian Commerce Clause gives Congress authority "[t]o regulate *Commerce* . . . with the Indian tribes." Art. I, §8, cl. 3 (emphasis added). "At the time the original Constitution was ratified, 'commerce' consisted of selling, buying, and bartering, as well as transporting for these purposes." *United States v. Lopez* (1995) (Thomas, J., concurring). See also 1 S. Johnson, A Dictionary of the English Language 361 (4th rev. ed. 1773) (reprint 1978) (defining commerce as "Intercourse; exchange of one thing for another; interchange of any thing; trade; traffick"). "[W]hen Federalists and Anti-Federalists discussed the Commerce Clause during the ratification period, they often used trade (in its selling/bartering sense) and commerce interchangeably." *Lopez* (Thomas, J., concurring). The term "commerce" did not include economic activity such as "manufacturing and agriculture," let alone noneconomic activity such as adoption of children.

Furthermore, the term "commerce with Indian tribes" was invariably used during the time of the founding to mean " 'trade with Indians.' " See, *e.g.,* Natelson (citing 18th-century sources); Report of Committee on Indian Affairs (Feb. 20, 1787), in 32 Journals of the Continental Congress 1774-1789 (R. Hill ed. 1936) (hereinafter J. Cont'l Cong.) (using the phrase "commerce with the Indians" to mean trade with the Indians). And regulation of Indian commerce generally referred to legal structures governing "the conduct of the merchants engaged in the Indian trade, the nature of the goods they sold, the prices charged, and similar matters." Natelson.

The Indian Commerce Clause contains an additional textual limitation relevant to this case: Congress is given the power to regulate Commerce "with the Indian *tribes*." The Clause does not give Congress the power to regulate commerce with all Indian *persons* any more than the Foreign Commerce Clause gives Congress the power to regulate commerce with all foreign nationals traveling within the United States. A straightforward reading of the text, thus, confirms that Congress may only regulate commercial interactions — "commerce" — taking place with established Indian communities — "tribes." That power is far from "plenary."

B

Congress' assertion of "plenary power" over Indian affairs is also inconsistent with the history of the Indian Commerce Clause. At the time of the founding, the Clause was understood to reserve to the States general police powers with respect to Indians who were citizens of the several States. The Clause instead conferred on Congress the much narrower power to regulate trade with Indian tribes — that is, Indians who had not been incorporated into the body-politic of any State.

1

Before the Revolution, most Colonies adopted their own regulations governing Indian trade. See Natelson (citing colonial laws). Such regulations were necessary because colonial traders all too often abused their Indian trading partners, through fraud, exorbitant prices, extortion, and physical invasion of Indian territory, among other things. See 1 F. Prucha, The Great Father (1984) (hereinafter Prucha). These abuses sometimes provoked violent Indian retaliation. To mitigate these conflicts, most Colonies extensively regulated traders engaged in commerce with Indian tribes. See *e.g.,* Ordinance to Regulate Indian Affairs, Statutes of South Carolina (Aug. 31, 1751), in 16 Early American Indian Documents: Treaties and Laws, 1607-1789 (A. Vaughan and D. Rosen eds. 1998).[1] Over time, commercial regulation at the colonial level proved largely ineffective, in part because "[t]here was no uniformity among the colonies, no two sets of like regulations." Prucha.

Recognizing the need for uniform regulation of trade with the Indians, Benjamin Franklin proposed his own "articles of confederation" to the Continental Congress on July 21, 1775, which reflected his view that central control over Indian affairs should predominate over local control. 2 J. Cont'l Cong. (W. Ford ed. 1905). Franklin's proposal was not enacted, but in November 1775, Congress empowered a committee to draft regulations for the Indian trade. On July 12, 1776, the committee submitted a draft of the Articles of Confederation to Congress, which incorporated many of Franklin's proposals. The draft prohibited States from waging offensive war against the Indians without congressional authorization and granted Congress the exclusive power to acquire land from the

---

1. South Carolina, for example, required traders to be licensed, to be of good moral character, and to post a bond. Ordinance to Regulate Indian Affairs. A potential applicant's name was posted publicly before issuing the license, so anyone with objections had an opportunity to raise them. Restrictions were placed on employing agents and names of potential agents had to be disclosed. Traders who violated these rules were subject to substantial penalties.

Indians outside state boundaries, once those boundaries had been established. This version also gave Congress "the sole and exclusive Right and Power of . . . Regulating the Trade, and managing all Affairs with the Indians."

On August 20, 1776, the Committee of the Whole presented to Congress a revised draft, which provided Congress with "the sole and exclusive right and power of . . . regulating the trade, and managing all affairs with the Indians." Some delegates feared that the Articles gave Congress excessive power to interfere with States' jurisdiction over affairs with Indians residing within state boundaries. After further deliberation, the final result was a clause that included a broad grant of congressional authority with two significant exceptions: "The United States in Congress assembled shall also have the sole and exclusive right and power of . . . regulating the trade and managing all affairs with the Indians, not members of any of the States, provided that the legislative right of any State within its own limits be not infringed or violated." Articles of Confederation, Art. IX, cl. 4. As a result, Congress retained exclusive jurisdiction over Indian affairs outside the borders of the States; the States retained exclusive jurisdiction over relations with Member-Indians;[2] and Congress and the States "exercise[d] concurrent jurisdiction over transactions with tribal Indians within state boundaries, but congressional decisions would have to be in compliance with local law." Natelson 230. The drafting of the Articles of Confederation reveals the delegates' concern with protecting the power of the States to regulate Indian persons who were politically incorporated into the States. This concern for state power reemerged during the drafting of the Constitution.

2

The drafting history of the Constitutional Convention also supports a limited construction of the Indian Commerce Clause. On July 24, 1787, the convention elected a drafting committee — the Committee of Detail — and charged it to "report a Constitution conformable to the Resolutions passed by the Convention." 2 Records of the Federal Convention of 1787 (M. Farrand rev. 1966) (J. Madison). During the Committee's deliberations, John Rutledge, the chairman, suggested incorporating an Indian affairs power into the Constitution. The first draft reported back to the convention, however, provided Congress with authority "[t]o regulate commerce with foreign nations, and among the several States," *id.* (Madison) (Aug. 6, 1787), but did not include any specific Indian affairs clause. On August 18, James Madison proposed that the Federal Government be granted several additional powers, including the power "[t]o regulate *affairs* with the Indians as well within as without the limits of the U. States." *Id.* (J. Madison) (emphasis added). On August 22, Rutledge delivered the Committee of Detail's

---

2. Although Indians were generally considered "members" of a State if they paid taxes or were citizens, see Natelson, the precise definition of the term was "not yet settled" at the time of the founding and was "a question of frequent perplexity and contention in the federal councils," The Federalist No. 42 (J. Madison).

second report, which modified Madison's proposed clause. The Committee proposed to add to Congress' power "[t]o regulate commerce with foreign nations, and among the several States" the words, "and with Indians, within the Limits of any State, not subject to the laws thereof." The Committee's version, which echoed the Articles of Confederation, was far narrower than Madison's proposal. On August 31, the revised draft was submitted to a Committee of Eleven for further action. That Committee recommended adding to the Commerce Clause the phrase, "and with the Indian tribes," which the Convention ultimately adopted.

It is, thus, clear that the Framers of the Constitution were alert to the difference between the power to regulate trade with the Indians and the power to regulate all Indian affairs. By limiting Congress' power to the former, the Framers declined to grant Congress the same broad powers over Indian affairs conferred by the Articles of Confederation. See Prakash, Against Tribal Fungibility, 89 Cornell L. Rev. 1069, 1090 (2004).

During the ratification debates, opposition to the Indian Commerce Clause was nearly nonexistent. See Natelson (noting that Robert Yates, a New York Anti-Federalist was "almost the only writer who objected to any part [of] of the Commerce Clause — a clear indication that its scope was understood to be fairly narrow"). Given the Anti-Federalists' vehement opposition to the Constitution's other grants of power to the Federal Government, this silence is revealing. The ratifiers almost certainly understood the Clause to confer a relatively modest power on Congress — namely, the power to regulate trade with Indian tribes living beyond state borders. And this feature of the Constitution was welcomed by Federalists and Anti-Federalists alike due to the considerable interest in expanding trade with such Indian tribes. See, *e.g.,* The Federalist No. 42 (J. Madison) (praising the Constitution for removing the obstacles that had existed under the Articles of Confederation to federal control over "*trade* with Indians" (emphasis added)); 3 J. Elliot, The Debates in the Several State Conventions on the Adoption of the Federal Constitution 580 (2d ed. 1863) (Adam Stephens, at the Virginia ratifying convention, June 23, 1788, describing the Indian tribes residing near the Mississippi and "the variety of articles which might be obtained to advantage by trading with these people"); The Federalist No. 24 (A. Hamilton) (arguing that frontier garrisons would "be keys to the trade with the Indian nations"); Brutus (Letter) X, N.Y. J., Jan. 24, 1788 (conceding that there must be a standing army for some purposes, including "trade with Indians"). There is little evidence that the ratifiers of the Constitution understood the Indian Commerce Clause to confer anything resembling plenary power over Indian affairs. See Natelson 247-250.

III

In light of the original understanding of the Indian Commerce Clause, the constitutional problems that would be created by application of the ICWA here are evident. First, the statute deals with "child custody proceedings," §1903(1), not "commerce." It was enacted in response to concerns that "an alarmingly high percentage of Indian families [were] broken up by the removal, often unwarranted, of their children from them by nontribal public and private agencies." §1901(4). The perceived problem was that many Indian children were "placed in non-Indian foster and adoptive homes and institutions." This problem, however, had nothing to do with commerce.

Second, the portions of the ICWA at issue here do not regulate Indian tribes as tribes. [They] apply to all child custody proceedings involving an Indian child, regardless of whether an Indian tribe is involved. This case thus does not directly implicate Congress' power to "legislate in respect to Indian *tribes*." *United States v. Lara* (2004) (emphasis added). Baby Girl was never domiciled on an Indian Reservation, and the Cherokee Nation had no jurisdiction over her. Although Birth Father is a registered member of The Cherokee Nation, he did not live on a reservation either. He was, thus, subject to the laws of the State in which he resided (Oklahoma) and of the State where his daughter resided during the custody proceedings (South Carolina). Nothing in the Indian Commerce Clause permits Congress to enact special laws applicable to Birth Father merely because of his status as an Indian.

Because adoption proceedings like this one involve neither "commerce" nor "Indian tribes," there is simply no constitutional basis for Congress' assertion of authority over such proceedings. Also, the notion that Congress can direct state courts to apply different rules of evidence and procedure merely because a person of Indian descent is involved raises absurd possibilities. Such plenary power would allow Congress to dictate specific rules of criminal procedure for state-court prosecutions against Indian defendants. Likewise, it would allow Congress to substitute federal law for state law when contract disputes involve Indians. But the Constitution does not grant Congress power to override state law whenever that law happens to be applied to Indians. Accordingly, application of the ICWA to these child custody proceedings would be unconstitutional.

* * *

Because the Court's plausible interpretation of the relevant sections of the ICWA avoids these constitutional problems, I concur.

JACK M. BALKIN, COMMERCE, 109 MICH. L. REV. 1 (2010): Some contemporary originalists like Justice Clarence Thomas have argued that the original meaning of "commerce" is very narrow, essentially limited to the trade or exchange of goods and commodities. Thus, it would not include manufacturing, mining, or agriculture, much less any noneconomic activities. This reading is anachronistic: by focusing on the disposition of commodities it reflects a modern conception of commerce viewed as a subset of economic activity; it completely misses the eighteenth-century dimensions of commerce as a form of social intercourse. . . .

If we view the Commerce Clause through the lens of the central reasons for forming the Constitution and the central questions that faced the new nation — foreign affairs and dealings with Indian tribes — reading "commerce" to mean "intercourse" or "interactions" makes the most sense. The Clause enabled "Congress to regulate all interactions (and altercations) with foreign nations and Indian tribes," which "if improperly handled by a single state acting on its own, might lead to needless wars or compromise the interests of sister states."

One of the first things the new government did, for example, was to regulate its interactions with the Indian tribes, through a series of Trade and Intercourse Acts beginning in 1790. The title of these acts was apt: they not only required licenses for trade with Indians, but also punished "any crime upon, or trespass against, the person or property of any peaceable and friendly Indian or Indians." These crimes did not necessarily involve trade or even economic activity; they could involve assault, murder, or rape. Note as well that even if the point of regulating these crimes was because of their likely effects on trade with the Indian tribes, the activities regulated were themselves not economic. And note finally that the 1790 and 1793 Trade and Intercourse Acts could not be justified as legislation designed to enforce treaties; they applied to crimes against Indians whether or not they had signed treaties with the United States. Congress clearly believed that it could reach both economic and noneconomic activity under the Indian Commerce Clause; at the very least it believed that it could regulate non-economic activity in order to protect trade and diplomatic relations that would further trade. This is hardly surprising. It was assumed in international law at the time of the founding that international intercourse included both commercial and noncommercial aspects that were inevitably intertwined.

Neither the trade theory nor the economic theory can explain why the early Trade and Intercourse Acts would be constitutional unless we assume that Congress has the auxiliary power to regulate noneconomic (or nontrade) activity that affects foreign or Indian commerce. That is, we must assume that Congress can reach activities that do not involve trade or are not economic in order to protect its powers to regulate trade or other economic activity, perhaps under the Necessary and Proper Clause. If so, then the two theories essentially merge into the interaction theory. Note, however, that the Clause says that Congress can regulate "commerce" with foreign nations and with the Indian tribes, not "activity that affects commerce" with foreign nations and with the Indian tribes. The interaction theory is therefore more consistent with the text.

ROBERT G. NATELSON, THE ORIGINAL UNDERSTANDING OF THE INDIAN COMMERCE CLAUSE, 85 DENV. U. L. REV. 201 (2007): In contending for an expansive view of the commerce power, some have argued that a portion of the Indian Intercourse Act of 1790 shows an intended meaning for Indian "commerce" that goes beyond mere trade. . . . [T]he fundamental problem with arguing that the Indian Intercourse Act sheds light on the Commerce Clause is this: the Indian Intercourse Act was not adopted pursuant to the Commerce Clause. It was adopted pursuant to the Treaty Power.

In 1785 and 1786 Congress entered into the three "Hopewell" treaties with the Cherokees, Chickasaws, and Choctaws. By the terms of all these treaties, the United States had promised to regulate trade between the United States and the Natives "[f]or the benefit and comfort of the Indians, and for the prevention of injuries or oppressions on the part of the citizens or Indians." The tribes, President Washington, and Secretary of War Henry Knox all were unhappy over white abuses that continued in defiance of the treaties, and became convinced that enforcement legislation was needed.

On August 22, 1789, the President entered the chamber of the Senate and consulted its members on Indian affairs. After reciting the tribes' dissatisfaction, he noted that the Cherokees lived primarily in North Carolina, which had not yet joined the union, and added:

> The commissioners for negotiating with the Southern Indians may be instructed to transmit a message to the Cherokees, stating to them, as far as may be proper, the difficulties arising from the local claims of North Carolina, and to assure them that the United States are not unmindful of the treaty at Hopewell. . . .
>
> The Commissioners may be instructed to transmit messages to the said tribes, containing our assurances of the continuance of the friendship of the United States, and that measures will soon be taken for extending a trade to them agreeably to the treaties of Hopewell.

The President then proceeded to impress upon his listeners the importance of an early agreement with the Creeks. He returned two days later for further consultation. Congress responded the following summer by enacting the Indian Intercourse Act.

Hence, the first three sections of the Act were designed to fulfill the promise of the United States to regulate trade for the benefit of the Indians. Section 4 was, by its terms, designed to effectuate Indian treaties. Section 5—the substantive criminal provision—loosely tracked the language in another provision of the Hopewell pacts, which required that United States citizens who committed crimes in Indian country be tried and punished as if they had committed those crimes against fellow citizens. Provisions in treaties that defined and provided for punishment of crimes were well precedented.

The trade and criminal portions of the Indian Intercourse Act applied to all Native Americans, not merely the Hopewell tribes. But that was because none of the treaties limited their primary benefits to members of the signatory tribes. The trade provisions in the treaties referred generally to "the Indians," and the criminal sections referred to "any Indian." Further, the broad statutory language was appropriate because the government apparently planned to apply the Hopewell language as a template for future agreements: very similar terms were contained in a fourth treaty, signed only a few days later with the Creeks, and in a fifth, concluded the following year with the Cherokees.

A law enacted to execute the Treaty Power cannot be said to represent an interpretation of the Commerce Clause. . . .

STUDY GUIDE:

- Does this case simply "graft [the] holding in *Raich* onto the commerce element of the Hobbs Act"? Or does it, as Justice Thomas writes in dissent, "expand" *Raich*.

- Is robbery an economic activity, separate and apart from whether robbery has a substantial effect on economic activity?
- How does Justice Thomas's dissent employ "necessary" and "proper" as separate legal inquiries?
- Does the majority's construction of the Hobbs Act provide the federal government with a general police power?

Taylor v. United States
136 S. Ct. 2074 (2016)

JUSTICE ALITO delivered the opinion of the Court.

The Hobbs Act makes it a crime for a person to affect commerce, or to attempt to do so, by robbery. The Act defines "commerce" broadly as interstate commerce "and all other commerce over which the United States has jurisdiction." This case requires us to decide what the Government must prove to satisfy the Hobbs Act's commerce element when a defendant commits a robbery that targets a marijuana dealer's drugs or drug proceeds.

The answer to this question is straightforward and dictated by our precedent. We held in *Gonzales v. Raich* (2005), that the Commerce Clause gives Congress authority to regulate the national market for marijuana, including the authority to proscribe the purely intrastate production, possession, and sale of this controlled substance. Because Congress may regulate these intrastate activities based on their aggregate effect on interstate commerce, it follows that Congress may also regulate intrastate drug *theft*. And since the Hobbs Act criminalizes robberies and attempted robberies that affect any commerce "over which the United States has jurisdiction," the prosecution in a Hobbs Act robbery case satisfies the Act's commerce element if it shows that the defendant robbed or attempted to rob a drug dealer of drugs or drug proceeds. By targeting a drug dealer in this way, a robber necessarily affects or attempts to affect commerce over which the United States has jurisdiction.

In this case, petitioner Anthony Taylor was convicted on two Hobbs Act counts based on proof that he attempted to rob marijuana dealers of their drugs and drug money. We hold that this evidence was sufficient to satisfy the Act's commerce element.

I

Beginning as early as 2009, an outlaw gang called the "Southwest Goonz" committed a series of home invasion robberies targeting drug dealers in the area of Roanoke, Virginia. For obvious reasons, drug dealers are more likely than ordinary citizens to keep large quantities of cash and illegal drugs in their homes and are less likely to report robberies to the police. For participating in two such home invasions, Taylor was convicted of two counts of Hobbs Act robbery, in violation of §1951(a), and one count of using a firearm in furtherance of a crime of violence, in violation of §924(c). . . .

The first attempted drug robbery for which Taylor was convicted occurred in August 2009. Taylor and others targeted the home of Josh Whorley, having obtained information that Whorley dealt "exotic and high grade" marijuana. "The robbers expected to find both drugs and money" in Whorley's home. Taylor and the others broke into the home, searched it, and assaulted Whorley and his girl-friend. They demanded to be told the location of money and drugs but, not locat-ing any, left with only jewelry, $40, two cell phones, and a marijuana cigarette.

The second attempted drug robbery occurred two months later in October 2009 at the home of William Lynch. A source informed the leader of the gang that, on a prior occasion, the source had robbed Lynch of 20 pounds of marijuana in front of Lynch's home. The gang also received information that Lynch con-tinued to deal drugs. Taylor and others broke into Lynch's home, held his wife and young children at gunpoint, assaulted his wife, and demanded to know the location of his drugs and money. Again largely unsuccessful, the robbers made off with only a cell phone.

For his participation in these two home invasions, Taylor was indicted under the Hobbs Act on two counts of affecting commerce or attempting to do so through robbery. His first trial resulted in a hung jury. On retrial, at the urging of the Government, the District Court precluded Taylor from introducing evidence that the drug dealers he targeted might be dealing in only locally grown mari-juana. During the second trial, Taylor twice moved for a judgment of acquittal on the ground that the prosecution had failed to meet its burden on the commerce element, but the District Court denied those motions, holding that the proof that Taylor attempted to rob drug dealers was sufficient as a matter of law to satisfy that element. The jury found Taylor guilty on both of the Hobbs Act counts and one of the firearms counts.

On appeal, Taylor challenged the sufficiency of the evidence to prove the com-merce element of the Hobbs Act, but the Fourth Circuit affirmed. "Because drug dealing in the aggregate necessarily affects interstate commerce," the court rea-soned, "the government was simply required to prove that Taylor depleted or attempted to deplete the assets of such an operation."

We granted certiorari to resolve a conflict in the Circuits regarding the demands of the Hobbs Act's commerce element in cases involving the theft of drugs and drug proceeds from drug dealers.

II

A

The Hobbs Act provides in relevant part as follows: "Whoever in any way or degree obstructs, delays, or affects commerce or the movement of any article or commodity in commerce, by robbery . . . or attempts or conspires so to do . . . shall be fined under this title or imprisoned not more than twenty years, or both."

The Act then defines the term "commerce" to mean

commerce within the District of Columbia, or any Territory or Possession of the United States; all commerce between any point in a State, Territory, Possession, or the District of Columbia and any point outside thereof; all commerce between points within the same State through any place outside such State; and all other commerce over which the United States has jurisdiction.

The language of the Hobbs Act is unmistakably broad. It reaches any obstruction, delay, or other effect on commerce, even if small, and the Act's definition of commerce encompasses "all . . . commerce over which the United States has jurisdiction." We have noted the sweep of the Act in past cases.

B

To determine how far this commerce element extends — and what the Government must prove to meet it — we look to our Commerce Clause cases. We have said that there are three categories of activity that Congress may regulate under its commerce power: (1) "the use of the channels of interstate commerce"; (2) "the instrumentalities of interstate commerce, or persons or things in interstate commerce, even though the threat may come only from intrastate activities"; and (3) "those activities having a substantial relation to interstate commerce, . . . *i.e.,* those activities that substantially affect interstate commerce." *United States v. Lopez* (1995). We have held that activities in this third category — those that "substantially affect" commerce — may be regulated so long as they substantially affect interstate commerce in the aggregate, even if their individual impact on interstate commerce is minimal. See *Wickard v. Filburn* (1942) ("[E]ven if appellee's activity be local and though it may not be regarded as commerce, it may still, whatever its nature, be reached by Congress if it exerts a substantial economic effect on interstate commerce").

While this final category is broad, "thus far in our Nation's history our cases have upheld Commerce Clause regulation of intrastate activity only where that activity is economic in nature." *United States v. Morrison* (2000).

In this case, the activity at issue, the sale of marijuana, is unquestionably an economic activity. It is, to be sure, a form of business that is illegal under federal law and the laws of most States. But there can be no question that marijuana trafficking is a moneymaking endeavor — and a potentially lucrative one at that.

In *Raich,* the Court addressed Congress's authority to regulate the marijuana market. The Court reaffirmed "Congress' power to regulate purely local activities that are part of an economic 'class of activities' that have a substantial effect on interstate commerce." The production, possession, and distribution of controlled substances constitute a "class of activities" that in the aggregate substantially affect interstate commerce, and therefore, the Court held, Congress possesses the authority to regulate (and to criminalize) the production, possession, and distribution of controlled substances even when those activities occur entirely within the boundaries of a single State. Any other outcome, we warned, would leave a gaping enforcement hole in Congress's regulatory scheme.

The case now before us requires no more than that we graft our holding in *Raich* onto the commerce element of the Hobbs Act. The Hobbs Act criminalizes robberies affecting "commerce over which the United States has jurisdiction." Under *Raich,* the market for marijuana, including its intrastate aspects, is "commerce over which the United States has jurisdiction." It therefore follows as a simple matter of logic that a robber who affects or attempts to affect even the intrastate sale of marijuana grown within the State affects or attempts to affect commerce over which the United States has jurisdiction.

C

Rejecting this logic, Taylor takes the position that the robbery or attempted robbery of a drug dealer's inventory violates the Hobbs Act only if the Government proves something more. This argument rests in part on the fact that *Raich* concerned the Controlled Substances Act (CSA), the criminal provisions of which lack a jurisdictional element. The Hobbs Act, by contrast, contains such an element—namely, the conduct criminalized must affect or attempt to affect commerce in some way or degree. Therefore, Taylor reasons, the prosecution must prove beyond a reasonable doubt either (1) that the particular drugs in question originated or were destined for sale out of State or (2) that the particular drug dealer targeted in the robbery operated an interstate business. The Second and Seventh Circuits have adopted this same argument.

This argument is flawed. It confuses the standard of proof with the meaning of the element that must be proved. There is no question that the Government in a Hobbs Act prosecution must prove beyond a reasonable doubt that the defendant engaged in conduct that satisfies the Act's commerce element, but the meaning of that element is a question of law. And, as noted, *Raich* established that the purely intrastate production and sale of marijuana is commerce over which the Federal Government has jurisdiction. Therefore, if the Government proves beyond a reasonable doubt that a robber targeted a marijuana dealer's drugs or illegal proceeds, the Government has proved beyond a reasonable doubt that commerce over which the United States has jurisdiction was affected.

The only way to escape that conclusion would be to hold that the Hobbs Act does not exercise the full measure of Congress's commerce power. But we reached the opposite conclusion more than 50 years ago, and it is not easy to see how the expansive language of the Act could be interpreted in any other way.

This conclusion does not make the commerce provision of the Hobbs Act superfluous. That statute, unlike the criminal provisions of the CSA, applies to forms of conduct that, even in the aggregate, may not substantially affect commerce. The Act's commerce element ensures that applications of the Act do not exceed Congress's authority. But in a case like this one, where the target of a robbery is a drug dealer, proof that the defendant's conduct in and of itself affected or threatened commerce is not needed. All that is needed is proof that the defendant's conduct fell within a category of conduct that, in the aggregate, had the requisite effect.

D

Contrary to the dissent, today's holding merely applies—it in no way expands—*Raich*'s interpretation of the scope of Congress's power under the Commerce Clause. The dissent resists the substantial-effects approach and the aggregation principle on which *Raich* is based. But we have not been asked to reconsider *Raich*. So our decision in *Raich* controls the outcome here. As long as Congress may regulate the purely intrastate possession and sale of illegal drugs, Congress may criminalize the theft or attempted theft of those same drugs.

We reiterate what this means. In order to obtain a conviction under the Hobbs Act for the robbery or attempted robbery of a drug dealer, the Government need not show that the drugs that a defendant stole or attempted to steal either traveled or were destined for transport across state lines. Rather, to satisfy the Act's commerce element, it is enough that a defendant knowingly stole or attempted to steal drugs or drug proceeds, for, as a matter of law, the market for illegal drugs is "commerce over which the United States has jurisdiction." And it makes no difference under our cases that any actual or threatened effect on commerce in a particular case is minimal. See *Perez v. United States* (1971) ("Where the class of activities is regulated and that class is within the reach of federal power, the courts have no power 'to excise, as trivial, individual instances' of the class" (emphasis deleted)).

E

In the present case, the Government met its burden by introducing evidence that Taylor's gang intentionally targeted drug dealers to obtain drugs and drug proceeds. One of the victims had been robbed of substantial quantities of drugs at his residence in the past, and the other was thought to possess high-grade marijuana. The robbers also made explicit statements in the course of the robberies revealing that they believed that the victims possessed drugs and drug proceeds. Both robberies were committed with the express intent to obtain illegal drugs and the proceeds from the sale of illegal drugs. Such proof is sufficient to meet the commerce element of the Hobbs Act.

Our holding today is limited to cases in which the defendant targets drug dealers for the purpose of stealing drugs or drug proceeds. We do not resolve what the Government must prove to establish Hobbs Act robbery where some other type of business or victim is targeted. . . .

JUSTICE THOMAS, dissenting.

The Hobbs Act makes it a federal crime to commit a robbery that "affects" "commerce over which the United States has jurisdiction." Under the Court's decision today, the Government can obtain a Hobbs Act conviction without proving that the defendant's robbery in fact affected interstate commerce—or any commerce. The Court's holding creates serious constitutional problems and extends our already expansive, flawed commerce-power precedents. I would construe the Hobbs Act in accordance with constitutional limits and hold that the

Act punishes a robbery only when the Government proves that the robbery itself affected interstate commerce.

I

In making it a federal crime to commit a robbery that "affects commerce," the Hobbs Act invokes the full reach of Congress' commerce power: The Act defines "commerce" to embrace "all . . . commerce over which the United States has jurisdiction." To determine the Hobbs Act's reach, I start by examining the limitations on Congress' authority to punish robbery under its commerce power. In light of those limitations and in accordance with the Hobbs Act's text, I would hold that the Government in a Hobbs Act case may obtain a conviction for robbery only if it proves, beyond a reasonable doubt, that the defendant's robbery itself affected interstate commerce. The Government may not obtain a conviction by proving only that the defendant's robbery affected intrastate commerce or other intrastate activity.

A

Congress possesses only limited authority to prohibit and punish robbery. "The Constitution creates a Federal Government of enumerated powers." *United States v. Lopez* (1995); see Art. I, §8; *Marbury v. Madison* (1803) (Marshall, C.J.) ("The powers of the legislature are defined, and limited; and that those limits may not be mistaken, or forgotten, the constitution is written"). As with its powers generally, Congress has only limited authority over crime. The Government possesses broad general authority in territories and federal enclaves. See Art. I, §8, cl. 17 (conferring power of "exclusive Legislation" over the District of Columbia); Art. IV, §3, cl. 2 ("The Congress shall have Power to dispose of and make all needful Rules and Regulations respecting the Territory or other Property belonging to the United States"). But its power over crimes committed in the States is very different. The Constitution expressly delegates to Congress authority over only four specific crimes: counterfeiting securities and coin of the United States, Art. I, §8, cl. 6; piracies and felonies committed on the high seas, Art. I, §8, cl. 10; offenses against the law of nations, *ibid.*; and treason, Art. III, §3, cl. 2. Given these limited grants of federal power, it is "clea[r] that Congress cannot punish felonies generally." *Cohens v. Virginia* (1821) (Marshall, C.J.). Congress has "no general right to punish murder committed within any of the States," for example, and no general right to punish the many crimes that fall outside of Congress' express grants of criminal authority. "The Constitution," in short, "withhold[s] from Congress a plenary police power." *Lopez.* see Art. I, §8; Amdt. 10.

Beyond the four express grants of federal criminal authority, then, Congress may validly enact criminal laws only to the extent that doing so is "necessary and proper for carrying into Execution" its enumerated powers or other powers that the Constitution vests in the Federal Government. Art. I, §8, cl. 18. As Chief Justice Marshall explained, "the [federal] government may, legitimately, punish any violation of its laws" as a necessary and proper means for carrying into execution Congress' enumerated powers. *McCulloch v. Maryland* (1819). But if these limitations are not respected, Congress will accumulate the general police power that the Constitution withholds.

The scope of Congress' power to punish robbery in the Hobbs Act — or in any federal statute — must be assessed in light of these principles. The Commerce Clause — the constitutional provision that the Hobbs Act most clearly invokes — does not authorize Congress to punish robbery. That Clause authorizes Congress to regulate "Commerce . . . among the several States." Art. I, §8, cl. 3. Robbery is not "Commerce" under that Clause. At the founding, "commerce" "consisted of selling, buying, and bartering, as well as transporting for these purposes." *Lopez* (Thomas, J., concurring). The Commerce Clause, as originally understood, thus "empowers Congress to regulate the buying and selling of goods and services trafficked across state lines." *Gonzales v. Raich* (Thomas, J., dissenting). Robbery is not buying, it is not selling, and it cannot plausibly be described as a commercial transaction ("trade or exchange for value").

Because Congress has no freestanding power to punish robbery and because robbery is not itself "Commerce," Congress may prohibit and punish robbery only to the extent that doing so is "necessary and proper for carrying into Execution" Congress' power to regulate commerce. Art. I, §8, cl. 18. To be "necessary," Congress' prohibition of robbery must be "plainly adapted" to regulating interstate commerce. *McCulloch.* This means that Congress' robbery prohibition must have an "obvious, simple, and direct relation" with the regulation of interstate commerce. *Raich* (Thomas, J., dissenting) (internal quotation marks omitted). And for Congress' robbery prohibition to be "proper," it cannot be "prohibited" by the Constitution or inconsistent with its "letter and spirit." see *United States v. Comstock* (2010) (Thomas, J., dissenting).

                                    B

With those principles in mind, I turn to the Hobbs Act. The Act provides,

> Whoever in any way or degree obstructs, delays, or affects commerce or the movement of any article or commodity in commerce, by robbery or extortion or attempts or conspires so to do, or commits or threatens physical violence to any person or property in furtherance of a plan or purpose to do anything in violation of this section shall be [punished].

In keeping with Congress' authority to regulate certain commerce — but not robbery generally — the central feature of a Hobbs Act crime is an effect on commerce. The Act begins by focusing on commerce and then carefully describes the required relationship between the proscribed conduct and commerce: The Act uses active verbs — "obstructs," "delays," "affects" — to describe how a robbery must relate to commerce, making clear that a defendant's robbery must affect commerce.

The Act's reach depends on the meaning of "commerce," which the Act defines as commerce within the District of Columbia, or any Territory or Possession of the United States; all commerce between any point in a State, Territory, Possession, or the District of Columbia and any point outside thereof; all commerce between points within the same State through any place outside such State; and all other commerce over which the United States has jurisdiction.

As noted above, this provision is comprehensive and appears to invoke all of Congress' commerce power. The first clause of the definition invokes Congress' broad police power, including power over internal commerce, in the District of Columbia and the Territories. See Art. I, §8, cl. 17 (District of Columbia); Art. IV, §3, cl. 2 (territories). The second and third clauses most clearly invoke those broad powers as well as Congress' power "[t]o regulate Commerce . . . among the several States." Art. I, §8, cl. 3. The final clause invokes all federal commerce power not covered in the previous clauses. It invokes (to the extent that the second and third clauses do not already do so) Congress' authority "[t]o regulate Commerce with foreign Nations . . . and with the Indian Tribes."

The critical question in this case is whether the commerce definition's final clause extends further, to some intrastate activity. Given the limitations imposed by the Constitution, I would construe this clause not to reach such activity.

As explained above, for the Hobbs Act to constitutionally prohibit robberies that interfere with intrastate activity, that prohibition would need to be "necessary and proper for carrying into Execution" Congress' power to regulate interstate commerce, Art. I, §8, cls. 3, 18. Punishing a local robbery — one that affects only intrastate commerce or other intrastate activity — cannot satisfy that standard. Punishing a local robbery does not bear a "direct relation" to the regulation of interstate commerce, so it would not be "necessary." *Raich* (Thomas, J., dissenting). Nor would punishing such a robbery be "proper." Permitting Congress to criminalize such robberies would confer on Congress a general police power over the Nation — even though the Constitution confers no such power on Congress. *Lopez; Raich* (Thomas, J., dissenting). Allowing the Federal Government to reach a simple home robbery, for example, would "encroac[h] on States' traditional police powers to define the criminal law and to protect . . . their citizens." This would "subvert basic principles of federalism and dual sovereignty," and would be inconsistent with the "letter and spirit" of the Constitution.

Thus, the Hobbs Act reaches a local robbery only when that particular robbery "obstructs, delays, or affects" *interstate* commerce. So construed, the Hobbs Act validly punishes robbery. Congress' power "[t]o regulate Commerce . . . among the several States," Art. I, §8, cl. 3, "would lack force or practical effect if Congress lacked the authority to enact criminal laws" prohibiting interference with interstate commerce or the movement of articles or goods in interstate commerce, *Comstock* (Thomas, J., dissenting). The Hobbs Act's prohibition on such interferences thus helps to "carr[y] into Execution" Congress' enumerated power to regulate interstate commerce. Art. I, §8, cls. 3, 18. A prohibition on such interference by robbery bears an "obvious, simple, and direct relation" to regulating interstate commerce: it allows commerce to flow between States unobstructed. *Raich* (Thomas, J., dissenting). It is therefore "necessary."

And such a prohibition accords with the limited nature of the powers that the Constitution confers on Congress, by adhering to the categories of commerce that the Constitution authorizes Congress to regulate and by keeping Congress from exercising a general police power. It is accordingly "proper" to that extent. If construed to reach a robbery that does not affect interstate commerce, however, the Hobbs Act exceeds Congress' authority because it is no longer "necessary and proper" to the execution of Congress' power "[t]o regulate Commerce . . . among the several States," Art. I, §8, cls. 3, 18.

Robberies that might satisfy these principles would be those that affect the channels of interstate commerce or instrumentalities of interstate commerce. A robbery that forces an interstate freeway to shut down thus may form the basis for a valid Hobbs Act conviction. So too might a robbery of a truck driver who is in the course of transporting commercial goods across state lines. But if the Government cannot prove that a robbery in a State affected interstate commerce, then the robbery is not punishable under the Hobbs Act. Sweeping in robberies that do not affect interstate commerce comes too close to conferring on Congress a general police power over the Nation.

Given the Hobbs Act's text and relevant constitutional principles, the Government in a Hobbs Act robbery case (at least one that involves only intrastate robbery) must prove, beyond a reasonable doubt, that the defendant's robbery itself affected interstate commerce.

C

On this interpretation of the Hobbs Act, petitioner David Anthony Taylor's convictions cannot stand. The Government cites no evidence that Taylor actually obstructed, delayed, or affected interstate commerce when he committed the two intrastate robberies here. The Government did not prove that Taylor affected any channel of interstate commerce, instrumentality of commerce, or person or thing in interstate commerce. Nor did the Government prove that Taylor affected an actual commercial transaction—let alone an interstate commercial transaction. At most, the Government proved instead that Taylor robbed two drug dealers in their homes in Virginia; that the marijuana that Taylor expected to (but did not) find in these robberies might possibly at some point have crossed state lines; and that Taylor expected to find large amounts of marijuana. Under the principles set forth above, that is not sufficient to bring Taylor's robberies within the Hobbs Act's reach. We should reverse Taylor's Hobbs Act convictions.

II

Upholding Taylor's convictions, the Court reads the Hobbs Act differently. The Court concludes that the "commerce over which the United States has jurisdiction," §1951(b)(3), includes intrastate activity. Under our modern precedents, as the Court notes, Congress may regulate not just the channels of interstate commerce, instrumentalities of interstate commerce, and persons or things moving in interstate commerce, but may also regulate "those activities having a substantial relation to interstate commerce, . . . *i.e.,* those activities that substantially affect interstate commerce." *Lopez, Wickard v. Filburn* (1942) ("[E]ven if appellee's activity be local and though it may not be regarded as commerce, it may still, whatever its nature, be reached by Congress if it exerts a substantial economic effect on interstate commerce"). The substantial-effects approach is broad, in part because of its "aggregation principle": Congress can regulate an activity — even an intrastate, noncommercial activity — if that activity falls within a "class of activities" that, "as a whole," "substantially affects interstate commerce," even if "any specific activity within the class" has no such effects "when considered in isolation." *Lopez* (Thomas, J., concurring). According to the Court, the final clause of the Hobbs Act's definition of commerce embraces this category of activities that, in the aggregate, substantially affect commerce. Any robbery that targets a marijuana dealer, the Court then holds, affects the type of intrastate activity that Congress may regulate under its commerce power. For at least three reasons, the Court's holding is in error.

A

Although our modern precedents (such as *Wickard*) embrace the substantial-effects approach, applying that approach to the Hobbs Act is tantamount to abandoning any limits on Congress' commerce power — even the slight limits recognized by our expansive modern precedents. As I have explained, if the Hobbs Act is construed to punish a robbery that by itself affects only intrastate activity, then the Act defies the constitutional design.

That is true even under our modern precedents. Even those precedents emphasize that "[t]he Constitution requires a distinction between what is truly national and what is truly local." *United States v. Morrison* (2000); see *Lopez.* The substantial-effects approach is at war with that principle. To avoid giving Congress a general police power, there must be some limit to what Congress can regulate. But the substantial-effects approach's aggregation principle "has no stopping point." "[O]ne *always* can draw the circle broadly enough to cover an activity that, when taken in isolation, would not have substantial effects on commerce." Under the substantial-effects approach, Congress could, under its commerce power, regulate *any* robbery: In the aggregate, any type of robbery could be deemed to substantially affect interstate commerce.

By applying the substantial-effects test to the criminal prohibition before us, the Court effectively gives Congress a police power. That is why the Court cannot identify any true limit on its understanding of the commerce power. Although the Court maintains that its holding "is limited to cases in which the defendant targets drug dealers for the purpose of stealing drugs or drug proceeds," its reasoning allows for unbounded regulation. Given that the Hobbs Act can be read in a way that does not give Congress a general police power, we should not construe the statute as the Court does today.

B

Applying the substantial-effects approach is especially unsound here because it effectively relieves the Government of its central burden in a criminal case—the burden to prove every element beyond a reasonable doubt—and because the Court's holding does not follow from even our broad precedents. The Court reasons that, under *Gonzales v. Raich*—a case that rests on substantial-effects reasoning—"the market for marijuana, including its intrastate aspects, is 'commerce over which the United States has jurisdiction.'" Therefore, "a robber who affects or attempts to affect even the intrastate sale of marijuana grown within the State affects or attempts to affect commerce over which the United States has jurisdiction." As the Court later states, "[W]here the target of a robbery is a drug dealer, proof that the defendant's conduct in and of itself affected or threatened commerce is not needed. All that is needed is proof that the defendant's conduct fell within a category of conduct that, in the aggregate, had the requisite effect." *Ante.*

Raich is too thin a reed to support the Court's holding. *Raich* upheld the federal Controlled Substances Act's regulation of "the intrastate manufacture and possession of marijuana" for personal medical use, on the view that Congress "had a rational basis for believing that failure to regulate the intrastate manufacture and possession of marijuana" would undercut federal regulation of the broader interstate marijuana market. The Court "stress[ed]" that it did not "need [to] determine whether [local cultivation and possession of marijuana], taken in the aggregate, substantially affect[ed] interstate commerce in fact, but only whether a 'rational basis' exist[ed] for so concluding."

As an initial matter, *Raich* did not, as the Court suggests, hold that "the market for marijuana, including its intrastate aspects, is '*commerce* over which the United States has jurisdiction.'" *Raich* held at most that the market for marijuana comprises *activities* that may substantially affect commerce over which the United States has jurisdiction. Those activities are not necessarily "commerce," so *Raich*'s holding does not establish what the Hobbs Act's text requires.

But even if *Raich* established that the intrastate aspects of the marijuana market are "commerce over which the United States has jurisdiction," *Raich* still would not establish the further point that the Court needs for its conclusion. Specifically, *Raich* would not establish that a robbery affecting a drug dealer establishes, beyond a reasonable doubt, that the robber actually "obstructs, delays, or affects" the marijuana market. §1951(a). *Raich* did not hold that any activity relating to the marijuana market *in fact* affects commerce. *Raich* instead disclaimed the need to "determine whether" activities relating to the marijuana market—even "taken in the aggregate"—"substantially affect interstate commerce in fact." *Raich* decided only that Congress had a rational basis—a merely "'conceivable'" basis, for thinking that it needed to regulate that activity as part of an effective regulatory regime. That is far from a finding, beyond a reasonable doubt, that a particular robbery relating to marijuana is an activity that affects interstate commerce. Grafting *Raich*'s "holding . . . onto the commerce element of the Hobbs Act" thus does not lead to the conclusion that "a robber who affects or attempts to affect . . . the intrastate sale of marijuana grown within [a] State affects or attempts to affect"—beyond a reasonable doubt—"commerce over which the United States has jurisdiction."

The Court's analysis thus provides no assurance that the Government has proved beyond a reasonable doubt that a Hobbs Act robbery defendant in fact affected commerce. And it unnecessarily extends our already broad precedents.

C

Finally, today's decision weakens longstanding protections for criminal defendants. And when a broad reading of a criminal statute would upset federalism, courts must be more careful still. "[U]nless Congress conveys its purpose clearly," we do not deem it "to have significantly changed the federal-state balance in the prosecution of crimes." *Jones v. United States* (2000).

The substantial-effects test is in tension with these principles. That test—and the deferential, rational-basis review to which it is subjected—puts virtually no burdens on the Government. That should not come as a surprise because the substantial-effects test gained momentum not in the criminal context, but instead in the context in which courts most defer to the Government: the regulatory arena. *E.g., Wickard* (relying on substantial-effects reasoning to uphold regulatory restrictions on wheat under the Agricultural Adjustment Act of 1938). Without adequate reflection, the Court later extended this approach to the criminal context. In *Perez v. United States* (1971), for example, the Court applied the substantial-effects approach to a criminal statute, holding that Congress could criminally punish loansharking under its commerce power because "[e]xtortionate credit transactions, though purely intrastate, may in the judgment of Congress affect interstate commerce" when judged as a "class of activities."

The Court takes that "dangerous" step—and other dangerous steps—today. It construes the Hobbs Act in a way that conflicts with the Constitution, with our precedents, and with longstanding protections for the accused. I would interpret the Hobbs Act in a way that is consistent with its text and with the Constitution.

For these reasons, I respectfully dissent.

Chapter 4

Federalism Limits on Congressional Power

STUDY GUIDE:

- Why exactly is PASPA unconstitutional? Does it violate the 10th Amendment? Does it exceed Congress's enumerated powers? Was this law both a "necessary" *and* "proper" exercise of federal power?
- Do all 9 Justices agree with the commandeering doctrine? Why exactly does Justice Ginsburg dissent?

Murphy et al. v. National Collegiate Athletic Assn. et al.
584 S. Ct. ___ (2018)

JUSTICE ALITO delivered the opinion of the Court.

The State of New Jersey wants to legalize sports gambling at casinos and horseracing tracks, but a federal law, the Professional and Amateur Sports Protection Act, generally makes it unlawful for a State to "authorize" sports gambling schemes. We must decide whether this provision is compatible with the system of "dual sovereignty" embodied in the Constitution.

I

A

Nevada . . . [is] the only state venue for legal sports gambling in casinos, and sports gambling is immensely popular. Sports gambling, however, has long had strong opposition. Opponents argue that it is particularly addictive and especially attractive to young people with a strong interest in sports, and in the past gamblers corrupted and seriously damaged the reputation of professional and amateur sports. Apprehensive about the potential effects of sports gambling, professional sports leagues and the National Collegiate Athletic Association (NCAA) long opposed legalization.

B

By the 1990s, there were signs that the trend that had brought about the legalization of many other forms of gambling might extend to sports gambling, and this sparked federal efforts to stem the tide. Opponents of sports gambling turned to the legislation now before us, the Professional and Amateur Sports Protection Act (PASPA). . . .

PASPA's most important provision, part of which is directly at issue in these cases, makes it "unlawful" for a State or any of its subdivisions "to sponsor, operate, advertise, promote, license, or authorize by law or compact . . . a lottery, sweepstakes, or other betting, gambling, or wagering scheme based . . . on" competitive sporting events. §3702(1). In parallel, §3702(2) makes it "unlawful" for "a person to sponsor, operate, advertise, or promote" those same gambling schemes—but only if this is done "pursuant to the law or compact of a governmental entity." PASPA does not make sports gambling a federal crime (and thus was not anticipated to impose a significant law enforcement burden on the Federal Government). Instead, PASPA allows the Attorney General, as well as professional and amateur sports organizations, to bring civil actions to enjoin violations. §3703.

At the time of PASPA's adoption, a few jurisdictions allowed some form of sports gambling. In Nevada, sports gambling was legal in casinos, and three States hosted sports lotteries or allowed sports pools. PASPA contains "grandfather" provisions allowing these activities to continue. Another provision gave New Jersey the option of legalizing sports gambling in Atlantic City—provided that it did so within one year of the law's effective date. §3704(a)(3).

New Jersey did not take advantage of this special option, but by 2011, with Atlantic City facing stiff competition, the State had a change of heart. New Jersey voters approved an amendment to the State Constitution making it lawful for the legislature to authorize sports gambling, and in 2012 the legislature enacted a law doing just that.

The 2012 Act quickly came under attack. The major professional sports leagues and the NCAA brought an action in federal court against the New Jersey Governor and other state officials (hereinafter New Jersey), seeking to enjoin the new law on the ground that it violated PASPA. In response, the State argued, among other things, that PASPA unconstitutionally infringed the State's sovereign authority to end its sports gambling ban.

In making this argument, the State relied primarily on two cases, *New York v. United States* (1992), and *Printz v. United States* (1997), in which we struck down federal laws based on what has been dubbed the "anticommandeering" principle. In *New York,* we held that a federal law unconstitutionally ordered the State to regulate in accordance with federal standards, and in *Printz,* we found that another federal statute unconstitutionally compelled state officers to enforce federal law.

Relying on these cases, New Jersey argued that PASPA is similarly flawed because it regulates a State's exercise of its lawmaking power by prohibiting it from modifying or repealing its laws prohibiting sports gambling. The plaintiffs countered that PASPA is critically different from the commandeering cases because it does not command the States to take any affirmative act. Without an affirmative federal command to *do* something, the plaintiffs insisted, there can be no claim of commandeering.

The District Court found no anticommandeering violation, and a divided panel of the Third Circuit affirmed. The panel thought it significant that PASPA does not impose any affirmative command. . . .

New Jersey filed a petition for a writ of certiorari, raising the anticommandeering issue. Opposing certiorari, the United States told this Court that PASPA does not require New Jersey "to leave in place the state-law prohibitions against sports gambling that it had chosen to adopt prior to PASPA's enactment. To the contrary, New Jersey is free to repeal those prohibitions in whole or in part." We denied review.

Picking up on the suggestion that a partial repeal would be allowed, the New Jersey Legislature enacted the law now before us. The 2014 Act declares that it is not to be interpreted as causing the State to authorize, license, sponsor, operate, advertise, or promote sports gambling. Instead, it is framed as a repealer. Specifically, it repeals the provisions of state law prohibiting sports gambling insofar as they concerned the "placement and acceptance of wagers" on sporting events by persons 21 years of age or older at a horseracing track or a casino or gambling house in Atlantic City. The new law also specified that the repeal was effective only as to wagers on sporting events not involving a New Jersey college team or a collegiate event taking place in the State.

Predictably, the same plaintiffs promptly commenced a new action in federal court. They won in the District Court, and the case was eventually heard by the Third Circuit sitting en banc. The en banc court affirmed. . . . Having found that the 2014 Act violates PASPA's prohibition of state authorization of sports gambling schemes, the court went on to hold that this prohibition does not contravene the anticommandeering principle because it "does not command states to take affirmative actions."

We granted review to decide the important constitutional question presented by these cases. . . .

III

A

The anticommandeering doctrine may sound arcane, but it is simply the expression of a fundamental structural decision incorporated into the Constitution, *i.e.,* the decision to withhold from Congress the power to issue orders directly to the States. When the original States declared their independence, they claimed the powers inherent in sovereignty—in the words of the Declaration of Independence, the authority "to do all . . . Acts and Things which Independent States may of right do." The Constitution limited but did not abolish the sovereign powers of the States, which retained "a residuary and inviolable sovereignty." The Federalist No. 39. Thus, both the Federal Government and the States wield sovereign powers, and that is why our system of government is said to be one of "dual sovereignty." *Gregory v. Ashcroft* (1991).

The Constitution limits state sovereignty in several ways. It directly prohibits the States from exercising some attributes of sovereignty. See, *e.g.,* Art. I, §10. Some grants of power to the Federal Government have been held to impose implicit restrictions on the States. And the Constitution indirectly restricts the States by granting certain legislative powers to Congress, see Art. I, §8, while providing in the Supremacy Clause that federal law is the "supreme Law of the Land . . . any Thing in the Constitution or Laws of any State to the Contrary not-withstanding," Art. VI, cl. 2. This means that when federal and state law conflict, federal law prevails and state law is preempted.

The legislative powers granted to Congress are sizable, but they are not unlimited. The Constitution confers on Congress not plenary legislative power but only certain enumerated powers. Therefore, all other legislative power is reserved for the States, as the Tenth Amendment confirms. And conspicuously absent from the list of powers given to Congress is the power to issue direct orders to the governments of the States. The anticommandeering doctrine simply represents the recognition of this limit on congressional authority.

Although the anticommandeering principle is simple and basic, it did not emerge in our cases until relatively recently, when Congress attempted in a few isolated instances to extend its authority in unprecedented ways. The pioneering case was *New York v. United States* (1992), which concerned a federal law that required a State, under certain circumstances, either to "take title" to low-level radioactive waste or to "regulat[e] according to the instructions of Congress." In enacting this provision, Congress issued orders to either the legislative or executive branch of state government (depending on the branch authorized by state law to take the actions demanded). Either way, the Court held, the provision was unconstitutional because "the Constitution does not empower Congress to subject state governments to this type of instruction." . . .

The opinion recalled that "no Member of the Court ha[d] ever suggested" that even "a particularly strong federal interest" "would enable Congress to command a state government to enact *state* regulation." . . . "Congress may not simply 'commandee[r] the legislative processes of the States by directly compelling them to enact and enforce a federal regulatory program.'"

Five years after *New York,* the Court applied the same principles to a federal statute requiring state and local law enforcement officers to perform background checks and related tasks in connection with applications for handgun licenses. *Printz.* Holding this provision unconstitutional, the Court put the point succinctly: "The Federal Government" may not "command the States' officers, or those of their political subdivisions, to administer or enforce a federal regulatory program." This rule applies, *Printz* held, not only to state officers with policy-making responsibility but also to those assigned more mundane tasks.

B

Our opinions in *New York* and *Printz* explained why adherence to the anticommandeering principle is important. Without attempting a complete survey, we mention several reasons that are significant here.

First, the rule serves as "one of the Constitution's structural protections of liberty." *Printz*. "The Constitution does not protect the sovereignty of States for the benefit of the States or state governments as abstract political entities." "To the contrary, the Constitution divides authority between federal and state governments for the protection of individuals." " '[A] healthy balance of power between the States and the Federal Government [reduces] the risk of tyranny and abuse from either front.' "

Second, the anticommandeering rule promotes political accountability. When Congress itself regulates, the responsibility for the benefits and burdens of the regulation is apparent. Voters who like or dislike the effects of the regulation know who to credit or blame. By contrast, if a State imposes regulations only because it has been commanded to do so by Congress, responsibility is blurred.

Third, the anticommandeering principle prevents Congress from shifting the costs of regulation to the States. If Congress enacts a law and requires enforcement by the Executive Branch, it must appropriate the funds needed to administer the program. It is pressured to weigh the expected benefits of the program against its costs. But if Congress can compel the States to enact and enforce its program, Congress need not engage in any such analysis.

IV

The PASPA provision at issue here — prohibiting state authorization of sports gambling — violates the anticommandeering rule. That provision unequivocally dictates what a state legislature may and may not do. And this is true under either our interpretation or that advocated by respondents and the United States. In either event, state legislatures are put under the direct control of Congress. It is as if federal officers were installed in state legislative chambers and were armed with the authority to stop legislators from voting on any offending proposals. A more direct affront to state sovereignty is not easy to imagine.

Neither respondents nor the United States contends that Congress can compel a State to enact legislation, but they say that prohibiting a State from enacting new laws is another matter. Noting that the laws challenged in *New York* and *Printz* "told states what they must do instead of what they must not do," respondents contend that commandeering occurs "only when Congress goes beyond precluding state action and affirmatively commands it."

This distinction is empty. It was a matter of happenstance that the laws challenged in *New York* and *Printz* commanded "affirmative" action as opposed to imposing a prohibition. The basic principle — that Congress cannot issue direct orders to state legislatures — applies in either event.

Here is an illustration. PASPA includes an exemption for States that permitted sports betting at the time of enactment, §3704, but suppose Congress did not adopt such an exemption. Suppose Congress ordered States with legalized sports betting to take the affirmative step of criminalizing that activity and ordered the remaining States to retain their laws prohibiting sports betting. There is no good reason why the former would intrude more deeply on state sovereignty than the latter. . . .

V

Respondents and the United States defend the anti-authorization prohibition on the ground that it constitutes a valid preemption provision, but it is no such thing. Preemption is based on the Supremacy Clause, and that Clause is not an independent grant of legislative power to Congress. Instead, it simply provides "a rule of decision." It specifies that federal law is supreme in case of a conflict with state law. Therefore, in order for the PASPA provision to preempt state law, it must satisfy two requirements. First, it must represent the exercise of a power conferred on Congress by the Constitution; pointing to the Supremacy Clause will not do. Second, since the Constitution "confers upon Congress the power to regulate individuals, not States," the PASPA provision at issue must be best read as one that regulates private actors. . . .

[I]t is clear that the PASPA provision prohibiting state authorization of sports gambling is not a preemption provision because there is no way in which this provision can be understood as a regulation of private actors. It certainly does not confer any federal rights on private actors interested in conducting sports gambling operations. (It does not give them a federal right to engage in sports gambling.) Nor does it impose any federal restrictions on private actors. If a private citizen or company started a sports gambling operation, either with or without state authorization, §3702(1) would not be violated and would not provide any ground for a civil action by the Attorney General or any other party. Thus, there is simply no way to understand the provision prohibiting state authorization as anything other than a direct command to the States. And that is exactly what the anticommandeering rule does not allow.

In so holding, we recognize that a closely related provision of PASPA, §3702(2), *does* restrict private conduct, but that is not the provision challenged by petitioners.

* * *

The legalization of sports gambling is a controversial subject. Supporters argue that legalization will produce revenue for the States and critically weaken illegal sports betting operations, which are often run by organized crime. Opponents contend that legalizing sports gambling will hook the young on gambling, encourage people of modest means to squander their savings and earnings, and corrupt professional and college sports.

The legalization of sports gambling requires an important policy choice, but the choice is not ours to make. Congress can regulate sports gambling directly, but if it elects not to do so, each State is free to act on its own. Our job is to interpret the law Congress has enacted and decide whether it is consistent with the Constitution. PASPA is not. PASPA "regulate[s] state governments' regulation" of their citizens, *New York*. The Constitution gives Congress no such power.

The judgment of the Third Circuit is reversed.

It is so ordered.

JUSTICE THOMAS, concurring.

I join the Court's opinion in its entirety. I write separately, however, to express my growing discomfort with our modern severability precedents.

I agree with the Court that the Professional and Amateur Sports Protection Act (PASPA) exceeds Congress' Article I authority to the extent it prohibits New Jersey from "authoriz[ing]" or "licens[ing]" sports gambling. Unlike the dissent, I do "doubt" that Congress can prohibit sports gambling that does not cross state lines. *Post* (opinion of Ginsburg, J.); see *License Tax Cases* (1867) (holding that Congress has "no power" to regulate "the internal commerce or domestic trade of the States," including the intrastate sale of lottery tickets); *United States v. Lopez* (1995) (Thomas, J., concurring) (documenting why the Commerce Clause does not permit Congress to regulate purely local activities that have a substantial effect on interstate commerce). But even assuming the Commerce Clause allows Congress to prohibit intrastate sports gambling "directly," it "does not authorize Congress to regulate state governments' regulation of interstate commerce." *New York v. United States* (1992). The Necessary and Proper Clause does not give Congress this power either, as a law is not "proper" if it "subvert[s] basic principles of federalism and dual sovereignty." *Gonzales v. Raich* (2005) (Thomas, J., dissenting). Commandeering the States, as PASPA does, subverts those principles. See *Printz v. United States* (1997).

Because PASPA is at least partially unconstitutional, our precedents instruct us to determine "which portions of the . . . statute we must sever and excise." *United States v. Booker* (2005). . . .

In sum, our modern severability precedents are in tension with longstanding limits on the judicial power. And, though no party in this case has asked us to reconsider these precedents, at some point, it behooves us to do so.

JUSTICE GINSBURG, with whom JUSTICE SOTOMAYOR joins, and with whom JUSTICE BREYER joins in part, dissenting.

The petition for certiorari filed by the Governor of New Jersey invited the Court to consider a sole question: "Does a federal statute that prohibits modification or repeal of state-law prohibitions on private conduct impermissibly commandeer the regulatory power of States in contravention of *New York v. United States?*"

Assuming, *arguendo,* a "yes" answer to that question, there would be no cause to deploy a wrecking ball destroying the Professional and Amateur Sports Protection Act (PASPA) in its entirety, as the Court does today. . . . Nor is there any doubt that Congress has power to regulate gambling on a nationwide basis, authority Congress exercised in PASPA. See *Gonzales v. Raich* (2005) ("Our case law firmly establishes Congress' power to regulate purely local activities that are part of an economic 'class of activities' that have a substantial effect on interstate commerce.").

Surely, the accountability concern that gave birth to the anticommandeering doctrine is not implicated in any federal proscription other than the bans on States' authorizing and licensing sports-gambling schemes. The concern triggering the doctrine arises only "where the Federal Government compels States to regulate" or to enforce federal law, thereby creating the appearance that state officials are responsible for policies Congress forced them to enact. *New York v. United States* (1992). If States themselves and private parties may not operate sports-gambling schemes, responsibility for the proscriptions is hardly blurred. It cannot be maintained credibly that state officials have anything to do with the restraints. Unmistakably, the foreclosure of sports-gambling schemes, whether state run or privately operated, is chargeable to congressional, not state, legislative action. . . . The Court wields an ax to cut down §3702 instead of using a scalpel to trim the statute. . . .

* * *

In PASPA, shorn of the prohibition on modifying or repealing state law, Congress permissibly exercised its authority to regulate commerce by instructing States and private parties to refrain from operating sports-gambling schemes. On no rational ground can it be concluded that Congress would have preferred no statute at all if it could not prohibit States from authorizing or licensing such schemes. Deleting the alleged "commandeering" directions would free the statute to accomplish just what Congress legitimately sought to achieve: stopping sports-gambling regimes while making it clear that the stoppage is attributable to federal, not state, action. I therefore dissent from the Court's determination to destroy PASPA rather than salvage the statute.

STUDY GUIDE:

- In 1990, Congress enacted the Copyright Remedy Clarification Act of 1990. This law purported to abrogate state sovereign immunity for copyright violations. Did Congress make sufficient findings to satisfy the test from *City of Boerne v. Flores* (1997)?
- The Rehnquist Court decided several sovereign immunity cases by a 5-4 vote. *Allen v. Cooper* (2020), however, was unanimous. Even Justices Breyer and Ginsburg, who dissented in *Seminole Tribe*, joined the majority. Has the Roberts Court acquiesced to this aspect of the Rehnquist Court's federalism jurisprudence?

Allen v. Cooper
589 U.S. ___ (2020)

JUSTICE KAGAN delivered the opinion of the Court.

In two basically identical statutes passed in the early 1990s, Congress sought to strip the States of their sovereign immunity from patent and copyright infringement suits. Not long after, this Court held in *Florida Prepaid Postsecondary Ed. Expense Bd. v. College Savings Bank* (1999), that the patent statute lacked a valid constitutional basis. Today, we take up the copyright statute. We find that our decision in *Florida Prepaid* compels the same conclusion.

I

In 1717, the pirate Edward Teach, better known as Blackbeard, captured a French slave ship in the West Indies and renamed her *Queen Anne's Revenge.*

The vessel became his flagship. Carrying some 40 cannons and 300 men, the *Revenge* took many prizes as she sailed around the Caribbean and up the North American coast. But her reign over those seas was short-lived. In 1718, the ship ran aground on a sandbar a mile off Beaufort, North Carolina. Blackbeard and most of his crew escaped without harm. Not so the *Revenge*. She sank beneath the waters, where she lay undisturbed for nearly 300 years.

In 1996, a marine salvage company named Intersal, Inc., discovered the shipwreck. Under federal and state law, the wreck belongs to North Carolina. But the State contracted with Intersal to take charge of the recovery activities. Intersal in turn retained petitioner Frederick Allen, a local videographer, to document the operation. For over a decade, Allen created videos and photos of divers' efforts to salvage the *Revenge*'s guns, anchors, and other remains. He registered copyrights in all those works.

This suit arises from North Carolina's publication of some of Allen's videos and photos. Allen first protested in 2013 that the State was infringing his copyrights by uploading his work to its website without permission. To address that allegation, North Carolina agreed to a settlement paying Allen $15,000 and laying out the parties' respective rights to the materials. But Allen and the State soon found themselves embroiled in another dispute. Allen complained that North Carolina had impermissibly posted five of his videos online and used one of his photos in a newsletter. When the State declined to admit wrongdoing, Allen filed this action in Federal District Court. It charges the State with copyright infringement (call it a modern form of piracy) and seeks money damages. . . .

II

North Carolina moved to dismiss the suit on the ground of sovereign immunity. It invoked the general rule that federal courts cannot hear suits brought by individuals against nonconsenting States. But Allen responded that an exception to the rule applied because Congress had abrogated the States' sovereign immunity from suits like his. The Copyright Remedy Clarification Act of 1990 (CRCA or Act) provides that a State "shall not be immune, under the Eleventh Amendment [or] any other doctrine of sovereign immunity, from suit in Federal court" for copyright infringement. And the Act specifies that in such a suit a State will be liable, and subject to remedies, "in the same manner and to the same extent as" a private party That meant, Allen contended, that his suit against North Carolina could go forward.

In our constitutional scheme, a federal court generally may not hear a suit brought by any person against a nonconsenting State. That bar is nowhere explicitly set out in the Constitution. The text of the Eleventh Amendment (the single most relevant provision) applies only if the plaintiff is not a citizen of the defendant State.[2] But this Court has long understood that Amendment to "stand not so

---

2. The Eleventh Amendment reads: "The Judicial Power of the United States shall not be construed to extend to any suit in law or equity, commenced or prosecuted against one of the United States by Citizens of another State, or by Citizens or Subjects of any Foreign State."

much for what it says" as for the broader "presupposition of our constitutional structure which it confirms." *Blatchford v. Native Village of Noatak* (1991). That premise, the Court has explained, has several parts. First, "each State is a sovereign entity in our federal system." *Seminole Tribe of Fla. v. Florida* (1996). Next, "[i]t is inherent in the nature of sovereignty not to be amenable to [a] suit" absent consent. *Id.*, at 54, n. 13 (quoting The Federalist No. 81 ((A. Hamilton)). And last, that fundamental aspect of sovereignty constrains federal "judicial authority." *Blatchford.*

But not entirely. This Court has permitted a federal court to entertain a suit against a nonconsenting State on two conditions. First, Congress must have enacted "unequivocal statutory language" abrogating the States' immunity from the suit. *Seminole Tribe* (internal quotation marks omitted); see *Dellmuth v. Muth* (1989) (requiring Congress to "mak[e] its intention unmistakably clear"). And second, some constitutional provision must allow Congress to have thus encroached on the States' sovereignty. Not even the most crystalline abrogation can take effect unless it is "a valid exercise of constitutional authority." *Kimel v. Florida Bd. of Regents* (2000).

No one here disputes that Congress used clear enough language to abrogate the States' immunity from copyright infringement suits. The CRCA provides that States "shall not be immune" from those actions in federal court. And the Act specifies that a State stands in the identical position as a private defendant— exposed to liability and remedies "in the same manner and to the same extent." So there is no doubt what Congress meant to accomplish. Indeed, this Court held in *Florida Prepaid* that the essentially verbatim provisions of the Patent Remedy Act "could not have [made] any clearer" Congress's intent to remove the States' immunity.

The contested question is whether Congress had authority to take that step. Allen maintains that it did, under either of two constitutional provisions. He first points to the clause in Article I empowering Congress to provide copyright protection. If that fails, he invokes Section 5 of the Fourteenth Amendment, which authorizes Congress to "enforce" the commands of the Due Process Clause. Neither contention can succeed. The slate on which we write today is anything but clean. *Florida Prepaid*, along with other precedent, forecloses each of Allen's arguments.

A

Congress has power under Article I "[t]o promote the Progress of Science and useful Arts, by securing for limited Times to Authors and Inventors the exclusive Right to their respective Writings and Discoveries." §8, cl. 8. That provision—call it the Intellectual Property Clause—enables Congress to grant both copyrights and patents. And the monopoly rights so given impose a corresponding duty (*i.e.,* not to infringe) on States no less than private parties.

In Allen's view, Congress's authority to abrogate sovereign immunity from copyright suits naturally follows. Abrogation is the single best—or maybe, he says, the only — way for Congress to "secur[e]" a copyright holder's "exclusive Right[s]" as against a State's intrusion. So, Allen contends, the authority to take that step must fall within the Article I grant of power to protect intellectual property.

The problem for Allen is that this Court has already rejected his theory. The Intellectual Property Clause, as just noted, covers copyrights and patents alike. So it was the first place the *Florida Prepaid* Court looked when deciding whether the Patent Remedy Act validly stripped the States of immunity from infringement suits. . . . Congress could not use its Article I power over patents to remove the States' immunity. We based that conclusion on *Seminole Tribe v. Florida*, decided three years earlier. There, the Court had held that "Article I cannot be used to circumvent" the limits sovereign immunity "place[s] upon federal jurisdiction." That proscription ended the matter. Because Congress could not "abrogate state sovereign immunity [under] Article I," *Florida Prepaid* explained, the Intellectual Property Clause could not support the Patent Remedy Act. And to extend the point to this case: if not the Patent Remedy Act, not its copyright equivalent either, and for the same reason. Here too, the power to "secur[e]" an intellectual property owner's "exclusive Right" under Article I stops when it runs into sovereign immunity.

Allen claims, however, that a later case offers an exit ramp from *Florida Prepaid*. In *Central Va. Community College v. Katz* (2006), we held that Article I's Bankruptcy Clause enables Congress to subject nonconsenting States to bankruptcy proceedings (there, to recover a preferential transfer). We thus exempted the Bankruptcy Clause from *Seminole Tribe*'s general rule that Article I cannot justify haling a State into federal court. In bankruptcy, we decided, sovereign immunity has no place. But if that is true, Allen asks, why not say the same thing here? Allen reads *Katz* as "adopt[ing] a clause-by-clause approach to evaluating whether a particular clause of Article I" allows the abrogation of sovereign immunity. And he claims that the Intellectual Property Clause "supplies singular warrant" for Congress to take that step. That is so, Allen reiterates, because "Congress could not 'secur[e]' authors' 'exclusive Right' to their works if [it] were powerless" to make States pay for infringing conduct.

But everything in *Katz* is about and limited to the Bankruptcy Clause; the opinion reflects what might be called bankruptcy exceptionalism. In part, *Katz* rested on the "singular nature" of bankruptcy jurisdiction. . . . The nation's first Bankruptcy Act, for example, empowered those courts to order that States release people they were holding in debtors' prisons. So through and through, we thought, the Bankruptcy Clause embraced the idea that federal courts could impose on state sovereignty. In that, it was *sui generis* — again, "unique" — among Article I's grants of authority. . . .

B

Section 5 of the Fourteenth Amendment, unlike almost all of Article I, can authorize Congress to strip the States of immunity. The Fourteenth Amendment "fundamentally altered the balance of state and federal power" that the original

Constitution and the Eleventh Amendment struck. *Seminole Tribe.* Its first section imposes prohibitions on the States, including (as relevant here) that none may "deprive any person of life, liberty, or property, without due process of law." Section 5 then gives Congress the "power to enforce, by appropriate legislation," those limitations on the States' authority. That power, the Court has long held, may enable Congress to abrogate the States' immunity and thus subject them to suit in federal court. See *Fitzpatrick v. Bitzer* (1976).

For an abrogation statute to be "appropriate" under Section 5, it must be tailored to "remedy or prevent" conduct infringing the Fourteenth Amendment's substantive prohibitions. *City of Boerne v. Flores* (1997). Congress can permit suits against States for actual violations of the rights guaranteed in Section 1. And to deter those violations, it can allow suits against States for "a somewhat broader swath of conduct," including acts constitutional in themselves. *Kimel.* But Congress cannot use its "power to enforce" the Fourteenth Amendment to alter what that Amendment bars. *Kimel* (prohibiting Congress from "substantively redefin[ing]" the Fourteenth Amendment's requirements). That means a congressional abrogation is valid under Section 5 only if it sufficiently connects to conduct courts have held Section 1 to proscribe.

To decide whether a law passes muster, this Court has framed a type of means-end test. For Congress's action to fall within its Section 5 authority, we have said, "[t]here must be a congruence and proportionality between the injury to be prevented or remedied and the means adopted to that end." *Boerne.* On the one hand, courts are to consider the constitutional problem Congress faced—both the nature and the extent of state conduct violating the Fourteenth Amendment. That assessment usually (though not inevitably) focuses on the legislative record, which shows the evidence Congress had before it of a constitutional wrong. See *Florida Prepaid.* On the other hand, courts are to examine the scope of the response Congress chose to address that injury. Here, a critical question is how far, and for what reasons, Congress has gone beyond redressing actual constitutional violations. Hard problems often require forceful responses and, as noted above, Section 5 allows Congress to "enact[] reasonably prophylactic legislation" to deter constitutional harm. *Kimel*; *Boerne* (Congress's conclusions on that score are "entitled to much deference"). But "[s]trong measures appropriate to address one harm may be an unwarranted response to another, lesser one." *Boerne.* Always, what Congress has done must be in keeping with the Fourteenth Amendment rules it has the power to "enforce."

All this raises the question: When does the Fourteenth Amendment care about copyright infringement? Sometimes, no doubt. Copyrights are a form of property. See *Fox Film Corp. v. Doyal* (1932). And the Fourteenth Amendment bars the States from "depriv[ing]" a person of property "without due process of law." But even if sometimes, by no means always. Under our precedent, a merely negligent act does not "deprive" a person of property. So an infringement must be intentional, or at least reckless, to come within the reach of the Due Process Clause. And more: A State cannot violate that Clause unless it fails to offer an adequate remedy for an infringement, because such a remedy itself satisfies the demand of "due process." That means within the broader world of state copyright infringement is a smaller one where the Due Process Clause comes into play.

Because the same is true of patent infringement, *Florida Prepaid* again serves as the critical precedent. That decision defined the scope of unconstitutional infringement in line with the caselaw cited above—as intentional conduct for which there is no adequate state remedy. It then searched for evidence of that sort of infringement in the legislative record of the Patent Remedy Act. And it determined that the statute's abrogation of immunity—again, the equivalent of the CRCA's—was out of all proportion to what it found. That analysis is the starting point of our inquiry here. And indeed, it must be the ending point too unless the evidence of unconstitutional infringement is materially different for copyrights than patents. Consider once more, then, *Florida Prepaid*, now not on Article I but on Section 5.

In enacting the Patent Remedy Act, *Florida Prepaid* found, Congress did not identify a pattern of unconstitutional patent infringement. To begin with, we explained, there was only thin evidence of States infringing patents at all— putting aside whether those actions violated due process. The House Report, recognizing that "many states comply with patent law," offered just two examples of patent infringement suits against the States. . . . What was more, there was no evidence that any instance of infringement by States crossed constitutional lines.

Given that absence of evidence, *Florida Prepaid* held, the Patent Remedy Act swept too far. Recall what the Patent Remedy Act did—and did not. It abrogated sovereign immunity for any and every patent suit, thereby "plac[ing] States on the same footing as private parties." It did not set any limits. . . . No, it exposed all States to the hilt—on a record that failed to show they had caused any discernible constitutional harm (or, indeed, much harm at all). That imbalance made it impossible to view the legislation "as responsive to, or designed to prevent, unconstitutional behavior." The statute's "indiscriminate scope" was too "out of proportion" to any due process problem. It aimed not to correct such a problem, but to "provide a uniform remedy for patent infringement" writ large. The Patent Remedy Act, in short, did not "enforce" Section 1 of the Fourteenth Amendment—and so was not "appropriate" under Section 5.

Could, then, this case come out differently? Given the identical scope of the CRCA and Patent Remedy Act, that could happen only if the former law responded to materially stronger evidence of infringement, especially of the unconstitutional kind. . . . As an initial matter, the concrete evidence of States infringing copyrights (even ignoring whether those acts violate due process) is scarcely more impressive than what the *Florida Prepaid* Court saw. . . . This is not, to put the matter charitably, the stuff from which Section 5 legislation ordinarily arises.

Under *Florida Prepaid*, the CRCA thus must fail our "congruence and proportionality" test. As just shown, the evidence of Fourteenth Amendment injury supporting the CRCA and the Patent Remedy Act is equivalent—for both, that is, exceedingly slight. And the scope of the two statutes is identical—extending to every infringement case against a State. It follows that the balance the laws strike between constitutional wrong and statutory remedy is correspondingly askew. In this case, as in *Florida Prepaid*, the law's "indiscriminate scope" is "out of pro-portion" to any due process problem. In this case, as in that one, the statute aims to "provide a uniform remedy" for statutory infringement, rather than to redress or prevent unconstitutional conduct. And so in this case, as in that one, the law is invalid under Section 5.

That conclusion, however, need not prevent Congress from passing a valid copyright abrogation law in the future. In doing so, Congress would presumably approach the issue differently than when it passed the CRCA. At that time, the Court had not yet decided *Seminole Tribe*, so Congress probably thought that Article I could support its all-out abrogation of immunity. And to the extent it relied on Section 5, Congress acted before this Court created the "congruence and proportionality" test. For that reason, Congress likely did not appreciate the importance of linking the scope of its abrogation to the redress or preven-tion of unconstitutional injuries — and of creating a legislative record to back up that connection. But going forward, Congress will know those rules. And under them, if it detects violations of due process, then it may enact a proportionate response. That kind of tailored statute can effectively stop States from behaving as copyright pirates. Even while respecting constitutional limits, it can bring digital Blackbeards to justice.

III

Florida Prepaid all but prewrote our decision today. That precedent made clear that Article I's Intellectual Property Clause could not provide the basis for an abrogation of sovereign immunity. And it held that Section 5 of the Fourteenth Amendment could not support an abrogation on a legislative record like the one here. For both those reasons, we affirm the judgment below.

It is so ordered.

JUSTICE THOMAS, concurring in part and concurring in the judgment.

I agree with the Court's conclusion that the Copyright Remedy Clarification Act of 1990 does not validly abrogate States' sovereign immunity. But I cannot join the Court's opinion in its entirety. I write separately to note two disagree-ments and one question that remains open for resolution in a future case.

First, although I agree that *Florida Prepaid Postsecondary Ed. Expense Bd. v. College Savings Bank* (1999), is binding precedent, I cannot join the Court's discussion of *stare decisis*. The Court claims we need " 'special justification[s]' " to overrule precedent because error alone "cannot overcome *stare decisis*." *Ante*, at 9–10. That approach "does not comport with our judicial duty under Article III." *Gamble v. United States* (2019) (Thomas, J., concurring). If our decision in *Florida Prepaid* were demonstrably erroneous, the Court would be obligated to "correct the error, regardless of whether other factors support overruling the precedent."

Here, adherence to our precedent is warranted because petitioners have not demonstrated that our decision in *Florida Prepaid* "is incorrect, much less demonstrably erroneous." *Gamble*. The Court in *Florida Prepaid* correctly concluded that "Congress may not abrogate state sovereign immunity pursuant to its Article I powers," including its powers under the Intellectual Property Clause. Petitioners' claims to the contrary are unpersuasive.*

Second, I do not join the Court's discussion regarding future copyright legislation. In my view, we should opine on "only the case before us in light of the record before us." *Manhattan Community Access Corp. v. Halleck* (2019). We should not purport to advise Congress on how it might exercise its legislative authority, nor give our blessing to hypothetical statutes or legislative records not at issue here.

Finally, I believe the question whether copyrights are property within the original meaning of the Fourteenth Amendment's Due Process Clause remains open. The Court relies on *Fox Film Corp. v. Doyal* (1932), to conclude that "[c]opyrights are a form of property." But *Fox Film Corp.* addressed "property" in the context of state tax laws, not the Due Process Clause. And although we stated in *Florida Prepaid* that patents are "property" for due process purposes, we did not analyze the Fourteenth Amendment's text, and neither of the cases we cited involved due process. see also Merrill, The Landscape of Constitutional Property, 86 Va. L. Rev. 885, 887 (2000) (noting that the "Court has not always been attentive to the 'property' threshold" of the Due Process Clauses). Because the parties agree that petitioners' copyrights are property, and because the Fourteenth Amendment does not authorize this statute's abrogation of state sovereign immunity either way, we need not resolve this open question today. I would, however, be willing to consider the matter in an appropriate case.

For these reasons, I join all of the Court's opinion except for the final paragraph in Part II–A and the final paragraph in Part II–B.

Justice BREYER, with whom Justice GINSBURG joins, concurring in the judgment.

. . . To subject nonconsenting States to private suits for copyright or patent infringement, says the Court, Congress must endeavor to pass a more "tailored statute" than the one before us, relying not on the Intellectual Property Clause, but on §5 of the Fourteenth Amendment. Whether a future legislative effort along those lines will pass constitutional muster is anyone's guess. But faced with the risk of unfairness to authors and inventors alike, perhaps Congress will venture into this great constitutional unknown.

That our sovereign-immunity precedents can be said to call for so uncertain a voyage suggests that something is amiss. Indeed, we went astray in *Seminole Tribe of Fla. v. Florida* (1996), as I have consistently maintained. See *College Savings Bank v. Florida Prepaid Postsecondary Ed. Expense Bd.*,

---

* Note: Because I adhere to our precedents regarding Article I and state sovereign immunity, I continue to believe that Central Va. Community College v. Katz (2006), was wrongly decided. The Court today rightfully limits that decision to the Bankruptcy Clause context, calling it a "good-for-one-clause-only holding". I would go a step further and recognize that the Court's decision in Katz is not good for even that clause.

(1999) (dissenting opinion); *Federal Maritime Comm'n v. South Carolina Ports Authority* (2002) (same). We erred again in *Florida Prepaid Postsecondary Ed. Expense Bd. v. College Savings Bank* (1999), by holding that Congress exceeded its §5 powers when it passed a patent counterpart to the copyright statute at issue here. But recognizing that my longstanding view has not carried the day, and that the Court's decision in *Florida Prepaid* controls this case, I concur in the judgment.

Chiafalo v. Washington
591 U.S. ___ (2020)

JUSTICE KAGAN delivered the opinion of the Court.

Every four years, millions of Americans cast a ballot for a presidential candidate. Their votes, though, actually go toward selecting members of the Electoral College, whom each State appoints based on the popular returns. Those few "electors" then choose the President.

The States have devised mechanisms to ensure that the electors they appoint vote for the presidential candidate their citizens have preferred. With two partial exceptions, every State appoints a slate of electors selected by the political party whose candidate has won the State's popular vote. Most States also compel electors to pledge in advance to support the nominee of that party. This Court upheld such a pledge requirement decades ago, rejecting the argument that the Constitution "demands absolute freedom for the elector to vote his own choice." *Ray* v. *Blair* (1952).

Today, we consider whether a State may also penalize an elector for breaking his pledge and voting for someone other than the presidential candidate who won his State's popular vote. We hold that a State may do so.

I

Our Constitution's method of picking Presidents emerged from an eleventh-hour compromise. The issue, one delegate to the Convention remarked, was "the most difficult of all [that] we have had to decide." 2 Records of the Federal Convention of 1787 (Farrand). Despite long debate and many votes, the delegates could not reach an agreement. In the dying days of summer, they referred the matter to the so-called Committee of Eleven to devise a solution. The Committee returned with a proposal for the Electoral College. Just two days later, the delegates accepted the recommendation with but a few tweaks. James Madison later wrote to a friend that the "difficulty of finding an unexceptionable [selection] process" was "deeply felt by the Convention." Because "the final arrangement of it took place in the latter stage of the Session," Madison continued, "it was not exempt from a degree of the hurrying influence produced by fatigue and impatience in all such Bodies: tho' the degree was much less than usually prevails in them." Whether less or not, the delegates soon finished their work and departed for home.

The provision they approved about presidential electors is fairly slim. Article II, §1, cl. 2 says:

> "Each State shall appoint, in such Manner as the Legislature thereof may direct, a Number of Electors, equal to the whole Number of Senators and Representatives to which the State may be entitled in the Congress: but no Senator or Representative, or Person holding an Office of Trust or Profit under the United States, shall be appointed an Elector."

The next clause (but don't get attached: it will soon be superseded) set out the procedures the electors were to follow in casting their votes. In brief, each member of the College would cast votes for two candidates in the presidential field. The candidate with the greatest number of votes, assuming he had a majority, would become President. The runner-up would become Vice President. If no one had a majority, the House of Representatives would take over and decide the winner.

That plan failed to anticipate the rise of political parties, and soon proved unworkable. The Nation's first contested presidential election occurred in 1796, after George Washington's retirement. John Adams came in first among the candidates, and Thomas Jefferson second. That meant the leaders of the era's two warring political parties—the Federalists and the Republicans—became President and Vice President respectively. (One might think of this as fodder for a new season of Veep.) Four years later, a different problem arose. Jefferson and Aaron Burr ran that year as a Republican Party ticket, with the former meant to be President and the latter meant to be Vice. For that plan to succeed, Jefferson had to come in first and Burr just behind him. Instead, Jefferson came in first and Burr . . . did too. Every elector who voted for Jefferson also voted for Burr, producing a tie. That threw the election into the House of Representatives, which took no fewer than 36 ballots to elect Jefferson. (Alexander Hamilton secured his place on the Broadway stage—but possibly in the cemetery too—by lobbying Federalists in the House to tip the election to Jefferson, whom he loathed but viewed as less of an existential threat to the Republic.) By then, everyone had had enough of the Electoral College's original voting rules.

The result was the Twelfth Amendment, whose main part provided that electors would vote separately for President and Vice President. The Amendment, ratified in 1804, says:

> "The Electors shall meet in their respective states and vote by ballot for President and Vice-President . . . ; they shall name in their ballots the person voted for as President, and in distinct ballots the person voted for as Vice-President, and they shall make distinct lists of all persons voted for as President, and of all persons voted for as Vice-President, and of the number of votes for each, which lists they shall sign and certify, and transmit sealed to [Congress, where] the votes shall then be counted."

The Amendment thus brought the Electoral College's voting procedures into line with the Nation's new party system.

Within a few decades, the party system also became the means of translating popular preferences within each State into Electoral College ballots. In the

Nation's earliest elections, state legislatures mostly picked the electors, with the majority party sending a delegation of its choice to the Electoral College. By 1832, though, all States but one had introduced popular presidential elections. At first, citizens voted for a slate of electors put forward by a political party, expecting that the winning slate would vote for its party's presidential (and vice presidential) nominee in the Electoral College. By the early 20th century, citizens in most States voted for the presidential candidate himself; ballots increasingly did not even list the electors. After the popular vote was counted, States appointed the electors chosen by the party whose presidential nominee had won statewide, again expecting that they would vote for that candidate in the Electoral College.[3]

In the 20th century, many States enacted statutes meant to guarantee that outcome — that is, to prohibit so-called faithless voting. Rather than just assume that party-picked electors would vote for their party's winning nominee, those States insist that they do so. As of now, 32 States and the District of Columbia have such statutes on their books. They are typically called pledge laws because most demand that electors take a formal oath or pledge to cast their ballot for their party's presidential (and vice presidential) candidate. Others merely impose that duty by law. Either way, the statutes work to ensure that the electors vote for the candidate who got the most statewide votes in the presidential election.

Most relevant here, States began about 60 years ago to back up their pledge laws with some kind of sanction. By now, 15 States have such a system. Almost all of them immediately remove a faithless elector from his position, substituting an alternate whose vote the State reports instead. A few States impose a monetary fine on any elector who flouts his pledge.

Washington is one of the 15 States with a sanctions-backed pledge law designed to keep the State's electors in line with its voting citizens. As all States now do, Washington requires political parties fielding presidential candidates to nominate a slate of electors. On Election Day, the State gives voters a ballot listing only the candidates themselves. When the vote comes in, Washington moves toward appointing the electors chosen by the party whose candidate won the statewide count. But before the appointment can go into effect, each elector must "execute [a] pledge" agreeing to "mark [her] ballots" for the presidential (and vice presidential) candidate of the party nominating her. And the elector must comply with that pledge, or else face a sanction. At the time relevant here, the punishment was a civil fine of up to $1,000.

This case involves three Washington electors who violated their pledges in the 2016 presidential election. That year, Washington's voters chose Hillary Clinton

---

3. Maine and Nebraska (which, for simplicity's sake, we will ignore after this footnote) developed a more complicated system in which two electors go to the winner of the statewide vote and one goes to the winner of each congressional district. So, for example, if the Republican candidate wins the popular vote in Nebraska as a whole but loses to the Democratic candidate in one of the State's three congressional districts, the Republican will get four electors and the Democrat will get one. Here too, though, the States use party slates to pick the electors, in order to reflect the relevant popular preferences (whether in the State or in an individual district).

over Donald Trump for President. The State thus appointed as its electors the nominees of the Washington State Democratic Party. Among those Democratic electors were petitioners Peter Chiafalo, Levi Guerra, and Esther John (the Electors). All three pledged to support Hillary Clinton in the Electoral College. But as that vote approached, they decided to cast their ballots for someone else. The three hoped they could encourage other electors—particularly those from States Donald Trump had carried—to follow their example. The idea was to deprive him of a majority of electoral votes and throw the election into the House of Representatives. So the three Electors voted for Colin Powell for President. But their effort failed. Only seven electors across the Nation cast faithless votes—the most in a century, but well short of the goal. Candidate Trump became President Trump. And, more to the point here, the State fined the Electors $1,000 apiece for breaking their pledges to support the same candidate its voters had. . . .

II

As the state court recognized, this Court has considered elector pledge requirements before. Some seventy years ago Edmund Blair tried to become a presidential elector in Alabama. Like all States, Alabama lodged the authority to pick electors in the political parties fielding presidential candidates. And the Alabama Democratic Party required a pledge phrased much like Washington's today. No one could get on the party's slate of electors without agreeing to vote in the Electoral College for the Democratic presidential candidate. Blair challenged the pledge mandate. He argued that the "intention of the Founders was that [presidential] electors should exercise their judgment in voting." *Ray*. The pledge requirement, he claimed, "interfere[d] with the performance of this constitutional duty to select [a president] according to the best judgment of the elector."

Our decision in *Ray* rejected that challenge. "Neither the language of Art. II, §1, nor that of the Twelfth Amendment," we explained, prohibits a State from appointing only electors committed to vote for a party's presidential candidate. Nor did the Nation's history suggest such a bar. To the contrary, "[h]istory teaches that the electors were expected to support the party nominees" as far back as the earliest contested presidential elections. "[L]ongstanding practice" thus "weigh[ed] heavily" against Blair's claim. And current voting procedures did too. The Court noted that by then many States did not even put electors' names on a presidential ballot. The whole system presupposed that the electors, because of either an "implied" or an "oral pledge," would vote for the candidate who had won the State's popular election.

Ray, however, reserved a question not implicated in the case: Could a State enforce those pledges through legal sanctions? Or would doing so violate an elector's "constitutional freedom" to "vote as he may choose" in the Electoral College? Today, we take up that question. We uphold Washington's penalty-backed pledge law for reasons much like those given in *Ray*. The Constitution's text and the Nation's history both support allowing a State to enforce an elector's pledge to support his party's nominee—and the state voters' choice—for President.

A

Article II, §1's appointments power gives the States far-reaching authority over presidential electors, absent some other constitutional constraint.[4] As noted earlier, each State may appoint electors "in such Manner as the Legislature thereof may direct." Art. II, §1, cl. 2. This Court has described that clause as "conveying the broadest power of determination" over who becomes an elector. *McPherson v. Blacker* (1892).[5] And the power to appoint an elector (in any manner) includes power to condition his appointment—that is, to say what the elector must do for the appointment to take effect. A State can require, for example, that an elector live in the State or qualify as a regular voter during the relevant time period. Or more substantively, a State can insist (as *Ray* allowed) that the elector pledge to cast his Electoral College ballot for his party's presidential nominee, thus tracking the State's popular vote. See *Ray* (A pledge requirement "is an exercise of the state's right to appoint electors in such manner" as it chooses). Or—so long as nothing else in the Constitution poses an obstacle—a State can add, as Washington did, an associated condition of appointment: It can demand that the elector actually live up to his pledge, on pain of penalty. Which is to say that the State's appointment power, barring some outside constraint, enables the enforcement of a pledge like Washington's.[6]

And nothing in the Constitution expressly prohibits States from taking away presidential electors' voting discretion as Washington does. The Constitution is barebones about electors. Article II includes only the instruction to each State to appoint, in whatever way it likes, as many electors as it has Senators and Representatives (except that the State may not appoint members of the Federal Government). The Twelfth Amendment then tells electors to meet in their States, to vote for President and Vice President separately, and to transmit lists of all their votes to the President of the United States Senate for counting. Appointments and procedures and . . . that is all. . . .

The Electors and their *amici* object that the Framers using those words expected the Electors' votes to reflect their own judgments. Hamilton praised the Constitution for entrusting the Presidency to "men most capable of analyzing the

---

4. Checks on a State's power to appoint electors, or to impose conditions on an appointment, can theoretically come from anywhere in the Constitution. A State, for example, cannot select its electors in a way that violates the Equal Protection Clause. And if a State adopts a condition on its appointments that effectively imposes new requirements on presidential candidates, the condition may conflict with the Presidential Qualifications Clause.

5. See also *U.S. Term Limits, Inc. v. Thornton* (1995) (describing Article II, §1 as an "express delegation[ ] of power to the States"); but see *post* (Thomas, J., concurring in judgment) (continuing to press the view, taken in the *Thornton* dissent, that Article II, §1 grants the States no power at all).

6. The concurring opinion would have us make fine distinctions among state laws punishing faithless voting—treating some as conditions of appointment and others not, depending on small semantic differences. See *post* (distinguishing, for example, between Oklahoma's law fining an elector for violating his oath (to vote for his party's candidate) and Washington's law fining an elector for not voting for his party's candidate (whom he took an oath to support)). The Electors themselves raised no such argument, and they were right not to do so. No matter the precise phrasing, a law penalizing faithless voting (like a law merely barring that practice) is an exercise of the State's power to impose conditions on the appointment of electors. See *Ray v. Blair* (1952).

qualities" needed for the office, who would make their choices "under circumstances favorable to deliberation." The Federalist No. 68. So too, John Jay predicted that the Electoral College would "be composed of the most enlightened and respectable citizens," whose choices would reflect "discretion and discernment." The Federalist No. 64.

But even assuming other Framers shared that outlook, it would not be enough. Whether by choice or accident, the Framers did not reduce their thoughts about electors' discretion to the printed page. All that they put down about the electors was what we have said: that the States would appoint them, and that they would meet and cast ballots to send to the Capitol. Those sparse instructions took no position on how independent from — or how faithful to — party and popular preferences the electors' votes should be. On that score, the Constitution left much to the future. And the future did not take long in coming. Almost immediately, presidential electors became trusty transmitters of other people's decisions.

B

"Long settled and established practice" may have "great weight in a proper interpretation of constitutional provisions." *The Pocket Veto Case* (1929). As James Madison wrote, "a regular course of practice" can "liquidate & settle the meaning of " disputed or indeterminate "terms & phrases." See The Federalist No. 37. The Electors make an appeal to that kind of practice in asserting their right to independence. But "our whole experience as a Nation" points in the opposite direction. *NLRB* v. *Noel Canning* (2014). Electors have only rarely exercised discretion in casting their ballots for President. From the first, States sent them to the Electoral College — as today Washington does — to vote for pre-selected candidates, rather than to use their own judgment. And electors (or at any rate, almost all of them) rapidly settled into that non-discretionary role.

Begin at the beginning — with the Nation's first contested election in 1796. Would-be electors declared themselves for one or the other party's presidential candidate. (Recall that in this election Adams led the Federalists against Jefferson's Republicans.) In some States, legislatures chose the electors; in others, ordinary voters did. But in either case, the elector's declaration of support for a candidate — essentially a pledge — was what mattered. Or said differently, the selectors of an elector knew just what they were getting — not someone who would deliberate in good Hamiltonian fashion, but someone who would vote for their party's candidate. "[T]he presidential electors," one historian writes, "were understood to be instruments for expressing the will of those who selected them, not independent agents authorized to exercise their own judgment." Whittington, Originalism, Constitutional Construction, and the Problem of Faithless Electors (2017). And when the time came to vote in the Electoral College, all but one elector did what everyone expected, faithfully representing their selectors' choice of presidential candidate. . . .

Courts and commentators throughout the 19th century recognized the electors as merely acting on other people's preferences. Justice Story wrote that "the electors are now chosen wholly with reference to particular candidates," having either "silently" or "publicly pledge[d]" how they will vote. "[N]othing is left to the electors," he continued, "but to register [their] votes, which are already pledged." Indeed, any "exercise of an independent judgment would be treated[ ] as a political usurpation, dishonourable to the individual, and a fraud upon his constituents." . . . The electors, the Court noted, were chosen "simply to register the will of the appointing power in respect of a particular candidate." *McPherson.*

State election laws evolved to reinforce that development, ensuring that a State's electors would vote the same way as its citizens. . . . Washington's law, penalizing a pledge's breach . . . reflects a tradition more than two centuries old. In that practice, electors are not free agents; they are to vote for the candidate whom the State's voters have chosen.

The history going the opposite way is one of anomalies only. The Electors stress that since the founding, electors have cast some 180 faithless votes for either President or Vice President. But that is 180 out of over 23,000. And more than a third of the faithless votes come from 1872, when the Democratic Party's nominee (Horace Greeley) died just after Election Day. Putting those aside, faithless votes represent just one-half of one percent of the total. Still, the Electors counter, Congress has counted all those votes. But because faithless votes have never come close to affecting an outcome, only one has ever been challenged. True enough, that one was counted. But the Electors cannot rest a claim of historical tradition on one counted vote in over 200 years. And anyway, the State appointing that elector had no law requiring a pledge or otherwise barring his use of discretion. Congress's deference to a state decision to tolerate a faithless vote is no ground for rejecting a state decision to penalize one.

III

The Electors' constitutional claim has neither text nor history on its side. Article II and the Twelfth Amendment give States broad power over electors, and give electors themselves no rights. Early in our history, States decided to tie electors to the presidential choices of others, whether legislatures or citizens. Except that legislatures no longer play a role, that practice has continued for more than 200 years. Among the devices States have long used to achieve their object are pledge laws, designed to impress on electors their role as agents of others. A State follows in the same tradition if, like Washington, it chooses to sanction an elector for breaching his promise. Then too, the State instructs its electors that they have no ground for reversing the vote of millions of its citizens. That direction accords with the Constitution—as well as with the trust of a Nation that here, We the People rule.

JUSTICE THOMAS, with whom JUSTICE GORSUCH joins as to Part II, concurring in the judgment.

The Court correctly determines that States have the power to require Presidential electors to vote for the candidate chosen by the people of the State. I disagree, however, with its attempt to base that power on Article II. In my view, the Constitution is silent on States' authority to bind electors in voting. I would resolve this case by simply recognizing that "[a]ll powers that the Constitution neither delegates to the Federal Government nor prohibits to the States are controlled by the people of each State." *U.S. Term Limits, Inc. v. Thornton* (1995) (Thomas, J., dissenting).

I

A

The Constitution does not address—expressly or by necessary implication— whether States have the power to require that Presidential electors vote for the candidates chosen by the people. Article II, §1, and the Twelfth Amendment provide for the election of the President through a body of electors. But neither speaks directly to a State's power over elector voting.

The only provision in the Constitution that arguably addresses a State's power over Presidential electors is Clause 2 of Article II, §1. That Clause provides, in relevant part, that "[e]ach State shall appoint, in such Manner as the Legislature thereof may direct, a Number of Electors." As I have previously explained, this language "imposes an affirmative obligation on the States" to establish the manner for appointing electors. By using the term "shall," "the Clause expressly requires action by the States." This obligation to provide the manner of appointing electors does not expressly delegate power to States; it simply imposes an affirmative duty.

B

In a somewhat cursory analysis, the Court concludes that the States' duty to appoint electors "in such Manner as the Legislature thereof may direct," Art. II, §1, cl. 2, provides an express grant of "power to appoint an elector." As explained above, this interpretation erroneously conflates the imposition of a duty with the granting of a power. But even setting that issue aside, I cannot agree with the Court's analysis. The Court appears to misinterpret Article II, §1, by over- reading its language as authorizing the broad power to impose and enforce sub- stantive conditions on appointment. The Court then misconstrues the State of Washington's law as enforcing a condition of appointment.

1

The Court's conclusion that the text of Article II, §1, expressly grants States the power to impose substantive conditions or qualifications on electors is highly questionable. Its interpretation appears to strain the plain meaning of the text, ignore historical evidence, and give the term "Manner" different meanings in parallel provisions of Article I and Article II. . . .

First, the Court's attempt to root its analysis in Article II, §1, seems to stretch the plain meaning of the Constitution's text. Article II, §1, provides that States shall appoint electors "in such Manner as the Legislature thereof may direct." At the time of the founding, the term "manner" referred to a "[f]orm" or "method." These definitions suggest that Article II requires state legislatures merely to set the approach for selecting Presidential electors, not to impose substantive limitations on whom may become an elector. And determining the "Manner" of appointment certainly does not include the power to impose requirements as to how the electors vote *after they are appointed*, which is what the Washington law addresses. . . .

Historical evidence from the founding also suggests that the "Manner" of appointment refers to the method for selecting electors, rather than the substantive limitations placed on the position. . . . In context, it is clear that the Framers understood "Manner" in Article II, §1, to refer to the mode of appointing electors — consistent with the plain meaning of the term.

This understanding of "Manner" was seemingly shared by those at the ratifying conventions. For instance, at the North Carolina ratifying convention, John Steele stated that "[t]he power over the *manner* of elections [under Article I, §4] does not include that of saying who shall vote." Rather "the power over the *manner* only enables [States] to determine how these electors shall elect." In short, the historical context and contemporaneous use of the term "Manner" seem to indicate that the Framers and the ratifying public both understood the term in accordance with its plain meaning.

Finally, the Court's interpretation gives the same term — "Manner" — different meanings in two parallel provisions of the Constitution. Article I, §4, states that "[t]he Times, Places and Manner of holding Elections for Senators and Representatives, shall be prescribed in each State by the Legislature thereof." In *U. S. Term Limits*, the Court concluded that the term "Manner" in Article I includes only "a grant of authority to issue procedural regulations," not "the broad power to set qualifications." Yet, today, the Court appears to take the exact opposite view. The Court interprets the term "Manner" in Article II, §1, to include the power to impose conditions or qualifications on the appointment of electors.

With respect, I demur. "When seeking to discern the meaning of a word in the Constitution, there is no better dictionary than the rest of the Constitution itself." *Arizona State Legislature v. Arizona Independent Redistricting Comm'n* (2015) (Roberts, C. J., dissenting). While terms may not always have the exact same meaning throughout the Constitution, here we are interpreting the same word ("Manner") in two provisions that the Court has already stated impose "paralle[l]" duties — setting the " 'Manner of holding Elections' " and setting the " 'Manner' " of " 'appoint[ing] a Number of Electors.' " *U. S. Term Limits*. Nothing in the Constitution's text or history indicates that the Court should take the strongly disfavored step of concluding that the term "Manner" has two different meanings in these closely aligned provisions. . . .

II

When the Constitution is silent, authority resides with the States or the people. This allocation of power is both embodied in the structure of our Constitution and expressly required by the Tenth Amendment. The application of this fundamental principle should guide our decision here.

"The ultimate source of the Constitution's authority is the consent of the people of each individual State." *U. S. Term Limits* (Thomas, J., dissenting). When the States ratified the Federal Constitution, the people of each State acquiesced in the transfer of limited power to the Federal Government. They ceded only those powers granted to the Federal Government by the Constitution. "The Federal Government and the States thus face different default rules: Where the Constitution is silent about the exercise of a particular power[,] the Federal Government lacks that power and the States enjoy it."

This allocation of power is apparent in the structure of our Constitution. The Federal Government "is acknowledged by all to be one of enumerated powers." *McCulloch v. Maryland* (1819). "[T]he powers delegated by the . . . Constitution to the federal government are few and defined," while those that belong to the States "remain . . . numerous and indefinite." The Federalist No. 45 (J. Madison). Article I, for example, enumerates various legislative powers in §8, but it specifically limits Congress' authority to the "legislative Powers herein granted," §1. States face no such constraint because the Constitution does not delineate the powers of the States. Article I, §10, contains a brief list of powers removed from the States, but States are otherwise "free to exercise all powers that the Constitution does not withhold from them."

This structural principle is explicitly enshrined in the Tenth Amendment. That Amendment states that "[t]he powers not delegated to the United States by the Constitution, nor prohibited by it to the States, are reserved to the States respectively, or to the people." As Justice Story explained, "[t]his amendment is a mere affirmation of what, upon any just reasoning, is a necessary rule of interpreting the constitution. Being an instrument of limited and enumerated powers, it follows irresistibly, that what is not conferred, is withheld, and belongs to the state authorities." J. Story, Commentaries on the Constitution of the United States (1833); *New York v. United States* (1992). In other words, the Tenth Amendment "states but a truism that all is retained which has not been surrendered," *United States v. Darby* (1941), "mak[ing] clear that powers reside at the state level except where the Constitution removes them from that level," *U. S. Term Limits* (Thomas, J., dissenting); see also *Garcia v. San Antonio Metropolitan Transit Authority* (1985).

Thus, "[w]here the Constitution is silent about the exercise of a particular power[,] that is, where the Constitution does not speak either expressly or by necessary implication," the power is "either delegated to the state government or retained by the people." *U. S. Term Limits* (Thomas, J., dissenting); cf. *Martin v. Hunter's Lessee* (1816) (stating that the Federal Government's powers under the Constitution must be "expressly given, or given by necessary implication").

B

This fundamental allocation of power applies in the context of the electoral college. Article II, §1, and the Twelfth Amendment address the election of the President through a body of electors. These sections of the Constitution provide the Federal Government with limited powers concerning the election, set various

requirements for the electors, and impose an affirmative obligation on States
to appoint electors. Art. II, §1; Amdt. 12. Each of these directives is consistent
with the general structure of the Constitution and the principle of reserved
powers. Put simply, nothing in the text or structure of Article II and the Twelfth
Amendment contradicts the fundamental distribution of power preserved by the
Tenth Amendment.

Of course, the powers reserved to the States concerning Presidential electors
cannot "be exercised in such a way as to violate express constitutional commands."
Williams v. Rhodes (1968). That is, powers related to electors reside
with States to the extent that the Constitution does not remove or restrict that
power. Thus, to invalidate a state law, there must be "something in the Federal
Constitution that deprives the [States of] the power to enact such [a] measur[e]."
U. S. Term Limits (THOMAS, J., dissenting).

As the Court recognizes, nothing in the Constitution prevents States from
requiring Presidential electors to vote for the candidate chosen by the people.
Petitioners ask us to infer a constitutional right to elector independence by interpreting
the terms "appoint," "Electors," "vote," and "by Ballot" to align with the
Framers' *expectations* of discretion in elector voting. But the Framers' expectations
aid our interpretive inquiry only to the extent that they provide evidence of
the original public meaning of the Constitution. They cannot be used to change
that meaning. As the Court explains, the plain meaning of the terms relied on by
petitioners do not appear to "connote independent choice." Thus, "the original
expectation[s]" of the Framers as to elector discretion provide "no reason for
holding that the power confided to the States by the Constitution has ceased to
exist."

* * *

"The people of the States, from whom all governmental powers stem, have
specified that all powers not prohibited to the States by the Federal Constitution
are reserved 'to the States respectively, or to the people.' " *U. S. Term Limits*
(Thomas, J., dissenting). Because I would decide this case based on that fundamental
principle, I concur only in the judgment.

Chapter 5

Federalism Limits on State Power

STUDY GUIDE:

- Are the Court's modern Dormant Commerce Clause precedents consistent with the original meaning of the Commerce Clause? How does Justice Alito make this case?

Tennessee Wine and Spirits Retailers Association v. Thomas
588 U.S. ___ (2019)

JUSTICE ALITO delivered the opinion of the Court.

The State of Tennessee imposes demanding durational-residency requirements on all individuals and businesses seeking to obtain or renew a license to operate a liquor store. One provision precludes the renewal of a license unless the applicant has resided in the State for 10 consecutive years. Another provides that a corporation cannot obtain a license unless all of its stockholders are residents. The Court of Appeals for the Sixth Circuit struck down these provisions as blatant violations of the Commerce Clause, and neither petitioner — an association of Tennessee liquor retailers — nor the State itself defends them in this Court.

The Sixth Circuit also invalidated a provision requiring applicants for an initial license to have resided in the State for the prior two years, and petitioner does challenge that decision. But while this requirement is less extreme than the others that the Sixth Circuit found to be unconstitutional, we now hold that it also violates the Commerce Clause and is not shielded by §2 of the Twenty-first Amendment. Section 2 was adopted as part of the scheme that ended prohibition on the national level. It gives each State leeway in choosing the alcohol-related public health and safety measures that its citizens find desirable. But §2 is not a license to impose all manner of protectionist restrictions on commerce in alcoholic beverages. Because Tennessee's 2-year residency requirement for retail license applicants blatantly favors the State's residents and has little relationship to public health and safety, it is unconstitutional.

I

A

Tennessee, like many other States, requires alcoholic beverages distributed in the State to pass through a specified three-tiered system. Acting through the Tennessee Alcoholic Beverage Commission (TABC), the State issues different types of licenses to producers, wholesalers, and retailers of alcoholic beverages. Producers may sell only to licensed wholesalers; wholesalers may sell only to licensed retailers or other wholesalers; and only licensed retailers may sell to consumers. No person may lawfully participate in the sale of alcohol without the appropriate license.

Included in the Tennessee scheme are onerous durational-residency requirements for all persons and companies wishing to operate "retail package stores" that sell alcoholic beverages for off-premises consumption (hereinafter liquor stores). To obtain an initial retail license, an individual must demonstrate that he or she has "been a bona fide resident" of the State for the previous two years. And to renew such a license — which Tennessee law requires after only one year of operation — an individual must show continuous residency in the State for a period of 10 consecutive years. . . .

II

A

The Court of Appeals held that Tennessee's 2-year residency requirement violates the Commerce Clause, which provides that "[t]he Congress shall have Power . . . [t]o regulate Commerce with foreign Nations, and among the several States, and with the Indian Tribes." Art. I, §8, cl. 3. "Although the Clause is framed as a positive grant of power to Congress," *Comptroller of Treasury of Md. v. Wynne* (2015), we have long held that this Clause also prohibits state laws that unduly restrict interstate commerce. See, *e.g.*, *ibid.*; *Philadelphia v. New Jersey* (1978); *Cooley v. Board of Wardens of Port of Philadelphia ex rel. Soc. for Relief of Distressed Pilots* (1852); *Willson v. Black Bird Creek Marsh Co.* (1829). "This 'negative' aspect of the Commerce Clause" prevents the States from adopting protectionist measures and thus preserves a national market for goods and services. *New Energy Co. of Ind. v. Limbach* (1988).

This interpretation, generally known as "the dormant Commerce Clause," has a long and complicated history. Its roots go back as far as *Gibbons v. Ogden* (1824), where Chief Justice Marshall found that a version of the dormant Commerce Clause argument had "great force." His successor disagreed, see *License Cases* (1847) (Taney, C. J.), but by the latter half of the 19th century the dormant Commerce Clause was firmly established, see, and it played an important role in the economic history of our Nation. See Cushman, *Formalism and Realism in Commerce Clause Jurisprudence*, 67 U. Chi. L. Rev. 1089, 1107 (2000).

In recent years, some Members of the Court have authored vigorous and thoughtful critiques of this interpretation. See, *e.g.*, *Camps Newfound/Owatonna*,

Inc. v. Town of Harrison (1997) (Thomas, J., dissenting); *Tyler Pipe Industries, Inc. v. Washington State Dept. of Revenue* (1987) (Scalia, J., concurring in part and dissenting in part). But the proposition that the Commerce Clause by its own force restricts state protectionism is deeply rooted in our case law. And without the dormant Commerce Clause, we would be left with a constitutional scheme that those who framed and ratified the Constitution would surely find surprising.

That is so because removing state trade barriers was a principal reason for the adoption of the Constitution. Under the Articles of Confederation, States notoriously obstructed the interstate shipment of goods. "Interference with the arteries of commerce was cutting off the very life-blood of the nation." M. Farrand, The Framing of the Constitution of the United States 7 (1913). The Annapolis Convention of 1786 was convened to address this critical problem, and it culminated in a call for the Philadelphia Convention that framed the Constitution in the summer of 1787. At that Convention, discussion of the power to regulate interstate commerce was almost uniformly linked to the removal of state trade barriers, and when the Constitution was sent to the state conventions, fostering free trade among the States was prominently cited as a reason for ratification. In The Federalist No. 7, Hamilton argued that state protectionism could lead to conflict among the States, and in No. 11, he touted the benefits of a free national market, In The Federalist No. 42, Madison sounded a similar theme.

In light of this background, it would be strange if the Constitution contained no provision curbing state protectionism, and at this point in the Court's history, no provision other than the Commerce Clause could easily do the job. The only other provisions that the Framers might have thought would fill that role, at least in part, are the Import-Export Clause, Art. I, §10, cl. 2, which generally prohibits a State from "lay[ing] any Imposts or Duties on Imports or Exports," and the Privileges and Immunities Clause, Art. IV, §2, which provides that "[t]he Citizens of each State shall be entitled to all Privileges and Immunities of Citizens in the several States." But the Import-Export Clause was long ago held to refer only to international trade. And the Privileges and Immunities Clause has been interpreted not to protect corporations, and may not guard against certain discrimination scrutinized under the dormant Commerce Clause, see Denning, Why the Privileges and Immunities Clause of Article IV Cannot Replace the Dormant Commerce Clause Doctrine, 88 Minn. L. Rev. 384, 393-397 (2003). So if we accept the Court's established interpretation of those provisions, that leaves the Commerce Clause as the primary safeguard against state protectionism.

It is not surprising, then, that our cases have long emphasized the connection between the trade barriers that prompted the call for a new Constitution and our dormant Commerce Clause jurisprudence. . . .

In light of this history and our established case law, we reiterate that the Commerce Clause by its own force restricts state protectionism.

B

Under our dormant Commerce Clause cases, if a state law discriminates against out-of-state goods or nonresident economic actors, the law can be sustained only on a showing that it is narrowly tailored to "advanc[e] a legitimate local purpose." *Department of Revenue of Ky. v. Davis* (2008).

Tennessee's 2-year durational-residency requirement plainly favors Tennesseans over nonresidents, and neither the Association nor the dissent below defends that requirement under the standard that would be triggered if the requirement applied to a person wishing to operate a retail store that sells a commodity other than alcohol. Instead, their arguments are based on §2 of the Twenty-first Amendment, to which we will now turn.

III

Section 2 of the Twenty-first Amendment provides as follows:

> The transportation or importation into any State, Territory, or possession of the United States for delivery or use therein of intoxicating liquors, in violation of the laws thereof, is hereby prohibited.

. . . In attempting to understand how §2 and other constitutional provisions work together, we have looked to history for guidance, and history has taught us that the thrust of §2 is to "constitutionaliz[e]" the basic structure of federal-state alcohol regulatory authority that prevailed prior to the adoption of the Eighteenth Amendment. *Craig v. Boren* (1976). . . .

IV

By 1933, support for Prohibition had substantially diminished but not vanished completely. Thirty-eight state conventions eventually ratified the Twenty-first Amendment, but 10 States either rejected or took no action on the Amendment. Section 1 of the Twenty-first Amendment repealed the Eighteenth Amendment[, which prohibited the manufacture, sale, transportation, and importation of alcoholic beverages anywhere in the country,] and thus ended nationwide Prohibition, but §2, the provision at issue here, gave each State the option of banning alcohol if its citizens so chose. . . .

[W]e have inferred that . . . §2 was meant to "constitutionaliz[e]" the basic understanding of the extent of the States' power to regulate alcohol that prevailed before Prohibition. [*Craig*] And as recognized during that period, the Commerce Clause did not permit the States to impose protectionist measures clothed as police-power regulations. . . .[15]

---

15. The dissent characterizes the Court as a "committee of nine" that has "stray[ed] from the text" of the Twenty-first Amendment and "impose[d] [its] own free-trade rules" on the States. This is empty rhetoric. The dissent itself strays from a blinkered reading of the Amendment. The dissent interprets §2 of the Amendment to mean more than it literally says, arguing that §2 covers the residency requirements at issue even though they are not tied in any way to what the Amendment actually addresses, namely, "the transportation or importation" of alcohol across state lines. And the dissent agrees that §2 cannot be read as broadly as one might think if its language were read in isolation and not as part of an integrated constitutional scheme. The dissent asserts that §2 does not

. . . The Court . . . [has] held that §2 does not entirely supersede Congress's power to regulate commerce. . . . As for the dormant Commerce Clause, the developments leading to the adoption of the Twenty-first Amendment have convinced us that the aim of §2 was not to give States a free hand to restrict the importation of alcohol for purely protectionist purposes. . . .

Most recently, in *Granholm* [*v. Heald (2005)*], we struck down a set of discriminatory direct-shipment laws that favored in-state wineries over out-of-state competitors. After surveying the history of §2, we affirmed that "the Twenty-first Amendment does not immunize all laws from Commerce Clause challenge." We therefore examined whether the challenged laws were reasonably necessary to protect the States' asserted interests in policing underage drinking and facilitating tax collection. Concluding that the answer to that question was no, we invalidated the laws as inconsistent with the dormant Commerce Clause's nondiscrimination principle.

To summarize, the Court has acknowledged that §2 grants States latitude with respect to the regulation of alcohol, but the Court has repeatedly declined to read §2 as allowing the States to violate the "nondiscrimination principle" that was a central feature of the regulatory regime that the provision was meant to constitutionalize. . . .

Recognizing that §2 was adopted to give each State the authority to address alcohol-related public health and safety issues in accordance with the preferences of its citizens, we ask whether the challenged requirement can be justified as a public health or safety measure or on some other legitimate nonprotectionist ground. Section 2 gives the States regulatory authority that they would not otherwise enjoy, but as we pointed out in *Granholm*, "mere speculation" or "unsupported assertions" are insufficient to sustain a law that would otherwise violate the Commerce Clause. Where the predominant effect of a law is protectionism, not the protection of public health or safety, it is not shielded by §2.

The provision at issue here expressly discriminates against nonresidents and has at best a highly attenuated relationship to public health or safety. During the course of this litigation, the Association relied almost entirely on the argument that Tennessee's residency requirements are simply "not subject to Commerce Clause challenge," and the State itself mounted no independent defense. As a result, the record is devoid of any "concrete evidence" showing that the 2-year residency requirement actually promotes public health or safety; nor is there evidence that nondiscriminatory alternatives would be insufficient to further those interests. . . .

Not only is the 2-year residency requirement ill suited to promote responsible sales and consumption practices (an interest that we recognize as legitimate,

---

abrogate all previously adopted constitutional provisions, just the dormant Commerce Clause. But the dissent does not say whether it thinks §2 allows the States to adopt alcohol regulations that serve no conceivable purpose other than protectionism. Even the dissent below did not go that far. If §2 gives the States *carte blanche* to engage in protectionism, we suppose that Tennessee could restrict licenses to persons who can show that their lineal ancestors have lived in the State since 1796 when the State entered the Union. Does the dissent really think that this is what §2 was meant to permit?

contrary to the dissent's suggestion), but there are obvious alternatives that better serve that goal without discriminating against nonresidents. State law empowers the relevant authorities to limit both the number of retail licenses and the amount of alcohol that may be sold to an individual. The State could also mandate more extensive training for managers and employees and could even demand that they demonstrate an adequate connection with and knowledge of the local community. And the State of course remains free to monitor the practices of retailers and to take action against those who violate the law.

Given all this, the Association has fallen far short of showing that the 2-year durational-residency requirement for license applicants is valid. Like the other discriminatory residency requirements that the Association is unwilling to defend, the predominant effect of the 2-year residency requirement is simply to protect the Association's members from out-of-state competition. We therefore hold that this provision violates the Commerce Clause and is not saved by the Twenty-first Amendment.

JUSTICE GORSUCH, with whom JUSTICE THOMAS joins, dissenting.

Alcohol occupies a complicated place in this country's history. Some of the founders were enthusiasts; Benjamin Franklin thought wine was "proof that God loves us." Many in the Prohibition era were decidedly less enamored; they saw "liquor [a]s a lawlessness unto itself." *Duckworth v. Arkansas* (1941) (Jackson, J., concurring in result). Over time, the people have adopted two separate constitutional Amendments to adjust and then readjust alcohol's role in our society. But through it all, one thing has always held true: States may impose residency requirements on those who seek to sell alcohol within their borders to ensure that retailers comply with local laws and norms. In fact, States have enacted residency requirements for at least 150 years, and the Tennessee law at issue before us has stood since 1939. Today and for the first time, the Court claims to have discovered a duty and power to strike down laws like these as unconstitutional. Respectfully, I do not see it. . . .

As judges, we may be sorely tempted to "rationalize" the law and impose our own free-trade rules for all goods and services in interstate commerce. Certainly, that temptation seems to have proven nearly irresistible for this Court when it comes to alcohol. And as Justice Cardozo once observed, "an intellectual passion . . . for symmetry of form and substance" is "an ideal which can never fail to exert some measure of attraction upon the professional experts who make up the lawyer class." B. Cardozo, The Nature of the Judicial Process 34 (1921). But real life is not always so tidy and satisfactory, and neither are the democratic compromises we are bound to respect as judges. Like it or not, those who adopted the Twenty-first Amendment took the view that reasonable people can disagree about the costs and benefits of free trade in alcohol. They left us with clear instructions that the free-trade rules this Court has devised for "cabbages and candlesticks" should not be applied to alcohol. *Carter v. Virginia* (1944) (Frankfurter, J., concurring). Under the terms of the compromise they hammered out, the regulation of alcohol wasn't left to the imagination of a committee of nine sitting in Washington, D. C., but to the judgment of the people themselves and their local elected representatives. State governments were supposed to serve as "laborator[ies]" of democracy, *New State Ice Co. v. Liebmann* (1932) (Brandeis, J., dissenting), with "broad power to regulate liquor under §2," *Granholm*. If the people wish to alter this arrangement, that is their sovereign right. But until then, I would enforce the Twenty-first Amendment as they wrote and originally understood it.

Chapter 6

The Executive Power

Study Guide:

- Does the majority opinion dispute that the "travel ban" originated as a ban on Muslims entering the United States? If not, how could the President possibly prevail?
- Why does the majority opinion not apply the Court's "Establishment Clause precedents concerning laws and policies applied domestically" to the travel ban?
- The majority opinion explains, "we must consider not only the statements of a particular President, but also the authority of the Presidency itself." What does this statement mean?
- Does the majority opinion actually overrule *Korematsu*? The dissent charges that "[b]y blindly accepting the Government's misguided invitation to sanction a discriminatory policy motivated by animosity toward a disfavored group, all in the name of a superficial claim of national security, the Court redeploys the same dangerous logic underlying *Korematsu* and merely replaces one 'gravely wrong' decision with another." Can *Hawaii v. Trump* be distinguished from *Korematsu*?
- Justice Kennedy's concurring opinion contends that "[t]here are numerous instances in which the statements and actions of Government officials are not subject to judicial scrutiny or intervention." Is the travel ban not "subject to judicial scrutiny"?

Trump v. Hawaii
138 S. Ct. 2392 (2018)

Chief Justice ROBERTS delivered the opinion of the Court.

Under the Immigration and Nationality Act, foreign nationals seeking entry into the United States undergo a vetting process to ensure that they satisfy the numerous requirements for admission. The Act also vests the President with authority to restrict the entry of aliens whenever he finds that their entry "would be detrimental to the interests of the United States." 8 U.S.C. §1182(f). Relying on that delegation, the President concluded that it was necessary to impose entry restrictions on nationals of countries that do not share adequate information for an informed entry determination, or that otherwise present national security risks. Presidential Proclamation. The plaintiffs in this litigation, respondents here, challenged the application of those entry restrictions to certain aliens abroad. We now decide whether the President had authority under the Act to issue the Proclamation, and whether the entry policy violates the Establishment Clause of the First Amendment.

I

A

Shortly after taking office, President Trump signed Executive Order No. 13769, Protecting the Nation From Foreign Terrorist Entry Into the United States. EO-1 directed the Secretary of Homeland Security to conduct a review to examine the adequacy of information provided by foreign governments about their nationals seeking to enter the United States. Pending that review, the order suspended for 90 days the entry of foreign nationals from seven countries — Iran, Iraq, Libya, Somalia, Sudan, Syria, and Yemen — that had been previously identified by Congress or prior administrations as posing heightened terrorism risks. The District Court for the Western District of Washington entered a temporary restraining order blocking the entry restrictions, and the Court of Appeals for the Ninth Circuit denied the Government's request to stay that order.

In response, the President revoked EO-1, replacing it with Executive Order No. 13780, which again directed a worldwide review. (EO-2). Citing investigative burdens on agencies and the need to diminish the risk that dangerous individuals would enter without adequate vetting, EO-2 also temporarily restricted the entry (with case-by-case waivers) of foreign nationals from six of the countries covered by EO-1: Iran, Libya, Somalia, Sudan, Syria, and Yemen. The order explained that those countries had been selected because each "is a state sponsor of terrorism, has been significantly compromised by terrorist organizations, or contains active conflict zones." The entry restriction was to stay in effect for 90 days, pending completion of the worldwide review.

These interim measures were immediately challenged in court. The District Courts for the Districts of Maryland and Hawaii entered nationwide preliminary injunctions barring enforcement of the entry suspension, and the respective Courts of Appeals upheld those injunctions, albeit on different grounds. This Court granted certiorari and stayed the injunctions — allowing the entry suspension to go into effect — with respect to foreign nationals who lacked a "credible claim of a bona fide relationship" with a person or entity in the United States. The temporary restrictions in EO-2 expired before this Court took any action, and we vacated the lower court decisions as moot.

On September 24, 2017, after completion of the worldwide review, the President issued the Proclamation before us. The Proclamation (as its title indicates) sought to improve vetting procedures by identifying ongoing deficiencies in the information needed to assess whether nationals of particular countries present "public safety threats." To further that purpose, the Proclamation placed entry restrictions on the nationals of eight foreign states whose systems for managing and sharing information about their nationals the President deemed inadequate.

The Proclamation described how foreign states were selected for inclusion based on the review undertaken pursuant to EO-2. As part of that review, the Department of Homeland Security (DHS), in consultation with the State Department and several intelligence agencies, developed a "baseline" for the information required from foreign governments to confirm the identity of individuals seeking entry into the United States, and to determine whether those individuals pose a security threat. . . .

[After the review process], the Acting Secretary of Homeland Security concluded that eight countries—Chad, Iran, Iraq, Libya, North Korea, Syria, Venezuela, and Yemen—remained deficient in terms of their risk profile and willingness to provide requested information. The Acting Secretary recommended that the President impose entry restrictions on certain nationals from all of those countries except Iraq. . . .

After consulting with multiple Cabinet members and other officials, the President adopted the Acting Secretary's recommendations and issued the Proclamation. Invoking his authority under 8 U.S.C. §§1182(f) and 1185(a), the President determined that certain entry restrictions were necessary to "prevent the entry of those foreign nationals about whom the United States Government lacks sufficient information"; "elicit improved identity management and information-sharing protocols and practices from foreign governments"; and otherwise "advance [the] foreign policy, national security, and counterterrorism objectives" of the United States. The President explained that these restrictions would be the "most likely to encourage cooperation" while "protect[ing] the United States until such time as improvements occur." . . .

The Proclamation exempts lawful permanent residents and foreign nationals who have been granted asylum. It also provides for case-by-case waivers when a foreign national demonstrates undue hardship, and that his entry is in the national interest and would not pose a threat to public safety. The Proclamation further directs DHS to assess on a continuing basis whether entry restrictions should be modified or continued, and to report to the President every 180 days. Upon completion of the first such review period, the President, on the recommendation of the Secretary of Homeland Security, determined that Chad had sufficiently improved its practices, and he accordingly lifted restrictions on its nationals. . . .

III

The INA establishes numerous grounds on which an alien abroad may be inadmissible to the United States and ineligible for a visa. Congress has also delegated to the President authority to suspend or restrict the entry of aliens in certain circumstances. The principal source of that authority, §1182(f), enables the President to "suspend the entry of all aliens or any class of aliens" whenever he "finds" that their entry "would be detrimental to the interests of the United States."

Plaintiffs argue that the Proclamation is not a valid exercise of the President's authority under the INA. In their view, §1182(f) confers only a residual power to temporarily halt the entry of a discrete group of aliens engaged in harmful conduct. They also assert that the Proclamation violates another provision of the INA—8 U.S.C. §1152(a)(1)(A)—because it discriminates on the basis of nationality in the issuance of immigrant visas.

By its plain language, §1182(f) grants the President broad discretion to suspend the entry of aliens into the United States. The President lawfully exercised that discretion based on his findings—following a worldwide, multi-agency review—that entry of the covered aliens would be detrimental to the national interest. And plaintiffs' attempts to identify a conflict with other provisions in the INA, and their appeal to the statute's purposes and legislative history, fail to overcome the clear statutory language. . . .

A

The text of §1182(f) states:

> "Whenever the President finds that the entry of any aliens or of any class of aliens into the United States would be detrimental to the interests of the United States, he may by proclamation, and for such period as he shall deem necessary, suspend the entry of all aliens or any class of aliens as immigrants or nonimmigrants, or impose on the entry of aliens any restrictions he may deem to be appropriate."

By its terms, §1182(f) exudes deference to the President in every clause. It entrusts to the President the decisions whether and when to suspend entry ("[w]henever [he] finds that the entry" of aliens "would be detrimental" to the national interest); whose entry to suspend ("all aliens or any class of aliens"); for how long ("for such period as he shall deem necessary"); and on what conditions ("any restrictions he may deem to be appropriate"). It is therefore unsurprising that we have previously observed that §1182(f) vests the President with "ample power" to impose entry restrictions in addition to those elsewhere enumerated in the INA.

The Proclamation falls well within this comprehensive delegation. The sole prerequisite set forth in §1182(f) is that the President "find [ ]" that the entry of the covered aliens "would be detrimental to the interests of the United States." The President has undoubtedly fulfilled that requirement here. He first ordered DHS and other agencies to conduct a comprehensive evaluation of every single country's compliance with the information and risk assessment baseline. The President then issued a Proclamation setting forth extensive findings describing how deficiencies in the practices of select foreign governments—several of which are state sponsors of terrorism—deprive the Government of "sufficient information to assess the risks [those countries' nationals] pose to the United States." Based on that review, the President found that it was in the national interest to restrict entry of aliens who could not be vetted with adequate information—both to protect national security and public safety, and to induce improvement by their home countries.

Plaintiffs believe that these findings are insufficient. They argue, as an initial matter, that the Proclamation fails to provide a persuasive rationale for why nationality alone renders the covered foreign nationals a security risk. And they further discount the President's stated concern about deficient vetting because the Proclamation allows many aliens from the designated countries to enter on nonimmigrant visas.

Such arguments are grounded on the premise that §1182(f) not only requires the President to *make* a finding that entry "would be detrimental to the interests of the United States," but also to explain that finding with sufficient detail to enable judicial review. That premise is questionable. But even assuming that some form of review is appropriate, plaintiffs' attacks on the sufficiency of the President's findings cannot be sustained. The 12-page Proclamation—which thoroughly describes the process, agency evaluations, and recommendations underlying the President's chosen restrictions—is more detailed than any prior order a President has issued under §1182(f). (Citing proclamations from Presidents Clinton and Reagan).

Moreover, plaintiffs' request for a searching inquiry into the persuasiveness of the President's justifications is inconsistent with the broad statutory text and the deference traditionally accorded the President in this sphere. "Whether the President's chosen method" of addressing perceived risks is justified from a policy perspective is "irrelevant to the scope of his [§1182(f)] authority." *Sale.* And when the President adopts "a preventive measure . . . in the context of international affairs and national security," he is "not required to conclusively link all of the pieces in the puzzle before [courts] grant weight to [his] empirical conclusions." *Holder v. Humanitarian Law Project* (2010).

The Proclamation also comports with the remaining textual limits in §1182(f). We agree with plaintiffs that the word "suspend" often connotes a "defer[ral] till later," Webster's Third New International Dictionary 2303 (1966). But that does not mean that the President is required to prescribe in advance a fixed end date for the entry restrictions. . . . In fact, not one of the 43 suspension orders issued prior to this litigation has specified a precise end date.

Like its predecessors, the Proclamation makes clear that its "conditional restrictions" will remain in force only so long as necessary to "address" the identified "inadequacies and risks" within the covered nations. To that end, the Proclamation establishes an ongoing process to engage covered nations and assess every 180 days whether the entry restrictions should be modified or terminated. Indeed, after the initial review period, the President determined that Chad had made sufficient improvements to its identity-management protocols, and he accordingly lifted the entry suspension on its nationals.

Finally, the Proclamation properly identifies a "class of aliens"—nationals of select countries—whose entry is suspended. Plaintiffs argue that "class" must refer to a well-defined group of individuals who share a common "characteristic" apart from nationality. But the text of §1182(f), of course, does not say that, and the word "class" comfortably encompasses a group of people linked by nationality. Plaintiffs also contend that the class cannot be "overbroad." But that simply amounts to an unspoken tailoring requirement found nowhere in

Congress's grant of authority to suspend entry of not only "any class of aliens" but "all aliens."

In short, the language of §1182(f) is clear, and the Proclamation does not exceed any textual limit on the President's authority.

B

Confronted with this "facially broad grant of power," plaintiffs focus their attention on statutory structure and legislative purpose. They seek support in, first, the immigration scheme reflected in the INA as a whole, and, second, the legislative history of §1182(f) and historical practice. Neither argument justifies departing from the clear text of the statute.

1

Plaintiffs' structural argument starts with the premise that §1182(f) does not give the President authority to countermand Congress's considered policy judgments. The President, they say, may supplement the INA, but he cannot supplant it. . . .

Although plaintiffs claim that their reading preserves for the President a flexible power to "supplement" the INA, their understanding of the President's authority is remarkably cramped: He may suspend entry by classes of aliens "similar in nature" to the existing categories of inadmissibility—but not too similar—or only in response to "some exigent circumstance" that Congress did not already touch on in the INA. see also Tr. of Oral Arg. 57 ("Presidents have wide berth in this area . . . if there's any sort of emergency."). In any event, no Congress that wanted to confer on the President only a residual authority to address emergency situations would ever use language of the sort in §1182(f). Fairly read, the provision vests authority in the President to impose additional limitations on entry beyond the grounds for exclusion set forth in the INA—including in response to circumstances that might affect the vetting system or other "interests of the United States."

Because plaintiffs do not point to any contradiction with another provision of the INA, the President has not exceeded his authority under §1182(f).

2

. . . Drawing on legislative debates over §1182(f), plaintiffs suggest that the President's suspension power should be limited to exigencies where it would be difficult for Congress to react promptly. Precursor provisions enacted during the First and Second World Wars confined the President's exclusion authority to times of "war" and "national emergency." When Congress enacted §1182(f) in 1952, plaintiffs note, it borrowed "nearly verbatim" from those predecessor statutes, and one of the bill's sponsors affirmed that the provision would apply only during a time of crisis. According to plaintiffs, it therefore follows that Congress sought to delegate only a similarly tailored suspension power in §1182(f).

If anything, the drafting history suggests the opposite. In borrowing "nearly verbatim" from the pre-existing statute, Congress made one critical altera- tion—it removed the national emergency standard that plaintiffs now seek to reintroduce in another form. Weighing Congress's conscious departure from its wartime statutes against an isolated floor statement, the departure is far more probative. When Congress wishes to condition an exercise of executive authority on the President's finding of an exigency or crisis, it knows how to say just that. Here, Congress instead chose to condition the President's exercise of the suspen- sion authority on a different finding: that the entry of an alien or class of aliens would be "detrimental to the interests of the United States."

Plaintiffs also strive to infer limitations from executive practice. By their count, every previous suspension order under §1182(f) can be slotted into one of two categories. The vast majority targeted discrete groups of for- eign nationals engaging in conduct "deemed harmful by the immigration laws." And the remaining entry restrictions that focused on entire nation- alities—namely, President Carter's response to the Iran hostage crisis and President Reagan's suspension of immigration from Cuba—were, in their view, designed as a response to diplomatic emergencies "that the immigration laws do not address."

Even if we were willing to confine expansive language in light of its past appli- cations, the historical evidence is more equivocal than plaintiffs acknowledge. Presidents have repeatedly suspended entry not because the covered nationals themselves engaged in harmful acts but instead to retaliate for conduct by their governments that conflicted with U.S. foreign policy interests. . . .

More significantly, plaintiffs' argument about historical practice is a double- edged sword. The more ad hoc their account of executive action—to fit the history into their theory—the harder it becomes to see such a refined delegation in a statute that grants the President sweeping authority to decide whether to suspend entry, whose entry to suspend, and for how long.

C

Plaintiffs' final statutory argument is that the President's entry suspension vio- lates §1152(a)(1)(A), which provides that "no person shall . . . be discriminated against in the issuance of an immigrant visa because of the person's race, sex, nationality, place of birth, or place of residence." They contend that we should interpret the provision as prohibiting nationality-based discrimination throughout the *entire* immigration process, despite the reference in §1152(a)(1)(A) to the act of visa issuance alone. Specifically, plaintiffs argue that §1152(a)(1)(A) applies to the predicate question of a visa applicant's eligibility for admission and the subsequent question whether the holder of a visa may in fact enter the country. Any other conclusion, they say, would allow the President to circumvent the protections against discrimination enshrined in §1152(a)(1)(A).

As an initial matter, this argument challenges only the validity of the entry restrictions on *immigrant* travel. Section 1152(a)(1)(A) is expressly limited to the issuance of "immigrant visa[s]" while §1182(f) allows the President to suspend entry of "immigrants or nonimmigrants." At a minimum, then, plaintiffs' reading would not affect any of the limitations on nonimmigrant travel in the Proclamation.

In any event, we reject plaintiffs' interpretation because it ignores the basic distinction between admissibility determinations and visa issuance that runs throughout the INA. Section 1182 defines the pool of individuals who are admissible to the United States. Its restrictions come into play at two points in the process of gaining entry (or admission) into the United States. First, any alien who is inadmissible under §1182 (based on, for example, health risks, criminal history, or foreign policy consequences) is screened out as "ineligible to receive a visa." 8 U.S.C. §1201(g). Second, even if a consular officer issues a visa, entry into the United States is not guaranteed. As every visa application explains, a visa does not entitle an alien to enter the United States "if, upon arrival," an immigration officer determines that the applicant is "inadmissible under this chapter, or any other provision of law"—including §1182(f).

Sections 1182(f) and 1152(a)(1)(A) thus operate in different spheres: Section 1182 defines the universe of aliens who are admissible into the United States (and therefore eligible to receive a visa). Once §1182 sets the boundaries of admissibility into the United States, §1152(a)(1)(A) prohibits discrimination in the allocation of immigrant visas based on nationality and other traits. The distinction between admissibility—to which §1152(a)(1)(A) does not apply—and visa issuance—to which it does—is apparent from the text of the provision, which specifies only that its protections apply to the "issuance" of "immigrant visa[s]," without mentioning admissibility or entry. Had Congress instead intended in §1152(a)(1)(A) to constrain the President's power to determine who may enter the country, it could easily have chosen language directed to that end. . . .

Common sense and historical practice confirm as much. Section 1152(a)(1)(A) has never been treated as a constraint on the criteria for admissibility in §1182. Presidents have repeatedly exercised their authority to suspend entry on the basis of nationality. As noted, President Reagan relied on §1182(f) to suspend entry "as immigrants by all Cuban nationals," subject to exceptions. Likewise, President Carter invoked §1185(a)(1) to deny and revoke visas to all Iranian nationals.

On plaintiffs' reading, those orders were beyond the President's authority. The entry restrictions in the Proclamation on North Korea (which plaintiffs do not challenge in this litigation) would also be unlawful. Nor would the President be permitted to suspend entry from particular foreign states in response to an epidemic confined to a single region, or a verified terrorist threat involving nationals of a specific foreign nation, or even if the United States were on the brink of war.

In a reprise of their §1182(f) argument, plaintiffs attempt to soften their position by falling back on an implicit exception for Presidential actions that are "closely drawn" to address "specific fast-breaking exigencies." Yet the absence of any textual basis for such an exception more likely indicates that Congress did not intend for §1152(a)(1)(A) to limit the President's flexible authority to suspend entry based on foreign policy interests. In addition, plaintiffs' proposed exigency test would require courts, rather than the President, to determine whether a foreign government's conduct rises to the level that would trigger a supposed implicit exception to a federal statute. The text of §1152(a)(1)(A) offers no standards that would enable courts to assess, for example, whether the situation in North Korea justifies entry restrictions while the terrorist threat in Yemen does not.

* * *

The Proclamation is squarely within the scope of Presidential authority under the INA. Indeed, neither dissent even attempts any serious argument to the contrary, despite the fact that plaintiffs' primary contention below and in their briefing before this Court was that the Proclamation violated the statute.

IV

A

We now turn to plaintiffs' claim that the Proclamation was issued for the unconstitutional purpose of excluding Muslims. Because we have an obligation to assure ourselves of jurisdiction under Article III, we begin by addressing the question whether plaintiffs have standing to bring their constitutional challenge.

Federal courts have authority under the Constitution to decide legal questions only in the course of resolving "Cases" or "Controversies." Art. III, §2. One of the essential elements of a legal case or controversy is that the plaintiff have standing to sue. Standing requires more than just a "keen interest in the issue." *Hollingsworth v. Perry* (2013). It requires allegations—and, eventually, proof—that the plaintiff "personal[ly]" suffered a concrete and particularized injury in connection with the conduct about which he complains. *Spokeo, Inc. v. Robins* (2016). In a case arising from an alleged violation of the Establishment Clause, a plaintiff must show, as in other cases, that he is "directly affected by the laws and practices against which [his] complaints are directed." *School Dist. of Abington Township v. Schempp* (1963). That is an issue here because the entry restrictions apply not to plaintiffs themselves but to others seeking to enter the United States.

Plaintiffs first argue that they have standing on the ground that the Proclamation "establishes a disfavored faith" and violates "their own right to be free from federal [religious] establishments." They describe such injury as "spiritual and dignitary."

We need not decide whether the claimed dignitary interest establishes an adequate ground for standing. The three individual plaintiffs assert another, more concrete injury: the alleged real-world effect that the Proclamation has had in keeping them separated from certain relatives who seek to enter the country.

We agree that a person's interest in being united with his relatives is sufficiently concrete and particularized to form the basis of an Article III injury in fact. This Court has previously considered the merits of claims asserted by United States citizens regarding violations of their personal rights allegedly caused by the Government's exclusion of particular foreign nationals. See *Kerry v. Din* (2015) (plurality opinion); *Kleindienst v. Mandel* (1972). Likewise, one of our prior stay orders in this litigation recognized that an American individual who has "a bona fide relationship with a particular person seeking to enter the country . . . can legitimately claim concrete hardship if that person is excluded."

The Government responds that plaintiffs' Establishment Clause claims are not justiciable because the Clause does not give them a legally protected interest in the admission of particular foreign nationals. But that argument — which depends upon the scope of plaintiffs' Establishment Clause rights — concerns the merits rather than the justiciability of plaintiffs' claims. We therefore conclude that the individual plaintiffs have Article III standing to challenge the exclusion of their relatives under the Establishment Clause.

B

The First Amendment provides, in part, that "Congress shall make no law respecting an establishment of religion, or prohibiting the free exercise thereof." Our cases recognize that "[t]he clearest command of the Establishment Clause is that one religious denomination cannot be officially preferred over another." *Larson v. Valente* (1982). Plaintiffs believe that the Proclamation violates this prohibition by singling out Muslims for disfavored treatment. The entry suspension, they contend, operates as a "religious gerrymander," in part because most of the countries covered by the Proclamation have Muslim-majority populations. And in their view, deviations from the information-sharing baseline criteria suggest that the results of the multi-agency review were "foreordained." Relying on Establishment Clause precedents concerning laws and policies applied domestically, plaintiffs allege that the primary purpose of the Proclamation was religious animus and that the President's stated concerns about vetting protocols and national security were but pretexts for discriminating against Muslims.

At the heart of plaintiffs' case is a series of statements by the President and his advisers casting doubt on the official objective of the Proclamation. For example, while a candidate on the campaign trail, the President published a "Statement on Preventing Muslim Immigration" that called for a "total and complete shutdown of Muslims entering the United States until our country's representatives can figure out what is going on." That statement remained on his campaign website until May 2017. Then-candidate Trump also stated that "Islam hates us" and asserted that the United States was "having problems with Muslims coming into the country." Shortly after being elected, when asked whether violence in Europe had affected his plans to "ban Muslim immigration," the President replied, "You know my plans. All along, I've been proven to be right."

One week after his inauguration, the President issued EO-1. In a television interview, one of the President's campaign advisers explained that when the President "first announced it, he said, 'Muslim ban.' He called me up. He said, 'Put a commission together. Show me the right way to do it legally.'" The adviser said he assembled a group of Members of Congress and lawyers that "focused on, instead of religion, danger . . . . [The order] is based on places where there [is] substantial evidence that people are sending terrorists into our country."

Plaintiffs also note that after issuing EO-2 to replace EO-1, the President expressed regret that his prior order had been "watered down" and called for a "much tougher version" of his "Travel Ban." Shortly before the release of the Proclamation, he stated that the "travel ban . . . should be far larger, tougher, and more specific," but "stupidly that would not be politically correct." More recently, on November 29, 2017, the President retweeted links to three anti-Muslim propaganda videos. In response to questions about those videos, the President's deputy press secretary denied that the President thinks Muslims are a threat to the United States, explaining that "the President has been talking about these security issues for years now, from the campaign trail to the White House" and "has addressed these issues with the travel order that he issued earlier this year and the companion proclamation." *IRAP v. Trump,* (C.A.4 2018). . . .

Plaintiffs argue that this President's words strike at fundamental standards of respect and tolerance, in violation of our constitutional tradition. But the issue before us is not whether to denounce the statements. It is instead the significance of those statements in reviewing a Presidential directive, neutral on its face, addressing a matter within the core of executive responsibility. In doing so, we must consider not only the statements of a particular President, but also the authority of the Presidency itself.

The case before us differs in numerous respects from the conventional Establishment Clause claim. Unlike the typical suit involving religious displays or school prayer, plaintiffs seek to invalidate a national security directive regulating the entry of aliens abroad. Their claim accordingly raises a number of delicate issues regarding the scope of the constitutional right and the manner of proof. The Proclamation, moreover, is facially neutral toward religion. Plaintiffs therefore ask the Court to probe the sincerity of the stated justifications for the policy by reference to extrinsic statements — many of which were made before the President took the oath of office. These various aspects of plaintiffs' challenge inform our standard of review.

C

For more than a century, this Court has recognized that the admission and exclusion of foreign nationals is a "fundamental sovereign attribute exercised by the Government's political departments largely immune from judicial control." *Fiallo v. Bell* (1977); see *Harisiades v. Shaughnessy* (1952) ("[A]ny policy toward aliens is vitally and intricately interwoven with contemporaneous policies in regard to the conduct of foreign relations [and] the war power."). Because decisions in these matters may implicate "relations with foreign powers," or involve "classifications defined in the light of changing political and economic circumstances," such judgments "are frequently of a character more appropriate to either the Legislature or the Executive." *Mathews v. Diaz* (1976).

Nonetheless, although foreign nationals seeking admission have no constitutional right to entry, this Court has engaged in a circumscribed judicial inquiry when the denial of a visa allegedly burdens the constitutional rights of a U.S. citizen. In *Kleindienst v. Mandel,* the Attorney General denied admission to a Belgian journalist and self-described "revolutionary Marxist," Ernest Mandel, who had been invited to speak at a conference at Stanford University. The professors who wished to hear Mandel speak challenged that decision under the First Amendment, and we acknowledged that their constitutional "right to receive information" was implicated. But we limited our review to whether the Executive gave a "facially legitimate and bona fide" reason for its action. Given the authority of the political branches over admission, we held that "when the Executive exercises this [delegated] power negatively on the basis of a facially legitimate and bona fide reason, the courts will neither look behind the exercise of that discretion, nor test it by balancing its justification" against the asserted constitutional interests of U.S. citizens.

The principal dissent suggests that *Mandel* has no bearing on this case, but our opinions have reaffirmed and applied its deferential standard of review across different contexts and constitutional claims. In *Din,* Justice Kennedy reiterated that "respect for the political branches' broad power over the creation and administration of the immigration system" meant that the Government need provide only a statutory citation to explain a visa denial. Likewise in *Fiallo,* we applied *Mandel* to a "broad congressional policy" giving immigration preferences to mothers of illegitimate children. Even though the statute created a "categorical" entry classification that discriminated on the basis of sex and legitimacy, the Court concluded that "it is not the judicial role in cases of this sort to probe and test the justifications" of immigration policies.

Mandel's narrow standard of review "has particular force" in admission and immigration cases that overlap with "the area of national security." *Din* (Kennedy, J., concurring in judgment). For one, "[j]udicial inquiry into the national-security realm raises concerns for the separation of powers" by intruding on the President's constitutional responsibilities in the area of foreign affairs. *Ziglar v. Abbasi* (2017). For another, "when it comes to collecting evidence and drawing inferences" on questions of national security, "the lack of competence on the part of the courts is marked." *Humanitarian Law Project.*

The upshot of our cases in this context is clear: "Any rule of constitutional law that would inhibit the flexibility" of the President "to respond to changing world conditions should be adopted only with the greatest caution," and our inquiry into matters of entry and national security is highly constrained. *Mathews.* We need not define the precise contours of that inquiry in this case. A conventional application of *Mandel,* asking only whether the policy is facially legitimate and bona fide, would put an end to our review. But the Government has suggested that it may be appropriate here for the inquiry to extend beyond the facial neutrality of the order. See Tr. of Oral Arg. (describing *Mandel* as "the starting point" of the analysis). For our purposes today, we assume that we may look behind the face of the Proclamation to the extent of applying rational basis review. That standard of review considers whether the entry policy is plausibly related to the Government's stated objective to protect the country and improve vetting processes. See *Railroad Retirement Bd. v. Fritz* (1980). As a result, we may consider plaintiffs' extrinsic evidence, but will uphold the policy so long as it can reasonably be understood to result from a justification independent of unconstitutional grounds.[5]

D

Given the standard of review, it should come as no surprise that the Court hardly ever strikes down a policy as illegitimate under rational basis scrutiny. On the few occasions where we have done so, a common thread has been that the laws at issue lack any purpose other than a "bare . . . desire to harm a politically unpopular group." *Department of Agriculture v. Moreno* (1973). In one case, we invalidated a local zoning ordinance that required a special permit for group homes for the intellectually disabled, but not for other facilities such as fraternity houses or hospitals. We did so on the ground that the city's stated concerns about (among other things) "legal responsibility" and "crowded conditions" rested on "an irrational prejudice" against the intellectually disabled. *Cleburne v. Cleburne Living Center, Inc.* (1985). And in another case, this Court overturned a state constitutional amendment that denied gays and lesbians access to the protection of antidiscrimination laws. The amendment, we held, was "divorced from any factual context from which we could discern a relationship to legitimate state interests," and "its sheer breadth [was] so discontinuous with the reasons offered for it" that the initiative seemed "inexplicable by anything but animus." *Romer v. Evans* (1996).

The Proclamation does not fit this pattern. It cannot be said that it is impossible to "discern a relationship to legitimate state interests" or that the policy is "inexplicable by anything but animus." Indeed, the dissent can only attempt to argue otherwise by refusing to apply anything resembling rational basis review. But because there is persuasive evidence that the entry suspension has a legitimate

---

5. The dissent finds "perplexing" the application of rational basis review in this context. Post, at 15. But what is far more problematic is the dissent's assumption that courts should review immigration policies, diplomatic sanctions, and military actions under the de novo "reasonable observer" inquiry applicable to cases involving holiday displays and graduation ceremonies. The dissent criticizes application of a more constrained standard of review as "throw[ing] the Establishment Clause out the window." Post, at 16, n. 6. But as the numerous precedents cited in this section make clear, such a circumscribed inquiry applies to any constitutional claim concerning the entry of foreign nationals. See Part IV–C, supra. The dissent can cite no authority for its proposition that the more free-ranging inquiry it proposes is appropriate in the national security and foreign affairs context.

grounding in national security concerns, quite apart from any religious hostility, we must accept that independent justification.

The Proclamation is expressly premised on legitimate purposes: preventing entry of nationals who cannot be adequately vetted and inducing other nations to improve their practices. The text says nothing about religion. Plaintiffs and the dissent nonetheless emphasize that five of the seven nations currently included in the Proclamation have Muslim-majority populations. Yet that fact alone does not support an inference of religious hostility, given that the policy covers just 8% of the world's Muslim population and is limited to countries that were previously designated by Congress or prior administrations as posing national security risks.

The Proclamation, moreover, reflects the results of a worldwide review process undertaken by multiple Cabinet officials and their agencies. Plaintiffs seek to discredit the findings of the review, pointing to deviations from the review's baseline criteria resulting in the inclusion of Somalia and omission of Iraq. But as the Proclamation explains, in each case the determinations were justified by the distinct conditions in each country. Although Somalia generally satisfies the information-sharing component of the baseline criteria, it "stands apart . . . in the degree to which [it] lacks command and control of its territory." Proclamation §2(h)(i). As for Iraq, the Secretary of Homeland Security determined that entry restrictions were not warranted in light of the close cooperative relationship between the U.S. and Iraqi Governments and the country's key role in combating terrorism in the region. §1(g). It is, in any event, difficult to see how exempting one of the largest predominantly Muslim countries in the region from coverage under the Proclamation can be cited as evidence of animus toward Muslims.

The dissent likewise doubts the thoroughness of the multi-agency review because a recent Freedom of Information Act request shows that the final DHS report "was a mere 17 pages." Yet a simple page count offers little insight into the actual substance of the final report, much less predecisional materials underlying it.

More fundamentally, plaintiffs and the dissent challenge the entry suspension based on their perception of its effectiveness and wisdom. They suggest that the policy is overbroad and does little to serve national security interests. But we cannot substitute our own assessment for the Executive's predictive judgments on such matters, all of which "are delicate, complex, and involve large elements of prophecy." *Chicago & Southern Air Lines, Inc. v. Waterman S.S. Corp.* (1948); see also *Regan v. Wald* (1984). While we of course "do not defer to the Government's reading of the First Amendment," the Executive's evaluation of the underlying facts is entitled to appropriate weight, particularly in the context of litigation involving "sensitive and weighty interests of national security and foreign affairs." *Humanitarian Law Project.*[6]

---

6. The dissent recycles much of plaintiffs' §1182(f) argument to assert that "Congress has already erected a statutory scheme that fulfills" the President's stated concern about deficient vetting. But for the reasons set forth earlier, Congress has not in any sense "stepped into the space and solved the exact problem." Neither the existing inadmissibility grounds nor the narrow Visa Waiver Program address the failure of certain high-risk countries to provide a minimum baseline of reliable information.

Three additional features of the entry policy support the Government's claim of a legitimate national security interest. First, since the President introduced entry restrictions in January 2017, three Muslim-majority countries—Iraq, Sudan, and Chad—have been removed from the list of covered countries. The Proclamation emphasizes that its "conditional restrictions" will remain in force only so long as necessary to "address" the identified "inadequacies and risks," and establishes an ongoing process to engage covered nations and assess every 180 days whether the entry restrictions should be terminated. . . .

Second, for those countries that remain subject to entry restrictions, the Proclamation includes significant exceptions for various categories of foreign nationals. The policy permits nationals from nearly every covered country to travel to the United States on a variety of nonimmigrant visas. These carveouts for nonimmigrant visas are substantial: Over the last three fiscal years—before the Proclamation was in effect—the majority of visas issued to nationals from the covered countries were nonimmigrant visas. The Proclamation also exempts permanent residents and individuals who have been granted asylum.

Third, the Proclamation creates a waiver program open to all covered foreign nationals seeking entry as immigrants or nonimmigrants. According to the Proclamation, consular officers are to consider in each admissibility determination whether the alien demonstrates that (1) denying entry would cause undue hardship; (2) entry would not pose a threat to public safety; and (3) entry would be in the interest of the United States. . . . The Proclamation also directs DHS and the State Department to issue guidance elaborating upon the circumstances that would justify a waiver.[7]

Finally, the dissent invokes *Korematsu v. United States* (1944). Whatever rhetorical advantage the dissent may see in doing so, *Korematsu* has nothing to do with this case. The forcible relocation of U.S. citizens to concentration camps, solely and explicitly on the basis of race, is objectively unlawful and outside the scope of Presidential authority. But it is wholly inapt to liken that morally repugnant order to a facially neutral policy denying certain foreign nationals the privilege of admission. The entry suspension is an act that is well within executive authority and could have been taken by any other President—the only question is evaluating the actions of this particular President in promulgating an otherwise valid Proclamation.

The dissent's reference to *Korematsu*, however, affords this Court the opportunity to make express what is already obvious: *Korematsu* was gravely wrong the day it was decided, has been overruled in the court of history, and—to be clear—"has no place in law under the Constitution." *Youngstown* (Jackson, J., dissenting).

* * *

---

7. JUSTICE BREYER focuses on only one aspect of our consideration—the waiver program and other exemptions in the Proclamation. Citing selective statistics, anecdotal evidence, and a declaration from unrelated litigation, JUSTICE BREYER suggests that not enough individuals are receiving waivers or exemptions. Yet even if such an inquiry were appropriate under rational basis review, the evidence he cites provides "but a piece of the picture," and does not affect our analysis.

Under these circumstances, the Government has set forth a sufficient national security justification to survive rational basis review. We express no view on the soundness of the policy. We simply hold today that plaintiffs have not demonstrated a likelihood of success on the merits of their constitutional claim. . . .

The judgment of the Court of Appeals is reversed, and the case is remanded for further proceedings consistent with this opinion.

It is so ordered.

JUSTICE KENNEDY, concurring.

I join the Court's opinion in full.

There may be some common ground between the opinions in this case, in that the Court does acknowledge that in some instances, governmental action may be subject to judicial review to determine whether or not it is "inexplicable by anything but animus," *Romer v. Evans* (1996), which in this case would be animosity to a religion. Whether judicial proceedings may properly continue in this case, in light of the substantial deference that is and must be accorded to the Executive in the conduct of foreign affairs, and in light of today's decision, is a matter to be addressed in the first instance on remand. And even if further proceedings are permitted, it would be necessary to determine that any discovery and other preliminary matters would not themselves intrude on the foreign affairs power of the Executive.

In all events, it is appropriate to make this further observation. There are numerous instances in which the statements and actions of Government officials are not subject to judicial scrutiny or intervention. That does not mean those officials are free to disregard the Constitution and the rights it proclaims and protects. The oath that all officials take to adhere to the Constitution is not confined to those spheres in which the Judiciary can correct or even comment upon what those officials say or do. Indeed, the very fact that an official may have broad discretion, discretion free from judicial scrutiny, makes it all the more imperative for him or her to adhere to the Constitution and to its meaning and its promise.

The First Amendment prohibits the establishment of religion and promises the free exercise of religion. From these safeguards, and from the guarantee of freedom of speech, it follows there is freedom of belief and expression. It is an urgent necessity that officials adhere to these constitutional guarantees and mandates in all their actions, even in the sphere of foreign affairs. An anxious world must know that our Government remains committed always to the liberties the Constitution seeks to preserve and protect, so that freedom extends outward, and lasts.

THOMAS, J., concurring.

I join the Court's opinion, which highlights just a few of the many problems with the plaintiffs' claims. There are several more. Section 1182(f) does not set forth any judicially enforceable limits that constrain the President. See *Webster v. Doe* (1988). Nor could it, since the President has *inherent* authority to exclude aliens from the country. See *United States ex rel. Knauff v. Shaughnessy* (1950); accord,

Sessions v. Dimaya (2018) (Thomas, J., dissenting). Further, the Establishment Clause does not create an individual right to be free from all laws that a "reasonable observer" views as religious or antireligious. See *Town of Greece v. Galloway* (2014) (Thomas, J., concurring in part and concurring in judgment); *Elk Grove Unified School Dist. v. Newdow* (2004) (Thomas, J., concurring in judgment). The plaintiffs cannot raise any other First Amendment claim, since the alleged religious discrimination in this case was directed at aliens abroad. See *United States v. Verdugo-Urquidez* (1990). And, even on its own terms, the plaintiffs' proffered evidence of anti-Muslim discrimination is unpersuasive. . . .

In sum, universal injunctions are legally and historically dubious. If federal courts continue to issue them, this Court is dutybound to adjudicate their authority to do so.

JUSTICE BREYER, with whom JUSTICE KAGAN joins, dissenting.

The question before us is whether Proclamation No. 9645 is lawful. If its promulgation or content was significantly affected by religious animus against Muslims, it would violate the relevant statute or the First Amendment itself. See 8 U.S.C. §1182(f) (requiring "find[ings]" that persons denied entry "would be detrimental to the interests of the United States"); *Church of Lukumi Babalu Aye, Inc. v. Hialeah* (1993) (First Amendment); *Masterpiece Cakeshop, Ltd. v. Colorado Civil Rights Comm'n* (2018) (same). If, however, its sole *ratio decidendi* was one of national security, then it would be unlikely to violate either the statute or the Constitution. Which is it? Members of the Court principally disagree about the answer to this question, *i.e.,* about whether or the extent to which religious animus played a significant role in the Proclamation's promulgation or content.

In my view, the Proclamation's elaborate system of exemptions and waivers can and should help us answer this question. That system provides for case-by-case consideration of persons who may qualify for visas despite the Proclamation's general ban. Those persons include lawful permanent residents, asylum seekers, refugees, students, children, and numerous others. There are likely many such persons, perhaps in the thousands. . . .

On the one hand, if the Government is applying the exemption and waiver provisions as written, then its argument for the Proclamation's lawfulness is strengthened. . . . For another thing, the Proclamation then follows more closely the basic statutory scheme, which provides for strict case-by-case scrutiny of applications. It would deviate from that system, not across the board, but where circumstances may require that deviation.

Further, since the case-by-case exemptions and waivers apply without regard to the individual's religion, application of that system would help make clear that the Proclamation does not deny visas to numerous Muslim individuals (from those countries) who do not pose a security threat. And that fact would help to rebut the First Amendment claim that the Proclamation rests upon anti-Muslim bias rather than security need. Finally, of course, the very fact that Muslims from those countries would enter the United States (under Proclamation-provided exemptions and waivers) would help to show the same thing.

On the other hand, if the Government is *not* applying the system of exemptions and waivers that the Proclamation contains, then its argument for the Proclamation's lawfulness becomes significantly weaker. . . .

And, perhaps most importantly, if the Government is not applying the Proclamation's exemption and waiver system, the claim that the Proclamation is a "Muslim ban," rather than a "security-based" ban, becomes much stronger. How could the Government successfully claim that the Proclamation rests on security needs if it is excluding Muslims who satisfy the Proclamation's own terms? At the same time, denying visas to Muslims who meet the Proclamation's own security terms would support the view that the Government excludes them for reasons based upon their religion.

Unfortunately there is evidence that supports the second possibility, *i.e.,* that the Government is not applying the Proclamation as written. . . .

[G]iven the importance of the decision in this case, the need for assurance that the Proclamation does not rest upon a "Muslim ban," and the assistance in deciding the issue that answers to the "exemption and waiver" questions may provide, I would send this case back to the District Court for further proceedings. And, I would leave the injunction in effect while the matter is litigated. Regardless, the Court's decision today leaves the District Court free to explore these issues on remand.

If this Court must decide the question without this further litigation, I would, on balance, find the evidence of antireligious bias, including statements on a website taken down only after the President issued the two executive orders preceding the Proclamation, along with the other statements also set forth in Justice Sotomayor's opinion, a sufficient basis to set the Proclamation aside. And for these reasons, I respectfully dissent.

JUSTICE SOTOMAYOR, with whom JUSTICE GINSBURG joins, dissenting.

The United States of America is a Nation built upon the promise of religious liberty. Our Founders honored that core promise by embedding the principle of religious neutrality in the First Amendment. The Court's decision today fails to safeguard that fundamental principle. It leaves undisturbed a policy first advertised openly and unequivocally as a "total and complete shutdown of Muslims entering the United States" because the policy now masquerades behind a facade of national-security concerns. But this repackaging does little to cleanse Presidential Proclamation No. 9645 of the appearance of discrimination that the President's words have created. Based on the evidence in the record, a reasonable observer would conclude that the Proclamation was motivated by anti-Muslim animus. That alone suffices to show that plaintiffs are likely to succeed on the merits of their Establishment Clause claim. The majority holds otherwise by ignoring the facts, misconstruing our legal precedent, and turning a blind eye to the pain and suffering the Proclamation inflicts upon countless families and individuals, many of whom are United States citizens. Because that troubling result runs contrary to the Constitution and our precedent, I dissent.

I

Plaintiffs challenge the Proclamation on various grounds, both statutory and constitutional. Ordinarily, when a case can be decided on purely statutory grounds, we strive to follow a "prudential rule of avoiding constitutional questions." *Zobrest v. Catalina Foothills School Dist.* (1993). But that rule of thumb is far from categorical, and it has limited application where, as here, the constitutional question proves far simpler than the statutory one. Whatever the merits of plaintiffs' complex statutory claims, the Proclamation must be enjoined for a more fundamental reason: It runs afoul of the Establishment Clause's guarantee of religious neutrality.

A

The Establishment Clause forbids government policies "respecting an establishment of religion." U.S. Const., Amdt. 1. The "clearest command" of the Establishment Clause is that the Government cannot favor or disfavor one religion over another. *Larson v. Valente* (1982); *Church of Lukumi Babalu Aye, Inc. v. Hialeah* (1993) ("[T]he First Amendment forbids an official purpose to disapprove of a particular religion"); *Edwards v. Aguillard* (1987) ("The Establishment Clause . . . forbids *alike* the preference of a religious doctrine *or* the prohibition of theory which is deemed antagonistic to a particular dogma" (internal quotation marks omitted)); *Lynch v. Donnelly* (1984) (noting that the Establishment Clause "forbids hostility toward any [religion]," because "such hostility would bring us into 'war with our national tradition as embodied in the First Amendmen[t]'"); *Epperson v. Arkansas* (1968) ("[T]he State may not adopt programs or practices . . . which aid or oppose any religion. This prohibition is absolute"). Consistent with that clear command, this Court has long acknowledged that governmental actions that favor one religion "inevitabl[y]" foster "the hatred, disrespect and even contempt of those who [hold] contrary beliefs." *Engel v. Vitale* (1962). That is so, this Court has held, because such acts send messages to members of minority faiths " 'that they are outsiders, not full members of the political community.'" *Santa Fe Independent School Dist. v. Doe* (2000). To guard against this serious harm, the Framers mandated a strict "principle of denominational neutrality." *Larson*; *Board of Ed. of Kiryas Joel Village School Dist. v. Grumet* (1994) (recognizing the role of courts in "safeguarding a principle at the heart of the Establishment Clause, that government should not prefer one religion to another, or religion to irreligion").

"When the government acts with the ostensible and predominant purpose" of disfavoring a particular religion, "it violates that central Establishment Clause value of official religious neutrality, there being no neutrality when the government's ostensible object is to take sides." *McCreary County v. American Civil Liberties Union of Ky.* (2005). To determine whether plaintiffs have proved an

Establishment Clause violation, the Court asks whether a reasonable observer would view the government action as enacted for the purpose of disfavoring a religion. *Town of Greece v. Galloway,* 572 (2014) (plurality opinion).

In answering that question, this Court has generally considered the text of the government policy, its operation, and any available evidence regarding "the historical background of the decision under challenge, the specific series of events leading to the enactment or official policy in question, and the legislative or administrative history, including contemporaneous statements made by" the decisionmaker. *Lukumi* (opinion of Kennedy, J.); *McCreary* (courts must evaluate "text, legislative history, and implementation . . . , or comparable official act" (internal quotation marks omitted)). At the same time, however, courts must take care not to engage in "any judicial psychoanalysis of a drafter's heart of hearts."

B

1

Although the majority briefly recounts a few of the statements and background events that form the basis of plaintiffs' constitutional challenge, that highly abridged account does not tell even half of the story. The full record paints a far more harrowing picture, from which a reasonable observer would readily conclude that the Proclamation was motivated by hostility and animus toward the Muslim faith.

During his Presidential campaign, then-candidate Donald Trump pledged that, if elected, he would ban Muslims from entering the United States. Specifically, on December 7, 2015, he issued a formal statement "calling for a total and complete shutdown of Muslims entering the United States." That statement, which remained on his campaign website until May 2017 (several months into his Presidency), read in full:

> "Donald J. Trump is calling for a total and complete shutdown of Muslims entering the United States until our country's representatives can figure out what is going on. According to Pew Research, among others, there is great hatred towards Americans by large segments of the Muslim population. Most recently, a poll from the Center for Security Policy released data showing '25% of those polled agreed that violence against Americans here in the United States is justified as a part of the global jihad' and 51% of those polled 'agreed that Muslims in America should have the choice of being governed according to Shariah.' Shariah authorizes such atrocities as murder against nonbelievers who won't convert, beheadings and more unthinkable acts that pose great harm to Americans, especially women.
>
> "Mr. Trum[p] stated, 'Without looking at the various polling data, it is obvious to anybody the hatred is beyond comprehension. Where this hatred comes from and why we will have to determine. Until we are able to determine and understand this problem and the dangerous threat it poses, our country cannot be the victims of the horrendous attacks by people that believe only in Jihad, and have no sense of reason or respect of human life. If I win the election for President, we are going to Make America Great Again.'—Donald J. Trump."

On December 8, 2015, Trump justified his proposal during a television interview by noting that President Franklin D. Roosevelt "did the same thing" with respect to the internment of Japanese Americans during World War II. In January 2016, during a Republican primary debate, Trump was asked whether he wanted to "rethink [his] position" on "banning Muslims from entering the country." He answered, "No." A month later, at a rally in South Carolina, Trump told an apocryphal story about United States General John J. Pershing killing a large group of Muslim insurgents in the Philippines with bullets dipped in pigs' blood in the early 1900's. *Id.,* at 163-164. In March 2016, he expressed his belief that "Islam hates us . . . . [W]e can't allow people coming into this country who have this hatred of the United States . . . [a]nd of people that are not Muslim." That same month, Trump asserted that "[w]e're having problems with the Muslims, and we're having problems with Muslims coming into the country." He therefore called for surveillance of mosques in the United States, blaming terrorist attacks on Muslims' lack of "assimilation" and their commitment to "sharia law." A day later, he opined that Muslims "do not respect us at all" and "don't respect a lot of the things that are happening throughout not only our country, but they don't respect other things."

As Trump's presidential campaign progressed, he began to describe his policy proposal in slightly different terms. In June 2016, for instance, he characterized the policy proposal as a suspension of immigration from countries "where there's a proven history of terrorism." He also described the proposal as rooted in the need to stop "importing radical Islamic terrorism to the West through a failed immigration system." Asked in July 2016 whether he was "pull[ing] back from" his pledged Muslim ban, Trump responded, "I actually don't think it's a rollback. In fact, you could say it's an expansion." He then explained that he used different terminology because "[p]eople were so upset when [he] used the word Muslim."

A month before the 2016 election, Trump reiterated that his proposed "Muslim ban" had "morphed into a[n] extreme vetting from certain areas of the world." Then, on December 21, 2016, President-elect Trump was asked whether he would "rethink" his previous "plans to create a Muslim registry or ban Muslim immigration." He replied: "You know my plans. All along, I've proven to be right."

On January 27, 2017, one week after taking office, President Trump signed EO-1, entitled "Protecting the Nation From Foreign Terrorist Entry Into the United States." As he signed it, President Trump read the title, looked up, and said "We all know what that means." That same day, President Trump explained to the media that, under EO-1, Christians would be given priority for entry as refugees into the United States. In particular, he bemoaned the fact that in the past, "[i]f you were a Muslim [refugee from Syria] you could come in, but if you were a Christian, it was almost impossible." Considering that past policy "very unfair," President Trump explained that EO-1 was designed "to help" the Christians in Syria. The following day, one of President Trump's key advisers candidly drew the connection between EO-1 and the "Muslim ban" that the President had pledged to implement if elected. According to that adviser, "[W]hen [Donald Trump] first announced it, he said, 'Muslim ban.' He called me up. He said, 'Put a commission together. Show me the right way to do it legally.'"

On February 3, 2017, the United States District Court for the Western District of Washington enjoined the enforcement of EO-1. The Ninth Circuit denied the Government's request to stay that injunction. Rather than appeal the Ninth Circuit's decision, the Government declined to continue defending EO-1 in court and instead announced that the President intended to issue a new executive order to replace EO-1.

On March 6, 2017, President Trump issued that new executive order, which, like its predecessor, imposed temporary entry and refugee bans. One of the President's senior advisers publicly explained that EO-2 would "have the same basic policy outcome" as EO-1, and that any changes would address "very technical issues that were brought up by the court." After EO-2 was issued, the White House Press Secretary told reporters that, by issuing EO-2, President Trump "continue[d] to deliver on . . . his most significant campaign promises." That statement was consistent with President Trump's own declaration that "I keep my campaign promises, and our citizens will be very happy when they see the result."

Before EO-2 took effect, federal District Courts in Hawaii and Maryland enjoined the order's travel and refugee bans. The Fourth and Ninth Circuits upheld those injunctions in substantial part. In June 2017, this Court granted the Government's petition for certiorari and issued a *per curiam* opinion partially staying the District Courts' injunctions pending further review. In particular, the Court allowed EO-2's travel ban to take effect except as to "foreign nationals who have a credible claim of a bona fide relationship with a person or entity in the United States."

While litigation over EO-2 was ongoing, President Trump repeatedly made statements alluding to a desire to keep Muslims out of the country. For instance, he said at a rally of his supporters that EO-2 was just a "watered down version of the first one" and had been "tailor[ed]" at the behest of "the lawyers." He further added that he would prefer "to go back to the first [executive order] and go all the way" and reiterated his belief that it was "very hard" for Muslims to assimilate into Western culture. During a rally in April 2017, President Trump recited the lyrics to a song called "The Snake," a song about a woman who nurses a sick snake back to health but then is attacked by the snake, as a warning about Syrian refugees entering the country. And in June 2017, the President stated on Twitter that the Justice Department had submitted a "watered down, politically correct version" of the "original Travel Ban" "to S[upreme] C[ourt]."[1] The President went on to tweet: "People, the lawyers and the courts can call it whatever they want, but I am calling it what we need and what it is, a TRAVEL BAN!" He added: "That's right, we need a TRAVEL BAN for certain DANGEROUS countries, not some politically correct term that won't help us protect our people!" Then, on August 17, 2017, President Trump issued yet another tweet about Islam, once more referencing the story about General Pershing's massacre of Muslims in the Philippines: "Study what General Pershing . . . did to terrorists when caught. There was no more Radical Islamic Terror for 35 years!"

In September 2017, President Trump tweeted that "[t]he travel ban into the United States should be far larger, tougher and more specific — but stupidly,

---

1. According to the White House, President Trump's statements on Twitter are "official statements."

that would not be politically correct!" Later that month, on September 24, 2017, President Trump issued [the] Presidential Proclamation, which restricts entry of certain nationals from six Muslim-majority countries. On November 29, 2017, President Trump "retweeted" three anti-Muslim videos, entitled "Muslim Destroys a Statue of Virgin Mary!", "Islamist mob pushes teenage boy off roof and beats him to death!", and "Muslim migrant beats up Dutch boy on crutches!"[2] Those videos were initially tweeted by a British political party whose mission is to oppose "all alien and destructive politic[al] or religious doctrines, including . . . Islam." *Ibid.* When asked about these videos, the White House Deputy Press Secretary connected them to the Proclamation, responding that the "President has been talking about these security issues for years now, from the campaign trail to the White House" and "has addressed these issues with the travel order that he issued earlier this year and the companion proclamation."

2

As the majority correctly notes, "the issue before us is not whether to denounce" these offensive statements. Rather, the dispositive and narrow question here is whether a reasonable observer, presented with all "openly available data," the text and "historical context" of the Proclamation, and the "specific sequence of events" leading to it, would conclude that the primary purpose of the Proclamation is to disfavor Islam and its adherents by excluding them from the country. See *McCreary.* The answer is unquestionably yes.

Taking all the relevant evidence together, a reasonable observer would conclude that the Proclamation was driven primarily by anti-Muslim animus, rather than by the Government's asserted national-security justifications. Even before being sworn into office, then-candidate Trump stated that "Islam hates us," warned that "[w]e're having problems with the Muslims, and we're having problems with Muslims coming into the country," promised to enact a "total and complete shutdown of Muslims entering the United States," and instructed one of his advisers to find a "lega[l]" way to enact a Muslim ban, *id.*[3] The

---

2. The content of these videos is highly inflammatory, and their titles are arguably misleading. For instance, the person depicted in the video entitled "Muslim migrant beats up Dutch boy on crutches!" was reportedly not a "migrant," and his religion is not publicly known.

3. The Government urges us to disregard the President's campaign statements. But nothing in our precedent supports that blinkered approach. To the contrary, courts must consider "the historical background of the decision under challenge, the specific series of events leading to the enactment or official policy in question, and the legislative or administrative history." Church of Lukumi Babalu Aye, Inc. v. Hialeah (1993) (opinion of Kennedy, J.). Moreover, President Trump and his advisers have repeatedly acknowledged that the Proclamation and its predecessors are an outgrowth of the President's campaign statements. For example, just last November, the Deputy White House Press Secretary reminded the media that the Proclamation addresses "issues" the President has been talking about "for years," including on "the campaign trail." In any case, as the Fourth Circuit correctly recognized, even without relying on any of the President's campaign statements, a reasonable observer would conclude that the Proclamation was enacted for the impermissible purpose of disfavoring Muslims.

President continued to make similar statements well after his inauguration, as detailed above.

Moreover, despite several opportunities to do so, President Trump has never disavowed any of his prior statements about Islam.[4] Instead, he has continued to make remarks that a reasonable observer would view as an unrelenting attack on the Muslim religion and its followers. Given President Trump's failure to correct the reasonable perception of his apparent hostility toward the Islamic faith, it is unsurprising that the President's lawyers have, at every step in the lower courts, failed in their attempts to launder the Proclamation of its discriminatory taint. See *United States v. Fordice* (1992). Notably, the Court recently found less pervasive official expressions of hostility and the failure to disavow them to be constitutionally significant. Cf. *Masterpiece Cakeshop, Ltd. v. Colorado Civil Rights Comm'n* (2018) ("The official expressions of hostility to religion in some of the commissioners' comments — comments that were not disavowed at the Commission or by the State at any point in the proceedings that led to the affirmance of the order — were inconsistent with what the Free Exercise Clause requires"). It should find the same here.

Ultimately, what began as a policy explicitly "calling for a total and complete shutdown of Muslims entering the United States" has since morphed into a "Proclamation" putatively based on national-security concerns. But this new window dressing cannot conceal an unassailable fact: the words of the President and his advisers create the strong perception that the Proclamation is contaminated by impermissible discriminatory animus against Islam and its followers.

II

Rather than defend the President's problematic statements, the Government urges this Court to set them aside and defer to the President on issues related to immigration and national security. The majority accepts that invitation and incorrectly applies a watered-down legal standard in an effort to short circuit plaintiffs' Establishment Clause claim.

---

4. At oral argument, the Solicitor General asserted that President Trump "made crystal-clear on September 25 that he had no intention of imposing the Muslim ban" and "has praised Islam as one of the great countries [sic] of the world." Because the record contained no evidence of any such statement made on September 25th, however, the Solicitor General clarified after oral argument that he actually intended to refer to President Trump's statement during a television interview on January 25, 2017. During that interview, the President was asked whether EO-1 was "the Muslim ban," and answered, "no it's not the Muslim ban." But that lone assertion hardly qualifies as a disavowal of the President's comments about Islam — some of which were spoken after January 25, 2017. Moreover, it strains credulity to say that President Trump's January 25th statement makes "crystal-clear" that he never intended to impose a Muslim ban given that, until May 2017, the President's website displayed the statement regarding his campaign promise to ban Muslims from entering the country.

The majority begins its constitutional analysis by noting that this Court, at times, "has engaged in a circumscribed judicial inquiry when the denial of a visa allegedly burdens the constitutional rights of a U.S. citizen." *Kleindienst v. Mandel* (1972). As the majority notes, *Mandel* held that when the Executive Branch provides "a facially legitimate and bona fide reason" for denying a visa, "courts will neither look behind the exercise of that discretion, nor test it by balancing its justification." *Id.*, at 770. In his controlling concurrence in *Kerry v. Din* (2015), Justice Kennedy applied *Mandel*'s holding and elaborated that courts can " 'look behind' the Government's exclusion of" a foreign national if there is "an affirmative showing of bad faith on the part of the consular officer who denied [the] visa." *Din*, 576 U.S., at ____ (opinion concurring in judgment) (slip op., at 5). The extent to which *Mandel* and *Din* apply at all to this case is unsettled, and there is good reason to think they do not.[5] Indeed, even the Government agreed at oral argument that where the Court confronts a situation involving "all kinds of denigrating comments about" a particular religion and a subsequent policy that is designed with the purpose of disfavoring that religion but that "dot[s] all the i's and . . . cross[es] all the t's," *Mandel* would not "pu[t] an end to judicial review of that set of facts."

In light of the Government's suggestion "that it may be appropriate here for the inquiry to extend beyond the facial neutrality of the order," the majority rightly declines to apply *Mandel*'s "narrow standard of review" and "assume[s] that we may look behind the face of the Proclamation." In doing so, however, the Court, without explanation or precedential support, limits its review of the Proclamation to rational-basis scrutiny. That approach is perplexing, given that in other Establishment Clause cases, including those involving claims of religious animus or discrimination, this Court has applied a more stringent standard

---

5. *Mandel* and *Din* are readily distinguishable from this case for a number of reasons. First, *Mandel* and *Din* each involved a constitutional challenge to an Executive Branch decision to exclude a single foreign national under a specific statutory ground of inadmissibility. Here, by contrast, President Trump is not exercising his discretionary authority to determine the admission or exclusion of a particular foreign national. He promulgated an executive order affecting millions of individuals on a categorical basis. Second, *Mandel* and *Din* did not purport to establish the framework for adjudicating cases (like this one) involving claims that the Executive Branch violated the Establishment Clause by acting pursuant to an unconstitutional purpose. Applying *Mandel*'s narrow standard of review to such a claim would run contrary to this Court's repeated admonition that "[f]acial neutrality is not determinative" in the Establishment Clause context. *Lukumi*. Likewise, the majority's passing invocation of *Fiallo v. Bell* is misplaced. Fiallo, unlike this case, addressed a constitutional challenge to a statute enacted by Congress, not an order of the President. *Fiallo*'s application of *Mandel* says little about whether *Mandel*'s narrow standard of review applies to the unilateral executive proclamation promulgated under the circumstances of this case. Finally, even assuming that Mandel and Din apply here, they would not preclude us from looking behind the face of the Proclamation because plaintiffs have made "an affirmative showing of bad faith, by the President who, among other things, instructed his subordinates to find a "lega[l]" way to enact a Muslim ban.

of review. See, *e.g., McCreary; Larson.*[6] As explained above, the Proclamation is plainly unconstitutional under that heightened standard.

But even under rational-basis review, the Proclamation must fall. That is so because the Proclamation is " 'divorced from any factual context from which we could discern a relationship to legitimate state interests,' and 'its sheer breadth [is] so discontinuous with the reasons offered for it'" that the policy is " 'inexplicable by anything but animus.'" *Ante* (quoting *Romer v. Evans* (1996)); see also *Cleburne v. Cleburne Living Center, Inc.* (1985) (recognizing that classifications predicated on discriminatory animus can never be legitimate because the Government has no legitimate interest in exploiting "mere negative attitudes, or fear" toward a disfavored group). The President's statements, which the majority utterly fails to address in its legal analysis, strongly support the conclusion that the Proclamation was issued to express hostility toward Muslims and exclude them from the country. Given the overwhelming record evidence of anti-Muslim animus, it simply cannot be said that the Proclamation has a legitimate basis.

The majority insists that the Proclamation furthers two interrelated national-security interests: "preventing entry of nationals who cannot be adequately vetted and inducing other nations to improve their practices." But the Court offers insufficient support for its view "that the entry suspension has a legitimate grounding in [those] national security concerns, quite apart from any religious hostility." Indeed, even a cursory review of the Government's asserted national-security rationale reveals that the Proclamation is nothing more than a " 'religious gerrymander.'" *Lukumi.*

The majority first emphasizes that the Proclamation "says nothing about religion." Even so, the Proclamation, just like its predecessors, overwhelmingly

---

6. The majority chides as "problematic" the importation of Establishment Clause jurisprudence "in the national security and foreign affairs context." As the majority sees it, this Court's Establishment Clause precedents do not apply to cases involving "immigration policies, diplomatic sanctions, and military actions." But just because the Court has not confronted the precise situation at hand does not render these cases (or the principles they announced) inapplicable. Moreover, the majority's complaint regarding the lack of direct authority is a puzzling charge, given that the majority itself fails to cite any "authority for its proposition" that a more probing review is inappropriate in a case like this one, where United States citizens allege that the Executive has violated the Establishment Clause by issuing a sweeping executive order motivated by animus. In any event, even if there is no prior case directly on point, it is clear from our precedent that "[w]hatever power the United States Constitution envisions for the Executive" in the context of national security and foreign affairs, "it most assuredly envisions a role for all three branches when individual liberties are at stake." Hamdi v. Rumsfeld (2004) (plurality opinion). This Court's Establishment Clause precedents require that, if a reasonable observer would understand an executive action to be driven by discriminatory animus, the action be invalidated. See *McCreary.* That reasonable-observer inquiry includes consideration of the Government's asserted justifications for its actions. The Government's invocation of a national-security justification, however, does not mean that the Court should close its eyes to other relevant information. Deference is different from unquestioning acceptance. Thus, what is "far more problematic" in this case is the majority's apparent willingness to throw the Establishment Clause out the window and forgo any meaningful constitutional review at the mere mention of a national-security concern.

targets Muslim-majority nations. Given the record here, including all the President's statements linking the Proclamation to his apparent hostility toward Muslims, it is of no moment that the Proclamation also includes minor restrictions on two non-Muslim majority countries, North Korea and Venezuela, or that the Government has removed a few Muslim-majority countries from the list of covered countries since EO-1 was issued. Consideration of the entire record supports the conclusion that the inclusion of North Korea and Venezuela, and the removal of other countries, simply reflect subtle efforts to start "talking territory instead of Muslim," precisely so the Executive Branch could evade criticism or legal consequences for the Proclamation's otherwise clear targeting of Muslims. The Proclamation's effect on North Korea and Venezuela, for example, is insubstantial, if not entirely symbolic. And prior sanctions order already restricts entry of North Korean nationals, and the Proclamation targets only a handful of Venezuelan government officials and their immediate family members. As such, the President's inclusion of North Korea and Venezuela does little to mitigate the anti-Muslim animus that permeates the Proclamation.

The majority next contends that the Proclamation "reflects the results of a worldwide review process undertaken by multiple Cabinet officials." . . . [T]he worldwide review does little to break the clear connection between the Proclamation and the President's anti-Muslim statements. The President campaigned on a promise to implement a "total and complete shutdown of Muslims" entering the country, translated that campaign promise into a concrete policy, and made several statements linking that policy (in its various forms) to anti-Muslim animus.

Ignoring all this, the majority empowers the President to hide behind an administrative review process that the Government refuses to disclose to the public. Furthermore, evidence of which we can take judicial notice indicates that the multiagency review process could not have been very thorough. Ongoing litigation under the Freedom of Information Act shows that the September 2017 report the Government produced after its review process was a mere 17 pages. That the Government's analysis of the vetting practices of hundreds of countries boiled down to such a short document raises serious questions about the legitimacy of the President's proclaimed national-security rationale.

Beyond that, Congress has already addressed the national-security concerns supposedly undergirding the Proclamation through an "extensive and complex" framework governing "immigration and alien status." *Arizona v. United States* (2012).[7] The Immigration and Nationality Act sets forth, in painstaking detail, a reticulated scheme regulating the admission of individuals to the United States.

---

7. It is important to note, particularly given the nature of this case, that many consider "using the term 'alien' to refer to other human beings" to be "offensive and demeaning." I use the term here only where necessary "to be consistent with the statutory language" that Congress has chosen and "to avoid any confusion in replacing a legal term of art with a more appropriate term." *Ibid.*

Generally, admission to the United States requires a valid visa or other travel document. . . .

In addition to vetting rigorously any individuals seeking admission to the United States, the Government also rigorously vets the information-sharing and identity-management systems of other countries, as evidenced by the Visa Waiver Program, which permits certain nationals from a select group of countries to skip the ordinary visa-application process. . . .

Put simply, Congress has already erected a statutory scheme that fulfills the putative national-security interests the Government now puts forth to justify the Proclamation. Tellingly, the Government remains wholly unable to articulate any credible national-security interest that would go unaddressed by the current statutory scheme absent the Proclamation. The Government also offers no evidence that this current vetting scheme, which involves a highly searching consideration of individuals required to obtain visas for entry into the United States and a highly searching consideration of which countries are eligible for inclusion in the Visa Waiver Program, is inadequate to achieve the Proclamation's proclaimed objectives of "preventing entry of nationals who cannot be adequately vetted and inducing other nations to improve their [vetting and information-sharing] practices." . . .

Equally unavailing is the majority's reliance on the Proclamation's waiver program. As several *amici* thoroughly explain, there is reason to suspect that the Proclamation's waiver program is nothing more than a sham. . . .

In sum, none of the features of the Proclamation highlighted by the majority supports the Government's claim that the Proclamation is genuinely and primarily rooted in a legitimate national-security interest. What the unrebutted evidence actually shows is that a reasonable observer would conclude, quite easily, that the primary purpose and function of the Proclamation is to disfavor Islam by banning Muslims from entering our country.

III

As the foregoing analysis makes clear, plaintiffs are likely to succeed on the merits of their Establishment Clause claim. . . .

First, plaintiffs have shown a likelihood of irreparable harm in the absence of an injunction. . . .

Second, plaintiffs have demonstrated that the balance of the equities tips in their favor. Against plaintiffs' concrete allegations of serious harm, the Government advances only nebulous national-security concerns. Although national security is unquestionably an issue of paramount public importance, it is not "a talisman" that the Government can use "to ward off inconvenient claims — a 'label' used to 'cover a multitude of sins.'" *Ziglar v. Abbasi* (2017). That is especially true here, because, as noted, the Government's other statutory tools, including the existing rigorous individualized vetting process, already address the Proclamation's purported national-security concerns.

Finally, plaintiffs and their *amici* have convincingly established that "an injunction is in the public interest."[13]

IV

The First Amendment stands as a bulwark against official religious prejudice and embodies our Nation's deep commitment to religious plurality and tolerance. That constitutional promise is why, "[f]or centuries now, people have come to this country from every corner of the world to share in the blessing of religious freedom." *Town of Greece v. Galloway* (Kagan, J., dissenting). Instead of vindicating those principles, today's decision tosses them aside. In holding that the First Amendment gives way to an executive policy that a reasonable observer would view as motivated by animus against Muslims, the majority opinion upends this Court's precedent, repeats tragic mistakes of the past, and denies countless individuals the fundamental right of religious liberty.

Just weeks ago, the Court rendered its decision in *Masterpiece Cakeshop,* which applied the bedrock principles of religious neutrality and tolerance in considering a First Amendment challenge to government action. *Masterpiece Cakeshop* ("The Constitution 'commits government itself to religious tolerance, and upon even slight suspicion that proposals for state intervention stem from animosity to religion or distrust of its practices, all officials must pause to remember their own high duty to the Constitution and to the rights it secures'" (quoting *Lukumi*)); *Masterpiece,* 584 U.S., at ____ (Kagan, J., concurring) ("[S]tate actors cannot show hostility to religious views; rather, they must give those views 'neutral and respectful consideration'"). Those principles should apply equally here. In both instances, the question is whether a government actor exhibited tolerance and neutrality in reaching a decision that affects individuals' fundamental religious freedom. But unlike in *Masterpiece,* where a state civil rights commission was found to have acted without "the neutrality that the Free Exercise Clause requires," the government actors in this case will not be held accountable for breaching the First Amendment's guarantee of religious neutrality and tolerance. Unlike in *Masterpiece,* where the majority considered the state commissioners' statements about religion to be persuasive evidence of unconstitutional government action, the majority here completely

---

13. Because the majority concludes that plaintiffs have failed to show a likelihood of success on the merits, it takes no position on "the propriety of the nationwide scope of the injunction issued by the District Court." The District Court did not abuse its discretion by granting nationwide relief. Given the nature of the Establishment Clause violation and the unique circumstances of this case, the imposition of a nationwide injunction was "'necessary to provide complete relief to the plaintiffs.'" *Madsen v. Women's Health Center, Inc.* (1994); see *Califano v. Yamasaki* (1979) ("[T]he scope of injunctive relief is dictated by the extent of the violation established, not by the geographical extent of the plaintiff class").

sets aside the President's charged statements about Muslims as irrelevant. That holding erodes the foundational principles of religious tolerance that the Court elsewhere has so emphatically protected, and it tells members of minority religions in our country " 'that they are outsiders, not full members of the political community.'" *Santa Fe.*

Today's holding is all the more troubling given the stark parallels between the reasoning of this case and that of *Korematsu v. United States* (1944). In *Korematsu,* the Court gave "a pass [to] an odious, gravely injurious racial classification" authorized by an executive order. *Adarand Constructors, Inc. v. Peña* (1995) (Ginsburg, J., dissenting). As here, the Government invoked an ill-defined national-security threat to justify an exclusionary policy of sweeping proportion. As here, the exclusion order was rooted in dangerous stereotypes about, *inter alia,* a particular group's supposed inability to assimilate and desire to harm the United States. See *Korematsu* (Murphy, J., dissenting). As here, the Government was unwilling to reveal its own intelligence agencies' views of the alleged security concerns to the very citizens it purported to protect. And as here, there was strong evidence that impermissible hostility and animus motivated the Government's policy.

Although a majority of the Court in *Korematsu* was willing to uphold the Government's actions based on a barren invocation of national security, dissenting Justices warned of that decision's harm to our constitutional fabric. Justice Murphy recognized that there is a need for great deference to the Executive Branch in the context of national security, but cautioned that "it is essential that there be definite limits to [the government's] discretion," as "[i]ndividuals must not be left impoverished of their constitutional rights on a plea of military necessity that has neither substance nor support." Justice Jackson lamented that the Court's decision upholding the Government's policy would prove to be "a far more subtle blow to liberty than the promulgation of the order itself," for although the executive order was not likely to be long lasting, the Court's willingness to tolerate it would endure.

In the intervening years since *Korematsu,* our Nation has done much to leave its sordid legacy behind. Today, the Court takes the important step of finally overruling *Korematsu,* denouncing it as "gravely wrong the day it was decided." This formal repudiation of a shameful precedent is laudable and long overdue. But it does not make the majority's decision here acceptable or right. By blindly accepting the Government's misguided invitation to sanction a discriminatory policy motivated by animosity toward a disfavored group, all in the name of a superficial claim of national security, the Court redeploys the same dangerous logic underlying *Korematsu* and merely replaces one "gravely wrong" decision with another.

Our Constitution demands, and our country deserves, a Judiciary willing to hold the coordinate branches to account when they defy our most sacred legal commitments. Because the Court's decision today has failed in that respect, with profound regret, I dissent.

Department of Homeland Security v. Thuraissigiam
591 U.S. ___ (2020)

On writ of certiorari to the United States Court of Appeals for the Ninth Circuit

JUSTICE ALITO delivered the opinion of the Court.

Every year, hundreds of thousands of aliens are apprehended at or near the border attempting to enter this country illegally. Many ask for asylum, claiming that they would be persecuted if returned to their home countries. Some of these claims are valid, and by granting asylum, the United States lives up to its ideals and its treaty obligations. Most asylum claims, however, ultimately fail, and some are fraudulent. In 1996, when Congress enacted the Illegal Immigration Reform and Immigrant Responsibility Act (IIRIRA), it crafted a system for weeding out patently meritless claims and expeditiously removing the aliens making such claims from the country. It was Congress's judgment that detaining all asylum seekers until the full-blown removal process is completed would place an unacceptable burden on our immigration system and that releasing them would present an undue risk that they would fail to appear for removal proceedings.

This case concerns the constitutionality of the system Congress devised. Among other things, IIRIRA placed restrictions on the ability of asylum seekers to obtain review under the federal habeas statute, but the United States Court of Appeals for the Ninth Circuit held that these restrictions are unconstitutional. According to the Ninth Circuit, they unconstitutionally suspend the writ of habeas corpus and violate asylum seekers' right to due process. We now review that decision and reverse.

Respondent's Suspension Clause argument fails because it would extend the writ of habeas corpus far beyond its scope "when the Constitution was drafted and ratified." *Boumediene v. Bush* (2008). Indeed, respondent's use of the writ would have been unrecognizable at that time. Habeas has traditionally been a means to secure *release* from unlawful detention, but respondent invokes the writ to achieve an entirely different end, namely, to obtain additional administrative review of his asylum claim and ultimately to obtain authorization to stay in this country.

Respondent's due process argument fares no better. While aliens who have established connections in this country have due process rights in deportation proceedings, the Court long ago held that Congress is entitled to set the conditions for an alien's lawful entry into this country and that, as a result, an alien at the threshold of initial entry cannot claim any greater rights under the Due Process Clause. See *Nishimura Ekiu v. United States* (1892). Respondent attempted to enter the country illegally and was apprehended just 25 yards from the border. He therefore has no entitlement to procedural rights other than those afforded by statute.

In short, under our precedents, neither the Suspension Clause nor the Due Process Clause of the Fifth Amendment requires any further review of respondent's claims, and IIRIRA's limitations on habeas review are constitutional as applied.

I

C

. . . Respondent Vijayakumar Thuraissigiam, a Sri Lankan national, crossed the southern border without inspection or an entry document at around 11 p.m. one night in January 2017. A Border Patrol agent stopped him within 25 yards of the border, and the Department detained him for expedited removal. He claimed a fear of returning to Sri Lanka because a group of men had once abducted and severely beaten him, but he said that he did not know who the men were, why they had assaulted him, or whether Sri Lankan authorities would protect him in the future. . . .

The asylum officer credited respondent's account of the assault but determined that he lacked a "credible" fear of persecution. . . . After hearing further testimony from respondent, an Immigration Judge affirmed on *de novo* review and returned the case to the Department for removal.

Respondent then filed a federal habeas petition. . . . The District Court dismissed the petition, holding that 8 U.S.C. §§1252(a)(2) and (e)(2)[5] and clear Ninth Circuit case law foreclosed review of the negative credible-fear determination that resulted in respondent's expedited removal order. The court also rejected respondent's argument "that the jurisdictional limitations of §1252(e) violate the Suspension Clause," again relying on Circuit precedent.

The Ninth Circuit reversed. It found that our Suspension Clause precedent demands "reference to the writ as it stood in 1789." But without citing any pre-1789 case about the scope of the writ, the court held that §1252(e)(2) violates the Suspension Clause. The court added that respondent "has procedural due process rights," specifically the right " 'to expedited removal proceedings that conformed to the dictates of due process.' " Although the decision applied only to respondent, petitioners across the Circuit have used it to obtain review outside the scope of §1252(e)(2), and petitioners elsewhere have attempted to follow suit.

II

A

The Suspension Clause provides that "[t]he Privilege of the Writ of Habeas Corpus shall not be suspended, unless when in Cases of Rebellion or Invasion the public Safety may require it." U. S. Const., Art. I, §9, cl. 2. In *INS* v. *St. Cyr*

---

5. "§1252(e)(2), limits the review that an alien in expedited removal may obtain via a petition for a writ of habeas corpus. That provision allows habeas review of three matters: first, 'whether the petitioner is an alien'; second, 'whether the petitioner was ordered removed'; and third, whether the petitioner has already been granted entry as a lawful permanent resident, refugee, or asylee."

we wrote that the Clause, at a minimum, "protects the writ as it existed in 1789," when the Constitution was adopted. And in this case, respondent agrees that "there is no reason" to consider whether the Clause extends any further. We therefore proceed on that basis.[12]

B

This principle dooms respondent's Suspension Clause argument, because neither respondent nor his *amici* have shown that the writ of habeas corpus was understood at the time of the adoption of the Constitution to permit a petitioner to claim the right to enter or remain in a country or to obtain administrative review potentially leading to that result. The writ simply provided a means of contesting the lawfulness of restraint and securing release.

In 1768, Blackstone's Commentaries—usually a "satisfactory exposition of the common law of England," *Schick v. United States* (1904)—made this clear. Blackstone wrote that habeas was a means to "remov[e] the injury of unjust and illegal confinement." 3 W. Blackstone, Commentaries on the Laws of England. Justice Story described the "common law" writ the same way. See 3 Commentaries on the Constitution of the United States (1833). Habeas, he explained, "is the appropriate remedy to ascertain . . . whether any person is rightfully in confinement or not." . . .

In this case, however, respondent did not ask to be released. Instead, he sought entirely different relief: vacatur of his "removal order" and "an order directing [the Department] to provide him with a new . . . opportunity to apply for asylum and other relief from removal." Such relief might fit an injunction or writ of mandamus—which tellingly, his petition also requested—but that relief falls outside the scope of the common-law habeas writ. . . .

III

Disputing this conclusion, respondent argues that the Suspension Clause guarantees a broader habeas right. To substantiate this claim, he points to three bodies of case law: British and American cases decided prior to or around the time of the adoption of the Constitution, decisions of this Court during the so-called "finality era" (running from the late 19th century to the mid-20th century), and two of our more recent cases. None of these sources support his argument.

---

12. The original meaning of the Suspension Clause is the subject of controversy. In *INS v. St. Cyr* (2001), the majority and dissent debated whether the Clause independently guarantees the availability of the writ or simply restricts the temporary withholding of its operation. We do not revisit that question. Nor do we consider whether the scope of the writ as it existed in 1789 defines the boundary of the constitutional protection to which the *St. Cyr* Court referred, since the writ has never encompassed respondent's claims. We also do not reconsider whether the common law allowed the issuance of a writ on behalf of an alien who lacked any allegiance to the country.

A

Respondent and *amici* supporting his position have done considerable research into the use of habeas before and around the time of the adoption of the Constitution, but they have not unearthed evidence that habeas was then used to obtain anything like what is sought here, namely, authorization for an alien to remain in a country other than his own or to obtain administrative or judicial review leading to that result. All that their research (and the dissent's) shows is that habeas was used to seek release from detention in a variety of circumstances. In fact, respondent and his *amici* do not argue that their cases show anything more.

Because respondent seeks to use habeas to obtain something far different from simple release, his cause is not aided by the many release cases that he and his *amici* have found. Thus, for present purposes, it is immaterial that habeas was used to seek release from confinement that was imposed for . . . other [causes]. What matters is that all these cases are about release from restraint. . . .[18]

[Respondent's] second case, *Somerset v. Stewart* (K. B. 1772), is celebrated but does not aid respondent. James Somerset was a slave who was "detain[ed]" on a ship bound for Jamaica, and Lord Mansfield famously ordered his release on the ground that his detention as a slave was unlawful in England. This relief, release from custody, fell within the historic core of habeas, and Lord Mansfield did not order anything else.

It may well be that a collateral consequence of Somerset's release was that he was allowed to remain in England, but if that is so, it was due not to the writ issued by Lord Mansfield, but to English law regarding entitlement to reside in the country. At the time, England had nothing like modern immigration restrictions. . . .[19]

For a similar reason, respondent cannot find support in early 19th-century American cases in which deserting foreign sailors used habeas to obtain their release from the custody of American officials. In none of the cases involving deserters that have been called to our attention did the court order anything more than simple release from custody. . . .

In these cases, as in *Somerset*, it may be that the released petitioners were able to remain in the United States as a collateral consequence of release, but if so, that was due not to the writs ordering their release, but to U.S. immigration law or the lack thereof. These decisions came at a time when an "open door to the immigrant was the . . . federal policy." *Harisiades v. Shaughnessy* (1952). So release may have had the side effect of enabling these individuals to remain in this country, but that is beside the point.

---

18. Whether the founding generation understood habeas relief more broadly than described by Blackstone, Justice Story, and our prior cases, cannot be settled by a single case or even a few obscure and possibly aberrant cases.

19. This regime lasted until after 1789, when the Aliens Act of 1793 authorized justices of the peace to imprison "without bail or mainprize" (*i.e.*, bond) any alien found without a passport, who could then be "sen[t] out of th[e] realm."

The relief that a habeas court may order and the collateral consequences of that relief are two entirely different things. Ordering an individual's release from custody may have the side effect of enabling that person to pursue all sorts of opportunities that the law allows. . . . Similarly, while the release of an alien may give the alien the opportunity to remain in the country if the immigration laws permit, we have no evidence that the writ as it was known in 1789 could be used to require that aliens be permitted to remain in a country other than their own, or as a means to seek that permission. . . .[20]

Despite pages of rhetoric, the dissent is unable to cite a single pre-1789 habeas case in which a court ordered relief that was anything like what respondent seeks here. The dissent instead contends that "the Suspension Clause inquiry does not require a close (much less precise) factual match with historical habeas precedent," and then discusses cases that are not even close to this one. The dissent reveals the true nature of its argument by suggesting that there are "inherent difficulties [in] a strict originalist approach in the habeas context because of, among other things, the dearth of reasoned habeas decisions at the founding." But respondent does not ask us to hold that the Suspension Clause guarantees the writ as it might have evolved since the adoption of the Constitution. On the contrary, as noted at the outset of this discussion, he rests his argument on "the writ as it existed in 1789."

What the dissent merely implies, one concurring opinion states expressly, arguing that the scope of the writ guaranteed by the Suspension Clause "may change 'depending upon the circumstances'" and thus may allow certain aliens to seek relief other than release. *Post* (Breyer, J., concurring in judgment) (quoting *Boumediene*). But that is not respondent's argument, and as a general rule "we rely on the parties to frame the issues for decision and assign to courts the role of neutral arbiter of matters the parties present." *United States v. Sineneng-Smith* (2020). In any event, the concurrence's snippets of quotations from *Boumediene* are taken entirely out of context. They relate to the question whether the statutory review procedures for Guantanamo detainees *seeking release from custody* provided an adequate substitute for a habeas petition *seeking release*. They do not suggest that any habeas writ guaranteed by the Suspension Clause permits a petitioner to obtain relief that goes far beyond the "core" of habeas as "a remedy for unlawful executive detention." *Munaf*.[21]

---

20. The role of federal courts under our Constitution is very different from that of those English judges. The English judges "were considered agents of the Crown, designed to assist the King in the exercise of his power." *Boumediene.* . . . Habeas was an exercise of the King's prerogative "to have an account . . . why the liberty of any of his subjects is restrained." J. Story, Commentaries;. In our federal courts, by contrast, the scope of habeas has been tightly regulated by statute, from the Judiciary Act of 1789 to the present day, and precedent is as binding in a habeas case as in any other. See, *e.g.*, *Jenkins v. Hutton* (2017).

21. This concurrence imagines three horrible possibilities that it fears could come to pass unless we interpret the Suspension Clause to protect the right to some undefined category of relief beyond release from custody. . . . Finally, there is the hypothetical alien denied asylum on the ground that Judaism is not a religion. Such a decision would of course be ridiculous, but why it would not raise a question of "brute fac[t]" that falls outside the concurrence's interpretation of the Suspension Clause,

B

We now proceed to consider the second body of case law on which respondent relies, decisions of this Court during the "finality era," which takes its name from a feature of the Immigration Act of 1891 making certain immigration decisions "final."

. . . This interpretation of the "finality era" cases is badly mistaken. Those decisions were based not on the Suspension Clause but on the habeas statute and the immigration laws then in force. The habeas statute in effect during this time was broad in scope. It authorized the federal courts to review whether a person was being held in custody in violation of any federal law, including immigration laws. Thus, when aliens claimed that they were detained in violation of immigration statutes, the federal courts considered whether immigration authorities had complied with those laws. This, of course, required that the immigration laws be interpreted, and at the start of the finality era, this Court interpreted the 1891 Act's finality provision to block review of only questions of fact. Accordingly, when writs of habeas corpus were sought by aliens who were detained on the ground that they were not entitled to enter this country, the Court considered whether, given the facts found by the immigration authorities, the detention was consistent with applicable federal law. But the Court exercised that review because it was authorized to do so by statute. The decisions did not hold that this review was required by the Suspension Clause.

In this country, the habeas authority of federal courts has been addressed by statute from the very beginning. The Judiciary Act of 1789, gave the federal courts the power to issue writs of habeas corpus under specified circumstances, but after the Civil War, Congress enacted a much broader statute. That law, the Habeas Corpus Act of 1867, provided that "the several courts of the United States . . . shall have power to grant writs of habeas corpus in all cases where any person may be restrained of his or her liberty in violation of the constitution, or of any treaty or law of the United States." The Act was "of the most comprehensive character," bringing "within the *habeas corpus* jurisdiction of every court and of every judge every possible case of privation of liberty contrary" to federal law. *Ex parte McCardle* (1868).

The Immigration Act of 1891, enacted during one of the country's great waves of immigration, required the exclusion of certain categories of aliens and established procedures for determining whether aliens fell within one of those categories of the 1867 Act]. The [1891] Act required the exclusion of "idiots, insane persons, paupers or persons likely to become a public charge," persons with infectious diseases, persons with convictions for certain crimes,

---

is again not clear. Whatever may be said about the concurrence's hypotheticals, it is possible to imagine all sorts of abuses not even remotely related to unauthorized executive detention that could be imposed on people in this country if the Constitution allowed Congress to deprive the courts of any jurisdiction to entertain claims regarding such abuses. If that were to happen, it would no doubt be argued that constitutional provisions other than the Suspension Clause guaranteed judicial review. We have no occasion to consider such arguments here.

some individuals whose passage had been paid for by a third party, and certain laborers. Inspection officers were authorized to board arriving vessels and inspect any aliens on board. And, in the provision of central importance here, the Act provided that "[a]ll decisions made by the inspection officers or their assistants touching the right of any alien to land, when adverse to such right, shall be final unless appeal be taken to the superintendent of immigration, whose action shall be subject to review by the Secretary of the Treasury." Later immigration Acts, which remained in effect until 1952, contained similar provisions.

The first of the finality era cases, *Nishimura Ekiu v. United States* (1892), required the Court to address the effect of the 1891 Act's finality provision in a habeas case. The Court interpreted the 1891 Act to preclude judicial review only with respect to questions of fact. And after interpreting the 1891 Act in this way, the Court found that "the act of 1891 is constitutional."

The Court's narrow interpretation of the 1891 Act's finality provision meant that the federal courts otherwise retained the full authority granted by the Habeas Corpus Act of 1867 to determine whether an alien was detained in violation of federal law. Turning to that question, the Court held that the only procedural rights of an alien seeking to enter the country are those conferred by statute. . . . What is critical for present purposes is that the Court did not hold that the Suspension Clause imposed any limitations on the authority of Congress to restrict the issuance of writs of habeas corpus in immigration matters.

. . . The *Nishimura Ekiu* Court had no occasion to decide whether the Suspension Clause would have tolerated a broader limitation, and there is not so much as a hint in the opinion that the Court considered this question. Indeed, the opinion never even mentions the Suspension Clause, and it is utterly implausible that the Court would hold *sub silentio* that Congress had violated that provision.

Holding that an Act of Congress unconstitutionally suspends the writ of habeas corpus is momentous. The Justices on the Court at the beginning of the finality era had seen historic occasions when the writ was suspended — during the Civil War by President Lincoln and then by Congress, and later during Reconstruction by President Grant. The suspension of habeas during this era played a prominent role in our constitutional history. See *Ex parte Merryman* (CC Md. 1861) (Taney, C. J.); *Ex parte Milligan* (1866). (Two of the Justices at the beginning of the finality era were on the Court when *Ex parte Milligan* was decided.) The Justices knew a suspension of the writ when they saw one, and it is impossible to believe that the *Nishimura Ekiu* Court identified another occasion when Congress had suspended the writ and based its decision on the Suspension Clause without even mentioning that provision.

The dissent's interpretation of *Nishimura Ekiu* is different from respondent's. According to the dissent, *Nishimura Ekiu* interpreted the 1891 Act as it did based on the doctrine of constitutional avoidance. This reading has no support in the Court's opinion, which never mentions the Suspension Clause or the avoidance doctrine and never explains why the Clause would allow Congress to preclude review of factual findings but nothing more. But even if there were some basis for this interpretation, it would not benefit respondent, and that is undoubtedly why he has not made the argument. IIRIRA unequivocally bars habeas review of respondent's claims, and he does not argue that it can be read any other way. The avoidance doctrine "has no application in the absence of ambiguity." *Warger v. Shauers* (2014). Thus, if *Nishimura Ekiu*'s interpretation were based on constitutional avoidance, it would still not answer the interpretive question here.

When we look to later finality era cases, any suggestion of a Suspension Clause foundation becomes even less plausible. None of those decisions mention the Suspension Clause or even hint that they are based on that provision, and these omissions are telling. . . . During World War II, the Court held that "enemy aliens" could utilize habeas "unless there was suspension of the writ." *In re Yamashita* (1946). And the Court invoked the Suspension Clause in holding that the Executive lacked authority to intern a Japanese-American citizen. See *Ex parte Endo* (1944). If the Justices during that time had thought that the Suspension Clause provided the authority they were exercising in the many cases involving habeas petitions by aliens detained prior to entry, it is hard to believe that this important fact would have escaped mention. . . .

Rather than relying on the Suspension Clause, those cases simply involved the exercise of the authority conferred by the habeas statute then in effect. This was true of *Nishimura Ekiu, Gegiow*, and every other finality era case that respondent cites in support of his Suspension Clause argument. . . . No majority opinion even mentioned the Suspension Clause. Indeed, any mention of the Constitution was rare — and unhelpful to respondent's arguments here.[26] And in all the cited cases concerning aliens detained at entry, unlike the case now before us, what was sought — and the only relief considered — was release. Indeed, in an early finality era case, the Court took pains to note that it did not "express any opinion" on whether an alien was entitled to enter. *Lem Moon Sing v. United States* (1895). . . .

In sum, the Court exercised habeas jurisdiction in the finality era cases because the habeas statute conferred that authority, not because it was required by the Suspension Clause. As a result, these cases cannot support respondent's argument that the writ of habeas corpus as it was understood when the Constitution was adopted would have allowed him to claim the right to administrative and judicial review while still in custody.

C

We come, finally, to the more recent cases on which respondent relies. The most recent, *Boumediene*, is not about immigration at all. It held that suspected foreign terrorists could challenge their detention at the naval base in Guantanamo Bay, Cuba. They had been "apprehended on the battlefield in Afghanistan" and elsewhere, not while crossing the border. They sought only to be released from Guantanamo, not to enter this country. And nothing in the Court's discussion of the Suspension Clause suggested that they could have used habeas as a means

---

26. In *Fong Yue Ting v. United States*, 149 U.S. 698, 713 (1893), and many other cases, the Court noted that the Constitution gives Congress plenary power to set requirements for admission.

of gaining entry. Rather, the Court reaffirmed that release is the habeas remedy though not the "exclusive" result of every writ, given that it is often "appropriate" to allow the executive to cure defects in a detention.

Respondent's other recent case is *St. Cyr*, in which the Court's pertinent holding rejected the argument that certain provisions of IIRIRA and the Antiterrorism and Effective Death Penalty Act of 1996 that did not refer expressly to habeas should nevertheless be interpreted as stripping the authority conferred by the habeas statute. . . . The writ of habeas corpus as it existed at common law provided a vehicle to challenge all manner of detention by government officials, and the Court had held long before that the writ could be invoked by aliens already in the country who were held in custody pending deportation. *St. Cyr* reaffirmed these propositions, and this statement in *St. Cyr* does not signify approval of respondent's very different attempted use of the writ, which the Court did not consider.

IV

In addition to his Suspension Clause argument, respondent contends that IIRIRA violates his right to due process by precluding judicial review of his allegedly flawed credible-fear proceeding. . . .

In 1892, the Court wrote that as to "foreigners who have never been naturalized, nor acquired any domicil or residence within the United States, nor even been admitted into the country pursuant to law," "the decisions of executive or administrative officers, acting within powers expressly conferred by Congress, are due process of law." *Nishimura Ekiu*. Since then, the Court has often reiterated this important rule. . . .

Respondent argues that this rule does not apply to him because he was not taken into custody the instant he attempted to enter the country (as would have been the case had he arrived at a lawful port of entry). Because he succeeded in making it 25 yards into U. S. territory before he was caught, he claims the right to be treated more favorably. The Ninth Circuit agreed with this argument.

We reject it. It disregards the reason for our century-old rule regarding the due process rights of an alien seeking initial entry. That rule rests on fundamental propositions: "[T]he power to admit or exclude aliens is a sovereign prerogative"; the Constitution gives "the political department of the government" plenary authority to decide which aliens to admit, *Nishimura Ekiu*; and a concomitant of that power is the power to set the procedures to be followed in determining whether an alien should be admitted, see *Knauff*.

This rule would be meaningless if it became inoperative as soon as an arriving alien set foot on U. S. soil. When an alien arrives at a port of entry — for example, an international airport — the alien is on U. S. soil, but the alien is not considered to have entered the country for the purposes of this rule. On the contrary, aliens who arrive at ports of entry — even those paroled elsewhere in the country for years pending removal — are "treated" for due process purposes "as if stopped at the border." *Mezei*.

The same must be true of an alien like respondent. . . . Like an alien detained after arriving at a port of entry, an alien like respondent is "on the threshold." *Mezei*. The rule advocated by respondent and adopted by the Ninth Circuit would undermine the "sovereign prerogative" of governing admission to this country and create a perverse incentive to enter at an unlawful rather than a lawful location. *Plasencia*.

For these reasons, an alien in respondent's position has only those rights regarding admission that Congress has provided by statute. . . . Because the Due Process Clause provides nothing more, it does not require review of that determination or how it was made. As applied here, therefore, §1252(e)(2) does not violate due process.

Justice THOMAS, concurring.

I join the Court's opinion, which correctly concludes that respondent's Suspension Clause argument fails because he does not seek a writ of habeas corpus. I write separately to address the original meaning of the Suspension Clause, which guarantees that "[t]he Privilege of the Writ of Habeas Corpus shall not be suspended, unless when in Cases of Rebellion or Invasion the public Safety may require it." Art. I, §9, cl. 2. The Founders appear to have understood "[t]he Privilege of the Writ of Habeas Corpus" to guarantee freedom from discretionary detention, and a "suspen[sion]" of that privilege likely meant a statute granting the executive the power to detain without bail or trial based on mere suspicion of a crime or dangerousness. Thus, the expedited removal procedure in the Illegal Immigration Reform and Immigrant Responsibility Act of 1996, 110 Stat. 3009–546, is likely not a suspension.[1]

I

The writ of habeas corpus began as a prerogative writ in the Court of King's Bench in the 16th century. Over time, however, it came to be understood both as a right to be free from arbitrary detention and as a procedural writ.

By the end of the 16th century, the English connected the common-law writ of habeas corpus to liberty. Specifically, it was associated with the guarantee in Magna Carta that "[n]o free person (*Nullus liber homo*) shall be taken or imprisoned, or disseised or outlawed or exiled, or in any way destroyed . . . except by the lawful judgment of his peers or by the law of the land." Perhaps most prominently, Edward Coke wrote in his Institutes that "if a man be taken, or committed to prison *contra legem terrae*, against the Law of the land," then "[h]e may have an *habeas corpus*." . . .

This association between habeas corpus and freedom from discretionary detention deepened after 1679 with the Habeas Corpus Act. . . . It required an officer served with a writ of habeas corpus to produce the prisoner within three

---

1. I express no view on the question whether respondent is even entitled to the privilege of the writ as an unadmitted alien.

days in "any such criminall or supposed criminall Matters." It also guaranteed bail to prisoners in cases of felony or high treason if they were not tried within one term of court. To protect these rights, Parliament created a special statutory remedy: All writs under the Habeas Corpus Act were marked as issuing pursuant to the statute. . . .

William Blackstone put it even more sweepingly, writing that the Habeas Corpus Act "is frequently considered as another *magna carta*."

II

The Founders inherited this understanding of habeas corpus. And they enshrined it in the Suspension Clause, which they understood to protect a substantive right.

The language of the Suspension Clause evinces this understanding. The Clause itself does not authorize courts to issue writs of habeas corpus. Nor does it refer simply to the writ of habeas corpus. Rather, it protects the *privilege of* the writ of habeas corpus. The word "privilege" was "used interchangeably with the words 'rights,' 'liberties,' and 'freedoms,' and had been since the time of Blackstone." *McDonald v. Chicago* (2010) (Thomas, J., concurring in part and concurring in judgment). By using this term, the Framers appear to have had a substantive right in mind.

Ratification debates reflect this understanding as well. Future Supreme Court Justice James Iredell said in the North Carolina convention that, "[b]y the privileges of the *habeas corpus*, no man can be confined without inquiry; and if it should appear that he has been committed contrary to law, he must be discharged."

This understanding is echoed in statements that the Constitution protects the Habeas Corpus Act, the writ of habeas corpus, or simply "the habeas corpus," all referring to a substantive right. Alexander Hamilton wrote in The Federalist No. 83 that "the *habeas corpus* act" was "provided for in the most ample manner in the plan of the convention." Again in No. 84, he wrote that the Constitution "establish[ed] the writ of *habeas corpus*." . . . In Virginia, Governor Edmund Randolph — a signer and future Attorney General — argued that "the habeas corpus is at least on as secure and good a footing as it is in England" because "[t]hat privilege is secured here by the Constitution." . . . In sum, it seems that the founding generation viewed the privilege of the writ of habeas corpus as a freedom from arbitrary detention.[2]

---

2. None of this is to say that the writ of habeas corpus involved a wide-ranging, ever-changing inquiry. As the Court today reaffirms, "the scope of habeas has been tightly regulated by statute, from the Judiciary Act of 1789 to the present day." *Ante*, at 21, n. 20. A writ of habeas corpus was "in the nature of a writ of error, to examine the legality of the commitment." *Ex parte Watkins* (1830) (Marshall, C. J.).

III

The remaining question is what it means for "[t]he Privilege of the Writ of Habeas Corpus" to "be suspended." U. S. Const., Art. I, §9, cl. 2. At the founding, suspension was a well-known term that meant "a [t]emporal [s]top of a [m]an's [r]ight." N. Bailey, An Universal Etymological English Dictionary (22d ed. 1770). In the context of habeas corpus, it appears to have specifically meant a grant of authority to the executive to detain without bail or trial based on suspicion of a crime or dangerousness.

The English understood the term this way. . . . Americans shared a similar understanding, as evidenced by the suspensions that States passed during the Revolutionary War. "By their common terms," these suspensions "bestowed authority on state executives to arrest and detain persons preventively based on suspicion of supporting the Crown." Tyler, Habeas Corpus in Wartime. . . .

Although the ratification debates are not especially illuminating on the meaning of a suspension, they provide further support for this understanding. Luther Martin wrote that the Government, upon "suspending the habeas corpus act may *seize* upon the persons of those *advocates of freedom*, who have had *virtue* and *resolution* enough to excite the opposition, and may *imprison* them during its pleasure." . . .

In sum, a suspension was not necessarily an express limitation on the availability of the writ of habeas corpus. Rather, it appears to have been a grant of power to detain based on suspicion of a crime or dangerousness without bail or trial.

IV

Under this interpretation, 8 U. S. C. §1252 likely does not suspend the writ of habeas corpus. . . . This statute bears little resemblance to a suspension as that term was understood at the founding. It does not allow the executive to detain based on mere suspicion of a crime or dangerousness. Rather, it requires a finding that the detainee lacks valid documentation and is not eligible for asylum. It even expressly permits habeas relief for a detainee who does not meet certain criteria for expedited removal.

Some may wish that the Suspension Clause were broader. Perhaps for this reason, our precedents have departed from the original understanding of the Suspension Clause. See, *e.g.*, *Boumediene v. Bush* (2008) (Scalia, J., dissenting); *St. Cyr* (Scalia, J., dissenting). But this understanding does contain an important guarantee of individual liberty by limiting the circumstances in which Congress may give the executive power to detain without bail or trial based on suspicion of a crime or dangerousness. In this case, that guarantee has not been violated.

Justice BREYER, with whom Justice Ginsburg joins, concurring in the judgment.

The statute at issue here, 8 U. S. C. §1252(e)(2), sets forth strict limits on what claims a noncitizen subject to expedited removal may present in federal habeas corpus proceedings. I agree that enforcing those limits *in this particular case* does not violate the Suspension Clause's constitutional command: "The Privilege of the Writ of Habeas Corpus shall not be suspended, unless when in Cases of Rebellion or Invasion the public Safety may require it." U. S. Const., Art. I, §9, cl. 2. But we need not, and should not, go further. . . .

Addressing more broadly whether the Suspension Clause protects people challenging removal decisions may raise a host of difficult questions in the immigration context. What review might the Suspension Clause assure, say, a person apprehended years after she crossed our borders clandestinely and started a life in this country? Under current law, noncitizens who have lived in the United States for up to two years may be placed in expedited-removal proceedings, but Congress might decide to raise that 2-year cap (or remove it altogether). Does the Suspension Clause let Congress close the courthouse doors to a long-term permanent resident facing removal?

Could Congress, for that matter, deny habeas review to someone ordered removed despite claiming to be a natural-born U.S. citizen? . . . What about foreclosing habeas review of a claim that rogue immigration officials forged the record of a credible-fear interview that, in truth, never happened? Or that such officials denied a refugee asylum based on the dead-wrong legal interpretation that Judaism does not qualify as a "religion" under governing law?

The answers to these and other "difficult questions about the scope of [Suspension Clause] protections" lurk behind the scenes here. *Lozman v. Riviera Beach* (2018). I would therefore avoid making statements about the Suspension Clause that sweep beyond the principles needed to decide this case—let alone come to conclusions about the Due Process Clause, a distinct constitutional provision that is not directly at issue here.

As for the resolution of the dispute before us, Congress, in my view, had the constitutional power to foreclose habeas review of the claims that respondent has pressed in this case. Habeas corpus, as we have said, is an "adaptable remedy," and the "precise application and scope" of the review it guarantees may change "depending upon the circumstances." *Boumediene v. Bush* (2008). So where the Suspension Clause applies, the "habeas court's role" may prove more "extensive," or less so, depending on the context at issue. Here, even assuming that the Suspension Clause guarantees respondent some form of habeas review—which is to say, even accepting for argument's sake that the relief respondent seeks *is* "release," the scope of that constitutionally required review would not extend to his claims.

Two features of this case persuade me.

First, respondent's status suggests that the constitutional floor set by the Suspension Clause here cannot be high. A Border Patrol agent apprehended respondent just 25 yards inside the border. Respondent was placed in expedited removal proceedings shortly thereafter, where he received the same consideration for relief from removal that Congress has afforded persons arriving at the border. Respondent has never lived in, or been lawfully admitted to, the United States.

To my mind, those are among the "circumstances" that inform the "scope" of any habeas review that the Suspension Clause might guarantee respondent. *Boumediene*. . . .

Second, our precedents demonstrate that respondent's claims are of the kind that Congress may, consistent with the Suspension Clause, make unreviewable in habeas proceedings. Even accepting respondent's argument that our "finality era" cases map out a constitutional minimum, his claims, on the facts presented here, differ significantly from those that we reviewed throughout this period. . . .

Mindful that the "Constitution deals with substance, not shadows," *Salazar v. Buono* (2010) (Roberts, C. J., concurring), I accordingly view both claims as factual in nature, notwithstanding respondent's contrary characterization. For that reason, Congress may foreclose habeas review of these claims without running afoul of the Suspension Clause. See, *e.g.*, *Nishimura Ekiu.* . . .

Reviewing claims hinging on procedural details of this kind would go beyond the traditionally "limited role" that habeas has played in immigration cases similar to this one — even during the finality era. *St. Cyr.* To interpret the Suspension Clause as insisting upon habeas review of these claims would require, by constitutional command, that the habeas court make indeterminate and highly record-intensive judgments on matters of degree. Respondent has not cited, and I have not found, any case of ours suggesting that the Suspension Clause demands parsing procedural compliance at so granular a level. Neither, apparently, has the Solicitor General.

Together with respondent's status, these characteristics convince me that Congress had the constitutional power to foreclose habeas review of respondent's procedural claims. Recasting those claims as an allegation that respondent's "due process rights were violated by" immigration officials makes no material difference. That alternative description changes none of the features that, in my view, put respondent's procedural claims beyond the scope of any minimum habeas review that the Suspension Clause might assure him under the circumstances.

JUSTICE SOTOMAYOR, with whom JUSTICE KAGAN joins, dissenting.

The majority declares that the Executive Branch's denial of asylum claims in expedited removal proceedings shall be functionally unreviewable through the writ of habeas corpus, no matter whether the denial is arbitrary or irrational or contrary to governing law. That determination flouts over a century of this Court's practice. In case after case, we have heard claims indistinguishable from those respondent raises here, which fall within the heartland of habeas jurisdiction going directly to the origins of the Great Writ.

The Court thus purges an entire class of legal challenges to executive detention from habeas review, circumscribing that foundational and "stable bulwark of our liberties," 1 W. Blackstone, Commentaries (1832). By self-imposing this limitation on habeas relief in the absence of a congressional suspension, the Court abdicates its constitutional duty and rejects precedent extending to the foundations of our common law.

Making matters worse, the Court holds that the Constitution's due process protections do not extend to noncitizens like respondent, who challenge the procedures used to determine whether they may seek shelter in this country or whether they may be cast to an unknown fate. The decision deprives them of any means to ensure the integrity of an expedited removal order, an order which, the Court has just held, is not subject to any meaningful judicial oversight as to its substance. In doing so, the Court upends settled constitutional law and paves the way toward transforming already summary expedited removal proceedings into arbitrary administrative adjudications.

Today's decision handcuffs the Judiciary's ability to perform its constitutional duty to safeguard individual liberty and dismantles a critical component of the separation of powers. It will leave significant exercises of executive discretion unchecked in the very circumstance where the writ's protections "have been strongest." *INS v. St. Cyr* (2001). And it increases the risk of erroneous immigration decisions that contravene governing statutes and treaties.

The Court appears to justify its decision by adverting to the burdens of affording robust judicial review of asylum decisions. But our constitutional protections should not hinge on the vicissitudes of the political climate or bend to accommodate burdens on the Judiciary. I respectfully dissent.

I

The as-applied challenge here largely turns on how the Court construes respondent's requests for relief. Its descriptions, as well as those of one of the concurrences, skew the essence of these claims. A proper reframing thus is in order. . . .

Fairly characterized, respondent's claims allege legal error (for violations of governing asylum law and for violations of procedural due process) and an open-ended request for habeas relief. It is "uncontroversial" that the writ encompasses such claims. See *Boumediene v. Bush* (2008) (concluding that release is but one form of relief available); see also *St. Cyr.* (citing cases predating the founding to show that the writ could challenge "the erroneous application or interpretation" of relevant law).

II

Only by recasting respondent's claims and precedents does the Court reach its decision on the merits. By its account, none of our governing cases, recent or centuries old, recognize that the Suspension Clause guards a habeas right to the type of release that respondent allegedly seeks.[1] *Ante*, at 13, n. 14 (finding no evidence that the writ was understood in 1789 to grant relief that would amount to "gaining a right to remain in this country"); *ante*, at 13 (characterizing a

---

1. The Court wisely declines to explore whether the Suspension Clause independently guarantees the availability of the writ or simply restricts the temporary withholding of its operation, a point of disagreement between the majority and dissent in *INS v. St. Cyr*, (2001) But no majority of this Court, at any time, has adopted that theory. Notably, moreover, even Justice Scalia appears to have abandoned his position just three years later in *Hamdi v. Rumsfeld* (2004).

" 'meaningful opportunity' " for review of asylum claims as falling outside of traditional notions of release from custody). An overview of cases starting from the colonial period to the present reveals that the Court is incorrect, even accepting its improper framing of respondent's claims.

A

The critical inquiry, the Court contends, is whether respondent's specific requests for relief (namely, admission into the United States or additional asylum procedures allowing for admission into the United States) fall within the scope of the kind of release afforded by the writ as it existed in 1789. This scope, it explains, is what the Suspension Clause protects "at a minimum." But as the Court implicitly acknowledges, its inquiry is impossible. The inquiry also runs headlong into precedent, which has never demanded the kind of precise factual match with pre-1789 case law that today's Court demands.

To start, the Court recognizes the pitfalls of relying on pre-1789 cases to establish principles relevant to immigration and asylum. . . . The Court nevertheless seems to require respondent to engage in an exercise in futility. It demands that respondent unearth cases predating comprehensive federal immigration regulation showing that noncitizens obtained release from federal custody onto national soil. But no federal statutes at that time spoke to the permissibility of their entry in the first instance; the United States lacked a comprehensive asylum regime until the latter half of the 20th century. Despite the limitations inherent in this exercise, the Court appears to insist on a wealth of cases mirroring the precise relief requested at a granular level; nothing short of that, in the Court's view, would demonstrate that a noncitizen in respondent's position is entitled to the writ. See also Neuman, Habeas Corpus, Executive Detention, and the Removal of Aliens (1998) (noting the inherent difficulties of a strict originalist approach in the habeas context because of, among other things, the dearth of reasoned habeas decisions at the founding).

But this Court has never rigidly demanded a one-to-one match between a habeas petition and a common-law habeas analog. *Boumediene* is even clearer that the Suspension Clause inquiry does not require a close (much less precise) factual match with historical habeas precedent. There, the Court concluded that the writ applied to noncitizen detainees held in Guantanamo, despite frankly admitting that a "[d]iligent search by all parties reveal[ed] no certain conclusions" about the relevant scope of the common-law writ in 1789. . . . But crucially, the Court declined to "infer too much, one way or the other, from the lack of historical evidence on point." Instead, it sought to find comparable common-law habeas cases by "analogy."

There is no squaring the Court's methodology today with *St. Cyr* or *Boumediene*. As those cases show, requiring near-complete equivalence between common-law habeas cases and respondent's habeas claim is out of step with this Court's longstanding approach in immigration cases.

B

1

Applying the correct (and commonsense) approach to defining the Great Writ's historic scope reveals that respondent's claims have long been recognized in habeas.

Respondent cites *Somerset v. Stewart*, (K. B. 1772), as an example on point. There, Lord Mansfield issued a writ ordering release of a slave bound for Jamaica, holding that there was no basis in English law for "sending . . . him over" to another country. Thus, the writ issued even though it "did not free [the] slave so much as it protected him from deportation." *Somerset* establishes the longstanding availability of the writ to challenge the legality of removal and to secure release into a country in which a petitioner sought shelter. . . .

The Court dismisses these examples outright. It acknowledges that the petitioner in *Somerset* may have been allowed to remain in England because of his release on habeas, yet declares that this was "due not to the wri[t] ordering [his] release" but rather to the existing state of the law. But the writ clearly did more than permit the petitioner to disembark from a vessel; it prevented him from being "sen[t] . . . over" to Jamaica. What England's immigration laws might have prescribed after the writ's issuance did not bear on the availability of the writ as a means to remain in the country in the first instance. . . .

The reasoning of *Somerset Case* carried over to the Colonies, where colonial governments presumed habeas available to noncitizens to secure their residence in a territory. . . .

Founding era courts accepted this view of the writ's scope. Rather than credit these decisions, the Court marches through an assorted selection of cases and throws up its hands, contending that the case law merely reflects a wide range of circumstances for which individuals were deprived of their liberty. Thus, the Court concludes, the common law simply did not speak to whether individuals could seek "release" that would allow them to enter a country (as opposed to being expelled from it).

At the same time, notwithstanding its professed keen interest in precedent, the Court seems to discount decisions supporting respondent's view that habeas permitted release from custody into the country. At least two other classes of cases demonstrate that the writ was available from around the founding onward to noncitizens who were detained, and wanted to remain, including those who were prevented from entering the United States at all.

First, common-law courts historically granted the writ to discharge deserting foreign sailors found and imprisoned in the United States. . . . Next, courts routinely granted the writ to release wrongfully detained noncitizens into Territories other than the detainees' "own." Many involved the release of fugitive or former slaves outside their home State. . . .

The weight of historical evidence demonstrates that common-law courts at and near the founding granted habeas to noncitizen detainees to enter Territories not considered their own, and thus ordered the kind of release that the Court claims falls outside the purview of the common-law writ.

The Court argues that none of this evidence is persuasive because the writ could not be used to compel authorization to enter the United States. *Ante*, at 20. But that analogy is inapt. Perhaps if respondent here sought to use the writ to grant naturalization, the comparison would be closer. But respondent sought only the proper interpretation and application of asylum law (which statutorily permits him to remain if he shows a credible fear of persecution), or in the alternative, release pursuant to the writ (despite being cognizant that he could be denied asylum or rearrested upon release if he were found within the country without legal authorization). But that consequence does not deprive respondent of the ability to invoke the writ in the first instance. . . . For these reasons, the Court is wrong to dispute that common-law habeas practice encompassed the kind of release respondent seeks here.

2

The Court also appears to contend that respondent sought merely additional procedures in his habeas adjudication and that this kind of relief does not fall within the traditional scope of the writ. That reflects a misunderstanding of the writ. Habeas courts regularly afforded the state additional opportunities to show that a detention was lawful before ordering what the Court now considers a release outright. . . .

These examples confirm that outright habeas release was not always immediately awarded. But they also show that common-law courts understood that relief short of release, such as ordering officials to comply with the law and to correct underlying errors, nevertheless fell within the scope of a request for habeas corpus. . . .

C

Next, the Court casually dismisses nearly 70 years of precedent from the finality era, the most relevant historic period for examining judicial review of immigration decisions. It concludes that, in case after case, this Court exercised habeas review over legal questions arising in immigration cases akin to those at issue here, not because the Constitution required it but only because a statute permitted it. That conclusion is both wrong in its own right and repeats arguments this Court rejected a half century ago when reviewing this same body of cases.

At the turn of the 20th century, immigration to the United States was relatively unrestricted. Public sentiment, however, grew hostile toward many recent entrants, particularly migrant laborers from China. In response, Congress enacted the so-called Chinese Exclusion Act of 1882, which prohibited the entry of Chinese laborers to the United States. The Scott Act, enacted in 1888, forbade reentry of Chinese laborers who had left after previously residing in this country.

Although immigration officials routinely denied entry to arriving migrants on the basis of these laws, many of these decisions were overturned by federal courts on habeas review.

This did not escape Congress' attention. Congress responded by enacting the Immigration Act of 1891, which stripped federal courts of their power to review immigration denials: By its terms, that restriction on federal judicial power was not limited to review of some undefined subset of issues, such as questions of law or fact; it made executive immigration decisions final in all respects.

The Court, however, quickly construed the statute in *Nishimura Ekiu v. United States* (1892) (*Ekiu*), to preclude only review of executive factfinding. Having so construed the statute, the Court in *Ekiu*, and in case after case following *Ekiu*, recognized the availability of habeas to review a range of legal and constitutional questions arising in immigration decisions. The crucial question here is whether the finality-era Courts adopted that construction of jurisdiction-stripping statutes because it was simply the correct interpretation of the statute's terms and nothing more or because that construction was constitutionally compelled to ensure the availability of habeas review. The better view is that *Ekiu*'s construction of the 1891 statute was constitutionally compelled. . . .

What, then, can *Ekiu* tell us? Today's Court finds significant that the brief opinion makes no explicit mention of the Suspension Clause. This omission, it concludes, can only mean that the *Ekiu* Court did not think that (or had no occasion to consider whether) the Suspension Clause "imposed any limitations on the authority of Congress to restrict the issuance of writs of habeas corpus in immigration matters." . . .

But this myopic interpretation ignores many salient facts. . . . These considerations all point in one direction: Even if the *Ekiu* Court did not explicitly hold that the Suspension Clause prohibits Congress from broadly limiting all judicial review in immigration proceedings, it certainly decided the case in a manner that avoided raising this constitutional question. Indeed, faced with a jurisdiction-stripping statute, the only review left for the *Ekiu* Court was that required by the Constitution and, by extension, protected by the guarantee of habeas corpus. . . .

In any event, we need not speculate now about whether the *Ekiu* Court, or the Courts that followed, had the constitutional right to habeas corpus in mind when they interpreted jurisdiction-stripping statutes only to preclude review of historic facts. This Court has already identified which view is correct. In *Heikkila* v. *Barber* (1953), the Court explained that *Ekiu* and its progeny had, in fact, construed the finality statutes to avoid serious constitutional questions about Congress' ability to strip federal courts of their habeas power. . . .

At bottom, the better view of the finality-era cases is that they understood the habeas right they sustained to be, or at least likely to be, constitutionally compelled. . . . Ignoring how past courts wrestled with this issue may make it easier for the Court to announce that there is no unconstitutional suspension today. But by sweeping aside most of our immigration history in service of its conclusion, the Court reopens a question that this Court put to rest decades ago, and now decides it differently. The cost of doing so is enormous. The

Court, on its own volition, limits a constitutional protection so respected by our Founding Fathers that they forbade its suspension except in the direst of circumstances.

D

Not only does the Court cast to one side our finality-era jurisprudence, it skims over recent habeas precedent. Perhaps that is because these cases undermine today's decision. Indeed, both *INS v. St. Cyr* (2001), and *Boumediene v. Bush* (2008), instruct that eliminating judicial review of legal and constitutional questions associated with executive detention, like the expedited-removal statute at issue here does, is unconstitutional.

The Court acknowledges *St. Cyr*'s holding but does not heed it. . . . Thus based on the same principles that the Court purports to apply in this case, the *St. Cyr* Court reached the opposite conclusion: The Suspension Clause likely prevents Congress from eliminating judicial review of discretionary executive action in the deportation context, even when the writ is used to challenge more than the fact of detention itself. *Boumediene* reprised many of the rules articulated in *St. Cyr*. . . .

The Court discounts these cases because it objects to the perceived direction of respondent's requested release. It similarly contends that respondent's attempted use of the writ is "very different" from that at issue in *St. Cyr.*

Neither rejoinder is sound. *St. Cyr* and *Boumediene* confirm that at minimum, the historic scope of the habeas power guaranteed judicial review of constitutional and legal challenges to executive action. They do not require release as an exclusive remedy, let alone a particular direction of release. Rather, both cases built on the legacy of the finality era where the Court, concerned about the constitutionality of limiting judicial review, unquestionably entertained habeas petitions from arriving migrants who raised the same types of questions respondent poses here.

As discussed above, respondent requests review of immigration officials' allegedly unlawful interpretation of governing asylum law, and seeks to test the constitutional adequacy of expedited removal procedures. As a remedy, he requests procedures affording a conditional release, but certainly did not so limit his prayer for relief. His constitutional and legal challenges fall within the heartland of what *St. Cyr* said the common-law writ encompassed, and *Boumediene* confirms he is entitled to additional procedures as a form of conditional habeas relief. These precedents themselves resolve this case.

* * *

Because §1252(e)(2) excludes his challenges from habeas proceedings, and because the INA does not otherwise provide for meaningful judicial review of the Executive's removal determination, respondent has no effective means of vindicating his right to habeas relief. Quite simply, the Constitution requires more.

III

Although the Court concludes that habeas relief is not available because of the particular kind of release that it thinks respondent requests, it also suggests that respondent's unlawful status independently prohibits him from challenging the constitutionality of the expedited removal proceedings. By determining that respondent, a recent unlawful entrant who was apprehended close in time and place to his unauthorized border crossing, has no procedural due process rights to vindicate through his habeas challenge, the Court unnecessarily addresses a constitutional question in a manner contrary to the text of the Constitution and to our precedents.

The Court stretches to reach the issue whether a noncitizen like respondent is entitled to due process protections in relation to removal proceedings, which the court below mentioned only in a footnote and as an aside. In so doing, the Court opines on a matter neither necessary to its holding nor seriously in dispute below.

The Court is no more correct on the merits. To be sure, our cases have long held that foreigners who had never come into the United States — those "on the threshold of initial entry" — are not entitled to any due process with respect to their admission. *Shaughnessy v. United States ex rel. Mezei* (1953) (citing *Ekiu*). That follows from this Courts' holdings that the political branches of Government have "plenary" sovereign power over regulating the admission of noncitizens to the United States.

Noncitizens in this country, however, undeniably have due process rights. In *Yick Wo v. Hopkins* (1886), the Court explained that "[t]he Fourteenth Amendment to the Constitution is not confined to the protection of citizens" but rather applies "to all persons within the territorial jurisdiction, without regard to any differences of race, of color, or of nationality."

In its early cases, the Court speculated whether a noncitizen could invoke due process protections when he entered the country without permission or had resided here for too brief a period to "have become, in any real sense, a part of our population." But the Court has since determined that presence in the country is the touchstone for at least some level of due process protections. As a noncitizen within the territory of the United States, respondent is entitled to invoke the protections of the Due Process Clause.

In order to reach a contrary conclusion, the Court assumes that those who do not enter the country legally have the same due process rights as those who do not enter the country at all. The Court deems that respondent possesses only the rights of noncitizens on the "threshold of initial entry," skirting binding precedent by assuming that individuals like respondent have " 'assimilated to [the] status' " of an arriving noncitizen for purposes of the constitutional analysis. *Mezei*. But that relies on a legal fiction. Respondent, of course, was actually within the territorial limits of the United States.

More broadly, by drawing the line for due process at legal admission rather than physical entry, the Court tethers constitutional protections to a noncitizen's legal status as determined under contemporary asylum and immigration law. But the Fifth Amendment, which of course long predated any admissions program, does not contain limits based on immigration status or duration in the country: It applies to "persons" without qualification. *Yick Wo*. The Court has repeatedly affirmed as much long after Congress began regulating entry to the country. The Court lacks any textual basis to craft an exception to this rule, let alone one hinging on dynamic immigration laws that may be amended at any time, to redefine when an "entry" occurs. Fundamentally, it is out of step with how this Court has conceived the scope of the Due Process Clause for over a century: Congressional policy in the immigration context does not dictate the scope of the Constitution. . . .

Perhaps recognizing the tension between its opinion today and those cases, the Court cabins its holding to individuals who are "in respondent's position." Presumably the rule applies to—and only to—individuals found within 25 feet of the border who have entered within the past 24 hours of their apprehension. Where its logic must stop, however, is hard to say. Taken to its extreme, a rule conditioning due process rights on lawful entry would permit Congress to constitutionally eliminate all procedural protections for any noncitizen the Government deems unlawfully admitted and summarily deport them no matter how many decades they have lived here, how settled and integrated they are in their communities, or how many members of their family are U. S. citizens or residents.

This judicially fashioned line-drawing is not administrable, threatens to create arbitrary divisions between noncitizens in this country subject to removal proceedings, and, most important, lacks any basis in the Constitution. Both the Constitution and this Court's cases plainly guarantee due process protections to all "persons" regardless of their immigration status, a guarantee independent of the whims of the political branches. This contrary proclamation by the Court unnecessarily decides a constitutional question in a manner contrary to governing law.

IV

The Court reaches its decision only by downplaying the nature of respondent's claims, ignoring a plethora of common-law immigration cases from a time of relatively open borders, and mischaracterizing the most relevant precedents from this Court. Perhaps to shore up this unstable foundation, the Court justifies its decision by pointing to perceived vulnerabilities and abuses in the asylum system. I address the Court's policy concerns briefly. . . .

It is universally acknowledged that the asylum regime is under strain. It is also clear that, while the reasons for the large pending caseload are complicated,[13] delays in adjudications are undesirable for a number of reasons.

---

13. The Court, meanwhile, insinuates that much of the burden on the asylum system can be attributed to frivolous or fraudulent asylum claims. But the magnitude of asylum fraud has long been debated.

But the political branches have numerous tools at their disposal to reform the asylum system, and debates over the best methods of doing so are legion in the Government, in the academy, and in the public sphere. Congress and the Executive are thus well equipped to enact a range of measures to reform asylum in a number of ways and routinely do so. Indeed, as the Court notes, the expedited removal process at issue here was created by law as one such measure to ease pressures on the immigration system.

In the face of these policy choices, the role of the Judiciary is minimal, yet crucial: to ensure that laws passed by Congress are consistent with the limits of the Constitution. The Court today ignores its obligation, going out of its way to restrict the scope of the Great Writ and the reach of the Due Process Clause. This may accommodate congressional policy concerns by easing the burdens under which the immigration system currently labors. But it is nothing short of a self-imposed injury to the Judiciary, to the separation of powers, and to the values embodied in the promise of the Great Writ.

Because I disagree with the Court's interpretation of the reach of our Constitution's protections, I respectfully dissent.

Chapter 7

The Separation of Powers

STUDY GUIDE:

- Why does Justice Kagan conclude that the SORNA registration requirement "easily passes constitutional muster" under the nondelegation doctrine?
- This case was argued during the brief period before Justice Kavanaugh was confirmed. Therefore, there were only eight members on the bench.
- Why does Justice Alito not join Justice Gorsuch's dissent? Had Justice Alito not concurred with the judgment, the case would have resulted in a 4-4 split. When this happens, the Court would have summarily affirmed the lower court ruling (without establishing any precedent) and none of the opinions that follow would have been published. Can you see why Justice Alito might have wanted to avoid that result?
- Are you persuaded that the nondelegation doctrine is supported by the text, history, and structure of the Constitution?
- How should a court determine that a statute unconstitutionally delegated a legislative power?

Gundy v. United States
588 U.S. ___ (2019)

JUSTICE KAGAN announced the judgment of the Court and delivered an opinion, in which JUSTICE GINSBURG, JUSTICE BREYER, and JUSTICE SOTOMAYOR join.

The nondelegation doctrine bars Congress from transferring its legislative power to another branch of Government. This case requires us to decide whether 34 U.S.C. §20913(d), enacted as part of the Sex Offender Registration and Notification Act (SORNA), violates that doctrine. We hold it does not. Under §20913(d), the Attorney General must apply SORNA's registration requirements as soon as feasible to offenders convicted before the statute's enactment. That delegation easily passes constitutional muster. . . .

II

Article I of the Constitution provides that "[a]ll legislative Powers herein granted shall be vested in a Congress of the United States." §1. Accompanying that assignment of power to Congress is a bar on its further delegation. Congress, this Court explained early on, may not transfer to another branch "powers which are strictly and exclusively legislative." *Wayman v. Southard* (1825). But the Constitution does not "deny[] to the Congress the necessary resources of flexibility and practicality [that enable it] to perform its function[s]." *Yakus v. United States* (1944). Congress may "obtain[] the assistance of its coordinate Branches" — and in particular, may confer substantial discretion on executive agencies to implement and enforce the laws. *Mistretta v. United States* (1989). "[I]n our increasingly complex society, replete with ever changing and more technical problems," this Court has understood that "Congress simply cannot do its job absent an ability to delegate power under broad general directives." So we have held, time and again, that a statutory delegation is constitutional as long as Congress "lay[s] down by legislative act an intelligible principle to which the person or body authorized to [exercise the delegated authority] is directed to conform." *J. W. Hampton, Jr., & Co. v. United States* (1928).

Given that standard, a nondelegation inquiry always begins (and often almost ends) with statutory interpretation. The constitutional question is whether Congress has supplied an intelligible principle to guide the delegee's use of discretion. So the answer requires construing the challenged statute to figure out what task it delegates and what instructions it provides. See, *e.g., Whitman v. American Trucking Assns.*, Inc (2001) (construing the text of a delegation to place constitutionally adequate "limits on the EPA's discretion"); *American Power & Light Co. v. SEC* (1946) (interpreting a statutory delegation, in light of its "purpose[,] factual background[, and] context," to provide sufficiently "definite" standards). Only after a court has determined a challenged statute's meaning can it decide whether the law sufficiently guides executive discretion to accord with Article I. And indeed, once a court interprets the statute, it may find that the constitutional question all but answers itself.

That is the case here, because §20913(d) does not give the Attorney General anything like the "unguided" and "unchecked" authority that Gundy says. The provision, in Gundy's view, "grants the Attorney General plenary power to determine SORNA's applicability to pre-Act offenders — to require them to register, or not, as she sees fit, and to change her policy for any reason and at any time." If that were so, we would face a nondelegation question. But it is not. This Court has already interpreted §20913(d) to say something different — to require the Attorney General to apply SORNA to all pre-Act offenders as soon as feasible. And revisiting that issue yet more fully today, we reach the same conclusion. The text, considered alongside its context, purpose, and history, makes clear that the Attorney General's discretion extends only to considering and addressing feasibility issues. Given that statutory meaning, Gundy's constitutional claim must fail. Section 20913(d)'s delegation falls well within permissible bounds. . . .

Now that we have determined what §20913(d) means, we can consider whether it violates the Constitution. The question becomes: Did Congress make an impermissible delegation when it instructed the Attorney General to apply SORNA's registration requirements to pre-Act offenders as soon as feasible? Under this Court's long-established law, that question is easy. Its answer is no.

As noted earlier, this Court has held that a delegation is constitutional so long as Congress has set out an "intelligible principle" to guide the delegee's exercise of authority. *J. W. Hampton, Jr., & Co.* Or in a related formulation, the Court has stated that a delegation is permissible if Congress has made clear to the delegee "the general policy" he must pursue and the "boundaries of [his] authority." *American Power & Light.* Those standards, the Court has made clear, are not demanding. "[W]e have 'almost never felt qualified to second-guess Congress regarding the permissible degree of policy judgment that can be left to those executing or applying the law.'" *Whitman* (quoting *Mistretta* (Scalia, J., dissenting)). Only twice in this country's history (and that in a single year) have we found a delegation excessive—in each case because "Congress had failed to articulate *any* policy or standard" to confine discretion. *Mistretta*; see *A. L. A. Schechter Poultry Corp. v. United States* (1935); *Panama Refining Co. v. Ryan* (1935). By contrast, we have over and over upheld even very broad delegations. Here is a sample: We have approved delegations to various agencies to regulate in the "public interest." We have sustained authorizations for agencies to set "fair and equitable" prices and "just and reasonable" rates. We more recently affirmed a delegation to an agency to issue whatever air quality standards are "requisite to protect the public health." *Whitman.* And so forth.

In that context, the delegation in SORNA easily passes muster (as all eleven circuit courts to have considered the question found . . .). The statute conveyed Congress's policy that the Attorney General require pre-Act offenders to register as soon as feasible. Under the law, the feasibility issues he could address were administrative—and, more specifically, transitional—in nature. . . .

Those issues arose, as *Reynolds* explained, from the need to "newly register[ ] or reregister[ ] 'a large number' of pre-Act offenders" not then in the system. 565 U.S. at 440, 132 S. Ct. 975; see *supra,* at 8. And they arose, more technically, from the gap between an initial registration requirement hinged on imprisonment and a set of pre-Act offenders long since released. See 565 U.S. at 441, 132 S. Ct. 975; see *supra,* at 8. Even for those limited matters, the Act informed the Attorney General that he did not have forever to work things out. By stating its demand for a "comprehensive" registration system and by defining the "sex offenders" required to register to include pre-Act offenders, Congress conveyed that the Attorney General had only temporary authority. Or again, in the words of *Reynolds*, that he could prevent "*instantaneous* registration" and impose some "implementation delay." 565 U.S. at 443, 132 S. Ct. 975. That statutory authority, as compared to the delegations we have upheld in the past, is distinctly small-bore. It falls well within constitutional bounds.[4]

Indeed, if SORNA's delegation is unconstitutional, then most of Government is unconstitutional—dependent as Congress is on the need to give discretion to executive officials to implement its programs. Consider again this Court's

---

4. Even Gundy conceded at oral argument that if the statute means what we have said, it "likely would be constitutional." Tr. of Oral Arg. 25. That is why all of his argument is devoted to showing that it means something else.

long-time recognition: "Congress simply cannot do its job absent an ability to delegate power under broad general directives." *Mistretta.* Or as the dissent in that case agreed: "[S]ome judgments . . . must be left to the officers executing the law." (opinion of Scalia, J.); ("[A] certain degree of discretion[ ] inheres in most executive" action (internal quotation marks omitted)). Among the judgments often left to executive officials are ones involving feasibility. In fact, standards of that kind are ubiquitous in the U.S. Code. In those delegations, Congress gives its delegee the flexibility to deal with real-world constraints in carrying out his charge. So too in SORNA.

It is wisdom and humility alike that this Court has always upheld such "necessities of government." *Mistretta* (Scalia, J., dissenting); see *ibid.* ("Since Congress is no less endowed with common sense than we are, and better equipped to inform itself of the 'necessities' of government; and since the factors bearing upon those necessities are both multifarious and (in the nonpartisan sense) highly political . . . it is small wonder that we have almost never felt qualified to second-guess Congress regarding the permissible degree of policy judgment that can be left to those executing or applying the law"). We therefore affirm the judgment of the Court of Appeals.

It is so ordered.

JUSTICE KAVANAUGH took no part in the consideration or decision of this case.

JUSTICE ALITO, concurring in the judgment.

The Constitution confers on Congress certain "legislative [p]owers," Art. I, §1, and does not permit Congress to delegate them to another branch of the Government. See *Whitman v. American Trucking Assns.*, Inc. (2001). Nevertheless, since 1935, the Court has uniformly rejected nondelegation arguments and has upheld provisions that authorized agencies to adopt important rules pursuant to extraordinarily capacious standards.

If a majority of this Court were willing to reconsider the approach we have taken for the past 84 years, I would support that effort. But because a majority is not willing to do that, it would be freakish to single out the provision at issue here for special treatment.

Because I cannot say that the statute lacks a discernable standard that is adequate under the approach this Court has taken for many years, I vote to affirm.

JUSTICE GORSUCH, with whom THE CHIEF JUSTICE and JUSTICE THOMAS join, dissenting.

The Constitution promises that only the people's elected representatives may adopt new federal laws restricting liberty. Yet the statute before us scrambles that design. It purports to endow the nation's chief prosecutor with the power to write his own criminal code governing the lives of a half-million citizens. Yes, those affected are some of the least popular among us. But if a single executive branch official can write laws restricting the liberty of this group of persons, what does that mean for the next?

Today, a plurality of an eight-member Court endorses this extraconstitutional arrangement but resolves nothing. Working from an understanding of the Constitution at war with its text and history, the plurality reimagines the terms of the statute before us and insists there is nothing wrong with Congress handing off so much power to the Attorney General. But Justice Alito supplies the fifth vote for today's judgment and he does not join either the plurality's constitutional or statutory analysis, indicating instead that he remains willing, in a future case with a full Court, to revisit these matters. Respectfully, I would not wait.

I

For individuals convicted of sex offenses *after* Congress adopted the Sex Offender Registration and Notification Act (SORNA) in 2006, the statute offers detailed instructions. It requires them "to provide state governments with (and to update) information, such as names and current addresses, for inclusion on state and federal sex offender registries." The law divides offenders into three tiers based on the seriousness of their crimes: Some must register for 15 years, others for 25 years, and still others for life. The statute proceeds to set registration deadlines: Offenders sentenced to prison must register before they're released, while others must register within three business days after sentencing. The statute explains when and how offenders must update their registrations. And the statute specifies particular penalties for failing to comply with its commands. On and on the statute goes for more than 20 pages of the U.S. Code.

But what about those convicted of sex offenses *before* the Act's adoption? At the time of SORNA's enactment, the nation's population of sex offenders exceeded 500,000, and Congress concluded that something had to be done about these "pre-Act" offenders too. But it seems Congress couldn't agree what that should be. The treatment of pre-Act offenders proved a "controversial issue with major policy significance and practical ramifications for states." Among other things, applying SORNA immediately to this group threatened to impose unpopular and costly burdens on States and localities by forcing them to adopt or overhaul their own sex offender registration schemes. So Congress simply passed the problem to the Attorney General. For all half-million pre-Act offenders, the law says only this, in 34 U.S.C. §20913(d):

> "The Attorney General shall have the authority to specify the applicability of the requirements of this subchapter to sex offenders convicted before the enactment of this chapter . . . and to prescribe rules for the registration of any such sex offender."

Yes, that's it. The breadth of the authority Congress granted to the Attorney General in these few words can only be described as vast. As the Department of Justice itself has acknowledged, SORNA "does not require the Attorney General" to impose registration requirements on pre-Act offenders "within a certain time frame or by a date certain; it does not require him to act at all." If the Attorney General does choose to act, he can require all pre-Act offenders to register, or he can "require some but not all to register." For those he requires to register, the Attorney General may impose "some but not all of [SORNA's] registration requirements," as he pleases. And he is free to change his mind on any of these matters "at any given time or over the course of different [political] administrations." Congress thus gave the Attorney General free rein to write the rules for virtually the entire existing sex offender population in this country — a situation that promised to persist for years or decades until pre-Act offenders passed away or fulfilled the terms of their registration obligations and post-Act offenders came to predominate.

Unsurprisingly, different Attorneys General have exercised their discretion in different ways. For six months after SORNA's enactment, Attorney General Gonzales left past offenders alone. Then the pendulum swung the other direction when the Department of Justice issued an interim rule requiring pre-Act offenders to follow all the same rules as post-Act offenders. A year later, Attorney General Mukasey issued more new guidelines, this time directing the States to register some but not all past offenders. Three years after that, Attorney General Holder required the States to register only those pre-Act offenders convicted of a new felony after SORNA's enactment. Various Attorneys General have also taken different positions on whether pre-Act offenders might be entitled to credit for time spent in the community before SORNA was enacted.

These unbounded policy choices have profound consequences for the people they affect. Take our case. Before SORNA's enactment, Herman Gundy pleaded guilty in 2005 to a sexual offense. After his release from prison five years later, he was arrested again, this time for failing to register as a sex offender according to the rules the Attorney General had then prescribed for pre-Act offenders. As a result, Mr. Gundy faced an additional 10-year prison term — 10 years more than if the Attorney General had, in his discretion, chosen to write the rules differently.

II

A

Our founding document begins by declaring that "We the People . . . ordain and establish this Constitution." At the time, that was a radical claim, an assertion that sovereignty belongs not to a person or institution or class but to the whole of the people. From that premise, the Constitution proceeded to vest the authority to exercise different aspects of the people's sovereign power in distinct entities. In Article I, the Constitution entrusted all of the federal government's legislative power to Congress. In Article II, it assigned the executive power to the President. And in Article III, it gave independent judges the task of applying the laws to cases and controversies.

To the framers, each of these vested powers had a distinct content. When it came to the legislative power, the framers understood it to mean the power to adopt generally applicable rules of conduct governing future actions by private persons — the power to "prescrib[e] the rules by which the duties and rights of every citizen are to be regulated,"[17] or the power to "prescribe general rules for the government of society."[18]

The framers understood, too, that it would frustrate "the system of government ordained by the Constitution" if Congress could merely announce vague aspirations and then assign others the responsibility of adopting legislation to realize its goals. Through the Constitution, after all, the people had vested the power to prescribe rules limiting their liberties in Congress alone. No one, not even Congress, had the right to alter that arrangement. As Chief Justice Marshall explained, Congress may not "delegate . . . powers which are strictly and exclusively legislative." Or as John Locke, one of the thinkers who most influenced the framers' understanding of the separation of powers, described it:

> "The legislative cannot transfer the power of making laws to any other hands; for it being but a delegated power from the people, they who have it cannot pass it over to others. The people alone can appoint the form of the commonwealth, which is by constituting the legislative, and appointing in whose hands that shall be. And when the people have said we will submit to rules, and be governed by laws made by such men, and in such forms, nobody else can say other men shall make laws for them; nor can the people be bound by any laws but such as are enacted by those whom they have chosen and authorised to make laws for them."

Why did the framers insist on this particular arrangement? They believed the new federal government's most dangerous power was the power to enact laws restricting the people's liberty.[22] An "excess of law-making" was, in their words, one of "the diseases to which our governments are most liable." To address that tendency, the framers went to great lengths to make lawmaking difficult. In Article I, by far the longest part of the Constitution, the framers insisted that any proposed law must win the approval of two Houses of Congress—elected at different times, by different constituencies, and for different terms in office—and either secure the President's approval or obtain enough support to override his veto. Some occasionally complain about Article I's detailed and arduous processes for new legislation, but to the framers these were bulwarks of liberty.

Nor was the point only to limit the government's capacity to restrict the people's freedoms. Article I's detailed processes for new laws were also designed to promote deliberation. "The oftener the measure is brought under examination," Hamilton explained, "the greater the diversity in the situations of those who are to examine it," and "the less must be the danger of those errors which flow from want of due deliberation, or of those missteps which proceed from the contagion of some common passion or interest."[24]

---

17. The Federalist No. 78 (A. Hamilton).

18. *Fletcher v. Peck* (1810); see also J. Locke, The Second Treatise of Civil Government and a Letter Concerning Toleration §22, p. 13 (1947); 1 W. Blackstone, Commentaries on the Laws of England 44 (1765).

22. The Federalist No. 48 (J. Madison).

24. The Federalist No. 73 (Hamilton).

Other purposes animated the framers' design as well. Because men are not angels[25] and majorities can threaten minority rights, the framers insisted on a legislature composed of different bodies subject to different electorates as a means of ensuring that any new law would have to secure the approval of a supermajority of the people's representatives. This, in turn, assured minorities that their votes would often decide the fate of proposed legislation. Indeed, some even thought a Bill of Rights would prove unnecessary in light of the Constitution's design; in their view, sound structures forcing "[a]mbition [to] . . . counteract ambition" would do more than written promises to guard unpopular minorities from the tyranny of the majority. Restricting the task of legislating to one branch characterized by difficult and deliberative processes was also designed to promote fair notice and the rule of law, ensuring the people would be subject to a relatively stable and predictable set of rules. And by directing that legislating be done only by elected representatives in a public process, the Constitution sought to ensure that the lines of accountability would be clear: The sovereign people would know, without ambiguity, whom to hold accountable for the laws they would have to follow.

If Congress could pass off its legislative power to the executive branch, the "[v]esting [c]lauses, and indeed the entire structure of the Constitution," would "make no sense."[29] Without the involvement of representatives from across the country or the demands of bicameralism and presentment, legislation would risk becoming nothing more than the will of the current President. And if laws could be simply declared by a single person, they would not be few in number, the product of widespread social consensus, likely to protect minority interests, or apt to provide stability and fair notice. Accountability would suffer too. Legislators might seek to take credit for addressing a pressing social problem by sending it to the executive for resolution, while at the same time blaming the executive for the problems that attend whatever measures he chooses to pursue. In turn, the executive might point to Congress as the source of the problem. These opportunities for finger-pointing might prove temptingly advantageous for the politicians involved, but they would also threaten to " 'disguise . . . responsibility for . . . the decisions.' "[31]

The framers warned us against permitting consequences like these. As Madison explained, " '[t]here can be no liberty where the legislative and executive powers are united in the same person, or body of magistrates.' " The framers knew, too, that the job of keeping the legislative power confined to the legislative branch couldn't be trusted to self-policing by Congress; often enough, legislators will face rational incentives to pass problems to the executive branch. Besides, enforcing the separation of powers isn't about protecting institutional prerogatives or governmental turf. It's about respecting the people's sovereign choice

---

25. The Federalist No. 51 (Madison)

29. Lawson, Delegation and Original Meaning, 88 Va. L. Rev. 327, 340 (2002).

31. Rao, Administrative Collusion: How Delegation Diminishes the Collective Congress, 90 N. Y. U. L. Rev. 1463, 1478 (2015).

to vest the legislative power in Congress alone. And it's about safeguarding a structure designed to protect their liberties, minority rights, fair notice, and the rule of law. So when a case or controversy comes within the judicial competence, the Constitution does not permit judges to look the other way; we must call foul when the constitutional lines are crossed. Indeed, the framers afforded us independence from the political branches in large part to encourage exactly this kind of "fortitude . . . to do [our] duty as faithful guardians of the Constitution."

B

Accepting, then, that we have an obligation to decide whether Congress has unconstitutionally divested itself of its legislative responsibilities, the question follows: What's the test? Madison acknowledged that "no skill in the science of government has yet been able to discriminate and define, with sufficient certainty, its three great provinces — the legislative, executive, and judiciary." Chief Justice Marshall agreed that policing the separation of powers "is a subject of delicate and difficult inquiry." Still, the framers took this responsibility seriously and offered us important guiding principles.

First, we know that as long as Congress makes the policy decisions when regulating private conduct, it may authorize another branch to "fill up the details." In *Wayman v. Southard*, this Court upheld a statute that instructed the federal courts to borrow state-court procedural rules but allowed them to make certain "alterations and additions." Writing for the Court, Chief Justice Marshall distinguished between those "important subjects, which must be entirely regulated by the legislature itself," and "those of less interest, in which a general provision may be made, and power given to those who are to act . . . to fill up the details." The Court upheld the statute before it because Congress had announced the controlling general policy when it ordered federal courts to follow state procedures, and the residual authority to make "alterations and additions" did no more than permit courts to fill up the details.

Later cases built on Chief Justice Marshall's understanding. In *In re Kollock*, for example, the Court upheld a statute that assigned the Commissioner of Internal Revenue the responsibility to design tax stamps for margarine packages. Later still, and using the same logic, the Court sustained other and far more consequential statutes, like a law authorizing the Secretary of Agriculture to adopt rules regulating the "use and occupancy" of public forests to protect them from "destruction" and "depredations." Through all these cases, small or large, runs the theme that Congress must set forth standards "sufficiently definite and precise to enable Congress, the courts, and the public to ascertain" whether Congress's guidance has been followed. Second, once Congress prescribes the rule governing private conduct, it may make the application of that rule depend on executive fact-finding. Here, too, the power extended to the executive may prove highly consequential. During the Napoleonic Wars, for example, Britain and France each tried to block the United States from trading with the other. Congress responded with a statute instructing that, if the President found that either Great Britain or France stopped interfering with American trade, a trade embargo would be imposed against the other country. . . .

Third, Congress may assign the executive and judicial branches certain non-legislative responsibilities. While the Constitution vests all federal legislative power in Congress alone, Congress's legislative authority sometimes overlaps with authority the Constitution separately vests in another branch.[42] So, for example, when a congressional statute confers wide discretion to the executive, no separation-of-powers problem may arise if "the discretion is to be exercised over matters already within the scope of executive power." . . .

C

Before the 1930s, federal statutes granting authority to the executive were comparatively modest and usually easily upheld. But then the federal government began to grow explosively. And with the proliferation of new executive programs came new questions about the scope of congressional delegations. Twice the Court responded by striking down statutes for violating the separation of powers.

In *A. L. A. Schechter Poultry Corp. v. United States*, the Court considered a statute that transferred to the President the power "to approve 'codes of fair competition'" for slaughterhouses and other industries. But Congress offered no meaningful guidance. It did not, for example, reference any pre-existing common law of fair competition that might have supplied guidance on the policy questions, as it arguably had done earlier with the Sherman Act. And it did not announce rules contingent on executive fact-finding. Nor was this assigned power one that anyone thought might inhere in the executive power. Proceeding without the need to convince a majority of legislators, the President adopted a lengthy fair competition code written by a group of (possibly self-serving) New York poultry butchers.

Included in the code was a rule that often made it a federal crime for butchers to allow customers to select which individual chickens they wished to buy. Kosher butchers such as the Schechters had a hard time following these rules. Yet the government apparently singled out the Schechters as a test case; inspectors repeatedly visited them and, at times, apparently behaved abusively toward their customers. When the Schechters finally kicked the inspectors out, they were greeted with a criminal indictment running to dozens of counts. After a trial in which the Schechters were found guilty of selling one allegedly "unfit" chicken and other miscellaneous counts, this Court agreed to hear the case and struck down the law as a violation of the separation of powers. If Congress could permit the President to write a new code of fair competition all his own, Justice Cardozo explained, then "anything that Congress may do within the limits of the commerce clause for the betterment of business [could] be done by the President . . . by calling it a code. This is delegation running riot."

---

42. *Youngstown Sheet & Tube Co. v. Sawyer* (1952) (Jackson, J., concurring).

The same year, in *Panama Refining Co. v. Ryan*, the Court struck down a statute that authorized the President to decide whether and how to prohibit the interstate transportation of "hot oil," petroleum produced or withdrawn from storage in excess of state-set quotas. As in *Schechter Poultry*, the law provided no notice to regulated parties about what the President might wind up prohibiting, leading the Court to observe that Congress "ha[d] declared no policy, ha[d] established no standard, ha[d] laid down no rule." The Court explained that the statute did not call for the executive to "ascertai[n] the existence of facts to which legislation is directed." Nor did it ask the executive to " 'fill up the details' " "within the framework of the policy which the legislature has sufficiently defined." "If [the statute] were held valid," the Court continued, "it would be idle to pretend that anything would be left of limitations upon the power of the Congress to delegate its law-making function."

After *Schechter Poultry* and *Panama Refining*, Congress responded by writing a second wave of New Deal legislation more "[c]arefully crafted" to avoid the kind of problems that sank these early statutes. And since that time the Court hasn't held another statute to violate the separation of powers in the same way. Of course, no one thinks that the Court's quiescence can be attributed to an unwavering new tradition of more scrupulously drawn statutes. Some lament that the real cause may have to do with a mistaken "case of death by association" because *Schechter Poultry* and *Panama Refining* happened to be handed down during the same era as certain of the Court's now-discredited substantive due process decisions. But maybe the most likely explanation of all lies in the story of the evolving "intelligible principle" doctrine.

This Court first used that phrase in 1928 in *J. W. Hampton, Jr., & Co. v. United States*, where it remarked that a statute "lay[ing] down by legislative act an intelligible principle to which the [executive official] is directed to conform" satisfies the separation of powers. No one at the time thought the phrase meant to effect some revolution in this Court's understanding of the Constitution. While the exact line between policy and details, lawmaking and fact-finding, and legislative and non-legislative functions had sometimes invited reasonable debate, everyone agreed these were the relevant inquiries. And when Chief Justice Taft wrote of an "intelligible principle," it seems plain enough that he sought only to explain the operation of these traditional tests; he gave no hint of a wish to overrule or revise them. Tellingly, too, he wrote the phrase seven years before *Schechter Poultry* and *Panama Refining*, and it did nothing to alter the analysis in those cases, let alone prevent those challenges from succeeding by lopsided votes. . . .

Still, it's undeniable that the "intelligible principle" remark eventually began to take on a life of its own. We sometimes chide people for treating judicial opinions as if they were statutes, divorcing a passing comment from its context, ignoring all that came before and after, and treating an isolated phrase as if it were controlling. But that seems to be exactly what happened here. For two decades, no one thought to invoke the "intelligible principle" comment as a basis to uphold a statute that would have failed more traditional separation-of-powers tests. In fact, the phrase sat more or less silently entombed until the late 1940s. Only then did lawyers begin digging it up in earnest and arguing to this Court that it had somehow displaced (*sub silentio* of course) all prior teachings in this area.

This mutated version of the "intelligible principle" remark has no basis in the original meaning of the Constitution, in history, or even in the decision from which it was plucked. Judges and scholars representing a wide and diverse range of views have condemned it as resting on "misunderst[ood] historical founda-tions." They have explained, too, that it has been abused to permit delegations of legislative power that on any other conceivable account should be held unconsti-tutional. Indeed, where some have claimed to see "intelligible principles" many "less discerning readers [have been able only to] find gibberish."[62] . . .

Still, the scope of the problem can be overstated. At least some of the results the Court has reached under the banner of the abused "intelligible principle" doctrine may be consistent with more traditional teachings. . . . More recently, too, we've sought to tame misunderstandings of the intelligible principle "test." . . . To determine whether a statute provides an intelligible principle, we must ask: Does the statute assign to the executive only the responsibility to make factual findings? Does it set forth the facts that the executive must consider and the criteria against which to measure them? And most importantly, did Congress, and not the Executive Branch, make the policy judgments? Only then can we fairly say that a statute contains the kind of intelligible principle the Constitution demands. . . .

Nor have we abandoned enforcing other sides of the separation-of-powers tri-angle between the legislative, executive, and judiciary. We have not hesitated to prevent Congress from "confer[ring] the Government's 'judicial Power' on entities outside Article III." We've forbidden the executive from encroaching on legislative functions by wielding a line-item veto.[78] We've prevented Congress

---

62. Lawson, 88 Va. L. Rev., at 329. See also *Mistretta v. United States*, 488 U.S. 361, 415-417, 109 S. Ct. 647, 102 L. Ed.2d 714 (1989) (Scalia, J., dissenting); Ely, *supra*, at 132 ("[B]y refusing to leg-islate, our legislators are escaping the sort of accountability that is crucial to the intelligible function-ing of a democratic republic"); Wright, Beyond Discretionary Justice, 81 Yale L. J. 575, 583 (1972) ("[T]he delegation doctrine retains an important potential as a check on the exercise of unbounded, standardless discretion by administrative agencies"); *Michigan Gambling Opposition v. Kempthorne*, 525 F.3d 23, 34 (CADC 2008) (Brown, J., dissenting) ("[The majority] conjures standards and limits from thin air to construct a supposed intelligible principle") (collecting cases); Schoenbrod, 83 Mich. L. Rev., at 1231 ("[T]he [intelligible principle] test has become so ephemeral and elastic as to lose its meaning"); Schwartz, Of Administrators and Philosopher-Kings: The Republic, the Laws, and Delegations of Power, 72 Nw. U. L. Rev. 443, 446 (1977) ("[T]he requirement of defined standards has . . . become all but a vestigial euphemism"); P. Hamburger, Is Administrative Law Unlawful? 378 (2014) ("[T]he notion of an 'intelligible principle' sets a ludicrously low standard for what Congress must supply"); M. Redish, The Constitution as Political Structure 138-139 (1995); Gewirtz, The Courts, Congress, and Executive Policy-Making: Notes on Three Doctrines, 40 Law & Contemp. Prob., pt. 2, pp. 46, 50-51 (Summer 1976); McGowan, Congress, Court, and Control of Delegated Power, 77 Colum. L. Rev. 1119, 1127-1128, and n. 33 (1977).

78. *Clinton v. City of New York* (1998).

from delegating its collective legislative power to a single House.[79] And we've policed legislative efforts to control executive branch officials. These cases show that, when the separation of powers is at stake, we don't just throw up our hands. In all these areas, we recognize that abdication is "not part of the constitutional design." And abdication here would be no more appropriate. To leave this aspect of the constitutional structure alone undefended would serve only to accelerate the flight of power from the legislative to the executive branch, turning the latter into a vortex of authority that was constitutionally reserved for the people's representatives in order to protect their liberties. . . .

In a future case with a full panel, I remain hopeful that the Court may yet recognize that, while Congress can enlist considerable assistance from the executive branch in filling up details and finding facts, it may never hand off to the nation's chief prosecutor the power to write his own criminal code. That "is delegation running riot."

STUDY GUIDE:

- What is an "officer of the United States"? How does the majority define that term? How does Justice Thomas's concurrence define that term?
- If the PROMESA members are not "officers of the United States," what are they?
- How does Justice Sotomayor characterize the PROMESA members? Who does she think should be responsible for appointing those positions? What role does Congress have over governing Puerto Rico?

Fin. Oversight and Management Bd. for Puerto Rico v. Aurelius Investment, LLC, et al.
590 U.S. ___ (2020)

JUSTICE BREYER delivered the opinion of the Court.

The Constitution's Appointments Clause says that the President "shall nominate, *and by and with the Advice and Consent of the Senate,* shall appoint Ambassadors, other public Ministers and Consuls, Judges of the supreme Court, and all other *Officers of the United States.* . . ." Art. II, §2, cl. 2 (emphasis added).

In 2016, Congress enacted the Puerto Rico Oversight, Management, and Economic Stability Act (PROMESA). That Act created a Financial Oversight and Management Board, and it provided, as relevant here, that the President could appoint its seven members without "the advice and consent of the Senate," *i.e.,* without Senate confirmation.

The question before us is whether this method of appointment violates the Constitution's Senate confirmation requirement. In our view, the Appointments

---

79. *INS v. Chadha* (1983).

Clause governs the appointments of all officers of the United States, including those located in Puerto Rico. Yet two provisions of the Constitution empower Congress to create local offices for the District of Columbia and for Puerto Rico and the Territories. See Art. I, §8, cl. 17; Art. IV, §3, cl. 2. And the Clause's term "Officers of the United States" has never been understood to cover those whose powers and duties are primarily local in nature and derive from these two constitutional provisions. The Board's statutory responsibilities consist of primarily local duties, namely, representing Puerto Rico in bankruptcy proceedings and supervising aspects of Puerto Rico's fiscal and budgetary policies. We therefore find that the Board members are not "Officers of the United States." For that reason, the Appointments Clause does not dictate how the Board's members must be selected.

I

. . . In 2016, in response to Puerto Rico's fiscal crisis, Congress enacted PROMESA.

PROMESA allows Puerto Rico and its entities to file for federal bankruptcy protection. . . . PROMESA also created the Financial Oversight and Management Board — with seven members appointed by the President and with the Governor serving as an ex officio member. PROMESA gives the Board authority to file for bankruptcy on behalf of Puerto Rico or its instrumentalities.

As we have just said, PROMESA gives the President of the United States the power to appoint the Board's seven members without Senate confirmation, so long as he selects six from lists prepared by congressional leaders. . . .

II

Congress created the Board pursuant to its power under Article IV of the Constitution to "make all needful Rules and Regulations respecting the Territory . . . belonging to the United States." Some have argued in these cases that the Appointments Clause simply does not apply in the context of Puerto Rico. But, like the Court of Appeals, we believe the Appointments Clause restricts the appointment of all officers of the United States, including those who carry out their powers and duties in or in relation to Puerto Rico.

The Constitution's structure provides strong reason to believe that is so. The Constitution separates the three basic powers of Government — legislative, executive, and judicial — with each branch serving different functions. But the Constitution requires cooperation among the three branches in specified areas. Thus, to become law, proposed legislation requires the agreement of both Congress and the President (or, a supermajority in Congress). See *INS v. Chadha* (1983) (noting that the Constitution prescribes only four specific actions that Congress can take without bicameralism and presentment). At the same time, legislation must be consistent with constitutional constraints, and we usually look to the Judiciary as the ultimate interpreter of those constraints.

The Appointments Clause reflects a similar allocation of responsibility, between President and Senate, in cases involving appointment to high federal office. That Clause reflects the Founders' reaction to "one of [their] generation's greatest grievances against [pre-Revolutionary] executive power," the manipulation of appointments. *Freytag v. Commissioner* (1991); see also The Federalist No. 76 (A. Hamilton) (the Appointments Clause helps to preserve democratic accountability). The Founders addressed their concerns with the appointment power by both concentrating it and distributing it. On the one hand, they ensured that primary responsibility for nominations would fall on the President, whom they deemed "less vulnerable to interest-group pressure and personal favoritism" than a collective body. *Edmond v. United States* (1997). See also The Federalist No. 76 ("The sole and undivided responsibility of one man will naturally beget a livelier sense of duty and a more exact regard to reputation"). On the other hand, they ensured that the Senate's advice and consent power would provide "an excellent check upon a spirit of favoritism in the President and a guard against the appointment of unfit characters." *NLRB v. SW General, Inc.* (2017). By "limiting the appointment power" in this fashion, the Clause helps to "ensure that those who wielded [the appointments power] were accountable to political force and the will of the people." *Freytag.* "The blame of a bad nomination would fall upon the president singly and absolutely," while "[t]he censure of rejecting a good one would lie entirely at the door of the senate."

These other structural constraints, designed in part to ensure political accountability, apply to all exercises of federal power, including those related to Article IV entities. Cf., *e.g.*, *Metropolitan Washington Airports Authority v. Citizens for Abatement of Aircraft Noise, Inc.* (1991) *(MWAA)* (separation-of-powers principles apply when Congress acts under its Article IV power to legislate "respecting . . . other Property"). See also, *e.g.*, Act of Aug. 7, 1789 (the First Congress using bicameralism and presentment to make rules and regulations for the Northwest Territory). The objectives advanced by the Appointments Clause counsel strongly in favor of that Clause applying to the appointment of all "Officers of the United States." Why should it be different when such an officer's duties relate to Puerto Rico or other Article IV entities?

Indeed, the Appointments Clause has no Article IV exception. The Clause says in part that the President "shall nominate, and by and with the Advice and Consent of the Senate, shall appoint Ambassadors, other public Ministers and Consuls, Judges of the supreme Court, and all other Officers of the United States, whose Appointments . . . shall be established by Law. . . ." Art. II, §2, cl. 2.

That text firmly indicates that it applies to the appointment of *all* "Officers of the United States." And history confirms this reading. Before the writing of the Constitution, Congress had enacted an ordinance that allowed Congress to appoint officers to govern the Northwest Territory. As soon as the Constitution became law, the First Congress "adapt[ed]" that ordinance "to the present Constitution of the United States," Act of Aug. 7, 1789, in large part by providing for an appointment process consistent with the constraints of the Appointments Clause. In particular, it provided for a Presidential-appointment, Senate-confirmation process for high-level territorial appointees who assumed federal, as well as local, duties. Later Congresses took a similar approach to later territorial Governors with federal duties. We do not mean to suggest that every time Congress chooses to require advice and consent procedures it does so because they are constitutionally required. At times, Congress may wish to require Senate confirmation for policy reasons. Even so, Congress' practice of requiring advice and consent for these Governors with important federal duties supports the inference that Congress expected the Appointments Clause to apply to at least some officials with supervisory authority over the Territories.

Given the Constitution's structure, this history, roughly analogous case law, and the absence of any conflicting authority, we conclude that the Appointments Clause constrains the appointments power as to all "Officers of the United States," even when those officers exercise power in or related to Puerto Rico.

III

A

The more difficult question before us is whether the Board members are officers of the United States such that the Appointments Clause requires Senate confirmation. If they are not officers of the United States, but instead are some other type of officer, the Appointments Clause says nothing about them. (No one suggests that they are "Ambassadors," "other public Ministers and Consuls," or "Judges of the supreme Court.") And as we shall see, the answer to this question turns on whether the Board members have primarily local powers and duties.

The language at issue does not offer us much guidance for understanding the key term "of the United States." The text suggests a distinction between federal officers — officers exercising power of the National Government — and nonfederal officers — officers exercising power of some other government. The Constitution envisions a federalist structure, with the National Government exercising limited federal power and other, local governments — usually state governments — exercising more expansive power. But the Constitution recognizes that for certain localities, there will be no state government capable of exercising local power. Thus, two provisions of the Constitution, Article I, §8, cl. 17, and Article IV, §3, cl. 2, give Congress the power to legislate for those localities in ways "that would exceed its powers, or at least would be very unusual" in other contexts. *Palmore v. United States* (1973). Using these powers, Congress has long legislated for entities that are not States — the District of Columbia and the Territories. See *District of Columbia v. John R. Thompson Co.* (1953). And, in doing so, Congress has both made local law directly and also created structures of local government, staffed by local officials, who themselves have made and enforced local law. This structure suggests that when Congress creates local offices using these two unique powers, the officers exercise power of the local government, not the Federal Government.

History confirms what the Constitution's text and structure suggest. See *NLRB v. Noel Canning* (2014) (relying on history and structure in interpreting the Recess Appointments Clause). See also *McCulloch v. Maryland* (1819) (emphasizing the utility of historical practice in interpreting constitutional provisions). Longstanding practice indicates that a federal law's creation of an office in this context does not automatically make its holder an "Officer of the United States." Rather, Congress has often used these two provisions to create local offices filled in ways other than those specified in the Appointments Clause. When the First Congress legislated for the Northwest Territories, for example, it created a House of Representatives for the Territory with members selected by election. It also created an upper house of the territorial legislature, whose members were appointed by the President (without Senate confirmation) from lists provided by the elected, lower house. And it created magistrates appointed by the Governor.

The practice of creating by federal law local offices for the Territories and District of Columbia that are filled through election or local executive appointment has continued unabated for more than two centuries. Like Justice Thomas, we think the practice of the First Congress is strong evidence of the original meaning of the Constitution. We find this subsequent history similarly illuminates the text's meaning. . . .

We thus conclude that while the Appointments Clause *does* restrict the appointment of "Officers of the United States" with duties in or related to the District of Columbia or an Article IV entity, it *does not* restrict the appointment of local officers that Congress vests with primarily local duties under Article IV, §3, or Article I, §8, cl. 17.

B

The question remains whether the Board members have primarily local powers and duties. We note that the Clause qualifies the phrase "Officers of the United States" with the words "whose Appointments . . . shall be established by Law." And we also note that PROMESA says that the Board is "an entity within the territorial government" and "shall not be considered a department, agency, establishment, or instrumentality of the Federal Government." But the most these words show is that Congress did not intend to make the Board members "Officers of the United States." It does not prove that, insofar as the Constitution is concerned, they succeeded.

But we think they have. Congress did not simply state that the Board is part of the local Puerto Rican government. Rather, Congress also gave the Board a structure, a set of duties, and related powers all of which are consistent with this statement. . . .

To repeat: The Board has broad investigatory powers: It can administer oaths, issue subpoenas, take evidence and demand data from governments and creditors alike. But these powers are backed by Puerto Rican, not federal, law: Subpoenas are governed by Puerto Rico's personal jurisdiction statute; false testimony is punishable under the law of Puerto Rico; the Board must seek enforcement of its subpoenas by filing in the courts of Puerto Rico These powers are primarily local in nature. . . .

In short, the Board possesses considerable power—including the authority to substitute its own judgment for the considered judgment of the Governor and other elected officials. But this power primarily concerns local matters. Congress' law thus substitutes a different process for determining certain local policies (related to local fiscal responsibility) in respect to local matters. And that is the critical point for current purposes. The local nature of the legislation's expressed purposes, the representation of local interests in bankruptcy proceedings, the focus of the Board's powers upon local expenditures, the local logistical support, the reliance on local laws in aid of the Board's procedural powers—all these features when taken together and judged in the light of Puerto Rico's history (and that of the Territories and the District of Columbia)—make clear that the Board's members have primarily local duties, such that their selection is not subject to the constraints of the Appointments Clause.

IV

The Court of Appeals, pointing to three of this Court's cases, reached the opposite conclusion. See *Buckley v. Valeo* (1976) (*per curiam*), *Freytag v. Commissioner*, and *Lucia v. SEC* (2018). It pointed out that the Court, in those cases, discussed the term "Officer of the United States," and it concluded that, for Appointments Clause purposes, an appointee is such an "officer" if "(1) the appointee occupies a 'continuing' position established by federal law; (2) the appointee 'exercis[es] significant authority'; and (3) the significant authority is exercised 'pursuant to the laws of the United States.'" The Court of Appeals concluded that the Board members satisfied this test.

We do not believe these three cases set forth the critical legal test relevant here, however, and we do not apply any test they might enunciate. Each of the cases considered an Appointments Clause problem concerning the importance or significance of duties that were indisputably *federal* or national in nature. In *Buckley*, the question was whether members of the Federal Election Commission—appointees carrying out federal-election related duties—were "officers" for Appointments Clause purposes. In *Freytag*, the Court asked the same question about special federal trial judges serving on federal tax courts. And in *Lucia* the Court asked the same question about federal administrative law judges carrying out Securities and Exchange Commission duties.

Here, PROMESA, a federal law, creates the Board and its duties, and no one doubts their significance. But we cannot stop there. To do so would ignore the history we have discussed—history stretching back to the founding. And failing to take account of the nature of an appointee's federally created duties, *i.e.*, whether they are *primarily local versus primarily federal*, would threaten interference with democratic (or local appointment) selection methods in numerous Article IV Territories and perhaps the District of Columbia as well. There is no reason to understand the Appointments Clause—which, at least in part, seeks to advance democratic accountability and broaden appointments-related responsibility,—as making it significantly more difficult for local residents of such areas to share responsibility for the implementation of (statutorily created) primarily local duties. Neither the text nor the history of the Clause commands such a result. . . .

While we have found no case from this Court directly on point, we believe that the Court's analysis in *O'Donoghue v. United States* (1933), and especially *Palmore v. United States* provides a rough analogy. In *O'Donoghue*, the Court considered whether Article III's tenure and salary protections applied to judges of the courts in the District of Columbia. The Court held that they did. Those courts, it believed, were " 'courts of the United States' " and "recipients of the judicial power of the United States." The judges' salaries consequently could not be reduced.

In *Palmore*, however, the Court reached what might seem the precisely opposite conclusion. A criminal defendant, invoking *O'Donoghue*, argued that the D. C. Superior Court Judge could not constitutionally preside over the case because the judge lacked Article III's tenure protection, namely, life tenure. But the Court rejected the defendant's argument. Why? How did it explain *O'Donoghue*?

The difference, said the Court, lies in the fact that, in the meantime, Congress had changed the nature of the District of Columbia court. Congress changed what had been a unified court system where judges adjudicated both local and federal issues into separate court systems, in one of which judges adjudicated primarily local issues. Courts in that category had criminal jurisdiction over only those cases brought " 'under any law applicable exclusively to the District of Columbia.' " Its judges served for 15-year terms.

This Court, in *Palmore*, considered a local judge presiding over a local court. Congress had created that court in the exercise of its Article I power to "exercise exclusive Legislation in all Cases whatsoever" over the District of Columbia. The "focus" of these courts was "primarily upon . . . matters of strictly local concern." Hence, the nature of those courts was a "far cry" from that of the courts at issue in *O'Donoghue*.

The Court added that Congress had created non-Article III courts under its Article IV powers. It wrote that Congress could also create non-Article III courts under its Article I powers. And it held that judges serving on those non-Article III courts lacked Article III protections.

Palmore concerned Article I of the Constitution, not Article IV. And it concerned "the judicial Power of the United States," not "Officers of the United States." But it provides a rough analogy. It holds that Article III protections do not apply to an Article I court "focus[ed]," unlike the courts at issue in *O'Donoghue*, primarily on local matters. Here, Congress expressly invoked a constitutional provision allowing it to make local debt-related law (Article IV); it expressly located the Board within the local government of Puerto Rico; it clearly indicated that it intended the Board's members to be local officials; and it gave them primarily local powers, duties, and responsibilities.

In his concurring opinion, Justice Thomas criticizes the inquiry we set out—whether an officer's duties are primarily local or primarily federal—as too "amorphous." But we think this is the test established by the Constitution's text, as illuminated by historical practice. And we cannot see how Congress could avoid the strictures of the Appointments Clause by adding to a federal officer's other obligations a large number of local duties. Indeed, we think that our test, tied as it is to both the text and the history of the Appointments Clause, is more rigorous than the bare inquiry into the "nature" of the officer's authority that Justice Thomas proposes, and we believe it is more faithful to the Clause's original meaning.

V

We conclude, for the reasons stated, that the Constitution's Appointments Clause applies to the appointment of officers of the United States with powers and duties in and in relation to Puerto Rico, but that the congressionally mandated process for selecting members of the Financial Oversight and Management Board for Puerto Rico does not violate that Clause. Given this conclusion, we need not consider the request by some of the parties that we overrule the much-criticized "Insular Cases" and their progeny. See, *e.g., Downes v. Bidwell* (1901) (opinion of Brown, J.); *Balzac v. Porto Rico* (1922); *Reid v. Covert* (1957) (plurality opinion) (indicating that the Insular Cases should not be further extended). Those cases did not reach this issue, and whatever their continued validity we will not extend them in these cases.

Neither, since we hold the appointment method valid, need we consider the application of the *de facto* officer doctrine. See *Ryder v. United States* (1995) (discussing the doctrine).

Finally, as Justice Sotomayor recognizes we need not, and therefore do not, decide questions concerning the application of the Federal Relations Act and Public Law 600. No party has argued that those Acts bear any significant relation to the answer to the Appointments Clause question now before us.

For these reasons, we reverse the judgment of the Court of Appeals and remand the cases for further proceedings consistent with this opinion.

It is so ordered.

JUSTICE THOMAS, concurring in the judgment.

The Court reaches the right conclusion: The appointment process for members of the Financial Oversight and Management Board for Puerto Rico (Board) does not violate the Appointments Clause. I cannot agree, however, with the ill-defined path that the Court takes to reach this result. I would resolve these cases based on the original public meaning of the phrase "Officers of the United States" in the Appointments Clause.

I

The Appointments Clause provides that the President "shall nominate, and by and with the Advice and Consent of the Senate, shall appoint Ambassadors, other public Ministers and Consuls, Judges of the supreme Court, and all other Officers of the United States, whose Appointments are not herein otherwise provided for, and which shall be established by Law." Art. II, §2, cl. 2. The Clause also permits Congress to vest the appointment of "inferior Officers" in "the President alone," "the Courts of Law," or "the Heads of Departments."

As I have previously explained, the original public meaning of the phrase "Officers of the United States" includes "all federal civil officials who perform an ongoing, statutory duty." *Lucia v. SEC* (2018) (Thomas, J., concurring) (citing Mascott, Who Are "Officers of the United States"? 70 Stan. L. Rev. 443, 454 (2018) (Mascott)). At the founding, the term "officer" referred to "anyone who performed a continuous public duty." And the phrase "of the United States" limited the Appointments Clause to "federal" officers.

II

Territorial officials performing duties created under Article IV of the Constitution are not federal officers within the original meaning of the phrase "Officers of the United States." Since the founding, this Court has recognized a distinction between Article IV power and the powers of the National Government in Articles I, II, and III. The founding generation understood the phrase "Officers of the United States" to refer to officers exercising the powers of the National Government, not officers solely exercising Article IV territorial power. Because the Board's members perform duties pursuant to Article IV, they do not qualify as "Officers of the United States."

A

The Territory Clause of Article IV provides Congress the "Power to dispose of and make all needful Rules and Regulations respecting the Territory . . . belonging to the United States." §3, cl. 2. This power is "absolute and undisputed." *Sere v. Pitot* (1810). Congress has "full and complete legislative authority over the people of the Territories and all the departments of the territorial governments." *National Bank v. County of Yankton* (1880).

"No one has ever doubted the authority of congress to erect territorial governments within the territory of the United States, under the general language of the clause, 'to make all needful rules and regulations.'" 3 J. Story, Commentaries on the Constitution of the United States (1833). These governments are "the creations, exclusively, of [Congress], and subject to its supervision and control." *Benner v. Porter* (1850).[1]

---

1. The Court of Appeals attempted to draw a distinction between power exercised pursuant to territorial laws enacted by Congress and power exercised pursuant to territorial laws enacted by a territorial legislature. There is no meaningful distinction in this context. While the legislature of the Territory may establish laws for the Territories, Article IV remains the "ultimate source" of territorial power. *Puerto Rico v. Sanchez Valle*. Congress is the source of the "entire dominion and sovereignty" of a Territory, *Simms v. Simms* (1899), and therefore all territorial laws, whether congressionally enacted or territorially enacted, derive from Article IV.

Because territorial governments "are not organized under the Constitution," they are not "subject to its complex distribution of the powers of government." Congress may give Territories "a legislative, an executive, and a judiciary, with such powers as it has been their will to assign." And, since the founding, Congress has done so in ways that do not comport with the Constitution's restrictions on the National Government. For example, Congress has delegated Article IV legislative authority to territorial officials and legislatures, which it could not do with Article I legislative power. See *Whitman v. American Trucking Assns., Inc.* (2001); *Department of Transportation v. Association of American Railroads* (2015) (Thomas, J., concurring in judgment). It has also established territorial courts that do not comply with Article III. See Baude, Adjudication Outside Article III (2020) (analyzing territorial courts in early Territories).

The powers vested in territorial governments are distinct from the powers of the National Government. Territorial legislatures exercise the legislative power of the Territory, not Article I legislative power. *Cincinnati Soap Co. v. United States* (1937). Territorial officials exercise the executive power of the Territory, not Article II executive power. *Snow v. United States* (1873). And territorial courts exercise the judicial power of the Territory, not the "judicial power of the United States" under Article III. *American Ins. Co. v. 356 Bales of Cotton* (1828).

B

Given the distinction between territorial and national powers, the question becomes whether officers exercising Article IV territorial power are officers "of the United States" under the original meaning of the Appointments Clause. They are not. Both the text of the Appointments Clause and historical practice support this conclusion.

1

The text of the Appointments Clause indicates that "Officers of the United States" refers to officers exercising the powers of the National Government, not officers exercising territorial power. The Clause applies to the appointment of "Ambassadors, other public Ministers and Consuls, Judges of the supreme Court, and all other Officers of the United States." Art. II, §2, cl. 2. Each of the officers specifically mentioned in the Clause—"Ambassadors," "public Ministers," "Consuls," and "Judges of the supreme Court"—holds an office that exercises national power. *Ibid.* Although not dispositive, this fact suggests that the phrase "and all other Officers of the United States" refers to "other" officers of the National Government. See *Beecham v. United States* (1994) ("That several items in a list share an attribute counsels in favor of interpreting the other items as possessing that attribute as well"); see also A. Scalia & B. Garner, Reading Law: The Interpretation of Legal Texts (2012) (discussing the "associated-words canon," also known as *noscitur a sociis*).

2

Historical evidence from the founding era confirms that officers exercising Article IV territorial power are not "Officers of the United States." The Court acknowledges some of this evidence and surveys the history of appointments in Puerto Rico. I, however, would give more weight and focus to the practices of the First Congress, which provide "powerful evidence of the original understanding of the Constitution." *Comptroller of Treasury of Md. v. Wynne* (2015) (Thomas, J., dissenting) (compiling cases relying on the practices of the First Congress to interpret the Constitution).

Before the Constitution's ratification, the Northwest Ordinance of 1787 set up a territorial government for the Northwest Territory. This ordinance granted Congress the power to appoint the Northwest Territory's Governor, secretary, judges, and general militia officers. And it provided the Governor the power to appoint "magistrates and other civil officers" of the Territory.

In 1789, after the ratification of the Constitution, the First Congress amended the Northwest Ordinance "to adapt [it] to the present Constitution of the United States." One of these amendments provided that "the President shall nominate, and by and with the advice and consent of the Senate, shall appoint all officers which by the said ordinance were to have been appointed by the United States in Congress assembled, and all officers so appointed shall be commissioned by him." The officers not previously designated for congressional appointment, including "magistrates and other civil officers," remained subject to appointment by the Governor. These amendments (and lack thereof) provide strong evidence that the First Congress understood the distinction between territorial officers and officers of the National Government.

As the Court recognizes, Congress revised the Northwest Ordinance to require "a Presidential-appointment, Senate-confirmation process for high-level territorial appointees who assumed *federal, as well as local, duties*." For example, Congress revised the appointment process for the Governor of the Northwest Territory, who performed duties under the powers of the National Government in addition to his Article IV territorial duties. . . . Thus, at least with respect to the Governor, who wielded powers of the National Government, the First Congress appears to have modified the Northwest Ordinance to ensure its compliance with the Appointments Clause.

In contrast, Congress did not revise the process for appointing "magistrates and other civil officers," who remained subject to appointment by the Governor. The "magistrates and other civil officers" of the Northwest Territory included justices of the peace, clerks of the court, sheriffs, coroners, surveyors, and notaries. If these officials were exercising a statutory duty under the powers of the National Government, they would have certainly been considered "Officers of the United States" under the Appointments Clause. See Mascott. "The Founders considered individuals to be officers even if they performed only ministerial statutory duties — including recordkeepers, clerks, and tidewaiters (individuals who watched goods land at a customhouse)." *Lucia* (Thomas, J., concurring). But "the powers and duties of magistrates and other civil officers [were] regulated and defined by the [territorial] assembly," and therefore were necessarily exercised pursuant to Article IV. It is evident that the First Congress did not consider these officials to be "Officers of the United States," because it allowed appointment by an official who is not the "hea[d] of a department." See *United States v. Germaine* (1879).

One cannot plausibly conclude that the First Congress—seeking to "adapt" the Northwest Ordinance to the Constitution—prescribed methods of appointing territorial officers that violated the Appointments Clause. Rather, the First Congress recognized the distinction between territorial and national powers, and understood that officers performing duties pursuant to only Article IV territorial powers are not officers "of the United States." For these reasons, I would hold that the original meaning of the phrase "Officers of the United States" does not include territorial officers exercising only powers conferred under Article IV.

C

Under the original meaning of the Appointments Clause, the Board's members are not "Officers of the United States." They are territorial officers exercising power granted under Article IV.

The Board is "an entity within the territorial government," created "pursuant to article IV, section 3 of the Constitution of the United States," and funded by the Territory. The members of the Board perform duties involving the oversight of Puerto Rico's finances and fiscal reform efforts, and the representation of Puerto Rico in debt restructuring proceedings. Because "they do not exercise the national executive power," "national judicial power," or national legislative power, the Board's members are "Article IV executives," not Officers of the United States under the Appointments Clause. See *Freytag* v. *Commissioner* (1991) (Scalia, J., concurring in part and concurring in judgment).

The Court rightfully acknowledges the territorial nature of the Board's duties. But in the process, the Court sets up a dichotomy between officers with "primarily local versus primarily federal" duties. I cannot agree with this amorphous test.

As an initial matter, the Court need not decide whether an officer exercising both national and Article IV powers qualifies as an "Officer of the United States." The Board's members have responsibility for ongoing statutory duties that are entirely within the scope of Article IV.

Resolving this unnecessary issue is especially problematic because the original meaning of the phrase "Officers of the United States" arguably includes all officers exercising the powers of the National Government, even if those officers also exercise power vested under Article IV. The Governor of the Northwest Territory, for example, seems to have performed "primarily local" duties, yet the First Congress believed the Governor was an "Officer of the United States" subject to the restrictions of the Appointments Clause.

The Court fails to engage with this point. Indeed, it fails to provide any foundation at all for its "primarily local" rule. The only analysis to be found is a conclusory statement that *Palmore* v. *United States* (1973), "provides a rough analogy." But drawing a rule from a case that is "no[t] . . . directly on point," without even analyzing the underlying reasoning of that case, is not sound constitutional interpretation. And favoring a tangentially related decision from 1973 over the practices of the First Congress is certainly not "more faithful to the [Appointment] Clause's original meaning,"

Finally, the Court fails to provide any explanation for what makes an officer's duties "primarily local." Is it the relative importance of the duties? Or is it the number of duties exercised pursuant to each power? And what ratio is required for duties to be primarily local? The Court's opinion has no answers and does not even acknowledge the questions. And, regardless of how these questions are resolved, the primarily local test allows Congress to evade the requirements of the Appointments Clause by supplementing an officer's federal duties with sufficient territorial duties, such that they become "primarily local," whatever that means.

* * *

Today's decision reaches the right outcome, but it does so in a roundabout way that departs from the original meaning of the Appointments Clause. I would hold that the Board's members are not "Officers of the United States" because they perform ongoing statutory duties under only Article IV. I therefore cannot join the Court's opinion and concur only in the judgment.

JUSTICE SOTOMAYOR, concurring in the judgment.

Nearly 60 years ago, the people of Puerto Rico "embark[ed] on [a] project of constitutional self-governance" after entering into a compact with the Federal Government. *Puerto Rico v. Sanchez Valle* (2016). At the conclusion of that endeavor, the people of Puerto Rico established, and the United States Congress recognized, a "republican form of government" "pursuant to a constitution of [the Puerto Rican population's] own adoption." One would think the Puerto Rican home rule that resulted from that mutual enterprise might affect whether officers later installed by the Federal Government are properly considered officers of Puerto Rico rather than "Officers of the United States" subject to the Appointments Clause. U.S. Const., Art. II, §2, cl. 2. Yet the parties do not address that weighty issue or any attendant questions it raises. I thus do not resolve those matters here and instead concur in the judgment.

I nevertheless write to explain why these unexplored issues may well call into doubt the Court's conclusion that the members of the Financial Oversight and Management Board for Puerto Rico are territorial officers not subject to the "significant structural safeguards" embodied in the Appointments Clause. *Edmond* v. *United States* (1997). Puerto Rico's compact with the Federal Government and its republican form of government may not alter its status as a Territory. But territorial status should not be wielded as a talismanic opt out of prior congressional commitments or constitutional constraints.

I

A

. . . With the passage of Public Law 600 and the adoption and recognition of the Puerto Rico Constitution, "the United States and Puerto Rico . . . forged a unique political relationship, built on the island's evolution into a constitutional democracy exercising local self-rule."

Of critical import here, the Federal Government "relinquished its control over [Puerto Rico's] local affairs[,] grant[ing] Puerto Rico a measure of autonomy comparable to that possessed by the States." *Examining Bd. of Engineers, Architects and Surveyors v. Flores de Otero* (1976). Indeed, the very "purpose of Congress in the 1950 and 1952 legislation was to accord Puerto Rico the degree of autonomy and independence normally associated with States of the Union." . . .

II

A

In concluding that the Board members are territorial officers not subject to the strictures of the Appointment Clause, the Court does not meaningfully address Puerto Rico's history or status. Nor need it, as the parties do not discuss the potential consequences that Congress' recognition of complete self-government decades ago may have on the Appointments Clause analysis. But in my view, however one distinguishes territorial officers from federal officers (whether under the Court's "primarily local" test or some other standard), the longstanding compact between the Federal Government and Puerto Rico raises grave doubts as to whether the Board members are territorial officers not subject to the Appointments Clause. When Puerto Rico and Congress entered into a compact and ratified a constitution of Puerto Rico's adoption, Congress explicitly left the authority to choose Puerto Rico's governmental officers to the people of Puerto Rico. That turn of events seems to give to Puerto Rico, through a voluntary concession by the Federal Government, the exclusive right to establish Puerto Rico's own territorial officers.

No less than the bedrock principles of government upon which this Nation was founded ground this proposition. When the Framers resolved to build this Nation on a republican form of government, they understood that the American people would have the authority to select their own governmental officers. See, *e.g.*, The Federalist No. 39 (J. Madison) ("[W]e may define a republic to be . . . a government which derives all its powers directly or indirectly from the great body of the people"). Core to the 1950s "compact" between the Federal Government and Puerto Rico was that Puerto Rico's eventual constitution "shall provide a republican form of government." Thus, "resonant of American founding principles," the Puerto Rico Constitution set forth a tripartite government " 'republican in form' and 'subordinate to the sovereignty of the people of Puerto Rico.' " *Sanchez Valle*. "[T]he distinguishing feature" of such "republican form of government," this Court has recognized over and again, "is the right of the people to choose their own officers for governmental administration, and pass their own laws in virtue of the legislative power reposed in representative bodies, whose legitimate acts may be said to be those of the people themselves." *In re Duncan* (1891).

Thus, whatever authority the Federal Government exercised to select territorial officers for Puerto Rico before Congress recognized Puerto Rico's republican form of government, the authority "to choose [Puerto Rico's] own officers for governmental administration" now seems to belong to the people of Puerto Rico. *Duncan.* Indeed, however directly responsible the Federal Government was for Puerto Rico's local affairs before Public Law 600, those matters might be said to "now procee[d]" in the first instance "from the Puerto Rico Constitution as 'ordain[ed] and establish[ed]' by 'the people.'". . .

There can be little question, then, that the compact altered the relationship between the Federal Government and Puerto Rico. At a minimum, the post-compact developments, including this Court's precedents, indicate that Congress placed in the hands of the Puerto Rican people the authority to establish their own government, replete with officers of their own choosing, and that this grant of self-government was not an empty promise. That history prompts serious questions as to whether the Board members may be territorial officers of Puerto Rico when they are not elected or approved, directly or indirectly, by the people of Puerto Rico.

B

Of course, it might be argued that Congress is nevertheless free to repeal its grant of self-rule, including the grant of authority to the island to select its own governmental officers. And perhaps, it might further be said, that is exactly what Congress has done in PROMESA by declaring the Board "an entity within the territorial government" of Puerto Rico. But that is not so certain. . . .

Further, there is a legitimate question whether Congress could validly repeal any element of its earlier compact with Puerto Rico on its own initiative, even if it had been abundantly explicit in its intention to do so. . . .

Plausible reasons may exist to treat Public Law 600 and the Federal Government's recognition of Puerto Rico's sovereignty as similarly irrevocable, at least in the absence of mutual consent. Congress made clear in Public Law 600 that the agreement between the Federal Government and Puerto Rico was "in the nature of a compact." . . .

All of this presses up against broader questions about Congress' power under the Territories Clause of Article IV, U.S. Const., Art. IV, §3, cl. 2, the purported source of legislative authority for enacting PROMESA. May Congress ever simply cede its power under that Clause to legislate for the Territories, and did it do so nearly 60 years ago with respect to Puerto Rico? If so, is PROMESA itself invalid, at least insofar as it holds itself out as an exercise of Territories Clause authority? This Court has never squarely addressed such questions, except perhaps to acknowledge that Congress' authority under the Territories Clause may "continu[e] until granted away." *National Bank v. County of Yankton* (1880).

After all, the Territories Clause provides Congress not only the power to "make all needful Rules and Regulations respecting the Territor[ies]," but also the power to "dispose of" them, which necessarily encompasses the power to relinquish authority to legislate for them. U.S. Const., Art. IV, §3, cl. 2. And some have insisted that the power to cede authority exists no less in the absence of full "dispos[al]" through independence or Statehood.

Still, the parties here do not dispute Congress' ability to enact PROMESA under the Territories Clause in the first place; nor does it seem strictly necessary to call that matter into question to resolve the Appointments Clause concern presented here. Despite the "full measure of self-government" the island supposedly enjoys, Puerto Rico can well remain a "Territory" subject to some measure of Congress' Territories Clause authority. But even assuming that the Territories Clause thus enables Congress to enact federal laws "respecting" Puerto Rico, U.S. Const., Art. IV, §3, cl. 2, still some things the Clause does not necessarily do: It does not necessarily allow Congress to repeal by mere implication its prior grant of authority to the people of Puerto Rico to choose their own governmental officers. It does not necessarily give Congress license to revoke unilaterally an instrument that may be altered only with mutual consent. And it does not necessarily permit Congress to declare by fiat that the law must treat its exercise of authority under the Territories Clause as territorial rather than federal, irrespective of the compact it entered with the people of Puerto Rico leaving complete territorial authority to them.

III

Nor is it significant that Congress has historically provided for the appointment of officers who perform duties related to the Territories through methods other than those prescribed by the Appointments Clause. Those methods may be permissible up to a point in a Territory's development. But that historical practice does not, in my view, resolve the far more complex question whether Congress can continue to act in that manner indefinitely or long after granting Territories complete self-government.

Essentially none (if any) of the allegedly nonconforming appointments referenced by the parties occurred in circumstances where, as in the case of Puerto Rico, Congress previously granted the Territories complete home rule. Instead, they largely occurred during the initial or transitional stages of a Territory's existence, when often the terms of the organic statute establishing the Territory expressly provided for the Federal Government to act on behalf of the Territory. (After all, in newly established Territories, no recognized territorial government existed until the organic statute established one.) Because in that state of affairs, an organic statute plainly contemplated that *Congress* had authority to establish offices for the Territory, such congressionally established offices could fairly—indeed, necessarily—be treated as "territorial" to the extent they were tasked with territorial duties.

Does that necessarily remain the case if Congress later grants or establishes complete territorial self-government? As Puerto Rico's history may demonstrate, it is seemingly at that point that Congress purports to recognize that the Territory itself (not the Federal Government) wields authority over matters of the Territory, including the ability to select its own territorial officers. Perhaps it is also at that point that a distinction between territorial officers and federal officers crystallizes: Territorial officers are those who derive their authority from the people of the Territory; federal officers are those who derive their authority from the Federal Government. And here, the Board members indisputably are selected by the Federal Government, under a statute passed by Congress that specifies not just their governance responsibilities but also the priorities of their decisionmaking. . . .

* * *

These cases raise serious questions about when, if ever, the Federal Government may constitutionally exercise authority to establish territorial officers in a Territory like Puerto Rico, where Congress seemingly ceded that authority long ago to Puerto Rico itself. The 1950s compact between the Federal Government and Puerto Rico undoubtedly carried ramifications for Puerto Rico's status under federal and international law; the same may be true of the Appointments Clause analysis here. After all, the long-awaited promise of Public Law 600's compact between Puerto Rico and the Federal Government seemed to be that the people of Puerto Rico may choose their own territorial officers, rather than have such officers foisted on the Territory by the Federal Government.

Viewed against that backdrop, the result of these cases seems anomalous. The Board members, tasked with determining the financial fate of a self-governing Territory, exist in a twilight zone of accountability, neither selected by Puerto Rico itself nor subject to the strictures of the Appointments Clause. I am skeptical that the Constitution countenances this freewheeling exercise of control over a population that the Federal Government has explicitly agreed to recognize as operating under a government of their own choosing, pursuant to a constitution of their own choosing. Surely our Founders, having labored to attain such recognition of self-determination, would not view that same recognition with respect to Puerto Rico as a mere act of grace. Nevertheless, because these issues are not properly presented in these cases, I reluctantly concur in the judgment.

STUDY GUIDE:

- Why does Chief Justice Roberts find the CFPB unconstitutional? What is unique about its structure? How does Roberts reconcile this case with *Humphrey's Executor* and *Morrison v. Olson*?
- Justice Thomas wrote a concurring opinion joined by Justice Gorsuch. Why do they disagree with the majority opinion? Do they think this decision can be reconciled with *Humphrey's Executor* and *Morrison v. Olson*?

- Justice Kagan dissented. She wrote that the majority opinion effectively rewrote *Humphrey's Executor* and *Morrison v. Olson*. Is she right? Is the structure of the CFPB novel?

Seila Law LLC v. Consumer Financial Protection Bureau
591 U.S. ___ (2020)

CHIEF JUSTICE ROBERTS delivered the opinion of the Court with respect to Parts I, II, and III.

In the wake of the 2008 financial crisis, Congress established the Consumer Financial Protection Bureau (CFPB), an independent regulatory agency tasked with ensuring that consumer debt products are safe and transparent. In organizing the CFPB, Congress deviated from the structure of nearly every other independent administrative agency in our history. Instead of placing the agency under the leadership of a board with multiple members, Congress provided that the CFPB would be led by a single Director, who serves for a longer term than the President and cannot be removed by the President except for inefficiency, neglect, or malfeasance. The CFPB Director has no boss, peers, or voters to report to. Yet the Director wields vast rulemaking, enforcement, and adjudicatory authority over a significant portion of the U.S. economy. The question before us is whether this arrangement violates the Constitution's separation of powers.

Under our Constitution, the "executive Power"—all of it—is "vested in a President," who must "take Care that the Laws be faithfully executed." Art. II, §1, cl. 1; *id.*, §3. Because no single person could fulfill that responsibility alone, the Framers expected that the President would rely on subordinate officers for assistance. Ten years ago, in *Free Enterprise Fund v. Public Company Accounting Oversight Bd.* (2010), we reiterated that, "as a general matter," the Constitution gives the President "the authority to remove those who assist him in carrying out his duties." "Without such power, the President could not be held fully accountable for discharging his own responsibilities; the buck would stop somewhere else."

The President's power to remove—and thus supervise—those who wield executive power on his behalf follows from the text of Article II, was settled by the First Congress, and was confirmed in the landmark decision *Myers v. United States* (1926). Our precedents have recognized only two exceptions to the President's unrestricted removal power. In *Humphrey's Executor v. United States* (1935), we held that Congress could create expert agencies led by a *group* of principal officers removable by the President only for good cause. And in *United States v. Perkins* (1886), and *Morrison v. Olson* (1988), we held that Congress could provide tenure protections to certain *inferior* officers with narrowly defined duties.

We are now asked to extend these precedents to a new configuration: an independent agency that wields significant executive power and is run by a single individual who cannot be removed by the President unless certain statutory criteria are met. We decline to take that step. While we need not and do not revisit our prior decisions allowing certain limitations on the President's removal power, there are compelling reasons not to extend those precedents to the novel context of an independent agency led by a single Director. Such an agency lacks a foundation in historical practice and clashes with constitutional structure by concentrating power in a unilateral actor insulated from Presidential control.

We therefore hold that the structure of the CFPB violates the separation of powers. We go on to hold that the CFPB Director's removal protection is severable from the other statutory provisions bearing on the CFPB's authority. The agency may therefore continue to operate, but its Director, in light of our decision, must be removable by the President at will.

I

A

. . . In 2010, Congress . . . created the Consumer Financial Protection Bureau (CFPB) as an independent financial regulator within the Federal Reserve System. Dodd-Frank Wall Street Reform and Consumer Protection Act (Dodd-Frank). Congress tasked the CFPB with "implement[ing]" and "enforc[ing]" a large body of financial consumer protection laws to "ensur[e] that all consumers have access to markets for consumer financial products and services and that markets for consumer financial products and services are fair, transparent, and competitive." Congress transferred the administration of 18 existing federal statutes to the CFPB, including the Fair Credit Reporting Act, the Fair Debt Collection Practices Act, and the Truth in Lending Act. . . .

Congress also vested the CFPB with potent enforcement powers. The agency has the authority to conduct investigations, issue subpoenas and civil investigative demands, initiate administrative adjudications, and prosecute civil actions in federal court. . . .

The CFPB's rulemaking and enforcement powers are coupled with extensive adjudicatory authority. The agency may conduct administrative proceedings to "ensure or enforce compliance with" the statutes and regulations it administers.

. . . Rather than create a traditional independent agency headed by a multimember board or commission, Congress elected to place the CFPB under the leadership of a single Director. The CFPB Director is appointed by the President with the advice and consent of the Senate. The Director serves for a term of five years, during which the President may remove the Director from office only for "inefficiency, neglect of duty, or malfeasance in office."

Unlike most other agencies, the CFPB does not rely on the annual appropriations process for funding. Instead, the CFPB receives funding directly from the Federal Reserve, which is itself funded outside the appropriations process through bank assessments. Each year, the CFPB requests an amount that the Director deems "reasonably necessary to carry out" the agency's duties, and the Federal Reserve grants that request so long as it does not exceed 12% of the total operating expenses of the Federal Reserve (inflation adjusted). . . .

III

We hold that the CFPB's leadership by a single individual removable only for inefficiency, neglect, or malfeasance violates the separation of powers.

A

Article II provides that "[t]he executive Power shall be vested in a President," who must "take Care that the Laws be faithfully executed." Art. II, §1, cl. 1; *id.*, §3. The entire "executive Power" belongs to the President alone. But because it would be "impossib[le]" for "one man" to "perform all the great business of the State," the Constitution assumes that lesser executive officers will "assist the supreme Magistrate in discharging the duties of his trust." Writings of George Washington (1939).

These lesser officers must remain accountable to the President, whose authority they wield. As Madison explained, "[I]f any power whatsoever is in its nature Executive, it is the power of appointing, overseeing, and controlling those who execute the laws." That power, in turn, generally includes the ability to remove executive officials, for it is "only the authority that can remove" such officials that they "must fear and, in the performance of [their] functions, obey." *Bowsher.*

The President's removal power has long been confirmed by history and precedent. It "was discussed extensively in Congress when the first executive departments were created" in 1789. *Free Enterprise Fund.* . . . The First Congress's recognition of the President's removal power in 1789 "provides contemporaneous and weighty evidence of the Constitution's meaning," *Bowsher*, and has long been the "settled and well understood construction of the Constitution," *Ex parte Hennen* (1839).

The Court recognized the President's prerogative to remove executive officials in *Myers v. United States.* Chief Justice Taft, writing for the Court, conducted an exhaustive examination of the First Congress's determination in 1789, the views of the Framers and their contemporaries, historical practice, and our precedents up until that point. He concluded that Article II "grants to the President" the "general administrative control of those executing the laws, including the power of appointment *and removal* of executive officers." Just as the President's "selection of administrative officers is essential to the execution of the laws by him, so must be his power of removing those for whom he cannot continue to be responsible." "[T]o hold otherwise," the Court reasoned, "would make it impossible for the President . . . to take care that the laws be faithfully executed."

We recently reiterated the President's general removal power in *Free Enterprise Fund.* "Since 1789," we recapped, "the Constitution has been understood to empower the President to keep these officers accountable—by removing them from office, if necessary." Although we had previously sustained congressional limits on that power in certain circumstances, we declined to extend those limits to "a new situation not yet encountered by the Court"—an official insulated by *two* layers of for-cause removal protection. In the face of that novel impediment to the President's oversight of the Executive Branch, we adhered to the general rule that the President possesses "the authority to remove those who assist him in carrying out his duties."

Free Enterprise Fund left in place two exceptions to the President's unrestricted removal power. First, in *Humphrey's Executor*, decided less than a decade after *Myers*, the Court upheld a statute that protected the Commissioners of the FTC from removal except for "inefficiency, neglect of duty, or malfeasance in office." In reaching that conclusion, the Court stressed that Congress's ability to impose such removal restrictions "will depend upon the character of the office."

Because the Court limited its holding "to officers of the kind here under consideration," the contours of the *Humphrey's Executor* exception depend upon the characteristics of the agency before the Court. Rightly or wrongly, the Court viewed the FTC (as it existed in 1935) as exercising "no part of the executive power." Instead, it was "an administrative body" that performed "specified duties as a legislative or as a judicial aid." It acted "as a legislative agency" in "making investigations and reports" to Congress and "as an agency of the judiciary" in making recommendations to courts as a master in chancery. "To the extent that [the FTC] exercise[d] any executive *function*[,] as distinguished from executive *power* in the constitutional sense," it did so only in the discharge of its "quasi-legislative or quasi-judicial powers." *Ibid.* (emphasis added).[2]

The Court identified several organizational features that helped explain its characterization of the FTC as non-executive. Composed of five members—no more than three from the same political party—the Board was designed to be "non-partisan" and to "act with entire impartiality." The FTC's duties were "neither political nor executive," but instead called for "the trained judgment of a body of experts" "informed by experience." And the Commissioners' staggered, seven-year terms enabled the agency to accumulate technical expertise and avoid a "complete change" in leadership "at any one time."

In short, *Humphrey's Executor* permitted Congress to give for-cause removal protections to a multimember body of experts, balanced along partisan lines, that performed legislative and judicial functions and was said not to exercise any executive power.

While recognizing an exception for multimember bodies with "quasi-judicial" or "quasi-legislative" functions, *Humphrey's Executor* reaffirmed the core holding of *Myers* that the President has "unrestrictable power . . . to remove purely executive officers." The Court acknowledged that between purely executive officers on the one hand, and officers that closely resembled the FTC Commissioners on the other, there existed "a field of doubt" that the Court left "for future consideration."

---

2. The Court's conclusion that the FTC did not exercise executive power has not withstood the test of time. As we observed in *Morrison* v. *Olson* (1988), "[I]t is hard to dispute that the powers of the FTC at the time of *Humphrey's Executor* would at the present time be considered 'executive,' at least to some degree." See also *Arlington* v. *FCC* (2013) (even though the activities of administrative agencies "take 'legislative' and 'judicial' forms," "they are exercises of—indeed, under our constitutional structure they *must be* exercises of—the 'executive Power' " (quoting Art. II, §1, cl. 1)).

We have recognized a second exception for *inferior* officers in two cases, *United States v. Perkins* and *Morrison v. Olson*.[3] In *Perkins*, we upheld tenure protections for a naval cadet-engineer. And, in *Morrison*, we upheld a provision granting good-cause tenure protection to an independent counsel appointed to investigate and prosecute particular alleged crimes by high-ranking Government officials. Backing away from the reliance in *Humphrey's Executor* on the concepts of "quasi-legislative" and "quasi-judicial" power, we viewed the ultimate question as whether a removal restriction is of "such a nature that [it] impede[s] the President's ability to perform his constitutional duty." Although the independent counsel was a single person and performed "law enforcement functions that typically have been undertaken by officials within the Executive Branch," we concluded that the removal protections did not unduly interfere with the functioning of the Executive Branch because "the independent counsel [was] an inferior officer under the Appointments Clause, with limited jurisdiction and tenure and lacking policymaking or significant administrative authority." *Ibid.*

These two exceptions — one for multimember expert agencies that do not wield substantial executive power, and one for inferior officers with limited duties and no policymaking or administrative authority — "represent what up to now have been the outermost constitutional limits of permissible congressional restrictions on the President's removal power." *PHH* (Kavanaugh, J., dissenting).

B

Neither *Humphrey's Executor* nor *Morrison* resolves whether the CFPB Director's insulation from removal is constitutional. Start with *Humphrey's Executor.* Unlike the New Deal-era FTC upheld there, the CFPB is led by a single Director who cannot be described as a "body of experts" and cannot be considered "non-partisan" in the same sense as a group of officials drawn from both sides of the aisle. Moreover, while the staggered terms of the FTC Commissioners prevented complete turnovers in agency leadership and guaranteed that there would always be some Commissioners who had accrued significant expertise, the CFPB's single-Director structure and five-year term guarantee abrupt shifts in agency leadership and with it the loss of accumulated expertise.

In addition, the CFPB Director is hardly a mere legislative or judicial aid. Instead of making reports and recommendations to Congress, as the 1935 FTC did, the Director possesses the authority to promulgate binding rules fleshing out 19 federal statutes, including a broad prohibition on unfair and deceptive practices in a major segment of the U.S. economy. And instead of submitting

---

3. Article II distinguishes between two kinds of officers — principal officers (who must be appointed by the President with the advice and consent of the Senate) and inferior officers (whose appointment Congress may vest in the President, courts, or heads of Departments). §2, cl. 2. While "[o]ur cases have not set forth an exclusive criterion for distinguishing between principal and inferior officers," we have in the past examined factors such as the nature, scope, and duration of an officer's duties. *Edmond v. United States* (1997). More recently, we have focused on whether the officer's work is "directed and supervised" by a principal officer.

recommended dispositions to an Article III court, the Director may unilaterally issue final decisions awarding legal and equitable relief in administrative adjudications. Finally, the Director's enforcement authority includes the power to seek daunting monetary penalties against private parties on behalf of the United States in federal court — a quintessentially executive power not considered in *Humphrey's Executor*.[4]

The logic of *Morrison* also does not apply. Everyone agrees the CFPB Director is not an inferior officer, and her duties are far from limited. Unlike the independent counsel, who lacked policymaking or administrative authority, the Director has the sole responsibility to administer 19 separate consumer-protection statutes that cover everything from credit cards and car payments to mortgages and student loans. It is true that the independent counsel in *Morrison* was empowered to initiate criminal investigations and prosecutions, and in that respect wielded core executive power. But that power, while significant, was trained inward to high-ranking Governmental actors identified by others, and was confined to a specified matter in which the Department of Justice had a potential conflict of interest. By contrast, the CFPB Director has the authority to bring the coercive power of the state to bear on millions of private citizens and businesses, imposing even billion-dollar penalties through administrative adjudications and civil actions.

In light of these differences, the constitutionality of the CFPB Director's insulation from removal cannot be settled by *Humphrey's Executor* or *Morrison* alone.

C

The question instead is whether to extend those precedents to the "new situation" before us, namely an independent agency led by a single Director and vested with significant executive power. *Free Enterprise Fund*. We decline to do so. Such an agency has no basis in history and no place in our constitutional structure.

1

"Perhaps the most telling indication of [a] severe constitutional problem" with an executive entity "is [a] lack of historical precedent" to support it. An agency with a structure like that of the CFPB is almost wholly unprecedented.

After years of litigating the agency's constitutionality, the Courts of Appeals, parties, and *amici* have identified "only a handful of isolated" incidents in which Congress has provided good-cause tenure to principal officers who wield power alone rather than as members of a board or commission. "[T]hese few scattered examples" — four to be exact — shed little light. *NLRB v. Noel Canning* (2014).

---

4. The dissent would have us ignore the reasoning of *Humphrey's Executor* and instead apply the decision only as part of a reimagined *Humphrey's*-through-*Morrison* framework. But we take the decision on its own terms, not through gloss added by a later Court in dicta. . . .

. . . With the exception of the one-year blip for the Comptroller of the Currency, these isolated examples are modern and contested. And they do not involve regulatory or enforcement authority remotely comparable to that exercised by the CFPB. The CFPB's single-Director structure is an innovation with no foothold in history or tradition.[8]

2

In addition to being a historical anomaly, the CFPB's single-Director configuration is incompatible with our constitutional structure. Aside from the sole exception of the Presidency, that structure scrupulously avoids concentrating power in the hands of any single individual.

"The Framers recognized that, in the long term, structural protections against abuse of power were critical to preserving liberty." *Bowsher*. Their solution to governmental power and its perils was simple: divide it. To prevent the "gradual concentration" of power in the same hands, they enabled "[a]mbition . . . to counteract ambition" at every turn. The Federalist No. 51 (J. Madison). At the highest level, they "split the atom of sovereignty" itself into one Federal Government and the States. *Gamble* v. *United States*, (2019). They then divided the "powers of the new Federal Government into three defined categories, Legislative, Executive, and Judicial." *Chadha*.

They did not stop there. Most prominently, the Framers bifurcated the federal legislative power into two Chambers: the House of Representatives and the Senate, each composed of multiple Members and Senators. Art. I, §§2, 3.

The Executive Branch is a stark departure from all this division. The Framers viewed the legislative power as a special threat to individual liberty, so they divided that power to ensure that "differences of opinion" and the "jarrings of parties" would "promote deliberation and circumspection" and "check excesses in the majority." See The Federalist No. 70 (A. Hamilton); see also *id.*, No. 51. By contrast, the Framers thought it necessary to secure the authority of the Executive so that he could carry out his unique responsibilities. See No. 70. As Madison put it, while "the weight of the legislative authority requires that it should be . . . divided, the weakness of the executive may require, on the other hand, that it should be fortified." *Id.*, No. 51.

The Framers deemed an energetic executive essential to "the protection of the community against foreign attacks," "the steady administration of the laws," "the protection of property," and "the security of liberty." *Id.*, No. 70. Accordingly, they chose not to bog the Executive down with the "habitual feebleness and dilatoriness" that comes with a "diversity of views and opinions." Instead, they gave

---

8. The dissent categorizes the CFPB as one of many "financial regulators" that have historically enjoyed some insulation from the President. But even assuming financial institutions like the Second Bank and the Federal Reserve can claim a special historical status, the CFPB is in an entirely different league. It acts as a mini legislature, prosecutor, and court, responsible for creating substantive rules for a wide swath of industries, prosecuting violations, and levying knee-buckling penalties against private citizens. And, of course, it is the only agency of its kind run by a single Director.

the Executive the "[d]ecision, activity, secrecy, and dispatch" that "characterise the proceedings of one man."

To justify and check *that* authority—unique in our constitutional structure—the Framers made the President the most democratic and politically account-able official in Government. Only the President (along with the Vice President) is elected by the entire Nation. And the President's political accountability is enhanced by the solitary nature of the Executive Branch, which provides "a single object for the jealousy and watchfulness of the people." The President "cannot delegate ultimate responsibility or the active obligation to supervise that goes with it," because Article II "makes a single President responsible for the actions of the Executive Branch." *Free Enterprise Fund*, (quoting *Clinton v. Jones* (1997) (Breyer, J., concurring in judgment)).

The resulting constitutional strategy is straightforward: divide power every-where except for the Presidency, and render the President directly accountable to the people through regular elections. In that scheme, individual executive officials will still wield significant authority, but that authority remains subject to the ongoing supervision and control of the elected President. Through the President's oversight, "the chain of dependence [is] preserved," so that "the low-est officers, the middle grade, and the highest" all "depend, as they ought, on the President, and the President on the community." 1 Annals of Cong. (J. Madison).

The CFPB's single-Director structure contravenes this carefully calibrated system by vesting significant governmental power in the hands of a single indi-vidual accountable to no one. The Director is neither elected by the people nor meaningfully controlled (through the threat of removal) by someone who is. The Director does not even depend on Congress for annual appropriations. See The Federalist No. 58 (J. Madison) (describing the "power over the purse" as the "most compleat and effectual weapon" in representing the interests of the people). Yet the Director may *unilaterally*, without meaningful supervision, issue final regulations, oversee adjudications, set enforcement priorities, initiate prosecutions, and determine what penalties to impose on private parties. With no colleagues to persuade, and no boss or electorate looking over her shoulder, the Director may dictate and enforce policy for a vital segment of the economy affecting millions of Americans.

The CFPB Director's insulation from removal by an accountable President is enough to render the agency's structure unconstitutional. But several other features of the CFPB combine to make the Director's removal protection even more problematic. In addition to lacking the most direct method of presidential control—removal at will—the agency's unique structure also forecloses certain indirect methods of Presidential control.

Because the CFPB is headed by a single Director with a five-year term, some Presidents may not have any opportunity to shape its leadership and thereby influ-ence its activities. A President elected in 2020 would likely not appoint a CFPB Director until 2023, and a President elected in 2028 may *never* appoint one. That means an unlucky President might get elected on a consumer-protection platform and enter office only to find herself saddled with a holdover Director from a competing political party who is dead set *against* that agenda. To make matters worse, the agency's single-Director structure means the President will not have the opportunity to appoint any other leaders — such as a chair or fellow members of a Commission or Board — who can serve as a check on the Director's authority and help bring the agency in line with the President's preferred policies.

The CFPB's receipt of funds outside the appropriations process further aggravates the agency's threat to Presidential control. The President normally has the opportunity to recommend or veto spending bills that affect the operation of administrative agencies. See Art. I, §7, cl. 2; Art. II, §3. And, for the past century, the President has annually submitted a proposed budget to Congress for approval. . . . But no similar opportunity exists for the President to influence the CFPB Director. Instead, the Director receives over $500 million per year to fund the agency's chosen priorities. And the Director receives that money from the Federal Reserve, which is itself funded outside of the annual appropriations process. This financial freedom makes it even more likely that the agency will "slip from the Executive's control, and thus from that of the people." *Free Enterprise Fund*, 561 U.S., at 499.

3

Amicus raises three principal arguments in the agency's defense. At the outset, *amicus* questions the textual basis for the removal power and highlights statements from Madison, Hamilton, and Chief Justice Marshall expressing "heterodox" views on the subject. Brief for Court-Appointed *Amicus Curiae* 4–5, 28–29. But those concerns are misplaced. It is true that "there is no 'removal clause' in the Constitution," but neither is there a "separation of powers clause" or a "federalism clause." These foundational doctrines are instead evident from the Constitution's vesting of certain powers in certain bodies. As we have explained many times before, the President's removal power stems from Article II's vesting of the "executive Power" in the President. *Free Enterprise Fund* (quoting Art. II, §1, cl. 1). As for the opinions of Madison, Hamilton, and Chief Justice Marshall, we have already considered the statements cited by *amicus* and discounted them in light of their context (Madison), the fact they reflect initial impressions later abandoned by the speaker (Hamilton), or their subsequent rejection as ill-considered dicta (Chief Justice Marshall).

. . . [T]ext, first principles, the First Congress's decision in 1789, *Myers*, and *Free Enterprise Fund* all establish that the President's removal power is the rule, not the exception. While we do not revisit *Humphrey's Executor* or any other precedent today, we decline to elevate it into a freestanding invitation for Congress to impose additional restrictions on the President's removal authority.[11]

---

11. Building on *amicus'* proposal, the dissent would endorse whatever "the times demand, so long as the President retains the ability to carry out his constitutional functions." But that amorphous test provides no real limiting principle. The "clearest" (and only) "example" the dissent can muster for what may be prohibited is a for-cause removal restriction placed on the President's "close military or diplomatic advisers." But that carveout makes no logical or constitutional sense. In the dissent's

. . . *Amicus* and the House also fail to engage with the Dodd-Frank Act as a whole, which makes plain that the CFPB is an "independent bureau." Neither *amicus* nor the House explains how the CFPB would be "independent" if its head were required to implement the President's policies upon pain of removal. The Constitution might of course compel the agency to be dependent on the President notwithstanding Congress's contrary intent, but that result cannot fairly be inferred from the statute Congress enacted.

Constitutional avoidance is not a license to rewrite Congress's work to say whatever the Constitution needs it to say in a given situation. Without a proffered interpretation that is rooted in the statutory text and structure, and would avoid the constitutional violation we have identified, we take Congress at its word that it meant to impose a meaningful restriction on the President's removal authority.

The dissent, for its part, largely reprises points that the Court has already considered and rejected: It notes the lack of an express removal provision, invokes Congress's general power to create and define executive offices, highlights isolated statements from individual Framers, downplays the decision of 1789, minimizes *Myers*, brainstorms methods of Presidential control short of removal, touts the need for creative congressional responses to technological and economic change, and celebrates a pragmatic, flexible approach to American governance.

If these arguments sound familiar, it's because they are. They were raised by the dissent in *Free Enterprise Fund*. The answers to these repeated concerns (beyond those we have already covered) are the same today as they were ten years ago. . . .

As we explained in *Free Enterprise Fund*, "One can have a government that functions without being ruled by functionaries, and a government that benefits from expertise without being ruled by experts." While "[n]o one doubts Congress's power to create a vast and varied federal bureaucracy," the expansion of that bureaucracy into new territories the Framers could scarcely have imagined only sharpens our duty to ensure that the Executive Branch is overseen by a President accountable to the people.

---

view, for-cause removal restrictions are permissible because they guarantee the President "meaningful control" over his subordinates. If that is the theory, then what is the harm in giving the President the same "meaningful control" over his close advisers? The dissent claims to see a constitutional distinction between the President's "own constitutional duties in foreign relations and war" and his duty to execute laws passed by Congress. But the same Article that establishes the President's foreign relations and war duties expressly entrusts him to take care that the laws be faithfully executed. And, from the perspective of the governed, it is far from clear that the President's core and traditional powers present greater cause for concern than peripheral and modern ones. If anything, "[t]he growth of the Executive Branch, which now wields vast power and touches almost every aspect of daily life, *heightens* the concern that it may slip from the Executive's control, and thus from that of the people." *Free Enterprise Fund.*

IV

. . . Because we find the Director's removal protection severable from the other provisions of Dodd-Frank that establish the CFPB, we remand for the Court of Appeals to consider whether the civil investigative demand was validly ratified.

* * *

A decade ago, we declined to extend Congress's authority to limit the President's removal power to a new situation, never before confronted by the Court. We do the same today. In our constitutional system, the executive power belongs to the President, and that power generally includes the ability to supervise and remove the agents who wield executive power in his stead. While we have previously upheld limits on the President's removal authority in certain contexts, we decline to do so when it comes to principal officers who, acting alone, wield significant executive power. The Constitution requires that such officials remain dependent on the President, who in turn is accountable to the people.

The judgment of the United States Court of Appeals for the Ninth Circuit is vacated, and the case is remanded for further proceedings consistent with this opinion.

It is so ordered.

JUSTICE THOMAS, with whom JUSTICE GORSUCH joins, concurring in part and dissenting in part.

I

The decision in *Humphrey's Executor* poses a direct threat to our constitutional structure and, as a result, the liberty of the American people. The Court concludes that it is not strictly necessary for us to overrule that decision. But with today's decision, the Court has repudiated almost every aspect of *Humphrey's Executor*. In a future case, I would repudiate what is left of this erroneous precedent.

A

"The Constitution does not vest the Federal Government with an undifferentiated 'governmental power.'" *Department of Transportation v. Association of American Railroads* (2015) (Thomas, J., concurring in judgment). It sets out three branches and vests a different form of power in each—legislative, executive, and judicial. See Art. I, §1; Art. II, §1, cl. 1; Art. III, §1.

Article II of the Constitution vests "[t]he executive Power" in the "President of the United States of America," §1, cl. 1, and directs that he shall "take Care that the Laws be faithfully executed," §3. Of course, the President cannot fulfill his role of executing the laws without assistance. See *Myers v. United States* (1926). He therefore must "select those who [are] to act for him under his direction in the execution of the laws." While these officers assist the President in carrying out his constitutionally assigned duties, "[t]he buck stops with the President." *Free Enterprise Fund v. Public Company Accounting Oversight Bd.* (2010). "Since 1789, the Constitution has been understood to empower the President to keep [his] officers accountable — by removing them from office, if necessary." The Framers "insist[ed]" upon "unity in the Federal Executive" to "ensure both vigor and accountability" to the people. *Printz v. United States* (1997).

Despite the defined structural limitations of the Constitution and the clear vesting of executive power in the President, Congress has increasingly shifted executive power to a *de facto* fourth branch of Government — independent agencies. These agencies wield considerable executive power without Presidential oversight. They are led by officers who are insulated from the President by removal restrictions, "reduc[ing] the Chief Magistrate to [the role of] cajoler-in-chief." *Free Enterprise Fund.* But "[t]he people do not vote for the Officers of the United States. They instead look to the President to guide the assistants or deputies subject to his superintendence." Because independent agencies wield substantial power with no accountability to either the President or the people, they "pose a significant threat to individual liberty and to the constitutional system of separation of powers and checks and balances." *PHH Corp. v. CFPB* (CADC 2018) (Kavanaugh, J., dissenting).

Unfortunately, this Court "ha[s] not always been vigilant about protecting the structure of our Constitution," at times endorsing a "more pragmatic, flexible approach" to our Government's design. *Perez v. Mortgage Bankers Assn.* (2015) (Thomas, J., concurring in judgment). Our tolerance of independent agencies in *Humphrey's Executor* is an unfortunate example of the Court's failure to apply the Constitution as written. That decision has paved the way for an ever-expanding encroachment on the power of the Executive, contrary to our constitutional design.

B

3

... *Humphrey's Executor* laid the foundation for a fundamental departure from our constitutional structure with nothing more than handwaving and obfuscating phrases such as "quasi-legislative" and "quasi-judicial." Unlike the thorough analysis in *Myers*, the Court's thinly reasoned decision is completely "devoid of textual or historical precedent for the novel principle it set forth." *Morrison v. Olson* (1988) (Scalia, J., dissenting). The exceptional weakness of the reasoning could be a product of the circumstances under which the case was decided — in the midst of a bitter standoff between the Court and President Roosevelt[3] — or it could be just another example of this Court departing from the strictures of the Constitution for a "more pragmatic, flexible approach" to our government's

---

3. A number of historical sources indicate that President Roosevelt saw *Humphrey's Executor v. United States*, 295 U.S. 602 (1935), as an attack on his administration.

design. *Perez* (opinion of Thomas, J.). But whatever the motivation, *Humphrey's Executor* does not comport with the Constitution.

Humphrey's Executor relies on one key premise: the notion that there is a category of "quasi-legislative" and "quasi-judicial" power that is not exercised by Congress or the Judiciary, but that is also not part of "the executive power vested by the Constitution in the President." *Humphrey's Executor*. Working from that premise, the Court distinguished the "illimitable" power of removal recognized in *Myers, Humphrey's Executor*, and upheld the FTC Act's removal restriction, while simultaneously acknowledging that the Constitution vests the President with the entirety of the executive power.

The problem is that the Court's premise was entirely wrong. The Constitution does not permit the creation of officers exercising "quasi-legislative" and "quasi-judicial powers" in "quasi-legislative" and "quasi-judicial agencies." *Id.*, at 628–629. No such powers or agencies exist. Congress lacks the authority to delegate its legislative power, *Whitman* v. *American Trucking Assns., Inc.* (2001), and it cannot authorize the use of judicial power by officers acting outside of the bounds of Article III, *Stern* v. *Marshall* (2011). Nor can Congress create agencies that straddle multiple branches of Government. The Constitution sets out three branches of Government and provides each with a different form of power—legislative, executive, and judicial. See Art. I, §1; Art. II, §1, cl. 1; Art. III, §1. Free-floating agencies simply do not comport with this constitutional structure. . . .

The Court upheld the FTC Act's removal restriction by using the "quasi" label to support its claim that the FTC "exercise[d] no part of the executive power vested by the Constitution in the President." *Humphrey's Executor*. But "it is hard to dispute that the powers of the FTC at the time of *Humphrey's Executor* would at the present time be considered 'executive,' at least to some degree." *Morrison*.

C

Today's decision constitutes the latest in a series of cases that have significantly undermined *Humphrey's Executor*. First, in *Morrison*, the Court repudiated the reasoning of the decision. Then, in *Free Enterprise Fund*, we returned to the principles set out in the "landmark case of *Myers*." And today, the Court rightfully limits *Humphrey's Executor* to "multimember expert agencies that do not wield substantial executive power." After these decisions, the foundation for *Humphrey's Executor* is not just shaky. It is nonexistent.

This Court's repudiation of *Humphrey's Executor* began with its decision in *Morrison*. . . . The lone dissenter, Justice Scalia, disagreed with much of the Court's analysis but noted that the Court had rightfully "swept" *Humphrey's Executor* "into the dustbin of repudiated constitutional principles." Thus, all nine Members of the Court in *Morrison* rejected the core rationale of *Humphrey's Executor*.

The reasoning of the Court's decision in *Free Enterprise Fund* created further tension (if not outright conflict) with *Humphrey's Executor*. . . . *Humphrey's*

Executor . . . ignores Article II's Vesting Clause, sidesteps the President's removal power, and encourages the exercise of executive power by unaccountable officers. The reasoning of the two decisions simply cannot be reconciled.

Finally, today's decision builds upon *Morrison* and *Free Enterprise Fund*, further eroding the foundation of *Humphrey's Executor*. The Court correctly notes that "[t]he entire 'executive Power' belongs to the President alone." The President therefore must have "power to remove—and thus supervise—those who wield executive power on his behalf." As a result, the Court concludes that *Humphrey's Executor* must be limited to "multimember expert agencies that *do not wield substantial executive power*." And, at the same time, it recognizes (as the Court did in *Morrison*) that "[t]he Court's conclusion that the FTC did not exercise executive power has not withstood the test of time." In other words, *Humphrey's Executor* does not even satisfy its own exception.

In light of these decisions, it is not clear what is left of *Humphrey's Executor*'s rationale.[4] But if any remnant of that decision is still standing, it certainly is not enough to justify the numerous, unaccountable independent agencies that currently exercise vast executive power outside the bounds of our constitutional structure.

* * *

Continued reliance on *Humphrey's Executor* to justify the existence of independent agencies creates a serious, ongoing threat to our Government's design. Leaving these unconstitutional agencies in place does not enhance this Court's legitimacy; it subverts political accountability and threatens individual liberty. We have a "responsibility to 'examin[e] without fear, and revis[e] without reluctance,' any 'hasty and crude decisions' rather than leaving 'the character of [the] law impaired, and the beauty and harmony of the [American constitutional] system destroyed by the perpetuity of error.'" *Gamble v. United States* (2019) (Thomas, J., concurring). We simply cannot compromise when it comes to our Government's structure. Today, the Court does enough to resolve this case, but in the future, we should reconsider *Humphrey's Executor in toto*. And I hope that we will have the will to do so. . . .

JUSTICE KAGAN, with whom JUSTICE GINSBURG, JUSTICE BREYER, and JUSTICE SOTOMAYOR join, concurring in the judgment with respect to severability and dissenting in part.

---

4. The dissent, while vigorously defending the holding of *Humphrey's Executor*, can muster no defense for the reasoning of the decision. The dissent does not defend the notion of "quasi" powers or "quasi" agencies, recognizing that the power exercised by the FTC was executive power. And, in 39 pages, it cannot explain how any aspect of *Humphrey's Executor* (other than its holding) survived *Morrison v. Olson*, and *Free Enterprise Fund v. Public Company Accounting Oversight Bd.* (2010). Instead, the dissent simply claims that *Humphrey's Executor* was "extended" and "clarified" in *Morrison*, attempting to breathe validity into *Humphrey's Executor* through the Court's *Morrison* decision. But the dissent's reading of *Morrison* as "extend[ing] *Humphrey's* domain" is baffling. *Morrison* expressly repudiated the substantive reasoning of *Humphrey's Executor*.

Throughout the Nation's history, this Court has left most decisions about how to structure the Executive Branch to Congress and the President, acting through legislation they both agree to. In particular, the Court has commonly allowed those two branches to create zones of administrative independence by limiting the President's power to remove agency heads. The Federal Reserve Board. The Federal Trade Commission (FTC). The National Labor Relations Board. Statute after statute establishing such entities instructs the President that he may not discharge their directors except for cause—most often phrased as inefficiency, neglect of duty, or malfeasance in office. Those statutes, whose language the Court has repeatedly approved, provide the model for the removal restriction before us today. If precedent were any guide, that provision would have survived its encounter with this Court—and so would the intended independence of the Consumer Financial Protection Bureau (CFPB).

Our Constitution and history demand that result. The text of the Constitution allows these common for-cause removal limits. Nothing in it speaks of removal. And it grants Congress authority to organize all the institutions of American governance, provided only that those arrangements allow the President to perform his own constitutionally assigned duties. Still more, the Framers' choice to give the political branches wide discretion over administrative offices has played out through American history in ways that have settled the constitutional meaning. From the first, Congress debated and enacted measures to create spheres of administration—especially of financial affairs—detached from direct presidential control. As the years passed, and governance became ever more complicated, Congress continued to adopt and adapt such measures—confident it had latitude to do so under a Constitution meant to "endure for ages to come." *McCulloch v. Maryland* (1819) (approving the Second Bank of the United States). Not every innovation in governance—not every experiment in administrative independence—has proved successful. And debates about the prudence of limiting the President's control over regulatory agencies, including through his removal power, have never abated.[1] But the Constitution—both as originally drafted and as practiced—mostly leaves disagreements about administrative structure to Congress and the President, who have the knowledge and experience needed to address them. Within broad bounds, it keeps the courts—who do not—out of the picture.

The Court today fails to respect its proper role. It recognizes that this Court has approved limits on the President's removal power over heads of agencies much like the CFPB. Agencies possessing similar powers, agencies charged with similar missions, agencies created for similar reasons. The majority's explanation is that the heads of those agencies fall within an "exception"—one for multimember bodies and another for inferior officers—to a "general

---

1. In the academic literature, compare, *e.g.*, Kagan, Presidential Administration, 114 Harv. L. Rev. 2245 (2001) (generally favoring presidential control over agencies), with, *e.g.*, Strauss, Overseer, or "The Decider"? The President in Administrative Law, 75 Geo. Wash. L. Rev. 696 (2007) (generally favoring administrative independence).

rule" of unrestricted presidential removal power. And the majority says the CFPB Director does not. That account, though, is wrong in every respect. The majority's general rule does not exist. Its exceptions, likewise, are made up for the occasion—gerrymandered so the CFPB falls outside them. And the distinction doing most of the majority's work—between multimember bodies and single directors—does not respond to the constitutional values at stake. If a removal provision violates the separation of powers, it is because the measure so deprives the President of control over an official as to impede his own constitutional functions. But with or without a for-cause removal provision, the President has at least as much control over an individual as over a commission—and possibly more. That means the constitutional concern is, if anything, ameliorated when the agency has a single head. Unwittingly, the majority shows why courts should stay their hand in these matters. "Compared to Congress and the President, the Judiciary possesses an inferior understanding of the realities of administration" and the way "political power[ ] operates." *Free Enterprise Fund v. Public Company Accounting Oversight Bd.* (2010) (Breyer, J., dissenting).

In second-guessing the political branches, the majority second-guesses as well the wisdom of the Framers and the judgment of history. It writes in rules to the Constitution that the drafters knew well enough not to put there. It repudiates the lessons of American experience, from the 18th century to the present day. And it commits the Nation to a static version of governance, incapable of responding to new conditions and challenges. Congress and the President established the CFPB to address financial practices that had brought on a devastating recession, and could do so again. Today's decision wipes out a feature of that agency its creators thought fundamental to its mission—a measure of independence from political pressure. I respectfully dissent.

I

The text of the Constitution, the history of the country, the precedents of this Court, and the need for sound and adaptable governance—all stand against the majority's opinion. They point not to the majority's "general rule" of "unrestricted removal power" with two grudgingly applied "exceptions." Rather, they bestow discretion on the legislature to structure administrative institutions as the times demand, so long as the President retains the ability to carry out his constitutional duties. And most relevant here, they give Congress wide leeway to limit the President's removal power in the interest of enhancing independence from politics in regulatory bodies like the CFPB.

A

What does the Constitution say about the separation of powers—and particularly about the President's removal authority? (Spoiler alert: about the latter, nothing at all.)

The majority offers the civics class version of separation of powers — call it the Schoolhouse Rock definition of the phrase. See Schoolhouse Rock! Three Ring Government (Mar. 13, 1979), ("Ring one, Executive. Two is Legislative, that's Congress. Ring three, Judiciary"). The Constitution's first three articles, the majority recounts, "split the atom of sovereignty" among Congress, the President, and the courts. And by that mechanism, the Framers provided a "simple" fix "to governmental power and its perils."

There is nothing wrong with that as a beginning (except the adjective "simple"). It is of course true that the Framers lodged three different kinds of power in three different entities. And that they did so for a crucial purpose — because, as James Madison wrote, "there can be no liberty where the legislative and executive powers are united in the same person[] or body" or where "the power of judging [is] not separated from the legislative and executive powers." The Federalist No. 47 (quoting Baron de Montesquieu).

The problem lies in treating the beginning as an ending too — in failing to recognize that the separation of powers is, by design, neither rigid nor complete. Blackstone, whose work influenced the Framers on this subject as on others, observed that "every branch" of government "supports and is supported, regulates and is regulated, by the rest." W. Blackstone, Commentaries on the Laws of England (1765). So as James Madison stated, the creation of distinct branches "did not mean that these departments ought to have no partial agency in, or no controul over the acts of each other." The Federalist No. 47.[2] To the contrary, Madison explained, the drafters of the Constitution — like those of then-existing state constitutions — opted against keeping the branches of government "absolutely separate and distinct." Or as Justice Story reiterated a half-century later: "[W]hen we speak of a separation of the three great departments of government," it is "not meant to affirm, that they must be kept wholly and entirely separate." J. Story, Commentaries on the Constitution of the United States (1833). Instead, the branches have — as they must for the whole arrangement to work — "common link[s] of connexion [and] dependence."

One way the Constitution reflects that vision is by giving Congress broad authority to establish and organize the Executive Branch. Article II presumes the existence of "Officer[s]" in "executive Departments." §2, cl. 1. But it does not, as you might think from reading the majority opinion, give the President authority to decide what kinds of officers — in what departments, with what responsibilities — the Executive Branch requires. See ante ("The entire 'executive Power' belongs to the President alone"). Instead, Article I's Necessary and Proper Clause puts those decisions in the legislature's hands. Congress has the power "[t]o make all Laws which shall be necessary and proper for carrying into Execution" not just its own enumerated powers but also "all other Powers vested by this Constitution in the Government of the United States, or in any Department or Officer thereof."

---

2. The principle of separation of powers, Madison continued, maintained only that "where the *whole* power of one department is exercised by the same hands which possess the *whole* power of another department, the fundamental principles of a free constitution[ ] are subverted." The Federalist No. 47.

§8, cl. 18. Similarly, the Appointments Clause reflects Congress's central role in structuring the Executive Branch. Yes, the President can appoint principal officers, but only as the legislature "shall . . . establish[ ] by Law" (and of course subject to the Senate's advice and consent). Art. II, §2, cl. 2. And Congress has plenary power to decide not only what inferior officers will exist but also who (the President or a head of department) will appoint them. So as Madison told the first Congress, the legislature gets to "create[ ] the office, define[ ] the powers, [and] limit[ ] its duration." The President, as to the construction of his own branch of government, can only try to work his will through the legislative process.[3]

The majority relies for its contrary vision on Article II's Vesting Clause, but the provision can't carry all that weight. Or as Chief Justice Rehnquist wrote of a similar claim in *Morrison v. Olson* (1988), "extrapolat[ing]" an unrestricted removal power from such "general constitutional language"—which says only that "[t]he executive Power shall be vested in a President"—is "more than the text will bear." Dean John Manning has well explained why, even were it not obvious from the Clause's "open-ended language." Separation of Powers as Ordinary Interpretation (2011). . . . For now, note two points about practice before the Constitution's drafting. First, in that era, Parliament often restricted the King's power to remove royal officers—and the President, needless to say, wasn't supposed to be a king. Second, many States at the time allowed limits on gubernatorial removal power even though their constitutions had similar vesting clauses. Historical understandings thus belie the majority's "general rule."

Nor can the Take Care Clause come to the majority's rescue. That Clause cannot properly serve as a "placeholder for broad judicial judgments" about presidential control. Goldsmith & Manning, The Protean Take Care Clause (2016). To begin with, the provision—"he shall take Care that the Laws be faithfully executed"—speaks of duty, not power. Art. II, §3. New scholarship suggests the language came from English and colonial oaths taken by, and placing fiduciary obligations on, all manner and rank of executive officers. . . . And yet more important, the text of the Take Care Clause requires only enough authority to make sure "the laws [are] faithfully executed"—meaning with fidelity to the law itself, not to every presidential policy preference. As this Court has held, a President can ensure " 'faithful execution' of the laws"—thereby satisfying his "take care" obligation—with a removal provision like the one here. *Morrison*. A for-cause standard gives him "ample authority to assure that [an official] is competently performing [his] statutory responsibilities in a manner that comports with the [relevant legislation's] provisions."

---

3. Article II's Opinions Clause also demonstrates the possibility of limits on the President's control over the Executive Branch. Under that Clause, the President "may require the Opinion, in writing, of the principal Officer in each of the executive Departments, upon any Subject relating to the Duties of their respective Offices." §2, cl. 1. For those in the majority's camp, that Clause presents a puzzle: If the President must always have the direct supervisory control they posit, including by threat of removal, why would he ever need a constitutional warrant to demand agency heads' opinions? The Clause becomes at least redundant—though really, inexplicable—under the majority's idea of executive power.

Finally, recall the Constitution's telltale silence: Nowhere does the text say anything about the President's power to remove subordinate officials at will. The majority professes unconcern. After all, it says, "neither is there a 'separation of powers clause' or a 'federalism clause.'" But those concepts are carved into the Constitution's text—the former in its first three articles separating powers, the latter in its enumeration of federal powers and its reservation of all else to the States. And anyway, at-will removal is hardly such a "foundational doctrine[].".You won't find it on a civics class syllabus. That's because removal is a *tool*—one means among many, even if sometimes an important one, for a President to control executive officials. See generally *Free Enterprise Fund* (Breyer, J., dissenting). To find that authority hidden in the Constitution as a "general rule" is to discover what is nowhere there.

B

History no better serves the majority's cause. As Madison wrote, "a regular course of practice" can "liquidate & settle the meaning of" disputed or indeterminate constitutional provisions. Letter to Spencer Roane (Sept. 2, 1819), see *NLRB v. Noel Canning* (2014). The majority lays claim to that kind of record, asserting that its muscular view of "[t]he President's removal power has long been confirmed by history." But that is not so. The early history—including the fabled Decision of 1789—shows mostly debate and division about removal authority. And when a "settle[ment of] meaning" at last occurred, it was not on the majority's terms. Instead, it supports wide latitude for Congress to create spheres of administrative independence.

1

Begin with evidence from the Constitution's ratification. And note that this moment is indeed the beginning: Delegates to the Constitutional Convention never discussed whether or to what extent the President would have power to remove executive officials. As a result, the Framers advocating ratification had no single view of the matter. In Federalist No. 77, Hamilton presumed that under the new Constitution "[t]he consent of [the Senate] would be necessary to displace as well as to appoint" officers of the United States. By contrast, Madison thought the Constitution allowed Congress to decide how any executive official could be removed. He explained in Federalist No. 39: "The tenure of the ministerial offices generally will be a subject of legal regulation, conformably to the reason of the case, and the example of the State Constitutions." Neither view, of course, at all supports the majority's story.[4]

---

4. The majority dismisses Federalist Nos. 77 and 39 as "reflect[ing] initial impressions later abandoned." But even Hamilton's and Madison's later impressions are less helpful to the majority than it suggests. Assuming Hamilton gave up on the Senate's direct participation in removal (the evidence is sketchy but plausible), there is no evidence to show he accepted the majority's view.

The second chapter is the Decision of 1789, when Congress addressed the removal power while considering the bill creating the Department of Foreign Affairs. Speaking through Chief Justice Taft—a judicial presidentialist if ever there was one—this Court in *Myers v. United States* (1926), read that debate as expressing Congress's judgment that the Constitution gave the President illimitable power to remove executive officials. The majority rests its own historical claim on that analysis (though somehow also finding room for its two exceptions). But Taft's historical research has held up even worse than *Myers'* holding (which was mostly reversed). As Dean Manning has concluded after reviewing decades' worth of scholarship on the issue, "the implications of the debate, properly understood, [are] highly ambiguous and prone to overreading."

The best view is that the First Congress was "deeply divided" on the President's removal power, and "never squarely addressed" the central issue here. Prakash, New Light on the Decision of 1789 (2006). The congressional debates revealed three main positions. Some shared Hamilton's Federalist No. 77 view: The Constitution required Senate consent for removal. At the opposite extreme, others claimed that the Constitution gave absolute removal power to the President. And a third faction maintained that the Constitution placed Congress in the driver's seat: The legislature could regulate, if it so chose, the President's authority to remove. In the end, Congress passed a bill saying nothing about removal, leaving the President free to fire the Secretary of Foreign Affairs at will. But the only one of the three views definitively rejected was Hamilton's theory of necessary Senate consent. As even strong proponents of executive power have shown, Congress never "endorse[d] the view that [it] lacked authority to modify" the President's removal authority when it wished to. The summer of 1789 thus ended without resolution of the critical question: Was the removal power "beyond the reach of congressional regulation?"

Contrary to the majority's view, then, the founding era closed without any agreement that Congress lacked the power to curb the President's removal authority. And as it kept that question open, Congress took the first steps—which would launch a tradition—of distinguishing financial regulators from diplomatic and military officers. The latter mainly helped the President carry out his own constitutional duties in foreign relations and war. The former chiefly carried out statutory duties, fulfilling functions Congress had assigned to their offices. In addressing the new Nation's finances, Congress had begun to use its powers under the Necessary and Proper Clause to design effective administrative institutions. And that included taking steps to insulate certain officers from political influence.

And while Madison opposed the first Congress's enactment of removal limits (as the majority highlights), he also maintained that the legislature had constitutional power to protect the Comptroller of the Treasury from at-will firing. In any event, such changing minds and inconstant opinions don't usually prove the existence of constitutional rules.

2

As the decades and centuries passed, those efforts picked up steam. Confronting new economic, technological, and social conditions, Congress—and often the President—saw new needs for pockets of independence within the federal bureaucracy. And that was especially so, again, when it came to financial regulation. I mention just a few highlights here—times when Congress decided that effective governance depended on shielding technical or expertise-based functions relating to the financial system from political pressure (or the moneyed interests that might lie behind it). Enacted under the Necessary and Proper Clause, those measures—creating some of the Nation's most enduring institutions—themselves helped settle the extent of Congress's power. "[A] regular course of practice," to use Madison's phrase, has "liquidate[d]" constitutional meaning about the permissibility of independent agencies. . . .

And then, nearly a century and a half ago, the floodgates opened. . . . So year by year by year, the broad sweep of history has spoken to the constitutional question before us: Independent agencies are everywhere.

C

What is more, the Court's precedents before today have accepted the role of independent agencies in our governmental system. To be sure, the line of our decisions has not run altogether straight. But we have repeatedly upheld provisions that prevent the President from firing regulatory officials except for such matters as neglect or malfeasance. In those decisions, we sounded a caution, insisting that Congress could not impede through removal restrictions the President's performance of his own constitutional duties. (So, to take the clearest example, Congress could not curb the President's power to remove his close military or diplomatic advisers.) But within that broad limit, this Court held, Congress could protect from at-will removal the officials it deemed to need some independence from political pressures. Nowhere do those precedents suggest what the majority announces today: that the President has an "unrestricted removal power" subject to two bounded exceptions.

The majority grounds its new approach in *Myers*, ignoring the way this Court has cabined that decision. *Myers*, the majority tells us, found an unrestrained removal power "essential to the [President's] execution of the laws." What the majority does not say is that within a decade the Court abandoned that view (much as later scholars rejected Taft's one-sided history). In *Humphrey's Executor v. United States*, the Court unceremoniously—and unanimously—confined *Myers* to its facts. . . . And *Humphrey's* found constitutional a statute identical to the one here, providing that the President could remove FTC Commissioners for "inefficiency, neglect of duty, or malfeasance in office.". . .

Another three decades on, *Morrison* both extended *Humphrey's* domain and clarified the standard for addressing removal issues. The *Morrison* Court, over a one-Justice dissent, upheld for-cause protections afforded to an independent counsel with power to investigate and prosecute crimes committed by high-ranking officials. . . . The key question in all the cases, *Morrison* saw, was whether such a restriction would "impede the President's ability to perform his constitutional duty." Only if it did so would it fall outside Congress's power. And the protection for the independent counsel, the Court found, did not. Even though the counsel's functions were "purely executive," the President's "need to control the exercise of [her] discretion" was not "so central to the functioning of the Executive Branch as to require" unrestricted removal authority. True enough, the Court acknowledged, that the for-cause standard prevented the President from firing the counsel for discretionary decisions or judgment calls. But it preserved "ample authority" in the President "to assure that the counsel is competently performing" her "responsibilities in a manner that comports with" all legal requirements. That meant the President could meet his own constitutional obligation "to ensure 'the faithful execution' of the laws."[9]

The majority's description of *Morrison*, is not true to the decision. (Mostly, it seems, the majority just wishes the case would go away.) First, *Morrison* is no "exception" to a broader rule from *Myers*. *Morrison* echoed all of *Humphrey's* criticism of the by-then infamous *Myers* "dicta." It again rejected the notion of an "all-inclusive" removal power. It yet further confined *Myers'* reach, making clear that Congress could restrict the President's removal of officials carrying out even the most traditional executive functions. And the decision, with care, set out the governing rule — again, that removal restrictions are permissible so long as they do not impede the President's performance of his own constitutionally assigned duties. Second, as all that suggests, *Morrison* is not limited to inferior officers. In the eight pages addressing the removal issue, the Court constantly spoke of "officers" and "officials" in general. By contrast, the Court there used the word "inferior" in just one sentence (which of course the majority quotes), when applying its general standard to the case's facts. Indeed, Justice Scalia's dissent emphasized that the counsel's inferior-office status played no role in the Court's decision.

Even *Free Enterprise Fund*, in which the Court recently held a removal provision invalid, operated within the framework of this precedent — and in so doing, left in place a removal provision just like the one here. . . .

So caselaw joins text and history in establishing the general permissibility of for-cause provisions giving some independence to agencies. Contrary to the

---

9. Pretending this analysis is mine rather than *Morrison*'s, the majority registers its disagreement. In its view, a test asking whether a for-cause provision impedes the President's ability to carry out his constitutional functions has "no real limiting principle." If the provision leaves the President with constitutionally sufficient control over some subordinates (like the independent counsel), the majority asks, why not over even his close military or diplomatic advisers? But the Constitution itself supplies the answer. If the only presidential duty at issue is the one to ensure faithful execution of the laws, a for-cause provision does not stand in the way: As *Morrison* recognized, it preserves authority in the President to ensure (just as the Take Care Clause requires) that an official is abiding by law. But now suppose an additional constitutional duty is implicated — relating, say, to the conduct of foreign affairs or war. To carry out those duties, the President needs advisers who will (beyond complying with law) help him devise and implement policy. And that means he needs the capacity to fire such advisers for disagreeing with his policy calls.

majority's view, those laws do not represent a suspicious departure from illimitable presidential control over administration. For almost a century, this Court has made clear that Congress has broad discretion to enact for-cause protections in pursuit of good governance.

D

The deferential approach this Court has taken gives Congress the flexibility it needs to craft administrative agencies. Diverse problems of government demand diverse solutions. . . . Rather than impose rigid rules like the majority's, they should let Congress and the President figure out what blend of independence and political control will best enable an agency to perform its intended functions.

Judicial intrusion into this field usually reveals only how little courts know about governance. Even everything I just said is an over-simplification. It suggests that agencies can easily be arranged on a spectrum, from the most to the least presidentially controlled. But that is not so. A given agency's independence (or lack of it) depends on a wealth of features, relating not just to removal standards, but also to appointments practices, procedural rules, internal organization, oversight regimes, historical traditions, cultural norms, and (inevitably) personal relationships. . . . Of course no court, as *Free Enterprise Fund* noted, can accurately assess the "bureaucratic minutiae" affecting a President's influence over an agency. But that is yet more reason for courts to defer to the branches charged with fashioning administrative structures, and to hesitate before ruling out agency design specs like for-cause removal standards.

Our Constitution, as shown earlier, entrusts such decisions to more accountable and knowledgeable actors. The document — with great good sense — sets out almost no rules about the administrative sphere. As Chief Justice Marshall wrote when he upheld the first independent financial agency: "To have prescribed the means by which government should, in all future time, execute its powers, would have been to change, entirely, the character of the instrument." *McCulloch*. That would have been, he continued, "an unwise attempt to provide, by immutable rules, for exigencies which, if foreseen at all, must have been seen dimly." And if the Constitution, for those reasons, does not lay out immutable rules, then neither should judges. This Court has usually respected that injunction. It has declined to second-guess the work of the political branches in creating independent agencies like the CFPB. In reversing course today — in spurning a "pragmatic, flexible approach to American governance" in favor of a dogmatic, inflexible one — the majority makes a serious error.

II

No one had a doubt that the [CFPB] should be independent. As explained already, Congress has historically given — with this Court's permission — a measure of independence to financial regulators like the Federal Reserve Board and the FTC. And agencies of that kind had administered most of the legislation whose enforcement the new statute transferred to the CFPB. The law thus included an ordinary for-cause provision—once again, that the President could fire the CFPB's Director only for "inefficiency, neglect of duty, or malfeasance in office." That standard would allow the President to discharge the Director for a failure to "faithfully execute[]" the law, as well as for basic incompetence. U.S. Const., Art. II, §3. But it would not permit removal for policy differences.

The question here, which by now you're well equipped to answer, is whether including that for-cause standard in the statute creating the CFPB violates the Constitution.

A

Applying our longstanding precedent, the answer is clear: It does not. This Court, as the majority acknowledges, has sustained the constitutionality of the FTC and similar independent agencies. The for-cause protections for the heads of those agencies, the Court has found, do not impede the President's ability to perform his own constitutional duties, and so do not breach the separation of powers. There is nothing different here. The CFPB wields the same kind of power as the FTC and similar agencies. And all of their heads receive the same kind of removal protection. No less than those other entities—by now part of the fabric of government—the CFPB is thus a permissible exercise of Congress's power under the Necessary and Proper Clause to structure administration. . . .

Second, the removal protection given the CFPB's Director is standard fare. The removal power rests with the President alone; Congress has no role to play, as it did in the laws struck down in *Myers* and *Bowsher*. The statute provides only one layer of protection, unlike the law in *Free Enterprise Fund*. And the clincher, which you have heard before: The for-cause standard used for the CFPB is identical to the one the Court upheld in *Humphrey's*. Both enable the President to fire an agency head for "inefficiency, neglect of duty, or malfeasance in office." A removal provision of that kind applied to a financial agency head, this Court has held, does not "unduly trammel[] on executive authority," even though it prevents the President from dismissing the official for a discretionary policy judgment. *Morrison*. Once again: The removal power has not been "completely stripped from the President," providing him with no means to "ensure the 'faithful execution' of the laws." Rather, this Court has explained, the for-cause standard gives the President "ample authority to assure that [the official] is competently performing his or her statutory responsibilities in a manner that comports with" all legal obligations. In other words—and contra today's majority—the President's removal power, though not absolute, gives him the "meaningful[] control[]" of the Director that the Constitution requires.

The analysis is as simple as simple can be. The CFPB Director exercises the same powers, and receives the same removal protections, as the heads of other, constitutionally permissible independent agencies. How could it be that this opinion is a dissent?

B

The majority focuses on one (it says sufficient) reason: The CFPB Director is singular, not plural. And a solo CFPB Director does not fit within either of the majority's supposed exceptions. He is not an inferior officer, so (the majority says) *Morrison* does not apply; and he is not a multimember board, so (the majority says) neither does *Humphrey's*. Further, the majority argues, "[a]n agency with a [unitary] structure like that of the CFPB" is "novel" — or, if not quite that, "almost wholly unprecedented." Finally, the CFPB's organizational form violates the "constitutional structure" because it vests power in a "single individual" who is "insulated from Presidential control."

I'm tempted at this point just to say: No. All I've explained about constitutional text, history, and precedent invalidates the majority's thesis. But I'll set out here some more targeted points, taking step by step the majority's reasoning.

First, as I'm afraid you've heard before, the majority's "exceptions" (like its general rule) are made up. To begin with, our precedents reject the very idea of such exceptions. "The analysis contained in our removal cases," *Morrison* stated, shuns any attempt "to define rigid categories" of officials who may (or may not) have job protection. Still more, the contours of the majority's exceptions don't connect to our decisions' reasoning. The analysis in *Morrison*, as I've shown, extended far beyond inferior officers. And of course that analysis had to apply to *individual* officers: The independent counsel was very much a person, not a committee. So the idea that *Morrison* is in a separate box from this case doesn't hold up.[12] Similarly, *Humphrey's* and later precedents give no support to the majority's view that the number of people at the apex of an agency matters to the constitutional issue. Those opinions mention the "groupness" of the agency head only in their background sections. The majority picks out that until-now-irrelevant fact to distinguish the CFPB, and constructs around it an until-now-unheard-of exception. So if the majority really wants to see something "novel," it need only look to its opinion.

By contrast, the CFPB's single-director structure has a fair bit of precedent behind it. The Comptroller of the Currency. The Office of the Special Counsel (OSC). The Social Security Administration (SSA). The Federal Housing Finance Agency (FHFA). Maybe four prior agencies is in the eye of the beholder, but it's hardly nothing. . . . Almost *all* independent agencies are controversial, no matter how many directors they have. Or at least controversial among Presidents and their lawyers. That's because whatever might be said in their favor, those agencies divest the President of some removal power. If signing statements and veto threats made independent agencies unconstitutional, quite a few wouldn't pass

---

12. The majority, seeking some other way to distinguish *Morrison*, asserts that the independent counsel's "duties" were more "limited" than the CFPB Director's. That's true in a sense: All (all?) the special counsel had to do was decide whether the President and his top advisers had broken the law. But I doubt (and I suspect Presidents would too) whether the need to control those duties was any less "central to the functioning of the Executive Branch" than the need to control the CFPB's. And in any event, as I've shown, *Morrison* did much more than approve a specific removal provision; it created a standard to govern all removal cases that is at complete odds with the majority's reasoning.

muster. Maybe that's what the majority really wants (I wouldn't know)—but it can't pretend the disputes surrounding these agencies had anything to do with whether their heads are singular or plural.

Still more important, novelty is not the test of constitutionality when it comes to structuring agencies. See *Mistretta v. United States* (1989) ("[M]ere anomaly or innovation" does not violate the separation of powers). Congress regulates in that sphere under the Necessary and Proper Clause, not (as the majority seems to think) a Rinse and Repeat Clause. The Framers understood that new times would often require new measures, and exigencies often demand innovation. See *McCulloch.* In line with that belief, the history of the administrative sphere—its rules, its practices, its institutions—is replete with experiment and change. . Indeed, each of the agencies the majority says now fits within its "exceptions" was once new; there is, as the saying goes, "a first time for everything." *National Federation of Independent Business v. Sebelius* (2012). So even if the CFPB differs from its forebears in having a single director, that departure is not itself "telling" of a "constitutional problem." In deciding what *this* moment demanded, Congress had no obligation to make a carbon copy of a design from a bygone era. . . .

But if the demand is for generalization, then the majority's distinction cuts the opposite way: More powerful control mechanisms are needed (if anything) for commissions. Holding everything else equal, those are the agencies more likely to "slip from the Executive's control." Just consider your everyday experience: It's easier to get one person to do what you want than a gaggle. So too, you know exactly whom to blame when an individual—but not when a group—does a job badly. The same is true in bureaucracies. A multimember structure reduces accountability to the President because it's harder for him to oversee, to influence—or to remove, if necessary—a group of five or more commissioners than a single director. Indeed, that is *why* Congress so often resorts to hydra-headed agencies. . . .

Because it has no answer on that score, the majority slides to a different question: Assuming presidential control of any independent agency is vanishingly slim, is a single-head or a multi-head agency more capable of exercising power, and so of endangering liberty? The majority says a single head is the greater threat because he may wield power "*unilaterally*" and "[w]ith no colleagues to persuade." So the CFPB falls victim to what the majority sees as a constitutional anti-power-concentration principle (with an exception for the President).

If you've never heard of a statute being struck down on that ground, you're not alone. It is bad enough to "extrapolat[e]" from the "general constitutional language" of Article II's Vesting Clause an unrestricted removal power constraining Congress's ability to legislate under the Necessary and Proper Clause. It is still worse to extrapolate from the Constitution's general structure (division of powers) and implicit values (liberty) a limit on Congress's express power to create administrative bodies. And more: to extrapolate from such sources a distinction as prosaic as that between the SEC and the CFPB—*i.e.*, between a multi-headed and single-headed agency. That is, to adapt a phrase (or two) from our precedent, "more than" the emanations of "the text will bear." By using abstract separation-of-powers arguments for such purposes, the Court "appropriate[s]" the "power delegated to Congress by the Necessary and Proper Clause" to compose the government. In deciding for itself what is "proper," the Court goes beyond its own proper bounds.

And in doing so, the majority again reveals its lack of interest in how agencies work. First, the premise of the majority's argument—that the CFPB head is a mini-dictator, not subject to meaningful presidential control—is wrong. As this Court has seen in the past, independent agencies are not fully independent. A for-cause removal provision, as noted earlier, leaves "ample" control over agency heads in the hands of the President. He can discharge them for failing to perform their duties competently or in accordance with law, and so ensure that the laws are "faithfully executed." U.S. Const., Art. II, §3. . . . Second, the majority has nothing but intuition to back up its essentially functionalist claim that the CFPB would be less capable of exercising power if it had more than one Director (even supposing that were a suitable issue for a court to address). Maybe the CFPB would be. Or maybe not. . . . At the least: If the Court is going to invalidate statutes based on empirical assertions like this one, it should offer some empirical support. It should not pretend that its assessment that the CFPB wields more power more dangerously than the SEC comes from someplace in the Constitution. But today the majority fails to accord even that minimal respect to Congress.

III

. . . And now consider how the dispute ends—with five unelected judges rejecting the result of that democratic process. The outcome today will not shut down the CFPB: A different majority of this Court, including all those who join this opinion, believes that *if* the agency's removal provision is unconstitutional, it should be severed. But the majority on constitutionality jettisons a measure Congress and the President viewed as integral to the way the agency should operate. The majority does so even though the Constitution grants to Congress, acting with the President's approval, the authority to create and shape administrative bodies. And even though those branches, as compared to courts, have far greater understanding of political control mechanisms and agency design.

Nothing in the Constitution requires that outcome; to the contrary. "While the Constitution diffuses power the better to secure liberty, it also contemplates that practice will integrate the dispersed powers into a workable government." *Youngstown Sheet & Tube Co. v. Sawyer* (1952) (Jackson, J., concurring). The Framers took pains to craft a document that would allow the structures of governance to change, as times and needs change. The Constitution says only a few words about administration. As Chief Justice Marshall wrote: Rather than prescribing "immutable rules," it enables Congress to choose "the means by which government should, in all future time, execute its powers." *McCulloch*. It authorizes Congress to meet new exigencies with new devices. So Article II does not generally prohibit independent agencies. Nor do any supposed structural principles. Nor do any odors wafting from the document. Save for when those agencies impede the President's performance of his own constitutional duties, the matter is left up to Congress.

Our history has stayed true to the Framers' vision. Congress has accepted their invitation to experiment with administrative forms — nowhere more so than in the field of financial regulation. And this Court has mostly allowed it to do so. The result is a broad array of independent agencies, no two exactly alike but all with a measure of insulation from the President's removal power. The Federal Reserve Board; the FTC; the SEC; maybe some you've never heard of. As to each, Congress thought that formal job protection for policymaking would produce regulatory outcomes in greater accord with the long-term public interest. Congress may have been right; or it may have been wrong; or maybe it was some of both. No matter — the branches accountable to the people have decided how the people should be governed.

The CFPB should have joined the ranks. Maybe it will still do so, even under today's opinion: The majority tells Congress that it may "pursu[e] alternative responses" to the identified constitutional defect — "for example, converting the CFPB into a multimember agency." *Ante*, at 36. But there was no need to send Congress back to the drawing board. The Constitution does not distinguish between single-director and multimember independent agencies. It instructs Congress, not this Court, to decide on agency design. Because this Court ignores that sensible — indeed, that obvious — division of tasks, I respectfully dissent.

Trump v. Vance
591 U.S. ___ (2020)

CHIEF JUSTICE ROBERTS delivered the opinion of the Court.

In our judicial system, "the public has a right to every man's evidence."[1] Since the earliest days of the Republic, "every man" has included the President of the United States. Beginning with Jefferson and carrying on through Clinton, Presidents have uniformly testified or produced documents in criminal proceedings when called upon by federal courts. This case involves — so far as we and the parties can tell — the first *state* criminal subpoena directed to a President. The President contends that the subpoena is unenforceable. We granted certiorari to decide whether Article II and the Supremacy Clause categorically preclude, or require a heightened standard for, the issuance of a state criminal subpoena to a sitting President.

I

In the summer of 2018, the New York County District Attorney's Office opened an investigation into what it opaquely describes as "business transactions

---

1. This maxim traces at least as far back as Lord Chancellor Hardwicke, in a 1742 parliamentary debate.

involving multiple individuals whose conduct may have violated state law." A year later, the office — acting on behalf of a grand jury — served a subpoena *duces tecum* (essentially a request to produce evidence) on Mazars USA, LLP, the personal accounting firm of President Donald J. Trump. The subpoena directed Mazars to produce financial records relating to the President and business organizations affiliated with him, including "[t]ax returns and related schedules," from "2011 to the present."[2] The President, acting in his personal capacity, sued the district attorney and Mazars in Federal District Court to enjoin enforcement of the subpoena. He argued that, under Article II and the Supremacy Clause, a sitting President enjoys absolute immunity from state criminal process. . . . Mazars, concluding that the dispute was between the President and the district attorney, took no position on the legal issues raised by the President. . . .

II

In the summer of 1807, all eyes were on Richmond, Virginia. Aaron Burr, the former Vice President, was on trial for treason. Fallen from political grace after his fatal duel with Alexander Hamilton, and with a murder charge pending in New Jersey, Burr followed the path of many down-and-out Americans of his day — he headed West in search of new opportunity. But Burr was a man with outsized ambitions. Together with General James Wilkinson, the Governor of the Louisiana Territory, he hatched a plan to establish a new territory in Mexico, then controlled by Spain.[4] Both men anticipated that war between the United States and Spain was imminent, and when it broke out they intended to invade Spanish territory at the head of a private army.

But while Burr was rallying allies to his cause, tensions with Spain eased and rumors began to swirl that Burr was conspiring to detach States by the Allegheny Mountains from the Union. Wary of being exposed as the principal co-conspirator, Wilkinson took steps to ensure that any blame would fall on Burr. He sent a series of letters to President Jefferson accusing Burr of plotting to attack New Orleans and revolutionize the Louisiana Territory.

Jefferson, who despised his former running mate Burr for trying to steal the 1800 presidential election from him, was predisposed to credit Wilkinson's version of events. The President sent a special message to Congress identifying Burr as the "prime mover" in a plot "against the peace and safety of the Union." According to Jefferson, Burr contemplated either the "severance of the Union" or an attack on Spanish territory. Jefferson acknowledged that his sources contained

---

2. The grand jury subpoena essentially copied a subpoena issued to Mazars in April 2019 by the Committee on Oversight and Reform of the U.S. House of Representatives, which is at issue in *Trump v. Mazars USA, LLP*. The principal difference is that the instant subpoena expressly requests tax returns.

4. Wilkinson was secretly being paid by Spain for information and influence. In the wake of Burr's trial, he was investigated by Congress and later court-martialed. But he was acquitted for want of evidence, and his duplicity was not confirmed until decades after his death, when Spanish archival material came to light.

a "mixture of rumors, conjectures, and suspicions" but, citing Wilkinson's letters, he assured Congress that Burr's guilt was "beyond question."

The trial that followed was "the greatest spectacle in the short history of the republic," complete with a Founder-studded cast. People flocked to Richmond to watch, massing in tents and covered wagons along the banks of the James River, nearly doubling the town's population of 5,000. Burr's defense team included Edmund Randolph and Luther Martin, both former delegates at the Constitutional Convention and renowned advocates. Chief Justice John Marshall, who had recently squared off with the Jefferson administration in *Marbury v. Madison* (1803), presided as Circuit Justice for Virginia. Meanwhile Jefferson, intent on conviction, orchestrated the prosecution from afar, dedicating Cabinet meetings to the case, peppering the prosecutors with directions, and spending nearly $100,000 from the Treasury on the five-month proceedings.

In the lead-up to trial, Burr, taking aim at his accusers, moved for a subpoena *duces tecum* directed at Jefferson. The draft subpoena required the President to produce an October 21, 1806 letter from Wilkinson and accompanying documents, which Jefferson had referenced in his message to Congress. The prosecution opposed the request, arguing that a President could not be subjected to such a subpoena and that the letter might contain state secrets. Following four days of argument, Marshall announced his ruling to a packed chamber.

The President, Marshall declared, does not "stand exempt from the general provisions of the constitution" or, in particular, the Sixth Amendment's guarantee that those accused have compulsory process for obtaining witnesses for their defense. *United States v. Burr* (CC Va. 1807). At common law the "single reservation" to the duty to testify in response to a subpoena was "the case of the king," whose "dignity" was seen as "incompatible" with appearing "under the process of the court." But, as Marshall explained, a king is born to power and can "do no wrong." The President, by contrast, is "of the people" and subject to the law. According to Marshall, the sole argument for exempting the President from testimonial obligations was that his "duties as chief magistrate demand his whole time for national objects." But, in Marshall's assessment, those demands were "not unremitting." And should the President's duties preclude his attendance at a particular time and place, a court could work that out upon return of the subpoena.

Marshall also rejected the prosecution's argument that the President was immune from a subpoena *duces tecum* because executive papers might contain state secrets. "A subpoena duces tecum," he said, "may issue to any person to whom an ordinary subpoena may issue." As he explained, no "fair construction" of the Constitution supported the conclusion that the right "to compel the attendance of witnesses[ ] does not extend" to requiring those witnesses to "bring[] with them such papers as may be material in the defence." And, as a matter of basic fairness, permitting such information to be withheld would "tarnish the reputation of the court." As for "the propriety of introducing any papers," that would "depend on the character of the paper, not on the character of the person who holds it." Marshall acknowledged that the papers sought by Burr could contain information "the disclosure of which would endanger the public safety," but stated that, again, such concerns would have "due consideration" upon the return of the subpoena.

While the arguments unfolded, Jefferson, who had received word of the motion, wrote to the prosecutor indicating that he would—subject to the prerogative to decide which executive communications should be withheld—"furnish on all occasions, whatever the purposes of justice may require." Letter from T. Jefferson to G. Hay (June 12, 1807). His "personal attendance," however, was out of the question, for it "would leave the nation without" the "sole branch which the constitution requires to be always in function." Letter from T. Jefferson to G. Hay (June 17, 1807).

Before Burr received the subpoenaed documents, Marshall rejected the prosecution's core legal theory for treason and Burr was accordingly acquitted. Jefferson, however, was not done. Committed to salvaging a conviction, he directed the prosecutors to proceed with a misdemeanor (yes, misdemeanor) charge for inciting war against Spain. Burr then renewed his request for Wilkinson's October 21 letter, which he later received a copy of, and subpoenaed a second letter, dated November 12, 1806, which the prosecutor claimed was privileged. Acknowledging that the President may withhold information to protect public safety, Marshall instructed that Jefferson should "state the particular reasons" for withholding the letter. The court, paying "all proper respect" to those reasons, would then decide whether to compel disclosure. But that decision was averted when the misdemeanor trial was cut short after it became clear that the prosecution lacked the evidence to convict.

In the two centuries since the Burr trial, successive Presidents have accepted Marshall's ruling that the Chief Executive is subject to subpoena. In 1818, President Monroe received a subpoena to testify in a court-martial against one of his appointees. See Rotunda, Presidents and Ex-Presidents as Witnesses: A Brief Historical Footnote. His Attorney General, William Wirt—who had served as a prosecutor during Burr's trial—advised Monroe that, per Marshall's ruling, a subpoena to testify may "be properly awarded to the President." Id., at 5–6. Monroe offered to sit for a deposition and ultimately submitted answers to written interrogatories.

Following Monroe's lead, his successors have uniformly agreed to testify when called in criminal proceedings, provided they could do so at a time and place of their choosing. In 1875, President Grant submitted to a three-hour deposition in the criminal prosecution of a political appointee embroiled in a network of tax-evading whiskey distillers. See 1 R. Rotunda & J. Nowak, Constitutional Law §7.1(b)(ii), p. 996 (5th ed. 2012) (Rotunda & Nowak). A century later, President Ford's attempted assassin subpoenaed him to testify in her defense. Ford obliged—from a safe distance—in the first videotaped deposition of a President. President Carter testified via the same means in the trial of two local officials who, while Carter was Governor of Georgia, had offered to contribute to his campaign in exchange for advance warning of any state gambling raids. Two years later, Carter gave videotaped testimony to a federal grand jury investigating whether a fugitive financier had entreated the White House to quash his extradition proceedings. President Clinton testified three times, twice via deposition pursuant to subpoenas in federal criminal trials of associates implicated during the Whitewater investigation, and once by video for a grand jury investigating possible perjury.

The bookend to Marshall's ruling came in 1974 when the question he never had to decide—whether to compel the disclosure of official communications over the objection of the President—came to a head. That spring, the Special Prosecutor appointed to investigate the break-in of the Democratic National Committee Headquarters at the Watergate complex filed an indictment charging seven defendants associated with President Nixon and naming Nixon as an unindicted co-conspirator. As the case moved toward trial, the Special Prosecutor secured a subpoena *duces tecum* directing Nixon to produce, among other things, tape recordings of Oval Office meetings. Nixon moved to quash the subpoena, claiming that the Constitution provides an absolute privilege of confidentiality to all presidential communications. This Court rejected that argument in *United States v. Nixon* (1974), a decision we later described as "unequivocally and emphatically endors[ing] Marshall's" holding that Presidents are subject to subpoena. *Clinton v. Jones* (1997).

The *Nixon* Court readily acknowledged the importance of preserving the confidentiality of communications "between high Government officials and those who advise and assist them." "Human experience," the Court explained, "teaches that those who expect public dissemination of their remarks may well temper candor with a concern for appearances and for their own interests to the detriment of the decisionmaking process." Confidentiality thus promoted the "public interest in candid, objective, and even blunt or harsh opinions in Presidential decisionmaking."

But, like Marshall two centuries prior, the Court recognized the countervailing interests at stake. Invoking the common law maxim that "the public has a right to every man's evidence," the Court observed that the public interest in fair and accurate judicial proceedings is at its height in the criminal setting, where our common commitment to justice demands that "guilt shall not escape" nor "innocence suffer." Because these dual aims would be "defeated if judgments" were "founded on a partial or speculative presentation of the facts," the *Nixon* Court recognized that it was "imperative" that "compulsory process be available for the production of evidence needed either by the prosecution or the defense."

The Court thus concluded that the President's "generalized assertion of privilege must yield to the demonstrated, specific need for evidence in a pending criminal trial." Two weeks later, President Nixon dutifully released the tapes.

III

The history surveyed above all involved *federal* criminal proceedings. Here we are confronted for the first time with a subpoena issued to the President by a local grand jury operating under the supervision of a *state* court.[4]

---

4. While the subpoena was directed to the President's accounting firm, the parties agree that the papers at issue belong to the President and that Mazars is merely the custodian. Thus, for purposes of immunity, it is functionally a subpoena issued to the President.

In the President's view, that distinction makes all the difference. He argues that the Supremacy Clause gives a sitting President absolute immunity from state criminal subpoenas because compliance with those subpoenas would categorically impair a President's performance of his Article II functions. The Solicitor General, arguing on behalf of the United States, agrees with much of the President's reasoning but does not commit to his bottom line. Instead, the Solicitor General urges us to resolve this case by holding that a state grand jury subpoena for a sitting President's personal records must, at the very least, "satisfy a heightened standard of need," which the Solicitor General contends was not met here.

A

We begin with the question of absolute immunity. No one doubts that Article II guarantees the independence of the Executive Branch. As the head of that branch, the President "occupies a unique position in the constitutional scheme." *Nixon v. Fitzgerald* (1982). His duties, which range from faithfully executing the laws to commanding the Armed Forces, are of unrivaled gravity and breadth. Quite appropriately, those duties come with protections that safeguard the President's ability to perform his vital functions. See, *e.g.*, *ibid.* (concluding that the President enjoys "absolute immunity from damages liability predicated on his official acts"); *Nixon* (recognizing that presidential communications are presumptively privileged).

In addition, the Constitution guarantees "the entire independence of the General Government from any control by the respective States." *Farmers and Mechanics Sav. Bank of Minneapolis v. Minnesota* (1914). As we have often repeated, "States have no power . . . to retard, impede, burden, or in any manner control the operations of the constitutional laws enacted by Congress." *McCulloch v. Maryland* (1819). It follows that States also lack the power to impede the President's execution of those laws.

Marshall's ruling in *Burr*, entrenched by 200 years of practice and our decision in *Nixon*, confirms that *federal* criminal subpoenas do not "rise to the level of constitutionally forbidden impairment of the Executive's ability to perform its constitutionally mandated functions." *Clinton*. But the President, joined in part by the Solicitor General, argues that *state* criminal subpoenas pose a unique threat of impairment and thus demand greater protection. To be clear, the President does not contend here that *this* subpoena, in particular, is impermissibly burdensome. Instead he makes a *categorical* argument about the burdens generally associated with state criminal subpoenas, focusing on three: diversion, stigma, and harassment. We address each in turn.

1

The President's primary contention, which the Solicitor General supports, is that complying with state criminal subpoenas would necessarily divert the Chief Executive from his duties. He grounds that concern in *Nixon v. Fitzgerald*, which recognized a President's "absolute immunity from damages liability predicated on his official acts." In explaining the basis for that immunity, this Court observed that the prospect of such liability could "distract a President from his public duties, to the detriment of not only the President and his office but also the Nation that the Presidency was designed to serve." The President contends that the diversion occasioned by a state criminal subpoena imposes an equally intolerable burden on a President's ability to perform his Article II functions.

But *Fitzgerald* did not hold that distraction was sufficient to confer absolute immunity. We instead drew a careful analogy to the common law absolute immunity of judges and prosecutors, concluding that a President, like those officials, must "deal fearlessly and impartially with the duties of his office" — not be made "unduly cautious in the discharge of [those] duties" by the prospect of civil liability for official acts. Indeed, we expressly rejected immunity based on distraction alone 15 years later in *Clinton v. Jones*. There, President Clinton argued that the risk of being "distracted by the need to participate in litigation" entitled a sitting President to absolute immunity from civil liability, not just for official acts, as in *Fitzgerald*, but for private conduct as well. We disagreed with that rationale, explaining that the "dominant concern" in *Fitzgerald* was not mere distraction but the distortion of the Executive's "decisionmaking process" with respect to official acts that would stem from "worry as to the possibility of damages." The Court recognized that Presidents constantly face myriad demands on their attention, "some private, some political, and some as a result of official duty." But, the Court concluded, "[w]hile such distractions may be vexing to those subjected to them, they do not ordinarily implicate constitutional . . . concerns."

The same is true of criminal subpoenas. Just as a "properly managed" civil suit is generally "unlikely to occupy any substantial amount of " a President's time or attention, two centuries of experience confirm that a properly tailored criminal subpoena will not normally hamper the performance of the President's constitutional duties. If anything, we expect that in the mine run of cases, where a President is subpoenaed during a proceeding targeting someone else, as Jefferson was, the burden on a President will ordinarily be lighter than the burden of defending against a civil suit.

The President, however, believes the district attorney is investigating him and his businesses. In such a situation, he contends, the "toll that criminal process . . . exacts from the President is even heavier" than the distraction at issue in *Fitzgerald* and *Clinton*, because "criminal litigation" poses unique burdens on the President's time and will generate a "considerable if not overwhelming degree of mental preoccupation."

But the President is not seeking immunity from the diversion occasioned by the prospect of future criminal *liability*. Instead he concedes — consistent with the position of the Department of Justice — that state grand juries are free to investigate a sitting President with an eye toward charging him after the completion of his term. The President's objection therefore must be limited to the *additional* distraction caused by the subpoena itself. But that argument runs up against the 200 years of precedent establishing that Presidents, and their official communications, are subject to judicial process, see *Burr*, even when the President is under investigation, see *Nixon*.

2

The President next claims that the stigma of being subpoenaed will undermine his leadership at home and abroad. Notably, the Solicitor General does not endorse this argument, perhaps because we have twice denied absolute immunity claims by Presidents in cases involving allegations of serious misconduct. See *Clinton*; *Nixon*. But even if a tarnished reputation were a cognizable impairment, there is nothing inherently stigmatizing about a President performing "the citizen's normal duty of . . . furnishing information relevant" to a criminal investigation. *Branzburg v. Hayes* (1972). Nor can we accept that the risk of association with persons or activities under criminal investigation can absolve a President of such an important public duty. Prior Presidents have weathered these associations in federal cases and there is no reason to think any attendant notoriety is necessarily greater in state court proceedings.

To be sure, the consequences for a President's public standing will likely increase if he is the one under investigation. But, again, the President concedes that such investigations are permitted under Article II and the Supremacy Clause, and receipt of a subpoena would not seem to categorically magnify the harm to the President's reputation.

Additionally, while the current suit has cast the Mazars subpoena into the spotlight, longstanding rules of grand jury secrecy aim to prevent the very stigma the President anticipates. Of course, disclosure restrictions are not perfect. See *Nixon*, (observing that news media reporting made the protective order shielding the fact that the President had been named as an unindicted co-conspirator "no longer meaningful"). But those who make unauthorized disclosures regarding a grand jury subpoena do so at their peril. See, *e.g.*, N. Y. Penal Law Ann. §215.70 (2010) (designating unlawful grand jury disclosure as a felony).

3

Finally, the President and the Solicitor General warn that subjecting Presidents to state criminal subpoenas will make them "easily identifiable target[s]" for harassment. *Fitzgerald*. But we rejected a nearly identical argument in *Clinton*, where then-President Clinton argued that permitting civil liability for unofficial acts would "generate a large volume of politically motivated harassing and frivolous litigation." *Clinton*. The President and the Solicitor General nevertheless argue that state criminal subpoenas pose a heightened risk and could undermine the President's ability to "deal fearlessly and impartially" with the States. *Fitzgerald*. They caution that, while federal prosecutors are accountable to and removable by the President, the 2,300 district attorneys in this country are responsive to local constituencies, local interests, and local prejudices, and might "use criminal process to register their dissatisfaction with" the President.

What is more, we are told, the state courts supervising local grand juries may not exhibit the same respect that federal courts show to the President as a coordinate branch of Government.

We recognize, as does the district attorney, that harassing subpoenas could, under certain circumstances, threaten the independence or effectiveness of the Executive. Even so, in *Clinton* we found that the risk of harassment was not "serious" because federal courts have the tools to deter and, where necessary, dismiss vexatious civil suits. And, while we cannot ignore the possibility that state prosecutors may have political motivations, see *post* (Alito, J., dissenting), here again the law already seeks to protect against the predicted abuse.

First, grand juries are prohibited from engaging in "arbitrary fishing expeditions" and initiating investigations "out of malice or an intent to harass." These protections, as the district attorney himself puts it, "apply with special force to a President, in light of the office's unique position as the head of the Executive Branch." And, in the event of such harassment, a President would be entitled to the protection of federal courts. The policy against federal interference in state criminal proceedings, while strong, allows "intervention in those cases where the District Court properly finds that the state proceeding is motivated by a desire to harass or is conducted in bad faith." *Huffman v. Pursue, Ltd.* (1975).

Second, contrary to Justice Alito's characterization, our holding does not allow States to "run roughshod over the functioning of [the Executive B]ranch." The Supremacy Clause prohibits state judges and prosecutors from interfering with a President's official duties. Any effort to manipulate a President's policy decisions or to "retaliat[e]" against a President for official acts through issuance of a subpoena, would thus be an unconstitutional attempt to "influence" a superior sovereign "exempt" from such obstacles, see *McCulloch*. We generally "assume[] that state courts and prosecutors will observe constitutional limitations." *Dombrowski v. Pfister*, 380 U.S. 479, 484 (1965). Failing that, federal law allows a President to challenge any allegedly unconstitutional influence in a federal forum, as the President has done here. See 42 U.S.C. §1983; *Ex parte Young* (1908) (holding that federal courts may enjoin state officials to conform their conduct to federal law).

Given these safeguards and the Court's precedents, we cannot conclude that absolute immunity is necessary or appropriate under Article II or the Supremacy Clause. Our dissenting colleagues agree. Justice Thomas reaches the same conclusion based on the original understanding of the Constitution reflected in Marshall's decision in *Burr*. And Justice Alito, also persuaded by *Burr*, "agree[s]" that "not all" state criminal subpoenas for a President's records "should be barred." On that point the Court is unanimous.

B

We next consider whether a state grand jury subpoena seeking a President's private papers must satisfy a heightened need standard. The Solicitor General would require a threshold showing that the evidence sought is "critical" for

"specific charging decisions" and that the subpoena is a "last resort," meaning the evidence is "not available from any other source" and is needed "now,
rather than at the end of the President's term." Justice Alito, largely embracing
those criteria, agrees that a state criminal subpoena to a President "should not be
allowed unless a heightened standard is met." *Post* (asking whether the information is "critical" and "necessary . . . now").

We disagree, for three reasons. First, such a heightened standard would extend
protection designed for official documents to the President's private papers.
As the Solicitor General And Justice Alito acknowledge, their proposed test is
derived from executive privilege cases that trace back to *Burr*. There, Marshall
explained that if Jefferson invoked presidential privilege over executive communications, the court would not "proceed against the president as against an
ordinary individual" but would instead require an affidavit from the defense that
"would clearly show the paper to be essential to the justice of the case." The
Solicitor General and Justice Alito would have us apply a similar standard to
a President's personal papers. But this argument does not account for the relevant passage from *Burr*: "If there be a paper in the possession of the executive,
which is *not of an official nature*, he must stand, as respects that paper, in nearly
the same situation with any other individual. And it is only "nearly"—and not
"entirely"—because the President retains the right to assert privilege over documents that, while ostensibly private, "partake of the character of an official
paper."

Second, neither the Solicitor General nor Justice Alito has established that
heightened protection against state subpoenas is necessary for the Executive to
fulfill his Article II functions. Beyond the risk of harassment, which we addressed
above, the only justification they offer for the heightened standard is protecting
Presidents from "unwarranted burdens." In effect, they argue that even if federal
subpoenas to a President are warranted whenever evidence is material, state subpoenas are warranted "only when [the] evidence is essential." But that double
standard has no basis in law. For [1] if the state subpoena is not issued to manipulate, [2] the documents themselves are not protected, and [3] the Executive is not
impaired, then nothing in Article II or the Supremacy Clause supports holding
state subpoenas to a higher standard than their federal counterparts.

Finally, in the absence of a need to protect the Executive, the public interest
in fair and effective law enforcement cuts in favor of comprehensive access to
evidence. Requiring a state grand jury to meet a heightened standard of need
would hobble the grand jury's ability to acquire "all information that might
possibly bear on its investigation." *R. Enterprises, Inc.* And, even assuming the
evidence withheld under that standard were preserved until the conclusion of
a President's term, in the interim the State would be deprived of investigative
leads that the evidence might yield, allowing memories to fade and documents
to disappear. This could frustrate the identification, investigation, and indictment of third parties (for whom applicable statutes of limitations might lapse).
More troubling, it could prejudice the innocent by depriving the grand jury of
exculpatory evidence.

Rejecting a heightened need standard does not leave Presidents with "no real protection." *Post* (opinion of Alito, J.). To start, a President may avail himself of the same protections available to every other citizen. These include the right to challenge the subpoena on any grounds permitted by state law, which usually include bad faith and undue burden or breadth. And, as in federal court, "[t]he high respect that is owed to the office of the Chief Executive . . . should inform the conduct of the entire proceeding, including the timing and scope of discovery." *Clinton.* See *id.* (Breyer, J., concurring in judgment) (stressing the need for courts presiding over suits against the President to "schedule proceedings so as to avoid significant interference with the President's ongoing discharge of his official responsibilities"); *Nixon* ("[W]here a subpoena is directed to a President . . . appellate review . . . should be particularly meticulous.").

Furthermore, although the Constitution does not entitle the Executive to absolute immunity or a heightened standard, he is not "relegate[d]" only to the challenges available to private citizens. A President can raise subpoena-specific constitutional challenges, in either a state or federal forum. As previously noted, he can challenge the subpoena as an attempt to influence the performance of his official duties, in violation of the Supremacy Clause. This avenue protects against local political machinations "interposed as an obstacle to the effective operation of a federal constitutional power." *United States v. Belmont* (1937).

In addition, the Executive can — as the district attorney concedes — argue that compliance with a particular subpoena would impede his constitutional duties. Incidental to the functions confided in Article II is "the power to perform them, without obstruction or impediment." 3 J. Story, Commentaries on the Constitution of the United States (1833). As a result, "once the President sets forth and explains a conflict between judicial proceeding and public duties," or shows that an order or subpoena would "significantly interfere with his efforts to carry out" those duties, "the matter changes." *Clinton* (opinion of Breyer, J.). At that point, a court should use its inherent authority to quash or modify the subpoena, if necessary to ensure that such "interference with the President's duties would not occur."

* * *

Two hundred years ago, a great jurist of our Court established that no citizen, not even the President, is categorically above the common duty to produce evidence when called upon in a criminal proceeding. We reaffirm that principle today and hold that the President is neither absolutely immune from state criminal subpoenas seeking his private papers nor entitled to a heightened standard of need. The "guard[] furnished to this high officer" lies where it always has — in "the conduct of a court" applying established legal and constitutional principles to individual subpoenas in a manner that preserves both the independence of the Executive and the integrity of the criminal justice system. *Burr.*

The arguments presented here and in the Court of Appeals were limited to absolute immunity and heightened need. The Court of Appeals, however, has directed that the case be returned to the District Court, where the President may raise further arguments as appropriate.[6]

We affirm the judgment of the Court of Appeals and remand the case for further proceedings consistent with this opinion.

JUSTICE KAVANAUGH, with whom JUSTICE GORSUCH joins, concurring in the judgment.

The Court today unanimously concludes that a President does not possess absolute immunity from a state criminal subpoena, but also unanimously agrees that this case should be remanded to the District Court, where the President may raise constitutional and legal objections to the subpoena as appropriate. I agree with those two conclusions.

* * *

The dispute over this grand jury subpoena reflects a conflict between a State's interest in criminal investigation and a President's Article II interest in performing his or her duties without undue interference. Although this case involves personal information of the President and is therefore not an executive privilege case, the majority opinion correctly concludes based on precedent that Article II and the Supremacy Clause of the Constitution supply some protection for the Presidency against state criminal subpoenas of this sort.

In our system of government, as this Court has often stated, no one is above the law. That principle applies, of course, to a President. At the same time, in light of Article II of the Constitution, this Court has repeatedly declared — and the Court indicates again today — that a court may not proceed against a President as it would against an ordinary litigant. . . . *United States v. Burr* (CC Va. 1807) (Marshall, C. J.) ("In no case of this kind would a court be required to proceed against the president as against an ordinary individual"); [*Cheney v. United States Dist. Court for D.C.* (2004) (same); *Clinton v. Jones* (1997) (same); *United States v. Nixon* (1974) (same)].

The question here, then, is how to balance the State's interests and the Article II interests. The longstanding precedent that has applied to federal criminal subpoenas for official, privileged Executive Branch information is *United States v. Nixon* (1974). That landmark case requires that a prosecutor establish a "demonstrated, specific need" for the President's information.

The *Nixon* "demonstrated, specific need" standard is a tried-and-true test that accommodates both the interests of the criminal process and the Article II interests of the Presidency. . . .

Because this case again entails a clash between the interests of the criminal process and the Article II interests of the Presidency, I would apply the longstanding

---

6. The daylight between our opinion and Justice Thomas's "dissent" is not as great as that label might suggest. We agree that Presidents are neither absolutely immune from state criminal subpoenas nor insulated by a heightened need standard. We agree that Presidents may challenge specific subpoenas as impeding their Article II functions. And, although we affirm while Justice Thomas would vacate, we agree that this case will be remanded to the District Court.

Nixon "demonstrated, specific need" standard to this case. The majority opinion does not apply the *Nixon* standard in this distinct Article II context, as I would have done. That said, the majority opinion appropriately takes account of some important concerns that also animate *Nixon* and the Constitution's balance of powers. . . . All nine Members of the Court agree, moreover, that a President may raise objections to a state criminal subpoena not just in state court but also in federal court. And the majority opinion indicates that, in light of the "high respect that is owed to the office of the Chief Executive," courts "should be particularly meticulous" in assessing a subpoena for a President's personal records.

In the end, much may depend on how the majority opinion's various standards are applied in future years and decades.[2] It will take future cases to determine precisely how much difference exists between (i) the various standards articulated by the majority opinion, (ii) the overarching *Nixon* "demonstrated, specific need" standard that I would adopt, and (iii) Justice Thomas's and Justice Alito's other proposed standards. In any event, in my view, lower courts in cases of this sort involving a President will almost invariably have to begin by delving into why the State wants the information; why and how much the State needs the information, including whether the State could obtain the information elsewhere; and whether compliance with the subpoena would unduly burden or interfere with a President's official duties.

* * *

I agree that the case should be remanded to the District Court for further proceedings, where the President may raise constitutional and legal objections to the state grand jury subpoena as appropriate.

JUSTICE THOMAS, dissenting.

Respondent Cyrus Vance, Jr., the district attorney for the County of New York, served a grand jury subpoena on the President's personal accounting firm. The subpoena, which is nearly identical to a subpoena issued by a congressional Committee, requests nearly 10 years of the President's personal financial records. . . .

The President argues that he is absolutely immune from the issuance of any subpoena, but that if the Court disagrees, we should remand so that the District Court can develop a record about this particular subpoena. I agree with the majority that the President is not entitled to absolute immunity from *issuance* of the subpoena. But he may be entitled to relief against its *enforcement*. I therefore agree with the President that the proper course is to vacate and remand. If the President can show that "his duties as chief magistrate demand his whole time for national objects," *United States v. Burr* (CC Va. 1807) (Marshall, C. J.), he is entitled to relief from enforcement of the subpoena.

---

2. The same point—namely, that much may depend on future application—is also true of the four considerations articulated by the Court today in *Trump v. Mazars USA, LLP.*

I

The President first argues that he has absolute immunity from the issuance of grand jury subpoenas during his term in office. This Court has recognized absolute immunity for the President from "damages liability predicated on his official acts." *Nixon v. Fitzgerald* (1982). But we have rejected absolute immunity from damages actions for a President's nonofficial conduct, *Clinton v. Jones* (1997), and we have never addressed the question of immunity from a grand jury subpoena.

I agree with the majority that the President does not have absolute immunity from the issuance of a grand jury subpoena. Unlike the majority, however, I do not reach this conclusion based on a primarily functionalist analysis. Instead, I reach it based on the text of the Constitution, which, as understood by the ratifying public and incorporated into an early circuit opinion by Chief Justice Marshall, does not support the President's claim of absolute immunity.[1]

A

1

The text of the Constitution explicitly addresses the privileges of some federal officials, but it does not afford the President absolute immunity. Members of Congress are "privileged from Arrest during their Attendance at the Session of their respective Houses, and in going to and returning from the same," except for "Treason, Felony and Breach of the Peace." Art. I, §6, cl. 1. The Constitution further specifies that, "for any Speech or Debate in either House, they shall not be questioned in any other Place." *Ibid.* By contrast, the text of the Constitution contains no explicit grant of absolute immunity from legal process for the President. As a Federalist essayist noted during ratification, the President's "person is not so much protected as that of a member of the House of Representatives" because he is subject to the issuance of judicial process "like any other man in the ordinary course of law."

Prominent defenders of the Constitution confirmed the lack of absolute Presidential immunity. James Wilson, a signer of the Constitution and future Justice of this Court, explained to his fellow Pennsylvanians that "far from being above the laws, [the President] is amenable to them in his private character as a citizen, and in his public character by *impeachment*." James Iredell, another future Justice, observed in the North Carolina ratifying convention that "[i]f [the President] commits any crime, he is punishable by the laws of his country." . . .

2

The sole authority that the President cites from the drafting or ratification process is The Federalist No. 69, but it provides him no real support. Alexander Hamilton

---

1. I do not address the continuing validity of *Nixon v. Fitzgerald* (1982), which no party asks us to revisit.

stated that "[t]he President of the United States would be liable to be impeached, tried, and upon conviction of treason, bribery, or other high crimes or misdemeanors, removed from office; and would afterwards be liable to prosecution and punishment in the ordinary course of law." The Federalist No. 69. Hamilton did not say that the President was temporarily immune from judicial process. Moreover, he made this comment to reassure readers that the President was "amenable to personal punishment and disgrace." For the President, this is at best ambiguous evidence that cannot overcome the clear evidence discussed above.

The President further relies on a private letter written by President Jefferson. In the letter, Jefferson worried that the Executive would lose his independence "if he were subject to the *commands* of the [judiciary], & to imprisonment for disobedience; if the several courts could bandy him from pillar to post, keep him constantly trudging from north to south & east to west, and withdraw him entirely from his constitutional duties." But President Jefferson never squarely argued for absolute immunity. And, the concern Jefferson had about demands on the President's time is addressed by the standard that Chief Justice Marshall articulated in *Burr*. . . .

B

This original understanding is reflected in an early circuit decision by Chief Justice Marshall, on which the majority partially relies. . . . Burr was arrested for treason and brought before a grand jury in Richmond, where Chief Justice Marshall presided.

During the grand jury proceedings, Burr moved for a *subpoena duces tecum* ordering President Jefferson to produce the correspondence concerning Burr. *Burr*. Chief Justice Marshall pre-emptively rejected any notion of absolute immunity, despite the fact that the Government did not so much as suggest it in court. He distinguished the President from the British monarch, who did have immunity, calling it an "essentia[l] . . . difference" in our system that the President "is elected from the mass of the people, and, on the expiration of the time for which he is elected, returns to the mass of the people again." Thus, the President was more like a state governor or a member of the British cabinet than a king. Chief Justice Marshall found no authority suggesting that these officials were immune from judicial process.

Based on the evidence of original meaning and Chief Justice Marshall's early interpretation in *Burr*, the better reading of the text of the Constitution is that the President has no absolute immunity from the issuance of a grand jury subpoena.

II

In addition to contesting the issuance of the subpoena, the President also seeks injunctive and declaratory relief against its enforcement. The majority recognizes that the President can seek relief from enforcement, but it does not vacate and remand for the lower courts to address this question. I would do so and instruct them to apply the standard articulated by Chief Justice Marshall in *Burr*: If the President is unable to comply because of his official duties, then he is entitled to injunctive and declaratory relief.

A

In *Burr*, after explaining that the President was not absolutely immune from issuance of a subpoena, Chief Justice Marshall proceeded to explain that the President might be excused from the enforcement of one. As he put it, "[t]he guard, furnished to this high officer, to protect him from being harassed by vexatious and unnecessary subpoenas, is to be looked for in the conduct of a court *after those subpoenas have issued*; not in any circumstance which is to precede their being issued." Chief Justice Marshall set out the pertinent standard: To avoid enforcement of the subpoena, the President must "sho[w]" that "his duties as chief magistrate demand his whole time for national objects."[2]

Although *Burr* involved a federal subpoena, the same principle applies to a state subpoena. The ability of the President to discharge his duties until his term expires or he is removed from office by the Senate is "integral to the structure of the Constitution." *Franchise Tax Bd. of Cal. v. Hyatt* (2019). The Constitution is the "supreme Law of the Land," Art. VI, cl. 2, so a state court can no more enforce a subpoena when national concerns demand the President's entire time than a federal court can. Accordingly, a federal court may provide injunctive and declaratory relief to stay enforcement of a state subpoena when the President meets the *Burr* standard.

B

The *Burr* standard places the burden on the President but also requires courts to take pains to respect the demands on the President's time. The Constitution vests the President with extensive powers and responsibilities, and courts are poorly situated to conduct a searching review of the President's assertion that he is unable to comply.

1

The President has vast responsibilities both abroad and at home. The Founders gave the President "primary responsibility — along with the necessary power — to protect the national security and to conduct the Nation's foreign relations." *Hamdi v. Rumsfeld* (2004) (Thomas, J., dissenting). The Constitution

---

2. This standard appears to be something that Chief Justice Marshall and President Jefferson, who were often at odds, could agree on. President Jefferson's concern was that the Executive would lose his independence if courts could "withdraw him entirely from his constitutional duties." Relief from enforcement when those duties preclude the President's compliance addresses these concerns.

"expressly identifies certain foreign affairs powers and vests them" in his office. *Zivotofsky v. Kerry* (2015) (Thomas, J.). He is "Commander in Chief of the Army and Navy of the United States, and of the Militia of the several States, when called into the actual Service of the United States." Art. II, §2, cl. 1. He has "Power, by and with the Advice and Consent of the Senate, to make Treaties." Cl. 2. He has the power to "nominate, and by and with the Advice and Consent of the Senate [to] appoint Ambassadors [and] other public Ministers and Consuls." *Ibid.* He has the power to fill vacancies that arise during a Senate recess until "the End of [the Senate's] next Session." Cl. 3. And he is responsible for "receiv[ing] Ambassadors and other public Ministers" from foreign countries. §3.

The President also has residual powers granted by Article II's Vesting Clause. "By omitting the words 'herein granted' in [the Vesting Clause of] Article II, the Constitution indicates that the 'executive Power' vested in the President is not confined to those powers expressly identified in the document." *Zivotofsky* (opinion of Thomas, J.). Rather, the Constitution "vests the residual foreign affairs powers of the Federal Government—*i.e.*, those not specifically enumerated in the Constitution—in the President." Evidence from both the founding and the early years of the Constitution confirms that the residual foreign affairs powers of the Government were part of the "executive Power."

The President has extensive domestic responsibilities as well. He is given "[t]he executive Power," Art. II, §1, cl. 1, and is directed to "take Care that the Laws be faithfully executed," §3. "The vesting of the executive power in the President was essentially a grant of the power to execute the laws." *Myers v. United States* (1926). Even under a proper understanding of the scope of federal power, the President could not possibly execute all of the laws himself. The President must accordingly appoint subordinates "to act for him under his direction in the execution of the laws." Once officers are selected, the President must "supervise and guide their construction of the statutes under which they act in order to secure that unitary and uniform execution of the laws which Article II of the Constitution evidently contemplated in vesting general executive power in the President alone." And, of course, the President has the power to remove officers as he sees fit. *Id.*; see also *Seila Law LLC v. Consumer Financial Protection Bureau*, (Thomas, J.).

In addition, the President has several specifically enumerated domestic powers. He has the "Power to Grant Reprieves and Pardons for Offenses against the United States, except in Cases of Impeachment." Art. II, §2, cl. 1. He also has the power to "nominate, and by and with the Advice and Consent of the Senate [to] appoint . . . Judges of the supreme Court, and all other Officers of the United States, whose Appointments are not herein otherwise provided for, and which shall be established by Law." Cl. 2. And he must "give to the Congress Information of the State of the Union, and recommend to their Consideration such Measures as he shall judge necessary and expedient." §3.

The founding generation debated whether it was prudent to vest so many powers in a single person. Supporters of ratification responded that the design of the Presidency was necessary to the success of the Constitution. . . .

In sum, the demands on the President's time and the importance of his tasks are extraordinary, and the office of the President cannot be delegated to subordinates. A subpoena imposes both demands on the President's limited time and a mental burden, even when the President is not directly engaged in complying. This understanding of the Presidency should guide courts in deciding whether to enforce a subpoena for the President's documents.

2

Courts must also recognize their own limitations. When the President asserts that matters of foreign affairs or national defense preclude his compliance with a subpoena, the Judiciary will rarely have a basis for rejecting that assertion. . . .

The President has at his disposal enormous amounts of classified intelligence regarding the Government's concerns around the globe. His decisionmaking is further informed by experience in matters of foreign affairs, national defense, and intelligence that judges almost always will not have. And his decisionmaking takes into account the full spectrum of the Government's operations, not just the matters directly related to a particular case. Even with perfect information, courts lack the institutional competence to engage in a searching review of the President's reasons for not complying with a subpoena.

Here, too, Chief Justice Marshall was correct. A court should "fee[l] many, perhaps, peculiar motives for manifesting as guarded a respect for the chief magistrate of the Union as is compatible with its official duties." *Burr.* Courts should have the same "circumspection" as Chief Justice Marshall before "tak[ing] any step which would in any manner relate to that high personage."[3]

* * *

I agree with the majority that the President has no absolute immunity from the issuance of this subpoena. The President also sought relief from enforcement of the subpoena, however, and he asked this Court to allow further proceedings on that question if we rejected his claim of absolute immunity. The Court inexplicably fails to address this request, although its decision leaves the President free to renew his request for an injunction against enforcement immediately on remand.

---

3. The President and the Solicitor General argue that the grand jury must make a showing of heightened need. I agree with the majority's decision not to adopt this standard, but for different reasons. The constitutional question in this case is whether the President is able to perform the duties of his office, whereas a heightened need standard addresses a logically independent issue. Under a heightened-need standard, a grand jury with only the usual need for particular information would be refused it when the President is perfectly able to comply, while a grand jury with a heightened need would be entitled to it even if compliance would place undue obligations on the President. This result makes little sense and lacks any basis in the original understanding of the Constitution. I would leave questions of the grand jury's need to state law.

I would vacate and remand to allow the District Court to determine whether enforcement of this subpoena should be enjoined because the President's "duties as chief magistrate demand his whole time for national objects." Accordingly, I respectfully dissent.

JUSTICE ALITO, dissenting.

This case is almost certain to be portrayed as a case about the current President and the current political situation, but the case has a much deeper significance. While the decision will of course have a direct effect on President Trump, what the Court holds today will also affect all future Presidents—which is to say, it will affect the Presidency, and that is a matter of great and lasting importance to the Nation.

The event that precipitated this case is unprecedented. Respondent Vance, an elected state prosecutor, launched a criminal investigation of a sitting President and obtained a grand jury subpoena for his records. The specific question before us—whether the subpoena may be enforced—cannot be answered adequately without considering the broader question that frames it: whether the Constitution imposes restrictions on a State's deployment of its criminal law enforcement powers against a sitting President. If the Constitution sets no such limits, then a local prosecutor may prosecute a sitting President. And if that is allowed, it follows *a fortiori* that the subpoena at issue can be enforced. On the other hand, if the Constitution does not permit a State to prosecute a sitting President, the next logical question is whether the Constitution restrains any other prosecutorial or investigative weapons.

These are important questions that go to the very structure of the Government created by the Constitution. In evaluating these questions, two important structural features must be taken into account.

I

A

The first is the nature and role of the Presidency. The Presidency, like Congress and the Supreme Court, is a permanent institution created by the Constitution. All three of these institutions are distinct from the human beings who serve in them at any point in time. In the case of Congress or the Supreme Court, the distinction is easy to perceive, since they have multiple Members. But because "[t]he President is the only person who alone composes a branch of government . . . , there is not always a clear line between his personal and official affairs." *Trump v. Mazars USA, LLP.* As a result, the law's treatment of the person who serves as President can have an important effect on the institution, and the institution of the Presidency plays an indispensable role in our constitutional system.

The Constitution entrusts the President with responsibilities that are essential to the country's safety and wellbeing. The President is Commander in Chief of the Armed Forces. Art. II, §2, cl. 1. He is responsible for the defense of the country from the moment he enters office until the moment he leaves.

The President also has the lead role in foreign relations. He "make[s]" treaties with the advice and consent of the Senate, Art. II, §2, cl. 2, decides whether to recognize foreign governments, *Zivotofsky v. Kerry* (2015), enters into and rescinds executive agreements with other countries, meets with foreign leaders, appoints ambassadors, Art. II, §2, cl. 2, oversees the work of the State Department and intelligence agencies, and exercises important foreign-relations powers under statutes and treaties that give him broad discretion in matters relating to subjects such as terrorism, trade, and immigration.

The Constitution vests the President with "the executive Power" of the United States, Art. II, §1, cl. 1, and entrusts him with the responsibility "to take Care that the Laws be faithfully executed," §3. As the head of the Executive Branch, the President is ultimately responsible for everything done by all the departments and agencies of the Federal Government and a federal civilian work force that includes millions of employees. These weighty responsibilities impose enormous burdens on the time and energy of any occupant of the Presidency. . . .

B

The second structural feature is the relationship between the Federal Government and the States. Just as our Constitution balances power against power among the branches of the Federal Government, it also divides power between the Federal Government and the States. The Constitution permitted the States to retain many of the sovereign powers that they previously possessed, see, *e.g.*, *Murphy* v. *National Collegiate Athletic Assn.* (2018), but it gave the Federal Government powers that were deemed essential for the Nation's well-being and, indeed, its survival. And it provided for the Federal Government to be independent of and, within its allotted sphere, supreme over the States. Art. VI, cl. 2. Accordingly, a State may not block or interfere with the lawful work of the National Government.

This was an enduring lesson of Chief Justice Marshall's landmark opinion for the Court in *McCulloch v. Maryland* (1819). As is well known, the case concerned the attempt by the State of Maryland to regulate and tax the federally chartered Second Bank of the United States. After holding that Congress had the authority to establish the bank, Marshall's opinion went on to conclude that the State could not tax it. . . . Marshall thus held, not simply that Maryland was barred from assessing a crushing tax that threatened the bank's ability to operate, but that the State could not tax the bank at all. . . .

Even a rule allowing a state tax that did not discriminate between the federally chartered bank and state banks was ruled out. Instead, he concluded that preservation of the Constitution's federal structure demanded that any state effort to tax a federal instrumentality be nipped in the bud.

Building on this principle of federalism, two centuries of case law prohibit the States from taxing, regulating, or otherwise interfering with the lawful work of federal agencies, instrumentalities, and officers. . . .

II

A

In *McCulloch*, Maryland's sovereign taxing power had to yield, and in a similar way, a State's sovereign power to enforce its criminal laws must accommodate the indispensable role that the Constitution assigns to the Presidency. This must be the rule with respect to a state prosecution of a sitting President. Both the structure of the Government established by the Constitution and the Constitution's provisions on the impeachment and removal of a President make it clear that the prosecution of a sitting President is out of the question. It has been aptly said that the President is the "sole indispensable man in government," and subjecting a sitting President to criminal prosecution would severely hamper his ability to carry out the vital responsibilities that the Constitution puts in his hands.

The constitutional provisions on impeachment provide further support for the rule that a President may not be prosecuted while in office. The Framers foresaw the need to provide for the possibility that a President might be implicated in the commission of a serious offense, and they did not want the country to be forced to endure such a President for the remainder of his term in office. But when a President has been elected by the people pursuant to the procedures set out in the Constitution, it is no small thing to overturn that choice. The Framers therefore crafted a special set of procedures to deal with that contingency. They put the charging decision in the hands of a body that represents all the people (the House of Representatives), not a single prosecutor or the members of a local grand jury. And they entrusted the weighty decision whether to remove a President to a supermajority of Senators, who were expected to exercise reasoned judgment and not the political passions of the day or the sentiments of a particular region. . .

In the proceedings below, neither respondent, nor the District Court, nor the Second Circuit was willing to concede the fundamental point that a sitting President may not be prosecuted by a local district attorney.

. . . If a sitting President were charged in New York County, would he be arrested and fingerprinted? He would presumably be required to appear for arraignment in criminal court, where the judge would set the conditions for his release. Could he be sent to Rikers Island or be required to post bail? Could the judge impose restrictions on his travel? If the President were scheduled to travel abroad—perhaps to attend a G-7 meeting—would he have to get judicial approval? If the President were charged with a complicated offense requiring a long trial, would he have to put his Presidential responsibilities aside for weeks on end while sitting in a Manhattan courtroom? While the trial was in progress, would aides be able to approach him and whisper in his ear about pressing matters? Would he be able to obtain a recess whenever he needed to speak with an aide at greater length or attend to an urgent matter, such as speaking with a foreign leader? Could he effectively carry out all his essential Presidential responsibilities after the trial day ended and at the same time adequately confer with his trial attorneys regarding his defense? Or should he be expected to give up the right to attend his own trial and be tried in absentia? And if he were convicted, could he be imprisoned? Would aides be installed in a nearby cell?

B

While the prosecution of a sitting President provides the most dramatic example of a clash between the indispensable work of the Presidency and a State's exercise of its criminal law enforcement powers, other examples are easy to imagine. Suppose state officers obtained and sought to execute a search warrant for a sitting President's private quarters in the White House. Suppose a state court authorized surveillance of a telephone that a sitting President was known to use. Or suppose that a sitting President was subpoenaed to testify before a state grand jury and, as is generally the rule, no Presidential aides, even those carrying the so-called "nuclear football," were permitted to enter the grand jury room. What these examples illustrate is a principle that this Court has recognized: legal proceedings involving a sitting President must take the responsibilities and demands of the office into account. See *Clinton v. Jones* (1997).

It is not enough to recite sayings like "no man is above the law" and "the public has a right to every man's evidence." These sayings are true—and important—but they beg the question. The law applies equally to all persons, including a person who happens for a period of time to occupy the Presidency. But there is no question that the nature of the office demands in some instances that the application of laws be adjusted at least until the person's term in office ends.

C

. . . I turn first to the question of the effect of a state grand jury subpoena for a President's records. When the issuance of such a subpoena is part of an investigation that regards the President as a "target" or "subject," the subpoena can easily impair a President's "energetic performance of [his] constitutional duties." *Cheney v. United States Dist. Court for D.C.* (2004). Few individuals will simply brush off an indication that they may be within a prosecutor's crosshairs. Few will put the matter out of their minds and go about their work unaffected. For many, the prospect of prosecution will be the first and last thing on their minds every day.

We have come to expect our Presidents to shoulder burdens that very few people could bear, but it is unrealistic to think that the prospect of possible criminal prosecution will not interfere with the performance of the duties of the office. See also Kavanaugh, Separation of Powers During the Forty-Fourth Presidency and Beyond (2009) ("[A] President who is concerned about an ongoing criminal investigation is almost inevitably going to do a worse job as President").

. . . There are more than 2,300 local prosecutors and district attorneys in the country. Many local prosecutors are elected, and many prosecutors have ambitions for higher elected office. . . . If a sitting President is intensely unpopular in a particular district—and that is a common condition—targeting the President may be an alluring and effective electoral strategy. But it is a strategy that would undermine our constitutional structure. . . .

D

In light of the above, a subpoena like the one now before us should not be enforced unless it meets a test that takes into account the need to prevent interference with a President's discharge of the responsibilities of the office. I agree with the Court that not all such subpoenas should be barred. There may be situations in which there is an urgent and critical need for the subpoenaed information. The situation in the Burr trial, where the documents at issue were sought by a criminal defendant to defend against a charge of treason, is a good example. But in a case like the one at hand, a subpoena should not be allowed unless a heightened standard is met.

Prior cases involving Presidential subpoenas have always applied special, heightened standards. In the Burr trial, Chief Justice Marshall was careful to note that "in no case of this kind would a court be required to proceed against the president as against an ordinary individual," and he held that the subpoena to President Jefferson was permissible only because the prosecutor had shown that the materials sought were "essential to the justice of the [pending criminal] case." *United States v. Burr* (CC Va. 1807).

In *United States v. Nixon*, 418 U.S. 683 (1974), where the Watergate Special Prosecutor subpoenaed tape recordings and documents under the control of President Nixon, this Court refused to quash the subpoena because there was a "demonstrated, specific need for [the] evidence in a pending criminal trial." . . .

The important point is not that the subpoena in this case should necessarily be governed by the particular tests used in these cases, most of which involved official records that were claimed to be privileged. Rather, the point is that we should not treat this subpoena like an ordinary grand jury subpoena and should not relegate a President to the meager defenses that are available when an ordinary grand jury subpoena is challenged. But that, at bottom, is the effect of the Court's decision.

The Presidency deserves greater protection. Thus, in a case like this one, a prosecutor should be required (1) to provide at least a general description of the possible offenses that are under investigation, (2) to outline how the subpoenaed records relate to those offenses, and (3) to explain why it is important that the records be produced and why it is necessary for production to occur while the President is still in office.

In the present case, the district attorney made a brief proffer, but important questions were left hanging. It would not be unduly burdensome to insist on answers before enforcing the subpoena. . . .

The district attorney should also explain why it is important that the information in question be obtained from the President's records rather than another source. And the district attorney should set out why he finds it necessary that the records be produced now as opposed to when the President leaves office. . . .

E

Unlike this rule, which would not undermine any legitimate state interests, the opinion of the Court provides no real protection for the Presidency. The Court discounts the risk of harassment and assumes that state prosecutors will observe constitutional limitations, and I also assume that the great majority of state prosecutors will carry out their responsibilities responsibly. But for the reasons noted, there is a very real risk that some will not.

The Court emphasizes the protection afforded by "longstanding rules of grand jury secrecy," but that is no answer to the burdens that subpoenas may inflict, and in any event, grand jury secrecy rules are of limited value as safeguards against harassment. . . .

The Court says that a President can "*argue* that compliance with a particular subpoena would impede his constitutional duties," but under the Court's opinions in this case and *Mazars*, it is not easy to see how such an argument could prevail. The Court makes clear that any stigma or damage to a President's reputation does not count, and in *Mazars*, the Court states that "burdens on the President's time and attention" are generally not of constitutional concern. Elsewhere in its opinion in this case, the Court takes the position that when a President's non-official records are subpoenaed, his treatment should be little different from that of any other subpoena recipient. The most that the Court holds out is the possibility that there might be some unspecified extraordinary circumstances under which a President might obtain relief.

Finally, the Court touts the ability of a President to challenge a subpoena by "'an affirmative showing of impropriety,' including 'bad faith'" or retaliation for official acts. But "such objections are almost universally overruled." Direct evidence of impropriety is rarely obtainable, and it will be a challenge to make a circumstantial case unless the prosecutor is required to provide the sort of showing outlined above.

For all practical purposes, the Court's decision places a sitting President in the same unenviable position as any other person whose records are subpoenaed by a grand jury.

Attempting to justify this approach, the Court relies on Marshall's ruling in the Burr trial, but the Court ignores important differences between the situation in that case and the situation here. First, the subpoena in *Burr* was not issued by a grand jury at the behest of a prosecutor who was investigating the President. Instead, a defendant who was initially on trial for his life sought to obtain exculpatory evidence from the very man who was orchestrating the prosecution. Marshall's ruling took note of the context in which the evidence was sought. He stated: "If there be a paper in the possession of the executive, which is not of an official nature, he must stand, as respects that paper, in nearly the same situation with any other individual who possesses a paper *which might be required for the defense.*"

Second, it is significant that Burr, unlike the prosecutor in the present case, did not have the option of postponing his request for information until the President's term ended. Burr had not chosen to be charged or tried while Jefferson was in office, and by the time Jefferson's tenure ended, his trial was history. Third, because the case was prosecuted in federal court under federal law, it entirely lacked the federalism concerns that lie at the heart of the present case.

The lesson we should take from Marshall's jurisprudence is the lesson of *McCulloch* — the importance of preventing a State from undermining the lawful exercise of authority conferred by the Constitution on the Federal Government. There is considerable irony in the Court's invocation of Marshall to defend a decision allowing a State's prosecutorial power to run roughshod over the functioning of a branch of the Federal Government. . . .

The Court turns to *United States v. Nixon*, but that case arose under markedly different circumstances. Because the trial was in federal court, there was no issue of federalism, and the Court refused to order that the subpoena be quashed because of "the demonstrated, specific need for evidence in a pending criminal trial." In the case now before us, a "demonstrated, specific need" is precisely what is lacking.

This Court's decision in *Clinton v. Jones*, 520 U.S. 681, provides no greater support for today's decision. In that case, as noted, the lawsuit was brought in federal, not state, court, and while the subject of that particular civil suit was embarrassing, the Court addressed the broad question whether a President is immune from civil suits "'in all but the most exceptional cases.'" There is no question that a criminal prosecution holds far greater potential for distracting a President and diminishing his ability to carry out his responsibilities than does the average civil suit.

* * *

The subpoena at issue here is unprecedented. Never before has a local prosecutor subpoenaed the records of a sitting President. The Court's decision threatens to impair the functioning of the Presidency and provides no real protection against the use of the subpoena power by the Nation's 2,300+ local prosecutors. Respect for the structure of Government created by the Constitution demands greater protection for an institution that is vital to the Nation's safety and well-being.

I therefore respectfully dissent.

Trump v. Mazars
591 U.S. ___ (2020)

CHIEF JUSTICE ROBERTS delivered the opinion of the Court.

Over the course of five days in April 2019, three committees of the U.S. House of Representatives issued four subpoenas seeking information about the finances of President Donald J. Trump, his children, and affiliated businesses. We have held that the House has authority under the Constitution to issue subpoenas to assist it in carrying out its legislative responsibilities. The House asserts that the financial information sought here—encompassing a decade's worth of transactions by the President and his family—will help guide legislative reform in areas ranging from money laundering and terrorism to foreign involvement in U.S. elections. The President contends that the House lacked a valid legislative aim and instead sought these records to harass him, expose personal matters, and conduct law enforcement activities beyond its authority. The question presented is whether the subpoenas exceed the authority of the House under the Constitution.

We have never addressed a congressional subpoena for the President's information. Two hundred years ago, it was established that Presidents may be subpoenaed during a federal criminal proceeding, *United States v. Burr* (CC Va. 1807) (Marshall, Cir. J.), and earlier today we extended that ruling to state criminal proceedings, *Trump v. Vance*. Nearly fifty years ago, we held that a federal prosecutor could obtain information from a President despite assertions of executive privilege, *United States v. Nixon* (1974), and more recently we ruled that a private litigant could subject a President to a damages suit and appropriate discovery obligations in federal court, *Clinton v. Jones* (1997).

This case is different. Here the President's information is sought not by prosecutors or private parties in connection with a particular judicial proceeding, but by committees of Congress that have set forth broad legislative objectives. Congress and the President—the two political branches established by the Constitution—have an ongoing relationship that the Framers intended to feature both rivalry and reciprocity. See The Federalist No. 51 (J. Madison); *Youngstown Sheet & Tube Co. v. Sawyer* (1952) (Jackson, J., concurring). That distinctive aspect necessarily informs our analysis of the question before us.

I

A

Each of the three committees sought overlapping sets of financial documents, but each supplied different justifications for the requests.

The House Committee on Financial Services issued two subpoenas, both on April 11, 2019. The first, issued to Deutsche Bank, seeks the financial information of the President, his children, their immediate family members, and several affiliated business entities. . . . The second, issued to Capital One, demands similar financial information with respect to more than a dozen business entities associated with the President. The Deutsche Bank subpoena requests materials from "2010 through the present," and the Capital One subpoena covers "2016 through the present," but both subpoenas impose no time limitations for certain documents, such as those connected to account openings and due diligence.

According to the House, the Financial Services Committee issued these subpoenas pursuant to House Resolution 206, which called for "efforts to close loopholes that allow corruption, terrorism, and money laundering to infiltrate our country's financial system.". . . The House also invokes the oversight plan of the Financial Services Committee, which stated that the Committee intends to review banking regulation and "examine the implementation, effectiveness, and enforcement" of laws designed to prevent money laundering and the financing of terrorism. . . .

On the same day as the Financial Services Committee, the Permanent Select Committee on Intelligence issued an identical subpoena to Deutsche Bank—albeit for different reasons. According to the House, the Intelligence Committee subpoenaed Deutsche Bank as part of an investigation into foreign efforts to undermine the U.S. political process. . . .

Four days after the Financial Services and Intelligence Committees, the House Committee on Oversight and Reform issued another subpoena, this time to the President's personal accounting firm, Mazars USA, LLP. The subpoena demanded information related to the President and several affiliated business entities from 2011 through 2018, including statements of financial condition, independent auditors' reports, financial reports, underlying source documents, and communications between Mazars and the President or his businesses. The subpoena also requested all engagement agreements and contracts "[w]ithout regard to time.". . .

B

Petitioners—the President in his personal capacity, along with his children and affiliated businesses—filed two suits challenging the subpoenas. They contested the subpoena issued by the Oversight Committee in the District Court for the District of Columbia (*Mazars*), and the subpoenas issued by the Financial Services and Intelligence Committees in the Southern District of New York (*Deutsche Bank*). In both cases, petitioners contended that the subpoenas lacked a legitimate legislative purpose and violated the separation of powers. The President did not, however, resist the subpoenas by arguing that any of the requested records were protected by executive privilege. For relief, petitioners asked for declaratory judgments and injunctions preventing Mazars and the banks from complying with the subpoenas. Although named as defendants, Mazars and the banks took no positions on the legal issues in these cases, and the House committees intervened to defend the subpoenas. . . .

II

A

The question presented is whether the subpoenas exceed the authority of the House under the Constitution. Historically, disputes over congressional demands for presidential documents have not ended up in court. Instead, they have been hashed out in the "hurly-burly, the give-and-take of the political process between the legislative and the executive." A. Scalia, Assistant Attorney General, Office of Legal Counsel (1975).

That practice began with George Washington and the early Congress. In 1792, a House committee requested Executive Branch documents pertaining to General St. Clair's campaign against the Indians in the Northwest Territory, which had concluded in an utter rout of federal forces when they were caught by surprise near the present-day border between Ohio and Indiana. Since this was the first such request from Congress, President Washington called a Cabinet meeting, wishing to take care that his response "be rightly conducted" because it could "become a precedent."

The meeting, attended by the likes of Alexander Hamilton, Thomas Jefferson, Edmund Randolph, and Henry Knox, ended with the Cabinet of "one mind": The House had authority to "institute inquiries" and "call for papers" but the President could "exercise a discretion" over disclosures, "communicat[ing] such papers as the public good would permit" and "refus[ing]" the rest. President Washington then dispatched Jefferson to speak to individual congressmen and "bring them by persuasion into the right channel." The discussions were apparently fruitful, as the House later narrowed its request and the documents were supplied without recourse to the courts.

Jefferson, once he became President, followed Washington's precedent. In early 1807, after Jefferson had disclosed that "sundry persons" were conspiring to invade Spanish territory in North America with a private army, the House requested that the President produce any information in his possession touching on the conspiracy (except for information that would harm the public interest). Jefferson chose not to divulge the entire "voluminous" correspondence on the subject, explaining that much of it was "private" or mere "rumors" and "neither safety nor justice" permitted him to "expos[e] names" apart from identifying the conspiracy's "principal actor": Aaron Burr. Instead of the entire correspondence, Jefferson sent Congress particular documents and a special message summarizing the conspiracy. See generally *Vance*. Neither Congress nor the President asked the Judiciary to intervene.[2]

Ever since, congressional demands for the President's information have been resolved by the political branches without involving this Court. . . .

---

2. By contrast, later that summer, the Judiciary *was* called on to resolve whether President Jefferson could be issued a subpoena *duces tecum* arising from Burr's criminal trial. See *United States v. Burr* (CC Va. 1807); see also *Trump v. Vance*.

Congress and the President maintained this tradition of negotiation and compromise—without the involvement of this Court—until the present dispute. Indeed, from President Washington until now, we have never considered a dispute over a congressional subpoena for the President's records. And, according to the parties, the appellate courts have addressed such a subpoena only once, when a Senate committee subpoenaed President Nixon during the Watergate scandal. In that case, the court refused to enforce the subpoena, and the Senate did not seek review by this Court.

This dispute therefore represents a significant departure from historical practice. Although the parties agree that this particular controversy is justiciable, we recognize that it is the first of its kind to reach this Court; that disputes of this sort can raise important issues concerning relations between the branches; that related disputes involving congressional efforts to seek official Executive Branch information recur on a regular basis, including in the context of deeply partisan controversy; and that Congress and the Executive have nonetheless managed for over two centuries to resolve such disputes among themselves without the benefit of guidance from us. Such longstanding practice " 'is a consideration of great weight' " in cases concerning "the allocation of power between [the] two elected branches of Government," and it imposes on us a duty of care to ensure that we not needlessly disturb "the compromises and working arrangements that [those] branches . . . themselves have reached." *NLRB v. Noel Canning* (2014) (quoting *The Pocket Veto Case* (1929)). With that in mind, we turn to the question presented.

B

Congress has no enumerated constitutional power to conduct investigations or issue subpoenas, but we have held that each House has power "to secure needed information" in order to legislate. *McGrain v. Daugherty* (1927). . . .

Because this power is "justified solely as an adjunct to the legislative process," it is subject to several limitations. Most importantly, a congressional subpoena is valid only if it is "related to, and in furtherance of, a legitimate task of the Congress." The subpoena must serve a "valid legislative purpose," *Quinn v. United States* (1955); it must "concern[] a subject on which legislation 'could be had,' " *Eastland v. United States Servicemen's Fund* (1975).

Furthermore, Congress may not issue a subpoena for the purpose of "law enforcement," because "those powers are assigned under our Constitution to the Executive and the Judiciary." *Quinn.* Thus Congress may not use subpoenas to "try" someone "before [a] committee for any crime or wrongdoing." *McGrain.* Congress has no " 'general' power to inquire into private affairs and compel disclosures," and "there is no congressional power to expose for the sake of exposure," *Watkins.* "Investigations conducted solely for the personal aggrandizement of the investigators or to 'punish' those investigated are indefensible."

C

The President contends, as does the Solicitor General appearing on behalf of the United States, that the usual rules for congressional subpoenas do not govern here because the President's papers are at issue. They argue for a more demanding standard based in large part on cases involving the Nixon tapes — recordings of conversations between President Nixon and close advisers discussing the break-in at the Democratic National Committee's headquarters at the Watergate complex. The tapes were subpoenaed by a Senate committee and the Special Prosecutor investigating the break-in, prompting President Nixon to invoke executive privilege and leading to two cases addressing the showing necessary to require the President to comply with the subpoenas. See *Nixon*; *Senate Select Committee* (CADC).

Those cases, the President and the Solicitor General now contend, establish the standard that should govern the House subpoenas here. Quoting *Nixon*, the President asserts that the House must establish a "demonstrated, specific need" for the financial information, just as the Watergate special prosecutor was required to do in order to obtain the tapes. And drawing on *Senate Select Committee* — the D.C. Circuit case refusing to enforce the Senate subpoena for the tapes — the President and the Solicitor General argue that the House must show that the financial information is "demonstrably critical" to its legislative purpose.

We disagree that these demanding standards apply here. Unlike the cases before us, *Nixon* and *Senate Select Committee* involved Oval Office communications over which the President asserted executive privilege. That privilege safeguards the public interest in candid, confidential deliberations within the Executive Branch; it is "fundamental to the operation of Government." *Nixon*. As a result, information subject to executive privilege deserves "the greatest protection consistent with the fair administration of justice." We decline to transplant that protection root and branch to cases involving nonprivileged, private information, which by definition does not implicate sensitive Executive Branch deliberations.

The standards proposed by the President and the Solicitor General — if applied outside the context of privileged information — would risk seriously impeding Congress in carrying out its responsibilities. The President and the Solicitor General would apply the same exacting standards to *all* subpoenas for the President's information, without recognizing distinctions between privileged and nonprivileged information, between official and personal information, or between various legislative objectives. Such a categorical approach would represent a significant departure from the longstanding way of doing business between the branches, giving short shrift to Congress's important interests in conducting inquiries to obtain the information it needs to legislate effectively. . . .

Legislative inquiries might involve the President in appropriate cases; as noted, Congress's responsibilities extend to "every affair of government." *United States v. Rumely* (1953). Because the President's approach does not take adequate account of these significant congressional interests, we do not adopt it.

D

The House meanwhile would have us ignore that these suits involve the President. Invoking our precedents concerning investigations that did not target the President's papers, the House urges us to uphold its subpoenas because they "relate[ ] to a valid legislative purpose" or "concern[] a subject on which legislation could be had." That approach is appropriate, the House argues, because the cases before us are not "momentous separation-of-powers disputes." Largely following the House's lead, the courts below treated these cases much like any other, applying precedents that do not involve the President's papers. . . .

The House's approach fails to take adequate account of the significant separation of powers issues raised by congressional subpoenas for the President's information. Congress and the President have an ongoing institutional relationship as the "opposite and rival" political branches established by the Constitution. The Federalist No. 51. As a result, congressional subpoenas directed at the President differ markedly from congressional subpoenas we have previously reviewed, and they bear little resemblance to criminal subpoenas issued to the President in the course of a specific investigation, see *Vance*; *Nixon*. Unlike those subpoenas, congressional subpoenas for the President's information unavoidably pit the political branches against one another.

Far from accounting for separation of powers concerns, the House's approach aggravates them by leaving essentially no limits on the congressional power to subpoena the President's personal records. Any personal paper possessed by a President could potentially "relate to" a conceivable subject of legislation, for Congress has broad legislative powers that touch a vast number of subjects. The President's financial records could relate to economic reform, medical records to health reform, school transcripts to education reform, and so on. Indeed, at argument, the House was unable to identify *any* type of information that lacks some relation to potential legislation.

Without limits on its subpoena powers, Congress could "exert an imperious controul" over the Executive Branch and aggrandize itself at the President's expense, just as the Framers feared. The Federalist No. 71 (A. Hamilton); see *id.*, No. 48 (J. Madison); *Bowsher v. Synar* (1986). And a limitless subpoena power would transform the "established practice" of the political branches. *Noel Canning*. Instead of negotiating over information requests, Congress could simply walk away from the bargaining table and compel compliance in court.

The House and the courts below suggest that these separation of powers concerns are not fully implicated by the particular subpoenas here, but we disagree. We would have to be "blind" not to see what "[a]ll others can see and understand": that the subpoenas do not represent a run-of-the-mill legislative effort but rather a clash between rival branches of government over records of intense political interest for all involved. *Rumely* (quoting *Child Labor Tax Case* (1922) (Taft, C. J.)).

The interbranch conflict here does not vanish simply because the subpoenas seek personal papers or because the President sued in his personal capacity. The President is the only person who alone composes a branch of government. As a result, there is not always a clear line between his personal and official affairs. "The interest of the man" is often "connected with the constitutional rights of the place." The Federalist No. 51. Given the close connection between the Office of the President and its occupant, congressional demands for the President's papers can implicate the relationship between the branches regardless whether those papers are personal or official. Either way, a demand may aim to harass the President or render him "complaisan[t] to the humors of the Legislature." The Federalist No. 71. In fact, a subpoena for personal papers may pose a heightened risk of such impermissible purposes, precisely because of the documents' personal nature and their less evident connection to a legislative task. No one can say that the controversy here is less significant to the relationship between the branches simply because it involves personal papers. Quite the opposite. That appears to be what makes the matter of such great consequence to the President and Congress.

In addition, separation of powers concerns are no less palpable here simply because the subpoenas were issued to third parties. Congressional demands for the President's information present an interbranch conflict no matter where the information is held — it is, after all, the President's information. Were it otherwise, Congress could sidestep constitutional requirements any time a President's information is entrusted to a third party — as occurs with rapidly increasing frequency. Cf. *Carpenter v. United States* (2018). Indeed, Congress could declare open season on the President's information held by schools, archives, internet service providers, e-mail clients, and financial institutions. The Constitution does not tolerate such ready evasion; it "deals with substance, not shadows." *Cummings v. Missouri* (1867).

E

Congressional subpoenas for the President's personal information implicate weighty concerns regarding the separation of powers. Neither side, however, identifies an approach that accounts for these concerns. For more than two centuries, the political branches have resolved information disputes using the wide variety of means that the Constitution puts at their disposal. The nature of such interactions would be transformed by judicial enforcement of either of the approaches suggested by the parties, eroding a "[d]eeply embedded traditional way[] of conducting government." *Youngstown Sheet & Tube Co.* (Frankfurter, J., concurring).

A balanced approach is necessary, one that takes a "considerable impression" from "the practice of the government," *McCulloch v. Maryland* (1819); see *Noel Canning*, and "resist[s]" the "pressure inherent within each of the separate Branches to exceed the outer limits of its power," *INS v. Chadha* (1983). We therefore conclude that, in assessing whether a subpoena directed at the President's personal information is "related to, and in furtherance of, a legitimate task of the Congress," courts must perform a careful analysis that takes adequate account of the separation of powers principles at stake, including both the significant legislative interests of Congress and the "unique position" of the President. Several special considerations inform this analysis.

First, courts should carefully assess whether the asserted legislative purpose warrants the significant step of involving the President and his papers. . . . Congress may not rely on the President's information if other sources could reasonably provide Congress the information it needs in light of its particular legislative objective. The President's unique constitutional position means that Congress may not look to him as a "case study" for general legislation.

. . . While we certainly recognize Congress's important interests in obtaining information through appropriate inquiries, those interests are not sufficiently powerful to justify access to the President's personal papers when other sources could provide Congress the information it needs.

Second, to narrow the scope of possible conflict between the branches, courts should insist on a subpoena no broader than reasonably necessary to support Congress's legislative objective. The specificity of the subpoena's request "serves as an important safeguard against unnecessary intrusion into the operation of the Office of the President." *Cheney.*

Third, courts should be attentive to the nature of the evidence offered by Congress to establish that a subpoena advances a valid legislative purpose. The more detailed and substantial the evidence of Congress's legislative purpose, the better. That is particularly true when Congress contemplates legislation that raises sensitive constitutional issues, such as legislation concerning the Presidency. In such cases, it is "impossible" to conclude that a subpoena is designed to advance a valid legislative purpose unless Congress adequately identifies its aims and explains why the President's information will advance its consideration of the possible legislation.

Fourth, courts should be careful to assess the burdens imposed on the President by a subpoena. We have held that burdens on the President's time and attention stemming from judicial process and litigation, without more, generally do not cross constitutional lines. See *Vance*; *Clinton*. But burdens imposed by a congressional subpoena should be carefully scrutinized, for they stem from a rival political branch that has an ongoing relationship with the President and incentives to use subpoenas for institutional advantage.

Other considerations may be pertinent as well; one case every two centuries does not afford enough experience for an exhaustive list.

When Congress seeks information "needed for intelligent legislative action," it "unquestionably" remains "the duty of *all* citizens to cooperate." *Watkins.* Congressional subpoenas for information from the President, however, implicate special concerns regarding the separation of powers. The courts below did not take adequate account of those concerns. The judgments of the Courts of Appeals for the D. C. Circuit and the Second Circuit are vacated, and the cases are remanded for further proceedings consistent with this opinion.

JUSTICE THOMAS, dissenting.

Three Committees of the U.S. House of Representatives issued subpoenas to several accounting and financial firms to obtain the personal financial records of the President, his family, and several of his business entities. The Committees do not argue that these subpoenas were issued pursuant to the House's impeachment power. Instead, they argue that the subpoenas are a valid exercise of their legislative powers.

Petitioners challenge the validity of these subpoenas. In doing so, they call into question our precedents to the extent that they allow Congress to issue legislative subpoenas for the President's private, nonofficial documents. I would hold that Congress has no power to issue a legislative subpoena for private, nonofficial documents — whether they belong to the President or not. Congress may be able to obtain these documents as part of an investigation of the President, but to do so, it must proceed under the impeachment power. Accordingly, I would reverse the judgments of the Courts of Appeals.

I

I begin with the Committees' claim that the House's legislative powers include the implied power to issue legislative subpoenas. Although the Founders understood that the enumerated powers in the Constitution included implied powers, the Committees' test for the scope of those powers is too broad.

"The powers of the legislature are defined, and limited; and that those limits may not be mistaken, or forgotten, the constitution is written." *Marbury v. Madison* (1803). The structure of limited and enumerated powers in our Constitution denotes that "[o]ur system of government rests on one overriding principle: All power stems from the consent of the people." *U.S. Term Limits, Inc. v. Thornton* (1995) (Thomas, J., dissenting). As a result, Congress may exercise only those powers given by the people of the States through the Constitution.

The Founders nevertheless understood that an enumerated power could necessarily bring with it implied powers. The idea of implied powers usually arises in the context of the Necessary and Proper Clause, which gives Congress the power to "make all Laws which shall be necessary and proper for carrying into Execution the foregoing Powers, and all other Powers vested by this Constitution in the Government of the United States, or in any Department or Officer thereof." Art. I, §8, cl. 18. As I have previously explained, the Necessary and Proper Clause simply "made explicit what was already implicit in the grant of each enumerated power." *United States v. Comstock* (2010) (dissenting opinion). That is, "the grant of a general power includes the grant of incidental powers for carrying it out." Bray, "Necessary and Proper" and "Cruel and Unusual": Hendiadys in the Constitution (2016).

The scope of these implied powers is very limited. The Constitution does not sweep in powers "of inferior importance, merely because they are inferior." *McCulloch v. Maryland* (1819). Instead, Congress "can claim no powers which are not granted to it by the constitution, and the powers actually granted, must be such as are expressly given, or given by necessary implication." *Martin v. Hunter's Lessee* (1816). In sum, while the Committees' theory of an implied power is not categorically wrong, that power must be necessarily implied from an enumerated power.

II

At the time of the founding, the power to subpoena private, nonofficial documents was not included by necessary implication in any of Congress' legislative powers. This understanding persisted for decades and is consistent with the Court's first decision addressing legislative subpoenas, *Kilbourn v. Thompson* (1881). The test that this Court created in *McGrain v. Daugherty*, 273 U.S. 135 (1927), and the majority's variation on that standard today, are without support as applied to private, nonofficial documents.[1]

A

The Committees argue that Congress wields the same investigatory powers that the British Parliament did at the time of the founding. But this claim overlooks one of the fundamental differences between our Government and the British Government: Parliament was supreme. Congress is not.

I have previously explained that "the founding generation did not subscribe to Blackstone's view of parliamentary supremacy." *Department of Transportation v. Association of American Railroads*, (2015) (opinion concurring in judgment). . . . This significant difference means that Parliament's powers and Congress' powers are not necessarily the same.

In fact, the plain text of the Constitution makes clear that they are not. The Constitution expressly denies to Congress some of the powers that Parliament exercised. Article I, for example, prohibits bills of attainder, §9, cl. 3, which Parliament used to "sentenc[e] to death one or more specific persons." *United States v. Brown* (1965). A legislature can hardly be considered supreme if it lacks the power to pass bills of attainder, which Justice Story called the "highest power of sovereignty." Relatedly, the Constitution prohibits *ex post facto* laws, §9, cl. 3, reinforcing the fact that Congress' power to punish is limited.[2] And in a system in which Congress is not supreme, the individual protections in the Bill of Rights, such as the prohibition on unreasonable searches and seizures, meaningfully constrain Congress' power to compel documents from private citizens.

. . . At bottom, *Kilbourn* recognized that legislative supremacy was decisively rejected in the framing and ratification of our Constitution, which casts doubt on the Committees' claim that they have power to issue legislative subpoenas to private parties. . . .

---

1. I express no opinion about the constitutionality of legislative subpoenas for other kinds of evidence.

2. The Constitution also enumerates a limited set of congressional privileges. Although I express no opinion on the question, at least one early commentator thought the canon of *expressio unius* meant that Congress had no unenumerated privileges, such as the power to hold nonmembers in contempt.

C

Given that Congress has no exact precursor in England or colonial America, founding-era congressional practice is especially informative about the scope of implied legislative powers. Thus, it is highly probative that no founding-era Congress issued a subpoena for private, nonofficial documents. Although respondents could not identify the first such legislative subpoena at oral argument, Congress began issuing them by the end of the 1830s. However, the practice remained controversial in Congress and this Court throughout the first century of the Republic.

1

In an attempt to establish the power of Congress to issue legislative subpoenas, the Committees point to an investigation of Government affairs and an investigation under one of Congress' enumerated privileges. Both precedents are materially different from the subpoenas here.

In 1792, the House authorized a Committee to investigate a failed military expedition led by General Arthur St. Clair. . . . But the Committee never subpoenaed private, nonofficial documents, which is telling. . . . Thus, the power to subpoena private documents, which the Committee did not exercise, is a far greater power and much less likely to be implied in Congress' legislative powers.

In 1832, the House investigated Representative Samuel Houston for assaulting Representative William Stanberry. . . . The House subpoenaed witnesses to testify, and one of them brought official correspondence between the Secretary of War and the President. But official documents are obviously different from nonofficial documents. Moreover, the subpoenas were issued pursuant to the House's enumerated privilege of punishing its own Members, Art. I, §5, not as part of its legislative powers. Because these subpoenas were not issued pursuant to a legislative power, they do not aid the Committees' case. . . .

3

By the end of the 1830s, Congress began issuing legislative subpoenas for private, nonofficial documents. Still, the power to demand information from private parties during legislative investigations remained controversial.

In 1832, the House authorized a Committee to "inspect the books, and to examine into the proceedings of the Bank of the United States, to report thereon, and to report whether the provisions of its charter have been violated or not." The investigation itself appears to have ranged more widely, however, leading Congressman John Quincy Adams to criticize . . . that such an investigation "bears all the exceptionable and odious properties of general warrants and domiciliary visits." He also objected that the Committee's investigation of the Bank was tantamount to punishment and thus was in tension with the constitutional prohibitions on "passing any bill of attainder [or] *ex post facto* law." Thus, even when Congress authorized a Committee to send for private papers, the constitutionality of doing so was questioned. . . .

4

When this Court first addressed a legislative subpoena, it refused to uphold it. After casting doubt on legislative subpoenas generally, the Court in *Kilbourn v. Thompson*, held that the subpoena at issue was unlawful because it sought to investigate private conduct. . . . The Court thus rejected the notion that Congress inherited from Parliament an implied power to issue legislative subpoenas.

The Court did not reach a conclusion on the second theory that a legislative subpoena power was necessary for Congress to carry out its legislative duties. But it observed that, based on British judicial opinions, not "much aid [is] given to the doctrine, that this power exists as one necessary to enable either House of Congress to exercise successfully their function of legislation." The Court referred to a collection of 18th- and 19th-century English decisions grounding the Parliamentary subpoena power in that body's judicial origins. . . .

. . . Although the Court did not have occasion to decide whether the legislative subpoena in that case was necessary to the exercise of Congress' legislative powers, its discussion strongly suggests the subpoena was unconstitutional.[3]

. . . Even though the Court decided *Kilbourn* narrowly, it clearly entertained substantial doubts about the constitutionality of legislative subpoenas for private documents.

D

Nearly half a century later, in *McGrain v. Daugherty*, the Court reached the question reserved in *Kilbourn*—whether Congress has the power to issue legislative subpoenas. It rejected *Kilbourn*'s reasoning and upheld the power to issue legislative subpoenas as long as they were relevant to a legislative power. Although *McGrain* involved oral testimony, the Court has since extended this test to subpoenas for private documents. The Committees rely on *McGrain*, but this line of cases misunderstands both the original meaning of Article I and the historical practice underlying it.

1

. . . The Court concluded that, "[i]n actual legislative practice[,] power to secure needed information by [investigating and compelling testimony] has long

---

3. According to Justice Miller's private letters, "a majority of the Court, including Miller himself, were of the opinion that neither House nor Senate had power to punish for contempt witnesses who refused to testify before investigating committees." Only Justice Miller's desire to " 'decid[e] no more than is necessary' " caused the Court to avoid the broader question.

been treated as an attribute of the power to legislate." *McGrain.* . . . But the authority cited by the Court did not support that proposition. The Court cited the 1792 investigation of St. Clair's defeat, in which it appears no subpoena was issued, and the 1859 Senate investigation of John Brown's raid on Harper's Ferry, which led to an impassioned debate. Thus, for the reasons explained above, the examples relied on in *McGrain* are materially different from issuing a legislative subpoena for private, nonofficial documents.[5]

The Court acknowledged *Kilbourn,* but erroneously distinguished its discussion regarding the constitutionality of legislative subpoenas as immaterial dicta. . . .

Instead of relying on *Kilbourn*'s analysis, *McGrain* developed a test that rested heavily on functional considerations. . . . The Court thus concluded that Congress could issue legislative subpoenas, provided that "the purpose for which the witness's testimony was sought was to obtain information in aid of the legislative function." The Court has since applied this test to subpoenas for papers without any further analysis of the text or history of the Constitution. See *Eastland v. United States Servicemen's Fund* (1975). The majority today modifies that test for cases involving the President, but it leaves the core of the power untouched.

2

The opinion in *McGrain* lacks any foundation in text or history with respect to subpoenas for private, nonofficial documents. It fails to recognize that Congress, unlike Parliament, is not supreme. It does not cite any specific precedent for issuing legislative subpoenas for private documents from 18th-century colonial or state practice. And it identifies no founding-era legislative subpoenas for private documents.

Since *McGrain,* the Court has pared back Congress' authority to compel testimony and documents. It has held that certain convictions of witnesses for contempt of Congress violated the Fifth Amendment. It has also affirmed the reversal of a conviction on the ground that the Committee lacked authority to issue the subpoena. See *United States v. Rumely* (1953). And today, it creates a new four-part, nonexhaustive test for cases involving the President. Rather than continue our trend of trying to compensate for *McGrain*, I would simply decline to apply it in these cases because it is readily apparent that the Committees have no constitutional authority to subpoena private, nonofficial documents.

---

5. The Court also cited decisions between 1858 and 1913 from state courts and a Canadian court, none of which are persuasive evidence about the original meaning of the U.S. Constitution.

III

If the Committees wish to investigate alleged wrongdoing by the President and obtain documents from him, the Constitution provides Congress with a special mechanism for doing so: impeachment.[7]

A

It is often acknowledged, "if only half-heartedly honored," that one of the motivating principles of our Constitution is the separation of powers. *Association of American Railroads* (Thomas, J., concurring in judgment). The Framers recognized that there are three forms of governmental power: legislative, executive and judicial. The Framers also created three branches: Congress, the President, and the Judiciary. The three powers largely align with the three branches. To a limited extent, however, the Constitution contains "a partial intermixture of those departments for special purposes." The Federalist No. 66 (A. Hamilton). One of those special purposes is the system of checks and balances, and impeachment is one of those checks.

The Constitution grants the House "the sole Power of Impeachment," Art. I, §2, cl. 5, and it specifies that the President may be impeached for "Treason, Bribery, or other high Crimes and Misdemeanors," Art. II, §4. The founding generation understood impeachment as a check on Presidential abuses. In response to charges that impeachment "confounds legislative and judiciary authorities in the same body," Alexander Hamilton called it "an essential check in the hands of [Congress] upon the encroachments of the executive." The Federalist No. 66. And, in the Virginia ratifying convention, James Madison identified impeachment as a check on Presidential abuse of the treaty power.

B

The power to impeach includes a power to investigate and demand documents. Impeachments in the States often involved an investigation. . . .

Other evidence from the 1790s confirms that the power to investigate includes the power to demand documents. When the House of Representatives sought documents related to the Jay Treaty from President George Washington, he refused to provide them on the ground that the House had no legislative powers relating to the ratification of treaties. But he carefully noted that "[i]t does not occur that the inspection of the papers asked for can be relative to any purpose under the cognizance of the House of Representatives, except that of an impeachment;

---

7. I express no view on whether there are any limitations on the impeachment power that would prevent the House from subpoenaing the documents at issue.

which the resolution has not expressed." In other words, he understood that the House can demand documents as part of its power to impeach. . . .

I express no view today on the boundaries of the power to demand documents in connection with impeachment proceedings. But the power of impeachment provides the House with authority to investigate and hold accountable Presidents who commit high crimes or misdemeanors. That is the proper path by which the Committees should pursue their demands.

IV

For nearly two centuries, until the 1970s, Congress never attempted to subpoena documents to investigate wrongdoing by the President outside the context of impeachment. Congress investigated Presidents without opening impeachment proceedings. But it never issued a subpoena for private, nonofficial documents as part of those non-impeachment inquiries. . . .

Insisting that the House proceed through its impeachment power is not a mere formality. Unlike contempt, which is governed by the rules of each chamber, impeachment and removal constitutionally requires a majority vote by the House and a two-thirds vote by the Senate. Art. I, §2, cl. 5; §3, cl. 6. In addition, Congress has long thought it necessary to provide certain procedural safeguards to officials facing impeachment and removal. Finally, initiating impeachment proceedings signals to the public the gravity of seeking the removal of a constitutional officer at the head of a coordinate branch. *Mazars* (CADC 2019) (Rao, J., dissenting).

* * *

Congress' legislative powers do not authorize it to engage in a nationwide inquisition with whatever resources it chooses to appropriate for itself. The majority's solution—a nonexhaustive four-factor test of uncertain origin—is better than nothing. But the power that Congress seeks to exercise here has even less basis in the Constitution than the majority supposes. I would reverse in full because the power to subpoena private, nonofficial documents is not a necessary implication of Congress' legislative powers. If Congress wishes to obtain these documents, it should proceed through the impeachment power. Accordingly, I respectfully dissent.

JUSTICE ALITO, dissenting.

Justice Thomas makes a valuable argument about the constitutionality of congressional subpoenas for a President's personal documents. In these cases, however, I would assume for the sake of argument that such subpoenas are not categorically barred. Nevertheless, legislative subpoenas for a President's personal documents are inherently suspicious. Such documents are seldom of any special value in considering potential legislation, and subpoenas for such documents can easily be used for improper non-legislative purposes. Accordingly, courts must be very sensitive to separation of powers issues when they are asked to approve the enforcement of such subpoenas.

In many cases, disputes about subpoenas for Presidential documents are fought without judicial involvement. If Congress attempts to obtain such documents by subpoenaing a President directly, those two heavyweight institutions can use their considerable weapons to settle the matter. But when Congress issues such a subpoena to a third party, Congress must surely appreciate that the Judiciary may be pulled into the dispute, and Congress should not expect that the courts will allow the subpoena to be enforced without seriously examining its legitimacy.

Whenever such a subpoena comes before a court, Congress should be required to make more than a perfunctory showing that it is seeking the documents for a legitimate legislative purpose and not for the purpose of exposing supposed Presidential wrongdoing. The House can inquire about possible Presidential wrongdoing pursuant to its impeachment power, but the Committees do not defend these subpoenas as ancillary to that power.

Instead, they claim that the subpoenas were issued to gather information that is relevant to legislative issues, but there is disturbing evidence of an improper law enforcement purpose. In addition, the sheer volume of documents sought calls out for explanation.

The Court recognizes that the decisions below did not give adequate consideration to separation of powers concerns. Therefore, after setting out a non-exhaustive list of considerations for the lower courts to take into account, the Court vacates the judgments of the Courts of Appeals and sends the cases back for reconsideration. I agree that the lower courts erred and that these cases must be remanded, but I do not think that the considerations outlined by the Court can be properly satisfied unless the House is required to show more than it has put forward to date.

Specifically, the House should provide a description of the type of legislation being considered, and while great specificity is not necessary, the description should be sufficient to permit a court to assess whether the particular records sought are of any special importance. The House should also spell out its constitutional authority to enact the type of legislation that it is contemplating, and it should justify the scope of the subpoenas in relation to the articulated legislative needs. In addition, it should explain why the subpoenaed information, as opposed to information available from other sources, is needed. Unless the House is required to make a showing along these lines, I would hold that enforcement of the subpoenas cannot be ordered. Because I find the terms of the Court's remand inadequate, I must respectfully dissent.

Chapter 8

The Political Question Doctrine

STUDY GUIDE:

- Why are *racial* gerrymandering claims justiciable, but partisan gerrymandering claims are not justiciable?
- Justice Kagan's dissent began "For the first time ever, this Court refuses to remedy a constitutional violation because it thinks the task beyond judicial capabilities." Can you think of other cases where the Court reached such a conclusion?
- What other remedies do the people have to reduce or eliminate partisan gerrmandering?

Rucho v. Common Cause
588 U.S. ___ (2019)

CHIEF JUSTICE ROBERTS delivered the opinion of the Court.

Voters and other plaintiffs in North Carolina and Maryland challenged their States' congressional districting maps as unconstitutional partisan gerrymanders. The North Carolina plaintiffs complained that the State's districting plan discriminated against Democrats; the Maryland plaintiffs complained that their State's plan discriminated against Republicans. The plaintiffs alleged that the gerrymandering violated the First Amendment, the Equal Protection Clause of the Fourteenth Amendment, the Elections Clause, and Article I, §2, of the Constitution. The District Courts in both cases ruled in favor of the plaintiffs, and the defendants appealed directly to this Court.

These cases require us to consider once again whether claims of excessive partisanship in districting are "justiciable"—that is, properly suited for resolution by the federal courts. This Court has not previously struck down a districting plan as an unconstitutional partisan gerrymander, and has struggled without success over the past several decades to discern judicially manageable standards for deciding such claims. The districting plans at issue here are highly partisan, by any measure. The question is whether the courts below appropriately exercised judicial power when they found them unconstitutional as well.

I

A

The first case involves a challenge to the congressional redistricting plan enacted by the Republican-controlled North Carolina General Assembly in 2016. The Republican legislators leading the redistricting effort instructed their mapmaker to use political data to draw a map that would produce a congressional delegation of ten Republicans and three Democrats. As one of the two Republicans chairing the redistricting committee stated, "I think electing Republicans is better than electing Democrats. So I drew this map to help foster what I think is better for the country." He further explained that the map was drawn with the aim of electing ten Republicans and three Democrats because he did "not believe it [would be] possible to draw a map with 11 Republicans and 2 Democrats." One Democratic state senator objected that entrenching the 10-3 advantage for Republicans was not "fair, reasonable, [or] balanced" because, as recently as 2012, "Democratic congressional candidates had received more votes on a statewide basis than Republican candidates." The General Assembly was not swayed by that objection and approved the 2016 Plan by a party-line vote. . . .

B

The second case before us is *Lamone v. Benisek.* In 2011, the Maryland Legislature — dominated by Democrats — undertook to redraw the lines of that State's eight congressional districts. The Governor at the time, Democrat Martin O'Malley, led the process. . . . The Governor later testified that his aim was to "use the redistricting process to change the overall composition of Maryland's congressional delegation to 7 Democrats and 1 Republican by flipping" one district. . . . Overall, the Plan reduced the number of registered Republicans in the Sixth District by about 66,000 and increased the number of registered Democrats by about 24,000. The map was adopted by a party-line vote. It was used in the 2012 election and succeeded in flipping the Sixth District. A Democrat has held the seat ever since. . . .

II

A

Article III of the Constitution limits federal courts to deciding "Cases" and "Controversies." We have understood that limitation to mean that federal courts can address only questions "historically viewed as capable of resolution through the judicial process." *Flast v. Cohen* (1968). In these cases we are asked to decide an important question of constitutional law. "But before we do so, we must find that the question is presented in a 'case' or 'controversy' that is, in James Madison's words, 'of a Judiciary Nature.'" 2 Records of the Federal Convention of 1787, p. 430 (M. Farrand ed. 1966).

Chief Justice Marshall famously wrote that it is "the province and duty of the judicial department to say what the law is." *Marbury v. Madison* (1803). Sometimes, however, "the law is that the judicial department has no business entertaining the claim of unlawfulness—because the question is entrusted to one of the political branches or involves no judicially enforceable rights." *Vieth v. Jubelirer* (2004). In such a case the claim is said to present a "political question" and to be nonjusticiable—outside the courts' competence and therefore beyond the courts' jurisdiction. *Baker v. Carr* (1962). Among the political question cases the Court has identified are those that lack "judicially discoverable and manageable standards for resolving [them]."

Last Term in *Gill v. Whitford*, we reviewed our partisan gerrymandering cases and concluded that those cases "leave unresolved whether such claims may be brought." This Court's authority to act, as we said in *Gill*, is "grounded in and limited by the necessity of resolving, according to legal principles, a plaintiff's particular claim of legal right." The question here is whether there is an "appropriate role for the Federal Judiciary" in remedying the problem of partisan gerrymandering—whether such claims are claims of *legal* right, resolvable according to *legal* principles, or political questions that must find their resolution elsewhere.

B

Partisan gerrymandering is nothing new. Nor is frustration with it. The practice was known in the Colonies prior to Independence, and the Framers were familiar with it at the time of the drafting and ratification of the Constitution. During the very first congressional elections, George Washington and his Federalist allies accused Patrick Henry of trying to gerrymander Virginia's districts against their candidates—in particular James Madison, who ultimately prevailed over fellow future President James Monroe.

In 1812, Governor of Massachusetts and future Vice President Elbridge Gerry notoriously approved congressional districts that the legislature had drawn to aid the Democratic-Republican Party. The moniker "gerrymander" was born when an outraged Federalist newspaper observed that one of the misshapen districts resembled a salamander.

The Framers addressed the election of Representatives to Congress in the Elections Clause. Art. I, §4, cl. 1. That provision assigns to state legislatures the power to prescribe the "Times, Places and Manner of holding Elections" for Members of Congress, while giving Congress the power to "make or alter" any such regulations. Whether to give that supervisory authority to the National Government was debated at the Constitutional Convention. When those opposed to such congressional oversight moved to strike the relevant language, Madison came to its defense:

> "[T]he State Legislatures will sometimes fail or refuse to consult the common interest at the expense of their local coveniency or prejudices. . . . Whenever the State Legislatures had a favorite measure to carry, they would take care so to mould their regulations as to favor the candidates they wished to succeed."

During the subsequent fight for ratification, the provision remained a subject of debate. Antifederalists predicted that Congress's power under the Elections Clause would allow Congress to make itself "omnipotent," setting the "time" of elections as never or the "place" in difficult to reach corners of the State. Federalists responded that, among other justifications, the revisionary power was necessary to counter state legislatures set on undermining fair representation, including through malapportionment. The Federalists were, for example, concerned that newly developing population centers would be deprived of their proper electoral weight, as some cities had been in Great Britain.

Congress has regularly exercised its Elections Clause power, including to address partisan gerrymandering. The Apportionment Act of 1842, which required single-member districts for the first time, specified that those districts be "composed of contiguous territory," in "an attempt to forbid the practice of the gerrymander." . . . Congress also used its Elections Clause power in 1870, enacting the first comprehensive federal statute dealing with elections as a way to enforce the Fifteenth Amendment. . . .

Appellants suggest that, through the Elections Clause, the Framers set aside electoral issues such as the one before us as questions that only Congress can resolve. We do not agree. In two areas — one-person, one-vote and racial gerrymandering — our cases have held that there is a role for the courts with respect to at least some issues that could arise from a State's drawing of congressional districts. See *Wesberry v. Sanders* (1964); *Shaw v. Reno* (1993).

But the history is not irrelevant. The Framers were aware of electoral districting problems and considered what to do about them. They settled on a characteristic approach, assigning the issue to the state legislatures, expressly checked and balanced by the Federal Congress. As Alexander Hamilton explained, "it will . . . not be denied that a discretionary power over elections ought to exist somewhere. It will, I presume, be as readily conceded that there were only three ways in which this power could have been reasonably modified and disposed: that it must either have been lodged wholly in the national legislature, or wholly in the State legislatures, or primarily in the latter, and ultimately in the former." The Federalist No. 59. At no point was there a suggestion that the federal courts had a role to play. Nor was there any indication that the Framers had ever heard of courts doing such a thing.

C

Courts have nevertheless been called upon to resolve a variety of questions surrounding districting. Early on, doubts were raised about the competence of the federal courts to resolve those questions.

In the leading case of *Baker v. Carr*, voters in Tennessee complained that the State's districting plan for state representatives "debase[d]" their votes, because the plan was predicated on a 60-year-old census that no longer reflected the distribution of population in the State. The plaintiffs argued that votes of people in overpopulated districts held less value than those of people in less-populated districts, and that this inequality violated the Equal Protection Clause of the Fourteenth Amendment. The District Court dismissed the action on the ground that the claim was not justiciable, relying on this Court's precedents, including *Colegrove*. This Court reversed. It identified various considerations relevant to determining whether a claim is a nonjusticiable political question, including whether there is "a lack of judicially discoverable and manageable standards for resolving it." The Court concluded that the claim of population inequality among districts did not fall into that category, because such a claim could be decided under basic equal protection principles. In *Wesberry v. Sanders*, the Court extended its ruling to malapportionment of congressional districts, holding that Article I, §2, required that "one man's vote in a congressional election is to be worth as much as another's."

Another line of challenges to districting plans has focused on race. Laws that explicitly discriminate on the basis of race, as well as those that are race neutral on their face but are unexplainable on grounds other than race, are of course presumptively invalid. The Court applied those principles to electoral boundaries in *Gomillion v. Lightfoot*, concluding that a challenge to an "uncouth twenty-eight sided" municipal boundary line that excluded black voters from city elections stated a constitutional claim. . . .

Partisan gerrymandering claims have proved far more difficult to adjudicate. The basic reason is that, while it is illegal for a jurisdiction to depart from the one-person, one-vote rule, or to engage in racial discrimination in districting, "a jurisdiction may engage in constitutional political gerrymandering." *Hunt v. Cromartie* (1999).

To hold that legislators cannot take partisan interests into account when drawing district lines would essentially countermand the Framers' decision to entrust districting to political entities. The "central problem" is not determining whether a jurisdiction has engaged in partisan gerrymandering. It is "determining when political gerrymandering has gone too far." . . .

III

A

In considering whether partisan gerrymandering claims are justiciable, we are mindful of Justice Kennedy's counsel in *Vieth*: Any standard for resolving such claims must be grounded in a "limited and precise rationale" and be "clear, manageable, and politically neutral." An important reason for those careful constraints is that, as a Justice with extensive experience in state and local politics put it, "[t]he opportunity to control the drawing of electoral boundaries through the legislative process of apportionment is a critical and traditional part of politics in the United States." *Bandemer* (O'Connor, J.). An expansive standard requiring "the correction of all election district lines drawn for partisan reasons would commit federal and state courts to unprecedented intervention in the American political process," *Vieth* (Kennedy, J.).

As noted, the question is one of degree: How to "provid[e] a standard for deciding how much partisan dominance is too much." *Vieth* (Kennedy, J.). And it is vital in such circumstances that the Court act only in accord with especially clear standards: "With uncertain limits, intervening courts—even when proceeding with best intentions—would risk assuming political, not legal, responsibility for a process that often produces ill will and distrust." *Vieth* (Kennedy, J.). If federal courts are to "inject [themselves] into the most heated partisan issues" by adjudicating partisan gerrymandering claims, *Bandemer*, (O'Connor, J.), they must be armed with a standard that can reliably differentiate unconstitutional from "constitutional political gerrymandering."

B

Partisan gerrymandering claims rest on an instinct that groups with a certain level of political support should enjoy a commensurate level of political power and influence. Explicitly or implicitly, a districting map is alleged to be unconstitutional because it makes it too difficult for one party to translate statewide support into seats in the legislature. But such a claim is based on a "norm that does not exist" in our electoral system—"statewide elections for representatives along party lines." *Bandemer* (O'Connor, J.).

Partisan gerrymandering claims invariably sound in a desire for proportional representation. . . . The Founders certainly did not think proportional representation was required. For more than 50 years after ratification of the Constitution, many States elected their congressional representatives through at-large or "general ticket" elections. Such States typically sent single-party delegations to Congress. That meant that a party could garner nearly half of the vote statewide and wind up without any seats in the congressional delegation. . . .

Unable to claim that the Constitution requires proportional representation outright, plaintiffs inevitably ask the courts to make their own political judgment about how much representation particular political parties *deserve*—based on the votes of their supporters—and to rearrange the challenged districts to achieve that end. But federal courts are not equipped to apportion political power as a matter of fairness, nor is there any basis for concluding that they were authorized to do so. . . .

The initial difficulty in settling on a "clear, manageable and politically neutral" test for fairness is that it is not even clear what fairness looks like in this context. There is a large measure of "unfairness" in any winner-take-all system. Fairness may mean a greater number of competitive districts. Such a claim seeks to undo packing and cracking so that supporters of the disadvantaged party have a better shot at electing their preferred candidates. But making as many districts as possible more competitive could be a recipe for disaster for the disadvantaged party. . . .

On the other hand, perhaps the ultimate objective of a "fairer" share of seats in the congressional delegation is most readily achieved by yielding to the gravitational pull of proportionality and engaging in cracking and packing, to ensure each party its "appropriate" share of "safe" seats. [A "cracked" district is one in which a party's supporters are divided among multiple districts, so that they fall short of a majority in each; a "packed" district is one in which a party's supporters are highly concentrated, so they win that district by a large margin, "wasting" many votes that would improve their chances in others.—Eds.] Such an approach, however, comes at the expense of competitive districts and of individuals in districts allocated to the opposing party.

Or perhaps fairness should be measured by adherence to "traditional" districting criteria, such as maintaining political subdivisions, keeping communities of interest together, and protecting incumbents. But protecting incumbents, for example, enshrines a particular partisan distribution. And the "natural political geography" of a State—such as the fact that urban electoral districts are often dominated by one political party—can itself lead to inherently packed districts. . . .

Deciding among just these different visions of fairness (you can imagine many others) poses basic questions that are political, not legal. There are no legal standards discernible in the Constitution for making such judgments, let alone limited and precise standards that are clear, manageable, and politically neutral. Any judicial decision on what is "fair" in this context would be an "unmoored determination" of the sort characteristic of a political question beyond the competence of the federal courts. *Zivotofsky v. Clinton* (2012).

And it is only after determining how to define fairness that you can even begin to answer the determinative question: "How much is too much?" At what point does permissible partisanship become unconstitutional? If compliance with traditional districting criteria is the fairness touchstone, for example, how much deviation from those criteria is constitutionally acceptable and how should mapdrawers prioritize competing criteria? Should a court "reverse gerrymander" other parts of a State to counteract "natural" gerrymandering caused, for example, by the urban concentration of one party? If a districting plan protected half of the incumbents but redistricted the rest into head to head races, would that be constitutional? A court would have to rank the relative importance of those traditional criteria and weigh how much deviation from each to allow.

If a court instead focused on the respective number of seats in the legislature, it would have to decide the ideal number of seats for each party and determine at what point deviation from that balance went too far. If a 5-3 allocation corresponds most closely to statewide vote totals, is a 6-2 allocation permissible, given that legislatures have the authority to engage in a certain degree of partisan gerrymandering? Which seats should be packed and which cracked? Or if the goal is as many competitive districts as possible, how close does the split need to be for the district to be considered competitive? Presumably not all districts could qualify, so how to choose? Even assuming the court knew which version of fairness to be looking for, there are no discernible and manageable standards for deciding whether there has been a violation. The questions are "unguided and ill suited to the development of judicial standards," *Vieth*, and "results from one gerrymandering case to the next would likely be disparate and inconsistent," *id.*

Appellees contend that if we can adjudicate one-person, one-vote claims, we can also assess partisan gerrymandering claims. But the one-person, one-vote rule is relatively easy to administer as a matter of math. The same cannot be said of partisan gerrymandering claims, because the Constitution supplies no objective measure for assessing whether a districting map treats a political party fairly. It hardly follows from the principle that each person must have an equal say in the election of representatives that a person is entitled to have his political party achieve representation in some way commensurate to its share of statewide support.

More fundamentally, "vote dilution" in the one-person, one-vote cases refers to the idea that each vote must carry equal weight. In other words, each representative must be accountable to (approximately) the same number of constituents. That requirement does not extend to political parties. It does not mean that each party must be influential in proportion to its number of supporters. . . .

Nor do our racial gerrymandering cases provide an appropriate standard for assessing partisan gerrymandering. Unlike partisan gerrymandering claims, a racial gerrymandering claim does not ask for a fair share of political power and influence, with all the justiciability conundrums that entails. It asks instead for the elimination of a racial classification. A partisan gerrymandering claim cannot ask for the elimination of partisanship.

IV

Appellees and the dissent propose a number of "tests" for evaluating partisan gerrymandering claims, but none meets the need for a limited and precise standard that is judicially discernible and manageable. And none provides a solid grounding for judges to take the extraordinary step of reallocating power and influence between political parties. . . . [A]after a prima facie showing of partisan vote dilution, the District Court shifted the burden to the defendants to prove that the discriminatory effects are "attributable to a legitimate state interest or other neutral explanation." *Id.* . . . It is hard to see what the District Court's third prong—providing the defendant an opportunity to show that the discriminatory effects were due to a "legitimate redistricting objective"—adds to the inquiry. The first prong already requires the plaintiff to prove that partisan advantage predominates. Asking whether a legitimate purpose other than partisanship was the motivation for a particular districting map just restates the question.

B

. . . Both District Courts concluded that the districting plans at issue violated the plaintiffs' First Amendment right to association. . . . To begin, there are no restrictions on speech, association, or any other First Amendment activities in the districting plans at issue. The plaintiffs are free to engage in those activities no matter what the effect of a plan may be on their district.

The plaintiffs' argument is that partisanship in districting should be regarded as simple discrimination against supporters of the opposing party on the basis of political viewpoint. Under that theory, any level of partisanship in districting would constitute an infringement of their First Amendment rights. . . . The First Amendment test simply describes the act of districting for partisan advantage. It provides no standard for determining when partisan activity goes too far. . . .

These cases involve blatant examples of partisanship driving districting decisions. But the First Amendment analysis below offers no "clear" and "manageable" way of distinguishing permissible from impermissible partisan motivation. . . .

C

The dissent proposes using a State's own districting criteria as a neutral baseline from which to measure how extreme a partisan gerrymander is. The dissent would have us line up all the possible maps drawn using those criteria according to the partisan distribution they would produce. Distance from the "median" map would indicate whether a particular districting plan harms supporters of one party to an unconstitutional extent.

As an initial matter, it does not make sense to use criteria that will vary from State to State and year to year as the baseline for determining whether a gerrymander violates the Federal Constitution. The degree of partisan advantage that the Constitution tolerates should not turn on criteria offered by the gerrymanderers themselves. It is easy to imagine how different criteria could move the median map toward different partisan distributions. As a result, the same map could be constitutional or not depending solely on what the mapmakers said they set out to do. That possibility illustrates that the dissent's proposed constitutional test is indeterminate and arbitrary.

Even if we were to accept the dissent's proposed baseline, it would return us to "the original unanswerable question (How much political motivation and effect is too much?)." *Vieth* . . . The dissent's answer says it all: "This much is too much." That is not even trying to articulate a standard or rule. . . . There is no way to tell whether the prohibited deviation from that map should kick in at 25 percent or 75 percent or some other point. The only provision in the Constitution that specifically addresses the matter assigns it to the political branches. See Art. I, §4, cl. 1.

D

The North Carolina District Court further concluded that the 2016 Plan violated the Elections Clause and Article I, §2. We are unconvinced by that novel approach.

Article I, §2, provides that "[t]he House of Representatives shall be composed of Members chosen every second Year by the People of the several States." The Elections Clause provides that "[t]he Times, Places and Manner of holding

Elections for Senators and Representatives, shall be prescribed in each State by the Legislature thereof; but the Congress may at any time by Law make or alter such Regulations, except as to the Places of chusing [sic] Senators." Art. I, §4, cl. 1.

The District Court concluded that the 2016 Plan exceeded the North Carolina General Assembly's Elections Clause authority because, among other reasons, "the Elections Clause did not empower State legislatures to disfavor the interests of supporters of a particular candidate or party in drawing congressional districts." The court further held that partisan gerrymandering infringes the right of "the People" to select their representatives. Before the District Court's decision, no court had reached a similar conclusion. In fact, the plurality in *Vieth* concluded—without objection from any other Justice—that neither §2 nor §4 of Article I "provides a judicially enforceable limit on the political considerations that the States and Congress may take into account when districting."

The District Court nevertheless asserted that partisan gerrymanders violate "the core principle of [our] republican government" preserved in Art. I, §2, "namely, that the voters should choose their representatives, not the other way around." That seems like an objection more properly grounded in the Guarantee Clause of Article IV, §4, which "guarantee[s] to every State in [the] Union a Republican Form of Government." This Court has several times concluded, however, that the Guarantee Clause does not provide the basis for a justiciable claim.

V

Excessive partisanship in districting leads to results that reasonably seem unjust. But the fact that such gerrymandering is "incompatible with democratic principles," does not mean that the solution lies with the federal judiciary. We conclude that partisan gerrymandering claims present political questions beyond the reach of the federal courts. Federal judges have no license to reallocate political power between the two major political parties, with no plausible grant of authority in the Constitution, and no legal standards to limit and direct their decisions. "[J]udicial action must be governed by *standard*, by *rule*," and must be "principled, rational, and based upon reasoned distinctions" found in the Constitution or laws. *Vieth.* Judicial review of partisan gerrymandering does not meet those basic requirements. . . .

What the appellees and dissent seek is an unprecedented expansion of judicial power. We have never struck down a partisan gerrymander as unconstitutional—despite various requests over the past 45 years. The expansion of judicial authority would not be into just any area of controversy, but into one of the most intensely partisan aspects of American political life. That intervention would be unlimited in scope and duration—it would recur over and over again around the country with each new round of districting, for state as well as federal representatives. Consideration of the impact of today's ruling on democratic principles cannot ignore the effect of the unelected and politically unaccountable branch of the Federal Government assuming such an extraordinary and unprecedented role.

Our conclusion does not condone excessive partisan gerrymandering. Nor does our conclusion condemn complaints about districting to echo into a void. The States, for example, are actively addressing the issue on a number of fronts. . . . Provisions in state statutes and state constitutions can provide standards and guidance for state courts to apply. Indeed, numerous other States are restricting partisan considerations in districting through legislation. One way they are doing so is by placing power to draw electoral districts in the hands of independent commissions. . . .

Other States have mandated at least some of the traditional districting criteria for their mapmakers. Some have outright prohibited partisan favoritism in redistricting. . . .

As noted, the Framers gave Congress the power to do something about partisan gerrymandering in the Elections Clause. The first bill introduced in the 116th Congress would require States to create 15-member independent commissions to draw congressional districts and would establish certain redistricting criteria, including protection for communities of interest, and ban partisan gerrymandering. H. R. 1 (2019). . . .

Another example is the Fairness and Independence in Redistricting Act, which was introduced in 2005 and has been reintroduced in every Congress since. That bill would require every State to establish an independent commission to adopt redistricting plans. . . .

We express no view on any of these pending proposals. We simply note that the avenue for reform established by the Framers, and used by Congress in the past, remains open.

* * *

No one can accuse this Court of having a crabbed view of the reach of its competence. But we have no commission to allocate political power and influence in the absence of a constitutional directive or legal standards to guide us in the exercise of such authority. "It is emphatically the province and duty of the judicial department to say what the law is." *Marbury v. Madison.* In this rare circumstance, that means our duty is to say "this is not law."

JUSTICE KAGAN, with whom JUSTICE GINSBURG, JUSTICE BREYER, and JUSTICE SOTOMAYOR join, dissenting.

For the first time ever, this Court refuses to remedy a constitutional violation because it thinks the task beyond judicial capabilities.

And not just any constitutional violation. The partisan gerrymanders in these cases deprived citizens of the most fundamental of their constitutional rights: the rights to participate equally in the political process, to join with others to advance political beliefs, and to choose their political representatives. In so doing, the partisan gerrymanders here debased and dishonored our democracy, turning upside-down the core American idea that all governmental power derives from the people. These gerrymanders enabled politicians to entrench themselves in office as against voters' preferences. They promoted partisanship above respect for the popular will. They encouraged a politics of polarization and dysfunction. If left unchecked, gerrymanders like the ones here may irreparably damage our system of government.

And checking them is *not* beyond the courts. The majority's abdication comes just when courts across the country, including those below, have coalesced around manageable judicial standards to resolve partisan gerrymandering claims. Those standards satisfy the majority's own benchmarks. They do not require—indeed, they do not permit—courts to rely on their own ideas of electoral fairness, whether proportional representation or any other. And they limit courts to correcting only egregious gerrymanders, so judges do not become omnipresent players in the political process. But yes, the standards used here do allow—as well they should—judicial intervention in the worst-of-the-worst cases of democratic subversion, causing blatant constitutional harms. In other words, they allow courts to undo partisan gerrymanders of the kind we face today from North Carolina and Maryland. In giving such gerrymanders a pass from judicial review, the majority goes tragically wrong. . . .

I

B

"Governments," the Declaration of Independence states, "deriv[e] their just Powers from the Consent of the Governed." The Constitution begins: "We the People of the United States." The Gettysburg Address (almost) ends: "[G]overnment of the people, by the people, for the people."* If there is a single idea that made our Nation (and that our Nation commended to the world), it is this one: The people are sovereign. The "power," James Madison wrote, "is in the people over the Government, and not in the Government over the people."

Free and fair and periodic elections are the key to that vision. The people get to choose their representatives. And then they get to decide, at regular intervals, whether to keep them. Madison again: "[R]epublican liberty" demands "not only, that all power should be derived from the people; but that those entrusted with it should be kept in dependence on the people." The Federalist No. 37. Members of the House of Representatives, in particular, are supposed to "recollect[] [that] dependence" every day. To retain an "intimate sympathy with the people," they must be "compelled to anticipate the moment" when their "exercise of [power] is to be reviewed." Election day—next year, and two years later, and two years after that—is what links the people to their representatives, and gives the people their sovereign power. That day is the foundation of democratic governance.

---

* [Abraham Lincoln may have drew inspiration from Chief Justice John Marshall's opinion in *McCulloch v. Maryland* (1819). He wrote, "The government of the Union, then (whatever may be the influence of this fact on the case), is, emphatically and truly, a government of the people. In form, and in substance, it emanates from them. Its powers are granted by them, and are to be exercised directly on them, and for their benefit."—Eds.]

And partisan gerrymandering can make it meaningless. At its most extreme—as in North Carolina and Maryland—the practice amounts to "rigging elections." *Vieth v. Jubelirer*, (2004) (Kennedy, J., concurring in judgment). By drawing districts to maximize the power of some voters and minimize the power of others, a party in office at the right time can entrench itself there for a decade or more, no matter what the voters would prefer. Just ask the people of North Carolina and Maryland. The "core principle of republican government," this Court has recognized, is "that the voters should choose their representatives, not the other way around." *Arizona State Legislature v. Arizona Independent Redistricting Comm'n* (2015) (internal quotation marks omitted). Partisan gerrymandering turns it the other way around. By that mechanism, politicians can cherry-pick voters to ensure their reelection. And the power becomes, as Madison put it, "in the Government over the people."

The majority disputes none of this. I think it important to underscore that fact: The majority disputes none of what I have said (or will say) about how gerrymanders undermine democracy. Indeed, the majority concedes (really, how could it not?) that gerrymandering is "incompatible with democratic principles." And therefore what? That recognition would seem to demand a response. The majority offers two ideas that might qualify as such. One is that the political process can deal with the problem—a proposition so dubious on its face that I feel secure in delaying my answer for some time. The other is that political gerrymanders have always been with us. To its credit, the majority does not frame that point as an originalist constitutional argument. After all (as the majority rightly notes), racial and residential gerrymanders were also once with us, but the Court has done something about that fact.[1] The majority's idea instead seems to be that if we have lived with partisan gerrymanders so long, we will survive.

That complacency has no cause. Yes, partisan gerrymandering goes back to the Republic's earliest days. (As does vociferous opposition to it.) But big data and modern technology—of just the kind that the mapmakers in North Carolina and Maryland used—make today's gerrymandering altogether different from the crude linedrawing of the past. Old-time efforts, based on little more than guesses, sometimes led to so-called dummymanders—gerrymanders that went spectacularly wrong. . . . While bygone mapmakers may have drafted three or four alternative districting plans, today's mapmakers can generate thousands of possibilities at the touch of a key—and then choose the one giving their party maximum advantage (usually while still meeting traditional districting requirements). The effect is to make gerrymanders far more effective and durable than before, insulating politicians against all but the most titanic shifts in the political tides. These are not your grandfather's—let alone the Framers'—gerrymanders. . . .

---

1. And even putting that aside, any originalist argument would have to deal with an inconvenient fact. The Framers originally viewed political parties themselves (let alone their most partisan actions) with deep suspicion, as fomenters of factionalism and "symptom[s] of disease in the body politic." G. Wood, Empire of Liberty: A History of the Early Republic, 1789-1815, p. 140 (2009).

And gerrymanders will only get worse (or depending on your perspective, better) as time goes on — as data becomes ever more fine-grained and data analysis techniques continue to improve. What was possible with paper and pen — or even with Windows 95 — doesn't hold a candle (or an LED bulb?) to what will become possible with developments like machine learning. And someplace along this road, "we the people" become sovereign no longer.

C

Partisan gerrymandering of the kind before us not only subverts democracy (as if that weren't bad enough). It violates individuals' constitutional rights as well. That statement is not the lonesome cry of a dissenting Justice. This Court has recognized extreme partisan gerrymandering as such a violation for many years.

Partisan gerrymandering operates through vote dilution — the devaluation of one citizen's vote as compared to others. . . . In short, the mapmaker has made some votes count for less, because they are likely to go for the other party.

That practice implicates the Fourteenth Amendment's Equal Protection Clause. The Fourteenth Amendment, we long ago recognized, "guarantees the opportunity for equal participation by all voters in the election" of legislators. *Reynolds v. Sims* (1964). . . . A State could not, we explained . . . "dilut[e] the weight of votes because of place of residence." The constitutional injury in a partisan gerrymandering case is much the same, except that the dilution is based on party affiliation. . . . As Justice Kennedy (in a controlling opinion) once hypothesized: If districters declared that they were drawing a map "so as most to burden [the votes of] Party X's" supporters, it would violate the Equal Protection Clause. *Vieth.* . . .

And partisan gerrymandering implicates the First Amendment too. That Amendment gives its greatest protection to political beliefs, speech, and association. Yet partisan gerrymanders subject certain voters to "disfavored treatment" — again, counting their votes for less — precisely because of "their voting history [and] their expression of political views." *Vieth* (Kennedy, J.). . . .

Though different Justices have described the constitutional harm in diverse ways, nearly all have agreed on this much: Extreme partisan gerrymandering (as happened in North Carolina and Maryland) violates the Constitution. . . . Once again, the majority never disagrees; it appears to accept the "principle that each person must have an equal say in the election of representatives." And indeed, without this settled and shared understanding that cases like these inflict constitutional injury, the question of whether there are judicially manageable standards for resolving them would never come up.

II

So the only way to understand the majority's opinion is as follows: In the face of grievous harm to democratic governance and flagrant infringements on individuals' rights — in the face of escalating partisan manipulation whose compatibility with this Nation's values and law no one defends — the majority declines to provide any remedy. For the first time in this Nation's history, the majority declares that it can do nothing about an acknowledged constitutional violation because it has searched high and low and cannot find a workable legal standard to apply.

The majority gives two reasons for thinking that the adjudication of partisan gerrymandering claims is beyond judicial capabilities. First and foremost, the majority says, it cannot find a neutral baseline — one not based on contestable notions of political fairness — from which to measure injury. . . .

I'll give the majority this one — and important — thing: It identifies some dangers everyone should want to avoid. Judges should not be apportioning political power based on their own vision of electoral fairness, whether proportional representation or any other. And judges should not be striking down maps left, right, and center, on the view that every smidgen of politics is a smidgen too much. Respect for state legislative processes — and restraint in the exercise of judicial authority — counsels intervention in only egregious cases.

But in throwing up its hands, the majority misses something under its nose: What it says can't be done *has* been done. Over the past several years, federal courts across the country — including, but not exclusively, in the decisions below — have largely converged on a standard for adjudicating partisan gerrymandering claims (striking down both Democratic and Republican districting plans in the process). And that standard does what the majority says is impossible. The standard does not use any judge-made conception of electoral fairness — either proportional representation or any other; instead, it takes as its baseline a State's *own* criteria of fairness, apart from partisan gain. And by requiring plaintiffs to make difficult showings relating to both purpose and effects, the standard invalidates the most extreme, but only the most extreme, partisan gerrymanders. . . .

As I lay out the lower courts' analyses, I consider two specific criticisms the majority levels — each of which reveals a saddening nonchalance about the threat such districting poses to self-governance. All of that lays the groundwork for then assessing the majority's more general view, described above, that judicial policing in this area cannot be either neutral or restrained. The lower courts' reasoning, as I'll show, proves the opposite. . . .

A

Start with the standard the lower courts used. . . . [B]oth courts (like others around the country) used basically the same three-part test to decide whether the plaintiffs had made out a vote dilution claim. . . : (1) intent; (2) effects; and (3) causation. First, the plaintiffs challenging a districting plan must prove that state officials' "predominant purpose" in drawing a district's lines was to "entrench [their party] in power" by diluting the votes of citizens favoring its rival. Second, the plaintiffs must establish that the lines drawn in fact have the intended effect by "substantially" diluting their votes. And third, if the plaintiffs make those showings, the State must come up with a legitimate, non-partisan justification to save its map. If you are a lawyer, you know that this test looks utterly ordinary. It is the sort of thing courts work with every day.

. . . The majority's response to the District Courts' purpose analysis is discomfiting. The majority does not contest the lower courts' findings; how could it? Instead, the majority says that state officials' intent to entrench their party in power is perfectly "permissible," even when it is the predominant factor in drawing district lines. But that is wrong. True enough, that the intent to inject "political considerations" into districting may not raise any constitutional concerns. . . . But when political actors have a specific and predominant intent to entrench themselves in power by manipulating district lines, that goes too far. . . . It cannot be permissible and thus irrelevant, as the majority claims, that state officials have as their purpose the kind of grotesquely gerrymandered map that, according to all this Court has ever said, violates the Constitution. . . .

On to the second step of the analysis, where the plaintiffs must prove that the districting plan substantially dilutes their votes. . . . The evidence reveals just how bad the two gerrymanders were (in case you had any doubts). And it shows how the same technologies and data that today facilitate extreme partisan gerrymanders also enable courts to discover them, by exposing just how much they dilute votes. . . . The majority claims all these findings are mere "prognostications" about the future, in which no one "can have any confidence." But the courts below did not gaze into crystal balls, as the majority tries to suggest. Their findings about these gerrymanders' effects on voters — both in the past and predictably in the future — were evidence-based, data-based, statistics-based. . . . They did not bet America's future — as today the majority does — on the idea that maps constructed with so much expertise and care to make electoral outcomes impervious to voting would somehow or other come apart. They looked at the evidence — at the facts about how these districts operated — and they could reach only one conclusion. By substantially diluting the votes of citizens favoring their rivals, the politicians of one party had succeeded in entrenching themselves in office. They had beat democracy. . . .

B

The majority's broadest claim, as I've noted, is that this is a price we must pay because judicial oversight of partisan gerrymandering cannot be "politically neutral" or "manageable." Courts, the majority argues, will have to choose among contested notions of electoral fairness. . . . And even once courts have chosen, the majority continues, they will have to decide "[h]ow much is too much?" — that is, how much deviation from the chosen "touchstone" to allow? . . . So the whole thing is impossible, the majority concludes. . . . But it never tries to analyze the serious question presented here — whether the kind of standard developed below falls prey to those objections, or instead allows for neutral and manageable oversight. The answer, as you've already heard enough to know, is the latter. That kind of oversight is not only possible; it's been done. Consider neutrality first. Contrary to the majority's suggestion, the District Courts did not have to—and in fact did not—choose among competing visions of electoral fairness. That is because they did not try to compare the State's actual map to an "ideally fair" one (whether based on proportional representation or some other criterion). Instead, they looked at the difference between what the State did and what the State would have done if politicians hadn't been intent on partisan gain. Or put differently, the comparator (or baseline or touchstone) is the result not of a judge's philosophizing but of the State's own characteristics and judgments. . . . All the courts did was determine how far the State had gone off that track because of its politicians' effort to entrench themselves in office. . . .

Using the criteria the State itself has chosen at the relevant time prevents any judicial predilections from affecting the analysis—exactly what the majority claims it wants. At the same time, using those criteria enables a court to measure just what it should: the extent to which the pursuit of partisan advantage—by these legislators at this moment—has distorted the State's districting decisions. . . . The majority's "how much is too much" critique fares no better than its neutrality argument. How about the following for a first-cut answer: This much is too much. By any measure, a map that produces a greater partisan skew than any of 3,000 randomly generated maps (all with the State's political geography and districting criteria built in) reflects "too much" partisanship. Think about what I just said: The absolute worst of 3,001 possible maps. The *only one* that could produce a 10-3 partisan split even as Republicans got a bare majority of the statewide vote. . . . If the majority had done nothing else, it could have set the line here. How much is too much? At the least, any gerrymanders as bad as these.

And if the majority thought that approach too case-specific, see *ante,* at 28, it could have used the lower courts' general standard—focusing on "predominant" purpose and "substantial" effects—without fear of indeterminacy. . . . Those inquiries would be no harder here than in other contexts. . . .

Illicit purpose was simple to show here only because politicians and mapmakers thought their actions could not be attacked in court. They therefore felt free to openly proclaim their intent to entrench their party in office. But if the Court today had declared that behavior justiciable, such smoking guns would all but disappear. Even assuming some officials continued to try implementing extreme partisan gerrymanders, they would not brag about their efforts. So plaintiffs would have to prove the intent to entrench through circumstantial evidence—essentially showing that no other explanation (no geographic feature or non-partisan districting objective) could explain the districting plan's vote dilutive effects. And that would be impossible unless those effects were even more than substantial—unless mapmakers had packed and cracked with abandon in unprecedented ways. As again, they did here. That the two courts below found constitutional violations does not mean their tests were unrigorous; it means that the conduct they confronted was constitutionally appalling—by even the strictest measure, inordinately partisan. . . .

The plaintiffs asked only that the courts bar politicians from entrenching themselves in power by diluting the votes of their rivals' supporters. And the courts, using neutral and manageable—and eminently legal—standards, provided that (and only that) relief. This Court should have cheered, not overturned, that restoration of the people's power to vote.

III

This Court has long understood that it has a special responsibility to remedy violations of constitutional rights resulting from politicians' districting decisions. Over 50 years ago, we committed to providing judicial review in that sphere, recognizing as we established the one-person-one-vote rule that "our oath and our office require no less." *Reynolds.* Of course, our oath and our office require us to vindicate all constitutional rights. But the need for judicial review is at its most urgent in cases like these. "For here, politicians' incentives conflict with voters' interests, leaving citizens without any political remedy for their constitutional harms." *Gill* (Kagan, J., concurring). Those harms arise because politicians want to stay in office. No one can look to them for effective relief.

No worries, the majority says; it has another idea. The majority notes that voters themselves have recently approved ballot initiatives to put power over districting in the hands of independent commissions or other non-partisan actors. Some Members of the majority, of course, once thought such initiatives unconstitutional. See *Arizona State Legislature* (Roberts, C. J., dissenting). But put that aside. Fewer than half the States offer voters an opportunity to put initiatives to direct vote; in all the rest (including North Carolina and Maryland), voters are dependent on legislators to make electoral changes (which for all the reasons already given, they are unlikely to do). . . .

The majority's most perplexing "solution" is to look to state courts. But what do those courts know that this Court does not? If they can develop and apply neutral and manageable standards to identify unconstitutional gerrymanders, why couldn't we? . . .

The gerrymanders here—and they are typical of many—violated the constitutional rights of many hundreds of thousands of American citizens. Those voters (Republicans in the one case, Democrats in the other) did not have an equal opportunity to participate in the political process. Their votes counted for far less than they should have because of their partisan affiliation. When faced with such constitutional wrongs, courts must intervene: "It is emphatically the province and duty of the judicial department to say what the law is." *Marbury v. Madison* (1803). That is what the courts below did. Their decisions are worth a read. They (and others that have recently remedied similar violations) are detailed, thorough, painstaking. They evaluated with immense care the factual evidence and legal arguments the parties presented. They used neutral and manageable and strict standards. They had not a shred of politics about them. Contra the majority this *was* law.

That is not to deny, of course, that these cases have great political consequence. . . . Gerrymandering . . . helps create the polarized political system so
many Americans loathe.

And gerrymandering is, as so many Justices have emphasized before, anti-
democratic in the most profound sense. In our government, "all political power
flows from the people." *Arizona State Legislature.* And that means, as Alexander
Hamilton once said, "that the people should choose whom they please to govern
them." But in Maryland and North Carolina they cannot do so. In Maryland,
election in and election out, there are 7 Democrats and 1 Republican in the congressional delegation. In North Carolina, however the political winds blow, there
are 10 Republicans and 3 Democrats. Is it conceivable that someday voters will
be able to break out of that prefabricated box? Sure. But everything possible has
been done to make that hard. To create a world in which power does not flow
from the people because they do not choose their governors.

Of all times to abandon the Court's duty to declare the law, this was not the
one. The practices challenged in these cases imperil our system of government.
Part of the Court's role in that system is to defend its foundations. None is more
important than free and fair elections. With respect but deep sadness, I dissent.

Chapter 9

Standing, Ripeness, and Mootness

ASSIGNMENT 1

Standing

STUDY GUIDE:

- What would have happened if, in addition to refusing to defend DOMA in court, the Department of Justice had also refused to enforce it? Would *Windsor* have still had standing? Does this raise any concerns?
- Can you identify a fundamental disagreement between Justices Kennedy and Scalia about the source and nature of "the judicial power" that explains their differing stances on standing?

United States v. Windsor
133 S. Ct. 2675 (2013)

JUSTICE KENNEDY delivered the opinion of the Court.

Two women then resident in New York were married in a lawful ceremony in Ontario, Canada, in 2007. Edith Windsor and Thea Spyer returned to their home in New York City. When Spyer died in 2009, she left her entire estate to Windsor. Windsor sought to claim the estate tax exemption for surviving spouses. She was barred from doing so, however, by a federal law, the Defense of Marriage Act, which excludes a same-sex partner from the definition of "spouse" as that term is used in federal statutes. Windsor paid the taxes but filed suit to challenge the constitutionality of this provision. The United States District Court and the Court of Appeals ruled that this portion of the statute is unconstitutional and ordered the United States to pay Windsor a refund. This Court granted certiorari and now affirms the judgment in Windsor's favor.

I

. . . While the tax refund suit was pending, the Attorney General of the United States notified the Speaker of the House of Representatives, pursuant to 28

U.S.C. §530D, that the Department of Justice would no longer defend the constitutionality of DOMA's §3. Noting that "the Department has previously defended DOMA against . . . challenges involving legally married same-sex couples," the Attorney General informed Congress that "the President has concluded that given a number of factors, including a documented history of discrimination, classifications based on sexual orientation should be subject to a heightened standard of scrutiny." The Department of Justice has submitted many §530D letters over the years refusing to defend laws it deems unconstitutional, when, for instance, a federal court has rejected the Government's defense of a statute and has issued a judgment against it. This case is unusual, however, because the §530D letter was not preceded by an adverse judgment. The letter instead reflected the Executive's own conclusion, relying on a definition still being debated and considered in the courts, that heightened equal protection scrutiny should apply to laws that classify on the basis of sexual orientation.

Although "the President . . . instructed the Department not to defend the statute in *Windsor*," he also decided "that Section 3 will continue to be enforced by the Executive Branch" and that the United States had an "interest in providing Congress a full and fair opportunity to participate in the litigation of those cases." The stated rationale for this dual-track procedure (determination of unconstitutionality coupled with ongoing enforcement) was to "recogniz[e] the judiciary as the final arbiter of the constitutional claims raised."

In response to the notice from the Attorney General, the Bipartisan Legal Advisory Group (BLAG) of the House of Representatives voted to intervene in the litigation to defend the constitutionality of §3 of DOMA. The Department of Justice did not oppose limited intervention by BLAG. . . .

On the merits of the tax refund suit, the District Court ruled against the United States. It held that §3 of DOMA is unconstitutional and ordered the Treasury to refund the tax with interest. Both the Justice Department and BLAG filed notices of appeal, and the Solicitor General filed a petition for certiorari before judgment. Before this Court acted on the petition, the Court of Appeals for the Second Circuit affirmed the District Court's judgment. It applied heightened scrutiny to classifications based on sexual orientation, as both the Department and Windsor had urged. The United States has not complied with the judgment. Windsor has not received her refund, and the Executive Branch continues to enforce §3 of DOMA. In granting certiorari on the question of the constitutionality of §3 of DOMA, the Court requested argument on two additional questions: whether the United States' agreement with Windsor's legal position precludes further review and whether BLAG has standing to appeal the case. All parties agree that the Court has jurisdiction to decide this case; and, with the case in that framework, the Court appointed Professor Vicki Jackson as *amicus curiae* to argue the position that the Court lacks jurisdiction to hear the dispute. She has ably discharged her duties. . . .

II

It is appropriate to begin by addressing whether either the Government or BLAG, or both of them, were entitled to appeal to the Court of Appeals and later to seek certiorari and appear as parties here. There is no dispute that when this case was in the District Court it presented a concrete disagreement between opposing parties, a dispute suitable for judicial resolution. "[A] taxpayer has standing to challenge the collection of a specific tax assessment as unconstitutional; being forced to pay such a tax causes a real and immediate economic injury to the individual taxpayer." *Hein v. Freedom From Religion Foundation, Inc.* (2007) (plurality opinion) (emphasis deleted). Windsor suffered a redressable injury when she was required to pay estate taxes from which, in her view, she was exempt but for the alleged invalidity of §3 of DOMA.

The decision of the Executive not to defend the constitutionality of §3 in court while continuing to deny refunds and to assess deficiencies does introduce a complication. Even though the Executive's current position was announced before the District Court entered its judgment, the Government's agreement with Windsor's position would not have deprived the District Court of jurisdiction to entertain and resolve the refund suit; for her injury (failure to obtain a refund allegedly required by law) was concrete, persisting, and unredressed. The Government's position—agreeing with Windsor's legal contention but refusing to give it effect—meant that there was a justiciable controversy between the parties, despite what the claimant would find to be an inconsistency in that stance. Windsor, the Government, BLAG, and the *amicus* appear to agree upon that point. The disagreement is over the standing of the parties, or aspiring parties, to take an appeal in the Court of Appeals and to appear as parties in further proceedings in this Court.

The *amicus'* position is that, given the Government's concession that §3 is unconstitutional, once the District Court ordered the refund the case should have ended; and the *amicus* argues the Court of Appeals should have dismissed the appeal. The *amicus* submits that once the President agreed with Windsor's legal position and the District Court issued its judgment, the parties were no longer adverse. From this standpoint the United States was a prevailing party below, just as Windsor was. Accordingly, the *amicus* reasons, it is inappropriate for this Court to grant certiorari and proceed to rule on the merits; for the United States seeks no redress from the judgment entered against it.

This position, however, elides the distinction between two principles: the jurisdictional requirements of Article III and the prudential limits on its exercise. See *Warth v. Seldin* (1975). The latter are "essentially matters of judicial self-governance." The Court has kept these two strands separate: "Article III standing, which enforces the Constitution's case-or-controversy requirement, see *Lujan v. Defenders of Wildlife* (1992); and prudential standing, which embodies 'judicially self-imposed limits on the exercise of federal jurisdiction,' *Allen v. Wright* (1984)." *Elk Grove Unified School Dist. v. Newdow* (2004).

The requirements of Article III standing are familiar:

> First, the plaintiff must have suffered an "injury in fact"—an invasion of a legally protected interest which is (a) concrete and particularized, and (b) "actual or imminent, not "conjectural or hypothetical." Second, there must be a causal connection between the injury and the conduct complained of—the injury has to be "fairly . . .

trace[able] to the challenged action of the defendant, and not . . . th[e] result [of] the independent action of some third party not before the court." Third, it must be "likely," as opposed to merely "speculative," that the injury will be "redressed by a favorable decision." *Lujan.*

Rules of prudential standing, by contrast, are more flexible "rule[s] . . . of federal appellate practice," *Deposit Guaranty Nat. Bank v. Roper* (1980), designed to protect the courts from "decid[ing] abstract questions of wide public significance even [when] other governmental institutions may be more competent to address the questions and even though judicial intervention may be unnecessary to protect individual rights." *Warth.*

In this case the United States retains a stake sufficient to support Article III jurisdiction on appeal and in proceedings before this Court. The judgment in question orders the United States to pay Windsor the refund she seeks. An order directing the Treasury to pay money is "a real and immediate economic injury," *Hein*, indeed as real and immediate as an order directing an individual to pay a tax. That the Executive may welcome this order to pay the refund if it is accompanied by the constitutional ruling it wants does not eliminate the injury to the national Treasury if payment is made, or to the taxpayer if it is not. The judgment orders the United States to pay money that it would not disburse but for the court's order. The Government of the United States has a valid legal argument that it is injured even if the Executive disagrees with §3 of DOMA, which results in Windsor's liability for the tax. Windsor's ongoing claim for funds that the United States refuses to pay thus establishes a controversy sufficient for Article III jurisdiction. It would be a different case if the Executive had taken the further step of paying Windsor the refund to which she was entitled under the District Court's ruling.

This Court confronted a comparable case in *INS v. Chadha* (1983). A statute by its terms allowed one House of Congress to order the Immigration and Naturalization Service (INS) to deport the respondent Chadha. There, as here, the Executive determined that the statute was unconstitutional, and "the INS presented the Executive's views on the constitutionality of the House action to the Court of Appeals." The INS, however, continued to abide by the statute, and "the INS brief to the Court of Appeals did not alter the agency's decision to comply with the House action ordering deportation of Chadha." This Court held "that the INS was sufficiently aggrieved by the Court of Appeals decision prohibiting it from taking action it would otherwise take," regardless of whether the agency welcomed the judgment. The necessity of a "case or controversy" to satisfy Article III was defined as a requirement that the Court's "decision will have real meaning: if we rule for Chadha, he will not be deported; if we uphold [the statute], the INS will execute its order and deport him." This conclusion was not dictum. It was a necessary predicate to the Court's holding that "prior to Congress' intervention, there was adequate Art. III adverseness." The holdings of cases are instructive, and the words of *Chadha* make clear its holding that the refusal of the Executive to provide the relief sought suffices to preserve a justiciable dispute as required by Article III. In short, even where "the Government largely agree[s] with the opposing party on the merits of the controversy," there is sufficient adverseness and an "adequate basis for jurisdiction in the fact that the Government intended to enforce the challenged law against that party."

It is true that "[a] party who receives all that he has sought generally is not aggrieved by the judgment affording the relief and cannot appeal from it." *Roper*. But this rule "does not have its source in the jurisdictional limitations of Art. III. In an appropriate case, appeal may be permitted . . . at the behest of the party who has prevailed on the merits, so long as that party retains a stake in the appeal satisfying the requirements of Art. III." *Roper*.

While these principles suffice to show that this case presents a justiciable controversy under Article III, the prudential problems inherent in the Executive's unusual position require some further discussion. The Executive's agreement with Windsor's legal argument raises the risk that instead of a "real, earnest and vital controversy," the Court faces a "friendly, non-adversary, proceeding . . . [in which] a party beaten in the legislature [seeks to] transfer to the courts an inquiry as to the constitutionality of the legislative act." *Ashwander v. TVA* (1936) (Brandeis, J., concurring). Even when Article III permits the exercise of federal jurisdiction, prudential considerations demand that the Court insist upon "that concrete adverseness which sharpens the presentation of issues upon which the court so largely depends for illumination of difficult constitutional questions." *Baker v. Carr* (1962).

There are, of course, reasons to hear a case and issue a ruling even when one party is reluctant to prevail in its position. Unlike Article III requirements — which must be satisfied by the parties before judicial consideration is appropriate — the relevant prudential factors that counsel against hearing this case are subject to "countervailing considerations [that] may outweigh the concerns underlying the usual reluctance to exert judicial power." *Warth*. One consideration is the extent to which adversarial presentation of the issues is assured by the participation of *amici curiae* prepared to defend with vigor the constitutionality of the legislative act. With respect to this prudential aspect of standing as well, the *Chadha* Court encountered a similar situation. It noted that "there may be prudential, as opposed to Art. III, concerns about sanctioning the adjudication of [this case] in the absence of any participant supporting the validity of [the statute]. The Court of Appeals properly dispelled any such concerns by inviting and accepting briefs from both Houses of Congress." *Chadha* was not an anomaly in this respect. The Court adopts the practice of entertaining arguments made by an *amicus* when the Solicitor General confesses error with respect to a judgment below, even if the confession is in effect an admission that an Act of Congress is unconstitutional.

In the case now before the Court the attorneys for BLAG present a substantial argument for the constitutionality of §3 of DOMA. BLAG's sharp adversarial presentation of the issues satisfies the prudential concerns that otherwise might counsel against hearing an appeal from a decision with which the principal parties agree. Were this Court to hold that prudential rules require it to dismiss the case, and, in consequence, that the Court of Appeals erred in failing to dismiss it as well, extensive litigation would ensue. The district courts in 94 districts throughout the Nation would be without precedential guidance not only in tax refund suits but also in cases involving the whole of DOMA's sweep involving over 1,000 federal statutes and a myriad of federal regulations. For instance, the opinion of the Court of Appeals for the First Circuit, addressing the validity of DOMA in a case involving regulations of the Department of Health and Human Services, likely would be vacated with instructions to dismiss, its ruling and guidance also then erased. Rights and privileges of hundreds of thousands of persons would be adversely affected, pending a case in which all prudential concerns about justiciability are absent. That numerical prediction may not be certain, but it is certain that the cost in judicial resources and expense of litigation for all persons adversely affected would be immense. True, the very extent of DOMA's mandate means that at some point a case likely would arise without the prudential concerns raised here; but the costs, uncertainties, and alleged harm and injuries likely would continue for a time measured in years before the issue is resolved. In these unusual and urgent circumstances, the very term "prudential" counsels that it is a proper exercise of the Court's responsibility to take jurisdiction. For these reasons, the prudential and Article III requirements are met here. . . .

The Court's conclusion that this petition may be heard on the merits does not imply that no difficulties would ensue if this were a common practice in ordinary cases. The Executive's failure to defend the constitutionality of an Act of Congress based on a constitutional theory not yet established in judicial decisions has created a procedural dilemma. On the one hand, as noted, the Government's agreement with Windsor raises questions about the propriety of entertaining a suit in which it seeks affirmance of an order invalidating a federal law and ordering the United States to pay money. On the other hand, if the Executive's agreement with a plaintiff that a law is unconstitutional is enough to preclude judicial review, then the Supreme Court's primary role in determining the constitutionality of a law that has inflicted real injury on a plaintiff who has brought a justiciable legal claim would become only secondary to the President's. This would undermine the clear dictate of the separation-of-powers principle that when an Act of Congress is alleged to conflict with the Constitution, "[i]t is emphatically the province and duty of the judicial department to say what the law is." *Marbury v. Madison* (1803). Similarly, with respect to the legislative power, when Congress has passed a statute and a President has signed it, it poses grave challenges to the separation of powers for the Executive at a particular moment to be able to nullify Congress' enactment solely on its own initiative and without any determination from the Court.

The Court's jurisdictional holding, it must be underscored, does not mean the arguments for dismissing this dispute on prudential grounds lack substance. Yet the difficulty the Executive faces should be acknowledged. When the Executive makes a principled determination that a statute is unconstitutional, it faces a difficult choice. Still, there is no suggestion here that it is appropriate for the Executive as a matter of course to challenge statutes in the judicial forum rather than making the case to Congress for their amendment or repeal. The integrity of the political process would be at risk if difficult constitutional issues were simply referred to the Court as a routine exercise. But this case is not routine. And the capable defense of the law by BLAG ensures that these prudential issues do not cloud the merits question, which is one of immediate importance to the Federal Government and to hundreds of thousands of persons. These circumstances support the Court's decision to proceed to the merits.

JUSTICE SCALIA, with whom JUSTICE THOMAS joins, and with whom THE CHIEF JUSTICE joins as to Part I, dissenting. . . .

This case is about power in several respects. It is about the power of our people to govern themselves, and the power of this Court to pronounce the law. Today's opinion aggrandizes the latter, with the predictable consequence of diminishing the former. We have no power to decide this case. And even if we did, we have no power under the Constitution to invalidate this democratically adopted legislation. The Court's errors on both points spring forth from the same diseased root: an exalted conception of the role of this institution in America.

I

A

The Court is eager—*hungry*—to tell everyone its view of the legal question at the heart of this case. Standing in the way is an obstacle, a technicality of little interest to anyone but the people of We the People, who created it as a barrier against judges' intrusion into their lives. They gave judges, in Article III, only the "judicial Power," a power to decide not abstract questions but real, concrete "Cases" and "Controversies." Yet the plaintiff and the Government agree entirely on what should happen in this lawsuit. They agree that the court below got it right; and they agreed in the court below that the court below that one got it right as well. What, then, are we *doing* here? The answer lies at the heart of the jurisdictional portion of today's opinion, where a single sentence lays bare the majority's vision of our role. The Court says that we have the power to decide this case because if we did not, then our "primary role in determining the constitutionality of a law" (at least one that "has inflicted real injury on a plaintiff") would "become only secondary to the President's." But wait, the reader wonders—Windsor won below, and so *cured* her injury, and the President was glad to see it. True, says the majority, but judicial review must march on regardless, lest we "undermine the clear dictate of the separation-of-powers principle that when an Act of Congress is alleged to conflict with the Constitution, it is emphatically the province and duty of the judicial department to say what the law is."

That is jaw-dropping. It is an assertion of judicial supremacy over the people's Representatives in Congress and the Executive. It envisions a Supreme Court standing (or rather enthroned) at the apex of government, empowered to decide all constitutional questions, always and everywhere "primary" in its role.

This image of the Court would have been unrecognizable to those who wrote and ratified our national charter. They knew well the dangers of "primary" power, and so created branches of government that would be "perfectly co-ordinate by the terms of their common commission," none of which branches could "pretend to an exclusive or superior right of settling the boundaries between their respective powers." The Federalist, No. 49 (J. Madison). The people did this to protect themselves. They did it to guard their right to self-rule against the black-robed supremacy that today's majority finds so attractive. So it was that Madison could confidently state, with no fear of contradiction, that there was nothing of "greater intrinsic value" or "stamped with the authority of more enlightened patrons of liberty" than a government of separate and coordinate powers. Id., No. 47.

For this reason we are quite forbidden to say what the law is whenever (as today's opinion asserts) "an Act of Congress is alleged to conflict with the Constitution." We can do so only when that allegation will determine the outcome of a lawsuit, and is contradicted by the other party. The "judicial Power" is not, as the majority believes, the power "to say what the law is," giving the Supreme Court the "primary role in determining the constitutionality of laws." The majority must have in mind one of the foreign constitutions that pronounces such primacy for its constitutional court and allows that primacy to be exercised in contexts other than a lawsuit. See, e.g., Basic Law for the Federal Republic of Germany, Art. 93. The judicial power as Americans have understood it (and their English ancestors before them) is the power to adjudicate, with conclusive effect, disputed government claims (civil or criminal) against private persons, and disputed claims by private persons against the government or other private persons. Sometimes (though not always) the parties before the court disagree not with regard to the facts of their case (or not only with regard to the facts) but with regard to the applicable law — in which event (and only in which event) it becomes the "province and duty of the judicial department to say what the law is."

In other words, declaring the compatibility of state or federal laws with the Constitution is not only not the "primary role" of this Court, it is not a separate, free-standing role at all. We perform that role incidentally — by accident, as it were — when that is necessary to resolve the dispute before us. Then, and only then, does it become "the province and duty of the judicial department to say what the law is." That is why, in 1793, we politely declined the Washington Administration's request to "say what the law is" on a particular treaty matter that was not the subject of a concrete legal controversy. And that is why, as our opinions have said, some questions of law will never be presented to this Court, because there will never be anyone with standing to bring a lawsuit. See Schlesinger v. Reservists Comm. to Stop the War (1974); United States v. Richardson (1974). As Justice Brandeis put it, we cannot "pass upon the constitutionality of legislation in a friendly, non-adversary, proceeding"; absent a "real, earnest and vital controversy between individuals," we have neither any work to do nor any power to do it. Ashwander v. TVA (1936) (concurring opinion). Our authority begins and ends with the need to adjudge the rights of an injured party who stands before us seeking redress. *Lujan v. Defenders of Wildlife* (1992). That is completely absent here. Windsor's injury was cured by the judgment in her favor. And while, in ordinary circumstances, the United States is injured by a directive to pay a tax refund, this suit is far from ordinary. Whatever injury the United States has suffered will surely not be redressed by the action that it, as a litigant, asks us to take. The final sentence of the Solicitor General's brief on the merits reads: "For the foregoing reasons, the judgment of the court of appeals *should be affirmed*." That will not cure the Government's injury, but carve it into stone. One could spend many fruitless afternoons ransacking our library for any other petitioner's brief seeking an affirmance of the judgment against it. What the petitioner United States asks us to do in the case before us is exactly what the respondent Windsor asks us to do: not to provide relief from the judgment below but to say that that judgment was correct. And the same was true in the Court of Appeals: Neither party sought to undo the judgment for Windsor, and so that court should have dismissed the appeal (just as we should dismiss) for lack of jurisdiction. Since both parties agreed with the judgment of the District Court for the Southern District of New York, the suit should have ended there. The further proceedings have been a contrivance, having no object in mind except to elevate a District Court judgment that has no precedential effect in other courts, to one that has precedential effect throughout the Second Circuit, and then (in this Court) precedential effect throughout the United States.

We have never before agreed to speak — to "say what the law is" — where there is no controversy before us. In the more than two centuries that this Court has existed as an institution, we have never suggested that we have the power to decide a question when every party agrees with both its nominal opponent *and the court below* on that question's answer. The United States reluctantly conceded that at oral argument. See Tr. of Oral Arg. 19-20.

The closest we have ever come to what the Court blesses today was our opinion in *INS v. Chadha* (1983). But in that case, two parties to the litigation disagreed with the position of the United States and with the court below: the House and Senate, which had intervened in the case. Because *Chadha* concerned the validity of a mode of congressional action — the one-house legislative veto — the House and Senate were threatened with destruction of what they claimed to be one of their institutional powers. The Executive choosing not to defend that power,[1] we permitted the House and Senate to intervene. Nothing like that is present here.

---

1. There the Justice Department's refusal to defend the legislation was in accord with its long-standing (and entirely reasonable) practice of declining to defend legislation that in its view infringes upon Presidential powers. There is no justification for the Justice Department's abandoning the law in the present case. The majority opinion makes a point of scolding the President for his "failure to defend the constitutionality of an Act of Congress based on a constitutional theory not yet established in judicial decisions." But the rebuke is tongue-in-cheek, for the majority gladly gives the President what he wants. Contrary to all precedent, it decides this case (and even decides it the way the President wishes) *despite* his abandonment of the defense and the consequent absence of a case or controversy.

To be sure, the Court in *Chadha* said that statutory aggrieved-party status was "not altered by the fact that the Executive may agree with the holding that the statute in question is unconstitutional." But in a footnote to that statement, the Court acknowledged Article III's separate requirement of a "justiciable case or controversy," and stated that *this* requirement was satisfied "because of the presence of the two Houses of Congress as adverse parties." . . . When a private party has a judicial decree safely in hand to prevent his injury, additional judicial action requires that a party injured by the decree *seek to undo it*. In *Chadha*, the intervening House and Senate fulfilled that requirement. Here no one does.

The majority's discussion of the requirements of Article III bears no resemblance to our jurisprudence. It accuses the *amicus* (appointed to argue against our jurisdiction) of "elid[ing] the distinction between . . . the jurisdictional requirements of Article III and the prudential limits on its exercise." It then proceeds to call the requirement of adverseness a "prudential" aspect of standing. *Of standing.* That is incomprehensible. A plaintiff (or appellant) can have all the standing in the world — satisfying all three standing requirements of *Lujan* that the majority so carefully quotes — and yet no Article III controversy may be before the court. Article III requires not just a plaintiff (or appellant) who has standing to complain but *an opposing party* who denies the validity of the complaint. It is not the *amicus* that has done the eliding of distinctions, but the majority, calling the quite separate Article III requirement of adverseness between the parties an element (which it then pronounces a "prudential" element) of standing. The question here is not whether, as the majority puts it, "the United States retains a stake sufficient to support Article III jurisdiction," the question is whether there is any controversy (which requires *contradiction*) between the United States and Ms. Windsor. There is not.

I find it wryly amusing that the majority seeks to dismiss the requirement of party-adverseness as nothing more than a "prudential" aspect of the sole Article III requirement of standing. (Relegating a jurisdictional requirement to "prudential" status is a wondrous device, enabling courts to ignore the requirement whenever they believe it "prudent" — which is to say, a good idea.) Half a century ago, a Court similarly bent upon announcing its view regarding the constitutionality of a federal statute achieved that goal by effecting a remarkably similar *but completely opposite* distortion of the principles limiting our jurisdiction. The Court's notorious opinion in *Flast v. Cohen* (1968), held that *standing* was merely an element (which it pronounced to be a "prudential" element) of the sole Article III requirement of *adverseness*. We have been living with the chaos created by that power-grabbing decision ever since, see *Hein v. Freedom From Religion Foundation, Inc.* (2007), as we will have to live with the chaos created by this one. . . .

It may be argued that if what we say is true some Presidential determinations that statutes are unconstitutional will not be subject to our review. That is as it should be, when both the President and the plaintiff agree that the statute is unconstitutional. Where the Executive is enforcing an unconstitutional law, suit will of course lie; but if, in that suit, the Executive admits the unconstitutional-ity of the law, the litigation should end in an order or a consent decree enjoining enforcement. This suit saw the light of day only because the President enforced the Act (and thus gave Windsor standing to sue) even though he believed it uncon-stitutional. He could have equally chosen (more appropriately, some would say) neither to enforce nor to defend the statute he believed to be unconstitutional, see Presidential Authority to Decline to Execute Unconstitutional Statutes, 18 Op. Off. Legal Counsel 199 (Nov. 2, 1994)—in which event Windsor would not have been injured, the District Court could not have refereed this friendly scrimmage, and the Executive's determination of unconstitutionality would have escaped this Court's desire to blurt out its view of the law. The matter would have been left, as so many matters ought to be left, to a tug of war between the President and the Congress, which has innumerable means (up to and including impeachment) of compelling the President to enforce the laws it has written. Or the President could have evaded presentation of the constitutional issue to this Court simply by declining to appeal the District Court and Court of Appeals dis-positions he agreed with. Be sure of this much: If a President wants to insulate his judgment of unconstitutionality from our review, he can. What the views urged in this dissent produce is not insulation from judicial review but insulation from Executive contrivance.

The majority brandishes the famous sentence from *Marbury v. Madison* (1803) that "[i]t is emphatically the province and duty of the judicial depart-ment to say what the law is." But that sentence neither says nor implies that it is *always* the province and duty of the Court to say what the law is—much less that its responsibility in that regard is a "primary" one. The very next sentence of Chief Justice Marshall's opinion makes the crucial qualification that today's majority ignores: "*Those who apply the rule to particular cases, must of neces-sity expound and interpret that rule.*" (emphasis added). Only when a "particular case" is before us—that is, a controversy that it is our business to resolve under Article III—do we have the province and duty to pronounce the law. For the views of our early Court more precisely addressing the question before us here, the majority ought instead to have consulted the opinion of Chief Justice Taney in *Lord v. Veazie* (1850):

> The objection in the case before us is . . . that the plaintiff and defendant have the same interest, and that interest adverse and in conflict with the interest of third persons, whose rights would be seriously affected if the question of law was decided in the manner that both of the parties to this suit desire it to be. A judgment entered under such circumstances, and for such purposes, is a mere form. The whole pro-ceeding was in contempt of the court, and highly reprehensible. . . . A judgment in form, thus procured, in the eye of the law is no judgment of the court. It is a nullity, and no writ of error will lie upon it. This writ is, therefore, dismissed.

There is, in the words of *Marbury*, no "necessity [to] expound and interpret" the law in this case; just a desire to place this Court at the center of the Nation's life. . . .

B

A few words in response to the theory of jurisdiction set forth in Justice Alito's dissent: Though less far reaching in its consequences than the majority's conversion of constitutionally required adverseness into a discretionary element of standing, the theory of that dissent similarly elevates the Court to the "primary" determiner of constitutional questions involving the separation of powers, and, to boot, increases the power of the most dangerous branch: the "legislative department," which by its nature "draw[s] all power into its impetuous vortex." The Federalist, No. 48, at 309 (J. Madison). Heretofore in our national history, the President's failure to "take Care that the Laws be faithfully executed," U.S. Const., Art. II, §3, could only be brought before a judicial tribunal by someone whose concrete interests were harmed by that alleged failure. Justice Alito would create a system in which Congress can hale the Executive before the courts not only to vindicate its own institutional powers to act, but to correct a perceived inadequacy in the execution of its laws.[2] This would lay to rest Tocqueville's praise of our judicial system as one which "intimately bind[s] the case made for the law with the case made for one man," one in which legislation is "no longer exposed to the daily aggression of the parties," and in which "[t]he political question that [the judge] must resolve is linked to the interest" of private litigants. A. de Tocqueville, Democracy in America 97 (H. Mansfield & D. Winthrop eds. 2000). That would be replaced by a system in which Congress and the Executive can pop immediately into court, in their institutional capacity, whenever the President refuses to implement a statute he believes to be unconstitutional, and whenever he implements a law in a manner that is not to Congress's liking.

Justice Alito's notion of standing will likewise enormously shrink the area to which "judicial censure, exercised by the courts on legislation, cannot extend." *ibid.* For example, a bare majority of both Houses could bring into court the assertion that the Executive's implementation of welfare programs is too generous—a failure that no other litigant would have standing to complain about. . . .

To be sure, if Congress cannot invoke our authority in the way that Justice Alito proposes, then its only recourse is to confront the President directly. Unimaginable evil this is not. Our system is *designed* for confrontation. That

---

2. Justice Alito attempts to limit his argument by claiming that Congress is injured (and can therefore appeal) when its statute is held unconstitutional without Presidential defense, but is *not* injured when its statute is held unconstitutional *despite* Presidential defense. I do not understand that line. The injury to Congress is the same whether the President has defended the statute or not. And if the injury is threatened, why should Congress not be able to participate in the suit from the beginning, just as the President can? And if having a statute declared unconstitutional (and therefore inoperative) by a court is an injury, why is it not an injury when a statute is declared unconstitutional by the President and rendered inoperative by his consequent failure to enforce it? Or when the President simply declines to enforce it without opining on its constitutionality? If it is the *inoperativeness* that constitutes the injury—the "impairment of [the legislative] function," as Justice Alito puts it—it should make no difference which of the other two branches inflicts it, and whether the Constitution is the pretext. A principled and predictable system of jurisprudence cannot rest upon a shifting concept of injury, designed to support standing when we would like it. . . .

is what "[a]mbition . . . counteract[ing] ambition," The Federalist, No. 51, at 322 (J. Madison), is all about. If majorities in both Houses of Congress care enough about the matter, they have available innumerable ways to compel executive action without a lawsuit — from refusing to confirm Presidential appointees to the elimination of funding. (Nothing says "enforce the Act" quite like ". . . or you will have money for little else.") But the condition is crucial; Congress must care enough to act against the President itself, not merely enough to instruct its lawyers to ask *us* to do so. Placing the Constitution's entirely anticipated political arm wrestling into permanent judicial receivership does not do the system a favor. And by the way, if the President loses the lawsuit but does not faithfully implement the Court's decree, just as he did not faithfully implement Congress's statute, what then? Only Congress can bring him to heel by . . . what do you think? Yes: a direct confrontation with the President.

JUSTICE ALITO . . . dissenting. . . .

In my view, the United States clearly is not a proper petitioner in this case. The United States does not ask us to overturn the judgment of the court below or to alter that judgment in any way. Quite to the contrary, the United States argues emphatically in favor of the correctness of that judgment. We have never before reviewed a decision at the sole behest of a party that took such a position, and to do so would be to render an advisory opinion, in violation of Article III's dictates. For the reasons given in Justice Scalia's dissent, I do not find the Court's arguments to the contrary to be persuasive. Whether the Bipartisan Legal Advisory Group of the House of Representatives (BLAG) has standing to petition is a much more difficult question. It is also a significantly closer question than whether the intervenors in *Hollingsworth v. Perry,* which the Court also decides today — have standing to appeal. It is remarkable that the Court has simultaneously decided that the United States, which "receive[d] all that [it] ha[d] sought" below, *Deposit Guaranty Nat. Bank v. Roper* (1980), is a proper petitioner in this case but that the intervenors in *Hollingsworth,* who represent the party that lost in the lower court, are not. In my view, both the *Hollingsworth* intervenors and BLAG have standing. . . .

A party invoking the Court's authority has a sufficient stake to permit it to appeal when it has " 'suffered an injury in fact' that is caused by 'the conduct complained of' and that 'will be redressed by a favorable decision.' " *Camreta v. Greene* (2011) (quoting *Lujan v. Defenders of Wildlife* (1992)). In the present case, the House of Representatives, which has authorized BLAG to represent its interests in this matter, suffered just such an injury. In *INS v. Chadha* (1983), the Court held that the two Houses of Congress were "proper parties" to file a petition in defense of the constitutionality of the one-house veto statute. Accordingly, the Court granted and decided petitions by both the Senate and the House, in addition to the Executive's petition. That the two Houses had standing to petition is not surprising: The Court of Appeals' decision in *Chadha,* by holding the one-house veto to be unconstitutional, had limited Congress' power to legislate. In discussing Article III standing, the Court suggested that Congress suffered a similar injury whenever federal legislation it had passed was struck down, noting that it had "long held that Congress is the proper party to defend the validity of a statute when an agency of government, as a defendant charged with enforcing the statute, agrees with plaintiffs that the statute is inapplicable or unconstitutional."

The United States attempts to distinguish *Chadha* on the ground that it "involved an unusual statute that vested the House and the Senate themselves each with special procedural rights—namely, the right effectively to veto Executive action." But that is a distinction without a difference: just as the Court of Appeals decision that the *Chadha* Court affirmed impaired Congress' power by striking down the one-house veto, so the Second Circuit's decision here impairs Congress' legislative power by striking down an Act of Congress. The United States has not explained why the fact that the impairment at issue in *Chadha* was "special" or "procedural" has any relevance to whether Congress suffered an injury. Indeed, because legislating is Congress' central function, any impairment of that function is a more grievous injury than the impairment of a procedural add-on. . . .

Both the United States and the Court-appointed *amicus* err in arguing that *Raines v. Byrd* (1997), is to the contrary. . . . *Raines* dealt with individual Members of Congress and specifically pointed to the individual Members' lack of institutional endorsement as a sign of their standing problem: "We attach some importance to the fact that appellees have not been authorized to represent their respective Houses of Congress in this action, and indeed both Houses actively oppose their suit." . . . Here, by contrast, passage by the House was needed for DOMA to become law. U.S. Const., Art. I, §7 (bicameralism and presentment requirements for legislation).

I appreciate the argument that the Constitution confers on the President alone the authority to defend federal law in litigation, but in my view, as I have explained, that argument is contrary to the Court's holding in *Chadha,* and it is certainly contrary to the *Chadha* Court's endorsement of the principle that "Congress is the proper party to defend the validity of a statute" when the Executive refuses to do so on constitutional grounds. Accordingly, in the narrow category of cases in which a court strikes down an Act of Congress and the Executive declines to defend the Act, Congress both has standing to defend the undefended statute and is a proper party to do so. . . .

STUDY GUIDE:

- In *Hollingsworth v. Perry*, Justices Kennedy and Alito argued in favor of standing as they had in *Windsor*. Chief Justice Roberts and Justice Scalia argued against standing in both cases. By contrast, Justices Breyer, Sotomayor, and Kagan switched from standing in *Windsor* to no standing here, while Justice Thomas switched from no standing in *Windsor* to standing here. Can these shifts in the line-ups be explained by differing philosophies on the doctrine of standing, as opposed to a desire to reach different outcomes in each case?

- If an initiative's proponents lack standing to defend it from constitutional challenge when the government refuses to do so, does this jurisprudence undermine the popular check on government that is supposed to be provided by popular initiatives? Should doctrine of federal standing reflect this difficulty?
- Is there any way for states with initiatives to fix this problem consistent with Chief Justice Roberts' opinion?
- Can you see the continuing relevance of the differing concepts of sovereignty we have seen discussed in previous chapters?

Hollingsworth v. Perry
133 S. Ct. 2652 (2013)

CHIEF JUSTICE ROBERTS delivered the opinion of the Court.

The public is currently engaged in an active political debate over whether same-sex couples should be allowed to marry. That question has also given rise to litigation. In this case, petitioners, who oppose same-sex marriage, ask us to decide whether the Equal Protection Clause "prohibits the State of California from defining marriage as the union of a man and a woman." Pet. for Cert. i. Respondents, same-sex couples who wish to marry, view the issue in somewhat different terms: For them, it is whether California—having previously recognized the right of same-sex couples to marry—may reverse that decision through a referendum. Federal courts have authority under the Constitution to answer such questions only if necessary to do so in the course of deciding an actual "case" or "controversy." As used in the Constitution, those words do not include every sort of dispute, but only those "historically viewed as capable of resolution through the judicial process." *Flast v. Cohen* (1968). This is an essential limit on our power: It ensures that we act *as judges,* and do not engage in policymaking properly left to elected representatives.

For there to be such a case or controversy, it is not enough that the party invoking the power of the court have a keen interest in the issue. That party must also have "standing," which requires, among other things, that it have suffered a concrete and particularized injury. Because we find that petitioners do not have standing, we have no authority to decide this case on the merits, and neither did the Ninth Circuit.

I

In 2008, the California Supreme Court held that limiting the official designation of marriage to opposite-sex couples violated the equal protection clause of the California Constitution. *In re Marriage Cases* (Cal. 2008) Later that year, California voters passed the ballot initiative at the center of this dispute, known as Proposition 8. That proposition amended the California Constitution to provide that "[o]nly marriage between a man and a woman is valid or recognized in

California." Cal. Const., Art. I, §7.5. Shortly thereafter, the California Supreme Court rejected a procedural challenge to the amendment, and held that the Proposition was properly enacted under California law. *Strauss v. Horton* (Cal. 2009). According to the California Supreme Court, Proposition 8 created a "narrow and limited exception" to the state constitutional rights otherwise guaranteed to same-sex couples. Under California law, same-sex couples have a right to enter into relationships recognized by the State as "domestic partnerships," which carry "the same rights, protections, and benefits, and shall be subject to the same responsibilities, obligations, and duties under law . . . as are granted to and imposed upon spouses." Cal. Fam. Code Ann. §297.5(a) (2004). In *In re Marriage Cases,* the California Supreme Court concluded that the California Constitution further guarantees same-sex couples "all of the constitutionally based incidents of marriage," including the right to have that marriage "officially recognized" as such by the State. Proposition 8, the court explained in *Strauss,* left those rights largely undisturbed, reserving only "the official *designation* of the term 'marriage' for the union of opposite-sex couples as a matter of state constitutional law."

Respondents, two same-sex couples who wish to marry, filed suit in federal court, challenging Proposition 8 under the Due Process and Equal Protection Clauses of the Fourteenth Amendment to the Federal Constitution. The complaint named as defendants California's Governor, attorney general, and various other state and local officials responsible for enforcing California's marriage laws. Those officials refused to defend the law, although they have continued to enforce it throughout this litigation. The District Court allowed petitioners—the official proponents of the initiative—to intervene to defend it. After a 12-day bench trial, the District Court declared Proposition 8 unconstitutional, permanently enjoining the California officials named as defendants from enforcing the law, and "directing the official defendants that all persons under their control or supervision" shall not enforce it. *Perry v. Schwarzenegger* (N.D. Cal. 2010). Those officials elected not to appeal the District Court order. When petitioners did, the Ninth Circuit asked them to address "why this appeal should not be dismissed for lack of Article III standing." *Perry v. Schwarzenegger* (CA9, Aug. 16, 2010). After briefing and argument, the Ninth Circuit certified a question to the California Supreme Court:

> Whether under Article II, Section 8 of the California Constitution, or otherwise under California law, the official proponents of an initiative measure possess either a particularized interest in the initiative's validity or the authority to assert the State's interest in the initiative's validity, which would enable them to defend the constitutionality of the initiative upon its adoption or appeal a judgment invalidating the initiative, when the public officials charged with that duty refuse to do so.

The California Supreme Court agreed to decide the certified question, and answered in the affirmative. Without addressing whether the proponents have a particularized interest of their own in an initiative's validity, the court concluded that "[i]n a postelection challenge to a voter-approved initiative measure, the official proponents of the initiative are authorized under California law to appear and assert the state's interest in the initiative's validity and to appeal a judgment invalidating the measure when the public officials who ordinarily defend the measure or appeal such a judgment decline to do so." *Perry v. Brown* (CA9, 2011).

Relying on that answer, the Ninth Circuit concluded that petitioners had standing under federal law to defend the constitutionality of Proposition 8. California, it reasoned, "'has standing to defend the constitutionality of its [laws],'" and States have the "prerogative, as independent sovereigns, to decide for themselves who may assert their interests." *Perry v. Brown* (CA9, 2012). "All a federal court need determine is that the state has suffered a harm sufficient to confer standing and that the party seeking to invoke the jurisdiction of the court is authorized by the state to represent its interest in remedying that harm."

On the merits, the Ninth Circuit affirmed the District Court. The court held the Proposition unconstitutional under the rationale of our decision in *Romer v. Evans* (1996). In the Ninth Circuit's view, *Romer* stands for the proposition that "the Equal Protection Clause requires the state to have a legitimate reason for withdrawing a right or benefit *from one group but not others,* whether or not it was required to confer that right or benefit in the first place." The Ninth Circuit concluded that "taking away the official designation" of "marriage" from same-sex couples, while continuing to afford those couples all the rights and obligations of marriage, did not further any legitimate interest of the State. Proposition 8, in the court's view, violated the Equal Protection Clause because it served no purpose "but to impose on gays and lesbians, through the public law, a majority's private disapproval of them and their relationships."

We granted certiorari to review that determination, and directed that the parties also brief and argue "Whether petitioners have standing under Article III, §2, of the Constitution in this case."

II

Article III of the Constitution confines the judicial power of federal courts to deciding actual "Cases" or "Controversies." §2. One essential aspect of this requirement is that any person invoking the power of a federal court must demonstrate standing to do so. This requires the litigant to prove that he has suffered a concrete and particularized injury that is fairly traceable to the challenged conduct, and is likely to be redressed by a favorable judicial decision. *Lujan v. Defenders of Wildlife* (1992). In other words, for a federal court to have authority under the Constitution to settle a dispute, the party before it must seek a remedy for a personal and tangible harm. "The presence of a disagreement, however sharp and acrimonious it may be, is insufficient by itself to meet Art. III's requirements." *Diamond v. Charles* (1986). The doctrine of standing, we recently explained, "serves to prevent the judicial process from being used to usurp the powers of the political branches." *Clapper v. Amnesty Int'l USA* (2013). In light of this "overriding and time-honored concern about keeping the Judiciary's power within its proper constitutional sphere, we must put aside the natural urge to proceed directly to the merits of [an] important dispute and to 'settle' it for the sake of convenience and efficiency." *Raines v. Byrd* (1997).

Most standing cases consider whether a plaintiff has satisfied the requirement when filing suit, but Article III demands that an "actual controversy" persist throughout all stages of litigation. *Already, LLC v. Nike, Inc.* (2013) (internal quotation marks omitted). That means that standing "must be met by persons seeking appellate review, just as it must be met by persons appearing in courts of first instance." *Arizonans for Official English v. Arizona* (1997). We therefore must decide whether petitioners had standing to appeal the District Court's order.

Respondents initiated this case in the District Court against the California officials responsible for enforcing Proposition 8. The parties do not contest that respondents had Article III standing to do so. Each couple expressed a desire to marry and obtain "official sanction" from the State, which was unavailable to them given the declaration in Proposition 8 that "marriage" in California is solely between a man and a woman.

After the District Court declared Proposition 8 unconstitutional and enjoined the state officials named as defendants from enforcing it, however, the inquiry under Article III changed. Respondents no longer had any injury to redress — they had won — and the state officials chose not to appeal.

The only individuals who sought to appeal that order were petitioners, who had intervened in the District Court. But the District Court had not ordered them to do or refrain from doing anything. To have standing, a litigant must seek relief for an injury that affects him in a "personal and individual way." *Defenders of Wildlife*. He must possess a "direct stake in the outcome" of the case. *Arizonans for Official English*. Here, however, petitioners had no "direct stake" in the outcome of their appeal. Their only interest in having the District Court order reversed was to vindicate the constitutional validity of a generally applicable California law.

We have repeatedly held that such a "generalized grievance," no matter how sincere, is insufficient to confer standing. A litigant "raising only a generally available grievance about government — claiming only harm to his and every citizen's interest in proper application of the Constitution and laws, and seeking relief that no more directly and tangibly benefits him than it does the public at large — does not state an Article III case or controversy." *Defenders of Wildlife.*

Petitioners argue that the California Constitution and its election laws give them a " 'unique,' 'special,' and 'distinct' role in the initiative process — one 'involving both authority and responsibilities that differ from other supporters of the measure.'" True enough — but only when it comes to the process of enacting the law. Upon submitting the proposed initiative to the attorney general, petitioners became the official "proponents" of Proposition 8. As such, they were responsible for collecting the signatures required to qualify the measure for the ballot. After those signatures were collected, the proponents alone had the right to file the measure with election officials to put it on the ballot. Petitioners also possessed control over the arguments in favor of the initiative that would appear in California's ballot pamphlets.

But once Proposition 8 was approved by the voters, the measure became "a duly enacted constitutional amendment or statute." *Perry*. Petitioners have no role — special or otherwise — in the enforcement of Proposition 8. See *id.* (petitioners do not "possess any official authority . . . to directly enforce the initiative measure in question"). They therefore have no "personal stake" in defending its enforcement that is distinguishable from the general interest of every citizen of California. *Defenders of Wildlife.*

Article III standing "is not to be placed in the hands of 'concerned bystanders,' who will use it simply as a 'vehicle for the vindication of value interests.'" *Diamond.* No matter how deeply committed petitioners may be to upholding Proposition 8 or how "zealous [their] advocacy," (Kennedy, J., dissenting), that is not a "particularized" interest sufficient to create a case or controversy under Article III.

III

A

Without a judicially cognizable interest of their own, petitioners attempt to invoke that of someone else. They assert that even if *they* have no cognizable interest in appealing the District Court's judgment, the State of California does, and they may assert that interest on the State's behalf. It is, however, a "fundamental restriction on our authority" that "[i]n the ordinary course, a litigant must assert his or her own legal rights and interests, and cannot rest a claim to relief on the legal rights or interests of third parties." *Powers v. Ohio* (1991). There are "certain, limited exceptions" to that rule. But even when we have allowed litigants to assert the interests of others, the litigants themselves still "must have suffered an injury in fact, thus giving [them] a sufficiently concrete interest in the outcome of the issue in dispute." In *Diamond v. Charles,* for example, we refused to allow Diamond, a pediatrician engaged in private practice in Illinois, to defend the constitutionality of the State's abortion law. In that case, a group of physicians filed a constitutional challenge to the Illinois statute in federal court. The State initially defended the law, and Diamond, a professed "conscientious object[or] to abortions," intervened to defend it alongside the State.

After the Seventh Circuit affirmed a permanent injunction against enforcing several provisions of the law, the State chose not to pursue an appeal to this Court. But when Diamond did, the state attorney general filed a "letter of interest," explaining that the State's interest in the proceeding was "essentially coterminous with the position on the issues set forth by [Diamond]." That was not enough, we held, to allow the appeal to proceed. As the Court explained, "[e]ven if there were circumstances in which a private party would have standing to defend the constitutionality of a challenged statute, this [was] not one of them," because Diamond was not able to assert an injury in fact of his own. And without "any judicially cognizable interest," Diamond could not "maintain the litigation abandoned by the State."

For the reasons we have explained, petitioners have likewise not suffered an injury in fact, and therefore would ordinarily have no standing to assert the State's interests.

B

Petitioners contend that this case is different, because the California Supreme Court has determined that they are "authorized under California law to appear and assert the state's interest" in the validity of Proposition 8. The court below agreed: "All a federal court need determine is that the state has suffered a harm sufficient to confer standing and that the party seeking to invoke the jurisdiction of the court is authorized by the state to represent its interest in remedying that harm." As petitioners put it, they "need no more show a personal injury, separate from the State's indisputable interest in the validity of its law, than would California's Attorney General or did the legislative leaders held to have standing in *Karcher v. May* (1987)." In *Karcher,* we held that two New Jersey state legislators—Speaker of the General Assembly Alan Karcher and President of the Senate Carmen Orechio—could intervene in a suit against the State to defend the constitutionality of a New Jersey law, after the New Jersey attorney general had declined to do so. "Since the New Jersey Legislature had authority under state law to represent the State's interests in both the District Court and the Court of Appeals," we held that the Speaker and the President, in their official capacities, could vindicate that interest in federal court on the legislature's behalf.

Far from supporting petitioners' standing, however, *Karcher* is compelling precedent against it. The legislators in that case intervened in their official capacities as Speaker and President of the legislature. No one doubts that a State has a cognizable interest "in the continued enforceability" of its laws that is harmed by a judicial decision declaring a state law unconstitutional. To vindicate that interest or any other, a State must be able to designate agents to represent it in federal court. See *Poindexter v. Greenhow* (1885) ("The State is a political corporate body [that] can act only through agents"). That agent is typically the State's attorney general. But state law may provide for other officials to speak for the State in federal court, as New Jersey law did for the State's presiding legislative officers in *Karcher*.

What is significant about *Karcher* is what happened after the Court of Appeals decision in that case. Karcher and Orechio lost their positions as Speaker and President, but nevertheless sought to appeal to this Court. We held that they could not do so. We explained that while they were able to participate in the lawsuit in their official capacities as presiding officers of the incumbent legislature, "since they no longer hold those offices, they lack authority to pursue this appeal."

The point of *Karcher* is not that a State could authorize *private parties* to represent its interests; Karcher and Orechio were permitted to proceed only because they were state officers, acting in an official capacity. As soon as they lost that capacity, they lost standing. Petitioners here hold no office and have always participated in this litigation solely as private parties. . . .

C

Both petitioners and respondents seek support from dicta in *Arizonans for Official English v. Arizona*. The plaintiff in *Arizonans for Official English* filed a constitutional challenge to an Arizona ballot initiative declaring English "the official language of the State of Arizona." After the District Court declared the initiative unconstitutional, Arizona's Governor announced that she would not pursue an appeal. Instead, the principal sponsor of the ballot initiative—the Arizonans for Official English Committee—sought to defend the measure in the Ninth Circuit. Analogizing the sponsors to the Arizona Legislature, the Ninth Circuit held that the Committee was "qualified to defend [the initiative] on appeal," and affirmed the District Court. Before finding the case mooted by other events, this Court expressed "grave doubts" about the Ninth Circuit's standing analysis. We reiterated that "[s]tanding to defend on appeal in the place of an original defendant . . . demands that the litigant possess 'a direct stake in the outcome.'" (quoting *Diamond*). We recognized that a legislator authorized by state law to represent the State's interest may satisfy standing requirements, as in *Karcher*, but noted that the Arizona committee and its members were "not elected representatives, and we [we]re aware of no Arizona law appointing initiative sponsors as agents of the people of Arizona to defend, in lieu of public officials, the constitutionality of initiatives made law of the State." *Arizonans for Official English.*

Petitioners argue that, by virtue of the California Supreme Court's decision, they *are* authorized to act " 'as agents of the people' of California." But that Court never described petitioners as "agents of the people," or of anyone else. Nor did the Ninth Circuit. The Ninth Circuit asked—and the California Supreme Court answered—only whether petitioners had "the authority to assert the State's interest in the initiative's validity." All that the California Supreme Court decision stands for is that, so far as California is concerned, petitioners may argue in defense of Proposition 8. This "does not mean that the proponents become de facto public officials"; the authority they enjoy is "simply the authority to participate as parties in a court action and to assert legal arguments in defense of the state's interest in the validity of the initiative measure." That interest is by definition a generalized one, and it is precisely because proponents assert such an interest that they lack standing under our precedents.

And petitioners are plainly not agents of the State—"formal" or otherwise. . . . [T]he point, the most basic features of an agency relationship are missing here. Agency requires more than mere authorization to assert a particular interest. "An essential element of agency is the principal's right to control the agent's actions." 1 Restatement (Third) of Agency §1.01, Comment *f* (2005) (hereinafter Restatement). Yet petitioners answer to no one; they decide for themselves, with no review, what arguments to make and how to make them. Unlike California's attorney general, they are not elected at regular intervals—or elected at all. No provision provides for their removal. As one *amicus* explains, "the proponents apparently have an unelected appointment for an unspecified period of time as defenders of the initiative, however and to whatever extent they choose to defend it." Brief for Walter Dellinger. "If the relationship between two persons is one of agency . . . , the agent owes a fiduciary obligation to the principal." 1 Restatement §1.01, Comment *e*. But petitioners owe nothing of the sort to the people of California. Unlike California's elected officials, they have taken no oath of office. As the California Supreme Court explained, petitioners are bound simply by "the same ethical constraints that apply to all other parties in a legal proceeding." They are free to pursue a purely ideological commitment to the law's constitutionality without the need to take cognizance of resource constraints, changes in public opinion, or potential ramifications for other state priorities. . . .

Neither the California Supreme Court nor the Ninth Circuit ever described the proponents as agents of the State, and they plainly do not qualify as such.

IV

The dissent eloquently recounts the California Supreme Court's reasons for deciding that state law authorizes petitioners to defend Proposition 8. . . . We do not "disrespect[ ]" or "disparage[ ]" those reasons. Nor do we question California's sovereign right to maintain an initiative process, or the right of initiative proponents to defend their initiatives in California courts, where Article III does not apply. But as the dissent acknowledges, standing in federal court is a question of federal law, not state law. And no matter its reasons, the fact that a State thinks a private party should have standing to seek relief for a generalized grievance cannot override our settled law to the contrary. The Article III requirement that a party invoking the jurisdiction of a federal court seek relief for a personal, particularized injury serves vital interests going to the role of the Judiciary in our system of separated powers. "Refusing to entertain generalized grievances ensures that . . . courts exercise power that is judicial in nature," *Lance*, and ensures that the Federal Judiciary respects "the proper—and properly limited—role of the courts in a democratic society," *DaimlerChrysler Corp. v. Cuno* (2006). States cannot alter that role simply by issuing to private parties who otherwise lack standing a ticket to the federal courthouse.

* * *

We have never before upheld the standing of a private party to defend the constitutionality of a state statute when state officials have chosen not to. We decline to do so for the first time here. Because petitioners have not satisfied their burden to demonstrate standing to appeal the judgment of the District Court, the Ninth Circuit was without jurisdiction to consider the appeal. The judgment of the Ninth Circuit is vacated, and the case is remanded with instructions to dismiss the appeal for lack of jurisdiction. It is so ordered.

JUSTICE KENNEDY, with whom JUSTICE THOMAS, JUSTICE ALITO, and JUSTICE SOTOMAYOR join, dissenting. . . .

In my view Article III does not require California, when deciding who may appear in court to defend an initiative on its behalf, to comply with the Restatement of Agency or with this Court's view of how a State should make its laws or structure its government. The Court's reasoning does not take into account the fundamental principles or the practical dynamics of the initiative system in California, which uses this mechanism to control and to bypass public officials—the same officials who would not defend the initiative, an injury the Court now leaves unremedied. The Court's decision also has implications for the 26 other States that use an initiative or popular referendum system and which, like California, may choose to have initiative proponents stand in for the State when public officials decline to defend an initiative in litigation. In my submission, the Article III requirement for a justiciable case or controversy does not prevent proponents from having their day in court.

These are the premises for this respectful dissent.

I

As the Court explains, the State of California sustained a concrete injury, sufficient to satisfy the requirements of Article III, when a United States District Court nullified a portion of its State Constitution. To determine whether justiciability continues in appellate proceedings after the State Executive acquiesced in the District Court's adverse judgment, it is necessary to ascertain what persons, if any, have "authority under state law to represent the State's interests" in federal court. *Karcher v. May* (1987). . . .

This Court, in determining the substance of state law, is "bound by a state court's construction of a state statute." *Wisconsin v. Mitchell* (1993). And the Supreme Court of California, in response to the certified question submitted to it in this case, has determined that State Elections Code provisions directed to initiative proponents do inform and instruct state law respecting the rights and status of proponents in post election judicial proceedings. Here, in reliance on these statutes and the California Constitution, the State Supreme Court has held that proponents do have authority "under California law to appear and assert the state's interest in the initiative's validity and appeal a judgment invalidating the measure when the public officials who ordinarily defend the measure or appeal such a judgment decline to do so." *Perry v. Brown* (Cal. 2011).

The reasons the Supreme Court of California gave for its holding have special relevance in the context of determining whether proponents have the authority to seek a federal-court remedy for the State's concrete, substantial, and continuing injury. As a class, official proponents are a small, identifiable group. Because many of their decisions must be unanimous, they are necessarily few in number. Their identities are public. Their commitment is substantial [including obtaining petition signatures, paying monetary fee, and drafting arguments for official ballot pamphlet]. They know and understand the purpose and operation of the proposed law, an important requisite in defending initiatives on complex matters such as taxation and insurance. Having gone to great lengths to convince voters to enact an initiative, they have a stake in the outcome and the necessary commitment to provide zealous advocacy.

Thus, in California, proponents play a "unique role . . . in the initiative process." They "have a unique relationship to the voter-approved measure that makes them especially likely to be reliable and vigorous advocates for the measure and to be so viewed by those whose votes secured the initiative's enactment into law." See also *id.* (because of "their special relationship to the initiative measure," proponents are "the most obvious and logical private individuals to ably and vigorously defend the validity of the challenged measure on behalf of the interests of the voters who adopted the initiative into law"). Proponents' authority under state law is not a contrivance. It is not a fictional construct. It is the product of the California Constitution and the California Elections Code. There is no basis for this Court to set aside the California Supreme Court's determination of state law. . . .

For these and other reasons, the Supreme Court of California held that the California Elections Code and Article II, §8, of the California Constitution afford proponents "the authority . . . to assert the state's interest in the validity of the initiative" when State officials decline to do so. The court repeated this unanimous holding more than a half-dozen times and in no uncertain terms. That should suffice to resolve the central issue on which the federal question turns.

II

A

The Court concludes that proponents lack sufficient ties to the state government. It notes that they "are not elected," "answer to no one," and lack "a fiduciary obligation" to the State (quoting 1 Restatement (Third) of Agency §1.01, Comments *e, f* (2005)). But what the Court deems deficiencies in the proponents' connection to the State government, the State Supreme Court saw as essential qualifications to defend the initiative system. The very object of the initiative system is to establish a lawmaking process that does not depend upon state officials. In California, the popular initiative is necessary to implement "the theory that all power of government ultimately resides in the people." The right to adopt initiatives has been described by the California courts as "one of the most precious rights of [the State's] democratic process." That historic role for the initiative system "grew out of dissatisfaction with the then governing public officials and a widespread belief that the people had lost control of the political process." The initiative's "primary purpose," then, "was to afford the people the ability to propose and to adopt constitutional amendments or statutory provisions that their elected public officials had refused or declined to adopt." The California Supreme Court has determined that this purpose is undermined if the very officials the initiative process seeks to circumvent are the only parties who can defend an enacted initiative when it is challenged in a legal proceeding. Giving the Governor and attorney general this *de facto* veto will erode one of the cornerstones of the State's governmental structure. And in light of the frequency with which initiatives' opponents resort to litigation, the impact of that veto could be substantial. As a consequence, California finds it necessary to vest the responsibility and right to defend a voter-approved initiative in the initiative's proponents when the State Executive declines to do so.

Yet today the Court demands that the State follow the Restatement of Agency. There are reasons, however, why California might conclude that a conventional agency relationship is inconsistent with the history, design, and purpose of the initiative process. The State may not wish to associate itself with proponents or their views outside of the "extremely narrow and limited" context of this litigation, or to bear the cost of proponents' legal fees. The State may also wish to avoid the odd conflict of having a formal agent of the State (the initiative's proponent) arguing in favor of a law's validity while state officials (*e.g.,* the attorney general) contend in the same proceeding that it should be found invalid.

Furthermore, it is not clear who the principal in an agency relationship would be. It would make little sense if it were the Governor or attorney general, for that would frustrate the initiative system's purpose of circumventing elected officials who fail or refuse to effect the public will. If there is to be a principal, then, it must be the people of California, as the ultimate sovereign in the State. See [Cal. Const., Art. II, §1] ("All political power is inherent in the people.") But the Restatement may offer no workable example of an agent representing a principal composed of nearly 40 million residents of a State. Cf. 1 Restatement (Second) of Agency, p. 2, Scope Note (1957) (noting that the Restatement "does not state the special rules applicable to public officers").

And if the Court's concern is that the proponents are unaccountable, that fear is neither well founded nor sufficient to overcome the contrary judgment of the State Supreme Court. It must be remembered that both elected officials and initiative proponents receive their authority to speak for the State of California directly from the people. The Court apparently believes that elected officials are acceptable "agents" of the State, but they are no more subject to ongoing supervision of their principal—*i.e.,* the people of the State—than are initiative proponents. At most, a Governor or attorney general can be recalled or voted out of office in a subsequent election, but proponents, too, can have their authority terminated or their initiative overridden by a subsequent ballot measure. Finally, proponents and their attorneys, like all other litigants and counsel who appear before a federal court, are subject to duties of candor, decorum, and respect for the tribunal and co-parties alike, all of which guard against the possibility that initiative proponents will somehow fall short of the appropriate standards for federal litigation.

B

Contrary to the Court's suggestion, this Court's precedents do not indicate that a formal agency relationship is necessary. In *Karcher v. May* (1987), the Speaker of the New Jersey Assembly (Karcher) and President of the New Jersey Senate (Orechio) intervened in support of a school moment-of-silence law that the State's Governor and attorney general declined to defend in court. In considering the question of standing, the Court looked to New Jersey law to determine whether Karcher and Orechio "had authority under state law to represent the State's interest in both the District Court and Court of Appeals." The Court concluded that they did. Because the "New Jersey Supreme Court ha[d] granted applications of the Speaker of the General Assembly and the President of the Senate to intervene as parties-respondent on behalf of the legislature in defense of a legislative enactment," the *Karcher* Court held that standing had been proper in the District Court and Court of Appeals. By the time the case arrived in this Court, Karcher and Orechio had lost their presiding legislative offices, without which they lacked the authority to represent the State under New Jersey law. This, the Court held, deprived them of standing. Here, by contrast, proponents' authority under California law is not contingent on officeholder status, so their standing is unaffected by the fact that they "hold no office" in California's Government. *Arizonans for Official English v. Arizona* (1997) is consistent with the premises of this dissent, not with the rationale of the Court's opinion. There, the Court noted its serious doubts as to the aspiring defenders' standing because there was "no Arizona law appointing initiative sponsors as agents of the people of Arizona to defend, in lieu of public officials, the constitutionality of initiatives made law of the State." The Court did use the word "agents"; but, read in context, it is evident that the Court's intention was not to demand a formal agency relationship in compliance with the Restatement. Rather, the Court used the term as shorthand for a party whom "state law authorizes" to "represent the State's interests" in court. . . .

III

There is much irony in the Court's approach to justiciability in this case. A prime purpose of justiciability is to ensure vigorous advocacy, yet the Court insists upon litigation conducted by state officials whose preference is to lose the case. The doctrine is meant to ensure that courts are responsible and constrained in their power, but the Court's opinion today means that a single district court can make a decision with far-reaching effects that cannot be reviewed. And rather than honor the principle that justiciability exists to allow disputes of public policy to be resolved by the political process rather than the courts, see, *e.g., Allen v. Wright* (1984), here the Court refuses to allow a State's authorized representatives to defend the outcome of a democratic election. The Court's opinion disrespects and disparages both the political process in California and the well-stated opinion of the California Supreme Court in this case. The California Supreme Court, not this Court, expresses concern for vigorous representation; the California Supreme Court, not this Court, recognizes the necessity to avoid conflicts of interest; the California Supreme Court, not this Court, comprehends the real interest at stake in this litigation and identifies the most proper party to defend that interest. The California Supreme Court's opinion reflects a better understanding of the dynamics and principles of Article III than does this Court's opinion. . . .

* * *

In the end, what the Court fails to grasp or accept is the basic premise of the initiative process. And it is this. The essence of democracy is that the right to make law rests in the people and flows to the government, not the other way around. Freedom resides first in the people without need of a grant from government. The California initiative process embodies these principles and has done so for over a century. . . . In California and the 26 other States that permit initiatives and popular referendums, the people have exercised their own inherent sovereign right to govern themselves. The Court today frustrates that choice by nullifying, for failure to comply with the Restatement of Agency, a State Supreme Court decision holding that state law authorizes an enacted initiative's proponents to defend the law if and when the State's usual legal advocates decline to do so. The Court's opinion fails to abide by precedent and misapplies basic principles of justiciability. Those errors necessitate this respectful dissent.

Chapter 10

Slavery, Citizenship, and the Due Process of Law

No new cases or readings.

Chapter 11

Contracting the Scope of the Thirteenth and Fourteenth Amendments

STUDY GUIDE:

- Did the Court find that the West Virginia law, limiting the composition of the jury to white males, deprived Strauder of the equal protection of the law, in violation of the 14th Amendment? If so, why did the Court not simply invalidate the West Virginia law? Rather, the Court's analysis is two-fold: (1) the West Virginia law deprives Strauder of the equal protection of the law; (2) therefore, Congress has the power to remedy that violation of the 14th Amendment under its Section 5 powers.
- Could an African-American defendant receive a fair trial from a jury that included only white men? Could a white defendant receive a fair trial from a jury that included only African-American men? Prior to the trial, Strauder's attorney gave the judge, but not the prosecutor, an affidavit indicating that "he had heard one of the jurors say, some three months before, that the prisoner ought to be hung."
- Is the exclusion of women from the jury pool a violation of the Equal Protection Clause? What about the exclusion of children from the jury pool?
- Justice Field's dissent in a companion case, *Ex Parte Virginia*, draws a distinction between "political rights" and "civil rights." How does he characterize jury service? Is it a right incident to citizenship?

Strauder v. West Virginia
100 U.S. 303 (1880)

MR. JUSTICE STRONG delivered the opinion of the court.

The plaintiff in error, a colored man, was indicted for murder [of his wife*] in the Circuit Court of Ohio County, in West Virginia, on the 20th of October,

---

* "A terrible murder was committed at an early hour yesterday morning. . . . The house was occupied by a colored man, Taylor Strauder, Anna Strauder, his wife, and Fanny Green, her daughter by a former husband, a little girl nine years old. . . . Strauder asked his wife where his shoes were. She replied that they were where he had left them the previous night. Thereupon, without further ceremony, Strauder reached and picked up a hatchet lying on the floor and dealt his wife two blows with

1874, and upon trial was convicted and sentenced. The record was then removed to the Supreme Court of the State, and there the judgment of the Circuit Court was affirmed. The present case is a writ of error to that court, and it is now, in substance, averred that at the trial in the State court the defendant (now plaintiff in error) was denied rights to which he was entitled under the Constitution and laws of the United States.

[Section 3 of the Civil Rights Act of 1866 provided a mechanism for a defendant to "remove" any "civil or criminal" case from state court, to federal court, if it involved a claim based on the Civil Rights Act, or the Freedmen's Bureau Act. For example, if a state prosecutor indicted a federal officer for protecting the rights of the freedmen, the federal officer could "remove" the case from state court to federal court, where, presumably the case would be dismissed. This removal provision, which expressed a deep distrust for state courts, could only have been based on Congress's powers under Section 2 of the 13th Amendment. Nine years later, and after the enactment of the Fourteenth Amendment, Congress expanded this removal provision in Section 641 of the Revised Statutes of the United States (1875). The statute allowed removal from state court to federal court in a far wider range of cases:

> When any civil suit or criminal prosecution is commenced in any State court for any cause whatsoever against any person who is denied, or cannot enforce, in the judicial tribunals of the State, or in the part of the State where such prosecution is pending, *any right secured to him by any law providing for the equal civil rights of citizens of the United States, or of all persons within the jurisdiction of the United States,* such suit or prosecution may, upon the petition of such defendant, filed in said State court at any time before the trial, or final hearing of the case, stating the facts, and verified by oath, be removed before trial into the next Circuit Court of the United States to be held in the district where it is pending.

Through this law, Congress explained that the state courts could not be trusted to protect the rights of the freedmen. It also could be based on both of Congress's enforcement powers: Section 2 of the 13th Amendment *and* Section 5 of the 14th Amendment. — Eds.]

In the Circuit Court of the State, before the trial of the indictment was commenced, the defendant presented his petition, verified by his oath, praying for a removal of the cause into the [federal] Circuit Court of the United States, assigning, as ground for the removal, that "by virtue of the laws of the State of West Virginia no colored man was eligible to be a member of the grand jury or to serve on a petit jury in the State; that white men are so eligible, and that

---

the poll of it, one on the temple, crushing it in, and another behind the ear. She appears to have been killed instantly, at least to have died without a struggle, as she was still sitting in the chair when found. While the awful tragedy was in progress the little girl became alarmed . . . Strauder commanded her to lie still and make no noise, on pain of death. She obeyed and Strauder left the house; but she not knowing but that he might return and execute his threat, did not stir from bed." *See* "Horrible Murder. A Colored Woman Tomahawked by Her Husband. He Brains Her With a Hatchet. The Murderer Escapes." Wheeling Daily Intelligencer (Apr. 19, 1872), https://perma.cc/3A37-Q47Q.

by reason of his being a colored man and having been a slave, he had reason to believe, and did believe, he could not have the full and equal benefit of all laws and proceedings in the State of West Virginia for the security of his person as is enjoyed by white citizens, and that he had less chance of enforcing in the courts of the State his rights on the prosecution, as a citizen of the United States, and that the probabilities of a denial of them to him as such citizen on every trial which might take place on the indictment in the courts of the State were much more enhanced than if he was a white man." [The West Virginia law provided: "All white male persons who are twenty-one years of age and who are citizens of this State shall be liable to serve as jurors, except as herein provided." — Eds.] This petition was denied by the State court, and the cause was forced to trial.

[The Defendant filed] motions to quash the *venire* [the composition of the jury — Eds.], "because the law under which [the jury] was issued was unconstitutional, null, and void." [The Defendant also made] successive motions to challenge the array of the [jury] panel, for a new trial, and in arrest of judgment. . . . [A]ll of [the motions] were overruled and made by exceptions parts of the record.

[The Supreme Court of West Virginia rejected the argument that removal was warranted: "We have seen that in the trial of a citizen of this State for an offense committed in the State against her laws, the prisoner could in no case have a right to have the trial removed to the Federal court; the fourteenth amendment not being intended to protect the citizens of any State against unjust legislation by their own State. In the particular case before us, I can not see why a jury of white men would not be quite as likely to do justice to the prisoner as a jury of negroes; but if it were otherwise, it would give him no right to have his case removed to the Federal court for trial." State v. Strauder, 11 W. Va. 745, 819 (1877) — Eds.]

In this court, several errors have been assigned, and the controlling questions underlying them all are, first, whether, by the Constitution and laws of the United States, every citizen of the United States has a right to a trial of an indictment against him by a jury selected and impanelled without discrimination against his race or color, because of race or color; and, second, if he has such a right, and is denied its enjoyment by the State in which he is indicted, may he cause the case to be removed into the Circuit Court of the United States?

It is to be observed that the first of these questions is not whether a colored man, when an indictment has been preferred against him, has a right to a grand or a petit jury composed in whole or in part of persons of his own race or color, but it is whether, in the composition or selection of jurors by whom he is to be indicted or tried, all persons of his race or color may be excluded by law, solely because of their race or color, so that by no possibility can any colored man sit upon the jury.

The questions are important, for they demand a construction of the recent amendments of the Constitution. If the defendant has a right to have a jury selected for the trial of his case without discrimination against all persons of his race or color, because of their race or color, the right, if not created, is protected by those amendments, and the legislation of Congress under them. The Fourteenth Amendment ordains that "all persons born or naturalized in the

United States and subject to the jurisdiction thereof are citizens of the United States and of the State wherein they reside. No State shall make or enforce any laws which shall abridge the privileges or immunities of citizens of the United States, nor shall any State deprive any person of life, liberty, or property, without due process of law, nor deny to any person within its jurisdiction the equal protection of the laws."

This is one of a series of constitutional provisions having a common purpose; namely, securing to a race recently emancipated, a race that through many generations had been held in slavery, all the civil rights that the superior race enjoy. The true spirit and meaning of the amendments, as we said in the *Slaughter-House Cases*, cannot be understood without keeping in view the history of the times when they were adopted, and the general objects they plainly sought to accomplish. At the time when they were incorporated into the Constitution, it required little knowledge of human nature to anticipate that those who had long been regarded as an inferior and subject race would, when suddenly raised to the rank of citizenship, be looked upon with jealousy and positive dislike, and that State laws might be enacted or enforced to perpetuate the distinctions that had before existed. Discriminations against them had been habitual. It was well known that in some States laws making such discriminations then existed, and others might well be expected. The colored race, as a race, was abject and ignorant, and in that condition was unfitted to command the respect of those who had superior intelligence. Their training had left them mere children, and as such they needed the protection which a wise government extends to those who are unable to protect themselves. They especially needed protection against unfriendly action in the States where they were resident. It was in view of these considerations the Fourteenth Amendment was framed and adopted. It was designed to assure to the colored race the enjoyment of all the civil rights that under the law are enjoyed by white persons, and to give to that race the protection of the general government, in that enjoyment, whenever it should be denied by the States. It not only gave citizenship and the privileges of citizenship to persons of color, but it denied to any State the power to withhold from them the equal protection of the laws, and authorized Congress to enforce its provisions by appropriate legislation. To quote the language used by us in the *Slaughter-House Cases* . . . "The existence of laws in the States where the newly emancipated negroes resided, which discriminated with gross injustice and hardship against them as a class, was the evil to be remedied, and by it [the Fourteenth Amendment] such laws were forbidden. If, however, the States did not conform their laws to its requirements, then, by the fifth section of the article of amendment, Congress was authorized to enforce it by suitable legislation." And it was added, "We doubt very much whether any action of a State, not directed by way of discrimination against the negroes, as a class, will ever be held to come within the purview of this provision."

If this is the spirit and meaning of the amendment, whether it means more or not, it is to be construed liberally, to carry out the purposes of its framers. It ordains that no State shall make or enforce any laws which shall abridge the privileges or immunities of citizens of the United States (evidently referring to the newly made citizens, who, being citizens of the United States, are declared to be also citizens of the State in which they reside). It ordains that no State shall deprive any person of life, liberty, or property, without due process of law, or deny to any person within its jurisdiction the equal protection of the laws. What is this but declaring that the law in the States shall be the same for the black as for the white; that all persons, whether colored or white, shall stand equal before the laws of the States, and, in regard to the colored race, for whose protection the amendment was primarily designed, that no discrimination shall be made against them by law because of their color? The words of the amendment, it is true, are prohibitory, but they contain a necessary implication of a positive immunity, or right, most valuable to the colored race — the right to exemption from unfriendly legislation against them distinctively as colored — exemption from legal discriminations, implying inferiority in civil society, lessening the security of their enjoyment of the rights which others enjoy, and discriminations which are steps towards reducing them to the condition of a subject race.

That the West Virginia statute respecting juries — the statute that controlled the selection of the grand and petit jury in the case of the plaintiff in error — is such a discrimination ought not to be doubted. Nor would it be if the persons excluded by it were white men. If in those States where the colored people constitute a majority of the entire population a law should be enacted excluding all white men from jury service, thus denying to them the privilege of participating equally with the blacks in the administration of justice, we apprehend no one would be heard to claim that it would not be a denial to white men of the equal protection of the laws. Nor if a law should be passed excluding all naturalized Celtic Irishmen, would there by any doubt of its inconsistency with the spirit of the amendment. The very fact that colored people are singled out and expressly denied by a statute all right to participate in the administration of the law, as jurors, because of their color, though they are citizens, and may be in other respects fully qualified, is practically a brand upon them, affixed by the law, an assertion of their inferiority, and a stimulant to that race prejudice which is an impediment to securing to individuals of the race that equal justice which the law aims to secure to all others.

The right to a trial by jury is guaranteed to every citizen of West Virginia by the Constitution of that State, and the constitution of juries is a very essential part of the protection such a mode of trial is intended to secure. . . . It is well known that prejudices often exist against particular classes in the community, which sway the judgment of jurors, and which, therefore, operate in some cases to deny to persons of those classes the full enjoyment of that protection which others enjoy. Prejudice in a local community is held to be a reason for a change of venue. The framers of the constitutional amendment must have known full well the existence of such prejudice and its likelihood to continue against the manumitted [that is, freed — Eds.] slaves and their race, and that knowledge was doubtless a motive that led to the amendment. By their manumission and citizenship the colored race became entitled to the equal protection of the laws of the

States in which they resided; and the apprehension that through prejudice they might be denied that equal protection, that is, that there might be discrimination against them, was the inducement to bestow upon the national government the power to enforce the provision that no State shall deny to them the equal protection of the laws. [That is, Section 5 of the 14th Amendment—Eds.] Without the apprehended existence of prejudice that portion of the amendment would have been unnecessary, and it might have been left to the States to extend equality of protection.

In view of these considerations, it is hard to see why the statute of West Virginia should not be regarded as discriminating against a colored man when he is put upon trial for an alleged criminal offence against the State. It is not easy to comprehend how it can be said that while every white man is entitled to a trial by a jury selected from persons of his own race or color, or, rather, selected without discrimination against his color, and a negro is not, the latter is equally protected by the law with the former. Is not protection of life and liberty against race or color prejudice, a right, a legal right, under the constitutional amendment? And how can it be maintained that compelling a colored man to submit to a trial for his life by a jury drawn from a panel from which the State has expressly excluded every man of his race, because of color alone, however well qualified in other respects, is not a denial to him of equal legal protection?

We do not say that within the limits from which it is not excluded by the amendment a State may not prescribe the qualifications of its jurors, and in so doing make discriminations. It may confine the selection to males, to freeholders, to citizens, to persons within certain ages, or to persons having educational qualifications. We do not believe the Fourteenth Amendment was ever intended to prohibit this. Looking at its history, it is clear it had no such purpose. Its aim was against discrimination because of race or color. As we have said more than once, its design was to protect an emancipated race, and to strike down all possible legal discriminations against those who belong to it. . . .

The Fourteenth Amendment makes no attempt to enumerate the rights it designed to protect. It speaks in general terms, and those are as comprehensive as possible. Its language is prohibitory; but every prohibition implies the existence of rights and immunities, prominent among which is an immunity from inequality of legal protection, either for life, liberty, or property. Any State action that denies this immunity to a colored man is in conflict with the Constitution.

Concluding, therefore, that the statute of West Virginia, discriminating in the selection of jurors, as it does, against negroes because of their color, amounts to a denial of the equal protection of the laws to a colored man when he is put upon trial for an alleged offence against the State, it remains only to be considered whether the power of Congress to enforce the provisions of the Fourteenth Amendment by appropriate legislation is sufficient to justify the enactment of sect. 641 of the Revised Statutes [that is, the removal statute—Eds.].

A right or an immunity, whether created by the Constitution or only guaranteed by it, even without any express delegation of power, may be protected by Congress. *Prigg* v. *The Commonwealth of Pennsylvania*. So in *United States* v.

Reese, it was said by the Chief Justice of this court: "Rights and immunities created by or dependent upon the Constitution of the United States can be protected by Congress. The form and manner of the protection may be such as Congress in the legitimate exercise of its legislative discretion shall provide. These may be varied to meet the necessities of the particular right to be protected." But there is express authority to protect the rights and immunities referred to in the Fourteenth Amendment, and to enforce observance of them by appropriate congressional legislation. And one very efficient and appropriate mode of extending such protection and securing to a party the enjoyment of the right or immunity, is a law providing for the removal of his case from a State court, in which the right is denied by the State law, into a Federal court, where it will be upheld. This is an ordinary mode of protecting rights and immunities conferred by the Federal Constitution and laws. Sect. 641 is such a provision. It enacts that "when any civil suit or criminal prosecution is commenced in any State court for any cause whatsoever against any person who is denied, or cannot enforce, in the judicial tribunals of the State, or in the part of the State where such prosecution is pending, any right secured to him by any law providing for the equal civil rights of citizens of the United States, or of all persons within the jurisdiction of the United States, such suit or prosecution may, upon the petition of such defendant, filed in said State court at any time before the trial, or final hearing of the case, stating the facts, and verified by oath, be removed before trial into the next Circuit Court of the United States to be held in the district where it is pending."

This act plainly has reference to sects. 1977 and 1978 of the statutes [in which Congress re-codified Section 1 of the Civil Rights Act of 1866] which partially enumerate the rights and immunities intended to be guaranteed by the Constitution, the first of which declares that "all persons within the jurisdiction of the United States shall have the same right in every State and Territory to make and enforce contracts, to sue, be parties, give evidence, and to the full and equal benefit of all laws and proceedings for the security of persons and property, as is enjoyed by white citizens, and shall be subject to like punishment, pains, penalties, taxes, licenses, and exactions of every kind, and to no other." This act puts in the form of a statute what had been substantially ordained by the constitutional amendment. It was a step towards enforcing the constitutional provisions. Sect. 641 was an advanced step, fully warranted, we think, by the fifth section of the Fourteenth Amendment.

We have heretofore considered and affirmed the constitutional power of Congress to authorize the removal from State courts into the circuit courts of the United States, before trial, of criminal prosecutions for alleged offences against the laws of the State, when the defence presents a Federal question, or when a right under the Federal Constitution or laws is involved. *Tennessee* v. *Davis*. It is unnecessary now to repeat what we there said.

That the petition of the plaintiff in error, filed by him in the State court before the trial of his case, made a case for removal into the Federal Circuit Court, under sect. 641, is very plain, if, by the constitutional amendment and sect. 1977 of the Revised Statutes, he was entitled to immunity from discrimination against him in the selection of jurors, because of their color, as we have endeavored to show that he was. It set forth sufficient facts to exhibit a denial of that immunity, and a denial by the statute law of the State.

There was error, therefore, in proceeding to the trial of the indictment against him after his petition was filed, as also in overruling his challenge to the array of the jury, and in refusing to quash the panel.

The judgment of the Supreme Court of West Virginia will be reversed, and the case remitted with instructions to reverse the judgment of the Circuit Court of Ohio county; and it is

So ordered.

MR. JUSTICE FIELD.

I dissent from the judgment of the court in this case, on the grounds stated in my opinion in *Ex parte Virginia*, and MR. JUSTICE CLIFFORD concurs with me. . . . Nothing, in my judgment, could have a greater tendency to destroy the independence and autonomy of the States; reduce them to a humiliating and degrading dependence upon the central government; engender constant irritation; and destroy that domestic tranquility which it was one of the objects of the Constitution to insure, than the doctrine asserted in this case, that Congress can exercise coercive authority over judicial officers of the States in the discharge of their duties under State laws. It will be only another step in the same direction towards consolidation, when it assumes to exercise similar coercive authority over governors and legislators of the States. . . .

The Thirteenth and Fourteenth Amendments are relied upon . . . to support the legislation in question. . . . To each of these amendments a clause is added, authorizing Congress to enforce its provisions by "appropriate legislation." . . . Aside from the extinction of slavery, and the declaration of citizenship, their provisions are merely prohibitory upon the States and there is nothing in their language or purpose which indicates that they are to be construed or enforced in any way different from that adopted with reference to previous restraints upon the States. The provision authorizing Congress to enforce them by appropriate legislation does not enlarge their scope, nor confer any authority which would not have existed independently of it. . . . Congress could not lay down rules for the guidance of the State judiciary, and prescribe to it the law and the motives by which it should be controlled, and if these were disregarded, direct criminal proceedings against its members; because a judiciary independent of external authority is essential to the independence of the State, and also, I may add, to a just and efficient administration of justice in her courts. . . . I cannot think I am mistaken in saying that a change so radical in the relation between the Federal and State authorities, as would justify legislation interfering with the independent action of the different departments of the State governments, in all matters over which the States retain jurisdiction, was never contemplated by the recent amendments. . . .

But the privilege or the duty, whichever it may be called, of acting as a juror in the courts of the country, is not an incident of citizenship. Women are citizens; so are the aged above sixty, and children in their minority; yet they are not allowed in Virginia to act as jurors. Though some of these are in all respects qualified for such service, no one will pretend that their exclusion by law from the jury list impairs their rights as citizens. . . .

[Justice Field turns to his analysis of the Equal Protection Clause—Eds.] All persons within the jurisdiction of the State, whether permanent residents or temporary sojourners, whether old or young, male or female, are to be equally protected. Yet no one will contend that equal protection to women, to children, to the aged, to aliens, can only be secured by allowing persons of the class to which they belong to act as jurors in cases affecting their interests. The equality of protection intended does not require that all persons shall be permitted to participate in the government of the State and the administration of its laws, to hold its offices, or be clothed with any public trusts. As already said, the universality of the protection assured repels any such conclusion. The equality of the protection secured extends only to civil rights as distinguished from those which are political, or arise from the form of the government and its mode of administration. . . .

The political rights which he may enjoy, such as holding office and discharging a public trust, are qualified because their possession depends on his fitness, to be adjudged by those whom society has clothed with the elective authority. The Thirteenth and Fourteenth Amendments were designed to secure the civil rights of all persons, of every race, color, and condition; but they left to the States to determine to whom the possession of political powers should be entrusted. This is manifest from the fact that when it was desired to confer political power upon the newly made citizens of the States, as was done by inhibiting the denial to them of the suffrage on account of race, color, or previous condition of servitude, a new amendment was required. . . .

The position that in cases where the rights of colored persons are concerned, justice will not be done to them unless they have a mixed jury, is founded upon the notion that in such cases white persons will not be fair and honest jurors. If this position be correct, there ought not to be any white persons on the jury where the interests of colored persons only are involved. That jury would not be an honest or fair one, of which any of its members should be governed in his judgment by other considerations than the law and the evidence; and that decision would hardly be considered just which should be reached by a sort of compromise, in which the prejudices of one race were set off against the prejudices of the other. To be consistent, those who hold this notion should contend that in cases affecting members of the colored race only, the juries should be composed entirely of colored persons, and that the presiding judge should be of the same race. . . .

If these views as to the purport and meaning of the Thirteenth and Fourteenth Amendments to the Constitution be correct, there is no warrant for the act of Congress under which the indictment in this case was found . . .

Those who regard the independence of the States in all their reserved powers—and this includes the independence of their legislative, judicial, and executive departments—as essential to the successful maintenance of our form of government, cannot fail to view with the gravest apprehension for the future, the indictment, in a court of the United States, of a judicial officer of a State for the manner in which he has discharged his duties under her laws, and of which she makes no complaint. . . . The legislation of Congress is founded, and is sustained by this court, as it seems to me, upon a theory as to what constitutes the equal protection of the laws, which is purely speculative, not warranted by any experience of the country, and not in accordance with the understanding of the people as to the meaning of those terms since the organization of the government.

Chapter 12

Expanding the Scope of the Due Process Clause

No new cases or readings.

Chapter 13

Equal Protection of the Law: Discrimination on the Basis of Race

STUDY GUIDE:

- *Schuette* (rhymes with duty) concerned not whether race-based "affirmative action" remedies are permissible but instead whether prohibiting its use by popular referendum constitutes a violation of the Equal Protection Clause.
- Even the dissent, however, did not contend that such a policy was mandated by the Equal Protection Clause. Instead, the issue was whether barring government officials from using this practice by state referendum violated the so-called political process doctrine.

Schuette v. Coalition to Defend Affirmative Action, Integration and Immigrant Rights and Fight for Equality by any Means Necessary (BAMN) (2014)
134 S. Ct. 1623

JUSTICE KENNEDY announced the judgment of the Court and delivered an opinion, in which THE CHIEF JUSTICE and JUSTICE ALITO join.

The Court in this case must determine whether an amendment to the Constitution of the State of Michigan, approved and enacted by its voters, is invalid under the Equal Protection Clause of the Fourteenth Amendment to the Constitution of the United States.

In 2003 the Court reviewed the constitutionality of two admissions systems at the University of Michigan, one for its undergraduate class and one for its law school. The undergraduate admissions plan was addressed in *Gratz v. Bollinger* (2003). The law school admission plan was addressed in *Grutter v. Bollinger* (2003). Each admissions process permitted the explicit consideration of an applicant's race. In *Gratz,* the Court invalidated the undergraduate plan as a violation of the Equal Protection Clause. In *Grutter,* the Court found no constitutional flaw in the law school admission plan's more limited use of race-based preferences.

In response to the Court's decision in *Gratz,* the university revised its undergraduate admissions process, but the revision still allowed limited use of race-based preferences. After a statewide debate on the question of racial preferences in the context of governmental decisionmaking, the voters, in 2006, adopted an amendment to the State Constitution prohibiting state and other governmental entities in Michigan from granting certain preferences, including race-based preferences, in a wide range of actions and decisions. Under the terms of the amendment, race-based preferences cannot be part of the admissions process for state universities. That particular prohibition is central to the instant case.

The ballot proposal was called Proposal 2 and, after it passed by a margin of 58 percent to 42 percent, the resulting enactment became Article I, §26, of the Michigan Constitution. . . .

A panel of the United States Court of Appeals for the Sixth Circuit . . . held that Proposal 2 had violated the principles elaborated by this Court in *Washington v. Seattle School Dist. No. 1* (1982) [and *Hunter v. Erickson* (1969)]. In *Hunter*, the Court for the first time elaborated what the Court of Appeals here styled the "political process" doctrine. There, the Akron City Council found that the citizens of Akron consisted of "people of different race[s], . . . many of whom live in circumscribed and segregated areas, under sub-standard unhealthful, unsafe, unsanitary and overcrowded conditions, because of discrimination in the sale, lease, rental and financing of housing." To address the problem, Akron enacted a fair housing ordinance to prohibit that sort of discrimination. In response, voters amended the city charter to overturn the ordinance and to require that any additional antidiscrimination housing ordinance be approved by referendum. But most other ordinances "regulating the real property market" were not subject to those threshold requirements. . . . *Hunter* rests on the unremarkable principle that the State may not alter the procedures of government to target racial minorities. The facts in *Hunter* established that invidious discrimination would be the necessary result of the procedural restructuring. Thus, in . . . *Hunter*, there was a demonstrated injury on the basis of race that, by reasons of state encouragement or participation, became more aggravated.

[In *Seattle*,] the school board adopted a mandatory busing program to alleviate racial isolation of minority students in local schools. Voters who opposed the school board's busing plan passed a state initiative that barred busing to desegregate. . . . *Seattle* is best understood as a case in which the state action in question (the bar on busing enacted by the State's voters) had the serious risk, if not purpose, of causing specific injuries on account of race. . . . *Seattle* involved a state initiative that "was carefully tailored to interfere only with desegregative busing." The *Seattle* Court . . . found that the State's disapproval of the school board's busing remedy was an aggravation of the very racial injury in which the State itself was complicit.

The broad language used in *Seattle,* however, went well beyond the analysis needed to resolve the case. . . . *Seattle* stated that where a government policy "inures primarily to the benefit of the minority" and "minorities . . . consider" the policy to be "in their interest," then any state action that "place[s] effective decisionmaking authority over" that policy "at a different level of government" must be reviewed under strict scrutiny. In essence, according to the broad reading of *Seattle*, any state action with a "racial focus" that makes it "more difficult for certain racial minorities than for other groups" to "achieve legislation that is in their interest" is subject to strict scrutiny. It is this reading of *Seattle* that the Court of Appeals found to be controlling here. And that reading must be rejected. . . . The expansive reading of *Seattle* has no principled limitation and raises serious questions of compatibility with the Court's settled equal protection jurisprudence. To the extent *Seattle* is read to require the Court to determine and declare which political policies serve the "interest" of a group defined in racial terms, that rationale was unnecessary to the decision in *Seattle*; it has no support in precedent; and it raises serious constitutional concerns. That expansive language does not provide a proper guide for decisions and should not be deemed authoritative or controlling. . . . There would be no apparent limiting standards defining what public policies should be included in what *Seattle* called policies that "inur[e] primarily to the benefit of the minority" and that "minorities . . . consider" to be "in their interest." Those who seek to represent the interests of particular racial groups could attempt to advance those aims by demanding an equal protection ruling that any number of matters be foreclosed from voter review or participation. In a nation in which governmental policies are wide ranging, those who seek to limit voter participation might be tempted, were this Court to adopt the *Seattle* formulation, to urge that a group they choose to define by race or racial stereotypes are advantaged or disadvantaged by any number of laws or decisions. Tax policy, housing subsidies, wage regulations, and even the naming of public schools, highways, and monuments are just a few examples of what could become a list of subjects that some organizations could insist should be beyond the power of voters to decide, or beyond the power of a legislature to decide when enacting limits on the power of local authorities or other governmental entities to address certain subjects. Racial division would be validated, not discouraged, were the *Seattle* formulation, and the reasoning of the Court of Appeals in this case, to remain in force. . . .

Perhaps, when enacting policies as an exercise of democratic self-government, voters will determine that race-based preferences should be adopted. The constitutional validity of some of those choices regarding racial preferences is not at issue here. The holding in the instant case is simply that the courts may not disempower the voters from choosing which path to follow. In the realm of policy discussions the regular give-and-take of debate ought to be a context in which rancor or discord based on race are avoided, not invited. And if these factors are to be interjected, surely it ought not to be at the invitation or insistence of the courts. . . .

By approving Proposal 2 and thereby adding §26 to their State Constitution, the Michigan voters exercised their privilege to enact laws as a basic exercise of their democratic power. In the federal system States "respond, through the enactment of positive law, to the initiative of those who seek a voice in shaping the destiny of their own times." [*Bond v. United States* (2011)], Michigan voters used the initiative system to bypass public officials who were deemed not responsive to the concerns of a majority of the voters with respect to a policy of granting race-based preferences that raises difficult and delicate issues.

The freedom secured by the Constitution consists, in one of its essential dimensions, of the right of the individual not to be injured by the unlawful exercise of governmental power. The mandate for segregated schools, *Brown v. Board of Education* (1954); a wrongful invasion of the home, *Silverman v. United States* (1961); or punishing a protester whose views offend others, *Texas v. Johnson* (1989); and scores of other examples teach that individual liberty has constitutional protection, and that liberty's full extent and meaning may remain yet to be discovered and affirmed. Yet freedom does not stop with individual rights. Our constitutional system embraces, too, the right of citizens to debate so they can learn and decide and then, through the political process, act in concert to try to shape the course of their own times and the course of a nation that must strive always to make freedom ever greater and more secure. Here Michigan voters acted in concert and statewide to seek consensus and adopt a policy on a difficult subject against a historical background of race in America that has been a source of tragedy and persisting injustice. That history demands that we continue to learn, to listen, and to remain open to new approaches if we are to aspire always to a constitutional order in which all persons are treated with fairness and equal dignity. Were the Court to rule that the question addressed by Michigan voters is too sensitive or complex to be within the grasp of the electorate; or that the policies at issue remain too delicate to be resolved save by university officials or faculties, acting at some remove from immediate public scrutiny and control; or that these matters are so arcane that the electorate's power must be limited because the people cannot prudently exercise that power even after a full debate, that holding would be an unprecedented restriction on the exercise of a fundamental right held not just by one person but by all in common. It is the right to speak and debate and learn and then, as a matter of political will, to act through a lawful electoral process.

. . . It is demeaning to the democratic process to presume that the voters are not capable of deciding an issue of this sensitivity on decent and rational grounds. The process of public discourse and political debate should not be foreclosed even if there is a risk that during a public campaign there will be those, on both sides, who seek to use racial division and discord to their own political advantage. An informed public can, and must, rise above this. The idea of democracy is that it can, and must, mature. Freedom embraces the right, indeed the duty, to engage in a rational, civic discourse in order to determine how best to form a consensus to shape the destiny of the Nation and its people. These First Amendment dynamics would be disserved if this Court were to say that the question here at issue is beyond the capacity of the voters to debate and then to determine. . . .

The electorate's instruction to governmental entities not to embark upon the course of race-defined and race-based preferences was adopted, we must assume, because the voters deemed a preference system to be unwise, on account of what voters may deem its latent potential to become itself a source of the very resentments and hostilities based on race that this Nation seeks to put behind it. Whether those adverse results would follow is, and should be, the subject of debate. Voters might likewise consider, after debate and reflection, that programs designed to increase diversity—consistent with the Constitution—are a necessary part of progress to transcend the stigma of past racism.

This case is not about how the debate about racial preferences should be resolved. It is about who may resolve it. There is no authority in the Constitution of the United States or in this Court's precedents for the Judiciary to set aside Michigan laws that commit this policy determination to the voters. Deliberative debate on sensitive issues such as racial preferences all too often may shade into rancor. But that does not justify removing certain court-determined issues from the voters' reach. Democracy does not presume that some subjects are either too divisive or too profound for public debate.

The judgment of the Court of Appeals for the Sixth Circuit is reversed.

It is so ordered.

JUSTICE KAGAN took no part in the consideration or decision of this case.

CHIEF JUSTICE ROBERTS, concurring.

The dissent devotes 11 pages to expounding its own policy preferences in favor of taking race into account in college admissions, while nonetheless concluding that it "do[es] not mean to suggest that the virtues of adopting race-sensitive admissions policies should inform the legal question before the Court." *Post* (opinion of Sotomayor, J.). The dissent concedes that the governing boards of the State's various universities could have implemented a policy making it illegal to "discriminate against, or grant preferential treatment to," any individual on the basis of race. On the dissent's view, if the governing boards conclude that drawing racial distinctions in university admissions is undesirable or counterproductive, they are permissibly exercising their policymaking authority. But others who might reach the same conclusion are failing to take race seriously.

The dissent states that "[t]he way to stop discrimination on the basis of race is to speak openly and candidly on the subject of race." And it urges that "[r]ace matters because of the slights, the snickers, the silent judgments that reinforce that most crippling of thoughts: 'I do not belong here.'" But it is not "out of touch with reality" to conclude that racial preferences may themselves have the debilitating effect of reinforcing precisely that doubt, and—if so—that the preferences do more harm than good. To disagree with the dissent's views on the costs and benefits of racial preferences is not to "wish away, rather than confront" racial inequality. People can disagree in good faith on this issue, but it similarly does more harm than good to question the openness and candor of those on either side of the debate.

JUSTICE SCALIA, with whom JUSTICE THOMAS joins, concurring in the judgment.

It has come to this. Called upon to explore the jurisprudential twilight zone between two errant lines of precedent, we confront a frighteningly bizarre question: Does the Equal Protection Clause of the Fourteenth Amendment *forbid* what its text plainly *requires*? Needless to say (except that this case obliges us to say it), the question answers itself. "The Constitution proscribes government discrimination on the basis of race, and state-provided education is no exception." *Grutter v. Bollinger* (2003) (Scalia, J., concurring in part and dissenting in part). It is precisely this understanding — the correct understanding — of the federal Equal Protection Clause that the people of the State of Michigan have adopted for their own fundamental law. By adopting it, they did not simultaneously *offend* it. . . .

But the battleground for this case is not the constitutionality of race-based admissions — at least, not quite. Rather, it is the so-called political-process doctrine, derived from this Court's opinions in *Washington v. Seattle School Dist. No. 1* (1982), and *Hunter v. Erickson* (1969). I agree with those parts of the plurality opinion that repudiate this doctrine. But I do not agree with its reinterpretation of *Seattle* and *Hunter*, which makes them stand in part for the cloudy and doctrinally anomalous proposition that whenever state action poses "the serious risk . . . of causing specific injuries on account of race," it denies equal protection. I would instead reaffirm that the "ordinary principles of our law [and] of our democratic heritage" require "plaintiffs alleging equal protection violations" stemming from facially neutral acts to "prove intent and causation and not merely the existence of racial disparity." *Freeman v. Pitts* (1992) (Scalia, J., concurring) (citing *Washington v. Davis* (1976)). I would further hold that a law directing state actors to provide equal protection is (to say the least) facially neutral, and cannot violate the Constitution. Section 26 of the Michigan Constitution (formerly Proposal 2) rightly stands. . . . Patently atextual, unadministrable, and contrary to our traditional equal-protection jurisprudence, Hunter and Seattle should be overruled. . . .

Generally, "a State is afforded wide leeway when experimenting with the appropriate allocation of state legislative power" and may create "political subdivisions such as cities and counties . . . 'as convenient agencies for exercising such of the governmental powers of the state as may be entrusted to them.' " *Holt Civic Club v. Tuscaloosa* (1978). Accordingly, States have "absolute discretion" to determine the "number, nature and duration of the powers conferred upon [municipal] corporations and the territory over which they shall be exercised." *Holt.* So it would seem to go without saying that a State may give certain powers to cities, later assign the same powers to counties, and even reclaim them for itself. . . .

I part ways with *Hunter, Seattle,* and (I think) the plurality for an additional reason: Each endorses a version of the proposition that a facially neutral law may deny equal protection solely because it has a disparate racial impact. Few equal-protection theories have been so squarely and soundly rejected. . . . Notwithstanding our dozens of cases confirming the exceptionless nature of the *Washington v. Davis* rule, the plurality opinion leaves ajar an effects-test escape hatch modeled after *Hunter* and *Seattle,* suggesting that state action denies equal protection when it "ha[s] the *serious risk,* if not purpose, of causing specific injuries on account of race," or is either "designed to be used, or . . . *likely to be used,* to encourage infliction of injury by reason of race." *Ante* (emphasis added). Since these formulations enable a determination of an equal-protection violation where there is no discriminatory intent, they are inconsistent with the long *Washington v. Davis* line of cases. . . .

Thus, the question in this case, as in every case in which neutral state action is said to deny equal protection on account of race, is whether the action reflects a racially discriminatory purpose. *Seattle* stresses that "singling out the political processes affecting racial issues for uniquely disadvantageous treatment inevitably raises dangers of impermissible motivation." True enough, but that motivation must be proved. And respondents do not have a prayer of proving it here. . . . In my view, any law expressly requiring state actors to afford all persons equal protection of the laws . . . does not — *cannot* — deny "to any person . . . equal protection of the laws," U.S. Const., Amdt. 14, §1, regardless of whatever evidence of seemingly foul purposes plaintiffs may cook up in the trial court.

* * *

As Justice Harlan observed over a century ago, "[o]ur Constitution is color-blind, and neither knows nor tolerates classes among citizens." *Plessy v. Ferguson* (1896) (dissenting opinion). The people of Michigan wish the same for their governing charter. It would be shameful for us to stand in their way.[11]

JUSTICE BREYER, concurring in the judgment. . . .

I continue to believe that the Constitution permits, though it does not require, the use of the kind of race-conscious programs that are now barred by the Michigan Constitution. The serious educational problems that faced Americans at the time this Court decided *Grutter* endure. . . . And low educational achievement continues to be correlated with income and race. . . .

The Constitution allows local, state, and national communities to adopt narrowly tailored race-conscious programs designed to bring about greater inclusion and diversity. But the Constitution foresees the ballot box, not the courts, as the normal instrument for resolving differences and debates about the merits of these programs. . . .

Hunter and *Seattle* involved efforts to manipulate the political process in a way not here at issue. Both cases involved a restructuring of the political process that changed the political level at which policies were enacted. In *Hunter*, decisionmaking was moved from the elected city council to the local electorate at large. And in *Seattle*, decisionmaking by an elected school board was replaced with decisionmaking by the state legislature and electorate at large.

This case, in contrast, does not involve a reordering of the *political* process; it does not in fact involve the movement of decisionmaking from one political level to another. Rather, here, Michigan law delegated broad policymaking authority to elected university boards, see Mich. Const., Art. VIII, §5, but those boards delegated admissions-related decisionmaking authority to unelected university faculty members and administrators. . . . Thus, unelected faculty members and administrators, not voters or their elected representatives, adopted the race-conscious admissions programs affected by Michigan's constitutional amendment. The amendment took decisionmaking authority away from these unelected actors and placed it in the hands of the voters. . . .

[T]o extend the holding of *Hunter* and *Seattle* to reach situations in which decisionmaking authority is moved from an administrative body to a political one would pose significant difficulties. The administrative process encompasses vast numbers of decisionmakers answering numerous policy questions in hosts of different fields. Administrative bodies modify programs in detail, and decisionmaking authority within the administrative process frequently moves around — due to amendments to statutes, new administrative rules, and evolving agency practice. It is thus particularly difficult in this context for judges to determine when a change in the locus of decisionmaking authority places a comparative structural burden on a racial minority. And to apply *Hunter* and *Seattle* to the administrative process would, by tending to hinder change, risk discouraging experimentation, interfering with efforts to see when and how race-conscious policies work.

Finally, the principle that underlies *Hunter* and *Seattle* runs up against a competing principle. . . . This competing principle favors decisionmaking though the democratic process. Just as this principle strongly supports the right of the people, or their elected representatives, to adopt race-conscious policies for reasons of inclusion, so must it give them the right to vote not to do so. . . .

Therefore, I concur in the judgment of the Court.

JUSTICE SOTOMAYOR, with whom JUSTICE GINSBURG joins, dissenting.

We are fortunate to live in a democratic society. But without checks, democratically approved legislation can oppress minority groups. For that reason, our Constitution places limits on what a majority of the people may do. This case implicates one such limit: the guarantee of equal protection of the laws. Although that guarantee is traditionally understood to prohibit intentional discrimination under existing laws, equal protection does not end there. Another fundamental strand of our equal protection jurisprudence focuses on process, securing to all citizens the right to participate meaningfully and equally in self-government. That right is the bedrock of our democracy, for it preserves all other rights.

Yet to know the history of our Nation is to understand its long and lamentable record of stymieing the right of racial minorities to participate in the political process. At first, the majority acted with an open, invidious purpose. Notwithstanding the command of the Fifteenth Amendment, certain States shut racial minorities out of the political process altogether by withholding the right to vote. This Court intervened to preserve that right. The majority tried again, replacing outright bans on voting with literacy tests, good character requirements, poll taxes, and gerrymandering. The Court was not fooled; it invalidated those measures, too. The majority persisted. This time, although it allowed the minority access to the political process, the majority changed the ground rules of the process so as to make it more difficult for the minority, and the minority alone, to obtain policies designed to foster racial integration. Although these political restructurings may not have been discriminatory in purpose, the Court reaffirmed the right of minority members of our society to participate meaningfully and equally in the political process.

This case involves this last chapter of discrimination: A majority of the Michigan electorate changed the basic rules of the political process in that State in a manner that uniquely disadvantaged racial minorities.[1] Prior to the enactment of the constitutional initiative at issue here, all of the admissions policies of Michigan's public colleges and universities—including race-sensitive admissions policies—were in the hands of each institution's governing board. The members of those boards are nominated by political parties and elected by the citizenry in statewide elections. After over a century of being shut out of Michigan's institutions of higher education, racial minorities in Michigan had succeeded in persuading the elected board representatives to adopt admissions policies that took into account the benefits of racial diversity. And this Court twice blessed such efforts—first in *Regents of Univ. of Cal.* and again in *Grutter,* a case that itself concerned a Michigan admissions policy.

In the wake of *Grutter,* some voters in Michigan set out to eliminate the use of race-sensitive admissions policies. Those voters were of course free to pursue this end in any number of ways. For example, they could have persuaded existing board members to change their minds through individual or grassroots lobbying efforts, or through general public awareness campaigns. Or they could have mobilized efforts to vote uncooperative board members out of office, replacing them with members who would share their desire to abolish race-sensitive admissions policies. When this Court holds that the Constitution permits a particular policy, nothing prevents a majority of a State's voters from choosing not to adopt that policy. Our system of government encourages—and indeed, depends on—that type of democratic action.

But instead, the majority of Michigan voters changed the rules in the middle of the game, reconfiguring the existing political process in Michigan in a manner that burdened racial minorities. They did so in the 2006 election by amending the Michigan Constitution to enact Art. I, §26, which provides in relevant part that Michigan's public universities "shall not discriminate against, or grant preferential treatment to, any individual or group on the basis of race, sex, color, ethnicity, or national origin in the operation of public employment, public education, or public contracting."

As a result of §26, there are now two very different processes through which a Michigan citizen is permitted to influence the admissions policies of the State's universities: one for persons interested in race-sensitive admissions policies and one for everyone else. A citizen who is a University of Michigan alumnus, for instance, can advocate for an admissions policy that considers an applicant's legacy status by meeting individually with members of the Board of Regents to

---

1. I of course do not mean to suggest that Michigan's voters acted with anything like the invidious intent of those who historically stymied the rights of racial minorities. Contra (Scalia, J., concurring in judgment). But like earlier chapters of political restructuring, the Michigan amendment at issue in this case changed the rules of the political process to the disadvantage of minority members of our society.

convince them of her views, by joining with other legacy parents to lobby the Board, or by voting for and supporting Board candidates who share her position. The same options are available to a citizen who wants the Board to adopt admissions policies that consider athleticism, geography, area of study, and so on. The one and only policy a Michigan citizen may not seek through this long-established process is a race-sensitive admissions policy that considers race in an individualized manner when it is clear that race-neutral alternatives are not adequate to achieve diversity. For that policy alone, the citizens of Michigan must undertake the daunting task of amending the State Constitution.

Our precedents do not permit political restructurings that create one process for racial minorities and a separate, less burdensome process for everyone else. This Court has held that the Fourteenth Amendment does not tolerate "a political structure that treats all individuals as equals, yet more subtly distorts governmental processes in such a way as to place special burdens on the ability of minority groups to achieve beneficial legislation." *Seattle*. Such restructuring, the Court explained, "is no more permissible than denying [the minority] the [right to] vote, on an equal basis with others." *Hunter*. In those cases — *Hunter* and *Seattle* — the Court recognized what is now known as the "political-process doctrine": When the majority reconfigures the political process in a manner that burdens only a racial minority, that alteration triggers strict judicial scrutiny.

Today, disregarding *stare decisis,* a majority of the Court effectively discards those precedents. The plurality does so, it tells us, because the freedom actually secured by the Constitution is the freedom of self-government — because the majority of Michigan citizens "exercised their privilege to enact laws as a basic exercise of their democratic power." It would be "demeaning to the democratic process," the plurality concludes, to disturb that decision in any way. This logic embraces majority rule without an important constitutional limit.

The plurality's decision fundamentally misunderstands the nature of the injustice worked by §26. This case is not, as the plurality imagines, about "who may resolve" the debate over the use of race in higher education admissions. I agree wholeheartedly that nothing vests the resolution of that debate exclusively in the courts or requires that we remove it from the reach of the electorate. Rather, this case is about *how* the debate over the use of race-sensitive admissions policies may be resolved — that is, it must be resolved in constitutionally permissible ways. While our Constitution does not guarantee minority groups victory in the political process, it does guarantee them meaningful and equal access to that process. It guarantees that the majority may not win by stacking the political process against minority groups permanently, forcing the minority alone to surmount unique obstacles in pursuit of its goals — here, educational diversity that cannot reasonably be accomplished through race-neutral measures. Today, by permitting a majority of the voters in Michigan to do what our Constitution forbids, the Court ends the debate over race-sensitive admissions policies in Michigan in a manner that contravenes constitutional protections long recognized in our precedents.

Like the plurality, I have faith that our citizenry will continue to learn from this Nation's regrettable history; that it will strive to move beyond those injustices towards a future of equality. And I, too, believe in the importance of public discourse on matters of public policy. But I part ways with the plurality when it suggests that judicial intervention in this case "impede[s]" rather than "advance[s]" the democratic process and the ultimate hope of equality. I firmly believe that our role as judges includes policing the process of self-government and stepping in when necessary to secure the constitutional guarantee of equal protection. Because I would do so here, I respectfully dissent. . . .

For much of its history, our Nation has denied to many of its citizens the right to participate meaningfully and equally in its politics. This is a history we strive to put behind us. But it is a history that still informs the society we live in, and so it is one we must address with candor. . . . This Court's landmark ruling in *Brown v. Board of Education* (1954), triggered a new era of political restructuring, this time in the context of education. . . . The Court remained true to its command in *Brown*. In Arkansas, for example, it enforced a desegregation order against the Little Rock school board. *Cooper v. Aaron* (1958). On the very day the Court announced that ruling, the Arkansas Legislature responded by changing the rules. It enacted a law permitting the Governor to close any public school in the State, and stripping local school districts of their decisionmaking authority so long as the Governor determined that local officials could not maintain " 'a general, suitable, and efficient educational system.' " *Aaron v. Cooper* (C.A.8 1958). The then-Governor immediately closed all of Little Rock's high schools. . . .

Hunter and *Seattle* vindicated a principle that is as elementary to our equal protection jurisprudence as it is essential: The majority may not suppress the minority's right to participate on equal terms in the political process. Under this doctrine, governmental action deprives minority groups of equal protection when it (1) has a racial focus, targeting a policy or program that "inures primarily to the benefit of the minority," *Seattle*; and (2) alters the political process in a manner that uniquely burdens racial minorities' ability to achieve their goals through that process. A faithful application of the doctrine resoundingly resolves this case in respondents' favor. . . . Section 26 restructures the political process in Michigan in a manner that places unique burdens on racial minorities. It establishes a distinct and more burdensome political process for the enactment of admissions plans that consider racial diversity. . . .

And what now of the political-process doctrine? After the plurality's revision of *Hunter* and *Seattle*, it is unclear what is left. The plurality certainly does not tell us. On this point, and this point only, I agree with Justice Scalia that the plurality has rewritten those precedents beyond recognition. . . .

The political process is the channel of change. It is the means by which citizens may both obtain desirable legislation and repeal undesirable legislation. Of course, we do not expect minority members of our society to obtain every single result they seek through the political process—not, at least, when their views conflict with those of the majority. The minority plainly does not have a right to prevail over majority groups in any given political contest. But the minority does have a right to play by the same rules as the majority. It is this right that *Hunter* and *Seattle* so boldly vindicated.

This right was hardly novel at the time of *Hunter* and *Seattle*. For example, this Court focused on the vital importance of safeguarding minority groups' access to the political process in *United States v. Carolene Products Co.* (1938), a case that predated *Hunter* by 30 years. In a now-famous footnote, the Court explained that while ordinary social and economic legislation carries a presumption of constitutionality, the same may not be true of legislation that offends fundamental rights or targets minority groups. Citing cases involving restrictions on the right to vote, restraints on the dissemination of information, interferences with political organizations, and prohibition of peaceable assembly, the Court recognized that "legislation which restricts those political processes which can ordinarily be expected to bring about repeal of undesirable legislation" could be worthy of "more exacting judicial scrutiny under the general prohibitions of the Fourteenth Amendment than are most other types of legislation." Id., at n.4. . . . The Court also noted that "prejudice against discrete and insular minorities may be a special condition, which tends seriously to curtail the operation of those political processes ordinarily to be relied upon to protect minorities, and which may call for a correspondingly more searching judicial inquiry." The values identified in *Carolene Products* lie at the heart of the political-process doctrine. Indeed, *Seattle* explicitly relied on *Carolene Products*. . . . These values are central tenets of our equal protection jurisprudence.

My colleagues are of the view that we should leave race out of the picture entirely and let the voters sort it out. We have seen this reasoning before. See *Parents Involved* ("The way to stop discrimination on the basis of race is to stop discriminating on the basis of race"). It is a sentiment out of touch with reality, one not required by our Constitution, and one that has properly been rejected as "not sufficient" to resolve cases of this nature. While "[t]he enduring hope is that race should not matter[,] the reality is that too often it does." *Parents Involved*.

Race matters. Race matters in part because of the long history of racial minorities' being denied access to the political process. And although we have made great strides, "voting discrimination still exists; no one doubts that." *Shelby County v. Holder* (2013).

Race also matters because of persistent racial inequality in society — inequality that cannot be ignored and that has produced stark socioeconomic disparities. See *Gratz* (Ginsburg, J., dissenting) (cataloging the many ways in which "the effects of centuries of law-sanctioned inequality remain painfully evident in our communities and schools," in areas like employment, poverty, access to health care, housing, consumer transactions, and education).

And race matters for reasons that really are only skin deep, that cannot be discussed any other way, and that cannot be wished away. Race matters to a young man's view of society when he spends his teenage years watching others tense up as he passes, no matter the neighborhood where he grew up. Race matters to a young woman's sense of self when she states her hometown, and then is pressed, "No, where are you *really* from?", regardless of how many generations her family has been in the country. Race matters to a young person addressed by a stranger in a foreign language, which he does not understand because only English was spoken at home. Race matters because of the slights, the snickers, the silent judgments that reinforce that most crippling of thoughts: "I do not belong here."

In my colleagues' view, examining the racial impact of legislation only perpetuates racial discrimination. This refusal to accept the stark reality that race matters is regrettable. The way to stop discrimination on the basis of race is to speak openly and candidly on the subject of race, and to apply the Constitution with eyes open to the unfortunate effects of centuries of racial discrimination. As members of the judiciary tasked with intervening to carry out the guarantee of equal protection, we ought not sit back and wish away, rather than confront, the racial inequality that exists in our society. It is this view that works harm, by perpetuating the facile notion that what makes race matter is acknowledging the simple truth that race *does* matter. . . .

To be clear, I do not mean to suggest that the virtues of adopting race-sensitive admissions policies should inform the legal question before the Court today regarding the constitutionality of §26. But I cannot ignore the unfortunate outcome of today's decision: Short of amending the State Constitution, a Herculean task, racial minorities in Michigan are deprived of even an opportunity to convince Michigan's public colleges and universities to consider race in their admissions plans when other attempts to achieve racial diversity have proved unworkable, and those institutions are unnecessarily hobbled in their pursuit of a diverse student body.

* * *

The Constitution does not protect racial minorities from political defeat. But neither does it give the majority free rein to erect selective barriers against racial minorities. The political-process doctrine polices the channels of change to ensure that the majority, when it wins, does so without rigging the rules of the game to ensure its success. Today, the Court discards that doctrine without good reason.

In doing so, it permits the decision of a majority of the voters in Michigan to strip Michigan's elected university boards of their authority to make decisions with respect to constitutionally permissible race-sensitive admissions policies, while preserving the boards' plenary authority to make all other educational decisions. "In a most direct sense, this implicates the judiciary's special role in safeguarding the interests of those groups that are relegated to such a position of political powerlessness as to command extraordinary protection from the majoritarian political process." *Seattle*. The Court abdicates that role, permitting the majority to use its numerical advantage to change the rules mid-contest and forever stack the deck against racial minorities in Michigan. The result is that Michigan's public colleges and universities are less equipped to do their part in ensuring that students of all races are "better prepare[d] . . . for an increasingly diverse workforce and society . . ." *Grutter.*

Today's decision eviscerates an important strand of our equal protection jurisprudence. For members of historically marginalized groups, which rely on the
federal courts to protect their constitutional rights, the decision can hardly bol-
ster hope for a vision of democracy that preserves for all the right to participate
meaningfully and equally in self-government.

I respectfully dissent.

Chapter 14

Equal Protection of the Law: Sex Discrimination and Other Types

Bostock v. Clayton County, Georgia
Altitude Express, Inc. v. Zarda et al., as Co-Independent
Executors of the Estate of Zarda
R. G. & G. R. Harris Funeral Homes, Inc. v. EEOC et al.
590 U.S. ___ (2020)

JUSTICE GORSUCH delivered the opinion of the Court.

Sometimes small gestures can have unexpected consequences. Major initiatives practically guarantee them. In our time, few pieces of federal legislation rank in significance with the Civil Rights Act of 1964. There, in Title VII, Congress outlawed discrimination in the workplace on the basis of race, color, religion, sex, or national origin. Today, we must decide whether an employer can fire someone simply for being homosexual or transgender. The answer is clear. An employer who fires an individual for being homosexual or transgender fires that person for traits or actions it would not have questioned in members of a different sex. Sex plays a necessary and undisguisable role in the decision, exactly what Title VII forbids.

Those who adopted the Civil Rights Act might not have anticipated their work would lead to this particular result. Likely, they weren't thinking about many of the Act's consequences that have become apparent over the years, including its prohibition against discrimination on the basis of motherhood or its ban on the sexual harassment of male employees. But the limits of the drafters' imagination supply no reason to ignore the law's demands. When the express terms of a statute give us one answer and extratextual considerations suggest another, it's no contest. Only the written word is the law, and all persons are entitled to its benefit.

I

Few facts are needed to appreciate the legal question we face. Each of the three cases before us started the same way: An employer fired a long-time employee shortly after the employee revealed that he or she is homosexual or transgender — and allegedly for no reason other than the employee's homosexuality or transgender status.

Gerald Bostock worked for Clayton County, Georgia, as a child welfare advocate. Under his leadership, the county won national awards for its work. After a decade with the county, Mr. Bostock began participating in a gay recreational softball league. Not long after that, influential members of the community allegedly made disparaging comments about Mr. Bostock's sexual orientation and participation in the league. Soon, he was fired for conduct "unbecoming" a county employee.

Donald Zarda worked as a skydiving instructor at Altitude Express in New York. After several seasons with the company, Mr. Zarda mentioned that he was gay and, days later, was fired.

Aimee Stephens worked at R. G. & G. R. Harris Funeral Homes in Garden City, Michigan. When she got the job, Ms. Stephens presented as a male. But two years into her service with the company, she began treatment for despair and loneliness. Ultimately, clinicians diagnosed her with gender dysphoria and recommended that she begin living as a woman. In her sixth year with the company, Ms. Stephens wrote a letter to her employer explaining that she planned to "live and work full-time as a woman" after she returned from an upcoming vacation. The funeral home fired her before she left, telling her "this is not going to work out."

While these cases began the same way, they ended differently. Each employee brought suit under Title VII alleging unlawful discrimination on the basis of sex. . . . During the course of the proceedings in these long-running disputes, both Mr. Zarda and Ms. Stephens have passed away. But their estates continue to press their causes for the benefit of their heirs. And we granted certiorari in these matters to resolve at last the disagreement among the courts of appeals over the scope of Title VII's protections for homosexual and transgender persons.

II

This Court normally interprets a statute in accord with the ordinary public meaning of its terms at the time of its enactment. After all, only the words on the page constitute the law adopted by Congress and approved by the President. If judges could add to, remodel, update, or detract from old statutory terms inspired only by extratextual sources and our own imaginations, we would risk amending statutes outside the legislative process reserved for the people's representatives. And we would deny the people the right to continue relying on the original meaning of the law they have counted on to settle their rights and obligations. See *New Prime Inc. v. Oliveira* (2019).

With this in mind, our task is clear. We must determine the ordinary public meaning of Title VII's command that it is "unlawful . . . for an employer to fail or refuse to hire or to discharge any individual, or otherwise to discriminate against any individual with respect to his compensation, terms, conditions, or privileges of employment, because of such individual's race, color, religion, sex, or national origin." To do so, we orient ourselves to the time of the statute's adoption, here 1964, and begin by examining the key statutory terms in turn before assessing their impact on the cases at hand and then confirming our work against this Court's precedents.

A

The only statutorily protected characteristic at issue in today's cases is "sex"—and that is also the primary term in Title VII whose meaning the parties dispute. Appealing to roughly contemporaneous dictionaries, the employers say that, as used here, the term "sex" in 1964 referred to "status as either male or female [as] determined by reproductive biology." The employees counter by submitting that, even in 1964, the term bore a broader scope, capturing more than anatomy and reaching at least some norms concerning gender identity and sexual orientation. But because nothing in our approach to these cases turns on the outcome of the parties' debate, and because the employees concede the point for argument's sake, we proceed on the assumption that "sex" signified what the employers suggest, referring only to biological distinctions between male and female.

Still, that's just a starting point. The question isn't just what "sex" meant, but what Title VII says about it. Most notably, the statute prohibits employers from taking certain actions "because of" sex. And, as this Court has previously explained, "the ordinary meaning of 'because of ' is 'by reason of' or 'on account of.'" *University of Tex. Southwestern Medical Center v. Nassar* (2013). In the language of law, this means that Title VII's "because of" test incorporates the "'simple'" and "traditional" standard of but-for causation. That form of causation is established whenever a particular outcome would not have happened "but for" the purported cause. In other words, a but-for test directs us to change one thing at a time and see if the outcome changes. If it does, we have found a but-for cause.

This can be a sweeping standard. . . . When it comes to Title VII, the adoption of the traditional but-for causation standard means a defendant cannot avoid liability just by citing some *other* factor that contributed to its challenged employment decision. So long as the plaintiff's sex was one but-for cause of that decision, that is enough to trigger the law. . . .

As sweeping as even the but-for causation standard can be, Title VII does not concern itself with everything that happens "because of " sex. The statute imposes liability on employers only when they "fail or refuse to hire," "discharge," "or otherwise . . . discriminate against" someone because of a statutorily protected characteristic like sex. The employers acknowledge that they discharged the plaintiffs in today's cases, but assert that the statute's list of verbs is qualified by the last item on it: "otherwise . . . discriminate against." By virtue of the word *otherwise*, the employers suggest, Title VII concerns itself not with every discharge, only with those discharges that involve discrimination.

Accepting this point, too, for argument's sake, the question becomes: What did "discriminate" mean in 1964? As it turns out, it meant then roughly what it means today: "To make a difference in treatment or favor (of one as compared with others)." Webster's New International Dictionary 745 (2d ed. 1954). To "discriminate against" a person, then, would seem to mean treating that individual worse than others who are similarly situated. See *Burlington N. & S. F. R. Co. v. White* (2006). In so-called "disparate treatment" cases like today's, this Court has also held that the difference in treatment based on sex must be intentional. See, *e.g., Watson v. Fort Worth Bank & Trust* (1988). So, taken together, an employer who intentionally treats a person worse because of sex — such as by firing the person for actions or attributes it would tolerate in an individual of another sex — discriminates against that person in violation of Title VII.

At first glance, another interpretation might seem possible. Discrimination sometimes involves "the act, practice, or an instance of discriminating categorically rather than individually." Webster's New Collegiate Dictionary 326 (1975); see (Alito, J., dissenting). On that understanding, the statute would require us to consider the employer's treatment of groups rather than individuals, to see how a policy affects one sex as a whole versus the other as a whole. That idea holds some intuitive appeal too. Maybe the law concerns itself simply with ensuring that employers don't treat women generally less favorably than they do men. So how can we tell which sense, individual or group, "discriminate" carries in Title VII?

The statute answers that question directly. It tells us three times — including immediately after the words "discriminate against" — that our focus should be on individuals, not groups: Employers may not "fail or refuse to hire or . . . discharge any *individual*, or otherwise . . . discriminate against any *individual* with respect to his compensation, terms, conditions, or privileges of employment, because of such *individual's* . . . sex." And the meaning of "individual" was as uncontroversial in 1964 as it is today: "A particular being as distinguished from a class, species, or collection." Webster's New International Dictionary, at 1267. . . .

This statute works to protect individuals of both sexes from discrimination, and does so equally. So an employer who fires a woman, Hannah, because she is insufficiently feminine and also fires a man, Bob, for being insufficiently masculine may treat men and women as groups more or less equally. But in *both* cases the employer fires an individual in part because of sex. Instead of avoiding Title VII exposure, this employer doubles it.

B

From the ordinary public meaning of the statute's language at the time of the law's adoption, a straightforward rule emerges: An employer violates Title VII when it intentionally fires an individual employee based in part on sex. It doesn't matter if other factors besides the plaintiff 's sex contributed to the decision. And it doesn't matter if the employer treated women as a group the same when compared to men as a group. If the employer intentionally relies in part on an individual employee's sex when deciding to discharge the employee — put differently, if changing the employee's sex would have yielded a different choice by the employer — a statutory violation has occurred. Title VII's message is "simple but momentous": An individual employee's sex is "not relevant to the selection, evaluation, or compensation of employees." *Price Waterhouse v. Hopkins* (1989).

The statute's message for our cases is equally simple and momentous: An individual's homosexuality or transgender status is not relevant to employment decisions. That's because it is impossible to discriminate against a person for being homosexual or transgender without discriminating against that individual based on sex. Consider, for example, an employer with two employees, both of whom are attracted to men. The two individuals are, to the employer's mind, materially identical in all respects, except that one is a man and the other a woman. If the employer fires the male employee for no reason other than the fact he is attracted to men, the employer discriminates against him for traits or actions it tolerates in his female colleague. Put differently, the employer intentionally singles out an employee to fire based in part on the employee's sex, and the affected employee's sex is a but-for cause of his discharge. Or take an employer who fires a transgender person who was identified as a male at birth but who now identifies as a female. If the employer retains an otherwise identical employee who was identified as female at birth, the employer intentionally penalizes a person identified as male at birth for traits or actions that it tolerates in an employee identified as female at birth. Again, the individual employee's sex plays an unmistakable and impermissible role in the discharge decision. . . .

[H]omosexuality and transgender status are inextricably bound up with sex. Not because homosexuality or transgender status are related to sex in some vague sense or because discrimination on these bases has some disparate impact on one sex or another, but because to discriminate on these grounds requires an employer to intentionally treat individual employees differently because of their sex. . . .

When an employer fires an employee because she is homosexual or transgender, two causal factors may be in play — *both* the individual's sex *and* something else (the sex to which the individual is attracted or with which the individual identifies). But Title VII doesn't care. If an employer would not have discharged an employee but for that individual's sex, the statute's causation standard is met, and liability may attach. . . .

At bottom, these cases involve no more than the straightforward application of legal terms with plain and settled meanings. For an employer to discriminate against employees for being homosexual or transgender, the employer must intentionally discriminate against individual men and women in part because of sex. That has always been prohibited by Title VII's plain terms — and that "should be the end of the analysis."

C

If more support for our conclusion were required, there's no need to look far. All that the statute's plain terms suggest, this Court's cases have already confirmed. Consider three of our leading precedents.

In *Phillips v. Martin Marietta Corp.* (1971), a company allegedly refused to hire women with young children, but did hire men with children the same age. Because its discrimination depended not only on the employee's sex as a female but also on the presence of another criterion — namely, being a parent of young children — the company contended it hadn't engaged in discrimination "because of" sex. . . . Unsurprisingly by now, these submissions did not sway the Court. That an employer discriminates intentionally against an individual only in part because of sex supplies no defense to Title VII. Nor does the fact an employer may happen to favor women as a class.

In *Los Angeles Dept. of Water and Power v. Manhart* (1978), an employer required women to make larger pension fund contributions than men. . . . [T]he Court recognized, a rule that appears evenhanded at the group level can prove discriminatory at the level of individuals. . . . Likewise, the Court dismissed as irrelevant the employer's insistence that its actions were motivated by a wish to achieve classwide equality between the sexes: An employer's intentional discrimination on the basis of sex is no more permissible when it is prompted by some further intention (or motivation), even one as prosaic as seeking to account for actuarial tables. . . .

In *Oncale v. Sundowner Offshore Services, Inc.* (1998), a male plaintiff alleged that he was singled out by his male co-workers for sexual harassment. The Court held it was immaterial that members of the same sex as the victim committed the alleged discrimination. Nor did the Court concern itself with whether men as a group were subject to discrimination or whether something in addition to sex contributed to the discrimination, like the plaintiff's conduct or personal attributes. "[A]ssuredly," the case didn't involve "the principal evil Congress was concerned with when it enacted Title VII." But, the Court unanimously explained, it is "the provisions of our laws rather than the principal concerns of our legislators by which we are governed." Because the plaintiff alleged that the harassment would not have taken place but for his sex — that is, the plaintiff would not have suffered similar treatment if he were female — a triable Title VII claim existed.

The lessons these cases hold for ours are by now familiar.

First, it's irrelevant what an employer might call its discriminatory practice, how others might label it, or what else might motivate it. . . . When an employer fires an employee for being homosexual or transgender, it necessarily and intentionally discriminates against that individual in part because of sex. And that is all Title VII has ever demanded to establish liability.

Second, the plaintiff's sex need not be the sole or primary cause of the employer's adverse action. . . .

Finally, an employer cannot escape liability by demonstrating that it treats males and females comparably as groups. . . . [A]n employer who intentionally fires an individual homosexual or transgender employee in part because of that individual's sex violates the law even if the employer is willing to subject all male and female homosexual or transgender employees to the same rule.

III

What do the employers have to say in reply? For present purposes, they do not dispute that they fired the plaintiffs for being homosexual or transgender. Sorting out the true reasons for an adverse employment decision is often a hard business, but none of that is at issue here. Rather, the employers submit that even intentional discrimination against employees based on their homosexuality or transgender status supplies no basis for liability under Title VII.

The employers' argument proceeds in two stages. Seeking footing in the statutory text, they begin by advancing a number of reasons why discrimination on the basis of homosexuality or transgender status doesn't involve discrimination because of sex. But each of these arguments turns out only to repackage errors we've already seen and this Court's precedents have already rejected. In the end, the employers are left to retreat beyond the statute's text, where they fault us for ignoring the legislature's purposes in enacting Title VII or certain expectations about its operation. They warn, too, about consequences that might follow a ruling for the employees. But none of these contentions about what the employers think the law was meant to do, or should do, allow us to ignore the law as it is.

A

. . . By discriminating against homosexuals, the employer intentionally penalizes men for being attracted to men and women for being attracted to women. By discriminating against transgender persons, the employer unavoidably discriminates against persons with one sex identified at birth and another today. Any way you slice it, the employer intentionally refuses to hire applicants in part because of the affected individuals' sex, even if it never learns any applicant's sex.

Next, the employers turn to Title VII's list of protected characteristics — race, color, religion, sex, and national origin. Because homosexuality and transgender status can't be found on that list and because they are conceptually distinct from sex, the employers reason, they are implicitly excluded from Title VII's reach. Put another way, if Congress had wanted to address these matters in Title VII, it would have referenced them specifically.

But that much does not follow. We agree that homosexuality and transgender status are distinct concepts from sex. But, as we've seen, discrimination based on homosexuality or transgender status necessarily entails discrimination based on sex; the first cannot happen without the second. Nor is there any such thing as a "canon of donut holes," in which Congress's failure to speak directly to a specific case that falls within a more general statutory rule creates a tacit exception. Instead, when Congress chooses not to include any exceptions to a broad rule, courts apply the broad rule. And that is exactly how this Court has always approached Title VII. . . .

The employers try the same point another way. Since 1964, they observe, Congress has considered several proposals to add sexual orientation to Title VII's list of protected characteristics, but no such amendment has become law. Meanwhile, Congress has enacted other statutes addressing other topics that do discuss sexual orientation. This postenactment legislative history, they urge, should tell us something.

But what? There's no authoritative evidence explaining why later Congresses adopted other laws referencing sexual orientation but didn't amend this one.

Maybe some in the later legislatures understood the impact Title VII's broad language already promised for cases like ours and didn't think a revision needed. Maybe others knew about its impact but hoped no one else would notice. Maybe still others, occupied by other concerns, didn't consider the issue at all. All we can know for certain is that speculation about why a later Congress declined to adopt new legislation offers a "particularly dangerous" basis on which to rest an interpretation of an existing law a different and earlier Congress did adopt. *Pension Benefit Guaranty Corporation v. LTV Corp.* (1990); see also *United States v. Wells* (1997); *Sullivan v. Finkelstein*, 496 U.S. 617, 632 (1990) (Scalia, J., concurring) ("Arguments based on subsequent legislative history . . . should not be taken seriously, not even in a footnote"). . . .

B

Ultimately, the employers are forced to abandon the statutory text and precedent altogether and appeal to assumptions and policy. Most pointedly, they contend that few in 1964 would have expected Title VII to apply to discrimination against homosexual and transgender persons. And whatever the text and our precedent indicate, they say, shouldn't this fact cause us to pause before recognizing liability?

It might be tempting to reject this argument out of hand. This Court has explained many times over many years that, when the meaning of the statute's terms is plain, our job is at an end. The people are entitled to rely on the law as written, without fearing that courts might disregard its plain terms based on some extratextual consideration. . . . And "it is ultimately the provisions of" those legislative commands "rather than the principal concerns of our legislators by which we are governed." *Oncale*; see also A. Scalia & B. Garner, Reading Law: The Interpretation of Legal Texts 101 (2012) (noting that unexpected applications of broad language reflect only Congress's "presumed point [to] produce general coverage — not to leave room for courts to recognize ad hoc exceptions").

Still, while legislative history can never defeat unambiguous statutory text, historical sources can be useful for a different purpose: Because the law's ordinary meaning at the time of enactment usually governs, we must be sensitive to the possibility a statutory term that means one thing today or in one context might have meant something else at the time of its adoption or might mean something different in another context. And we must be attuned to the possibility that a statutory phrase ordinarily bears a different meaning than the terms do when viewed individually or literally. To ferret out such shifts in linguistic usage or subtle distinctions between literal and ordinary meaning, this Court has sometimes consulted the understandings of the law's drafters as some (not always conclusive) evidence. . . .

The employers, however, advocate nothing like that here. They do not seek to use historical sources to illustrate that the meaning of any of Title VII's language has changed since 1964 or that the statute's terms, whether viewed individually or as a whole, ordinarily carried some message we have missed. To the contrary, as we have seen, the employers *agree* with our understanding of all the statutory language — "discriminate against any individual . . . because of such individual's . . . sex." Nor do the competing dissents offer an alternative account about what these terms mean either when viewed individually or in the aggregate. Rather than suggesting that the statutory language bears some other *meaning*, the employers and dissents merely suggest that, because few in 1964 expected today's *result*, we should not dare to admit that it follows ineluctably from the statutory text. When a new application emerges that is both unexpected and important, they would seemingly have us merely point out the question, refer the subject back to Congress, and decline to enforce the plain terms of the law in the meantime.

That is exactly the sort of reasoning this Court has long rejected. Admittedly, the employers take pains to couch their argument in terms of seeking to honor the statute's "expected applications" rather than vindicate its "legislative intent." But the concepts are closely related. One could easily contend that legislators only intended expected applications or that a statute's purpose is limited to achieving applications foreseen at the time of enactment. However framed, the employer's logic impermissibly seeks to displace the plain meaning of the law in favor of something lying beyond it. . . .

If anything, the employers' new framing may only add new problems. The employers assert that "no one" in 1964 or for some time after would have anticipated today's result. But is that really true? Not long after the law's passage, gay and transgender employees began filing Title VII complaints, so at least *some* people foresaw this potential application. See, *e.g.*, *Smith v. Liberty Mut. Ins. Co.* (N.D. Ga. 1975) (addressing claim from 1969); *Holloway v. Arthur Andersen & Co.* (9th Cir. 1977) (addressing claim from 1974). And less than a decade after Title VII's passage, during debates over the Equal Rights Amendment, others counseled that its language — which was strikingly similar to Title VII's — might also protect homosexuals from discrimination. See, *e.g.*, Note, The Legality of Homosexual Marriage, 82 Yale L.J. 573 (1973).

Why isn't that enough to demonstrate that today's result isn't totally unexpected? How many people have to foresee the application for it to qualify as "expected"? Do we look only at the moment the statute was enacted, or do we allow some time for the implications of a new statute to be worked out? Should we consider the expectations of those who had no reason to give a particular application any thought or only those with reason to think about the question? How do we account for those who change their minds over time, after learning new facts or hearing a new argument? How specifically or generally should we frame the "application" at issue? None of these questions have obvious answers, and the employers don't propose any. . . .

The employer's position also proves too much. If we applied Title VII's plain text only to applications some (yet-to-be-determined) group expected in 1964, we'd have more than a little law to overturn. Start with *Oncale*. How many people in 1964 could have expected that the law would turn out to protect male employees? Let alone to protect them from harassment by other male employees? As we acknowledged at the time, "male-on-male sexual harassment in the workplace was assuredly not the principal evil Congress was concerned with when it enacted Title VII." Yet the Court did not hesitate to recognize that Title VII's plain terms forbade it. Under the employer's logic, it would seem this was a mistake.

That's just the beginning of the law we would have to unravel. As one Equal Employment Opportunity Commission (EEOC) Commissioner observed shortly after the law's passage, the words of " 'the sex provision of Title VII [are] difficult to . . . control.' " The "difficult[y]" may owe something to the initial proponent of the sex discrimination rule in Title VII, Representative Howard Smith. On some accounts, the congressman may have wanted (or at least was indifferent to the possibility of) broad language with wide-ranging effect. Not necessarily because he was interested in rooting out sex discrimination in all its forms, but because he may have hoped to scuttle the whole Civil Rights Act and thought that adding language covering sex discrimination would serve as a poison pill. Certainly nothing in the meager legislative history of this provision suggests it was meant to be read narrowly.

Whatever his reasons, thanks to the broad language Representative Smith introduced, many, maybe most, applications of Title VII's sex provision were "unanticipated" at the time of the law's adoption. . . .

The weighty implications of the employers' argument from expectations also reveal why they cannot hide behind the no-elephants-in-mouseholes canon. That canon recognizes that Congress "does not alter the fundamental details of a regulatory scheme in vague terms or ancillary provisions." *Whitman v. American Trucking Assns., Inc.* (2001). But it has no relevance here. We can't deny that today's holding—that employers are prohibited from firing employees on the basis of homosexuality or transgender status—is an elephant. But where's the mousehole? Title VII's prohibition of sex discrimination in employment is a major piece of federal civil rights legislation. It is written in starkly broad terms. It has repeatedly produced unexpected applications, at least in the view of those on the receiving end of them. Congress's key drafting choices—to focus on discrimination against individuals and not merely between groups and to hold employers liable whenever sex is a but-for cause of the plaintiff's injuries— virtually guaranteed that unexpected applications would emerge over time. This elephant has never hidden in a mousehole; it has been standing before us all along.

With that, the employers are left to abandon their concern for expected applications and fall back to the last line of defense for all failing statutory interpretation arguments: naked policy appeals. If we were to apply the statute's plain language, they complain, any number of undesirable policy consequences would follow. Gone here is any pretense of statutory interpretation; all that's left is a suggestion we should proceed without the law's guidance to do as we think best. But that's an invitation no court should ever take up. The place to make new legislation, or address unwanted consequences of old legislation, lies in Congress. When it comes to statutory interpretation, our role is limited to applying the law's demands as faithfully as we can in the cases that come before us. As judges we possess no special expertise or authority to declare for ourselves what a self-governing people should consider just or wise. And the same judicial humility that requires us to refrain from adding to statutes requires us to refrain from diminishing them.

What are these consequences anyway? The employers worry that our decision will sweep beyond Title VII to other federal or state laws that prohibit sex discrimination. And, under Title VII itself, they say sex-segregated bathrooms, locker rooms, and dress codes will prove unsustainable after our decision today. But none of these other laws are before us; we have not had the benefit of adversarial testing about the meaning of their terms, and we do not prejudge any such question today. Under Title VII, too, we do not purport to address bathrooms, locker rooms, or anything else of the kind. The only question before us is whether an employer who fires someone simply for being homosexual or transgender has discharged or otherwise discriminated against that individual "because of such individual's sex." As used in Title VII, the term " 'discriminate against'" refers to "distinctions or differences in treatment that injure protected individuals." *Burlington N. & S. F. R.* Firing employees because of a statutorily protected trait surely counts. Whether other policies and practices might or might not qualify as unlawful discrimination or find justifications under other provisions of Title VII are questions for future cases, not these.

Separately, the employers fear that complying with Title VII's requirement in cases like ours may require some employers to violate their religious convictions. We are also deeply concerned with preserving the promise of the free exercise of religion enshrined in our Constitution; that guarantee lies at the heart of our pluralistic society. But worries about how Title VII may intersect with religious liberties are nothing new; they even predate the statute's passage. As a result of its deliberations in adopting the law, Congress included an express statutory exception for religious organizations. This Court has also recognized that the First Amendment can bar the application of employment discrimination laws "to claims concerning the employment relationship between a religious institution and its ministers." *Hosanna-Tabor Evangelical Lutheran Church and School v. EEOC* (2012). And Congress has gone a step further yet in the Religious Freedom Restoration Act of 1993 (RFRA). That statute prohibits the federal government from substantially burdening a person's exercise of religion unless it demonstrates that doing so both furthers a compelling governmental interest and represents the least restrictive means of furthering that interest. Because RFRA operates as a kind of super statute, displacing the normal operation of other federal laws, it might supersede Title VII's commands in appropriate cases.

But how these doctrines protecting religious liberty interact with Title VII are questions for future cases too. Harris Funeral Homes did unsuccessfully pursue a RFRA-based defense in the proceedings below. In its certiorari petition, however, the company declined to seek review of that adverse decision, and no other religious liberty claim is now before us. So while other employers in other cases may raise free exercise arguments that merit careful consideration, none of the employers before us today represent in this Court that compliance with Title VII will infringe their own religious liberties in any way.

*

Some of those who supported adding language to Title VII to ban sex discrimination may have hoped it would derail the entire Civil Rights Act. Yet, contrary to those intentions, the bill became law. Since then, Title VII's effects have unfolded with far-reaching consequences, some likely beyond what many in Congress or elsewhere expected.

But none of this helps decide today's cases. Ours is a society of written laws. Judges are not free to overlook plain statutory commands on the strength of nothing more than suppositions about intentions or guesswork about expectations. In Title VII, Congress adopted broad language making it illegal for an employer to rely on an employee's sex when deciding to fire that employee. We do not hesitate to recognize today a necessary consequence of that legislative choice: An employer who fires an individual merely for being gay or transgender defies the law.

It is so ordered.

JUSTICE ALITO, with whom JUSTICE THOMAS joins, dissenting.

There is only one word for what the Court has done today: legislation. The document that the Court releases is in the form of a judicial opinion interpreting a statute, but that is deceptive.

Title VII of the Civil Rights Act of 1964 prohibits employment discrimination on any of five specified grounds: "race, color, religion, sex, [and] national origin." Neither "sexual orientation" nor "gender identity" appears on that list. For the past 45 years, bills have been introduced in Congress to add "sexual orientation" to the list, and in recent years, bills have included "gender identity" as well. But to date, none has passed both Houses.

Last year, the House of Representatives passed a bill that would amend Title VII by defining sex discrimination to include both "sexual orientation" and "gender identity," but the bill has stalled in the Senate. An alternative bill would add similar prohibitions but contains provisions to protect religious liberty. This bill remains before a House Subcommittee.

Because no such amendment of Title VII has been enacted in accordance with the requirements in the Constitution (passage in both Houses and presentment to the President, Art. I, §7, cl. 2), Title VII's prohibition of discrimination because of "sex" still means what it has always meant. But the Court is not deterred by these constitutional niceties. Usurping the constitutional authority of the other branches, the Court has essentially taken H. R. 5's provision on employment discrimination and issued it under the guise of statutory interpretation. A more brazen abuse of our authority to interpret statutes is hard to recall.

The Court tries to convince readers that it is merely enforcing the terms of the statute, but that is preposterous. Even as understood today, the concept of discrimination because of "sex" is different from discrimination because of "sexual orientation" or "gender identity." And in any event, our duty is to interpret statutory terms to "mean what they conveyed to reasonable people *at the time they were written.*" A. Scalia & B. Garner, Reading Law: The Interpretation of Legal Texts (2012). If every single living American had been surveyed in 1964, it would have been hard to find any who thought that discrimination because of sex meant discrimination because of sexual orientation — not to mention gender identity, a concept that was essentially unknown at the time.

The Court attempts to pass off its decision as the inevitable product of the textualist school of statutory interpretation championed by our late colleague Justice Scalia, but no one should be fooled. The Court's opinion is like a pirate ship. It sails under a textualist flag, but what it actually represents is a theory of statutory interpretation that Justice Scalia excoriated — the theory that courts should "update" old statutes so that they better reflect the current values of society. See A. Scalia, A Matter of Interpretation (1997). If the Court finds it appropriate to adopt this theory, it should own up to what it is doing.[5]

Many will applaud today's decision because they agree on policy grounds with the Court's updating of Title VII. But the question in these cases is not whether discrimination because of sexual orientation or gender identity *should be* outlawed. The question is *whether Congress did that in 1964.*

It indisputably did not.

I

A

Title VII, as noted, prohibits discrimination "because of . . . sex," and in 1964, it was as clear as clear could be that this meant discrimination because of the genetic and anatomical characteristics that men and women have at the time of birth. Determined searching has not found a single dictionary from that time that defined "sex" to mean sexual orientation, gender identity, or "transgender status."

In all those dictionaries, the primary definition of "sex" was essentially the same as that in the then-most recent edition of Webster's New International Dictionary (2d ed. 1953): "[o]ne of the two divisions of organisms formed on the distinction of male and female." . . .

The Court does not dispute that this is what "sex" means in Title VII, although it coyly suggests that there is at least some support for a different and potentially relevant definition. But the Court declines to stand on that ground and instead

---

5. That is what Judge Posner did in the Seventh Circuit case holding that Title VII prohibits discrimination because of sexual orientation. See *Hively* v. *Ivy Tech Community College of Ind.* (2017) (en banc). Judge Posner agreed with that result but wrote: "I would prefer to see us acknowledge openly that today we, who are judges rather than members of Congress, are imposing on a half-century-old statute a meaning of 'sex discrimination' that the Congress that enacted it would not have accepted."

"proceed[s] on the assumption that 'sex' . . . refer[s] only to biological distinctions between male and female."

If that is so, it should be perfectly clear that Title VII does not reach discrimination because of sexual orientation or gender identity. If "sex" in Title VII means biologically male or female, then discrimination because of sex means discrimination because the person in question is biologically male or biologically female, not because that person is sexually attracted to members of the same sex or identifies as a member of a particular gender.

How then does the Court claim to avoid that conclusion? The Court tries to cloud the issue by spending many pages discussing matters that are beside the point. The Court observes that a Title VII plaintiff need not show that "sex" was the sole or primary motive for a challenged employment decision or its sole or primary cause; that Title VII is limited to discrimination with respect to a list of specified actions (such as hiring, firing, etc.); and that Title VII protects individual rights, not group rights.

All that is true, but so what? In cases like those before us, a plaintiff must show that sex was a "motivating factor" in the challenged employment action, so the question we must decide comes down to this: if an individual employee or applicant for employment shows that his or her sexual orientation or gender identity was a "motivating factor" in a hiring or discharge decision, for example, is that enough to establish that the employer discriminated "because of . . . sex"? Or, to put the same question in different terms, if an employer takes an employment action solely because of the sexual orientation or gender identity of an employee or applicant, has that employer necessarily discriminated because of biological sex?

The answers to those questions must be no, unless discrimination because of sexual orientation or gender identity inherently constitutes discrimination because of sex. The Court attempts to prove that point, and it argues, not merely that the terms of Title VII *can* be interpreted that way but that they *cannot reasonably be interpreted any other way*. According to the Court, the text is unambiguous.

The arrogance of this argument is breathtaking. As I will show, there is not a shred of evidence that any Member of Congress interpreted the statutory text that way when Title VII was enacted. See Part III–B, *infra*. But the Court apparently thinks that this was because the Members were not "smart enough to realize" what its language means. *Hively v. Ivy Tech Community College of Ind.* (7th Cir. 2017) (Posner, J., concurring). The Court seemingly has the same opinion about our colleagues on the Courts of Appeals, because until 2017, every single Court of Appeals to consider the question interpreted Title VII's prohibition against sex discrimination to mean discrimination on the basis of biological sex. And for good measure, the Court's conclusion that Title VII unambiguously reaches discrimination on the basis of sexual orientation and gender identity necessarily means that the EEOC failed to see the obvious for the first 48 years after Title VII became law. Day in and day out, the Commission enforced Title VII but did not grasp what discrimination "because of . . . sex" unambiguously means.

The Court's argument is not only arrogant, it is wrong. It fails on its own terms. "Sex," "sexual orientation," and "gender identity" are different concepts, as the Court concedes. And neither "sexual orientation" nor "gender identity" is tied to either of the two biological sexes. Both men and women may be attracted to members of the opposite sex, members of the same sex, or members of both sexes. And individuals who are born with the genes and organs of either biological sex may identify with a different gender.

Using slightly different terms, the Court asserts again and again that discrimination because of sexual orientation or gender identity inherently or necessarily entails discrimination because of sex. But repetition of an assertion does not make it so, and the Court's repeated assertion is demonstrably untrue.

Contrary to the Court's contention, discrimination because of sexual orientation or gender identity does not in and of itself entail discrimination because of sex. We can see this because it is quite possible for an employer to discriminate on those grounds without taking the sex of an individual applicant or employee into account. . . . In fact, at the time of the enactment of Title VII, the United States military had a blanket policy of refusing to enlist gays or lesbians, and under this policy for years thereafter, applicants for enlistment were required to complete a form that asked whether they were "homosexual."

At oral argument, the attorney representing the employees, [Pam Karlan] a prominent professor of constitutional law, was asked if there would be discrimination because of sex if an employer with a blanket policy against hiring gays, lesbians, and transgender individuals implemented that policy without knowing the biological sex of any job applicants. Her candid answer was that this would "not" be sex discrimination. And she was right.

The attorney's concession was necessary, but it is fatal to the Court's interpretation, for if an employer discriminates against individual applicants or employees without even knowing whether they are male or female, it is impossible to argue that the employer intentionally discriminated because of sex. An employer cannot intentionally discriminate on the basis of a characteristic of which the employer has no knowledge. And if an employer does not violate Title VII by discriminating on the basis of sexual orientation or gender identity without knowing the sex of the affected individuals, there is no reason why the same employer could not lawfully implement the same policy even if it knows the sex of these individuals. If an employer takes an adverse employment action for a perfectly legitimate reason — for example, because an employee stole company property — that action is not converted into sex discrimination simply because the employer knows the employee's sex. As explained, a disparate treatment case requires proof of intent — *i.e.,* that the employee's sex motivated the firing. In short, what this example shows is that discrimination because of sexual orientation or gender identity does not inherently or necessarily entail discrimination because of sex, and for that reason, the Court's chief argument collapses. . . .

[T]he Court makes two other arguments, more or less in passing. The first of these is essentially that sexual orientation and gender identity are closely related to sex. The Court argues that sexual orientation and gender identity are "inextricably bound up with sex," and that discrimination on the basis of sexual orientation or gender identity involves the application of "sex-based rules." . . . All these varian s stress that sex, sexual orientation, and gender identity are related concepts. . . .

It is curious to see this argument in an opinion that purports to apply the purest and highest form of textualism because the argument effectively amends the statutory text. Title VII prohibits discrimination because of *sex itself,* not everything that is related to, based on, or defined with reference to, "sex." Many things are related to sex. Think of all the nouns other than "orientation" that are commonly modified by the adjective "sexual." Some examples yielded by a quick computer search are "sexual harassment," "sexual assault," "sexual violence," "sexual intercourse," and "sexual content."

Does the Court really think that Title VII prohibits discrimination on all these grounds? Is it unlawful for an employer to refuse to hire an employee with a record of sexual harassment in prior jobs? Or a record of sexual assault or violence?. . . .

The Court's remaining argument is based on a hypothetical that the Court finds instructive. In this hypothetical, an employer has two employees who are "attracted to men," and *"to the employer's mind"* the two employees are "materially identical" except that one is a man and the other is a woman. The Court reasons that if the employer fires the man but not the woman, the employer is necessarily motivated by the man's biological sex. After all, if two employees are identical in every respect but sex, and the employer fires only one, what other reason could there be?

The problem with this argument is that the Court loads the dice. That is so because in the mind of an employer who does not want to employ individuals who are attracted to members of the same sex, these two employees are not materially identical in every respect but sex. On the contrary, they differ in another way that the employer thinks is quite material. And until Title VII is amended to add sexual orientation as a prohibited ground, this is a view that an employer is permitted to implement. . . .

The Court tries to avoid this inescapable conclusion by arguing that sex is really the only difference between the two employees. This is so, the Court maintains, because both employees "are attracted to men." Of course, the employer would couch its objection to the man differently. It would say that its objection was his sexual orientation. So this may appear to leave us with a battle of labels. . . .

The Court insists that its label is the right one, and that presumably is why it makes such a point of arguing that an employer cannot escape liability under Title VII by giving sex discrimination some other name. That is certainly true, but so is the opposite. Something that is *not* sex discrimination cannot be converted into sex discrimination by slapping on that label. So the Court cannot prove its point simply by labeling the employer's objection as "attract[ion] to men." Rather, the Court needs to show that its label is the correct one.

And a labeling standoff would not help the Court because that would mean that the bare text of Title VII does not unambiguously show that its interpretation is right. The Court would have no justification for its stubborn refusal to look any further.

As it turns out, however, there is no standoff. It can easily be shown that the employer's real objection is not "attract[ion] to men" but homosexual orientation. . . .

In sum, the Court's textual arguments fail on their own terms. The Court tries to prove that "it is impossible to discriminate against a person for being homosexual or transgender without discriminating against that individual based on sex," but as has been shown, it is entirely possible for an employer to do just that. "[H]omosexuality and transgender status are distinct concepts from sex" and discrimination because of sexual orientation or transgender status does not inherently or necessarily constitute discrimination because of sex. The Court's arguments are squarely contrary to the statutory text.

But even if the words of Title VII did not definitively refute the Court's interpretation, that would not justify the Court's refusal to consider alternative interpretations. The Court's excuse for ignoring everything other than the bare statutory text is that the text is unambiguous and therefore no one can reasonably interpret the text in any way other than the Court does. Unless the Court has met that high standard, it has no justification for its blinkered approach. And to say that the Court's interpretation is the only possible reading is indefensible.

B

Although the Court relies solely on the arguments discussed above, several other arguments figure prominently in the decisions of the lower courts and in briefs submitted by or in support of the employees. The Court apparently finds these arguments unpersuasive, and so do I, but for the sake of completeness, I will address them briefly. . . .

A second prominent argument made in support of the result that the Court now reaches analogizes discrimination against gays and lesbians to discrimination against a person who is married to or has an intimate relationship with a person of a different race. Several lower court cases have held that discrimination on this ground violates Title VII. And the logic of these decisions, it is argued, applies equally where an employee or applicant is treated unfavorably because he or she is married to, or has an intimate relationship with, a person of the same sex.

This argument totally ignores the historically rooted reason why discrimination on the basis of an interracial relationship constitutes race discrimination. And without taking history into account, it is not easy to see how the decisions in question fit the terms of Title VII.

Recall that Title VII makes it unlawful for an employer to discriminate against an individual "because of *such individual's race*." So if an employer is happy to employ whites and blacks but will not employ any employee in an interracial relationship, how can it be said that the employer is discriminating against either whites or blacks "because of such individual's race"? This employer would be applying the same rule to all its employees regardless of their race.

The answer is that this employer is discriminating on a ground that history tells us is a core form of race discrimination. Discrimination because of sexual orientation is different. It cannot be regarded as a form of sex discrimination on the ground that applies in race cases since discrimination because of sexual orientation is not historically tied to a project that aims to subjugate either men or women. An employer who discriminates on this ground might be called "homophobic" or "transphobic," but not sexist. See *Wittmer v. Phillips 66 Co.* (5th Cir. 2019) (Ho, J., concurring). . . .

II

A

So far, I have not looked beyond dictionary definitions of "sex," but textualists like Justice Scalia do not confine their inquiry to the scrutiny of dictionaries. Dictionary definitions are valuable because they are evidence of what people at the time of a statute's enactment would have understood its words to mean. But they are not the only source of relevant evidence, and what matters in the end is the answer to the question that the evidence is gathered to resolve: How would the terms of a statute have been understood by ordinary people at the time of enactment? Justice Scalia was perfectly clear on this point. The words of a law, he insisted, "mean *what they conveyed to reasonable people at the time.*" . . .

Thus, when textualism is properly understood, it calls for an examination of the social context in which a statute was enacted because this may have an important bearing on what its words were understood to mean at the time of enactment. Textualists do not read statutes as if they were messages picked up by a powerful radio telescope from a distant and utterly unknown civilization. Statutes consist of communications between members of a particular linguistic community, one that existed in a particular place and at a particular time, and these communications must therefore be interpreted as they were understood by that community at that time.

For this reason, it is imperative to consider how Americans in 1964 would have understood Title VII's prohibition of discrimination because of sex. To get a picture of this, we may imagine this scene. Suppose that, while Title VII was under consideration in Congress, a group of average Americans decided to read the text of the bill with the aim of writing or calling their representatives in Congress and conveying their approval or disapproval. What would these ordinary citizens have taken "discrimination because of sex" to mean? Would they have thought that this language prohibited discrimination because of sexual orientation or gender identity?

B

The answer could not be clearer. In 1964, ordinary Americans reading the text of Title VII would not have dreamed that discrimination because of sex meant discrimination because of sexual orientation, much less gender identity. The *ordinary meaning* of discrimination because of "sex" was discrimination because of a person's biological sex, not sexual orientation or gender identity. The possibility that discrimination on either of these grounds might fit within some exotic understanding of sex discrimination would not have crossed their minds.

1

In 1964, the concept of prohibiting discrimination "because of sex" was no novelty. It was a familiar and well-understood concept, and what it meant was equal treatment for men and women. . . .

The most prominent example of a provision using this language was the Nineteenth Amendment, ratified in 1920, which bans the denial or abridgment of the right to vote "on account of sex." Similar language appeared in the proposal of the National Woman's Party for an Equal Rights Amendment. As framed in 1921, this proposal forbade all "political, civil or legal disabilities or inequalities *on account of sex,* [o]r on account of marriage." . . .

In short, the concept of discrimination "because of," "on account of," or "on the basis of " sex was well understood. It was part of the campaign for equality that had been waged by women's rights advocates for more than a century, and what it meant was equal treatment for men and women.[22]

2

Discrimination "because of sex" was not understood as having anything to do with discrimination because of sexual orientation or transgender status. Any such notion would have clashed in spectacular fashion with the societal norms of the day.

For most 21st-century Americans, it is painful to be reminded of the way our society once treated gays and lesbians, but any honest effort to understand what the terms of Title VII were understood to mean when enacted must take into account the societal norms of that time. And the plain truth is that in 1964 homosexuality was thought to be a mental disorder, and homosexual conduct was regarded as morally culpable and worthy of punishment. . . .

Homosexuals were also excluded from entry into the United States. The Immigration and Nationality Act of 1952 (INA) excluded aliens "afflicted with psychopathic personality." In *Boutilier v. INS*, 387 U.S. (1967), this Court, relying

---

22. Analysis of the way Title VII's key language was used in books and articles during the relevant time period supports this conclusion. A study searched a vast database of documents from that time to determine how the phrase "discriminate against . . . because of [some trait]" was used. Phillips, The Overlooked Evidence in the Title VII Cases: The Linguistic (and Therefore Textualist) Principle of Compositionality (2020). The study found that the phrase was used to denote discrimination against "someone . . . motivated by prejudice, or biased ideas or attitudes . . . directed at people with that trait in particular." . . . Thus, as used in 1964, "discrimination because of sex" would have been understood to mean discrimination against a woman or a man based on "unfair beliefs or attitudes" about members of that particular sex.

on the INA's legislative history, interpreted that term to encompass homosexuals and upheld an alien's deportation on that ground. Three Justices disagreed with the majority's interpretation of the phrase "psychopathic personality."[27] But it apparently did not occur to anyone to argue that the Court's interpretation was inconsistent with the INA's express prohibition of discrimination "because of sex." That was how our society—and this Court—saw things a half century ago. Discrimination because of sex and discrimination because of sexual orientation were viewed as two entirely different concepts.

To its credit, our society has now come to recognize the injustice of past practices, and this recognition provides the impetus to "update" Title VII. But that is not our job. Our duty is to understand what the terms of Title VII were understood to mean when enacted, and in doing so, we must take into account the societal norms of that time. We must therefore ask whether ordinary Americans in 1964 would have thought that discrimination because of "sex" carried some exotic meaning under which private-sector employers would be prohibited from engaging in a practice that represented the official policy of the Federal Government with respect to its own employees. We must ask whether Americans at that time would have thought that Title VII banned discrimination against an employee for engaging in conduct that Congress had made a felony and a ground for civil commitment.

The questions answer themselves. Even if discrimination based on sexual orientation or gender identity could be squeezed into some arcane understanding of sex discrimination, the context in which Title VII was enacted would tell us that this is not what the statute's terms were understood to mean at that time. To paraphrase something Justice Scalia once wrote, "our job is not to scavenge the world of English usage to discover whether there is any possible meaning" of discrimination because of sex that might be broad enough to encompass discrimination because of sexual orientation or gender identity. *Chisom v. Roemer* (1991) (dissenting opinion). Without strong evidence to the contrary (and there is none here), our job is to ascertain and apply the "*ordinary* meaning" of the statute. And in 1964, ordinary Americans most certainly would not have understood Title VII to ban discrimination because of sexual orientation or gender identity.

The Court makes a tiny effort to suggest that at least some people in 1964 might have seen what Title VII really means. What evidence does it adduce? One complaint filed in 1969, another filed in 1974, and arguments made in the mid-1970s about the meaning of the Equal Rights Amendment. To call this evidence merely feeble would be generous.

C

While Americans in 1964 would have been shocked to learn that Congress had enacted a law prohibiting sexual orientation discrimination, they would have

---

27. Justices Douglas and Fortas thought that a homosexual is merely "one, who by some freak, is the product of an arrested development."

been bewildered to hear that this law also forbids discrimination on the basis of "transgender status" or "gender identity," terms that would have left people at the time scratching their heads. The term "transgender" is said to have been coined "'in the early 1970s,'" and the term "gender identity," now understood to mean "[a]n internal sense of being male, female or something else," apparently first appeared in an academic article in 1964. Certainly, neither term was in common parlance; indeed, dictionaries of the time still primarily defined the word "gender" by reference to grammatical classifications.

While it is likely true that there have always been individuals who experience what is now termed "gender dysphoria," *i.e.*, "[d]iscomfort or distress related to an incongruence between an individual's gender identity and the gender assigned at birth," the current understanding of the concept postdates the enactment of Title VII. . . . It defies belief to suggest that the public meaning of discrimination because of sex in 1964 encompassed discrimination on the basis of a concept that was essentially unknown to the public at that time.

D

1

The Court's main excuse for entirely ignoring the social context in which Title VII was enacted is that the meaning of Title VII's prohibition of discrimination because of sex is clear, and therefore it simply does not matter whether people in 1964 were "smart enough to realize" what its language means. *Hively* (Posner, J., concurring). According to the Court, an argument that looks to the societal norms of those times represents an impermissible attempt to displace the statutory language.

The Court's argument rests on a false premise. As already explained at length, the text of Title VII does not prohibit discrimination because of sexual orientation or gender identity. And what the public thought about those issues in 1964 is relevant and important, not because it provides a ground for departing from the statutory text, but because it helps to explain what the text was understood to mean when adopted.

In arguing that we must put out of our minds what we know about the time when Title VII was enacted, the Court relies on Justice Scalia's opinion for the Court in *Oncale v. Sundowner Offshore Services, Inc.* (1998). But *Oncale* is nothing like these cases, and no one should be taken in by the majority's effort to enlist Justice Scalia in its updating project.*

The Court's unanimous decision in *Oncale* was thoroughly unremarkable. The Court held that a male employee who alleged that he had been sexually harassed at work by other men stated a claim under Title VII. Although the

---

* Note. [Eds: Bryan Garner, Justice Scalia's frequent co-author, tweeted "Scalia J. would have been with Alito J. in dissent because the nobody-ever-thought-it-meant-that line of reasoning carried a lot of weight with him."]

impetus for Title VII's prohibition of sex discrimination was to protect women, anybody reading its terms would immediately appreciate that it applies equally to both sexes, and by the time *Oncale* reached the Court, our precedent already established that sexual harassment may constitute sex discrimination within the meaning of Title VII. See *Meritor Savings Bank, FSB v. Vinson* (1986). Given these premises, syllogistic reasoning dictated the holding.

What today's decision latches onto are *Oncale*'s comments about whether " 'male-on-male sexual harassment' " was on Congress's mind when it enacted Title VII. The Court in *Oncale* observed that this specific type of behavior "was assuredly not the *principal evil* Congress was concerned with when it enacted Title VII," but it found that immaterial because "statutory prohibitions often go beyond the *principal evil* to cover reasonably comparable evils, and it is ultimately the provisions of our laws rather than the *principal concerns* of our legislators by which we are governed."

It takes considerable audacity to read these comments as committing the Court to a position on deep philosophical questions about the meaning of language and their implications for the interpretation of legal rules. These comments are better understood as stating mundane and uncontroversial truths. Who would argue that a statute applies only to the "principal evils" and not lesser evils that fall within the plain scope of its terms? Would even the most ardent "purposivists" and fans of legislative history contend that congressional intent is restricted to Congress's "*principal* concerns"?

Properly understood, *Oncale* does not provide the slightest support for what the Court has done today. For one thing, it would be a wild understatement to say that discrimination because of sexual orientation and transgender status was not the "principal evil" on Congress's mind in 1964. Whether we like to admit it now or not, in the thinking of Congress and the public at that time, such discrimination would not have been evil at all.

But the more important difference between these cases and *Oncale* is that here the interpretation that the Court adopts does not fall within the ordinary meaning of the statutory text as it would have been understood in 1964. To decide for the defendants in *Oncale*, it would have been necessary to carve out an exception to the statutory text. Here, no such surgery is at issue. Even if we totally disregard the societal norms of 1964, the text of Title VII does not support the Court's holding. And the reasoning of *Oncale* does not preclude or counsel against our taking those norms into account. They are relevant, not for the purpose of creating an exception to the terms of the statute, but for the purpose of better appreciating how those terms would have been understood at the time. . . .

III

A

Because the opinion of the Court flies a textualist flag, I have taken pains to show that it cannot be defended on textualist grounds. But even if the Court's textualist argument were stronger, that would not explain today's decision. Many Justices of this Court, both past and present, have not espoused or practiced a method of statutory interpretation that is limited to the analysis of statutory text. Instead, when there is ambiguity in the terms of a statute, they have found it appropriate to look to other evidence of "congressional intent," including legislative history.

So, why in these cases are congressional intent and the legislative history of Title VII totally ignored? Any assessment of congressional intent or legislative history seriously undermines the Court's interpretation. . . . For those who regard congressional intent as the touchstone of statutory interpretation, the message of Title VII's legislative history cannot be missed.

C

Post-enactment events only clarify what was apparent when Title VII was enacted. As noted, bills to add "sexual orientation" to Title VII's list of prohibited grounds were introduced in every Congress beginning in 1975, and two such bills were before Congress in 1991 when it made major changes in Title VII. At that time, the three Courts of Appeals to reach the issue had held that Title VII does not prohibit discrimination because of sexual orientation, two other Circuits had endorsed that interpretation in dicta, and no Court of Appeals had held otherwise. Similarly, the three Circuits to address the application of Title VII to . transgender persons had all rejected the argument that it covered discrimination on this basis. These were also the positions of the EEOC. In enacting substantial changes to Title VII, the 1991 Congress abrogated numerous judicial decisions with which it disagreed. If it also disagreed with the decisions regarding sexual orientation and transgender discrimination, it could have easily overruled those as well, but it did not do so.

After 1991, six other Courts of Appeals reached the issue of sexual orientation discrimination, and until 2017, every single Court of Appeals decision understood Title VII's prohibition of "discrimination because of sex" to mean discrimination because of biological sex. Similarly, the other Circuit to formally address whether Title VII applies to claims of discrimination based on transgender status had also rejected the argument, creating unanimous consensus prior to the Sixth Circuit's decision below.

The Court observes that "[t]he people are entitled to rely on the law as written, without fearing that courts might disregard its plain terms," but it has no qualms about disregarding over 50 years of uniform judicial interpretation of Title VII's plain text. Rather, the Court makes the jaw-dropping statement that its decision exemplifies "judicial humility." Is it humble to maintain, not only that Congress did not understand the terms it enacted in 1964, but that all the Circuit Judges on all the pre-2017 cases could not see what the phrase discrimination "because of sex" really means? If today's decision is humble, it is sobering to imagine what the Court might do if it decided to be bold.

IV

What the Court has done today — interpreting discrimination because of "sex" to encompass discrimination because of sexual orientation or gender identity — is virtually certain to have far-reaching consequences. Over 100 federal statutes prohibit discrimination because of sex. The briefs in these cases have called to our attention the potential effects that the Court's reasoning may have under some of these laws, but the Court waves those considerations aside. As to Title VII itself, the Court dismisses questions about "bathrooms, locker rooms, or anything else of the kind." And it declines to say anything about other statutes whose terms mirror Title VII's.

The Court's brusque refusal to consider the consequences of its reasoning is irresponsible. If the Court had allowed the legislative process to take its course, Congress would have had the opportunity to consider competing interests and might have found a way of accommodating at least some of them. In addition, Congress might have crafted special rules for some of the relevant statutes. But by intervening and proclaiming categorically that employment discrimination based on sexual orientation or gender identity is simply a form of discrimination because of sex, the Court has greatly impeded — and perhaps effectively ended — any chance of a bargained legislative resolution. Before issuing today's radical decision, the Court should have given some thought to where its decision would lead.

As the briefing in these cases has warned, the position that the Court now adopts will threaten freedom of religion, freedom of speech, and personal privacy and safety. No one should think that the Court's decision represents an unalloyed victory for individual liberty.

I will briefly note some of the potential consequences of the Court's decision, but I do not claim to provide a comprehensive survey or to suggest how any of these issues should necessarily play out under the Court's reasoning.[43]

"[B]athrooms, locker rooms, [and other things] of [that] kind." The Court may wish to avoid this subject, but it is a matter of concern to many people who are reticent about disrobing or using toilet facilities in the presence of individuals whom they regard as members of the opposite sex. For some, this may simply be a question of modesty, but for others, there is more at stake. For women who have been victimized by sexual assault or abuse, the experience of seeing an unclothed person with the anatomy of a male in a confined and sensitive location such as a bathroom or locker room can cause serious psychological harm.

Under the Court's decision, however, transgender persons will be able to argue that they are entitled to use a bathroom or locker room that is reserved for persons of the sex with which they identify, and while the Court does not define what it means by a transgender person, the term may apply to individuals who are "gender fluid," that is, individuals whose gender identity is mixed or changes over time. Thus, a person who has not undertaken any physical transitioning

---

43. Contrary to the implication in the Court's opinion, I do not label these potential consequences "undesirable." I mention them only as possible implications of the Court's reasoning.

may claim the right to use the bathroom or locker room assigned to the sex with which the individual identifies at that particular time. The Court provides no clue why a transgender person's claim to such bathroom or locker room access might not succeed.

A similar issue has arisen under Title IX, which prohibits sex discrimination by any elementary or secondary school and any college or university that receives federal financial assistance. . . .

Women's sports. Another issue that may come up under both Title VII and Title IX is the right of a transgender individual to participate on a sports team or in an athletic competition previously reserved for members of one biological sex. . . . The effect of the Court's reasoning may be to force young women to compete against students who have a very significant biological advantage, including students who have the size and strength of a male but identify as female and students who are taking male hormones in order to transition from female to male.

Housing. The Court's decision may lead to Title IX cases against any college that resists assigning students of the opposite biological sex as roommates. . . . Similar claims may be brought under the Fair Housing Act. See 42 U.S.C. §3604.

Employment by religious organizations. Briefs filed by a wide range of religious groups—Christian, Jewish, and Muslim—express deep concern that the position now adopted by the Court "will trigger open conflict with faith-based employment practices of numerous churches, synagogues, mosques, and other religious institutions." They argue that "[r]eligious organizations need employees who actually live the faith," and that compelling a religious organization to employ individuals whose conduct flouts the tenets of the organization's faith forces the group to communicate an objectionable message.

This problem is perhaps most acute when it comes to the employment of teachers. . . . Thus, if a religious school teaches that sex outside marriage and sex reassignment procedures are immoral, the message may be lost if the school employs a teacher who is in a same-sex relationship or has undergone or is undergoing sex reassignment. Yet today's decision may lead to Title VII claims by such teachers and applicants for employment.

At least some teachers and applicants for teaching positions may be blocked from recovering on such claims by the "ministerial exception" recognized in *Hosanna-Tabor Evangelical Lutheran Church and School v. EEOC* (2012). Two cases now pending before the Court present the question whether teachers who provide religious instruction can be considered to be "ministers." But even if teachers with those responsibilities qualify, what about other very visible school employees who may not qualify for the ministerial exception?

Healthcare. Healthcare benefits may emerge as an intense battleground under the Court's holding. Transgender employees have brought suit under Title VII to challenge employer-provided health insurance plans that do not cover costly sex reassignment surgery. Similar claims have been brought under the Affordable Care Act (ACA), which broadly prohibits sex discrimination in the provision of healthcare.

Such claims present difficult religious liberty issues because some employers and healthcare providers have strong religious objections to sex reassignment procedures, and therefore requiring them to pay for or to perform these procedures will have a severe impact on their ability to honor their deeply held religious beliefs.

Freedom of speech. The Court's decision may even affect the way employers address their employees and the way teachers and school officials address students. Under established English usage, two sets of sex-specific singular personal pronouns are used to refer to someone in the third person (he, him, and his for males; she, her, and hers for females). But several different sets of gender-neutral pronouns have now been created and are preferred by some individuals who do not identify as falling into either of the two traditional categories.[58] Some jurisdictions, such as New York City, have ordinances making the failure to use an individual's preferred pronoun a punishable offense, and some colleges have similar rules. After today's decision, plaintiffs may claim that the failure to use their preferred pronoun violates one of the federal laws prohibiting sex discrimination.

The Court's decision may also pressure employers to suppress any statements by employees expressing disapproval of same-sex relationships and sex reassignment procedures. Employers are already imposing such restrictions voluntarily, and after today's decisions employers will fear that allowing employees to express their religious views on these subjects may give rise to Title VII harassment claims.

Constitutional claims. Finally, despite the important differences between the Fourteenth Amendment and Title VII, the Court's decision may exert a gravitational pull in constitutional cases. Under our precedents, the Equal Protection Clause prohibits sex-based discrimination unless a "heightened" standard of review is met. *Sessions* v. *Morales-Santana* (2017); *United States* v. *Virginia* (1996). By equating discrimination because of sexual orientation or gender identity with discrimination because of sex, the Court's decision will be cited as a ground for subjecting all three forms of discrimination to the same exacting standard of review.

Under this logic, today's decision may have effects that extend well beyond the domain of federal anti-discrimination statutes. This potential is illustrated by pending and recent lower court cases in which transgender individuals have challenged a variety of federal, state, and local laws and policies on constitutional grounds.

Although the Court does not want to think about the consequences of its decision, we will not be able to avoid those issues for long. The entire Federal Judiciary will be mired for years in disputes about the reach of the Court's reasoning.

* * *

---

58. See, *e.g.*, University of Wisconsin LGBTQ+ Resource Center, Gender Pronouns (2020): (f)ae, (f)aer, (f)aers; e/ey, em, eir, eirs; per, pers; ve, ver, vis; xe, xem, xyr, xyrs; ze/zie, hir, hirs.

The updating desire to which the Court succumbs no doubt arises from humane and generous impulses. Today, many Americans know individuals who are gay, lesbian, or transgender and want them to be treated with the dignity, consideration, and fairness that everyone deserves. But the authority of this Court is limited to saying what the law *is*.

The Court itself recognizes this: "The place to make new legislation . . . lies in Congress. When it comes to statutory interpretation, our role is limited to applying the law's demands as faithfully as we can in the cases that come before us." It is easy to utter such words. If only the Court would live by them.

I respectfully dissent.

JUSTICE KAVANAUGH, dissenting.

Like many cases in this Court, this case boils down to one fundamental question: Who decides? Title VII of the Civil Rights Act of 1964 prohibits employment discrimination "because of " an individual's "race, color, religion, sex, or national origin." The question here is whether Title VII should be expanded to prohibit employment discrimination because of sexual orientation. Under the Constitution's separation of powers, the responsibility to amend Title VII belongs to Congress and the President in the legislative process, not to this Court.

The political branches are well aware of this issue. In 2007, the U.S. House of Representatives voted 235 to 184 to prohibit employment discrimination on the basis of sexual orientation. In 2013, the U.S. Senate voted 64 to 32 in favor of a similar ban. In 2019, the House again voted 236 to 173 to outlaw employment discrimination on the basis of sexual orientation. Although both the House and Senate have voted at different times to prohibit sexual orientation discrimination, the two Houses have not yet come together with the President to enact a bill into law.

The policy arguments for amending Title VII are very weighty. The Court has previously stated, and I fully agree, that gay and lesbian Americans "cannot be treated as social outcasts or as inferior in dignity and worth." *Masterpiece Cakeshop, Ltd. v. Colorado Civil Rights Comm'n* (2018).

But we are judges, not Members of Congress. And in Alexander Hamilton's words, federal judges exercise "neither Force nor Will, but merely judgment." The Federalist No. 78. Under the Constitution's separation of powers, our role as judges is to interpret and follow the law as written, regardless of whether we like the result. Cf. *Texas v. Johnson* (1989) (Kennedy, J., concurring). Our role is not to make or amend the law. As written, Title VII does not prohibit employment discrimination because of sexual orientation.[1]

I

Title VII makes it unlawful for employers to discriminate because of "race, color, religion, sex, or national origin." As enacted in 1964, Title VII did not

---

1. Although this opinion does not separately analyze discrimination on the basis of gender identity, this opinion's legal analysis of discrimination on the basis of sexual orientation would apply in much the same way to discrimination on the basis of gender identity.

prohibit other forms of employment discrimination, such as age discrimination, disability discrimination, or sexual orientation discrimination.

Over time, Congress has enacted new employment discrimination laws. . . . For several decades, Congress has considered numerous bills to prohibit employment discrimination based on sexual orientation. But as noted above, although Congress has come close, it has not yet shouldered a bill over the legislative finish line.

In the face of the unsuccessful legislative efforts (so far) to prohibit sexual orientation discrimination, judges may not rewrite the law simply because of their own policy views. Judges may not update the law merely because they think that Congress does not have the votes or the fortitude. Judges may not predictively amend the law just because they believe that Congress is likely to do it soon anyway.

If judges could rewrite laws based on their own policy views, or based on their own assessments of likely future legislative action, the critical distinction between legislative authority and judicial authority that undergirds the Constitution's separation of powers would collapse, thereby threatening the impartial rule of law and individual liberty. As James Madison stated: "Were the power of judging joined with the legislative, the life and liberty of the subject would be exposed to arbitrary controul, for *the judge* would then be *the legislator.*" The Federalist No. 47, at 326 (citing Montesquieu). If judges could, for example, rewrite or update securities laws or healthcare laws or gun laws or environmental laws simply based on their own policy views, the Judiciary would become a democratically illegitimate super-legislature—unelected, and hijacking the important policy decisions reserved by the Constitution to the people's elected representatives.

Because judges interpret the law as written, not as they might wish it were written, the first 10 U.S. Courts of Appeals to consider whether Title VII prohibits sexual orientation discrimination all said no. Some 30 federal judges considered the question. All 30 judges said no, based on the text of the statute. 30 out of 30.

But in the last few years, a new theory has emerged. To end-run the bedrock separation-of-powers principle that courts may not unilaterally rewrite statutes, the plaintiffs here (and, recently, two Courts of Appeals) have advanced a novel and creative argument. They contend that discrimination "because of sexual orientation" and discrimination "because of sex" are actually not separate categories of discrimination after all. Instead, the theory goes, discrimination because of sexual orientation always qualifies as discrimination because of sex: When a gay man is fired because he is gay, he is fired because he is attracted to men, even though a similarly situated woman would not be fired just because she is attracted to men. According to this theory, it follows that the man has been fired, at least as a literal matter, because of his sex.

Under this literalist approach, sexual orientation discrimination automatically qualifies as sex discrimination, and Title VII's prohibition against sex discrimination therefore also prohibits sexual orientation discrimination—and actually has done so since 1964, unbeknownst to everyone. Surprisingly, the Court today buys into this approach.

For the sake of argument, I will assume that firing someone because of their sexual orientation may, as a very literal matter, entail making a distinction based on sex. But to prevail in this case with their literalist approach, the plaintiffs must *also* establish one of two other points. The plaintiffs must establish that courts, when interpreting a statute, adhere to literal meaning rather than ordinary meaning. Or alternatively, the plaintiffs must establish that the ordinary meaning of "discriminate because of sex"—not just the literal meaning—encompasses sexual orientation discrimination. The plaintiffs fall short on both counts.

First, courts must follow ordinary meaning, not literal meaning. And courts must adhere to the ordinary meaning of phrases, not just the meaning of the words in a phrase.

There is no serious debate about the foundational interpretive principle that courts adhere to ordinary meaning, not literal meaning, when interpreting statutes. As Justice Scalia explained, "the good textualist is not a literalist." A. Scalia, A Matter of Interpretation (1997). . . . The ordinary meaning that counts is the ordinary public meaning at the time of enactment—although in this case, that temporal principle matters little because the ordinary meaning of "discriminate because of sex" was the same in 1964 as it is now.

Judges adhere to ordinary meaning for two main reasons: rule of law and democratic accountability. A society governed by the rule of law must have laws that are known and understandable to the citizenry. And judicial adherence to ordinary meaning facilitates the democratic accountability of America's elected representatives for the laws they enact. Citizens and legislators must be able to ascertain the law by reading the words of the statute. Both the rule of law and democratic accountability badly suffer when a court adopts a hidden or obscure interpretation of the law, and not its ordinary meaning.

Consider a simple example of how ordinary meaning differs from literal meaning. A statutory ban on "vehicles in the park" would literally encompass a baby stroller. But no good judge would interpret the statute that way because the word "vehicle," in its ordinary meaning, does not encompass baby strollers. . . . Those cases exemplify a deeply rooted principle: When there is a divide between the literal meaning and the ordinary meaning, courts must follow the ordinary meaning.

Next is a critical point of emphasis in this case. The difference between literal and ordinary meaning becomes especially important when—as in this case— judges consider *phrases* in statutes. (Recall that the shorthand version of the phrase at issue here is "discriminate because of sex.") Courts must heed the ordinary meaning of the *phrase as a whole*, not just the meaning of the words in the phrase. That is because a phrase may have a more precise or confined meaning than the literal meaning of the individual words in the phrase. . . .

Justice Scalia explained the extraordinary importance of hewing to the ordinary meaning of a phrase: "Adhering to the *fair meaning* of the text (the textualist's touchstone) does not limit one to the hyperliteral meaning of each word in the text. In the words of Learned Hand: 'a sterile literalism . . . loses sight of the forest for the trees.' The full body of a text contains implications that can alter the literal meaning of individual words." A. Scalia & B. Garner, Reading Law (2012). . . .

If the usual evidence indicates that a statutory phrase bears an ordinary meaning different from the literal strung-together definitions of the individual words in the phrase, we may not ignore or gloss over that discrepancy.

In other words, this Court's precedents and longstanding principles of statutory interpretation teach a clear lesson: Do not simply split statutory phrases into their component words, look up each in a dictionary, and then mechanically put them together again, as the majority opinion today mistakenly does. To reiterate Justice Scalia's caution, that approach misses the forest for the trees. . . .

Bottom line: Statutory Interpretation 101 instructs courts to follow ordinary meaning, not literal meaning, and to adhere to the ordinary meaning of phrases, not just the meaning of the words in a phrase.

Second, in light of the bedrock principle that we must adhere to the ordinary meaning of a phrase, the question in this case boils down to the ordinary meaning of the phrase "discriminate because of sex." Does the ordinary meaning of that phrase encompass discrimination because of sexual orientation? The answer is plainly no.

On occasion, it can be difficult for judges to assess ordinary meaning. Not here. Both common parlance and common legal usage treat sex discrimination and sexual orientation discrimination as two distinct categories of discrimination — back in 1964 and still today.

. . . Seneca Falls was not Stonewall. The women's rights movement was not (and is not) the gay rights movement, although many people obviously support or participate in both. So to think that sexual orientation discrimination is just a form of sex discrimination is not just a mistake of language and psychology, but also a mistake of history and sociology.

Importantly, an overwhelming body of federal law reflects and reinforces the ordinary meaning and demonstrates that sexual orientation discrimination is distinct from, and not a form of, sex discrimination. Since enacting Title VII in 1964, Congress has *never* treated sexual orientation discrimination the same as, or as a form of, sex discrimination. Instead, Congress has consistently treated sex discrimination and sexual orientation discrimination as legally distinct categories of discrimination.

Many federal statutes prohibit sex discrimination, and many federal statutes also prohibit sexual orientation discrimination. But those sexual orientation statutes expressly prohibit sexual orientation discrimination in addition to expressly prohibiting sex discrimination. *Every single one.* To this day, Congress has never defined sex discrimination to encompass sexual orientation discrimination. Instead, when Congress wants to prohibit sexual orientation discrimination in addition to sex discrimination, Congress explicitly refers to sexual orientation discrimination.

That longstanding and widespread congressional practice matters. When interpreting statutes, as the Court has often said, we "usually presume differences in language" convey "differences in meaning." *Wisconsin Central.* . . .

As demonstrated by all of the statutes covering sexual orientation discrimination, Congress knows how to prohibit sexual orientation discrimination. So courts should not read that specific concept into the general words "discriminate because of sex." We cannot close our eyes to the indisputable fact that

Congress—for several decades in a large number of statutes—has identified sex discrimination and sexual orientation discrimination as two distinct categories.

Where possible, we also strive to interpret statutes so as not to create undue surplusage. It is not uncommon to find some scattered redundancies in statutes. But reading sex discrimination to encompass sexual orientation discrimination would cast aside as surplusage the numerous references to sexual orientation discrimination sprinkled throughout the U.S. Code in laws enacted over the last 25 years.

In short, an extensive body of federal law both reflects and reinforces the widespread understanding that sexual orientation discrimination is distinct from, and not a form of, sex discrimination.

The story is the same with bills proposed in Congress. Since the 1970s, Members of Congress have introduced many bills to prohibit sexual orientation discrimination in the workplace. Until very recently, all of those bills would have expressly established sexual orientation as a separately proscribed category of discrimination. The bills did not define sex discrimination to encompass sexual orientation discrimination.

The proposed bills are telling not because they are relevant to congressional intent regarding Title VII. See *Central Bank of Denver, N. A. v. First Interstate Bank of Denver, N. A.* (1994). Rather, the proposed bills are telling because they, like the enacted laws, further demonstrate the widespread usage of the English language in the United States: Sexual orientation discrimination is distinct from, and not a form of, sex discrimination. . . .

The States have proceeded in the same fashion. A majority of States prohibit sexual orientation discrimination in employment, either by legislation applying to most workers, an executive order applying to public employees, or both. Almost every state statute or executive order proscribing sexual orientation discrimination expressly prohibits sexual orientation discrimination separately from the State's ban on sex discrimination.

That common usage in the States underscores that sexual orientation discrimination is commonly understood as a legal concept distinct from sex discrimination.

And it is the common understanding in this Court as well. Since 1971, the Court has employed rigorous or heightened constitutional scrutiny of laws that classify on the basis of sex. See *United States v. Virginia* (1996); *J. E. B. v. Alabama ex rel. T. B.* (1994); *Craig* v. *Boren* (1976); *Frontiero v. Richardson* (1973) (plurality opinion); *Reed v. Reed* (1971). Over the last several decades, the Court has also decided many cases involving sexual orientation. But in those cases, the Court never suggested that sexual orientation discrimination is just a form of sex discrimination. All of the Court's cases from *Bowers* to *Romer* to *Lawrence* to *Windsor* to *Obergefell* would have been far easier to analyze and decide if sexual orientation discrimination were just a form of sex discrimination and therefore received the same heightened scrutiny as sex discrimination under the Equal Protection Clause. See *Bowers v. Hardwick* (1986); *Romer v. Evans* (1996); *Lawrence v. Texas* (2003); *United States v. Windsor* (2013); *Obergefell v. Hodges* (2015).

Did the Court in all of those sexual orientation cases just miss that obvious answer—and overlook the fact that sexual orientation discrimination is actually a form of sex discrimination? That seems implausible. Nineteen Justices have participated in those cases. Not a single Justice stated or even hinted that sexual orientation discrimination was just a form of sex discrimination and therefore entitled to the same heightened scrutiny under the Equal Protection Clause. The opinions in those five cases contain no trace of such reasoning. That is presumably because everyone on this Court, too, has long understood that sexual orientation discrimination is distinct from, and not a form of, sex discrimination.

In sum, all of the usual indicators of ordinary meaning—common parlance, common usage by Congress, the practice in the Executive Branch, the laws in the States, and the decisions of this Court—overwhelmingly establish that sexual orientation discrimination is distinct from, and not a form of, sex discrimination. The usage has been consistent across decades, in both the federal and state contexts. . . .

To tie it all together, the plaintiffs have only two routes to succeed here. Either they can say that literal meaning overrides ordinary meaning when the two conflict. Or they can say that the ordinary meaning of the phrase "discriminate because of sex" encompasses sexual orientation discrimination. But the first flouts long-settled principles of statutory interpretation. And the second contradicts the widespread ordinary use of the English language in America.

II

Until the last few years, every U.S. Court of Appeals to address this question concluded that Title VII does not prohibit discrimination because of sexual orientation. As noted above, in the first 10 Courts of Appeals to consider the issue, all 30 federal judges agreed that Title VII does not prohibit sexual orientation discrimination. 30 out of 30 judges.

The unanimity of those 30 federal judges shows that the question as a matter of law, as compared to as a matter of policy, was not deemed close. Those 30 judges realized a seemingly obvious point: Title VII is not a general grant of authority for judges to fashion an evolving common law of equal treatment in the workplace. Rather, Title VII identifies certain specific categories of prohibited discrimination. And under the separation of powers, Congress—not the courts—possesses the authority to amend or update the law, as Congress has done with age discrimination and disability discrimination, for example.

So what changed from the situation only a few years ago when 30 out of 30 federal judges had agreed on this question? Not the text of Title VII. The law has not changed. Rather, the judges' decisions have evolved.

To be sure, the majority opinion today does not openly profess that it is judicially updating or amending Title VII. Cf. *Hively* (Posner, J., concurring). But the majority opinion achieves the same outcome by seizing on literal meaning and overlooking the ordinary meaning of the phrase "discriminate because of sex." Although the majority opinion acknowledges that the meaning of a phrase and the meaning of a phrase's individual words *could* differ, it dismisses phrasal meaning for purposes of this case. The majority opinion repeatedly seizes on the meaning of the statute's individual terms, mechanically puts them back together, and generates an interpretation of the phrase "discriminate because of sex" that is literal. But to reiterate, that approach to statutory interpretation is fundamentally flawed. Bedrock principles of statutory interpretation dictate that we look to ordinary meaning, not literal meaning, and that we likewise adhere to the ordinary meaning of phrases, not just the meaning of words in a phrase. And the ordinary meaning of the phrase "discriminate because of sex" does not encompass sexual orientation discrimination.

The majority opinion deflects that critique by saying that courts should base their interpretation of statutes on the text as written, not on the legislators' subjective intentions. Of course that is true. No one disagrees. It is "the provisions of our laws rather than the principal concerns of our legislators by which we are governed." *Oncale v. Sundowner Offshore Services, Inc.* (1998).

But in my respectful view, the majority opinion makes a fundamental mistake by confusing ordinary meaning with subjective intentions. To briefly explain: In the early years after Title VII was enacted, some may have wondered whether Title VII's prohibition on sex discrimination protected male employees. After all, covering male employees may not have been the intent of some who voted for the statute. Nonetheless, discrimination on the basis of sex against women and discrimination on the basis of sex against men are both understood as discrimination because of sex (back in 1964 and now) and are therefore encompassed within Title VII. So too, regardless of what the intentions of the drafters might have been, the ordinary meaning of the law demonstrates that harassing an employee because of her sex is discriminating against the employee because of her sex with respect to the "terms, conditions, or privileges of employment," as this Court rightly concluded. *Meritor Savings Bank, FSB v. Vinson* (1986).[10]

---

10. An amicus brief supporting the plaintiffs suggests that the plaintiffs' interpretive approach is supported by the interpretive approach employed by the Court in its landmark decision in *Brown v. Board of Education* (1954). See Brief for Anti-Discrimination Scholars as Amici Curiae 4. That suggestion is incorrect. *Brown* is a correct decision as a matter of original public meaning. There were two analytical components of *Brown*. One issue was the meaning of "equal protection." The Court determined that black Americans — like all Americans — have an individual equal protection right against state discrimination on the basis of race. (That point is also directly made in *Bolling v. Sharpe* (1954).) Separate but equal is not equal. The other issue was whether that racial nondiscrimination principle applied to public schools, even though public schools did not exist in any comparable form in 1868. The answer was yes. The Court applied the equal protection principle to public schools in the same way that the Court applies, for example, the First Amendment to the Internet and the Fourth Amendment to cars. This case raises the same kind of inquiry as the first question in *Brown*. There, the question was what equal protection meant. Here, the question is what "discriminate because of sex" means. If this case raised the question whether the sex discrimination principle in Title VII applied to some category of employers unknown in 1964, such as to social media companies, it might be a case in Brown's second category, akin to the question whether the racial nondiscrimination principle applied to public schools. But that is not this case.

By contrast, this case involves sexual orientation discrimination, which has long and widely been understood as distinct from, and not a form of, sex discrimination. Until now, federal law has always reflected that common usage and recognized that distinction between sex discrimination and sexual orientation discrimination. To fire one employee because she is a woman and another employee because he is gay implicates two distinct societal concerns, reveals two distinct biases, imposes two distinct harms, and falls within two distinct statutory prohibitions. . . .

The majority opinion insists that it is not rewriting or updating Title VII, but instead is just humbly reading the text of the statute as written. But that assertion is tough to accept. Most everyone familiar with the use of the English language in America understands that the ordinary meaning of sexual orientation discrimination is distinct from the ordinary meaning of sex discrimination. Federal law distinguishes the two. State law distinguishes the two. This Court's cases distinguish the two. Statistics on discrimination distinguish the two. History distinguishes the two. Psychology distinguishes the two. Sociology distinguishes the two. Human resources departments all over America distinguish the two. Sports leagues distinguish the two. Political groups distinguish the two. Advocacy groups distinguish the two. Common parlance distinguishes the two. Common sense distinguishes the two.

As a result, many Americans will not buy the novel interpretation unearthed and advanced by the Court today. Many will no doubt believe that the Court has unilaterally rewritten American vocabulary and American law — a "statutory amendment courtesy of unelected judges." *Hively* (Sykes, J., dissenting). Some will surmise that the Court succumbed to "the natural desire that beguiles judges along with other human beings into imposing their own views of goodness, truth, and justice upon others." *Furman v. Georgia* (1972) (Rehnquist, J., dissenting).

I have the greatest, and unyielding, respect for my colleagues and for their good faith. But when this Court usurps the role of Congress, as it does today, the public understandably becomes confused about who the policymakers really are in our system of separated powers, and inevitably becomes cynical about the oft-repeated aspiration that judges base their decisions on law rather than on personal preference. The best way for judges to demonstrate that we are deciding cases based on the ordinary meaning of the law is to walk the walk, even in the hard cases when we might prefer a different policy outcome.

* * *

In judicially rewriting Title VII, the Court today cashiers an ongoing legislative process, at a time when a new law to prohibit sexual orientation discrimination was probably close at hand. . . . It was therefore easy to envision a day, likely just in the next few years, when the House and Senate took historic votes on a bill that would prohibit employment discrimination on the basis of sexual orientation. It was easy to picture a massive and celebratory Presidential signing ceremony in the East Room or on the South Lawn.

It is true that meaningful legislative action takes time — often too much time, especially in the unwieldy morass on Capitol Hill. But the Constitution does not put the Legislative Branch in the "position of a television quiz show contestant so that when a given period of time has elapsed and a problem remains unsolved by them, the federal judiciary may press a buzzer and take its turn at fashioning a solution." Rehnquist, The Notion of a Living Constitution, 54 Texas L. Rev. 693 (1976). The proper role of the Judiciary in statutory interpretation cases is "to apply, not amend, the work of the People's representatives," even when the judges might think that "Congress should reenter the field and alter the judgments it made in the past." *Henson*.

Instead of a hard-earned victory won through the democratic process, today's victory is brought about by judicial dictate—judges latching on to a novel form of living literalism to rewrite ordinary meaning and remake American law. Under the Constitution and laws of the United States, this Court is the wrong body to change American law in that way. The Court's ruling "comes at a great cost to representative self-government." *Hively* (Sykes, J., dissenting). And the implications of this Court's usurpation of the legislative process will likely reverberate in unpredictable ways for years to come.

Notwithstanding my concern about the Court's transgression of the Constitution's separation of powers, it is appropriate to acknowledge the important victory achieved today by gay and lesbian Americans. Millions of gay and lesbian Americans have worked hard for many decades to achieve equal treatment in fact and in law. They have exhibited extraordinary vision, tenacity, and grit—battling often steep odds in the legislative and judicial arenas, not to mention in their daily lives. They have advanced powerful policy arguments and can take pride in today's result. Under the Constitution's separation of powers, however, I believe that it was Congress's role, not this Court's, to amend Title VII. I therefore must respectfully dissent from the Court's judgment.

Chapter 15

Modern Substantive Due Process

STUDY GUIDE:

- Justice Ginsburg cited *McDonald* for the proposition that "[a] Bill of Rights protection is incorporated, we have explained, if it is 'fundamental to our scheme of ordered liberty,' or 'deeply rooted in this Nation's history and tradition.'" That is, a right can be incorporated if it is either (a) "fundamental" or (b) "deeply rooted." Is Justice Ginsburg's summary the best reading of *McDonald*?
- Why didn't Justice Gorsuch join Justice Thomas's concurrence?
- Justice Thomas considers the original public meaning of the Excessive Fines Clause both at the time of the 8th Amendment's ratification (1791) and at the time of the 14th Amendment's ratification (1868). Why does he look to both time periods?

Timbs v. Indiana
586 U.S. ___ (2019)

JUSTICE GINSBURG delivered the opinion of the Court.

Tyson Timbs pleaded guilty in Indiana state court to dealing in a controlled substance and conspiracy to commit theft. The trial court sentenced him to one year of home detention and five years of probation, which included a court-supervised addiction-treatment program. The sentence also required Timbs to pay fees and costs totaling $1,203. At the time of Timbs's arrest, the police seized his vehicle, a Land Rover SUV Timbs had purchased for about $42,000. Timbs paid for the vehicle with money he received from an insurance policy when his father died.

The State engaged a private law firm to bring a civil suit for forfeiture of Timbs's Land Rover, charging that the vehicle had been used to transport heroin. After Timbs's guilty plea in the criminal case, the trial court held a hearing on the forfeiture demand. Although finding that Timbs's vehicle had been used to facilitate violation of a criminal statute, the court denied the requested forfeiture, observing that Timbs had recently purchased the vehicle for $42,000, more than four times the maximum $10,000 monetary fine assessable against him for his drug conviction. Forfeiture of the Land Rover, the court determined, would be grossly disproportionate to the gravity of Timbs's offense, hence unconstitutional under the Eighth Amendment's Excessive Fines Clause. The Court of Appeals of Indiana affirmed that determination, but the Indiana Supreme Court reversed. The Indiana Supreme Court did not decide whether the forfeiture would be excessive. Instead, it held that the Excessive Fines Clause constrains only federal action and is inapplicable to state impositions. We granted certiorari.

The question presented: Is the Eighth Amendment's Excessive Fines Clause an "incorporated" protection applicable to the States under the Fourteenth Amendment's Due Process Clause? Like the Eighth Amendment's proscriptions of "cruel and unusual punishment" and "[e]xcessive bail," the protection against excessive fines guards against abuses of government's punitive or criminal-law-enforcement authority. This safeguard, we hold, is "fundamental to our scheme of ordered liberty," with "dee[p] root[s] in [our] history and tradition." *McDonald v. Chicago* (2010). The Excessive Fines Clause is therefore incorporated by the Due Process Clause of the Fourteenth Amendment.

I

A

When ratified in 1791, the Bill of Rights applied only to the Federal Government. *Barron ex rel. Tiernan v. Mayor of Baltimore* (1833). "The constitutional Amendments adopted in the aftermath of the Civil War," however, "fundamentally altered our country's federal system." *McDonald*. With only "a handful" of exceptions, this Court has held that the Fourteenth Amendment's Due Process Clause incorporates the protections contained in the Bill of Rights, rendering them applicable to the States. A Bill of Rights protection is incorporated, we have explained, if it is "fundamental to our scheme of ordered liberty," or "deeply rooted in this Nation's history and tradition." *Id.*

Incorporated Bill of Rights guarantees are "enforced against the States under the Fourteenth Amendment according to the same standards that protect those personal rights against federal encroachment." Thus, if a Bill of Rights protection is incorporated, there is no daylight between the federal and state conduct it prohibits or requires.[1]

B

Under the Eighth Amendment, "[e]xcessive bail shall not be required, nor excessive fines imposed, nor cruel and unusual punishments inflicted." Taken

---

1. The sole exception is our holding that the Sixth Amendment requires jury unanimity in federal, but not state, criminal proceedings. *Apodaca v. Oregon* (1972). As we have explained, that "exception to th[e] general rule . . . was the result of an unusual division among the Justices," and it "does not undermine the well-established rule that incorporated Bill of Rights protections apply identically to the States and the Federal Government." *McDonald*.

together, these Clauses place "parallel limitations" on "the power of those entrusted with the criminal-law function of government." *Browning-Ferris Industries of Vt., Inc. v. Kelco Disposal, Inc.* (1989). Directly at issue here is the phrase "nor excessive fines imposed," which "limits the government's power to extract payments, whether in cash or in kind, 'as punishment for some offense.'" *United States v. Bajakajian* (1998) (quoting *Austin v. United States,* (1993)). The Fourteenth Amendment, we hold, incorporates this protection.

The Excessive Fines Clause traces its venerable lineage back to at least 1215, when Magna Carta guaranteed that "[a] Free-man shall not be amerced for a small fault, but after the manner of the fault; and for a great fault after the greatness thereof, saving to him his contenement. . . ." §20, 9 Hen. III, ch. 14, in 1 Eng. Stat. at Large 5 (1225).[2] As relevant here, Magna Carta required that economic sanctions "be proportioned to the wrong" and "not be so large as to deprive [an offender] of his livelihood." *Browning-Ferris.* See also 4 W. Blackstone, Commentaries on the Laws of England 372 (1769) ("[N]o man shall have a larger amercement imposed upon him, than his circumstances or personal estate will bear. . . .").

Despite Magna Carta, imposition of excessive fines persisted. The 17th century Stuart kings, in particular, were criticized for using large fines to raise revenue, harass their political foes, and indefinitely detain those unable to pay. When James II was overthrown in the Glorious Revolution, the attendant English Bill of Rights reaffirmed Magna Carta's guarantee by providing that "excessive Bail ought not to be required, nor excessive Fines imposed; nor cruel and unusual Punishments inflicted."

Across the Atlantic, this familiar language was adopted almost verbatim, first in the Virginia Declaration of Rights, then in the Eighth Amendment, which states: "Excessive bail shall not be required, nor excessive fines imposed, nor cruel and unusual punishments inflicted."

Adoption of the Excessive Fines Clause was in tune not only with English law; the Clause resonated as well with similar colonial-era provisions. . . . In 1787, the constitutions of eight States—accounting for 70% of the U.S. population—forbade excessive fines. Calabresi, Agudo, & Dore, State Bills of Rights in 1787 and 1791, 85 S. Cal. L. Rev. 1451, 1517 (2012).

An even broader consensus obtained in 1868 upon ratification of the Fourteenth Amendment. By then, the constitutions of 35 of the 37 States—accounting for over 90% of the U.S. population—expressly prohibited excessive fines. Calabresi & Agudo, Individual Rights Under State Constitutions When the Fourteenth Amendment Was Ratified in 1868, 87 Texas L. Rev. 7, 82 (2008).

Notwithstanding the States' apparent agreement that the right guaranteed by the Excessive Fines Clause was fundamental, abuses continued. Following the

---

2. "Amercements were payments to the Crown, and were required of individuals who were 'in the King's mercy,' because of some act offensive to the Crown." *Browning-Ferris.* "[T]hough fines and amercements had distinct historical antecedents, they served fundamentally similar purposes—and, by the seventeenth and eighteenth centuries, the terms were often used interchangeably." Brief for Eighth Amendment Scholars as *Amici Curiae.*

Civil War, Southern States enacted Black Codes to subjugate newly freed slaves and maintain the prewar racial hierarchy. Among these laws' provisions were draconian fines for violating broad proscriptions on "vagrancy" and other dubious offenses. When newly freed slaves were unable to pay imposed fines, States often demanded involuntary labor instead. Congressional debates over the Civil Rights Act of 1866, the joint resolution that became the Fourteenth Amendment, and similar measures repeatedly mentioned the use of fines to coerce involuntary labor.

Today, acknowledgment of the right's fundamental nature remains widespread. As Indiana itself reports, all 50 States have a constitutional provision prohibiting the imposition of excessive fines either directly or by requiring proportionality. Indeed, Indiana explains that its own Supreme Court has held that the Indiana Constitution should be interpreted to impose the same restrictions as the Eighth Amendment. . . .

In short, the historical and logical case for concluding that the Fourteenth Amendment incorporates the Excessive Fines Clause is overwhelming. Protection against excessive punitive economic sanctions secured by the Clause is, to repeat, both "fundamental to our scheme of ordered liberty" and "deeply rooted in this Nation's history and tradition." *McDonald.* . . . For the reasons stated, the judgment of the Indiana Supreme Court is vacated, and the case is remanded for further proceedings not inconsistent with this opinion.

It is so ordered.

JUSTICE GORSUCH, concurring.

The majority faithfully applies our precedent and, based on a wealth of historical evidence, concludes that the Fourteenth Amendment incorporates the Eighth Amendment's Excessive Fines Clause against the States. I agree with that conclusion. As an original matter, I acknowledge, the appropriate vehicle for incorporation may well be the Fourteenth Amendment's Privileges or Immunities Clause, rather than, as this Court has long assumed, the Due Process Clause. See, *e.g.,* *McDonald v. Chicago* (2010) (Thomas, J., concurring in part and concurring in judgment) (documenting evidence that the "privileges or immunities of citizens of the United States" include, at minimum, the individual rights enumerated in the Bill of Rights); Wildenthal, Nationalizing the Bill of Rights: Revisiting the Original Understanding of the Fourteenth Amendment in 1866-67, 68 Ohio St. L.J. 1509 (2007); A. Amar, The Bill of Rights: Creation and Reconstruction 163-214 (1998); M. Curtis, No State Shall Abridge: The Fourteenth Amendment and the Bill of Rights (1986). But nothing in this case turns on that question, and, regardless of the precise vehicle, there can be no serious doubt that the Fourteenth Amendment requires the States to respect the freedom from excessive fines enshrined in the Eighth Amendment.

JUSTICE THOMAS, concurring in the judgment.

I agree with the Court that the Fourteenth Amendment makes the Eighth Amendment's prohibition on excessive fines fully applicable to the States. But I cannot agree with the route the Court takes to reach this conclusion. Instead of reading the Fourteenth Amendment's Due Process Clause to encompass a substantive right that has nothing to do with "process," I would hold that the right to be free from excessive fines is one of the "privileges or immunities of citizens of the United States" protected by the Fourteenth Amendment.

I

The Fourteenth Amendment provides that "[n]o State shall make or enforce any law which shall abridge the privileges or immunities of citizens of the United States." "On its face, this appears to grant . . . United States citizens a certain collection of rights — *i.e.*, privileges or immunities — attributable to that status." *McDonald v. Chicago* (2010) (Thomas, J., concurring in part and concurring in judgment). But as I have previously explained, this Court "marginaliz[ed]" the Privileges or Immunities Clause in the late 19th century by defining the collection of rights covered by the Clause "quite narrowly." Litigants seeking federal protection of substantive rights against the States thus needed "an alternative fount of such rights," and this Court "found one in a most curious place," the Fourteenth Amendment's Due Process Clause, which prohibits "any State" from "depriv[ing] any person of life, liberty, or property, without due process of law."

Because this Clause speaks only to "process," the Court has "long struggled to define" what substantive rights it protects. *McDonald* (opinion of Thomas, J.). The Court ordinarily says, as it does today, that the Clause protects rights that are "fundamental." Sometimes that means rights that are " 'deeply rooted in this Nation's history and tradition.' " *McDonald* (majority opinion). Other times, when that formulation proves too restrictive, the Court defines the universe of "fundamental" rights so broadly as to border on meaningless. See, *e.g.*, *Obergefell v. Hodges* (2015) ("rights that allow persons, within a lawful realm, to define and express their identity"); *Planned Parenthood of Southeastern Pa. v. Casey* (1992) ("At the heart of liberty is the right to define one's own concept of existence, of meaning, of the universe, and of the mystery of human life"). Because the oxymoronic "substantive" "due process" doctrine has no basis in the Constitution, it is unsurprising that the Court has been unable to adhere to any "guiding principle to distinguish 'fundamental' rights that warrant protection from nonfundamental rights that do not." *McDonald, supra*, at 811, 130 S.Ct. 3020 (opinion of Thomas, J.). And because the Court's substantive due process precedents allow the Court to fashion fundamental rights without any textual constraints, it is equally unsurprising that among these precedents are some of the Court's most notoriously incorrect decisions. *E.g.*, *Roe v. Wade* (1973); *Dred Scott v. Sandford* (1857).

The present case illustrates the incongruity of the Court's due process approach to incorporating fundamental rights against the States. Petitioner argues that the forfeiture of his vehicle is an excessive punishment. He does not argue that the Indiana courts failed to "proceed according to the 'law of the land' — that is, according to written constitutional and statutory provisions," or that the State failed to provide "some baseline procedures." *Nelson v. Colorado* (2017) (Thomas, J., dissenting). His claim has nothing to do with any "process" "due" him. I therefore decline to apply the "legal fiction" of substantive due process. *McDonald* (opinion of Thomas, J.).

II

When the Fourteenth Amendment was ratified, "the terms 'privileges' and 'immunities' had an established meaning as synonyms for 'rights.'" *Id.* Those "rights" were the "inalienable rights" of citizens that had been "long recognized," and "the ratifying public understood the Privileges or Immunities Clause to protect constitutionally enumerated rights" against interference by the States. *Id.* Many of these rights had been adopted from English law into colonial charters, then state constitutions and bills of rights, and finally the Constitution. "Consistent with their English heritage, the founding generation generally did not consider many of the rights identified in [the Bill of Rights] as new entitlements, but as inalienable rights of all men, given legal effect by their codification in the Constitution's text." *Id.*

The question here is whether the Eighth Amendment's prohibition on excessive fines was considered such a right. The historical record overwhelmingly demonstrates that it was.

A

The Excessive Fines Clause "was taken verbatim from the English Bill of Rights of 1689," *United States v. Bajakajian* (1998), which itself formalized a longstanding English prohibition on disproportionate fines. The Charter of Liberties of Henry I, issued in 1101, stated that "[i]f any of my barons or men shall have committed an offence he shall not give security to the extent of forfeiture of his money, as he did in the time of my father, or of my brother, but *according to the measure of the offence so shall he pay*. . . ." Expanding this principle, Magna Carta required that "amercements (the medieval predecessors of fines) should be proportioned to the offense and that they should not deprive a wrongdoer of his livelihood," *Bajakajian*:

> "A free man shall be amerced for a small fault only according to the measure thereof, and for a great crime according to its magnitude, saving his position; and in like manner, a merchant saving his trade, and a villein saving his tillage, if they should fall under Our mercy." Magna Carta, ch. 20 (1215).

. . . During the reign of the Stuarts in the period leading up to the Glorious Revolution of 1688-1689, fines were a flashpoint "in the constitutional and political struggles between the king and his parliamentary critics." From 1629 to 1640, Charles I attempted to govern without convening Parliament, but "in the absence of parliamentary grants," he needed other ways of raising revenue. He thus turned "to exactions, some odious and obsolete, some of very questionable legality, and others clearly against law."

The Court of Star Chamber, for instance, "imposed heavy fines on the king's enemies," in disregard "of the provision of the Great Charter, that no man shall be amerced even to the full extent of his means. . . ." "[T]he strong interest of th[is] court in these fines . . . had a tendency to aggravate the punishment. . . ." "The statute abolishing" the Star Chamber in 1641 "specifically prohibited any court thereafter from . . . levying . . . excessive fines." . . .

Shortly after the English Bill of Rights was enacted, Parliament addressed several excessive fines imposed before the Glorious Revolution. For example, the House of Lords overturned a £30,000 fine against the Earl of Devonshire as "excessive and exorbitant, against Magna Charta, the common right of the subject, and against the law of the land." Although the House of Lords refused to reverse the judgments against Titus Oates, a minority argued that his punishments were "contrary to Law and ancient Practice" and violated the prohibition on "excessive Fines." The House of Commons passed a bill to overturn Oates's conviction, and eventually, after a request from Parliament, the King pardoned Oates.

Writing a few years before our Constitution was adopted, Blackstone — "whose works constituted the preeminent authority on English law for the founding generation," *Alden v. Maine* (1999) — explained that the prohibition on excessive fines contained in the English Bill of Rights "had a retrospect to some unprecedented proceedings in the court of king's bench." Blackstone confirmed that this prohibition was "only declaratory . . . of the old constitutional law of the land," which had long "regulated" the "discretion" of the courts in imposing fines.

In sum, at the time of the founding, the prohibition on excessive fines was a longstanding right of Englishmen.

B

"As English subjects, the colonists considered themselves to be vested with the same fundamental rights as other Englishmen," *McDonald* (opinion of Thomas, J.), including the prohibition on excessive fines. Thus, the text of the Eighth Amendment was " 'based directly on . . . the Virginia Declaration of Rights,' which 'adopted verbatim the language of the English Bill of Rights.' " *Browning-Ferris Industries of Vt., Inc. v. Kelco Disposal, Inc.* (1989); see *Jones v. Commonwealth*, 5 Va. 555, 557 (1799) (opinion of Carrington, J.) (explaining that the clause in the Virginia Declaration of Rights embodied the traditional legal understanding that any "fine or amercement ought to be according to the degree of the fault and the estate of the defendant").

When the States were considering whether to ratify the Constitution, advocates for a separate bill of rights emphasized the need for an explicit prohibition on excessive fines mirroring the English prohibition. In colonial times, fines were "the drudge-horse of criminal justice," "probably the most common form of punishment." To some, this fact made a constitutional prohibition on excessive fines all the more important. As the well-known Anti-Federalist Brutus argued in an essay, a prohibition on excessive fines was essential to "the security of liberty" and was "as necessary under the general government as under that of the individual states; for the power of the former is as complete to the purpose of requiring bail, imposing fines, inflicting punishments, . . . and seizing . . . property . . . as the other." Similarly, during Virginia's ratifying convention, Patrick Henry pointed to Virginia's own prohibition on excessive fines and said that it would "depart from the genius of your country" for the Federal Constitution to omit a similar prohibition. Henry continued: "[W]hen we come to punishments, no latitude ought to be left, nor dependence put on the virtue of representatives" to "define punishments without this control."

Governor Edmund Randolph responded to Henry, arguing that Virginia's charter was "nothing more than an investiture, in the hands of the Virginia citizens, of those rights which belonged to British subjects." According to Randolph, "the exclusion of excessive bail and fines . . . would follow of itself without a bill of rights," for such fines would never be imposed absent "corruption in the House of Representatives, Senate, and President," or judges acting "contrary to justice."

For all the debate about whether an explicit prohibition on excessive fines was necessary in the Federal Constitution, all agreed that the prohibition on excessive fines was a well-established and fundamental right of citizenship. When the Excessive Fines Clause was eventually considered by Congress, it received hardly any discussion before "it was agreed to by a considerable majority." And when the Bill of Rights was ratified, most of the States had a prohibition on excessive fines in their constitutions.

Early commentary on the Clause confirms the widespread agreement about the fundamental nature of the prohibition on excessive fines. Justice Story, writing a few decades before the ratification of the Fourteenth Amendment, explained that the Eighth Amendment was "adopted, as an admonition to all departments of the national government, to warn them against such violent proceedings, as had taken place in England in the arbitrary reigns of some of the Stuarts," when "[e]normous fines and amercements were . . . sometimes imposed." Story included the prohibition on excessive fines as a right, along with the "right to bear arms" and others protected by the Bill of Rights, that "operates, as a qualification upon powers, actually granted by the people to the government"; without such a "restrict[ion]," the government's "exercise or abuse" of its power could be "dangerous to the people."

Chancellor Kent likewise described the Eighth Amendment as part of the "right of personal security . . . guarded by provisions which have been transcribed into the constitutions in this country from *magna carta*, and other fundamental acts of the English Parliament." He understood the Eighth Amendment to "guard against abuse and oppression," and emphasized that "the constitutions of almost every state in the Unio[n] contain the same declarations in substance, and nearly in the same language." Accordingly, "they must be regarded as fundamental doctrines in every state, for all the colonies were parties to the national declaration of rights in 1774, in which the . . . rights and liberties of English subjects were peremptorily claimed as their undoubted inheritance and birthright."

C

The prohibition on excessive fines remained fundamental at the time of the Fourteenth Amendment. In 1868, 35 of 37 state constitutions "expressly prohibited excessive fines." Nonetheless, as the Court notes, abuses of fines continued, especially through the Black Codes adopted in several States. The "centerpiece" of the Codes was their "attempt to stabilize the black work force and limit its economic options apart from plantation labor." E. Foner, Reconstruction: America's Unfinished Revolution 1863-1877 (1988). Under the Codes, "the state would enforce labor agreements and plantation discipline, punish those who refused to contract, and prevent whites from competing among themselves for black workers." The Codes also included " 'antienticement' measures punishing anyone offering higher wages to an employee already under contract."

The 39th Congress focused on these abuses during its debates over the Fourteenth Amendment, the Civil Rights Act of 1866, and the Freedmen's Bureau Act. During those well-publicized debates, Members of Congress consistently highlighted and lamented the "severe penalties" inflicted by the Black Codes and similar measures, Cong. Globe, 39th Cong., 1st Sess., 474 (1866) (Sen. Trumbull), suggesting that the prohibition on excessive fines was understood to be a basic right of citizenship.

For example, under Mississippi law, adult "freedmen, free negroes and mulattoes" "without lawful employment" faced $ 50 in fines and 10 days' imprisonment for vagrancy. Those convicted had five days to pay or they would be arrested and leased to "any person who will, for the shortest period of service, pay said fine and forfeiture and all costs." Members of Congress criticized such laws "for selling [black] men into slavery in punishment of crimes of the slightest magnitude." Cong. Globe, 39th Cong., 1st Sess., (1866) (Rep. Cook) ("It is idle to say these men will be protected by the States").

Similar examples abound. One congressman noted that Alabama's "aristocratic and anti-republican laws, almost reenacting slavery, among other harsh inflictions impose . . . a fine of fifty dollars and six months' imprisonment on any servant or laborer (white or black) who loiters away his time or is stubborn or refractory." He also noted that Florida punished vagrants with "a fine not exceeding $500 and imprison[ment] for a term not exceeding twelve months, or by being sold for a term not exceeding twelve months, at the discretion of the court." At the time, such fines would have been ruinous for laborers. Cf. *id.* (Sen. Howe) ("A thousand dollars! That sells a negro for his life").

These and other examples of excessive fines from the historical record informed the Nation's consideration of the Fourteenth Amendment. Even those opposed to civil-rights legislation understood the Privileges or Immunities Clause to guarantee those "fundamental principles" "fixed" by the Constitution, including "immunity from . . . excessive fines." And every post-1855 state constitution banned excessive fines. S. Calabresi & S. Agudo, Individual Rights Under State Constitutions When the Fourteenth Amendment Was Ratified in 1868, 87 Texas L. Rev. 7, 82 (2008). The attention given to abusive fines at the time of the Fourteenth Amendment, along with the ubiquity of state excessive-fines provisions, demonstrates that the public continued to understand the prohibition on excessive fines to be a fundamental right of American citizenship.

* * *

The right against excessive fines traces its lineage back in English law nearly a millennium, and from the founding of our country, it has been consistently recognized as a core right worthy of constitutional protection. As a constitutionally enumerated right understood to be a privilege of American citizenship, the Eighth Amendment's prohibition on excessive fines applies in full to the States.

June Medical Services LLC v. Russo
591 U.S. ___ (2020)

JUSTICE BREYER announced the judgment of the Court and delivered an opinion, in which JUSTICE GINSBURG, JUSTICE SOTOMAYOR, and JUSTICE KAGAN join.

In *Whole Woman's Health v. Hellerstedt* (2016), we held that " '[u]nnecessary health regulations that have the purpose or effect of presenting a substantial obstacle to a woman seeking an abortion impose an undue burden on the right' " and are therefore "constitutionally invalid." *Id.* (quoting *Planned Parenthood of Southeastern Pa. v. Casey* (1992). We explained that this standard requires courts independently to review the legislative findings upon which an abortion-related statute rests and to weigh the law's "asserted benefits against the burdens" it imposes on abortion access. *Id.* (citing *Gonzales v. Carhart* (2007)).

The Texas statute at issue in *Whole Woman's Health* required abortion providers to hold " 'active admitting privileges at a hospital' " within 30 miles of the place where they perform abortions. Reviewing the record for ourselves, we found ample evidence to support the District Court's finding that the statute did not further the State's asserted interest in protecting women's health. The evidence showed, moreover, that conditions on admitting privileges that served no "relevant credentialing function," "help[ed] to explain" the closure of half of Texas' abortion clinics. Those closures placed a substantial obstacle in the path of Texas women seeking an abortion. And that obstacle, "when viewed in light of the virtual absence of any health benefit," imposed an "undue burden" on abortion access in violation of the Federal Constitution.

In this case, we consider the constitutionality of a Louisiana statute, Act 620, that is almost word-for-word identical to Texas' admitting-privileges law. As in *Whole Woman's Health,* the District Court found that the statute offers no significant health benefit. It found that conditions on admitting privileges common to hospitals throughout the State have made and will continue to make it impossible for abortion providers to obtain conforming privileges for reasons that have nothing to do with the State's asserted interests in promoting women's health and safety. And it found that this inability places a substantial obstacle in the path of women seeking an abortion. As in *Whole Woman's Health*, the substantial

obstacle the Act imposes, and the absence of any health-related benefit, led the District Court to conclude that the law imposes an undue burden and is therefore unconstitutional.

The Court of Appeals agreed with the District Court's interpretation of the standards we have said apply to regulations on abortion. It thought, however, that the District Court was mistaken on the facts. We disagree. We have examined the extensive record carefully and conclude that it supports the District Court's findings of fact. Those findings mirror those made in *Whole Woman's Health* in every relevant respect and require the same result. We consequently hold that the Louisiana statute is unconstitutional.

I

A

. . . Act 620 requires any doctor who performs abortions to hold "active admitting privileges at a hospital that is located not further than thirty miles from the location at which the abortion is performed or induced and that provides obstetrical or gynecological health care services." The statute defines "active admitting privileges" to mean that the doctor must be "a member in good standing" of the hospital's "medical staff . . . with the ability to admit a patient and to provide diagnostic and surgical services to such patient." . . .

II

We initially consider a procedural argument that the State raised for the first time in its cross-petition for certiorari. As we have explained, the plaintiff abortion providers and clinics in this case have challenged Act 620 on the ground that it infringes their patients' rights to access an abortion. The State contends that the proper parties to assert these rights are the patients themselves. We think that the State has waived that argument.

The State's argument rests on the rule that a party cannot ordinarily " 'rest his claim to relief on the legal rights or interests of third parties.' " *Kowalski v. Tesmer* (2004) (quoting *Warth v. Seldin* (1975)). This rule is "prudential." It does not involve the Constitution's "case-or-controversy requirement. See *Craig v. Boren* (1976). And so, we have explained, it can be forfeited or waived.

. . . The State did not mention its current objection until it filed its cross-petition—more than five years after it argued that the plaintiffs' standing was beyond question.

The State's unmistakable concession of standing as part of its effort to obtain a quick decision from the District Court on the merits of the plaintiffs' undue-burden claims bars our consideration of it here. . . .

In any event, the rule the State invokes is hardly absolute. We have long permitted abortion providers to invoke the rights of their actual or potential patients in challenges to abortion-related regulations. See, *e.g., Whole Woman's Health*; *Gonzales, Ayotte v. Planned Parenthood of Northern New Eng.* (2006); *Stenberg* v. *Carhart* (2000); *Casey*; *Akron* v. *Akron Center for Reproductive Health, Inc.* (1983); *Planned Parenthood of Central Mo. v. Danforth* (1976); *Doe v. Bolton* (1973).

And we have generally permitted plaintiffs to assert third-party rights in cases where the " 'enforcement of the challenged restriction *against the litigant* would result indirectly in the violation of third parties' rights.' "; *Craig* (convenience store raising rights of young men to challenge sex-based restriction on beer sales); *Doe* (abortion provider raising the rights of pregnant women to access an abortion); *Carey v. Population Services Int'l* (1977) (distributors of contraceptives raising rights of prospective purchasers to challenge restrictions on sales of contraceptives); *Eisenstadt v. Baird* (1972) (similar); *Griswold v. Connecticut* (1965) (similar). In such cases, we have explained, "the obvious claimant" and "the least awkward challenger" is the party upon whom the challenged statute imposes "legal duties and disabilities."

The case before us lies at the intersection of these two lines of precedent. The plaintiffs are abortion providers challenging a law that regulates their conduct. . . . Our dissenting colleagues suggest that this case is different because the plaintiffs have challenged a law ostensibly enacted to protect the women whose rights they are asserting. But that is a common feature of cases in which we have found third-party standing. . . .

In short, the State's strategic waiver and a long line of well-established precedents foreclose its belated challenge to the plaintiffs' standing. We consequently proceed to consider the merits of the plaintiffs' claims.

IV

The District Court's Substantial-Obstacle
Determination

The District Court found that enforcing the admitting-privileges requirement would "result in a drastic reduction in the number and geographic distribution of abortion providers." In light of demographic, economic, and other evidence, the court concluded that this reduction would make it impossible for "many women seeking a safe, legal abortion in Louisiana . . . to obtain one" and that it would impose "substantial obstacles" on those who could. We consider each of these findings in turn.

A

Act 620's Effect on Abortion Providers

We begin with the District Court's findings in respect to Act 620's impact on abortion providers. As we have said, the court found that the Act would prevent

Does 1, 2, and 6 from providing abortions.* And it found that the Act would bar Doe 5 from working in his Baton Rouge-based clinic, relegating him to New Orleans. . . .

In *Whole Woman's Health*, we said that, by presenting "direct testimony" from doctors who had been unable to secure privileges, and "plausible inferences to be drawn from the timing of the clinic closures" around the law's effective date, the plaintiffs had "satisfied their burden" to establish that the Texas admitting-privileges requirement caused the closure of those clinics. . . .

The evidence on which the District Court relied in this case is even stronger and more detailed. The District Court supervised Does 1, 2, 5, and 6 for over a year and a half as they tried, and largely failed, to obtain conforming privileges from 13 relevant hospitals. . . .

The evidence also shows that many providers, even if they could initially obtain admitting privileges, would be unable to keep them. That is because, unless they have a practice that requires regular in-hospital care, they will lose the privileges for failing to use them. . . .

The evidence also shows that opposition to abortion played a significant role in some hospitals' decisions to deny admitting privileges. Some hospitals expressly bar anyone with privileges from performing abortions. . . .

Just as in *Whole Woman's Health*, the experiences of the individual doctors in this case support the District Court's factual finding that Louisiana's admitting-privileges requirement, like that in Texas' law, serves no " 'relevant credentialing function.' " . . .

Finally, Justice Alito and Justice Gorsuch suggest that the District Court failed to account for the possibility that new abortion providers might eventually replace Does 1, 2, 3, 5, and 6. But the Court of Appeals did not dispute, and the record supports, the District Court's additional finding that, for "the same reasons that Does 1, 2, 4, 5, and 6 have had difficulties getting active admitting privileges, reasons unrelated to their competence . . . it is unlikely that the [a]ffected clinics will be able to comply with the Act by recruiting new physicians who have or can obtain admitting privileges."

B

Act 620's Impact on Abortion Access

The District Court drew from the record evidence, including the factual findings we have just discussed, several conclusions in respect to the burden that Act 620 is likely to impose upon women's ability to access abortions in Louisiana. To better understand the significance of these conclusions, the reader should keep in mind the geographic distribution of the doctors and their clinics. . . .

---

* Note "(Like the courts below, we shall refer to the two doctors in the first case as Doe 1 and Doe 2; we shall refer to the two doctors in the second case as Doe 5 and Doe 6; and we shall refer to two other doctors then practicing in Louisiana as Doe 3 and Doe 4.").

Those women not altogether prevented from obtaining an abortion would face other burdens. As in *Whole Woman's Health*, the reduction in abortion providers caused by Act 620 would inevitably mean "longer waiting times, and increased crowding." The District Court heard testimony that delays in obtaining an abortion increase the risk that a woman will experience complications from the procedure and may make it impossible for her to choose a noninvasive medication abortion.

Even if they obtain an appointment at a clinic, women who might previously have gone to a clinic in Baton Rouge or Shreveport would face increased driving distances. New Orleans is nearly a five hour drive from Shreveport; it is over an hour from Baton Rouge; and Baton Rouge is more than four hours from Shreveport. The impact of those increases would be magnified by Louisiana's requirement that every woman undergo an ultrasound and receive mandatory counseling at least 24 hours before an abortion. A Shreveport resident seeking an abortion who might previously have obtained care at one of that city's local clinics would either have to spend nearly 20 hours driving back and forth to Doe 5's clinic twice, or else find overnight lodging in New Orleans. As the District Court stated, both experts and laypersons testified that the burdens of this increased travel would fall disproportionately on poor women, who are least able to absorb them. . . .

Taken together, we think that these findings and the evidence that underlies them are sufficient to support the District Court's conclusion that Act 620 would place substantial obstacles in the path of women seeking an abortion in Louisiana.

V

Benefits

We turn finally to the law's asserted benefits. The District Court found that there was " 'no significant health-related problem that the new law helped to cure.' " It found that the admitting-privileges requirement "[d]oes [n]ot [p]rotect [w]omen's [h]ealth," provides "no significant health benefits," and makes no improvement to women's health "compared to prior law." Our examination of the record convinces us that these findings are not "clearly erroneous."

First, the District Court found that the admitting-privileges requirement serves no "relevant credentialing function." As we have seen, hospitals can, and do, deny admitting privileges for reasons unrelated to a doctor's ability safely to perform abortions. And Act 620's requirement that physicians obtain privileges at a hospital within 30 miles of the place where they perform abortions further constrains providers for reasons that bear no relationship to competence.

Moreover, while "competency is a factor" in credentialing decisions, hospitals primarily focus upon a doctor's ability to perform the inpatient, hospital-based procedures for which the doctor seeks privileges — not outpatient abortions. . . .

Second, the District Court found that the admitting-privileges requirement "does not conform to prevailing medical standards and will not improve the safety of abortion in Louisiana." . . . For those patients who do experience complications at the clinic, the transfer agreement required by existing law is "sufficient to ensure continuity of care for patients in an emergency." . . .

As in *Whole Woman's Health*, the State introduced no evidence "showing that patients have better outcomes when their physicians have admitting privileges" or "of any instance in which an admitting privileges requirement would have helped even one woman obtain better treatment." . . .

VI

Conclusion

We conclude, in light of the record, that the District Court's significant factual findings — both as to burdens and as to benefits — have ample evidentiary support. None is "clearly erroneous." Given the facts found, we must also uphold the District Court's related factual and legal determinations. These include its determination that Louisiana's law poses a "substantial obstacle" to women seeking an abortion; its determination that the law offers no significant health-related benefits; and its determination that the law consequently imposes an "undue burden" on a woman's constitutional right to choose to have an abortion. We also agree with its ultimate legal conclusion that, in light of these findings and our precedents, Act 620 violates the Constitution.

VII

As a postscript, we explain why we have found unconvincing several further arguments that the State has made. . . .

Second, the State says that the record does not show that Act 620 will burden *every* woman in Louisiana who seeks an abortion. True, but beside the point. As we stated in *Casey*, a State's abortion-related law is unconstitutional on its face if "it will operate as a substantial obstacle to a woman's choice to undergo an abortion" in "a large fraction of the cases in which [it] is relevant." In *Whole Woman's Health*, we reaffirmed that standard. We made clear that the phrase refers to a large fraction of "those women for whom the provision is an actual rather than an irrelevant restriction." That standard, not an "every woman" standard, is the standard that must govern in this case.

Third, the State argues that Act 620 would not make it "nearly impossible" for a woman to obtain an abortion. But, again, the words "nearly impossible" do not describe the legal standard that governs here. Since *Casey*, we have repeatedly reiterated that the plaintiff's burden in a challenge to an abortion regulation is to show that the regulation's "purpose or effect" is to "plac[e] a substantial obstacle in the path of a woman seeking an abortion of a nonviable fetus." . . .

* * *

This case is similar to, nearly identical with, *Whole Woman's Health.* And the law must consequently reach a similar conclusion. Act 620 is unconstitutional. The Court of Appeals' judgment is erroneous. It is

Reversed.

CHIEF JUSTICE ROBERTS, concurring in the judgment.

. . . I joined the dissent in *Whole Woman's Health* and continue to believe that the case was wrongly decided. The question today however is not whether *Whole Woman's Health* was right or wrong, but whether to adhere to it in deciding the present case.

Today's case is a challenge from several abortion clinics and providers to a Louisiana law nearly identical to the Texas law struck down four years ago in *Whole Woman's Health.* Just like the Texas law, the Louisiana law requires physicians performing abortions to have "active admitting privileges at a hospital . . . located not further than thirty miles from the location at which the abortion is performed." Following a six-day bench trial, the District Court found that Louisiana's law would "result in a drastic reduction in the number and geographic distribution of abortion providers." The law would reduce the number of clinics from three to "one, or at most two," and the number of physicians providing abortions from five to "one, or at most two," and "therefore cripple women's ability to have an abortion in Louisiana."

The legal doctrine of *stare decisis* requires us, absent special circumstances, to treat like cases alike. The Louisiana law imposes a burden on access to abortion just as severe as that imposed by the Texas law, for the same reasons. Therefore Louisiana's law cannot stand under our precedents.

I

Stare decisis ("to stand by things decided") is the legal term for fidelity to precedent. It has long been "an established rule to abide by former precedents, where the same points come again in litigation; as well to keep the scale of justice even and steady, and not liable to waver with every new judge's opinion." W. Blackstone, Commentaries on the Laws of England (1765). This principle is grounded in a basic humility that recognizes today's legal issues are often not so different from the questions of yesterday and that we are not the first ones to try to answer them. Because the "private stock of reason . . . in each man is small, . . . individuals would do better to avail themselves of the general bank and capital of nations and of ages." E. Burke, Reflections on the Revolution in France (1790).

Adherence to precedent is necessary to "avoid an arbitrary discretion in the courts." The Federalist No. 78 (A. Hamilton). The constraint of precedent distinguishes the judicial "method and philosophy from those of the political and legislative process." [Justice Robert H.] Jackson, Decisional Law and Stare Decisis (1944).

The doctrine also brings pragmatic benefits. Respect for precedent "promotes the evenhanded, predictable, and consistent development of legal principles, fosters reliance on judicial decisions, and contributes to the actual and perceived integrity of the judicial process." *Payne v. Tennessee* (1991). It is the "means by which we ensure that the law will not merely change erratically, but will develop in a principled and intelligible fashion." *Vasquez v. Hillery* (1986). In that way, "*stare decisis* is an old friend of the common lawyer." Jackson.

Stare decisis is not an "inexorable command." *Ramos v. Louisiana* (2020) (slip op., at 20). But for precedent to mean anything, the doctrine must give way only to a rationale that goes beyond whether the case was decided correctly. The Court accordingly considers additional factors before overruling a precedent, such as its adminstrability, its fit with subsequent factual and legal developments, and the reliance interests that the precedent has engendered. See *Janus v. State, County, and Municipal Employees* (2018).

Stare decisis principles also determine how we handle a decision that itself departed from the cases that came before it. In those instances, "[r]emaining true to an 'intrinsically sounder' doctrine established in prior cases better serves the values of *stare decisis* than would following" the recent departure. *Adarand Constructors, Inc. v. Peña* (1995). *Stare decisis* is pragmatic and contextual, not "a mechanical formula of adherence to the latest decision." *Helvering v. Hallock* (1940).

II

A

Both Louisiana and the providers agree that the undue burden standard announced in *Casey* provides the appropriate framework to analyze Louisiana's law. Neither party has asked us to reassess the constitutional validity of that standard. . . .

Under *Casey*, the State may not impose an undue burden on the woman's ability to obtain an abortion. "A finding of an undue burden is a shorthand for the conclusion that a state regulation has the purpose or effect of placing a substantial obstacle in the path of a woman seeking an abortion of a nonviable fetus." Laws that do not pose a substantial obstacle to abortion access are permissible, so long as they are "reasonably related" to a legitimate state interest.

After faithfully reciting this standard, the Court in *Whole Woman's Health* added the following observation: "The rule announced in *Casey* . . . requires that courts consider the burdens a law imposes on abortion access together with the benefits those laws confer." The plurality repeats today that the undue burden standard requires courts "to weigh the law's asserted benefits against the burdens it imposes on abortion access."

Read in isolation from *Casey*, such an inquiry could invite a grand "balancing test in which unweighted factors mysteriously are weighed." *Marrs v. Motorola, Inc.* (7th Cir. 2009) (Posner, J.). Under such tests, "equality of treatment is . . . impossible to achieve; predictability is destroyed; judicial arbitrariness is facilitated; judicial courage is impaired." Scalia, The Rule of Law as a Law of Rules (1989).

In this context, courts applying a balancing test would be asked in essence to weigh the State's interests in "protecting the potentiality of human life" and the health of the woman, on the one hand, against the woman's liberty interest in defining her "own concept of existence, of meaning, of the universe, and of the mystery of human life" on the other. There is no plausible sense in which anyone, let alone this Court, could objectively assign weight to such imponderable values and no meaningful way to compare them if there were. Attempting to do so would be like "judging whether a particular line is longer than a particular rock is heavy," *Bendix Autolite Corp. v. Midwesco Enterprises, Inc.* (1988) (Scalia, J., concurring in judgment). Pretending that we could pull that off would require us to act as legislators, not judges, and would result in nothing other than an "unanalyzed exercise of judicial will" in the guise of a "neutral utilitarian calculus." *New Jersey v. T.L.O.* (1985) (Brennan, J., concurring in part and dissenting in part).

Nothing about *Casey* suggested that a weighing of costs and benefits of an abortion regulation was a job for the courts. On the contrary, we have explained that the "traditional rule" that "state and federal legislatures [have] wide discretion to pass legislation in areas where there is medical and scientific uncertainty" is "consistent with *Casey*." *Gonzales v. Carhart* (2007). *Casey* instead focuses on the existence of a substantial obstacle, the sort of inquiry familiar to judges across a variety of contexts. . . .

The only restriction *Casey* found unconstitutional was Pennsylvania's spousal notification requirement. . . . The upshot of *Casey* is clear: The several restrictions that did not impose a substantial obstacle were constitutional, while the restriction that did impose a substantial obstacle was unconstitutional.

To be sure, the Court at times discussed the benefits of the regulations, including when it distinguished spousal notification from parental consent. But in the context of *Casey*'s governing standard, these benefits were not placed on a scale opposite the law's burdens. Rather, *Casey* discussed benefits in considering the threshold requirement that the State have a "legitimate purpose" and that the law be "reasonably related to that goal."

So long as that showing is made, the only question for a court is whether a law has the "effect of placing a substantial obstacle in the path of a woman seeking an abortion of a nonviable fetus." *Casey* repeats that "substantial obstacle" standard nearly verbatim no less than 15 times.[2]

---

2. Justice Gorsuch correctly notes that *Casey* "expressly disavowed any test as strict as strict scrutiny." But he certainly is wrong to suggest that my position is in any way inconsistent with that disavowal. Applying strict scrutiny would require "any regulation touching upon the abortion decision" to be the least restrictive means to further a compelling state interest. *Casey* however recognized that such a test would give "too little acknowledgement and implementation" to the State's "legitimate interests in the health of the woman and in protecting the potential life within her." Under *Casey*, abortion regulations are valid so long as they do not pose a substantial obstacle and meet the threshold requirement of being "reasonably related" to a "legitimate purpose."

. . . We should respect the statement in *Whole Woman's Health* that it was applying the undue burden standard of *Casey*. The opinion in *Whole Woman's Health* began by saying, "We must here decide whether two provisions of [the Texas law] violate the Federal Constitution as interpreted in *Casey*." Nothing more. The Court explicitly stated that it was applying "the standard, as described in *Casey*," and reversed the Court of Appeals for applying an approach that did "not match the standard that this Court laid out in *Casey*."

Here the plurality expressly acknowledges that we are not considering how to analyze an abortion regulation that does not present a substantial obstacle. "That," the plurality explains, "is not this case." In this case, *Casey*'s requirement of finding a substantial obstacle before invalidating an abortion regulation is therefore a sufficient basis for the decision, as it was in *Whole Woman's Health*. In neither case, nor in *Casey* itself, was there call for consideration of a regulation's benefits, and nothing in *Casey* commands such consideration. Under principles of *stare decisis*, I agree with the plurality that the determination in *Whole Woman's Health* that Texas's law imposed a substantial obstacle requires the same determination about Louisiana's law. Under those same principles, I would adhere to the holding of *Casey*, requiring a substantial obstacle before striking down an abortion regulation.

B

Whole Woman's Health held that Texas's admitting privileges requirement placed "a substantial obstacle in the path of women seeking a previability abortion," independent of its discussion of benefits.[3] Because Louisiana's admitting privileges requirement would restrict women's access to abortion to the same degree as Texas's law, it also cannot stand under our precedent.[4]

To begin, the two laws are nearly identical. . . . Crucially, the District Court findings indicate that Louisiana's law would restrict access to abortion in just the same way as Texas's law, to the same degree or worse. In Texas, "as of the time the admitting-privileges requirement began to be enforced, the number of facilities providing abortions dropped in half, from about 40 to about 20." *Whole Woman's Health*. Eight abortion clinics closed in the months prior to the law's effective date. Another 11 clinics closed on the day the law took effect. . . .

---

3. Justice Gorsuch considers this is a "nonexistent ruling" nowhere to be found in *Whole Woman's Health*. I disagree. *Whole Woman's Health* first surveyed the benefits of Texas's admitting privileges requirement. The Court then transitioned to examining the law's burdens: "*At the same time*, the record evidence indicates that the admitting-privileges requirement places a substantial obstacle in the path of a woman's choice." And the Court made clear that a law which has the purpose or effect of placing "a substantial obstacle in the path of a woman seeking an abortion before the fetus attains viability" imposes an "undue burden" and therefore violates the Constitution. Thus the discussion of benefits in *Whole Woman's Health* was not necessary to its holding.

4. For the reasons the plurality explains, *ante*, at 11–16, I agree that the abortion providers in this case have standing to assert the constitutional rights of their patients.

In Texas, "common prerequisites to obtaining admitting privileges that [had] nothing to do with ability to perform medical procedures," including "clinical data requirements, residency requirements, and other discretionary factors," made it difficult for well-credentialed abortion physicians to obtain such privileges.

So too here. "While a physician's competency is a factor in assessing an applicant for admitting privileges" in Louisiana, "it is only one factor that hospitals consider in whether to grant privileges.". . .[5]

And . . . "[b]ecause, by all accounts, abortion complications are rare, an abortion provider is unlikely to have a consistent need to admit patients." *Id.*, at 50 (citations omitted).[6]

* * *

Stare decisis instructs us to treat like cases alike. The result in this case is controlled by our decision four years ago invalidating a nearly identical Texas law. The Louisiana law burdens women seeking previability abortions to the same extent as the Texas law, according to factual findings that are not clearly erroneous. For that reason, I concur in the judgment of the Court that the Louisiana law is unconstitutional.

JUSTICE THOMAS, dissenting.

Today a majority of the Court perpetuates its ill-founded abortion jurisprudence by enjoining a perfectly legitimate state law and doing so without jurisdiction. As is often the case with legal challenges to abortion regulations, this suit was brought by abortionists and abortion clinics. Their sole claim before this Court is that Louisiana's law violates the purported substantive due process right of a woman to abort her unborn child. But they concede that this right does not belong to them, and they seek to vindicate no private rights of their own. Under a proper understanding of Article III, these plaintiffs lack standing to invoke our jurisdiction.

Despite the fact that we granted Louisiana's petition specifically to address whether "abortion providers [can] be presumed to have third-party standing to challenge health and safety regulations on behalf of their patients," a majority of the Court all but ignores the question. The plurality and The Chief Justice ultimately cast aside this jurisdictional barrier to conclude that Louisiana's law is unconstitutional under our precedents. But those decisions created the right to abortion out of whole cloth, without a shred of support from the Constitution's text. Our abortion precedents are grievously wrong and should be overruled.

---

5. Justice Alito misunderstands my discussion of credentials as focusing on the law's lack of benefits. But my analysis, like *Casey*, is limited to the law's effect on the availability of abortion.

6. I agree with Justice Alito that the validity of admitting privileges laws "depend[s] on numerous factors that may differ from State to State." And I agree with Justice Gorsuch that "[w]hen it comes to the factual record, litigants normally start the case on a clean slate." Appreciating that others may in good faith disagree, however, I cannot view the record here as in any pertinent respect sufficiently different from that in *Whole Woman's Health* to warrant a different outcome.

Because we have neither jurisdiction nor constitutional authority to declare Louisiana's duly enacted law unconstitutional, I respectfully dissent.

I

For most of its history, this Court maintained that private parties could not bring suit to vindicate the constitutional rights of individuals who are not before the Court. But in the 20th century, the Court began to deviate from this traditional rule against third-party standing. See *Pierce v. Society of Sisters* (1925). From these deviations emerged our prudential third-party standing doctrine, which allows litigants to vicariously assert the constitutional rights of others when "the party asserting the right has a 'close' relationship with the person who possesses the right" and "there is a 'hindrance' to the possessor's ability to protect his own interests."[1]

The plurality feints toward this doctrine, claiming that third-party standing for abortionists is well settled by our precedents. But, ultimately, it dodges the question, claiming that Louisiana's standing challenge was waived below. Both assertions are erroneous. First, there is no controlling precedent that sets forth the blanket rule advocated for by plaintiffs here—*i.e.*, abortionists may challenge health and safety regulations based solely on their role in the abortion process. Second, I agree with Justice Alito that Louisiana did not waive its standing challenge below.

But even if there were a waiver, it would not be relevant. Louisiana argues that the abortionists and abortion clinics lack standing under Article III to assert the putative rights of their potential clients. No waiver, however explicit, could relieve us of our independent obligation to ensure that we have jurisdiction before addressing the merits of a case. And under a proper understanding of Article III's case-or-controversy requirement, plaintiffs lack standing to invoke our jurisdiction because they assert no private rights of their own, seeking only to vindicate the putative constitutional rights of individuals not before the Court.

A

. . . As an initial matter, this Court has never provided a coherent explanation for why the rule against third-party standing is properly characterized as prudential. . . . Thus, the "prudential" label for the rule against third-party standing remains a bit of a mystery. . . .

---

1. Today, the plurality reaffirms our precedent allowing beer vendors to assert the Fourteenth Amendment rights of their potential customers. *Ante* (citing *Craig v. Boren* (1976)). But it is fair to wonder whether gun vendors could expect to receive the same privilege if they seek to vindicate the Second Amendment rights of their customers. Given this Court's ad hoc approach to third-party standing and its tendency to treat the Second Amendment as a second-class right, their time would be better spent waiting for Godot.

The Court's previous statements on the rule against third-party standing have long suggested that the "proper place" for that rule is in Article III's case-or-controversy requirement. The Court has acknowledged that the traditional rule against third-party standing is "closely related to Art[icle] III concerns." *Warth v. Seldin* (1975). . . .

And most recently, in *Spokeo, Inc. v. Robins* (2016), the Court appeared to incorporate the rule against third-party standing into its understanding of Article III's injury-in-fact requirement. There, the Court stated that to establish an injury-in-fact a plaintiff must "show that he or she suffered 'an invasion of a legally protected interest' that is 'concrete and particularized' and 'actual or imminent, not conjectural or hypothetical.'" *Id.* (quoting *Lujan v. Defenders of Wildlife* (1992)). The Court further explained that whether a plaintiff "alleges that [the defendant] violated *his* statutory rights" rather than "the statutory rights of other people" was a question of "particularization" for an Article III injury. It is hard to reconcile this language in *Spokeo* with the plurality's assertion that third-party standing is permitted under Article III. . . .

C

Applying these principles to the case at hand, plaintiffs lack standing under Article III and we, in turn, lack jurisdiction to decide these cases. Thus, "[i]n light of th[e] 'overriding and time-honored concern about keeping the Judiciary's power within its proper constitutional sphere, we must put aside the natural urge to proceed directly to the merits of [an] important dispute and to "settle" it for the sake of convenience and efficiency.'" *Hollingsworth v. Perry* (2013) (Roberts, C. J., for the Court) (quoting *Raines v. Byrd* (1997)).

1

Contrary to the plurality's assertion otherwise, abortionists' standing to assert the putative rights of their clients has not been settled by our precedents. It is true that this Court has reflexively allowed abortionists and abortion clinics to vicariously assert a woman's putative right to abortion. But oftentimes the Court has not so much as addressed standing in those cases. . . . Specifically, when it comes "to our own judicial power or jurisdiction, this Court has followed the lead of Chief Justice Marshall who held that this Court is not bound by a prior exercise of jurisdiction in a case where it was not questioned and it was passed *sub silentio.*" *United States v. L. A. Tucker Truck Lines, Inc.* (1952) (citing *United States v. More* (1805)). . . .

2

Under a proper understanding of Article III, plaintiffs lack standing. As explained above, in suits seeking to vindicate private rights, the owners of those rights can establish a sufficient injury simply by asserting that their rights have been violated. Constitutional rights are generally considered "private rights" to the extent they " 'belon[g] to individuals, considered as individuals.' " *Spokeo* (Thomas, J., concurring). And the purported substantive due process right to abort an unborn child is no exception — it is an individual right that is inherently personal. After all, the Court "creat[ed the] right" based on the notion that abortion " 'involv[es] the most intimate and personal choices a person may make in a lifetime, choices central to personal dignity and autonomy.' " *Whole Women's Health* (Thomas, J., dissenting). Because this right belongs to the woman making that choice, not to those who provide abortions, plaintiffs cannot establish a personal legal injury by asserting that this right has been violated.[5]

The only injury asserted by plaintiffs in this suit is the possibility of facing criminal sanctions if the abortionists conduct abortions without admitting privileges in violation of the law. But plaintiffs do not claim any right to provide abortions, nor do they contest that the State has authority to regulate such procedures.[6] They have therefore demonstrated only real-world damages (or more accurately, the *possibility* of real-world damages), but no legal injury, or "invasion of a legally protected interest," that belongs to them. Thus, under a proper understanding of Article III, plaintiffs lack standing and, consequently, this Court lacks jurisdiction.

II

Even if the plaintiffs had standing, the Court would still lack the authority to enjoin Louisiana's law, which represents a constitutionally valid exercise of the State's traditional police powers. The plurality and The Chief Justice claim that the Court's judgment is dictated by "our precedents," particularly *Whole Woman's Health.* For the detailed reasons explained by Justice Alito, this is not true.

But today's decision is wrong for a far simpler reason: The Constitution does not constrain the States' ability to regulate or even prohibit abortion. This Court created the right to abortion based on an amorphous, unwritten right to privacy, which it grounded in the "legal fiction" of substantive due process, *McDonald v. Chicago* (2010) (Thomas, J., concurring in part and concurring in judgment). As the origins of this jurisprudence readily demonstrate, the putative right to abortion is a creation that should be undone.

---

5. Notably, plaintiffs point to no evidence in the record of women who seek abortions in Louisiana actually opposing this law on the ground that it violates their constitutional rights.

6. Although plaintiffs initially argued that Louisiana's law also violated their procedural due process rights by requiring them to obtain admitting privileges in an unreasonably short time, they have since abandoned that claim. And even if they had asserted violations of their own rights before this Court, those legal injuries would be insufficient to establish standing for a distinct claim based on their clients' putative rights.

A

The Court first conceived a free-floating constitutional right to privacy in *Griswold v. Connecticut*, 381 U.S. 479 (1965). In that case, the Court declared unconstitutional a state law prohibiting the use of contraceptives, finding that it violated a married couple's "right of privacy." The Court explained that this right could be found in the "penumbras" of *five* different Amendments to the Constitution—the First, Third, Fourth, Fifth, and Ninth. Rather than explain what free speech or the quartering of troops had to do with contraception, the Court simply declared that these rights had created "zones of privacy" with their "penumbras," which were "formed by emanations from those guarantees that help give them life and substance." This reasoning is as mystifying as it is baseless.

As Justice Black observed in his dissent, this general "right of privacy" was never before considered a constitutional guarantee protecting citizens from governmental intrusion. Rather, the concept was one of tort law, championed by Samuel Warren and the future Justice Louis Brandeis in their 1890 Harvard Law Review article entitled, "The Right to Privacy." 4 Harv. L. Rev. 193. Over 20 years after the Fourteenth Amendment was ratified and a century after the Bill of Rights was adopted, Warren and Brandeis were among the first to advocate for this privacy right in the context of tort relief for those whose personal information and private affairs were exploited by others. By "exalting a phrase . . . used in discussing grounds for tort relief, to the level of a constitutional rule," the Court arrogated to itself the "power to invalidate any legislative act which [it] find[s] irrational, unreasonable[,] or offensive" as an impermissible "interfere[nce] with 'privacy.'"

Just eight years later, the Court utilized its newfound power in *Roe v. Wade*, There, the Court struck down a Texas law restricting abortion as a violation of a woman's constitutional "right of privacy," which it grounded in the "concept of personal liberty" purportedly protected by the Due Process Clause of the Fourteenth Amendment. The Court began its legal analysis by openly acknowledging that the Constitution's text does not "mention any right of privacy." The Court nevertheless concluded that it need not bother with our founding document's text, because the Court's prior decisions—chief among them *Griswold*—had already divined such a right from constitutional penumbras. Without any legal explanation, the Court simply concluded that this unwritten right to privacy was "broad enough to encompass a woman's [abortion] decision."

B

Roe is grievously wrong for many reasons, but the most fundamental is that its core holding—that the Constitution protects a woman's right to abort her unborn child—finds no support in the text of the Fourteenth Amendment. *Roe* suggests that the Due Process Clause's reference to "liberty" could provide a textual basis for its novel privacy right. But that Clause does not guarantee liberty *qua* liberty.

Rather, it expressly contemplates the *deprivation* of liberty and requires only that such deprivations occur through "due process of law." Amdt. 14, §1. As I have previously explained, there is " 'considerable historical evidence support[ing] the position that "due process of law" was [originally understood as] a separation-of-powers concept . . . forbidding only deprivations not authorized by legislation or common law.' " *Johnson v. United States*,(2015) (opinion concurring in judgment). Others claim that the original understanding of this Clause requires that "statutes that purported to empower the other branches to deprive persons of rights without adequate procedural guarantees [be] subject to judicial review." Chapman & McConnell, Due Process as Separation of Powers, (2012). But, whatever the precise requirements of the Due Process Clause, "the notion that a constitutional provision that guarantees only 'process' before a person is deprived of life, liberty, or property could define the substance of those rights strains credulity for even the most casual user of words." *McDonald* (opinion of Thomas, J.).

More specifically, the idea that the Framers of the Fourteenth Amendment understood the Due Process Clause to protect a right to abortion is farcical. See *Roe* (Rehnquist, J., dissenting). In 1868, when the Fourteenth Amendment was ratified, a majority of the States and numerous Territories had laws on the books that limited (and in many cases nearly prohibited) abortion. It would no doubt shock the public at that time to learn that one of the new constitutional Amendments contained hidden within the interstices of its text a right to abortion. The fact that it took this Court over a century to find that right all but proves that it was more than hidden — it simply was not (and is not) there.

C

Despite the readily apparent illegitimacy of *Roe*, "the Court has doggedly adhered to [its core holding] again and again, often to disastrous ends." In doing so, the Court has repeatedly invoked *stare decisis*. And today, a majority of the Court insists that this doctrine compels its result.

The Court's current "formulation of the *stare decisis* standard does not comport with our judicial duty under Article III," which requires us to faithfully interpret the Constitution. *Gamble*. Rather, when our prior decisions clearly conflict with the text of the Constitution, we are required to "privilege [the] text over our own precedents." Because *Roe* and its progeny are premised on a "demonstrably erroneous interpretation of the Constitution," we should not apply them here.

Even under The Chief Justice's approach to *stare decisis*, continued adherence to these precedents cannot be justified. *Stare decisis* is "not an inexorable command," and this Court has recently overruled a number of poorly reasoned precedents that have proved themselves to be unworkable, see *Knick v. Township of Scott* (2019) (Roberts, C. J., for the Court); *Franchise Tax Bd. of Cal. v. Hyatt* (2019); *Janus v. State, County, and Municipal Employees* (2018). As I have already demonstrated, *Roe*'s reasoning is utterly deficient — in fact, not a single Justice today attempts to defend it.

Moreover, the fact that no five Justices can agree on the proper interpretation of our precedents today evinces that our abortion jurisprudence remains in a state of utter entropy. Since the Court decided *Roe*, Members of this Court have decried the unworkability of our abortion case law and repeatedly called for course corrections of varying degrees. In *Casey*, the majority claimed to clarify this "jurisprudence of doubt," but our decisions in the decades since then have only demonstrated the folly of that assertion. They serve as further evidence that this Court's abortion jurisprudence has failed to deliver the " 'principled and intelligible' " development of the law that *stare decisis* purports to secure. *Ante,* (opinion of Roberts, C. J.) (quoting *Vasquez v. Hillery* (1986)).

The Chief Justice advocates for a Burkean approach to the law that favors adherence to " 'the general bank and capital of nations and of ages.' " *Ante* (quoting E. Burke, Reflections on the Revolution in France (1790)). But such adherence to precedent was conspicuously absent when the Court broke new ground with its decisions in *Griswold* and *Roe*. And no one could seriously claim that these revolutionary decisions — or *Whole Woman's Health*, decided just four Terms ago — are part of the *"inheritance from our forefathers,"* fidelity to which demonstrates "reverence to antiquity." E. Burke, Reflections on the Revolution in France.

More importantly, we exceed our constitutional authority whenever we "appl[y] demonstrably erroneous precedent instead of the relevant law's text." *Gamble.* Because we can reconcile neither *Roe* nor its progeny with the text of our Constitution, those decisions should be overruled.

* * *

Because we lack jurisdiction and our abortion jurisprudence finds no basis in the Constitution, I respectfully dissent.[8]

Justice Alito, with whom Justice Gorsuch joins, with whom Justice Thomas joins except as to Parts III–C and IV–F, and with whom Justice Kavanaugh joins as to Parts I, II, and III, dissenting.

The majority bills today's decision as a facsimile of *Whole Woman's Health v. Hellerstedt* (2016), and it's true they have something in common. In both, the abortion right recognized in this Court's decisions is used like a bulldozer to flatten legal rules that stand in the way.

In *Whole Woman's Health*, res judicata and our standard approach to severability were laid low. Even *Planned Parenthood of Southeastern Pa. v. Casey* (1992), was altered.

---

8. I agree with Justice Alito's application of our precedents except in Part IV–F of his opinion, but I would not remand for further proceedings. Because plaintiffs lack standing under Article III, I would instead remand with instructions to dismiss for lack of jurisdiction. Alternatively, if I were to reach the merits because a majority of the Court concludes we have jurisdiction, I would affirm, as plaintiffs have failed to carry their burden of demonstrating that Act 620 is unconstitutional, even under our precedents.

Today's decision claims new victims. The divided majority cannot agree on what the abortion right requires, but it nevertheless strikes down a Louisiana law, Act 620, that the legislature enacted for the asserted purpose of protecting women's health. To achieve this end, the majority misuses the doctrine of *stare decisis*, invokes an inapplicable standard of appellate review, and distorts the record.

The plurality eschews the constitutional test set out in *Casey* and instead employs the balancing test adopted in *Whole Woman's Health*. The plurality concludes that the Louisiana law does nothing to protect the health of women, but that is disproved by substantial evidence in the record. And the plurality upholds the District Court's finding that the Louisiana law would cause a drastic reduction in the number of abortion providers in the State even though this finding was based on an erroneous legal standard and a thoroughly inadequate factual inquiry.

The Chief Justice stresses the importance of *stare decisis* and thinks that precedent, namely *Whole Woman's Health,* dooms the Louisiana law. But at the same time, he votes to overrule *Whole Woman's Health* insofar as it changed the *Casey* test.

Both the plurality and The Chief Justice hold that abortion providers can invoke a woman's abortion right when they attack state laws that are enacted to protect a woman's health. Neither waiver nor *stare decisis* can justify this holding, which clashes with our general rule on third-party standing. And the idea that a regulated party can invoke the right of a third party for the purpose of attacking legislation enacted to protect the third party is stunning. Given the apparent conflict of interest, that concept would be rejected out of hand in a case not involving abortion.

For these reasons, I cannot join the decision of the Court. I would remand the case to the District Court and instruct that court, before proceeding any further, to require the joinder of a plaintiff with standing. If a proper plaintiff is added, the District Court should conduct a new trial and determine, based on proper evidence, whether enforcement of Act 620 would diminish the number of abortion providers in the State to such a degree that women's access to abortions would be substantially impaired. In making that determination, the court should jettison the nebulous "good faith" test that it used in judging whether the physicians who currently lack admitting privileges would be able to obtain privileges and thus continue to perform abortions if Act 620 were permitted to take effect. Because the doctors in question (many of whom are or were plaintiffs in this case) stand to lose, not gain, by obtaining privileges, the court should require the plaintiffs to show that these doctors sought admitting privileges with the degree of effort that they would expend if their personal interests were at stake.

I

Under our precedent, the critical question in this case is whether the challenged Louisiana law places a "substantial obstacle in the path of a woman seeking an abortion of a nonviable fetus." *Casey.* . . .

The petitioners urge us to adopt a rule that is more favorable to abortion providers. At oral argument, their attorney maintained that a law that has no effect on women's access to abortion is nevertheless unconstitutional if it is not needed to protect women's health. Of course, that is precisely the argument one would expect from a business that wishes to be free from burdensome regulations. But unless an abortion law has an adverse effect *on women*, there is no reason why the law should face greater constitutional scrutiny than any other measure that burdens a regulated entity in the name of health or safety. Many state and local laws that are justified as safety measures rest on debatable empirical grounds. But when a party saddled with such restrictions challenges them as a violation of due process, our cases call for the restrictions to be sustained if "it might be thought that the particular legislative measure was a rational way" to serve a valid interest. See *Williamson v. Lee Optical of Okla., Inc.* (1955). The test that petitioners advocate would give abortion providers an unjustifiable advantage over all other regulated parties, and for that reason, it was rejected in *Casey*.

Casey also rules out the balancing test adopted in *Whole Woman's Health*. *Whole Woman's Health* simply misinterpreted *Casey*, and I agree that *Whole Woman's Health* should be overruled insofar as it changed the *Casey* test. Unless *Casey* is reexamined—and Louisiana has not asked us to do that—the test it adopted should remain the governing standard.

II

Because the plurality adheres to the balancing test adopted in *Whole Woman's Health*, it considers whether the Louisiana law helps to protect the health of women seeking abortions, and it concludes that "nothing in the record indicates that the background vetting for admitting privileges adds significantly to the vetting that the State Board of Medical Examiners already provides." The Chief Justice seems to agree, although it is unclear why this issue matters under the test he favors.

In any event, contrary to the view taken by the plurality and (seemingly) by The Chief Justice, there is ample evidence in the record showing that admitting privileges help to protect the health of women by ensuring that physicians who perform abortions meet a higher standard of competence than is shown by the mere possession of a license to practice. . . .

Louisiana adopted Act 620 in the aftermath of the Kermit Gosnell grand jury report, which expounded on the failures of regulatory oversight that allowed Gosnell's practices to continue for an extended period. The grand jury concluded that closer supervision would have uncovered Gosnell's egregious health and safety violations. Gosnell had a medical license, but it is doubtful that any hospital would have given him admitting privileges.

In sum, contrary to the plurality's assertion, there is ample evidence in the record showing that requiring admitting privileges has health and safety benefits. There is certainly room for debate about the need for this requirement, but under our case law, this Court's task is not to ascertain whether a law "adds significantly" to the existing regulatory framework. Instead, when confronted with a genuine dispute about a law's benefits, we have afforded legislatures "wide discretion" in assessing whether a regulation serves a legitimate medical need and is medically reasonable even in the face of medical and scientific uncertainty. Louisiana easily satisfied this standard.

For these reasons, both the plurality and The Chief Justice err in concluding that the admitting-privileges requirement serves no valid purpose.

III

They also err in their assessment of Act 620's likely effect on access to abortion. They misuse the doctrine of *stare decisis* and the standard of appellate review for findings of fact.

A

Stare decisis is a major theme in the plurality opinion and that of The Chief Justice. Both opinions try to create the impression that this case is the same as *Whole Woman's Health* and that *stare decisis* therefore commands the same result. In truth, however, the two cases are very different. While it is certainly true that the Texas and Louisiana *statutes* are largely the same, the two cases are not. The decision in *Whole Woman's Health* was not based on the face of the Texas statute, but on an empirical question, namely, the effect of the statute on access to abortion in that State. The Court's answer to that question depended on numerous factors that may differ from State to State, including the demand for abortions, the number and location of abortion clinics and physicians, the geography of the State, the distribution of the population, and the ability of physicians to obtain admitting privileges. There is no reason to think that a law requiring admitting privileges will necessarily have the same effect in every state. As a result, just because the Texas admitting privileges requirement was found by this Court, based on evidence in the record of that case, to have substantially reduced access to abortion in that State, it does not follow that Act 620 would have comparable effects in Louisiana. The two States are neighbors, but they are not the same. Accordingly, the record-based empirical determination in *Whole Woman's Health* is not controlling here. . . .

B

1

Aside from suggesting that *Whole Woman's Health* is dispositive, the plurality and The Chief Justice provide one other reason for concluding that Act 620, if allowed to go into effect, would create a substantial obstacle for women seeking abortions. Pointing to the District Court's finding that the Louisiana law would have a drastic effect on abortion access, the plurality and The Chief Justice note that findings of fact may be overturned only if clearly erroneous, and they see no such error here. In taking this approach, they overlook the flawed legal standard on which the District Court's finding depends, and they ignore the gross deficiencies of the evidence in the record.

Because the Louisiana law was not allowed to go into effect for any appreciable time, it was necessary for the District Court to predict what its effects would be. Attempting to do that, the court apparently concluded that none of the doctors who currently perform abortions in the State would be replaced if the admitting privileges requirement forced them to leave abortion practice. That inference is debatable, as it primarily rests on the anecdotal testimony of June Medical's administrator. Neither the plurality nor The Chief Justice explains why it should be accepted. That alone casts doubt on the finding to which the majority defers, but the problems with the finding do not stop there.

The finding was based on a fundamentally flawed test. In attempting to ascertain how many of the doctors who perform abortions in the State would have to leave abortion practice for lack of admitting privileges, the District Court received evidence in a variety of forms—some live testimony, but also deposition transcripts, declarations, and even letters from counsel—about the doctors' unsuccessful efforts to obtain privileges. The District Court considered whether these doctors had proceeded in "good faith"; it found that they all met that standard; and it therefore concluded that the law would leave the State with very few abortion providers.

2

Under the reasoning just described, the factual finding on which the plurality and The Chief Justice rely—that the Louisiana law would drastically reduce access to abortion in the State—depends on the District Court's finding that the doctors in question exercised "good faith" in their quest for privileges, but that test is woefully deficient. . . .

When the District Court made its assessment of the doctors' "good faith," enforcement of Act 620 had been preliminarily enjoined, and the doctors surely knew that enforcement would be permanently barred if the lawsuit was successful. Thus, the doctors had everything to lose and nothing to gain by obtaining privileges. . . .

If these doctors had secured privileges, that would have tended to defeat the lawsuit. Not only that, acquiring privileges would have subjected all the doctors to the previously described hospital monitoring, as well as any other obligations that a hospital imposed on doctors with privileges, such as providing unpaid care for the indigent. Thus, in light of the situation at the time when the doctors made their attempts to get privileges, they had an incentive to do as little as they thought the District Court would demand, not as much as they would if they stood to benefit from success.

Given this incentive structure, the District Court's "good faith" test was not up to the task. . . . In light of the doctors' incentives, more should have been required. The court should have asked whether the doctors' efforts to acquire privileges were equal to the efforts they would have made if they knew that their ability to continue to perform abortions was at stake. The District Court did not do that, and because its finding on abortion access rests on the wrong legal standard, it cannot stand.[8]

3

Not only did the District Court apply the wrong test, but the evidence in the record fails to show that the doctors made anything more than perfunctory efforts to obtain privileges. . . .

There are three abortion clinics in Louisiana: June Medical, d/b/a Hope Clinic, in Shreveport; Delta Clinic in Baton Rouge; and Women's Clinic in New Orleans. Five doctors perform abortions at those three locations: Doe 1, Doe 2, and Doe 3 at June Medical; Doe 5 at Delta Clinic and Women's Clinic; and Doe 6 at Women's Clinic. For purposes of the analysis that follows, I assume that Doe 1 could not get privileges.[9] If we also assume that none of these doctors would be replaced if they ceased to perform abortions, the impact of the challenged law on abortion access in the State depends on the ability of four doctors to secure such privileges: Doe 2 (June Medical, Shreveport), Doe 3 (June Medical, Shreveport), Doe 5 (Delta Clinic, Baton Rouge, and Women's Clinic, New Orleans), and Doe 6 (Women's Clinic, New Orleans). As I will show, under the correct legal standard, June Medical failed to prove that Act 620 would drive these four doctors out of the abortion practice. . . .

. . . In sum, Doe 2 all but admitted in his e-mails that his efforts to obtain privileges were perfunctory; he declined to apply at a hospital where he previously had privileges; at the only hospital where he made a formal application, he sought a position he knew he could not get for lack of a sufficient number of admissions; and at one other hospital (where he already had consulting privileges) he did no more than make an informal inquiry. The District Court should have considered whether Doe 2's efforts were consistent with the conduct of a person who really wanted to get privileges.

. . . The plurality justifies Doe 5's meager effort based on pure speculation. Because the one doctor Doe 5 asked had a transfer agreement with the Baton Rouge abortion clinic, the plurality reasons that "Doe 5 could have reasonably thought that, if this doctor wouldn't serve as his covering physician, no one

---

8. The plurality claims that my criticism of the District Court's "good faith" standard "is not a legal argument," and instead reflects a view of the facts—namely that the Does acted in "bad faith." But the District Court used "good faith" as the legal standard to assess whether Act 620 would cause the Does to stop performing abortions. Neither the District Court nor the plurality has defined "good faith." Unless that term reflects what the doctors would have done if the incentives had been reversed—and the plurality does not argue that it does—there is a legal issue.

9. Under the correct legal standard, however, it is not at all clear that Doe 1 made the effort required, at least with respect to Christus Health in Shreveport. . . .

would." The plurality goes on to say that "it was well within the District Court's discretion to credit that reading of the record."

This argument shows how far the plurality is willing to go to strike down the Louisiana law. The plurality relies on speculation about why Doe 5 made only one inquiry and why the District Court found this one inquiry sufficient. In fact, however, Doe 5 never explained why he asked only one doctor, and he never intimated that he gave up because that doctor had a transfer agreement with the clinic. Nor did the District Court rely on that inference in finding that Doe 5 exhibited good faith. And in any event, even if Doe 5 had a particularly strong reason to hope that the doctor he asked would agree to cover for him, it hardly follows that other inquiries would necessarily fail. . . .

To sum up Doe 5's situation: The challenged law would have no effect on him if he could find a covering doctor in Baton Rouge, but he asked only one doctor. He did little to pursue applications at two other hospitals because he was not optimistic about his chances and those hospitals required a certain amount of unpaid service to the poor. . . .

Putting all this together, it is apparent that the record does not come close to showing that Doe 2, Doe 5, and Doe 6 made the sort of effort that one would expect if their ability to continue performing abortions had depended on success. These doctors had an incentive to do the bare minimum that they thought the judge would demand—and as it turned out, the judge did not demand much, not even an appearance in his courtroom. In short, the record does not show that Act 620 would drive any of these doctors out of abortion practice, and therefore the Act would not lead Doe 3 to leave either. It follows that the District Court's finding on Act 620's likely effects cannot stand.

C

The Court should remand this case for a new trial under the correct legal standards. The District Court should apply *Casey*'s "substantial obstacle" test, not the *Whole Woman's Health* balancing test. And it should require those challenging Act 620 to demonstrate that the doctors who lack admitting privileges attempted to obtain them with the same zeal they would have exhibited if the Act were in effect and they stood to lose by failing in those efforts.

IV

On remand, the District Court should not permit June Medical to assert the rights of women wishing to obtain an abortion. The court should require the joinder of a plaintiff whose own rights are at stake. Our precedents rarely permit a plaintiff to assert the rights of a third party, and June Medical cannot satisfy our established test for third-party standing. Indeed, what June Medical seeks is something we have never allowed. It wants to rely on the rights of third parties whose interests conflict with its own.

A

The plurality holds that Louisiana waived any objection to June Medical's third-party standing, but that is a misreading of the record. The plurality relies on a passing statement in a brief filed by the State in District Court in connection with the plaintiffs' request for a temporary restraining order, but the statement is simply an accurate statement of circuit precedent on the standing of abortion providers. It does not constitute a waiver. . . .

We have a strong reason to decide the question of third-party standing because it implicates the integrity of future proceedings that should occur in this case. This case should be remanded for a new trial, and we should not allow that to occur without a proper plaintiff. Nothing compels us to forbear from addressing this issue.

B

This case features a blatant conflict of interest between an abortion provider and its patients. Like any other regulated entity, an abortion provider has a financial interest in avoiding burdensome regulations such as Act 620's admitting privileges requirement. Applying for privileges takes time and energy, and maintaining privileges may impose additional burdens. Women seeking abortions, on the other hand, have an interest in the preservation of regulations that protect their health. The conflict inherent in such a situation is glaring.

Some may not see the conflict in this case because they are convinced that the admitting privileges requirement does nothing to promote safety and is really just a ploy. But an abortion provider's ability to assert the rights of women when it challenges ostensible safety regulations should not turn on the merits of its claim. . . .

When an abortion regulation is enacted for the asserted purpose of protecting the health of women, an abortion provider seeking to strike down that law should not be able to rely on the constitutional rights of women. Like any other party unhappy with burdensome regulation, the provider should be limited to its own rights. . . .

D

The conflict of interest inherent in a case like this is reason enough to reject third-party standing, and our standard rules on third-party standing provide a second, independent reason. As a general rule, a plaintiff "must assert his own legal rights and interests, and cannot rest his claim to relief on the legal rights or interests of third parties." *Warth v. Seldin* (1975). We have recognized a "limited" exception to this rule, but in order to qualify, a litigant must demonstrate (1) closeness to the third party and (2) a hindrance to the third party's ability to bring suit. *Kowalski v. Tesmer* (2004).

The record shows that abortion providers cannot satisfy either prong of this test. First, a woman who obtains an abortion typically does not develop a close relationship with the doctor who performs the procedure. On the contrary, their relationship is generally brief and very limited. . . .

Nor can the second [prong], which requires that there be a hindrance to the ability of the third party to bring suit. . . . First, a woman who challenges an abortion restriction can sue under a pseudonym, and many have done so. Other precautions may be taken during the course of litigation to avoid revealing their identities.[1]

Second, if a woman seeking an abortion brings suit, her claim will survive the end of her pregnancy under the capable-of-repetition-yet-evading-review exception to mootness. See *Roe* v. *Wade* (1973) ("Pregnancy provides a classic justification for a conclusion of nonmootness"). To be sure, when the pregnancy terminates, an individual plaintiff's immediate interest in prosecuting the case may diminish. But this is generally true whenever the capable-of-repetition-yet-evading-review exception applies. . . .

F

As The Chief Justice points out, *stare decisis* generally counsels adherence to precedent, and in deciding whether to overrule a prior decision, we consider factors beyond the strength of the precedent's reasoning. But here, such factors weigh in favor of overruling.

Reexamination of a precedent may be appropriate when it is an "outlier" and its reasoning cannot be reconciled with other established precedents, see *Franchise Tax Bd. of Cal. v. Hyatt* (2019); *Janus* v. *State, County, and Municipal Employees* (2018); *United States v. Gaudin* (1995); *Rodriguez de Quijas v. Shearson/American Express, Inc.* (1989), and that is true of the rule allowing abortion providers to assert their patients' rights. The parties have not brought to our attention any other situation in which a party is allowed to invoke the right of a third party with blatantly adverse interests. The rule that the majority applies here is an abortion-only rule. . . .

The presence or absence of reliance is often a critical factor in applying the doctrine of stare decisis, see, *e.g., Franchise Tax Bd.*; *Janus*; *South Dakota v. Wayfair, Inc.* (2018); *Hilton v. South Carolina Public Railways Comm'n* (1991), but neither the plurality nor The Chief Justice claims that any reliance interests are at stake here. Women wishing to obtain abortions have not taken any action in reliance on the ability of abortion providers to sue on their behalf, and eliminating third-party standing for providers would not interfere with the ability of

---

1. Four cases to reach this Court have featured exclusively women plaintiffs. But there are a number of cases in which women have been co-plaintiffs along with abortion clinics or providers. More recently, abortion patients have litigated in the lower courts using their names, those of legal guardians, or pseudonyms.

women to sue. Nor does it appear that abortion providers have done anything in reliance on the special third-party standing rule they have enjoyed. If that rule were abrogated, they could still ask to intervene or appear as an *amicus curiae* in a suit brought by a woman, but it is deeply offensive to our rules of standing to permit them to sue in the name of their patients when they challenge laws enacted to protect their patients' safety.

On remand, the District Court should permit the joinder of a plaintiff with standing and should not proceed until such a plaintiff appears.

* * *

The decision in this case, like that in *Whole Woman's Health*, twists the law, and I therefore respectfully dissent.

JUSTICE GORSUCH, dissenting.

The judicial power is constrained by an array of rules. Rules about the deference due the legislative process, the standing of the parties before us, the use of facial challenges to invalidate democratically enacted statutes, and the award of prospective relief. Still more rules seek to ensure that any legal tests judges may devise are capable of neutral and principled administration. Individually, these rules may seem prosaic. But, collectively, they help keep us in our constitutionally assigned lane, sure that we are in the business of saying what the law is, not what we wish it to be.

Today's decision doesn't just overlook one of these rules. It overlooks one after another. And it does so in a case touching on one of the most controversial topics in contemporary politics and law, exactly the context where this Court should be leaning most heavily on the rules of the judicial process. In truth, *Roe v. Wade* (1973), is not even at issue here. The real question we face concerns our willingness to follow the traditional constraints of the judicial process when a case touching on abortion enters the courtroom.

*

When confronting a constitutional challenge to a law, this Court ordinarily reviews the legislature's factual findings under a "deferential" if not "[u]ncritical" standard. *Gonzales v. Carhart* (2007). When facing such a challenge, too, this Court usually accepts that "the public interest has been declared in terms well-nigh conclusive" by the legislature's adoption of the law — so we may review the law only for its constitutionality, not its wisdom. *Berman v. Parker* (1954). Today, however, the plurality declares that the law before us holds no benefits for the public and bears too many social costs. All while sharing virtually nothing about the facts that led the legislature to conclude otherwise. The law might as well have fallen from the sky.

Of course, that's hardly the case. In Act 620, Louisiana's legislature found that requiring abortion providers to hold admitting privileges at a hospital within 30 miles of the clinic where they perform abortions would serve the public interest by protecting women's health and safety. Those in today's majority never bother to say so, but it turns out that Act 620's admitting privileges requirement for abortion providers tracks longstanding state laws governing physicians who perform relatively low-risk procedures like colonoscopies, Lasik eye surgeries, and steroid injections at ambulatory surgical centers. In fact, the Louisiana legislature passed Act 620 only after extensive hearings at which experts detailed how the Act would promote safer abortion treatment—by providing "a more thorough evaluation mechanism of physician competency," promoting "continuity of care" following abortion, enhancing inter-physician communication, and preventing patient abandonment. . . .

The legislature also heard testimony that Louisiana's clinics and the physicians who work in them have racked up dozens of citations for safety and ethical violations in recent years. . . . The legislature heard, too, from affected women and emergency room physicians about clinic doctors' record of abandoning their patients. One woman testified that, while she was hemorrhaging, her abortion provider told her, " 'You're on your own. Get out.' " Eventually, the woman went to a hospital where an emergency room physician removed fetal body parts that the abortion provider had left in her body. Another patient who complained of severe pain following her abortion was told simply to go home and lie down. When she decided for herself to go to the emergency room, physicians discovered a tear in her uterus and a large hematoma containing a fetal head. The woman required an emergency hysterectomy. In another case, a clinic physician allowed a patient to bleed for three hours, yet a clinic employee testified that the physician would not let her call 911 because of possible media involvement. In the end, the employee called anyway and emergency room personnel discovered that the woman had a perforated uterus and a needed a hysterectomy. A different physician explained that she routinely treats abortion complications in the emergency room when the physician who performed the abortion lacks admitting privileges. In her experience, that situation "puts a woman's health at an unnecessary, unacceptable risk that results from a delay of care . . . and a lack of continuity of care." Admitting privileges would mitigate these risks, she testified, because "the physician who performed the procedure would be the one best equipped to evaluate and treat the patient."

Nor did the legislature neglect to consider the law's potential burdens. As witnesses explained, the admitting privileges requirement in Act 620 for abortion clinic providers would parallel existing requirements for many physicians who work at ambulatory surgical centers. And there is no indication this parallel admitting privileges requirement has led to the closing of any surgical centers or otherwise presented obstacles to quality care in Louisiana. Further, legislators learned that at least one Louisiana abortion provider already had qualifying admitting privileges, suggesting other competent abortion providers would be able to comply with the new regulation as well. . . .

*

After overlooking so many facts and the deference owed to the legislative process, today's decision misapplies many of the rules that normally constrain the judicial process. Start with the question who can sue. To establish standing in federal court, a plaintiff typically must assert an injury to her own legally protected interests — not the rights of someone else. . . .

No one even attempts to suggest this usual prerequisite is satisfied here. The plaintiffs before us are abortion providers. They do not claim a constitutional right to perform that procedure, and no one on the Court contends they hold such a right. Instead, the abortion providers before us seek only to assert the constitutional rights of an undefined, unnamed, indeed unknown, group of women who they hope will be their patients in the future.

In narrow circumstances, to be sure, this Court has allowed cases to proceed based on "third-party standing." But to qualify, the plaintiff must demonstrate both that he has a " 'close' relationship" with the person whose rights he wishes to assert *and* that some " 'hindrance' " hampers the right-holder's "ability to protect his own interests." *Kowalski v. Tesmer*, 543 U.S. 125, 130 (2004).

Nothing like that exists here. In the first place, the plaintiff abortion providers identify no reason to think affected women are unable to assert their own rights if they wish. . . . Separately and additionally, the abortion providers cannot claim a "close relationship" with the women whose rights they assert. . . .

*

. . . What's more, as this suit was in progress, the State discovered two additional Louisiana abortion providers not reflected in the district court's opinion. No one disputes the accuracy of the State's information about these two providers. Nor could anyone deny the importance of this information, when so much of today's decision seems to turn on the exact quantity and distribution of a relatively small number of abortion providers. Normally, this Court might hesitate to deliver a fact-bound decision premised on facts we know to be incorrect. But today's decision, assuming the worst once more, simply proceeds as if these providers didn't exist.

If there is a silver lining, though, it may be here. This Court generally recognizes that facts can change over time — and that, when they do, legal conclusions based on them may have to change as well. Even so-called "permanent injunctions" are actually provisional — open to modification "to prevent the possibility that [they] may operate injuriously in the future." *Glenn v. Field Packing Co.* (1933). After all, when the facts change, the law cannot pretend nothing has happened. For that reason, we have instructed lower courts to reconsider injunctions "when the party seeking relief . . . can show a significant change either in factual conditions or in law." *Agostini v. Felton* (1997). And, given the fact-intensive nature of today's analysis, the relief directed might well need to be reconsidered below if, for example, hospitals start offering qualifying admitting privileges to abortion providers, a handful of abortion providers relocate from other States, or even a tiny fraction of Louisiana's existing OB/GYNs decide to begin performing abortions. Given the post-trial developments Louisiana has already identified but no court has yet considered, there's every reason to think the factual context here is prone to significant changes.

*

. . . From beginning to end, the plurality treats *Whole Woman's Health*'s fact-laden predictions about how a Texas law would impact the availability of abortion in that State in 2016 as if they obviously and necessarily applied to Louisiana in 2020. Most notably, the plurality cites *Whole Woman's Health* for the proposition that admitting privileges requirements offer no benefit when it comes to patient safety or otherwise. But *Whole Woman's Health* found an absence of benefit based only on the particular factual record before it. Nothing in the decision suggested that its conclusions about the costs and benefits of the Texas statute were universal principles of law, medicine, or economics true in all places and at all times. Yet that is exactly how the plurality treats those conclusions—all while leaving unmentioned the facts Louisiana amassed in an effort to show that its law promises patient benefits in this place at this time.

. . . The plurality defers not only to the district court's findings about the extent of the law's benefits, but also to the lower court's judgment that the benefits are so limited that the law's burden on abortion access is "undue." By declining to apply our normal *de novo* standard of review to questions of law like these, today's decision proceeds on the remarkable premise that, even if the district court was wrong on the law, a duly enacted statute must fall because the lower court wasn't *clearly* wrong.

*

. . .The legal standard the plurality applies when it comes to admitting privileges for abortion clinics turns out to be exactly the sort of all-things-considered balancing of benefits and burdens this Court has long rejected. Really, it's little more than the judicial version of a hunter's stew: Throw in anything that looks interesting, stir, and season to taste. . . .

What was true there turns out to be no less true here. The plurality sides with the district court in concluding that the time and cost some women might have to endure to obtain an abortion outweighs the benefits of Act 620. Perhaps the plurality sees that answer as obvious, given its apparent conclusion that the Act would offer the public no benefits of any kind. But for its test to provide any helpful guidance, it must be capable of resolving cases the plurality can't so easily dismiss. Suppose, for example, a factfinder credited the State's evidence of medical benefit, finding that a small number of women would obtain safer medical care if the law went into effect. But suppose the same factfinder *also* credited a plaintiff's evidence of burden, finding that a large number of women would have to endure longer wait times and farther drives, and that a very small number of women would be unable to obtain an abortion at all. How is a judge supposed to balance, say, a few women's emergency hysterectomies against many women spending extra hours travelling to a clinic? The plurality's test offers no guidance. Nor can it. The benefits and burdens are incommensurable, and they do not teach such things in law school.

When judges take it upon themselves to assess the raw costs and benefits of a new law or regulation, it can come as no surprise that "[s]ome courts wind up attaching the same significance to opposite facts," and even attaching the opposite significance to the same facts. It can come as no surprise, either, that judges retreat to their underlying assumptions or moral intuitions when deciding whether a burden is undue. For what else is left?

Some judges have thrown up their hands at the task put to them by the Court in this area. If everything comes down to balancing costs against benefits, they have observed, "the only institution that can give an authoritative answer" is this Court, because the question isn't one of law at all and the only "balance" that matters is the one this Court strikes. *Planned Parenthood of Ind. & Ky. v. Box* (7th Cir. 2019) (Easterbrook, J., concurring in denial of rehearing en banc). The lament is understandable. Missing here is exactly what judges usually depend on when asked to make tough calls: an administrable legal rule to follow, a neutral principle, something outside themselves to guide their decision.

*

Setting aside the other departures from the judicial process on display today, the concurrence suggests it can remedy at least this one. We don't need to resort to a raw balancing test to resolve today's dispute. A deeper respect for *stare decisis* and existing precedents, the concurrence assures us, supplies the key to a safe way out. Unfortunately, however, the reality proves more complicated.

Start with the concurrence's discussion of *Whole Woman's Health*. Immediately after paying homage to *stare decisis*, the concurrence *refuses* to follow the all-things-considered balancing test that decision employed when striking down Texas's admitting privileges law. In the process, the concurrence rightly recounts many of the problems with raw balancing tests. But then, switching directions again, the concurrence insists we are bound by an *alternative* holding in *Whole Woman's Health*. According to the concurrence, this alternative holding declared that the Texas law imposed an impermissible "substantial obstacle" to abortion access in light *only* of the burdens the law imposed—"independent of [any] discussion of [the law's] benefits. And, the concurrence concludes, because the facts of this suit look like those in *Whole Woman's Health*, we must find an impermissible substantial obstacle here too.

But in this footwork lie at least two missteps. For one, the facts of this suit cannot be so neatly reduced to *Whole Woman's Health* redux. See *ante* (ALITO, J. dissenting). For another, *Whole Woman's Health* nowhere issued the alternative holding on which the concurrence pins its argument. At no point did the Court hold that the burdens imposed by the Texas law alone—divorced from any consideration of the law's benefits—could suffice to establish a substantial obstacle. To the contrary, *Whole Woman's Health* insisted that the substantial obstacle test "*requires* that courts consider the burdens a law imposes on abortion access together with the benefits th[e] la[w] confer[s]." And whatever else respect for *stare decisis* might suggest, it cannot demand allegiance to a nonexistent ruling inconsistent with the approach actually taken by the Court.

The concurrence's fallback argument doesn't solve the problem either. So what if *Whole Woman's Health* rejected the benefits-free version of the "substantial obstacle" test the concurrence endorses? The concurrence assures us that *Planned Parenthood of Southeastern Pa. v. Casey*, 505 U.S. 833 (1992), specified this form of the test, so we must (or at least may) do the same, whatever *Whole Woman's Health* says.

But here again, the concurrence rests on at least one mistaken premise. In the context of laws implicating only the State's interest in fetal life previability, the *Casey* plurality did describe its "undue burden" test as asking whether the law in question poses a substantial obstacle to abortion access. But when a State enacts a law "to further the health or safety of a woman seeking an abortion," the *Casey* plurality added a key qualification: Only "*[u]nnecessary* health regulations that have the purpose or effect of presenting a substantial obstacle to a woman seeking an abortion impose an undue burden on the right." That qualification is clearly applicable here, yet the concurrence nowhere addresses it, applying instead a new test of its own creation. In the context of medical regulations, too, the concurrence's new test might even prove stricter than strict scrutiny. After all, it's possible for a regulation to survive strict scrutiny if it is narrowly tailored to advance a compelling state interest. And no one doubts that women's health can be such an interest. Yet, under the concurrence's test it seems possible that even the most compelling and narrowly tailored medical regulation would have to fail if it placed a substantial obstacle in the way of abortion access. Such a result would appear to create yet another discontinuity with *Casey*, which expressly disavowed any test as strict as strict scrutiny.

*

To arrive at today's result, rules must be brushed aside and shortcuts taken. While the concurrence parts ways with the plurality at the last turn, the road both travel leads us to a strangely open space, unconstrained by many of the neutral principles that normally govern the judicial process. The temptation to proceed this direction, closer with each step toward an unobstructed exercise of will, may be always with us, a danger inherent in judicial review. But it is an impulse this Court normally strives mightily to resist. Today, in a highly politicized and contentious arena, we prove unwilling, or perhaps unable, to resist that temptation. Either way, respectfully, it is a sign we have lost our way.

JUSTICE KAVANAUGH, dissenting.

I join Parts I, II, and III of Justice Alito's dissent. A threshold question in this case concerns the proper standard for evaluating state abortion laws. The Louisiana law at issue here requires doctors who perform abortions to have admitting privileges at a hospital within 30 miles of the abortion clinic. The State asks us to assess the law by applying the undue burden standard of *Planned Parenthood of Southeastern Pa. v. Casey* (1992).[1] The plaintiffs ask us to apply the cost-benefit standard of *Whole Woman's Health v. Hellerstedt* (2016).

---

1. The State has not asked the Court to depart from the *Casey* standard.

Today, five Members of the Court reject the *Whole Woman's Health* cost-benefit standard. *Ante* (Roberts, C. J., concurring in judgment); *ante* (Thomas, J., dissenting); *ante* (Alito, J., joined by Thomas, Gorsuch, and Kavanaugh, JJ., dissenting); *ante* (Gorsuch, J., dissenting). A different five Members of the Court conclude that Louisiana's admitting-privileges law is unconstitutional because it "would restrict women's access to abortion to the same degree as" the Texas law in *Whole Woman's Health*. *Ante* (opinion of Roberts, C. J.); see also *ante* (opinion of Breyer, J., joined by Ginsburg, Sotomayor, and Kagan, JJ.).

I agree with the first of those two conclusions. But I respectfully dissent from the second because, in my view, additional factfinding is necessary to properly evaluate Louisiana's law. As Justice Alito thoroughly and carefully explains, the factual record at this stage of plaintiffs' facial, pre-enforcement challenge does not adequately demonstrate that the three relevant doctors (Does 2, 5, and 6) cannot obtain admitting privileges or, therefore, that any of the three Louisiana abortion clinics would close as a result of the admitting-privileges law. I expressed the same concern about the incomplete factual record more than a year ago during the stay proceedings, and the factual record has not changed since then. See *June Medical Services, L.L.C. v. Gee*, (2019) (opinion dissenting from grant of application for stay). In short, I agree with Justice Alito that the Court should remand the case for a new trial and additional factfinding under the appropriate legal standards.[2]

---

2. In my view, the District Court on remand should also address the State's new argument (raised for the first time in this Court) that these doctors and clinics lack third-party standing.

Chapter 16

Freedoms of Speech and Press

ASSIGNMENT 2

STUDY GUIDE:

- The next case concerns whether the regulation of "conduct" constitutes a restriction on "speech." The doctrines governing "time, place, and manner" regulations of speech are complex and are not covered in the casebook.
- The next case provides a brief introduction to those doctrines in the context of a recent controversy.

McCullen v. Coakley
134 S. Ct. 2518 (2014)

CHIEF JUSTICE ROBERTS delivered the opinion of the Court.

A Massachusetts statute makes it a crime to knowingly stand on a "public way or sidewalk" within 35 feet of an entrance or driveway to any place, other than a hospital, where abortions are performed. Petitioners are individuals who approach and talk to women outside such facilities, attempting to dissuade them from having abortions. The statute prevents petitioners from doing so near the facilities' entrances. The question presented is whether the statute violates the First Amendment.

I

A

In 2000, the Massachusetts Legislature enacted the Massachusetts Reproductive Health Care Facilities Act. The law was designed to address clashes between abortion opponents and advocates of abortion rights that were occurring outside clinics where abortions were performed. The Act established a defined area with an 18-foot radius around the entrances and driveways of such facilities. Anyone could enter that area, but once within it, no one (other than certain exempt individuals) could knowingly approach within six feet of another person — unless that person consented — "for the purpose of passing a leaflet or handbill to, displaying a sign to, or engaging in oral protest, education, or counseling with such other person." A separate provision subjected to criminal punishment anyone who "knowingly obstructs, detains, hinders, impedes or blocks another person's entry to or exit from a reproductive health care facility."

The statute was modeled on a similar Colorado law that this Court had upheld in *Hill v. Colorado* (2000). Relying on *Hill,* the United States Court of Appeals for the First Circuit sustained the Massachusetts statute against a First Amendment challenge.

By 2007, some Massachusetts legislators and law enforcement officials had come to regard the 2000 statute as inadequate. At legislative hearings, multiple witnesses recounted apparent violations of the law. Massachusetts Attorney General Martha Coakley, for example, testified that protestors violated the statute "on a routine basis." . . .

To address these concerns, the Massachusetts Legislature amended the statute in 2007, replacing the six-foot no-approach zones (within the 18-foot area) with a 35-foot fixed buffer zone from which individuals are categorically excluded. The statute now provides:

> No person shall knowingly enter or remain on a public way or sidewalk adjacent to a reproductive health care facility within a radius of 35 feet of any portion of an entrance, exit or driveway of a reproductive health care facility or within the area within a rectangle created by extending the outside boundaries of any entrance, exit or driveway of a reproductive health care facility in straight lines to the point where such lines intersect the sideline of the street in front of such entrance, exit or driveway. Mass. Gen. Laws, ch. 266, §120E½(b).

A "reproductive health care facility," in turn, is defined as "a place, other than within or upon the grounds of a hospital, where abortions are offered or performed."

The 35-foot buffer zone applies only "during a facility's business hours," and the area must be "clearly marked and posted." In practice, facilities typically mark the zones with painted arcs and posted signs on adjacent sidewalks and streets. A first violation of the statute is punishable by a fine of up to $500, up to three months in prison, or both, while a subsequent offense is punishable by a fine of between $500 and $5,000, up to two and a half years in prison, or both.

The Act exempts four classes of individuals: (1) "persons entering or leaving such facility"; (2) "employees or agents of such facility acting within the scope of their employment"; (3) "law enforcement, ambulance, firefighting, construction, utilities, public works and other municipal agents acting within the scope of their employment"; and (4) "persons using the public sidewalk or street right-of-way adjacent to such facility solely for the purpose of reaching a destination other than such facility." The legislature also retained the separate provision from the 2000 version that proscribes the knowing obstruction of access to a facility.

B

Some of the individuals who stand outside Massachusetts abortion clinics are fairly described as protestors, who express their moral or religious opposition to abortion through signs and chants or, in some cases, more aggressive methods such as face-to-face confrontation. Petitioners take a different tack. They attempt to engage women approaching the clinics in what they call "sidewalk counseling," which involves offering information about alternatives to abortion and help pursuing those options. . . .

The buffer zones have displaced petitioners from their previous positions outside the clinics. . . . Before the Act was amended to create the buffer zones, petitioners stood near the entryway to the foyer. Now a buffer zone — marked by a painted arc and a sign — surrounds the entrance. This zone extends 23 feet down the sidewalk in one direction, 26 feet in the other, and outward just one foot short of the curb. The clinic's entrance adds another seven feet to the width of the zone. The upshot is that petitioners are effectively excluded from a 56-foot-wide expanse of the public sidewalk in front of the clinic.

Petitioners at all three clinics claim that the buffer zones have considerably hampered their counseling efforts. Although they have managed to conduct some counseling and to distribute some literature outside the buffer zones — particularly at the Boston clinic — they say they have had many fewer conversations and distributed many fewer leaflets since the zones went into effect.

The second statutory exemption allows clinic employees and agents acting within the scope of their employment to enter the buffer zones. Relying on this exemption, the Boston clinic uses "escorts" to greet women as they approach the clinic, accompanying them through the zones to the clinic entrance. Petitioners claim that the escorts sometimes thwart petitioners' attempts to communicate with patients by blocking petitioners from handing literature to patients, telling patients not to "pay any attention" or "listen to" petitioners, and disparaging petitioners as "crazy." . . .

I

By its very terms, the Massachusetts Act regulates access to "public way[s]" and "sidewalk[s]." Such areas occupy a "special position in terms of First Amendment protection" because of their historic role as sites for discussion and debate. *United States v. Grace* (1983). These places — which we have labeled "traditional public fora" — "have immemorially been held in trust for the use of the public and, time out of mind, have been used for purposes of assembly, communicating thoughts between citizens, and discussing public questions." *Pleasant Grove City v. Summum* (2009).

It is no accident that public streets and sidewalks have developed as venues for the exchange of ideas. Even today, they remain one of the few places where a speaker can be confident that he is not simply preaching to the choir. With respect to other means of communication, an individual confronted with an uncomfortable message can always turn the page, change the channel, or leave the Web site. Not so on public streets and sidewalks. There, a listener often encounters speech he might otherwise tune out. In light of the First Amendment's purpose "to preserve an uninhibited marketplace of ideas in which truth will ultimately prevail," *FCC v. League of Women Voters of Cal.* (1984), this aspect of traditional public fora is a virtue, not a vice.

In short, traditional public fora are areas that have historically been open to the public for speech activities. Thus, even though the Act says nothing about speech on its face, there is no doubt—and respondents do not dispute—that it restricts access to traditional public fora and is therefore subject to First Amendment scrutiny.

Consistent with the traditionally open character of public streets and sidewalks, we have held that the government's ability to restrict speech in such locations is "very limited." *Grace.* In particular, the guiding First Amendment principle that the "government has no power to restrict expression because of its message, its ideas, its subject matter, or its content" applies with full force in a traditional public forum. *Police Dept. of Chicago v. Mosley* (1972). As a general rule, in such a forum the government may not "selectively . . . shield the public from some kinds of speech on the ground that they are more offensive than others." *Erznoznik v. Jacksonville* (1975).

We have, however, afforded the government somewhat wider leeway to regulate features of speech unrelated to its content. "[E]ven in a public forum the government may impose reasonable restrictions on the time, place, or manner of protected speech, provided the restrictions 'are justified without reference to the content of the regulated speech, that they are narrowly tailored to serve a significant governmental interest, and that they leave open ample alternative channels for communication of the information.'" *Ward v. Rock Against Racism* (1989).

While the parties agree that this test supplies the proper framework for assessing the constitutionality of the Massachusetts Act, they disagree about whether the Act satisfies the test's three requirements.

III

Petitioners contend that the Act is not content neutral for two independent reasons: First, they argue that it discriminates against abortion-related speech because it establishes buffer zones only at clinics that perform abortions. Second, petitioners contend that the Act, by exempting clinic employees and agents, favors one viewpoint about abortion over the other. If either of these arguments is correct, then the Act must satisfy strict scrutiny—that is, it must be the least restrictive means of achieving a compelling state interest. Respondents do not argue that the Act can survive this exacting standard. . . .

A

The Act applies only at a "reproductive health care facility," defined as "a place, other than within or upon the grounds of a hospital, where abortions are offered or performed." Given this definition, petitioners argue, "virtually all speech affected by the Act is speech concerning abortion," thus rendering the Act content based.

We disagree. To begin, the Act does not draw content-based distinctions on its face. The Act would be content based if it required "enforcement authorities" to "examine the content of the message that is conveyed to determine whether" a violation has occurred. But it does not. Whether petitioners violate the Act "depends" not "on what they say," *Holder v. Humanitarian Law Project* (2010), but simply on where they say it. Indeed, petitioners can violate the Act merely by standing in a buffer zone, without displaying a sign or uttering a word.

It is true, of course, that by limiting the buffer zones to abortion clinics, the Act has the "inevitable effect" of restricting abortion-related speech more than speech on other subjects. Brief for Petitioners (quoting *United States v. O'Brien* (1968)). But a facially neutral law does not become content based simply because it may disproportionately affect speech on certain topics. On the contrary, "[a] regulation that serves purposes unrelated to the content of expression is deemed neutral, even if it has an incidental effect on some speakers or messages but not others." *Ward.* The question in such a case is whether the law is " 'justified without reference to the content of the regulated speech.' " *Renton v. Playtime Theatres, Inc.* (1986) (quoting *Virginia Pharmacy Board v. Virginia Citizens Consumer Council, Inc.* (1976)).

The Massachusetts Act is. Its stated purpose is to "increase forthwith public safety at reproductive health care facilities." . . .

We have previously deemed the foregoing concerns to be content neutral. Obstructed access and congested sidewalks are problems no matter what caused them. A group of individuals can obstruct clinic access and clog sidewalks just as much when they loiter as when they protest abortion or counsel patients.

To be clear, the Act would not be content neutral if it were concerned with undesirable effects that arise from "the direct impact of speech on its audience" or "[l]isteners' reactions to speech." If, for example, the speech outside Massachusetts abortion clinics caused offense or made listeners uncomfortable, such offense or discomfort would not give the Commonwealth a content-neutral justification to restrict the speech. All of the problems identified by the Commonwealth here, however, arise irrespective of any listener's reactions. Whether or not a single person reacts to abortion protestors' chants or petitioners' counseling, large crowds outside abortion clinics can still compromise public safety, impede access, and obstruct sidewalks.

Petitioners do not really dispute that the Commonwealth's interests in ensuring safety and preventing obstruction are, as a general matter, content neutral. But petitioners note that these interests "apply outside every building in the State that hosts any activity that might occasion protest or comment," not just abortion clinics. By choosing to pursue these interests only at abortion clinics, petitioners argue, the Massachusetts Legislature evinced a purpose to "single[] out for regulation speech about one particular topic: abortion."

We cannot infer such a purpose from the Act's limited scope. The broad reach of a statute can help confirm that it was not enacted to burden a narrower category of disfavored speech. See Kagan, Private Speech, Public Purpose: The Role of Governmental Motive in First Amendment Doctrine, 63 U. Chi. L. Rev. 413, 451-452 (1996). At the same time, however, "States adopt laws to address the problems that confront them. The First Amendment does not require States to regulate for problems that do not exist." *Burson v. Freeman* (1992) (plurality opinion). The Massachusetts Legislature amended the Act in 2007 in response to a problem that was, in its experience, limited to abortion clinics. There was a record of crowding, obstruction, and even violence outside such clinics. There were apparently no similar recurring problems associated with other kinds of healthcare facilities, let alone with "every building in the State that hosts any activity that might occasion protest or comment." In light of the limited nature of the problem, it was reasonable for the Massachusetts Legislature to enact a limited solution. When selecting among various options for combating a particular problem, legislatures should be encouraged to choose the one that restricts less speech, not more.

B

Petitioners also argue that the Act is content based because it exempts four classes of individuals, one of which comprises "employees or agents of [a reproductive healthcare] facility acting within the scope of their employment." This exemption, petitioners say, favors one side in the abortion debate and thus constitutes viewpoint discrimination — an "egregious form of content discrimination," *Rosenberger v. Rector and Visitors of Univ. of Va.* (1995). In particular, petitioners argue that the exemption allows clinic employees and agents — including the volunteers who "escort" patients arriving at the Boston clinic — to speak inside the buffer zones.

It is of course true that "an exemption from an otherwise permissible regulation of speech may represent a governmental 'attempt to give one side of a debatable public question an advantage in expressing its views to the people.'" *City of Ladue v. Gilleo* (1994). At least on the record before us, however, the statutory exemption for clinic employees and agents acting within the scope of their employment does not appear to be such an attempt.

There is nothing inherently suspect about providing some kind of exemption to allow individuals who work at the clinics to enter or remain within the buffer zones. In particular, the exemption cannot be regarded as simply a carve-out for the clinic escorts; it also covers employees such as the maintenance worker shoveling a snowy sidewalk or the security guard patrolling a clinic entrance.

Given the need for an exemption for clinic employees, the "scope of their employment" qualification simply ensures that the exemption is limited to its purpose of allowing the employees to do their jobs. It performs the same function as the identical "scope of their employment" restriction on the exemption for "law enforcement, ambulance, fire-fighting, construction, utilities, public works and other municipal agents." . . . The limitation . . . makes clear — with respect to both clinic employees and municipal agents — that exempted individuals are allowed inside the zones only to perform those acts authorized by their employers. There is no suggestion in the record that any of the clinics authorize their employees to speak about abortion in the buffer zones. The "scope of their employment" limitation thus seems designed to protect against exactly the sort of conduct that petitioners and Justice Scalia fear.

Petitioners did testify in this litigation about instances in which escorts at the Boston clinic had expressed views about abortion to the women they were accompanying, thwarted petitioners' attempts to speak and hand literature to the women, and disparaged petitioners in various ways. It is unclear from petitioners' testimony whether these alleged incidents occurred within the buffer zones. There is no viewpoint discrimination problem if the incidents occurred outside the zones because petitioners are equally free to say whatever they would like in that area.

Even assuming the incidents occurred inside the zones, the record does not suggest that they involved speech within the scope of the escorts' employment. If the speech was beyond the scope of their employment, then each of the alleged incidents would violate the Act's express terms. Petitioners' complaint would then be that the police were failing to *enforce* the Act equally against clinic escorts. . . .

It would be a very different question if it turned out that a clinic authorized escorts to speak about abortion inside the buffer zones. In that case, the escorts would not seem to be violating the Act because the speech would be within the scope of their employment. The Act's exemption for clinic employees would then facilitate speech on only one side of the abortion debate — a clear form of viewpoint discrimination that would support an as-applied challenge to the buffer zone at that clinic. But the record before us contains insufficient evidence to show that the exemption operates in this way at any of the clinics, perhaps because the clinics do not want to doom the Act by allowing their employees to speak about abortion within the buffer zones.[4]

We thus conclude that the Act is neither content nor viewpoint based and therefore need not be analyzed under strict scrutiny.

IV

Even though the Act is content neutral, it still must be "narrowly tailored to serve a significant governmental interest." *Ward.* . . . For a content-neutral time, place, or manner regulation to be narrowly tailored, it must not "burden substantially more

---

4. Of course we do not hold that "[s]peech restrictions favoring one viewpoint over another are not content based unless it can be shown that the favored viewpoint has actually been expressed." *Post.* We instead apply an uncontroversial principle of constitutional adjudication: that a plaintiff generally cannot prevail on an *as-applied* challenge without showing that the law has in fact been (or is sufficiently likely to be) unconstitutionally *applied* to him. Specifically, when someone challenges a law as viewpoint discriminatory but it is not clear from the face of the law which speakers will be allowed to speak, he must show that he was prevented from speaking while someone espousing another viewpoint was permitted to do so. Justice Scalia can decry this analysis as "astonishing" only by quoting a sentence that is explicitly limited to as-applied challenges and treating it as relevant to facial challenges. *Ibid.*

speech than is necessary to further the government's legitimate interests." *Ward*. Such a regulation, unlike a content-based restriction of speech, "need not be the least restrictive or least intrusive means of" serving the government's interests. But the government still "may not regulate expression in such a manner that a substantial portion of the burden on speech does not serve to advance its goals."

A

As noted, respondents claim that the Act promotes "public safety, patient access to healthcare, and the unobstructed use of public sidewalks and roadways." . . . The buffer zones clearly serve these interests.

At the same time, the buffer zones impose serious burdens on petitioners' speech. At each of the three Planned Parenthood clinics where petitioners attempt to counsel patients, the zones carve out a significant portion of the adjacent public sidewalks, pushing petitioners well back from the clinics' entrances and driveways. The zones thereby compromise petitioners' ability to initiate the close, personal conversations that they view as essential to "sidewalk counseling." . . .

The buffer zones have also made it substantially more difficult for petitioners to distribute literature to arriving patients. As explained, because petitioners in Boston cannot readily identify patients before they enter the zone, they often cannot approach them in time to place literature near their hands — the most effective means of getting the patients to accept it. In Worcester and Springfield, the zones have pushed petitioners so far back from the clinics' driveways that they can no longer even attempt to offer literature as drivers turn into the parking lots. In short, the Act operates to deprive petitioners of their two primary methods of communicating with patients. . . .

In the context of petition campaigns, we have observed that "one-on-one communication" is "the most effective, fundamental, and perhaps economical avenue of political discourse." *Meyer v. Grant* (1988). And "handing out leaflets in the advocacy of a politically controversial viewpoint . . . is the essence of First Amendment expression"; "[n]o form of speech is entitled to greater constitutional protection." *McIntyre v. Ohio Elections Comm'n* (1995). When the government makes it more difficult to engage in these modes of communication, it imposes an especially significant First Amendment burden.

Respondents also emphasize that the Act does not prevent petitioners from engaging in various forms of "protest" — such as chanting slogans and displaying signs — outside the buffer zones. That misses the point. Petitioners are not protestors. They seek not merely to express their opposition to abortion, but to inform women of various alternatives and to provide help in pursuing them. Petitioners believe that they can accomplish this objective only through personal, caring, consensual conversations. And for good reason: It is easier to ignore a strained voice or a waving hand than a direct greeting or an outstretched arm. While the record indicates that petitioners have been able to have a number of quiet conversations outside the buffer zones, respondents have not refuted petitioners' testimony that the conversations have been far less frequent and far less successful since the buffer zones were instituted. It is thus no answer to say that petitioners can still be "seen and heard" by women within the buffer zones. If all that the women can see and hear are vociferous opponents of abortion, then the buffer zones have effectively stifled petitioners' message.

Finally, respondents suggest that, at the Worcester and Springfield clinics, petitioners are prevented from communicating with patients not by the buffer zones but by the fact that most patients arrive by car and park in the clinics' private lots. It is true that the layout of the two clinics would prevent petitioners from approaching the clinics' *doorways,* even without the buffer zones. But petitioners do not claim a right to trespass on the clinics' property. They instead claim a right to stand on the public sidewalks by the driveway as cars turn into the parking lot. Before the buffer zones, they could do so. Now they must stand a substantial distance away. The Act alone is responsible for that restriction on their ability to convey their message.

B

1

The buffer zones burden substantially more speech than necessary to achieve the Commonwealth's asserted interests. At the outset, we note that the Act is truly exceptional: Respondents and their *amici* identify no other State with a law that creates fixed buffer zones around abortion clinics. That of course does not mean that the law is invalid. It does, however, raise concern that the Commonwealth has too readily forgone options that could serve its interests just as well, without substantially burdening the kind of speech in which petitioners wish to engage.

That is the case here. The Commonwealth's interests include ensuring public safety outside abortion clinics, preventing harassment and intimidation of patients and clinic staff, and combating deliberate obstruction of clinic entrances. The Act itself contains a separate provision, subsection (e)—unchallenged by petitioners—that prohibits much of this conduct. . . .

The Commonwealth points to a substantial public safety risk created when protestors obstruct driveways leading to the clinics. That is, however, an example of its failure to look to less intrusive means of addressing its concerns. Any such obstruction can readily be addressed through existing local ordinances.

All of the foregoing measures are, of course, in addition to available generic criminal statutes forbidding assault, breach of the peace, trespass, vandalism, and the like. . . .

The Commonwealth also asserts an interest in preventing congestion in front of abortion clinics. According to respondents, even when individuals do not deliberately obstruct access to clinics, they can inadvertently do so simply by gathering in large numbers. But the Commonwealth could address that problem through more targeted means. Some localities, for example, have ordinances that require crowds blocking a clinic entrance to disperse when ordered to do so by the police, and that forbid the individuals to reassemble within a certain distance of the clinic for a certain period. . . .

And to the extent the Commonwealth argues that even these types of laws are ineffective, it has another problem. The portions of the record that respondents cite to support the anticongestion interest pertain mainly to one place at one time: the Boston Planned Parenthood clinic on Saturday mornings. Respondents point us to no evidence that individuals regularly gather at other clinics, or at other times in Boston, in sufficiently large groups to obstruct access. For a problem shown to arise only once a week in one city at one clinic, creating 35-foot buffer zones at every clinic across the Commonwealth is hardly a narrowly tailored solution. . . .

2

Respondents have but one reply: "We have tried other approaches, but they do not work." Respondents emphasize the history in Massachusetts of obstruction at abortion clinics, and the Commonwealth's allegedly failed attempts to combat such obstruction with injunctions and individual prosecutions. They also point to the Commonwealth's experience under the 2000 version of the Act, during which the police found it difficult to enforce the six-foot no-approach zones given the "frenetic" activity in front of clinic entrances. According to respondents, this history shows that Massachusetts has tried less restrictive alternatives to the buffer zones, to no avail.

We cannot accept that contention. Although respondents claim that Massachusetts "tried other laws already on the books," they identify not a single prosecution brought under those laws within at least the last 17 years. And while they also claim that the Commonwealth "tried injunctions," the last injunctions they cite date to the 1990s. In short, the Commonwealth has not shown that it seriously undertook to address the problem with less intrusive tools readily available to it. Nor has it shown that it considered different methods that other jurisdictions have found effective. . . .

To meet the requirement of narrow tailoring, the government must demonstrate that alternative measures that burden substantially less speech would fail to achieve the government's interests, not simply that the chosen route is easier. A painted line on the sidewalk is easy to enforce, but the prime objective of the First Amendment is not efficiency. In any case, we do not think that showing intentional obstruction is nearly so difficult in this context as respondents suggest. To determine whether a protestor intends to block access to a clinic, a police officer need only order him to move. If he refuses, then there is no question that his continued conduct is knowing or intentional. . . .

Given the vital First Amendment interests at stake, it is not enough for Massachusetts simply to say that other approaches have not worked.[9]

* * *

---

9. Because we find that the Act is not narrowly tailored, we need not consider whether the Act leaves open ample alternative channels of communication. Nor need we consider petitioners' overbreadth challenge.

Petitioners wish to converse with their fellow citizens about an important subject on the public streets and sidewalks — sites that have hosted discussions about the issues of the day throughout history. Respondents assert undeniably significant interests in maintaining public safety on those same streets and side-walks, as well as in preserving access to adjacent healthcare facilities. But here the Commonwealth has pursued those interests by the extreme step of closing a substantial portion of a traditional public forum to all speakers. It has done so without seriously addressing the problem through alternatives that leave the forum open for its time-honored purposes. The Commonwealth may not do that consistent with the First Amendment.

The judgment of the Court of Appeals for the First Circuit is reversed, and the case is remanded for further proceedings consistent with this opinion.

It is so ordered.

JUSTICE SCALIA, with whom JUSTICE KENNEDY and JUSTICE THOMAS join, concurring in the judgment.

Today's opinion carries forward this Court's practice of giving abortion-rights advocates a pass when it comes to suppressing the free-speech rights of their opponents. There is an entirely separate, abridged edition of the First Amendment applicable to speech against abortion.

The second half of the Court's analysis today, invalidating the law at issue because of inadequate "tailoring," is certainly attractive to those of us who oppose an abortion-speech edition of the First Amendment. But think again. This is an opinion that has Something for Everyone, and the more significant portion continues the onward march of abortion-speech-only jurisprudence. That is the first half of the Court's analysis, which concludes that a statute of this sort is not content based and hence not subject to so-called strict scrutiny. The Court reaches out to decide that question unnecessarily — or at least unnecessarily insofar as legal analysis is concerned.

I disagree with the Court's dicta (Part III) and hence see no reason to opine on its holding (Part IV).

I. THE COURT'S CONTENT-NEUTRALITY DISCUSSION IS UNNECESSARY

The gratuitous portion of today's opinion is Part III, which concludes — in seven pages of the purest dicta — that subsection (b) of the Massachusetts Reproductive Health Care Facilities Act is not specifically directed at speech opposing (or even concerning) abortion and hence need not meet the strict-scrutiny standard applicable to content-based speech regulations. . . .

II. THE STATUTE IS CONTENT BASED AND FAILS STRICT SCRUTINY

Having eagerly volunteered to take on the level-of-scrutiny question, the Court provides the wrong answer. Petitioners argue for two reasons that subsection (b) articulates a content-based speech restriction — and that we must therefore evaluate it through the lens of strict scrutiny.

A.　APPLICATION TO ABORTION CLINICS ONLY

First, petitioners maintain that the Act targets abortion-related — for practical purposes, abortion-opposing — speech because it applies outside abortion clinics only (rather than outside other buildings as well). . . . Every objective indication shows that the provision's primary purpose is to restrict speech that opposes abortion.

I begin, as suggested above, with the fact that the Act burdens only the public spaces outside abortion clinics. . . . [A]lthough the statute applies to all abortion clinics in Massachusetts, only one is known to have been beset by the problems that the statute supposedly addresses. The Court uses this striking fact (a smoking gun, so to speak) as a basis for concluding that the law is insufficiently "tailored" to safety and access concerns (Part IV) rather than as a basis for concluding that it is not *directed* to those concerns at all, but to the suppression of antiabortion speech. That is rather like invoking the eight missed human targets of a shooter who has killed one victim to prove, not that he is guilty of attempted mass murder, but that *he has bad aim.*

Whether the statute "restrict[s] more speech than necessary" in light of the problems that it allegedly addresses is, to be sure, relevant to the tailoring component of the First Amendment analysis (the shooter doubtless did have bad aim), but it is also relevant — powerfully relevant — to whether the law is really directed to safety and access concerns or rather to the suppression of a particular type of speech. Showing that a law that suppresses speech on a specific subject is so far-reaching that it applies even when the asserted non-speech-related problems are not present is persuasive evidence that the law is content based. In its zeal to treat abortion-related speech as a special category, the majority distorts not only the First Amendment but also the ordinary logic of probative inferences.

The structure of the Act also indicates that it rests on content-based concerns. The goals of "public safety, patient access to healthcare, and the unobstructed use of public sidewalks and roadways," are already achieved by an earlier-enacted subsection of the statute, which provides criminal penalties for "[a]ny person who knowingly obstructs, detains, hinders, impedes or blocks another person's entry to or exit from a reproductive health care facility." As the majority recognizes, that provision is easy to enforce. Thus, the speech-free zones carved out by subsection (b) add nothing to safety and access; what they achieve, and what they were obviously designed to achieve, is the suppression of speech opposing abortion.

Further contradicting the Court's fanciful defense of the Act is the fact that sub-section (b) was enacted as a more easily enforceable substitute for a prior provision. That provision did not exclude people entirely from the restricted areas around abortion clinics; rather, it forbade people in those areas to approach within six feet of another person *without that person's consent* "for the purpose of passing a leaflet or handbill to, displaying a sign to, or engaging in oral protest, education or counseling with such other person." As the majority acknowledges, that provision was "modeled on a . . . Colorado law that this Court had

upheld in *Hill*." And in that case, the Court recognized that the statute in question was directed at the suppression of unwelcome speech, vindicating what *Hill*
called "[t]he unwilling listener's interest in avoiding unwanted communication."
The Court held that interest to be content neutral.

The provision at issue here was indisputably meant to serve the same interest
in protecting citizens' supposed right to avoid speech that they would rather
not hear. For that reason, we granted a second question for review in this case
(though one would not know that from the Court's opinion, which fails to mention it): whether *Hill* should be cut back or cast aside. The majority avoids that
question by declaring the Act content neutral on other (entirely unpersuasive)
grounds. In concluding that the statute is content based and therefore subject
to strict scrutiny, I necessarily conclude that *Hill* should be overruled. Reasons
for doing so are set forth in the dissents in that case, and in the abundance of
scathing academic commentary describing how *Hill* stands in contradiction to
our First Amendment jurisprudence.[4] Protecting people from speech they do not
want to hear is not a function that the First Amendment allows the government
to undertake in the public streets and sidewalks. . . .

B.   EXEMPTION FOR ABORTION-CLINIC EMPLOYEES OR AGENTS

Petitioners contend that the Act targets speech opposing abortion (and thus
constitutes a presumptively invalid viewpoint-discriminatory restriction) for
another reason as well: It exempts "employees or agents" of an abortion clinic
"acting within the scope of their employment."

It goes without saying that "[g]ranting waivers to favored speakers (or . . .
denying them to disfavored speakers) would of course be unconstitutional."
Thomas v. Chicago Park Dist. (2002). The majority opinion . . . jumps right over
the prong that asks whether the provision "draw[s] . . . distinctions on its face,"
and instead proceeds directly to the purpose-related prong asking whether the
exemption "represent[s] a governmental attempt to give one side of a debatable
public question an advantage in expressing its views to the people," (internal
quotation marks omitted). I disagree with the majority's negative answer to that
question, but that is beside the point if the text of the statute—whatever its
purposes might have been—"license[s] one side of a debate to fight freestyle,
while requiring the other to follow Marquis of Queensberry rules." *R.A.V. v.
St. Paul* (1992).

Is there any serious doubt that *abortion-clinic employees or agents* "acting
within the scope of their employment" near clinic entrances may—indeed,
often will—speak in favor of abortion ("You are doing the right thing")? Or

---

4. *Hill* . . . is inexplicable on standard free-speech grounds[,] and . . . it is shameful the Supreme
Court would have upheld this piece of legislation on the reasoning that it gave." Constitutional Law
Symposium, Professor Michael W. McConnell's Response, 28 Pepperdine L. Rev. 747 (2001). "I
don't think [*Hill*] was a difficult case. I think it was slam-dunk simple and slam-dunk wrong." *Id.,* at
750 (remarks of Laurence Tribe). The list could go on.

speak in opposition to the message of abortion opponents — saying, for example, that "this is a safe facility" to rebut the statement that it is not? See Tr. of Oral Arg. The Court's contrary assumption is simply incredible. And the majority makes no attempt to establish the further necessary proposition that abortion-clinic employees and agents do not engage in nonspeech activities directed to the suppression of antiabortion speech by hampering the efforts of counselors to speak to prospective clients. Are we to believe that a clinic employee sent out to "escort" prospective clients into the building would not seek to prevent a counselor like Eleanor McCullen from communicating with them? He could pull a woman away from an approaching counselor, cover her ears, or make loud noises to drown out the counselor's pleas. . . .

The Court takes the peculiar view that, so long as the clinics have not specifically authorized their employees to speak in favor of abortion (or, presumably, to impede antiabortion speech), there is no viewpoint discrimination. But it is axiomatic that "where words are employed in a statute which had at the time a well-known meaning at common law or in the law of this country[,] they are presumed to have been used in that sense unless the context compels to the contrary." *Standard Oil Co. of N.J. v. United States* (1911). The phrase "scope of employment" is a well-known common-law concept that includes "[t]he range of reasonable and foreseeable activities that an employee engages in while carrying out the employer's business." Black's Law Dictionary (9th ed. 2009). The employer need not specifically direct or sanction each aspect of an employee's conduct for it to qualify. Indeed, employee conduct can qualify even if the employer specifically forbids it. In any case, it is implausible that clinics would bar escorts from engaging in the sort of activity mentioned above. Moreover, a statute that forbids one side but not the other to convey its message does not become viewpoint neutral simply because the favored side chooses voluntarily to abstain from activity that the statute permits.

There is not a shadow of a doubt that the assigned or foreseeable conduct of a clinic employee or agent can include both speaking in favor of abortion rights and countering the speech of people like petitioners. Indeed, as the majority acknowledges, the trial record includes testimony that escorts at the Boston clinic "expressed views about abortion to the women they were accompanying, thwarted petitioners' attempts to speak and hand literature to the women, and disparaged petitioners in various ways," including by calling them " 'crazy.' " What a surprise! The Web site for the Planned Parenthood League of Massachusetts (which operates the three abortion facilities where petitioners attempt to counsel women), urges readers to "Become a Clinic Escort Volunteer" in order to "provide a safe space for patients by escorting them through protestors to the health center." The dangers that the Web site attributes to "protestors" are related entirely to speech, not to safety or access. "Protestors," it reports, "hold signs, try to speak to patients entering the building, and distribute literature that can be misleading." The "safe space" provided by escorts is protection from that speech.

Going from bad to worse, the majority's opinion contends that "the record before us contains insufficient evidence to show" that abortion-facility escorts have actually spoken in favor of abortion (or, presumably, hindered antiabortion speech) while acting within the scope of their employment. Here is a brave new

First Amendment test: Speech restrictions favoring one viewpoint over another are not content based unless it can be shown that the favored viewpoint has actually been expressed. A city ordinance closing a park adjoining the Republican National Convention to all speakers except those whose remarks have been approved by the Republican National Committee is thus not subject to strict scrutiny unless it can be shown that someone has given committee-endorsed remarks. For this Court to suggest such a test is astonishing.[5]

C. CONCLUSION

In sum, the Act should be reviewed under the strict-scrutiny standard applicable to content-based legislation. That standard requires that a regulation represent "the least restrictive means" of furthering "a compelling Government interest." *United States v. Playboy Entertainment Group, Inc.* (2000) (internal quotation marks omitted). Respondents do not even attempt to argue that subsection (b) survives this test. "Suffice it to say that if protecting people from unwelcome communications"—the actual purpose of the provision—"is a compelling state interest, the First Amendment is a dead letter." *Hill* (Scalia, J., dissenting).

III. NARROW TAILORING

. . . The obvious purpose of the challenged portion of the Massachusetts Reproductive Health Care Facilities Act is to "protect" prospective clients of abortion clinics from having to hear abortion-opposing speech on public streets and sidewalks. The provision is thus unconstitutional root and branch and cannot be saved, as the majority suggests, by limiting its application to the single facility that has experienced the safety and access problems to which it is quite obviously not addressed. I concur only in the judgment that the statute is unconstitutional under the First Amendment.

JUSTICE ALITO, concurring in the judgment.

I agree that the Massachusetts statute at issue in this case violates the First Amendment. As the Court recognizes, if the Massachusetts law discriminates

---

5. The Court states that I can make this assertion "only by quoting a sentence that is explicitly limited to as-applied challenges and treating it as relevant to facial challenges." That is not so. The sentence in question appears in a paragraph immediately following rejection of the facial challenge, which begins: "It would be a very different question if it turned out that a clinic authorized escorts to speak about abortion inside the buffer zones." And the prior discussion regarding the facial challenge points to the fact that "[t]here is no suggestion in the record that any of the clinics authorize their employees to speak about abortion in the buffer zones." To be sure, the paragraph in question then goes on to concede only that the statute's constitutionality *as applied* would depend upon explicit clinic authorization. Even that seems to me wrong. Saying that voluntary action by a third party can cause an otherwise valid statute to violate the First Amendment as applied seems to me little better than saying it can cause such a statute to violate the First Amendment facially. A statute that punishes me for speaking unless *x* chooses to speak is unconstitutional facially and as applied, without reference to *x*'s action.

on the basis of viewpoint, it is unconstitutional, and I believe the law clearly discriminates on this ground. . . .

It is clear on the face of the Massachusetts law that it discriminates based on viewpoint. Speech in favor of the clinic and its work by employees and agents is permitted; speech criticizing the clinic and its work is a crime. This is blatant viewpoint discrimination. . . .

In this case, I do not think that it is possible to reach a judgment about the intent of the Massachusetts Legislature without taking into account the fact that the law that the legislature enacted blatantly discriminates based on viewpoint. In light of this feature, as well as the overbreadth that the Court identifies, it cannot be said, based on the present record, that the law would be content neutral even if the exemption for clinic employees and agents were excised. However, if the law were truly content neutral, I would agree with the Court that the law would still be unconstitutional on the ground that it burdens more speech than is necessary to serve the Commonwealth's asserted interests.

STUDY GUIDE:

- Why does the majority find that the California Reproductive Freedom, Accountability, Comprehensive Care, and Transparency Act violates the First Amendment? Does the law require the petitioners to endorse a message, or simply post a message approved by the government?
- Does *NIFLA v. Becerra* call into doubt other types of commercial regulations?
- Why does Justice Breyer's dissent compare the majority's opinion to *Lochner v. New York* (1905)? Did *Lochner* involve the First Amendment, or a liberty interest under the 14th Amendment's Due Process Clause?

National Institute of Family and Life Advocates v. Becerra
385 S. Ct. 236 (2018)

JUSTICE THOMAS delivered the opinion of the Court.

The California Reproductive Freedom, Accountability, Comprehensive Care, and Transparency Act (FACT Act) requires clinics that primarily serve pregnant women to provide certain notices. Licensed clinics must notify women that California provides free or low-cost services, including abortions, and give them a phone number to call. Unlicensed clinics must notify women that California has not licensed the clinics to provide medical services. The question in this case is whether these notice requirements violate the First Amendment.

I

A

The California State Legislature enacted the FACT Act to regulate crisis pregnancy centers. Crisis pregnancy centers — according to a report commissioned by the California State Assembly, are "pro-life (largely Christian belief-based) organizations that offer a limited range of free pregnancy options, counseling, and other services to individuals that visit a center." "[U]nfortunately," the author of the FACT Act stated, "there are nearly 200 licensed and unlicensed" crisis pregnancy centers in California. These centers "aim to discourage and prevent women from seeking abortions." The author of the FACT Act observed that crisis pregnancy centers "are commonly affiliated with, or run by organizations whose stated goal" is to oppose abortion—including "the National Institute of Family and Life Advocates," one of the petitioners here. To address this perceived problem, the FACT Act imposes two notice requirements on facilities that provide pregnancy-related services—one for licensed facilities and one for unlicensed facilities.

1

The first notice requirement applies to "licensed covered facilit[ies]." . . .

If a clinic is a licensed covered facility, the FACT Act requires it to disseminate a government-drafted notice on site. The notice states that "California has public programs that provide immediate free or low-cost access to comprehensive family planning services (including all FDA-approved methods of contraception), prenatal care, and abortion for eligible women. To determine whether you qualify, contact the county social services office at [insert the telephone number]." This notice must be posted in the waiting room, printed and distributed to all clients, or provided digitally at check-in. The notice must be in English and any additional languages identified by state law. In some counties, that means the notice must be spelled out in 13 different languages.

The stated purpose of the FACT Act, including its licensed notice requirement, is to "ensure that California residents make their personal reproductive health care decisions knowing their rights and the health care services available to them." The Legislature posited that "thousands of women remain unaware of the public programs available to provide them with contraception, health education and counseling, family planning, prenatal care, abortion, or delivery." Citing the "time sensitive" nature of pregnancy-related decisions, the Legislature concluded that requiring licensed facilities to inform patients themselves would be "[t]he most effective" way to convey this information.

2

The second notice requirement in the FACT Act applies to "unlicensed covered facilit[ies]." . . . Unlicensed covered facilities must provide a government-drafted notice stating that "[t]his facility is not licensed as a medical facility by the State of California and has no licensed medical provider who provides or directly supervises the provision of services." This notice must be provided on site and in all advertising materials. Onsite, the notice must be posted "conspicuously" at the entrance of the facility and in at least one waiting area. It must be "at least 8.5 inches by 11 inches and written in no less than 48-point type." In

advertisements, the notice must be in the same size or larger font than the surrounding text, or otherwise set off in a way that draws attention to it. Like the
licensed notice, the unlicensed notice must be in English and any additional
languages specified by state law. Its stated purpose is to ensure "that pregnant
women in California know when they are getting medical care from licensed
professionals."

B

After the Governor of California signed the FACT Act, petitioners—a
licensed pregnancy center, an unlicensed pregnancy center, and an organization
composed of crisis pregnancy centers—filed this suit. Petitioners alleged that
the licensed and unlicensed notices abridge the freedom of speech protected by
the First Amendment. The District Court denied their motion for a preliminary
injunction.

The Court of Appeals for the Ninth Circuit affirmed. After concluding that
petitioners' challenge to the FACT Act was ripe, the Ninth Circuit held that petitioners could not show a likelihood of success on the merits. It concluded that the
licensed notice survives the "lower level of scrutiny" that applies to regulations
of "professional speech." And it concluded that the unlicensed notice satisfies
any level of scrutiny.

We granted certiorari to review the Ninth Circuit's decision. We reverse with
respect to both notice requirements.

II

We first address the licensed notice.[2]

A

The First Amendment, applicable to the States through the Fourteenth
Amendment, prohibits laws that abridge the freedom of speech. When enforcing
this prohibition, our precedents distinguish between content-based and content-
neutral regulations of speech. Content-based regulations "target speech based
on its communicative content." *Reed v. Town of Gilbert* (2015). As a general
matter, such laws "are presumptively unconstitutional and may be justified only
if the government proves that they are narrowly tailored to serve compelling
state interests." This stringent standard reflects the fundamental principle that
governments have " 'no power to restrict expression because of its message, its

---

2. Petitioners raise serious concerns that both the licensed and unlicensed notices discriminate
based on viewpoint. Because the notices are unconstitutional either way, as explained below, we
need not reach that issue.

ideas, its subject matter, or its content.'" *Ibid.* (quoting *Police Dept. of Chicago v. Mosley* (1972)).

The licensed notice is a content-based regulation of speech. By compelling individuals to speak a particular message, such notices "alte[r] the content of [their] speech." *Riley v. National Federation of Blind of N. C., Inc.* (1988); accord, *Turner Broadcasting System, Inc. v. FCC* (1994); *Miami Herald Publishing Co. v. Tornillo* (1974). Here, for example, licensed clinics must provide a government-drafted script about the availability of state-sponsored services, as well as contact information for how to obtain them. One of those services is abortion—the very practice that petitioners are devoted to opposing. By requiring petitioners to inform women how they can obtain state-subsidized abortions—at the same time petitioners try to dissuade women from choosing that option—the licensed notice plainly "alters the content" of petitioners' speech. *Riley.*

B

Although the licensed notice is content based, the Ninth Circuit did not apply strict scrutiny because it concluded that the notice regulates "professional speech." Some Courts of Appeals have recognized "professional speech" as a separate category of speech that is subject to different rules. These courts define "professionals" as individuals who provide personalized services to clients and who are subject to "a generally applicable licensing and regulatory regime." "Professional speech" is then defined as any speech by these individuals that is based on "[their] expert knowledge and judgment," or that is "within the confines of [the] professional relationship." So defined, these courts except professional speech from the rule that content-based regulations of speech are subject to strict scrutiny.

But this Court has not recognized "professional speech" as a separate category of speech. Speech is not unprotected merely because it is uttered by "professionals." This Court has "been reluctant to mark off new categories of speech for diminished constitutional protection." *Denver Area Ed. Telecommunications Consortium, Inc. v. FCC* (1996) (Kennedy, J., concurring). And it has been especially reluctant to "exemp[t] a category of speech from the normal prohibition on content-based restrictions." *United States v. Alvarez* (2012). This Court's precedents do not permit governments to impose content-based restrictions on speech without "'persuasive evidence . . . of a long (if heretofore unrecognized) tradition'" to that effect. *Ibid.* (quoting *Brown v. Entertainment Merchants Assn.* (2011)).

This Court's precedents do not recognize such a tradition for a category called "professional speech." This Court has afforded less protection for professional speech in two circumstances—neither of which turned on the fact that professionals were speaking. First, our precedents have applied more deferential review to some laws that require professionals to disclose factual, noncontroversial information in their "commercial speech." See, *e.g., Zauderer v. Office of Disciplinary Counsel of Supreme Court of Ohio* (1985). Second, under our precedents, States may regulate professional conduct, even though that conduct incidentally involves speech. See, *Planned Parenthood of Southeastern Pa. v. Casey* (1992) (opinion of O'Connor, Kennedy, and Souter, JJ.). But neither line of precedents is implicated here.

1

This Court's precedents have applied a lower level of scrutiny to laws that compel disclosures in certain contexts. In *Zauderer*, for example, this Court upheld a rule requiring lawyers who advertised their services on a contingency-fee basis to disclose that clients might be required to pay some fees and costs. Noting that the disclosure requirement governed only "commercial advertising" and required the disclosure of "purely factual and uncontroversial information about the terms under which . . . services will be available," the Court explained that such requirements should be upheld unless they are "unjustified or unduly burdensome."

The *Zauderer* standard does not apply here. Most obviously, the licensed notice is not limited to "purely factual and uncontroversial information about the terms under which . . . services will be available." see also *Hurley v. Irish-American Gay, Lesbian and Bisexual Group of Boston, Inc.* (1995) (explaining that *Zauderer* does not apply outside of these circumstances). The notice in no way relates to the services that licensed clinics provide. Instead, it requires these clinics to disclose information about *state*-sponsored services — including abortion, anything but an "uncontroversial" topic. Accordingly, *Zauderer* has no application here.

2

In addition to disclosure requirements under *Zauderer*, this Court has upheld regulations of professional conduct that incidentally burden speech. "[T]he First Amendment does not prevent restrictions directed at commerce or conduct from imposing incidental burdens on speech," *Sorrell v. IMS Health Inc.* (2011), and professionals are no exception to this rule. Longstanding torts for professional malpractice, for example, "fall within the traditional purview of state regulation of professional conduct." *NAACP v. Button* (1963). While drawing the line between speech and conduct can be difficult, this Court's precedents have long drawn it.

In *Planned Parenthood of Southeastern Pa. v. Casey*, for example, this Court upheld a law requiring physicians to obtain informed consent before they could perform an abortion. Pennsylvania law required physicians to inform their patients of "the nature of the procedure, the health risks of the abortion and childbirth, and the 'probable gestational age of the unborn child.'" The law also required physicians to inform patients of the availability of printed materials from the State, which provided information about the child and various forms of assistance.

The joint opinion in *Casey* rejected a free-speech challenge to this informed-consent requirement. It described the Pennsylvania law as "a requirement that a doctor give a woman certain information as part of obtaining her consent to an abortion," which "for constitutional purposes, [was] no different from a requirement that a doctor give certain specific information about any medical procedure." The joint opinion explained that the law regulated speech only "as part of the *practice* of medicine, subject to reasonable licensing and regulation by the State." Indeed, the requirement that a doctor obtain informed consent to perform an operation is "firmly entrenched in American tort law." *Cruzan v. Director, Mo. Dept. of Health* (1990); see, e.g., *Schloendorff v. Society of N.Y. Hospital* (1914) (Cardozo, J.) (explaining that "a surgeon who performs an operation without his patient's consent commits an assault").

The licensed notice at issue here is not an informed-consent requirement or any other regulation of professional conduct. The notice does not facilitate informed consent to a medical procedure. In fact, it is not tied to a procedure at all. It applies to all interactions between a covered facility and its clients, regardless of whether a medical procedure is ever sought, offered, or performed. If a covered facility does provide medical procedures, the notice provides no information about the risks or benefits of those procedures. Tellingly, many facilities that provide the exact same services as covered facilities — such as general practice clinics, see §123471(a) — are not required to provide the licensed notice. The licensed notice regulates speech as speech.

3

Outside of the two contexts discussed above — disclosures under *Zauderer* and professional conduct — this Court's precedents have long protected the First Amendment rights of professionals. For example, this Court has applied strict scrutiny to content-based laws that regulate the noncommercial speech of lawyers, professional fundraisers, and organizations that provided specialized advice about international law. And the Court emphasized that the lawyer's statements in *Zauderer* would have been "fully protected" if they were made in a context other than advertising. Moreover, this Court has stressed the danger of content-based regulations "in the fields of medicine and public health, where information can save lives." *Sorrell.*

The dangers associated with content-based regulations of speech are also present in the context of professional speech. As with other kinds of speech, regulating the content of professionals' speech "pose[s] the inherent risk that the Government seeks not to advance a legitimate regulatory goal, but to suppress unpopular ideas or information." *Turner Broadcasting.* . . .

Further, when the government polices the content of professional speech, it can fail to " 'preserve an uninhibited marketplace of ideas in which truth will ultimately prevail.' " *McCullen v. Coakley* (2014). Professionals might have a host of good-faith disagreements, both with each other and with the government, on many topics in their respective fields. Doctors and nurses might disagree about the ethics of assisted suicide or the benefits of medical marijuana; lawyers and marriage counselors might disagree about the prudence of prenuptial agreements or the wisdom of divorce; bankers and accountants might disagree about the amount of money that should be devoted to savings or the benefits of tax reform. "[T]he best test of truth is the power of the thought to get itself accepted in the competition of the market," *Abrams v. United States* (1919) (Holmes, J., dissenting), and the people lose when the government is the one deciding which ideas should prevail.

"Professional speech" is also a difficult category to define with precision. See *Entertainment Merchants Assn.* As defined by the courts of appeals, the professional-speech doctrine would cover a wide array of individuals—doctors, lawyers, nurses, physical therapists, truck drivers, bartenders, barbers, and many others. One court of appeals has even applied it to fortune tellers. All that is required to make something a "profession," according to these courts, is that it involves personalized services and requires a professional license from the State. But that gives the States unfettered power to reduce a group's First Amendment rights by simply imposing a licensing requirement. States cannot choose the protection that speech receives under the First Amendment, as that would give them a powerful tool to impose "invidious discrimination of disfavored subjects." *Cincinnati v. Discovery Network, Inc.* (1993); see also *Riley* ("[S]tate labels cannot be dispositive of [the] degree of First Amendment protection.").

C

In sum, neither California nor the Ninth Circuit has identified a persuasive reason for treating professional speech as a unique category that is exempt from ordinary First Amendment principles. We do not foreclose the possibility that some such reason exists. We need not do so because the licensed notice cannot survive even intermediate scrutiny. California asserts a single interest to justify the licensed notice: providing low-income women with information about state-sponsored services. Assuming that this is a substantial state interest, the licensed notice is not sufficiently drawn to achieve it.

If California's goal is to educate low-income women about the services it provides, then the licensed notice is "wildly underinclusive." *Entertainment Merchants Assn.* The notice applies only to clinics that have a "primary purpose" of "providing family planning or pregnancy-related services" and that provide two of six categories of specific services. Other clinics that have another primary purpose, or that provide only one category of those services, also serve low-income women and could educate them about the State's services. According to the legislative record, California has "nearly 1,000 community clinics"—including "federally designated community health centers, migrant health centers, rural health centers, and frontier health centers"—that "serv[e] more than 5.6 million patients . . . annually through over 17 million patient encounters." But most of those clinics are excluded from the licensed notice requirement without explanation. Such "[u]nderinclusiveness raises serious doubts about whether the government is in fact pursuing the interest it invokes, rather than disfavoring a particular speaker or viewpoint." *Entertainment Merchants Assn.*

The FACT Act also excludes, without explanation, federal clinics and Family PACT providers from the licensed-notice requirement. California notes that those clinics can enroll women in California's programs themselves, but California's stated interest is informing women that these services exist in the first place. California has identified no evidence that the exempted clinics are more likely to provide this information than the covered clinics. In fact, the exempted clinics have long been able to enroll women in California's programs, but the FACT Act was premised on the notion that "thousands of women remain unaware of [them]." If the goal is to maximize women's awareness of these programs, then it would seem that California would ensure that the places that can immediately enroll women also provide this information. The FACT Act's exemption for these clinics, which serve many women who are pregnant or could become pregnant in the future, demonstrates the disconnect between its stated purpose and its actual scope. Yet "[p]recision . . . must be the touchstone" when it comes to regulations of speech, which "so closely touc[h] our most precious freedoms." *Button.*

Further, California could inform low-income women about its services "without burdening a speaker with unwanted speech." *Riley.* Most obviously, it could inform the women itself with a public-information campaign. California could even post the information on public property near crisis pregnancy centers. California argues that it has already tried an advertising campaign, and that many women who are eligible for publicly-funded healthcare have not enrolled. But California has identified no evidence to that effect. And regardless, a "tepid response" does not prove that an advertising campaign is not a sufficient alternative. *United States v. Playboy Entertainment Group, Inc.* (2000). Here, for example, individuals might not have enrolled in California's services because they do not want them, or because California spent insufficient resources on the advertising campaign. Either way, California cannot co-opt the licensed facilities to deliver its message for it. "[T]he First Amendment does not permit the State to sacrifice speech for efficiency." *Riley*; accord, *Arizona Free Enterprise Club's Freedom Club PAC v. Bennett* (2011).

In short, petitioners are likely to succeed on the merits of their challenge to the licensed notice. Contrary to the suggestion in the dissent, we do not question the legality of health and safety warnings long considered permissible, or purely factual and uncontroversial disclosures about commercial products.

III

We next address the unlicensed notice. The parties dispute whether the unlicensed notice is subject to deferential review under *Zauderer*. We need not decide whether the *Zauderer* standard applies to the unlicensed notice. Even under *Zauderer,* a disclosure requirement cannot be "unjustified or unduly burdensome." Our precedents require disclosures to remedy a harm that is "potentially real not purely hypothetical," *Ibanez v. Florida Dept. of Business and Professional Regulation, Bd. of Accountancy* (1994), and to extend "no broader than reasonably necessary," *In re R.M. J.* (1982); accord, *Virginia Bd. of Pharmacy v. Virginia Citizens Consumer Council, Inc.* (1976). Otherwise, they risk "chilling" protected speech." Importantly, California has the burden to prove that the unlicensed notice is neither unjustified nor unduly burdensome. It has not met its burden.

We need not decide what type of state interest is sufficient to sustain a disclosure requirement like the unlicensed notice. California has not demonstrated any justification for the unlicensed notice that is more than "purely hypothetical." *Ibid.* The only justification that the California Legislature put forward was ensuring that "pregnant women in California know when they are getting medical care from licensed professionals." At oral argument, however, California denied that the justification for the FACT Act was that women "go into [crisis pregnancy centers] and they don't realize what they are." Indeed, California points to nothing suggesting that pregnant women do not already know that the covered facilities are staffed by unlicensed medical professionals. The services that trigger the unlicensed notice—such as having "volunteers who collect health information from clients," "advertis[ing] . . . pregnancy options counseling," and offering over-the-counter "pregnancy testing," do not require a medical license. And California already makes it a crime for individuals without a medical license to practice medicine. At this preliminary stage of the litigation, we agree that petitioners are likely to prevail on the question whether California has proved a justification for the unlicensed notice.[4]

Even if California had presented a nonhypothetical justification for the unlicensed notice, the FACT Act unduly burdens protected speech. The unlicensed notice imposes a government-scripted, speaker-based disclosure requirement that is wholly disconnected from California's informational interest. It requires covered facilities to post California's precise notice, no matter what the facilities say on site or in their advertisements. And it covers a curiously narrow subset of speakers. While the licensed notice applies to facilities that provide "family planning" services and "contraception or contraceptive methods," the California Legislature dropped these triggering conditions for the unlicensed notice. The unlicensed notice applies only to facilities that primarily provide "pregnancy-related" services. Thus, a facility that advertises and provides pregnancy tests is covered by the unlicensed notice, but a facility across the street that advertises and provides nonprescription contraceptives is excluded—even though the latter is no less likely to make women think it is licensed. This Court's precedents are deeply skeptical of laws that "distinguis[h] among different speakers, allowing speech by some but not others." *Citizens United v. Federal Election Comm'n* (2010). Speaker-based laws run the risk that "the State has left unburdened those speakers whose messages are in accord with its own views." *Sorrell.*

---

4. Nothing in our opinion should be read to foreclose the possibility that California will gather enough evidence in later stages of this litigation.

The application of the unlicensed notice to advertisements demonstrates just how burdensome it is. The notice applies to all "print and digital advertising materials" by an unlicensed covered facility. These materials must include a government-drafted statement that "[t]his facility is not licensed as a medical facility by the State of California and has no licensed medical provider who provides or directly supervises the provision of services." An unlicensed facility must call attention to the notice, instead of its own message, by some method such as larger text or contrasting type or color. This scripted language must be posted in English and as many other languages as California chooses to require. As California conceded at oral argument, a billboard for an unlicensed facility that says "Choose Life" would have to surround that two-word statement with a 29-word statement from the government, in as many as 13 different languages. In this way, the unlicensed notice drowns out the facility's own message. More likely, the "detail required" by the unlicensed notice "effectively rules out" the possibility of having such a billboard in the first place.

For all these reasons, the unlicensed notice does not satisfy *Zauderer*, assuming that standard applies. California has offered no justification that the notice plausibly furthers. It targets speakers, not speech, and imposes an unduly burdensome disclosure requirement that will chill their protected speech. Taking all these circumstances together, we conclude that the unlicensed notice is unjustified and unduly burdensome under *Zauderer*. We express no view on the legality of a similar disclosure requirement that is better supported or less burdensome.

IV

We hold that petitioners are likely to succeed on the merits of their claim that the FACT Act violates the First Amendment. We reverse the judgment of the Court of Appeals and remand the case for further proceedings consistent with this opinion.

It is so ordered.

JUSTICE KENNEDY, with whom THE CHIEF JUSTICE, JUSTICE ALITO, and JUSTICE GORSUCH join, concurring.

I join the Court's opinion in all respects.

This separate writing seeks to underscore that the apparent viewpoint discrimination here is a matter of serious constitutional concern. The Court, in my view, is correct not to reach this question. It was not sufficiently developed, and the rationale for the Court's decision today suffices to resolve the case. And had the Court's analysis been confined to viewpoint discrimination, some legislators might have inferred that if the law were reenacted with a broader base and broader coverage it then would be upheld.

It does appear that viewpoint discrimination is inherent in the design and structure of this Act. This law is a paradigmatic example of the serious threat presented when government seeks to impose its own message in the place of individual speech, thought, and expression. For here the State requires primarily pro-life pregnancy centers to promote the State's own preferred message advertising abortions. This compels individuals to contradict their most deeply held beliefs, beliefs grounded in basic philosophical, ethical, or religious precepts, or all of these. And the history of the Act's passage and its underinclusive application suggest a real possibility that these individuals were targeted because of their beliefs.

The California Legislature included in its official history the congratulatory statement that the Act was part of California's legacy of "forward thinking." But it is not forward thinking to force individuals to "be an instrument for fostering public adherence to an ideological point of view [they] fin[d] unacceptable." *Wooley v. Maynard* (1977). It is forward thinking to begin by reading the First Amendment as ratified in 1791; to understand the history of authoritarian government as the Founders then knew it; to confirm that history since then shows how relentless authoritarian regimes are in their attempts to stifle free speech; and to carry those lessons onward as we seek to preserve and teach the necessity of freedom of speech for the generations to come. Governments must not be allowed to force persons to express a message contrary to their deepest convictions. Freedom of speech secures freedom of thought and belief. This law imperils those liberties.

JUSTICE BREYER, with whom JUSTICE GINSBURG, JUSTICE SOTOMAYOR, and JUSTICE KAGAN join, dissenting.

The petitioners ask us to consider whether two sections of a California statute violate the First Amendment. The first section requires licensed medical facilities (that provide women with assistance involving pregnancy or family planning) to tell those women where they might obtain help, including financial help, with comprehensive family planning services, prenatal care, and abortion. The second requires *un*licensed facilities offering somewhat similar services to make clear that they are unlicensed. In my view both statutory sections are likely constitutional, and I dissent from the Court's contrary conclusions.

I

A

... Before turning to the specific law before us, I focus upon the general interpretation of the First Amendment that the majority says it applies. It applies heightened scrutiny to the Act because the Act, in its view, is "content based." "By compelling individuals to speak a particular message," it adds, "such notices 'alte[r] the content of [their] speech.'" "As a general matter," the majority concludes, such laws are "presumptively unconstitutional" and are subject to "stringent" review.

The majority recognizes exceptions to this general rule: It excepts laws that "require professionals to disclose factual, noncontroversial information in their 'commercial speech,'" *provided that* the disclosure "relates to the services that [the regulated entities] provide." It also excepts laws that "regulate professional conduct" *and* only "incidentally burden speech."

This constitutional approach threatens to create serious problems. Because much, perhaps most, human behavior takes place through speech and because much, perhaps most, law regulates that speech in terms of its content, the majority's approach at the least threatens considerable litigation over the constitutional validity of much, perhaps most, government regulation. Virtually every disclosure law could be considered "content based," for virtually every disclosure law requires individuals "to speak a particular message." See *Reed v. Town of Gilbert* (2015) (Breyer, J., concurring in judgment) (listing regulations that inevitably involve content discrimination, ranging from securities disclosures to signs at petting zoos). Thus, the majority's view, if taken literally, could radically change prior law, perhaps placing much securities law or consumer protection law at constitutional risk, depending on how broadly its exceptions are interpreted. . . .

The majority, at the end of Part II of its opinion, perhaps recognizing this problem, adds a general disclaimer. It says that it does not "question the legality of health and safety warnings long considered permissible, or purely factual and uncontroversial disclosures about commercial products." But this generally phrased disclaimer would seem more likely to invite litigation than to provide needed limitation and clarification. The majority, for example, does not explain why the Act here, which is justified in part by health and safety considerations, does not fall within its "health" category . . . see also *Planned Parenthood of Southeastern Pa. v. Casey* (1992) (joint opinion of O'Connor, Kennedy, and Souter, JJ.) (reasoning that disclosures related to fetal development and childbirth are related to the health of a woman seeking an abortion). Nor does the majority opinion offer any reasoned basis that might help apply its disclaimer for distinguishing lawful from unlawful disclosures. In the absence of a reasoned explanation of the disclaimer's meaning and rationale, the disclaimer is unlikely to withdraw the invitation to litigation that the majority's general broad "content-based" test issues. That test invites courts around the Nation to apply an unpredictable First Amendment to ordinary social and economic regulation, striking down disclosure laws that judges may disfavor, while upholding others, all without grounding their decisions in reasoned principle.

Notably, the majority says nothing about limiting its language to the kind of instance where the Court has traditionally found the First Amendment wary of content-based laws, namely, in cases of viewpoint discrimination. "Content-based laws merit this protection because they present, albeit sometimes in a subtler form, the same dangers as laws that regulate speech based on viewpoint." *Reed* (Alito, J., concurring). Accordingly, "[l]imiting speech based on its 'topic' or 'subject'" can favor "those who do not want to disturb the status quo." But the mine run of disclosure requirements do nothing of that sort. They simply alert the public about child seat belt laws, the location of stairways, and the process to have their garbage collected, among other things.

Precedent does not require a test such as the majority's. Rather, in saying the Act is not a longstanding health and safety law, the Court substitutes its own approach — without a defining standard — for an approach that was reasonably clear. Historically, the Court has been wary of claims that regulation of business activity, particularly health-related activity, violates the Constitution. Ever since this Court departed from the approach it set forth in *Lochner v. New York* (1905), ordinary economic and social legislation has been thought to raise little constitutional concern. As Justice Brandeis wrote, typically this Court's function in such cases "is only to determine the reasonableness of the Legislature's belief in the existence of evils and in the effectiveness of the remedy provided." *New State Ice Co. v. Liebmann* (1932) (dissenting opinion); see *Williamson v. Lee Optical of Okla., Inc.* (1955) (adopting the approach of Justice Brandeis).

The Court has taken this same respectful approach to economic and social legislation when a First Amendment claim like the claim present here is at issue. See, *e.g., Zauderer v. Office of Disciplinary Counsel of Supreme Court of Ohio* (1985) (upholding reasonable disclosure requirements for attorneys); cf. *Central Hudson Gas & Elec. Corp. v. Public Serv. Comm'n of N. Y.* (1980) (applying intermediate scrutiny to other restrictions on commercial speech); *In re R.M. J.,* (1982) (no First Amendment protection for misleading or deceptive commercial speech). But see *Sorrell v. IMS Health Inc.* (2011) (striking down regulation of pharmaceutical drug-related information).

Even during the *Lochner* era, when this Court struck down numerous economic regulations concerning industry, this Court was careful to defer to state legislative judgments concerning the medical profession. The Court took the view that a State may condition the practice of medicine on any number of requirements, and physicians, in exchange for following those reasonable requirements, could receive a license to practice medicine from the State. Medical professionals do not, generally speaking, have a right to use the Constitution as a weapon allowing them rigorously to control the content of those reasonable conditions. In the name of the First Amendment, the majority today treads into territory where the pre-New Deal, as well as the post-New Deal, Court refused to go.

The Court, in justification, refers to widely accepted First Amendment goals, such as the need to protect the Nation from laws that " 'suppress unpopular ideas or information'" or inhibit the " 'marketplace of ideas in which truth will ultimately prevail.'" *New York Times Co. v. Sullivan* (1964). The concurrence highlights similar First Amendment interests. I, too, value this role that the First Amendment plays—in an appropriate case. But here, the majority enunciates a general test that reaches far beyond the area where this Court has examined laws closely in the service of those goals. And, in suggesting that heightened scrutiny applies to much economic and social legislation, the majority pays those First Amendment goals a serious disservice through dilution. Using the First Amendment to strike down economic and social laws that legislatures long would have thought themselves free to enact will, for the American public, obscure, not clarify, the true value of protecting freedom of speech.

B

Still, what about this specific case? The disclosure at issue here concerns speech related to abortion. It involves health, differing moral values, and differing points of view. Thus, rather than set forth broad, new, First Amendment principles, I believe that we should focus more directly upon precedent more closely related to the case at hand. This Court has more than once considered disclosure laws relating to reproductive health. Though those rules or holdings have changed over time, they should govern our disposition of this case. . . .

In *Planned Parenthood of Southeastern Pa. v. Casey* (1992), the Court . . . considered a state law that required doctors to provide information to a woman deciding whether to proceed with an abortion. That law required the doctor to tell the woman about the nature of the abortion procedure, the health risks of abortion and of childbirth, the " 'probable gestational age of the unborn child,'" and the availability of printed materials describing the fetus, medical assistance for childbirth, potential child support, and the agencies that would provide adoption services (or other alternatives to abortion).

This time a joint opinion of the Court, in judging whether the State could impose these informational requirements, asked whether doing so imposed an "undue burden" upon women seeking an abortion. *Casey.* It held that it did not. Hence the statute was constitutional. The joint opinion stated that the statutory requirements amounted to "reasonable measure[s] to ensure an informed choice, one which might cause the woman to choose childbirth over abortion." . . .

Thus, the Court considered the State's statutory requirements, including the requirement that the doctor must inform his patient about where she could learn how to have the newborn child adopted (if carried to term) and how she could find related financial assistance. To repeat the point, the Court then held that the State's requirements did *not* violate either the Constitution's protection of free speech or its protection of a woman's right to choose to have an abortion.

C

. . . If a State can lawfully require a doctor to tell a woman seeking an abortion about adoption services, why should it not be able, as here, to require a medical counselor to tell a woman seeking prenatal care or other reproductive healthcare about childbirth and abortion services? As the question suggests, there is no convincing reason to distinguish between information about adoption and information about abortion in this context. After all, the rule of law embodies even-handedness, and "what is sauce for the goose is normally sauce for the gander." *Heffernan v. City of Paterson* (2016).

1

The majority tries to distinguish *Casey* as concerning a regulation of professional conduct that only incidentally burdened speech. *Casey,* in its view, applies only when obtaining "informed consent" to a medical procedure is directly at issue.

This distinction, however, lacks moral, practical, and legal force. The individuals at issue here are all medical personnel engaging in activities that directly affect a woman's health—not significantly different from the doctors at issue in *Casey.* . . .

The Act requires these medical professionals to disclose information about the possibility of abortion (including potential financial help) that is as likely helpful to granting "informed consent" as is information about the possibility of adoption and childbirth (including potential financial help). That is why I find it impossible to drive any meaningful legal wedge between the law, as interpreted in *Casey,* and the law as it should be applied in this case. If the law in *Casey* regulated speech "only 'as part of the *practice* of medicine,'" so too here.

The majority contends that the disclosure here is unrelated to a "medical procedure," unlike that in *Casey,* and so the State has no reason to inform a woman about alternatives to childbirth (or, presumably, the health risks of childbirth). Really? No one doubts that choosing an abortion is a medical procedure that involves certain health risks. See *Whole Woman's Health v. Hellerstedt* (2016) (identifying the mortality rate in Texas as 1 in 120,000 to 144,000 abortions). But the same is true of carrying a child to term and giving birth. That is why prenatal care often involves testing for anemia, infections, measles, chicken pox, genetic disorders, diabetes, pneumonia, urinary tract infections, preeclampsia, and hosts of other medical conditions. Childbirth itself, directly or through pain management, risks harms of various kinds, some connected with caesarean or surgery-related deliveries, some related to more ordinary methods of delivery. Indeed, nationwide "childbirth is 14 times more likely than abortion to result in" the woman's death. Health considerations do not favor disclosure of alternatives and risks associated with the latter but not those associated with the former. . . .

The majority also finds it "[t]ellin[g]" that general practice clinics — *i.e.,* paid clinics — are not required to provide the licensed notice. But the lack-of-information problem that the statute seeks to ameliorate is a problem that the State explains is commonly found among low-income women. That those with low income might lack the time to become fully informed and that this circumstance might prove disproportionately correlated with income is not intuitively surprising. Nor is it surprising that those with low income, whatever they choose in respect to pregnancy, might find information about financial assistance particularly useful. There is "nothing inherently suspect" about this distinction, *McCullen v. Coakley* (2014), which is not "based on the content of [the advocacy] each group offers," *Turner Broadcasting System, Inc. v. FCC* (1994), but upon the patients the group generally serves and the needs of that population.

2

Separately, finding no First Amendment infirmity in the licensed notice is consistent with earlier Court rulings. For instance, in *Zauderer* we upheld a requirement that attorneys disclose in their advertisements that clients might be liable for significant litigation costs even if their lawsuits were unsuccessful. We refused to apply heightened scrutiny, instead asking whether the disclosure requirements were "reasonably related to the State's interest in preventing deception of consumers." . . . Where a State's requirement to speak "purely factual and uncontroversial information" does not attempt "to 'prescribe what shall be orthodox in politics, nationalism, religion, or other matters of opinion or force citizens to confess by word or act their faith therein,'" it does not warrant heightened scrutiny. *West Virginia Bd. of Ed. v. Barnette,* (1943). . . .

Abortion is a controversial topic and a source of normative debate, but the availability of state resources is not a normative statement or a fact of debatable truth. The disclosure includes information about resources available should a woman seek to continue her pregnancy or terminate it, and it expresses no official preference for one choice over the other. Similarly, the majority highlights an interest that often underlies our decisions in respect to speech prohibitions — the marketplace of ideas. But that marketplace is fostered, not hindered, by providing information to patients to enable them to make fully informed medical decisions in respect to their pregnancies.

Of course, one might take the majority's decision to mean that speech about abortion is special, that it involves in this case not only professional medical matters, but also views based on deeply held religious and moral beliefs about the nature of the practice. To that extent, arguably, the speech here is different from that at issue in *Zauderer.* But assuming that is so, the law's insistence upon treating like cases alike should lead us to reject the petitioners' arguments that I have discussed. This insistence, the need for evenhandedness, should prove particularly weighty in a case involving abortion rights. That is because Americans hold strong, and differing, views about the matter. Some Americans believe that abortion involves the death of a live and innocent human being. Others believe that the ability to choose an abortion is "central to personal dignity and autonomy," *Casey,* and note that the failure to allow women to choose an abortion involves the deaths of innocent women. We have previously noted that we cannot try to adjudicate who is right and who is wrong in this moral debate. But we can do our best to interpret American constitutional law so that it applies fairly within a Nation whose citizens strongly hold these different points of view. That is one reason why it is particularly important to interpret the First Amendment so that it applies evenhandedly as between those who disagree so strongly. For this reason too a Constitution that allows States to insist that medical providers tell women about the possibility of adoption should also allow States similarly to insist that medical providers tell women about the possibility of abortion.

D

It is particularly unfortunate that the majority, through application of so broad and obscure a standard, declines to reach remaining arguments that the Act discriminates on the basis of viewpoint. The petitioners argue that it unconstitutionally discriminates on the basis of viewpoint because it primarily covers facilities with supporters, organizers, and employees who are likely to hold strong pro-life views. They contend that the statute does not cover facilities likely to hold neutral or pro-choice views, because it exempts facilities that enroll patients in publicly funded programs that include abortion. In doing so, they say, the statute unnecessarily imposes a disproportionate burden upon facilities with pro-life views, the very facilities most likely to find the statute's references to abortion morally abhorrent.

The problem with this argument lies in the record. Numerous *amicus* briefs advance the argument. Some add that women who use facilities that are exempt from the statute's requirements (because they enroll patients in two California state-run medical programs that provide abortions) may still need the information provided by the disclosure, Brief for Cato Institute as *Amicus Curiae*, a point the majority adopts in concluding that the Act is underinclusive. But the key question is whether these exempt clinics are significantly more likely than are the pro-life clinics to tell or to have told their pregnant patients about the existence of these programs—in the absence of any statutory compulsion. If so, it may make sense—in terms of the statute's informational objective—to exempt them, namely if there is no need to cover them. But, if there are not good reasons to exempt these clinics from coverage, *i.e.,* if, for example, they too frequently do not tell their patients about the availability of abortion services, the petitioners' claim of viewpoint discrimination becomes much stronger.

The petitioners, however, did not develop this point in the record below. They simply stated in their complaint that the Act exempts "facilities which provide abortion services, freeing them from the Act's disclosure requirements, while leaving pro-life facilities subject to them." And in the District Court they relied solely on the allegations of their complaint, provided no supporting declarations, and contended that discovery was unnecessary. The District Court concluded that the reason for the Act's exemptions was that those clinics "provide the entire spectrum of services required of the notice," and that absent discovery, "there is no evidence to suggest the Act burdens only" pro-life conduct. Similarly, the petitioners pressed the claim in the Court of Appeals. But they did not supplement the record. Consequently, that court reached the same conclusion. Given the absence of evidence in the record before the lower courts, the "viewpoint discrimination" claim could not justify the issuance of a preliminary injunction.

II

The second statutory provision covers pregnancy-related facilities that provide women with certain medical-type services (such as obstetric ultrasounds or sonograms, pregnancy diagnosis, counseling about pregnancy options, or prenatal care), are not licensed as medical facilities by the State, and do not have a licensed medical provider on site. The statute says that such a facility must disclose that it is not "licensed as a medical facility." And it must make this disclosure in a posted notice and in advertising. *Ibid.*

The majority does not question that the State's interest (ensuring that "pregnant women in California know when they are getting medical care from licensed professionals") is the type of informational interest that *Zauderer* encompasses. . . . Nevertheless, the majority concludes that the State's interest is "purely hypothetical" because unlicensed clinics provide innocuous services that do not require a medical license. To do so, it applies a searching standard of review based on our precedents that deal with speech *restrictions,* not *disclosures.* This approach is incompatible with *Zauderer.*

There is no basis for finding the State's interest "hypothetical." The legislature heard that information-related delays in qualified healthcare negatively affect women seeking to terminate their pregnancies as well as women carrying their pregnancies to term, with delays in qualified prenatal care causing life-long health problems for infants. Even without such testimony, it is "self-evident" that patients might think they are receiving qualified medical care when they enter facilities that collect health information, perform obstetric ultrasounds or sonograms, diagnose pregnancy, and provide counseling about pregnancy options or other prenatal care. *Milavetz.* The State's conclusion to that effect is certainly reasonable. . . .

Relatedly, the majority suggests that the Act is suspect because it covers some speakers but not others. I agree that a law's exemptions can reveal viewpoint discrimination (although the majority does not reach this point). "[A]n exemption from an otherwise permissible regulation of speech may represent a governmental attempt to give one side of a debatable public question an advantage in expressing its views to the people." *McCullen.* Such speaker-based laws warrant heightened scrutiny "when they reflect the Government's preference for the substance of what the favored speakers have to say (or aversion to what the disfavored speakers have to say)." *Turner Broadcasting System, Inc.* Accordingly, where a law's exemptions "facilitate speech on only one side of the abortion debate," there is a "clear form of viewpoint discrimination." *McCullen.*

There is no cause for such concern here. The Act does not, on its face, distinguish between facilities that favor pro-life and those that favor pro-choice points of view. Nor is there any convincing evidence before us or in the courts below that discrimination was the purpose or the effect of the statute. Notably, California does not single out pregnancy-related facilities for this type of disclosure requirement. And it is unremarkable that the State excluded the provision of family planning and contraceptive services as triggering conditions. After all, the State was seeking to ensure that "pregnant women in California know when they are getting medical care from licensed professionals," and pregnant women generally do not need contraceptive services. . . .

For these reasons I would not hold the California statute unconstitutional on its face, I would not require the District Court to issue a preliminary injunction forbidding its enforcement, and I respectfully dissent from the majority's contrary conclusions.

STUDY GUIDE:

- What is the difference between a "content-based" and a "viewpoint-based" restriction on speech?
- What makes a trademark "scandalous"?
- Why did Justice Sotomayor apply a "narrowing" construction to the Lanham Act? Why did the majority opinion not applying such a saving construction?

Iancu v. Brunetti
588 U.S. ___ (2019)

Justice Kagan delivered the opinion of the Court.

Two terms ago, in *Matal v. Tam* (2017), this Court invalidated the Lanham Act's bar on the registration of "disparag[ing]" trademarks. Although split between two non-majority opinions, all Members of the Court agreed that the provision violated the First Amendment because it discriminated on the basis of viewpoint. Today we consider a First Amendment challenge to a neighboring provision of the Act, prohibiting the registration of "immoral[] or scandalous" trademarks. We hold that this provision infringes the First Amendment for the same reason: It too disfavors certain ideas.

I

Respondent Erik Brunetti is an artist and entrepreneur who founded a clothing line that uses the trademark FUCT. According to Brunetti, the mark (which functions as the clothing's brand name) is pronounced as four letters, one after the other: F-U-C-T. But you might read it differently and, if so, you would hardly be alone. See Tr. of Oral Arg. 5 (describing the brand name as "the equivalent of [the] past participle form of a well-known word of profanity"). That common perception caused difficulties for Brunetti when he tried to register his mark with the U. S. Patent and Trademark Office (PTO).

Under the Lanham Act, the PTO administers a federal registration system for trademarks. Registration of a mark is not mandatory. The owner of an unregistered mark may still use it in commerce and enforce it against infringers. But registration gives trademark owners valuable benefits. For example, registration constitutes "prima facie evidence" of the mark's validity. . . . [T]he Act directs the PTO to "refuse[] registration" of certain marks. For instance, the PTO cannot register a mark that "so resembles" another mark as to create a likelihood of confusion. . . . There are five or ten more (depending on how you count). And until we invalidated the criterion two years ago, the PTO could not register a mark that "disparage[d]" a "person[], living or dead."

This case involves another of the Lanham Act's prohibitions on registration — one applying to marks that "[c]onsist[] of or comprise[] immoral[] or scandalous matter." The PTO applies that bar as a "unitary provision," rather than treating the two adjectives in it separately. To determine whether a mark fits in the category, the PTO asks whether a "substantial composite of the general public" would find the mark "shocking to the sense of truth, decency, or propriety"; "giving offense to the conscience or moral feelings"; "calling out for condemnation"; "disgraceful"; "offensive"; "disreputable"; or "vulgar."

Both a PTO examining attorney and the PTO's Trademark Trial and Appeal Board decided that Brunetti's mark flunked that test. The attorney determined that FUCT was "a total vulgar" and "therefore[] unregistrable." App. 27-28. On review, the Board stated that the mark was "highly offensive" and "vulgar," and that it had "decidedly negative sexual connotations." As part of its review, the

Board also considered evidence of how Brunetti used the mark. It found that Brunetti's website and products contained imagery, near the mark, of "extreme nihilism" and "anti-social" behavior. In that context, the Board thought, the mark communicated "misogyny, depravity, [and] violence." The Board concluded: "Whether one considers [the mark] as a sexual term, or finds that [Brunetti] has used [the mark] in the context of extreme misogyny, nihilism or violence, we have no question but that [the term is] extremely offensive."

Brunetti then brought a facial challenge to the "immoral or scandalous" bar in the Court of Appeals for the Federal Circuit. That court found the prohibition to violate the First Amendment. As usual when a lower court has invalidated a federal statute, we granted certiorari.

II

This Court first considered a First Amendment challenge to a trademark registration restriction in *Tam*, just two Terms ago. There, the Court declared unconstitutional the Lanham Act's ban on registering marks that "disparage" any "person[], living or dead." §1052(a). The eight-Justice Court divided evenly between two opinions and could not agree on the overall framework for deciding the case. (In particular, no majority emerged to resolve whether a Lanham Act bar is a condition on a government benefit or a simple restriction on speech.) But all the Justices agreed on two propositions. First, if a trademark registration bar is viewpoint-based, it is unconstitutional. And second, the disparagement bar was viewpoint-based.

The Justices thus found common ground in a core postulate of free speech law: The government may not discriminate against speech based on the ideas or opinions it conveys. See *Rosenberger v. Rector and Visitors of Univ. of Va* (1995) (explaining that viewpoint discrimination is an "egregious form of content discrimination" and is "presumptively unconstitutional"). In Justice Kennedy's explanation, the disparagement bar allowed a trademark owner to register a mark if it was "positive" about a person, but not if it was "derogatory." That was the "essence of viewpoint discrimination," he continued, because "[t]he law thus reflects the Government's disapproval of a subset of messages it finds offensive." Justice Alito emphasized that the statute "denie[d] registration to any mark" whose disparaging message was "offensive to a substantial percentage of the members of any group." The bar thus violated the "bedrock First Amendment principle" that the government cannot discriminate against "ideas that offend." Slightly different explanations, then, but a shared conclusion: Viewpoint discrimination doomed the disparagement bar.

If the "immoral or scandalous" bar similarly discriminates on the basis of viewpoint, it must also collide with our First Amendment doctrine. The Government does not argue otherwise. In briefs and oral argument, the Government offers a theory for upholding the bar if it is viewpoint-neutral (essentially, that the bar would then be a reasonable condition on a government benefit). But the Government agrees that under *Tam* it may not "deny registration based on the views expressed" by a mark. "As the Court's *Tam* decision establishes," the

Government says, "the criteria for federal trademark registration" must be "viewpoint-neutral to survive Free Speech Clause review." So the key question becomes: Is the "immoral or scandalous" criterion in the Lanham Act viewpoint-neutral or viewpoint-based?

It is viewpoint-based. The meanings of "immoral" and "scandalous" are not mysterious, but resort to some dictionaries still helps to lay bare the problem. When is expressive material "immoral"? According to a standard definition, when it is "inconsistent with rectitude, purity, or good morals"; "wicked"; or "vicious." Or again, when it is "opposed to or violating morality"; or "morally evil." So the Lanham Act permits registration of marks that champion society's sense of rectitude and morality, but not marks that denigrate those concepts. And when is such material "scandalous"? Says a typical definition, when it "giv[es] offense to the conscience or moral feelings"; "excite[s] reprobation"; or "call[s] out condemnation." Or again, when it is "shocking to the sense of truth, decency, or propriety"; "disgraceful"; "offensive"; or "disreputable." So the Lanham Act allows registration of marks when their messages accord with, but not when their messages defy, society's sense of decency or propriety. Put the pair of overlapping terms together and the statute, on its face, distinguishes between two opposed sets of ideas: those aligned with conventional moral standards and those hostile to them; those inducing societal nods of approval and those provoking offense and condemnation. The statute favors the former, and disfavors the latter. "Love rules"? "Always be good"? Registration follows. "Hate rules"? "Always be cruel"? Not according to the Lanham Act's "immoral or scandalous" bar.

The facial viewpoint bias in the law results in viewpoint-discriminatory application. Recall that the PTO itself describes the "immoral or scandalous" criterion using much the same language as in the dictionary definitions recited above. The PTO, for example, asks whether the public would view the mark as "shocking to the sense of truth, decency, or propriety"; "calling out for condemnation"; "offensive"; or "disreputable." Using those guideposts, the PTO has refused to register marks communicating "immoral" or "scandalous" views about (among other things) drug use, religion, and terrorism. But all the while, it has approved registration of marks expressing more accepted views on the same topics.

Here are some samples. The PTO rejected marks conveying approval of drug use (YOU CAN'T SPELL HEALTHCARE WITHOUT THC for pain-relief medication, MARIJUANA COLA and KO KANE for beverages) because it is scandalous to "inappropriately glamoriz[e] drug abuse." But at the same time, the PTO registered marks with such sayings as D.A.R.E. TO RESIST DRUGS AND VIOLENCE and SAY NO TO DRUGS—REALITY IS THE BEST TRIP IN LIFE. Similarly, the PTO disapproved registration for the mark BONG HITS 4 JESUS because it "suggests that people should engage in an illegal activity [in connection with] worship" and because "Christians would be morally outraged by a statement that connects Jesus Christ with illegal drug use."* And the

---

* [*Morse v. Frederick* (2007) held that a student could be punished for displaying a banner with the message "Bong Hits 4 Jesus" at a school-supervised event.—Eds.]

PTO refused to register trademarks associating religious references with products (AGNUS DEI for safes and MADONNA for wine) because they would be "offensive to most individuals of the Christian faith" and "shocking to the sense of propriety." But once again, the PTO approved marks—PRAISE THE LORD for a game and JESUS DIED FOR YOU on clothing—whose message suggested religious faith rather than blasphemy or irreverence. Finally, the PTO rejected marks reflecting support for al-Qaeda (BABY AL QAEDA and AL-QAEDA on t-shirts) "because the bombing of civilians and other terrorist acts are shocking to the sense of decency and call out for condemnation." Yet it approved registration of a mark with the words WAR ON TERROR MEMORIAL. Of course, all these decisions are understandable. The rejected marks express opinions that are, at the least, offensive to many Americans. But as the Court made clear in *Tam*, a law disfavoring "ideas that offend" discriminates based on viewpoint, in violation of the First Amendment.

How, then, can the Government claim that the "immoral or scandalous" bar is viewpoint-neutral? The Government basically asks us to treat decisions like those described above as PTO examiners' mistakes. Still more, the Government tells us to ignore how the Lanham Act's language, on its face, disfavors some ideas. In urging that course, the Government does not dispute that the statutory language—and words used to define it—have just that effect. At oral argument, the Government conceded: "[I]f you just looked at the words like 'shocking' and 'offensive' on their face and gave them their ordinary meanings[,] they could easily encompass material that was shocking [or offensive] because it expressed an outrageous point of view or a point of view that most members" of society reject. But no matter, says the Government, because the statute is "susceptible of" a limiting construction that would remove this viewpoint bias. The Government's idea, abstractly phrased, is to narrow the statutory bar to "marks that are offensive [or] shocking to a substantial segment of the public because of their *mode* of expression, independent of any views that they may express." More concretely, the Government explains that this reinterpretation would mostly restrict the PTO to refusing marks that are "vulgar"—meaning "lewd," "sexually explicit or profane." Such a reconfigured bar, the Government says, would not turn on viewpoint, and so we could uphold it.

But we cannot accept the Government's proposal, because the statute says something markedly different. This Court, of course, may interpret "ambiguous statutory language" to "avoid serious constitutional doubts." *FCC v. Fox Television Stations, Inc.* (2009). But that canon of construction applies only when ambiguity exists. "We will not rewrite a law to conform it to constitutional requirements." *United States v. Stevens* (2010). So even assuming the Government's reading would eliminate First Amendment problems, we may adopt it only if we can see it in the statutory language. And we cannot. The "immoral or scandalous" bar stretches far beyond the Government's proposed construction. The statute as written does not draw the line at lewd, sexually explicit, or profane marks. Nor does it refer only to marks whose "mode of expression," independent of viewpoint, is particularly offensive. It covers the universe of immoral or scandalous — or (to use some PTO synonyms) offensive or disreputable — material. Whether or not lewd or profane. Whether the scandal and immorality comes from mode or instead from viewpoint. To cut the statute off where the Government urges is not to interpret the statute Congress enacted, but to fashion a new one.*

And once the "immoral or scandalous" bar is interpreted fairly, it must be invalidated. The Government just barely argues otherwise. In the last paragraph of its brief, the Government gestures toward the idea that the provision is salvageable by virtue of its constitutionally permissible applications (in the Government's view, its applications to lewd, sexually explicit, or profane marks). In other words, the Government invokes our First Amendment overbreadth doctrine, and asks us to uphold the statute against facial attack because its unconstitutional applications are not "substantial" relative to "the statute's plainly legitimate sweep." But to begin with, this Court has never applied that kind of analysis to a viewpoint-discriminatory law. In *Tam*, for example, we did not pause to consider whether the disparagement clause might admit some permissible applications (say, to certain libelous speech) before striking it down. The Court's finding of viewpoint bias ended the matter. And similarly, it seems unlikely we would compare permissible and impermissible applications if Congress outright banned "offensive" (or to use some other examples, "divisive" or "subversive") speech. Once we have found that a law "aim[s] at the suppression of" views, why would it matter that Congress could have captured some of the same speech through a viewpoint-neutral statute? But in any event, the "immoral or scandalous" bar is substantially overbroad. There are a great many immoral and scandalous ideas in the world (even more than there are swearwords), and the Lanham Act covers them all. It therefore violates the First Amendment.

JUSTICE ALITO, concurring.

For the reasons explained in the opinion of the Court, the provision of the Lanham Act at issue in this case violates the Free Speech Clause of the First Amendment because it discriminates on the basis of viewpoint and cannot be fixed without rewriting the statute. Viewpoint discrimination is poison to a free society. But in many countries with constitutions or legal traditions that claim to protect freedom of speech, serious viewpoint discrimination is now tolerated, and such discrimination has become increasingly prevalent in this country. At a

---

* We reject the dissent's statutory surgery for the same reason. Although conceding that the term "immoral" cannot be saved, the dissent thinks that the term "scandalous" can be read as the Government proposes. But that term is not "ambiguous," as the dissent argues; it is just broad. Remember that the dictionaries define it to mean offensive, disreputable, exciting reprobation, and so forth. Even if hived off from "immoral" marks, the category of scandalous marks thus includes *both* marks that offend by the ideas they convey *and* marks that offend by their mode of expression. And its coverage of the former means that it discriminates based on viewpoint. We say nothing at all about a statute that covers only the latter — or, in the Government's more concrete description, a statute limited to lewd, sexually explicit, and profane marks. Nor do we say anything about how to evaluate viewpoint-neutral restrictions on trademark registration, because the "scandalous" bar (whether or not attached to the "immoral" bar) is not one.

time when free speech is under attack, it is especially important for this Court to remain firm on the principle that the First Amendment does not tolerate viewpoint discrimination. We reaffirm that principle today.

Our decision is not based on moral relativism but on the recognition that a law banning speech deemed by government officials to be "immoral" or "scandalous" can easily be exploited for illegitimate ends. Our decision does not prevent Congress from adopting a more carefully focused statute that precludes the registration of marks containing vulgar terms that play no real part in the expression of ideas. The particular mark in question in this case could be denied registration under such a statute. The term suggested by that mark is not needed to express any idea and, in fact, as commonly used today, generally signifies nothing except emotion and a severely limited vocabulary. The registration of such marks serves only to further coarsen our popular culture. But we are not legislators and cannot substitute a new statute for the one now in force.

CHIEF JUSTICE ROBERTS, concurring in part and dissenting in part. . . .

I agree with the majority that the "immoral" portion of the provision is not susceptible of a narrowing construction that would eliminate its viewpoint bias. As Justice Sotomayor explains, however, the "scandalous" portion of the provision is susceptible of such a narrowing construction. Standing alone, the term "scandalous" need not be understood to reach marks that offend because of the ideas they convey; it can be read more narrowly to bar only marks that offend because of their mode of expression—marks that are obscene, vulgar, or profane. That is how the PTO now understands the term, in light of our decision in *Matal v. Tam* (2017). I agree with Justice Sotomayor that such a narrowing construction is appropriate in this context.

I also agree that, regardless of how exactly the trademark registration system is best conceived under our precedents—a question we left open in *Tam*—refusing registration to obscene, vulgar, or profane marks does not offend the First Amendment. Whether such marks can be registered does not affect the extent to which their owners may use them in commerce to identify goods. No speech is being restricted; no one is being punished. The owners of such marks are merely denied certain additional benefits associated with federal trademark registration. The Government, meanwhile, has an interest in not associating itself with trademarks whose content is obscene, vulgar, or profane. The First Amendment protects the freedom of speech; it does not require the Government to give aid and comfort to those using obscene, vulgar, and profane modes of expression. For those reasons, I concur in part and dissent in part.

JUSTICE BREYER, concurring in part and dissenting in part.

Our precedents warn us against interpreting statutes in ways that would likely render them unconstitutional. . . . Following these precedents, I agree with Justice Sotomayor that, for the reasons she gives, we should interpret the word "scandalous" in the present statute to refer only to certain highly "vulgar" or "obscene" modes of expression.

The question, then, is whether the First Amendment permits the Government to rely on this statute, as narrowly construed, to deny the benefits of federal trademark registration to marks like the one at issue here, which involves the use of the term "FUCT" in connection with a clothing line that includes apparel for children and infants. Like Justice Sotomayor, I believe the answer is "yes," though my reasons differ slightly from hers.

I

In my view, a category-based approach to the First Amendment cannot adequately resolve the problem before us. I would place less emphasis on trying to decide whether the statute at issue should be categorized as an example of "viewpoint discrimination," "content discrimination," "commercial speech," "government speech," or the like. Rather, as I have written before, I believe we would do better to treat this Court's speech-related categories not as outcome-determinative rules, but instead as rules of thumb. See *Reed v. Town of Gilbert* (2015) (Breyer, J., concurring). . . .

This case illustrates the limits of relying on rigid First Amendment categories, for the statute at issue does not fit easily into any of these categories. . . . Rather than puzzling over categorization, I believe we should focus on the interests the First Amendment protects and ask a more basic proportionality question: Does "the regulation at issue wor[k] harm to First Amendment interests that is disproportionate in light of the relevant regulatory objectives"? *Reed* (opinion of Breyer, J.).

II

Based on this proportionality analysis, I would conclude that the statute at issue here, as interpreted by Justice Sotomayor, does not violate the First Amendment.

How much harm to First Amendment interests does a bar on registering highly vulgar or obscene trademarks work? Not much. The statute leaves businesses free to use highly vulgar or obscene words on their products, and even to use such words directly next to other registered marks. Indeed, a business owner might even use a vulgar word as a trademark, provided that he or she is willing to forgo the benefits of registration. . . .

These attention-grabbing words, though financially valuable to some businesses that seek to attract interest in their products, threaten to distract consumers and disrupt commerce. And they may lead to the creation of public spaces that many will find repellant, perhaps on occasion creating the risk of verbal altercations or even physical confrontations. (Just think about how you might react if you saw someone wearing a t-shirt or using a product emblazoned with an odious racial epithet.) The Government thus has an interest in seeking to disincentivize the use of such words in commerce by denying the benefit of trademark registration. Cf. *Brandenburg v. Ohio* (1969) (permitting regulation of words "directed to inciting or producing imminent lawless action" and "likely to incite or produce such action").

Finally, although some consumers may be attracted to products labeled with highly vulgar or obscene words, others may believe that such words should not be displayed in public spaces where goods are sold and where children are likely to be present. They may believe that trademark registration of such words could make it more likely that children will be exposed to public displays involving such words. To that end, the Government may have an interest in protecting the sensibilities of children by barring the registration of such words.

The upshot of this analysis is that the narrowing construction articulated by Justice Sotomayor risks some harm to First Amendment interests, but not very much. And applying that interpretation seems a reasonable way—perhaps the only way—to further legitimate government interests. Of course, there is a risk that the statute might be applied in a manner that stretches it beyond the few vulgar words that are encompassed by the narrow interpretation Justice Sotomayor sets forth. That risk, however, could be mitigated by internal agency review to ensure that agency officials do not stray beyond their mandate. In any event, I do not believe that this risk alone warrants the facial invalidation of this statute.

I would conclude that the prohibition on registering "scandalous" marks does not "wor[k] harm to First Amendment interests that is disproportionate in light of the relevant regulatory objectives." I would therefore uphold this part of the statute. I agree with the Court, however, that the bar on registering "immoral" marks violates the First Amendment. Because Justice Sotomayor reaches the same conclusions, using roughly similar reasoning, I join her opinion insofar as it is consistent with the views set forth here.

JUSTICE SOTOMAYOR, with whom JUSTICE BREYER joins, concurring in part and dissenting in part.

The Court's decision today will beget unfortunate results. With the Lanham Act's scandalous-marks provision struck down as unconstitutional viewpoint discrimination, the Government will have no statutory basis to refuse (and thus no choice but to begin) registering marks containing the most vulgar, profane, or obscene words and images imaginable.

The coming rush to register such trademarks—and the Government's immediate powerlessness to say no—is eminently avoidable. Rather than read the relevant text as the majority does, it is equally possible to read that provision's bar on the registration of "scandalous" marks to address only obscenity, vulgarity, and profanity. Such a narrowing construction would save that duly enacted legislative text by rendering it a reasonable, viewpoint-neutral restriction on speech that is permissible in the context of a beneficial governmental initiative like the trademark-registration system. I would apply that narrowing construction to the term "scandalous" and accordingly reject petitioner Erik Brunetti's facial challenge. . . .

I

It is with regard to the word "scandalous" that I part ways with the majority. Unquestionably, "scandalous" can mean something similar to "immoral" and thus favor some viewpoints over others. See *ante*, at 6. But it does not have to be read that way. To say that a word or image is "scandalous" can instead mean that it is simply indecent, shocking, or generally offensive. See Funk & Wagnalls New Standard Dictionary 2186 (1944) (Funk & Wagnalls) ("shocking to the sense of truth, decency, *or* propriety; disgraceful, offensive" (emphasis added)); Webster's New International Dictionary 2229 (1942) ("exciting reprobation; calling out condemnation"); 9 Oxford English Dictionary 175 (1933) ("Of the nature of, or causing, a 'stumbling-block' or occasion of offence"); 8 Century Dictionary and Cyclopedia 5374 (1911) (Century Dictionary) ("Causing scandal or offense; exciting reproach or reprobation; extremely offensive to the sense of duty or propriety; shameful; shocking"); see also Webster's New College Dictionary 1008 (3d ed. 2005) ("shocking or offensive"). That offensiveness could result from the views expressed, but it could also result from the way in which those views are expressed: using a manner of expression that is "shocking to [one's] sense of . . . decency," Funk & Wagnalls 2186, or "extremely offensive to the sense of . . . propriety," 8 Century Dictionary 5374.

The word "scandalous" on its own, then, is ambiguous: It can be read broadly (to cover both offensive ideas and offensive manners of expressing ideas), or it can be read narrowly (to cover only offensive modes of expression). That alone raises the possibility that a limiting construction might be appropriate. But the broader text confirms the reasonableness of the narrower reading, because the word "scandalous" appears in the statute alongside other words that can, and should, be read to constrain its scope. . . .

Here, Congress used not only the word "scandalous," but also the words "immoral" and "disparage," in the same block of statutory text — each as a separate feature that could render a mark unregistrable. . . . The text of §1052 . . . is a grab bag: It bars the registration of marks featuring "immoral, deceptive, or scandalous matter," as well as, *inter alia*, disparaging marks, flags, insignias, mislabeled wines, and deceased Presidents. This is not, in other words, a situation in which Congress was simply . . . using two synonyms in rapid-fire succession when one would have done fine. Instead, "scandalous" and "immoral" are separated by an unrelated word ("deceptive") and mixed in with a lengthy series of other, unrelated concepts. . . .

For that reason, while the majority offers a reasonable reading of "scandalous," it also unnecessarily and ill-advisedly collapses the words "scandalous" and "immoral." Instead, it should treat them as each holding a distinct, nonredundant meaning, with "immoral" covering marks that are offensive because they transgress social norms, and "scandalous" covering marks that are offensive because of the mode in which they are expressed.

What would it mean for "scandalous" in §1052(a) to cover only offensive modes of expression? The most obvious ways — indeed, perhaps the only conceivable ways — in which a trademark can be expressed in a shocking or offensive manner are when the speaker employs obscenity, vulgarity, or profanity.[3] Obscenity has long been defined by this Court's decision in *Miller v. California* (1973). As for what constitutes "scandalous" vulgarity or profanity, I do not offer a list, but I do interpret the term to allow the PTO to restrict (and potentially promulgate guidance to clarify) the small group of lewd words or "swear" words that cause a visceral reaction, that are not commonly used around children, and that are prohibited in comparable settings. *FCC v. Pacifica Foundation* (1978) (opinion of Stevens, J.) (regulator's objection to a monologue containing various "four-letter words" was not to its "point of view, but to the way in which it [wa]s expressed"). Of course, "scandalous" offers its own limiting principle: if a word, though not exactly polite, cannot be said to be "scandalous"—e.g., "shocking" or "extremely offensive"—it is clearly not the kind of vulgarity or profanity that Congress intended to target. Everyone can think of a small number of words (including the apparent homonym of Brunetti's mark) that would, however, plainly qualify.[5] . . .

II

Adopting a narrow construction for the word "scandalous"—interpreting it to regulate only obscenity, vulgarity, and profanity—would save it from unconstitutionality. Properly narrowed, "scandalous" is a viewpoint-neutral form of content discrimination that is permissible in the kind of discretionary governmental program or limited forum typified by the trademark-registration system.

A

Content discrimination occurs whenever a government regulates "particular speech because of the topic discussed or the idea or message expressed." *Reed v. Town of Gilbert* (2015). Viewpoint discrimination is "an egregious form of content discrimination" in which "the government targets not subject matter, but particular views taken by speakers on a subject." *Rosenberger v. Rector and Visitors of Univ. of Va.* (1995). . . .

---

3. Other modes of expression, such as fighting words or extremely loud noises, could also be called shocking or offensive in certain contexts, see *R. A. V. v. St. Paul* (1992), but it is hard to see how they would apply in the context of a trademark.

5. There is at least one particularly egregious racial epithet that would fit this description as well. While *Matal v. Tam* (2017), removed a statutory basis to deny the registration of racial epithets in general, the Government represented at oral argument that it is holding in abeyance trademark applications that use that particular epithet. See Tr. of Oral Arg. 61. ["... the PTO views *Tam* as prohibiting a denial of registration for racial slurs, but, with respect to the single-most offensive racial slur, the PTO is currently holding in abeyance applications that incorporate that word, pending this Court's decision on . . . [whether] that word might be viewed as scandalous."] As a result of today's ruling, the Government will now presumably be compelled to register marks containing that epithet as well rather than treating it as a "scandalous" form of profanity under §1052(a).

Restrictions on particular modes of expression do not inherently qualify as viewpoint discrimination; they are not by nature examples of "the government target[ing] . . . particular views taken by speakers on a subject." *Rosenberger.* For example, a ban on lighting fires in the town square does not facially violate the First Amendment simply because it makes it marginally harder for would-be flag-burners to express their views in that place. See *R. A. V. v. St. Paul* (1992). By the same token, "fighting words are categorically excluded from the protection of the First Amendment" not because they have no content or express no viewpoint (often quite the opposite), but because "their content embodies a particularly intolerable (and socially unnecessary) *mode* of expressing *whatever* idea the speaker wishes to convey." *Id.*

A restriction on trademarks featuring obscenity, vulgarity, or profanity is similarly viewpoint neutral, though it is naturally content-based.[6] See *R. A. V.* (kinds of speech like "obscenity, defamation, etc." may "be regulated because of their constitutionally proscribable content."). . . . To treat a restriction on vulgarity, profanity, or obscenity as viewpoint discrimination would upend decades of precedent.

Brunetti invokes *Cohen v. California* (1971) to argue that the restriction at issue here is viewpoint discriminatory. But *Cohen*—which did not employ the precise taxonomy that is more common today—does not reach as far as Brunetti wants. *Cohen* arose in the criminal context: Cohen had been arrested and imprisoned under a California criminal statute targeting disturbances of the peace because he was "wearing a jacket bearing the words 'F[***] the Draft.'" The Court held that applying that statute to Cohen because of his jacket violated the First Amendment. But the Court did not suggest that the State had targeted Cohen to suppress his view itself (*i.e.,* his sharp distaste for the draft), such that it would have accepted an equally colorful statement of praise for the draft (or hostility toward war protesters). Rather, the Court suggested that the State had simply engaged in what later courts would more precisely call viewpoint-neutral content discrimination—it had regulated "the form or content of individual expression." . . .

Cohen therefore does not resolve this case in Brunetti's favor. Yes, Brunetti has been, as Cohen was, subject to content discrimination, but that content discrimination is properly understood as viewpoint neutral. And whereas even viewpoint-neutral content discrimination is (in all but the most compelling cases, such as threats) impermissible in the context of a criminal prosecution like the one that Cohen faced, Brunetti is subject to such regulation only in the context of the federal trademark-registration system. . . .

---

6. Of course, obscenity itself is subject to a longstanding exception to First Amendment protection, so it is proscribable in any event. As for vulgarity and profanity, however, they are not subject to any such exception, and a regulation like §1052(a)'s ban on the registration of scandalous marks is not "'justified without reference to the content of the regulated speech'" in the way that a simple regulation of time, place, or manner is. *Ward v. Rock Against Racism* (1989).

III

"The cardinal principle of statutory construction is to save and not to destroy."
Jones & Laughlin Steel Corp. In directing the PTO to deny the ancillary benefit
of registration to trademarks featuring "scandalous" content, Congress used a
word that is susceptible of different meanings. The majority's reading would
render the provision unconstitutional; mine would save it. Under these circumstances, the Court ought to adopt the narrower construction, rather than permit
a rush to register trademarks for even the most viscerally offensive words and
images that one can imagine.[13] . . .

Freedom of speech is a cornerstone of our society, and the First Amendment
protects Brunetti's right to use words like the one at issue here. The Government
need not, however, be forced to confer on Brunetti's trademark (and some more
extreme) the ancillary benefit of trademark registration, when "scandalous" in
§1052(a) can reasonably be read to bar the registration of only those marks that
are obscene, vulgar, or profane. Though I concur as to the unconstitutionality
of the term "immoral" in §1052(a), I respectfully dissent as to the term "scandalous" in the same statute and would instead uphold it under the narrow construction discussed here.

---

13. As noted above, I agree with the majority that §1052(a)'s bar on the registration of "immoral"
marks is unconstitutional viewpoint discrimination. I would simply sever that provision and uphold
the bar on "scandalous" marks.

Chapter 17

Freedom of Association

ASSIGNMENT 2

STUDY GUIDE:

- Why does requiring an employee to pay agency fees constitute compelled speech? Is the employee required to say, or not say, any particular message?
- Why does the majority find that stare decisis does not justify maintaining *Abood v. Detroit Board of Education* (1977)?
- Justice Kagan's dissent accuses the majority of serving as "black-robed rulers overriding citizens' choices" and refers to the Court's "6-year crusade to ban agency fees." Would this criticism apply to other cases where the Court overturns precedent?
- Does the majority "weaponiz[e] the First Amendment, in a way that unleashes judges, now and in the future, to intervene in economic and regulatory policy"?

Janus v. American Federation of State, County, and Municipal Employees, Council 31, et al.
138 S. Ct. 2448 (2018)

ALITO, J., delivered the opinion of the Court, in which ROBERTS, C.J., and KENNEDY, THOMAS, and, GORSUCH, JJ., joined. SOTOMAYOR, J., filed a dissenting opinion. KAGAN, J., filed a dissenting opinion, in which GINSBURG, BREYER, and SOTOMAYOR, JJ., joined.

JUSTICE ALITO delivered the opinion of the Court.

Under Illinois law, public employees are forced to subsidize a union, even if they choose not to join and strongly object to the positions the union takes in collective bargaining and related activities. We conclude that this arrangement violates the free speech rights of nonmembers by compelling them to subsidize private speech on matters of substantial public concern.

We upheld a similar law in *Abood v. Detroit Bd. of Ed.* (1977), and we recognize the importance of following precedent unless there are strong reasons for not doing so. But there are very strong reasons in this case. Fundamental free speech rights are at stake. *Abood* was poorly reasoned. It has led to practical problems and abuse. It is inconsistent with other First Amendment cases and has been undermined by more recent decisions. Developments since *Abood* was handed down have shed new light on the issue of agency fees, and no reliance interests on the part of public-sector unions are sufficient to justify the perpetuation of the free speech violations that *Abood* has countenanced for the past 41 years. *Abood* is therefore overruled.

I

A

Under the Illinois Public Labor Relations Act (IPLRA), employees of the State and its political subdivisions are permitted to unionize. If a majority of the employees in a bargaining unit vote to be represented by a union, that union is designated as the exclusive representative of all the employees. Employees in the unit are not obligated to join the union selected by their co-workers, but whether they join or not, that union is deemed to be their sole permitted representative.

Once a union is so designated, it is vested with broad authority. Only the union may negotiate with the employer on matters relating to "pay, wages, hours [,] and other conditions of employment." And this authority extends to the negotiation of what the IPLRA calls "policy matters," such as merit pay, the size of the work force, layoffs, privatization, promotion methods, and non-discrimination policies.

Designating a union as the employees' exclusive representative substantially restricts the rights of individual employees. Among other things, this designation means that individual employees may not be represented by any agent other than the designated union; nor may individual employees negotiate directly with their employer. Protection of the employees' interests is placed in the hands of the union, and therefore the union is required by law to provide fair representation for all employees in the unit, members and nonmembers alike.

Employees who decline to join the union are not assessed full union dues but must instead pay what is generally called an "agency fee," which amounts to a percentage of the union dues. Under *Abood*, nonmembers may be charged for the portion of union dues attributable to activities that are "germane to [the union's] duties as collective-bargaining representative," but nonmembers may not be required to fund the union's political and ideological projects. In labor-law parlance, the outlays in the first category are known as "chargeable" expenditures, while those in the latter are labeled "nonchargeable."

Illinois law does not specify in detail which expenditures are chargeable and which are not. The IPLRA provides that an agency fee may compensate a union for the costs incurred in "the collective bargaining process, contract administration[,] and pursuing matters affecting wages, hours[,] and conditions of employment." Excluded from the agency-fee calculation are union expenditures "related to the election or support of any candidate for political office."

Applying this standard, a union categorizes its expenditures as chargeable or nonchargeable and thus determines a nonmember's "proportionate share," this determination is then audited; the amount of the "proportionate share" is certified to the employer; and the employer automatically deducts that amount from the nonmembers' wages. Nonmembers need not be asked, and they are not required to consent before the fees are deducted.

After the amount of the agency fee is fixed each year, the union must send nonmembers what is known as a *Hudson* notice. This notice is supposed to provide nonmembers with "an adequate explanation of the basis for the [agency] fee." If nonmembers "suspect that a union has improperly put certain expenses in the [chargeable] category," they may challenge that determination.

As illustrated by the record in this case, unions charge nonmembers, not just for the cost of collective bargaining *per se,* but also for many other supposedly connected activities. Here, the nonmembers were told that they had to pay for "[l]obbying," "[s]ocial and recreational activities," "advertising," "[m]embership meetings and conventions," and "litigation," as well as other unspecified "[s]ervices" that "may ultimately inure to the benefit of the members of the local bargaining unit." The total chargeable amount for nonmembers was 78.06% of full union dues.

B

Petitioner Mark Janus is employed by the Illinois Department of Healthcare and Family Services as a child support specialist. The employees in his unit are among the 35,000 public employees in Illinois who are represented by respondent American Federation of State, County, and Municipal Employees, Council 31 (Union). Janus refused to join the Union because he opposes "many of the public policy positions that [it] advocates," including the positions it takes in collective bargaining. . . . Under his unit's collective-bargaining agreement, however, he was required to pay an agency fee of $44.58 per month, which would amount to about $535 per year.

Janus's concern about Illinois' current financial situation is shared by the Governor of the State, and it was the Governor who initially challenged the statute authorizing the imposition of agency fees. The Governor commenced an action in federal court, asking that the law be declared unconstitutional, and the Illinois attorney general (a respondent here) intervened to defend the law. . . .

Janus then sought review in this Court, asking us to overrule *Abood* and hold that public-sector agency-fee arrangements are unconstitutional. We granted certiorari to consider this important question. . . .

III

In *Abood,* the Court upheld the constitutionality of an agency-shop arrangement like the one now before us, 431 U.S., at 232, but in more recent cases we have recognized that this holding is "something of an anomaly," *Knox v. Service Employees* (2012), and that *Abood*'s "analysis is questionable on several grounds," *Harris*. We have therefore refused to extend *Abood* to situations where it does not squarely control, see *Harris*, while leaving for another day the question whether *Abood* should be overruled, *Harris*,; see *Knox*.

We now address that question. We first consider whether *Abood*'s holding is consistent with standard First Amendment principles.

A

The First Amendment, made applicable to the States by the Fourteenth Amendment, forbids abridgment of the freedom of speech. We have held time and again that freedom of speech "includes both the right to speak freely and the right to refrain from speaking at all." *Wooley v. Maynard* (1977); see *Riley v. National Federation of Blind of N. C., Inc.* (1988); *Harper & Row, Publishers, Inc. v. Nation Enterprises* (1985); *Miami Herald Publishing Co. v. Tornillo* (1974); accord, *Pacific Gas & Elec. Co. v. Public Util. Comm'n of Cal.* (1986) (plurality opinion). The right to eschew association for expressive purposes is likewise protected. *Roberts v. United States Jaycees* (1984) ("Freedom of association . . . plainly presupposes a freedom not to associate"); see *Pacific Gas & Elec.* ("[F]orced associations that burden protected speech are impermissible"). As Justice Jackson memorably put it: "If there is any fixed star in our constitutional constellation, it is that no official, high or petty, can prescribe what shall be orthodox in politics, nationalism, religion, or other matters of opinion or *force citizens to confess by word or act their faith therein*." *West Virginia Bd. of Ed. v. Barnette* (1943) (emphasis added).

Compelling individuals to mouth support for views they find objectionable violates that cardinal constitutional command, and in most contexts, any such effort would be universally condemned. Suppose, for example, that the State of Illinois required all residents to sign a document expressing support for a particular set of positions on controversial public issues — say, the platform of one of the major political parties. No one, we trust, would seriously argue that the First Amendment permits this.

[Perhaps because such compulsion so plainly violates the Constitution, most of our free speech cases have involved restrictions on what can be said, rather than laws compelling speech. But measures compelling speech are at least as threatening.

Free speech serves many ends. It is essential to our democratic form of government, and it furthers the search for truth. Whenever the Federal Government or a State prevents individuals from saying what they think on important matters or compels them to voice ideas with which they disagree, it undermines these ends.

When speech is compelled, however, additional damage is done. In that situation, individuals are coerced into betraying their convictions. Forcing free and independent individuals to endorse ideas they find objectionable is always demeaning, and for this reason, one of our landmark free speech cases said that a law commanding "involuntary affirmation" of objected-to beliefs would require "even more immediate and urgent grounds" than a law demanding silence.

Compelling a person to *subsidize* the speech of other private speakers raises similar First Amendment concerns. As Jefferson famously put it, "to compel a man to furnish contributions of money for the propagation of opinions which he disbelieves and abhor[s] is sinful and tyrannical." A Bill for Establishing Religious Freedom, in 2 Papers of Thomas Jefferson 545 (J. Boyd ed.1950). We have therefore recognized that a "'significant impingement on First Amendment rights'" occurs when public employees are required to provide financial support for a union that "takes many positions during collective bargaining that have powerful political and civic consequences." *Knox*.

Because the compelled subsidization of private speech seriously impinges on First Amendment rights, it cannot be casually allowed. Our free speech cases have identified "levels of scrutiny" to be applied in different contexts, and in three recent cases, we have considered the standard that should be used in judging the constitutionality of agency fees.

In *Knox*, the first of these cases, we found it sufficient to hold that the conduct in question was unconstitutional under even the test used for the compulsory subsidization of commercial speech. Even though commercial speech has been thought to enjoy a lesser degree of protection, see, e.g., *Central Hudson Gas & Elec. Corp. v. Public Serv. Comm'n of N. Y.* (1980), prior precedent in that area, specifically *United Foods,* had applied what we characterized as "exacting" scrutiny, a less demanding test than the "strict" scrutiny that might be thought to apply outside the commercial sphere. Under "exacting" scrutiny, we noted, a compelled subsidy must "serve a compelling state interest that cannot be achieved through means significantly less restrictive of associational freedoms."

In *Harris,* the second of these cases, we again found that an agency-fee requirement failed "exacting scrutiny." But we questioned whether that test provides sufficient protection for free speech rights, since "it is apparent that the speech compelled" in agency-fee cases "is not commercial speech."

Picking up that cue, petitioner in the present case contends that the Illinois law at issue should be subjected to "strict scrutiny." The dissent, on the other hand, proposes that we apply what amounts to rational-basis review, that is, that we ask only whether a government employer could reasonably believe that the exaction of agency fees serves its interests. See *post* (Kagan, J., dissenting) ("A government entity could reasonably conclude that such a clause was needed"). This form of minimal scrutiny is foreign to our free-speech jurisprudence, and we reject it here. At the same time, we again find it unnecessary to decide the issue of strict scrutiny because the Illinois scheme cannot survive under even the more permissive standard applied in *Knox* and *Harris*. . . .

C

In addition to the promotion of "labor peace," *Abood* cited "the risk of 'free riders'" as justification for agency fees, Respondents and some of their *amici* endorse this reasoning, contending that agency fees are needed to prevent non-members from enjoying the benefits of union representation without shouldering the costs.

Petitioner strenuously objects to this free-rider label. He argues that he is not a free rider on a bus headed for a destination that he wishes to reach but is more like a person shanghaied for an unwanted voyage.

Whichever description fits the majority of public employees who would not subsidize a union if given the option, avoiding free riders is not a compelling interest. As we have noted, "free-rider arguments . . . are generally insufficient to overcome First Amendment objections." To hold otherwise across the board would have startling consequences. Many private groups speak out with the objective of obtaining government action that will have the effect of benefiting nonmembers. May all those who are thought to benefit from such efforts be compelled to subsidize this speech?

Suppose that a particular group lobbies or speaks out on behalf of what it thinks are the needs of senior citizens or veterans or physicians, to take just a few examples. Could the government require that all seniors, veterans, or doctors pay for that service even if they object? It has never been thought that this is permissible. "[P]rivate speech often furthers the interests of nonspeakers," but "that does not alone empower the state to compel the speech to be paid for." In simple terms, the First Amendment does not permit the government to compel a person to pay for another party's speech just because the government thinks that the speech furthers the interests of the person who does not want to pay. . . .

. . .

In sum, we do not see any reason to treat the free-rider interest any differently in the agency-fee context than in any other First Amendment context. We therefore hold that agency fees cannot be upheld on free-rider grounds.

IV

Implicitly acknowledging the weakness of *Abood*'s own reasoning, proponents of agency fees have come forward with alternative justifications for the decision, and we now address these arguments.

A

The most surprising of these new arguments is the Union respondent's originalist defense of *Abood*. According to this argument, *Abood* was correctly decided because the First Amendment was not originally understood to provide *any* protection for the free speech rights of public employees.

As an initial matter, we doubt that the Union — or its members — actually want us to hold that public employees have "*no* [free speech] rights."

It is particularly discordant to find this argument in a brief that trumpets the importance of *stare decisis*. Taking away free speech protection for public employees would mean overturning decades of landmark precedent. Under the

Union's theory, *Pickering v. Board of Ed. of Township High School Dist. 205, Will Cty,* (1968), and its progeny would fall. Yet *Pickering,* as we will discuss, is now the foundation for respondents' chief defense of *Abood.* And indeed, *Abood* itself would have to go if public employees have no free speech rights, since *Abood* holds that the First Amendment prohibits the exaction of agency fees for political or ideological purposes. . . . Respondents presumably want none of this, desiring instead that we apply the Constitution's supposed original meaning only when it suits them — to retain the part of *Abood* that they like. We will not engage in this halfway originalism.

Nor, in any event, does the First Amendment's original meaning support the Union's claim. The Union offers no persuasive founding-era evidence that public employees were understood to lack free speech protections. While it observes that restrictions on federal employees' activities have existed since the First Congress, most of its historical examples involved limitations on public officials' outside business dealings, not on their speech. See *Ex parte Curtis* (1882). The only early *speech* restrictions the Union identifies are an 1806 statute prohibiting military personnel from using "'contemptuous or disrespectful words against the President'" and other officials, and an 1801 directive limiting electioneering by top government employees. But those examples at most show that the government was understood to have power to limit employee speech that threatened important governmental interests (such as maintaining military discipline and preventing corruption) — not that public employees' speech was entirely unprotected. Indeed, more recently this Court has upheld similar restrictions even while recognizing that government employees possess First Amendment rights. See, *e.g., Brown v. Glines* (1980) (upholding military restriction on speech that threatened troop readiness); *Civil Service Comm'n v. Letter Carriers,* (1973) (upholding limits on public employees' political activities).

Ultimately, the Union relies, not on founding-era evidence, but on dictum from a 1983 opinion of this Court stating that, "[f]or most of th[e 20th] century, the unchallenged dogma was that a public employee had no right to object to conditions placed upon the terms of employment — including those which restricted the exercise of constitutional rights." *Connick v. Myers.* Even on its own terms, this dictum about 20th-century views does not purport to describe how the First Amendment was understood in 1791. And a careful examination of the decisions by this Court that *Connick* cited to support its dictum, reveals that none of them rested on the facile premise that public employees are unprotected by the First Amendment. Instead, they considered (much as we do today) whether particular speech restrictions were "necessary to protect" fundamental government interests.

The Union has also failed to show that, even if public employees enjoyed free speech rights, the First Amendment was nonetheless originally understood to allow forced subsidies like those at issue here. We can safely say that, at the time of the adoption of the First Amendment, no one gave any thought to whether public-sector unions could charge nonmembers agency fees. Entities resembling labor unions did not exist at the founding, and public-sector unions did not emerge until the mid-20th century. The idea of public-sector unionization and agency fees would astound those who framed and ratified the Bill of Rights.[7] Thus, the Union cannot point to any accepted founding-era practice that even remotely resembles the compulsory assessment of agency fees from public-sector employees. We do know, however, that prominent members of the founding generation condemned laws requiring public employees to affirm or support beliefs with which they disagreed. As noted, Jefferson denounced compelled support for such beliefs as "'sinful and tyrannical,'" and others expressed similar views.

In short, the Union has offered no basis for concluding that *Abood* is supported by the original understanding of the First Amendment.

B

The principal defense of *Abood* advanced by respondents and the dissent is based on our decision in *Pickering*, which held that a school district violated the First Amendment by firing a teacher for writing a letter critical of the school administration. Under *Pickering* and later cases in the same line, employee speech is largely unprotected if it is part of what the employee is paid to do, see *Garcetti v. Ceballos* (2006), or if it involved a matter of only private concern. On the other hand, when a public employee speaks as a citizen on a matter of public concern, the employee's speech is protected unless "'the interest of the state, as an employer, in promoting the efficiency of the public services it performs through its employees' outweighs 'the interests of the [employee], as a citizen, in commenting upon matters of public concern.'" *Harris* (quoting *Pickering*). *Pickering* was the centerpiece of the defense of *Abood* in *Harris*, and we found the argument unpersuasive. The intervening years have not improved its appeal.

As we pointed out in *Harris, Abood* was not based on *Pickering*. The *Abood* majority cited the case exactly once—in a footnote—and then merely to acknowledge that "there may be limits on the extent to which an employee in a sensitive or policymaking position may freely criticize his superiors and the policies they espouse." That aside has no bearing on the agency-fee issue here.

Respondents' reliance on *Pickering* is thus "an effort to find a new justification for the decision in *Abood*." And we have previously taken a dim view of similar attempts to recast problematic First Amendment decisions. See, *e.g., Citizens United v. Federal Election Comm'n* (2010) (rejecting efforts to recast *Austin v. Michigan Chamber of Commerce* (1990)). We see no good reason, at this late date, to try to shoehorn *Abood* into the *Pickering* framework. . . .

---

7. Indeed, under common law, "collective bargaining was unlawful," *Teamsters v. Terry* (1990) (plurality opinion); see N. Citrine, Trade Union Law 4–7, 9–10 (2d ed.1960); Notes, Legality of Trade Unions at Common Law, 25 Harv. L.Rev. 465, 466 (1912), and into the 20th century, every individual employee had the "liberty of contract" to "sell his labor upon such terms as he deem[ed] proper," *Adair v. United States* (1908). So even the concept of a private third-party entity with the power to bind employees on the terms of their employment likely would have been foreign to the Founders. We note this only to show the problems inherent in the Union respondent's argument; we are not in any way questioning the foundations of modern labor law.

VI

For the reasons given above, we conclude that public-sector agency-shop arrangements violate the First Amendment, and *Abood* erred in concluding otherwise. There remains the question whether *stare decisis* nonetheless counsels against overruling *Abood*. It does not.

"*Stare decisis* is the preferred course because it promotes the evenhanded, predictable, and consistent development of legal principles, fosters reliance on judicial decisions, and contributes to the actual and perceived integrity of the judicial process." *Payne v. Tennessee* (1991). We will not overturn a past decision unless there are strong grounds for doing so. *United States v. International Business Machines Corp.* (1996); *Citizens United* (Roberts, C. J., concurring). But as we have often recognized, *stare decisis* is "'not an inexorable command.'" *Pearson v. Callahan* (2009); see also *Lawrence v. Texas* (2003); *State Oil Co. v. Khan* (1997); *Agostini v. Felton* (1997); *Seminole Tribe of Fla. v. Florida* (1996); *Payne.*

The doctrine "is at its weakest when we interpret the Constitution because our interpretation can be altered only by constitutional amendment or by overruling our prior decisions." *Agostini.* And *stare decisis* applies with perhaps least force of all to decisions that wrongly denied First Amendment rights: "This Court has not hesitated to overrule decisions offensive to the First Amendment (a fixed star in our constitutional constellation, if there is one)." *Federal Election Comm'n v. Wisconsin Right to Life, Inc.* (2007) (Scalia, J., concurring in part and concurring in judgment); see also *Citizens United* (overruling *Austin*); *Barnette* (overruling *Minersville School Dist. v. Gobitis* (1940)).

Our cases identify factors that should be taken into account in deciding whether to overrule a past decision. Five of these are most important here: the quality of *Abood*'s reasoning, the workability of the rule it established, its consistency with other related decisions, developments since the decision was handed down, and reliance on the decision. After analyzing these factors, we conclude that *stare decisis* does not require us to retain *Abood*.

A

An important factor in determining whether a precedent should be overruled is the quality of its reasoning, see *Citizens United* (Roberts, C. J., concurring); *Lawrence,* and as we explained in *Harris, Abood* was poorly reasoned, We will summarize, but not repeat, *Harris*'s lengthy discussion of the issue.

Abood went wrong at the start when it concluded that two prior decisions, *Railway Employes v. Hanson,* (1956), and *Machinists v. Street* (1961), "appear[ed] to require validation of the agency-shop agreement before [the Court]." Properly understood, those decisions did no such thing. Both cases involved Congress's "*bare authorization*" of *private-sector* union shops under the Railway Labor Act. *Abood* failed to appreciate that a very different First Amendment question arises when a State *requires* its employees to pay agency fees. . . .

Abood's unwarranted reliance on *Hanson* and *Street* appears to have contributed to another mistake: *Abood* judged the constitutionality of public-sector agency fees under a deferential standard that finds no support in our free speech cases. (As noted, today's dissent makes the same fundamental mistake.) *Abood* did not independently evaluate the strength of the government interests that were said to support the challenged agency-fee provision; nor did it ask how well that provision actually promoted those interests or whether they could have been adequately served without impinging so heavily on the free speech rights of nonmembers. Rather, *Abood* followed *Hanson* and *Street,* which it interpreted as having deferred to *"the legislative assessment* of the important contribution of the union shop to the system of labor relations established by Congress." But *Hanson* deferred to that judgment in deciding the Commerce Clause and substantive due process questions that were the focus of the case. Such deference to legislative judgments is inappropriate in deciding free speech issues. . . .

Abood* also did not sufficiently take into account the difference between the effects of agency fees in public- and private-sector collective bargaining. The challengers in *Abood* argued that collective bargaining with a government employer, unlike collective bargaining in the private sector, involves "inherently 'political'" speech. 431 U.S., at 226. The Court did not dispute that characterization, and in fact conceded that "decisionmaking by a public employer is above all a political process" driven more by policy concerns than economic ones. But (again invoking *Hanson*), the *Abood* Court asserted that public employees do not have "weightier First Amendment interest[s]" against compelled speech than do private employees. That missed the point. Assuming for the sake of argument that the First Amendment applies at all to private-sector agency-shop arrangements, the individual interests at stake still differ. "In the public sector, core issues such as wages, pensions, and benefits are important political issues, but that is generally not so in the private sector." *Harris.* . . .

In sum, as detailed in *Harris, Abood* was not well reasoned.[25]

B

Another relevant consideration in the *stare decisis* calculus is the workability of the precedent in question, *Montejo v. Louisiana* (2009), and that factor also weighs against *Abood.*

Abood's* line between chargeable and nonchargeable union expenditures has proved to be impossible to draw with precision. . . . Respondents agree that *Abood's* chargeable-nonchargeable line suffers from "a vagueness problem," that it sometimes "allows what it shouldn't allow," and that "a firm[er] line c[ould] be drawn." They therefore argue that we should "consider revisiting" this part of *Abood.* This concession only underscores the reality that *Abood* has proved

---

25. Contrary to the dissent's claim, see *post,* the fact that "[t]he rationale of [*Abood*] does not withstand careful analysis" *is* a reason to overrule it, *e.g., Lawrence v. Texas* (2003). And that is even truer when, as here, the defenders of the precedent do not attempt to "defend [its actual] reasoning." *Citizens United v. Federal Election Comm'n* (2010) (Roberts, C. J., concurring).

unworkable: Not even the parties defending agency fees support the line that it has taken this Court over 40 years to draw. . . .

Objecting employees also face a daunting and expensive task if they wish to challenge union chargeability determinations.

C

Developments since *Abood,* both factual and legal, have also "eroded" the decision's "underpinnings" and left it an outlier among our First Amendment cases. *United States v. Gaudin* (1995) . . .These developments, and the political debate over public spending and debt they have spurred, have given collective-bargaining issues a political valence that *Abood* did not fully appreciate.

Abood is also an "anomaly" in our First Amendment jurisprudence, as we recognized in *Harris* and *Knox.* This is not an altogether new observation. In *Abood* itself, Justice Powell faulted the Court for failing to perform the "'exacting scrutiny'" applied in other cases involving significant impingements on First Amendment rights. Our later cases involving compelled speech and association have also employed exacting scrutiny, if not a more demanding standard. See, e.g., *Roberts.* And we have more recently refused, even in agency-fee cases, to extend *Abood* beyond circumstances where it directly controls.

Abood particularly sticks out when viewed against our cases holding that public employees generally may not be required to support a political party. The Court reached that conclusion despite a "long tradition" of political patronage in government. It is an odd feature of our First Amendment cases that political patronage has been deemed largely unconstitutional, while forced subsidization of union speech (which has no such pedigree) has been largely permitted. As Justice Powell observed: "I am at a loss to understand why the State's decision to adopt the agency shop in the public sector should be worthy of *greater* deference, when challenged on First Amendment grounds, than its decision to adhere to the *tradition* of political patronage." *Abood.* We have no occasion here to reconsider our political patronage decisions, but Justice Powell's observation is sound as far as it goes. By overruling *Abood,* we end the oddity of privileging compelled union support over compelled party support and bring a measure of greater coherence to our First Amendment law.

D

In some cases, reliance provides a strong reason for adhering to established law, and this is the factor that is stressed most strongly by respondents, their *amici,* and the dissent. They contend that collective-bargaining agreements now in effect were negotiated with agency fees in mind and that unions may have given up other benefits in exchange for provisions granting them such fees. In this case, however, reliance does not carry decisive weight.

For one thing, it would be unconscionable to permit free speech rights to be abridged in perpetuity in order to preserve contract provisions that will expire on their own in a few years' time. "The fact that [public-sector unions] may view [agency fees] as an entitlement does not establish the sort of reliance interest that could outweigh the countervailing interest that [nonmembers] share in having their constitutional rights fully protected." *Arizona v. Gant* (2009).

For another, *Abood* does not provide "a clear or easily applicable standard, so arguments for reliance based on its clarity are misplaced." *South Dakota v. Wayfair, Inc.*

This is especially so because public-sector unions have been on notice for years regarding this Court's misgivings about *Abood*. In *Knox,* decided in 2012, we described *Abood* as a First Amendment "anomaly." Two years later in *Harris,* we were asked to overrule *Abood,* and while we found it unnecessary to take that step, we cataloged *Abood*'s many weaknesses. In 2015, we granted a petition for certiorari asking us to review a decision that sustained an agency-fee arrangement under *Abood. Friedrichs v. California Teachers Assn.* After exhaustive briefing and argument on the question whether *Abood* should be overruled, we affirmed the decision below by an equally divided vote. During this period of time, any public-sector union seeking an agency-fee provision in a collective-bargaining agreement must have understood that the constitutionality of such a provision was uncertain. . . .

Because public-sector collective-bargaining agreements are generally of rather short duration, a great many of those now in effect probably began or were renewed since *Knox* (2012) or *Harris* (2014). . . .

In short, the uncertain status of *Abood*, the lack of clarity it provides, the short-term nature of collective-bargaining agreements, and the ability of unions to protect themselves if an agency-fee provision was crucial to its bargain all work to undermine the force of reliance as a factor supporting *Abood*.[27]

* * *

We recognize that the loss of payments from nonmembers may cause unions to experience unpleasant transition costs in the short term, and may require unions to make adjustments in order to attract and retain members. But we must weigh these disadvantages against the considerable windfall that unions have received under *Abood* for the past 41 years. It is hard to estimate how many billions of dollars have been taken from nonmembers and transferred to public-sector unions in violation of the First Amendment. Those unconstitutional exactions cannot be allowed to continue indefinitely.

---

27. The dissent emphasizes another type of reliance, namely, that "[o]ver 20 States have by now enacted statutes authorizing [agency-fee] provisions." But as we explained in *Citizens United,* "[t]his is not a compelling interest for *stare decisis*. If it were, legislative acts could prevent us from overruling our own precedents, thereby interfering with our duty 'to say what the law is.'" *Citizens United* (quoting *Marbury v. Madison* (1803)). Nor does our decision "'require an extensive legislative response.'" States can keep their labor-relations systems exactly as they are — only they cannot force nonmembers to subsidize public-sector unions. In this way, these States can follow the model of the federal government and 28 other States.

All these reasons—that *Abood*'s proponents have abandoned its reasoning, that the precedent has proved unworkable, that it conflicts with other First Amendment decisions, and that subsequent developments have eroded its underpinnings—provide the "'special justification[s]'" for overruling *Abood*.[28]

VII

For these reasons, States and public-sector unions may no longer extract agency fees from nonconsenting employees. Under Illinois law, if a public-sector collective-bargaining agreement includes an agency-fee provision and the union certifies to the employer the amount of the fee, that amount is automatically deducted from the nonmember's wages. §315/6(e). No form of employee consent is required.

This procedure violates the First Amendment and cannot continue. Neither an agency fee nor any other payment to the union may be deducted from a nonmember's wages, nor may any other attempt be made to collect such a payment, unless the employee affirmatively consents to pay. . . . Unless employees clearly and affirmatively consent before any money is taken from them, this standard cannot be met.

* * *

Abood was wrongly decided and is now overruled. The judgment of the United States Court of Appeals for the Seventh Circuit is reversed, and the case is remanded for further proceedings consistent with this opinion.

It is so ordered.

JUSTICE KAGAN, with whom JUSTICE GINSBURG, JUSTICE BREYER, and JUSTICE SOTOMAYOR join, dissenting.

For over 40 years, *Abood v. Detroit Bd. of Ed.* (1977), struck a stable balance between public employees' First Amendment rights and government entities' interests in running their workforces as they thought proper. Under that decision, a government entity could require public employees to pay a fair share of the cost that a union incurs when negotiating on their behalf over terms of employment. But no part of that fair-share payment could go to any of the union's political or ideological activities.

---

28. Unfortunately, the dissent sees the need to resort to accusations that we are acting like "black-robed rulers" who have shut down an "energetic policy debate." We certainly agree that judges should not "overrid[e] citizens' choices" or "pick the winning side,"—unless the Constitution commands that they do so. But when a federal or state law violates the Constitution, the American doctrine of judicial review requires us to enforce the Constitution. Here, States with agency-fee laws have abridged fundamental free speech rights. In holding that these laws violate the Constitution, we are simply enforcing the First Amendment as properly understood, "[t]he very purpose of [which] was to withdraw certain subjects from the vicissitudes of political controversy, to place them beyond the reach of majorities and officials and to establish them as legal principles to be applied by the courts." *West Virginia Bd. of Ed. v. Barnette* (1943).

That holding fit comfortably with this Court's general framework for evaluating claims that a condition of public employment violates the First Amendment. The Court's decisions have long made plain that government entities have substantial latitude to regulate their employees' speech—especially about terms of employment—in the interest of operating their workplaces effectively. *Abood* allowed governments to do just that. While protecting public employees' expression about non-workplace matters, the decision enabled a government to advance important managerial interests—by ensuring the presence of an exclusive employee representative to bargain with. Far from an "anomaly," the *Abood* regime was a paradigmatic example of how the government can regulate speech in its capacity as an employer.

Not any longer. Today, the Court succeeds in its 6-year campaign to reverse *Abood.* See *Friedrichs v. California Teachers Assn.* (2016) (*per curiam*); *Harris v. Quinn* (2014); *Knox v. Service Employees* (2012). Its decision will have large-scale consequences. Public employee unions will lose a secure source of financial support. State and local governments that thought fair-share provisions furthered their interests will need to find new ways of managing their workforces. Across the country, the relationships of public employees and employers will alter in both predictable and wholly unexpected ways.

Rarely if ever has the Court overruled a decision—let alone one of this import—with so little regard for the usual principles of *stare decisis*. There are no special justifications for reversing *Abood.* It has proved workable. No recent developments have eroded its underpinnings. And it is deeply entrenched, in both the law and the real world. More than 20 States have statutory schemes built on the decision. Those laws underpin thousands of ongoing contracts involving millions of employees. Reliance interests do not come any stronger than those surrounding *Abood.* And likewise, judicial disruption does not get any greater than what the Court does today. I respectfully dissent.

I

I begin with *Abood*, the 41-year-old precedent the majority overrules. That case involved a union that had been certified as the exclusive representative of Detroit's public school teachers. . . .

[T]he Court acknowledged . . . the "First Amendment interests" of dissenting employees. *Ibid.* It recognized that some workers might oppose positions the union takes in collective bargaining, or even "unionism itself." And still more, it understood that unions often advance "political and ideological" views outside the collective-bargaining context—as when they "contribute to political candidates." Employees might well object to the use of their money to support such "ideological causes."

So the Court struck a balance, which has governed this area ever since. On the one hand, employees could be required to pay fees to support the union in "collective bargaining, contract administration, and grievance adjustment." There, the Court held, the "important government interests" in having a stably funded bargaining partner justify "the impingement upon" public employees' expression. But on the other hand, employees could not be compelled to fund the union's political and ideological activities. Outside the collective-bargaining sphere, the Court determined, an employee's First Amendment rights defeated any conflicting government interest.

II

Unlike the majority, I see nothing "questionable" about *Abood*'s analysis. The decision's account of why some government entities have a strong interest in agency fees (now often called fair-share fees) is fundamentally sound. And the balance *Abood* struck between public employers' interests and public employees' expression is right at home in First Amendment doctrine.

A

Abood's reasoning about governmental interests has three connected parts. First, exclusive representation arrangements benefit some government entities because they can facilitate stable labor relations. In particular, such arrangements eliminate the potential for inter-union conflict and streamline the process of negotiating terms of employment. Second, the government may be unable to avail itself of those benefits unless the single union has a secure source of funding. The various tasks involved in representing employees cost money; if the union doesn't have enough, it can't be an effective employee representative and bargaining partner. And third, agency fees are often needed to ensure such stable funding. That is because without those fees, employees have every incentive to free ride on the union dues paid by others.

The majority does not take issue with the first point. The majority claims that the second point never appears in *Abood,* but is willing to assume it for the sake of argument. So the majority stakes everything on the third point — the conclusion that maintaining an effective system of exclusive representation often entails agency fees.

But basic economic theory shows why a government would think that agency fees are necessary for exclusive representation to work. What ties the two together, as *Abood* recognized, is the likelihood of free-riding when fees are absent. Remember that once a union achieves exclusive-representation status, the law compels it to fairly represent all workers in the bargaining unit, whether or not they join or contribute to the union. Because of that legal duty, the union cannot give special advantages to its own members. And that in turn creates a collective action problem of nightmarish proportions. Everyone — not just those who oppose the union, but also those who back it — has an economic incentive to withhold dues; only altruism or loyalty — as *against* financial self-interest — can explain why an employee would pay the union for its services. And so emerged *Abood*'s rule allowing fair-share agreements: That rule ensured that a union would receive sufficient funds, despite its legally imposed disability, to effectively carry out its duties as exclusive representative of the government's employees.

The majority's initial response to this reasoning is simply to dismiss it. "[F]ree rider arguments," the majority pronounces, "are generally insufficient to overcome First Amendment objections." "To hold otherwise," it continues, "would have startling consequences" because "[m]any private groups speak out" in ways that will "benefit[ ] nonmembers." But that disregards the defining characteristic of *this* free-rider argument — that unions, unlike those many other private groups, must serve members and non-members alike. Groups advocating for "senior citizens or veterans" (to use the majority's examples) have no legal duty to provide benefits to all those individuals: They can spur people to pay dues by conferring all kinds of special advantages on their dues-paying members. Unions are — by law — in a different position, as this Court has long recognized. Justice Scalia, responding to the same argument as the majority's, may have put the point best. In a way that is true of no other private group, the "law *requires* the union to carry" non-members — "indeed, requires the union to *go out of its way* to benefit [them], even at the expense of its other interests." *Lehnert v. Ferris Faculty Assn.* (1991) (opinion concurring in part and dissenting in part). That special feature was what justified *Abood*: "Where the state imposes upon the union a duty to deliver services, it may permit the union to demand reimbursement for them." . . .

Of course, not all public employers will share that view. Some would rather not bargain with an exclusive representative. Others would prefer that representative to be poorly funded — to serve more as a front than an effectual bargaining partner. But as reflected in the number of fair-share statutes and contracts across the Nation, many government entities think that effective exclusive representation makes for good labor relations — and recognize, just as *Abood* did, that representation of that kind often depends on agency fees. *Abood* respected that state interest; today's majority fails even to understand it. Little wonder that the majority's First Amendment analysis, which involves assessing the government's reasons for imposing agency fees, also comes up short.

B

1

In many cases over many decades, this Court has addressed how the First Amendment applies when the government, acting not as sovereign but as employer, limits its workers' speech. Those decisions have granted substantial latitude to the government, in recognition of its significant interests in managing its workforce so as to best serve the public. *Abood* fit neatly with that caselaw, in both reasoning and result. Indeed, its reversal today creates a significant anomaly — an exception, applying to union fees alone, from the usual rules governing public employees' speech.

"Time and again our cases have recognized that the Government has a much freer hand" in dealing with its employees than with "citizens at large." *NASA v.*

Nelson (2011). The government, we have stated, needs to run "as effectively and efficiently as possible." *Engquist v. Oregon Dept. of Agriculture* (2008). That means it must be able, much as a private employer is, to manage its workforce as it thinks fit. A public employee thus must submit to "certain limitations on his or her freedom." *Garcetti v. Ceballos* (2006). Government workers, of course, do not wholly "lose their constitutional rights when they accept their positions." *Engquist.* But under our precedent, their rights often yield when weighed "against the realities of the employment context." If it were otherwise — if every employment decision were to "bec[o]me a constitutional matter" — "the Government could not function." *NASA,* 562 U.S., at 149.

Those principles apply with full force when public employees' expressive rights are at issue. As we have explained: "Government employers, like private employers, need a significant degree of control over their employees' words" in order to "efficient[ly] provi[de] public services." *Garcetti.* Again, significant control does not mean absolute authority. In particular, the Court has guarded against government efforts to "leverage the employment relationship" to shut down its employees' speech as private citizens. But when the government imposes speech restrictions relating to workplace operations, of the kind a private employer also would, the Court reliably upholds them. . . .

[The] majority's distinction between compelling and restricting speech also lacks force. The majority posits that compelling speech always works a greater injury, and so always requires a greater justification. But the only case the majority cites for that reading of our precedent is possibly (thankfully) the most exceptional in our First Amendment annals: It involved the state forcing children to swear an oath contrary to their religious beliefs. *West Virginia Bd. of Ed. v. Barnette* (1943). Regulations challenged as compelling expression do not usually look anything like that — and for that reason, the standard First Amendment rule is that the "difference between compelled speech and compelled silence" is "without constitutional significance." *Riley v. National Federation of Blind of N. C., Inc.* (1988); see *Wooley v. Maynard* (1977) (referring to "[t]he right to speak and the right to refrain from speaking" as "complementary components" of the First Amendment). And if anything, the First Amendment scales tip the opposite way when (as here) the government is not compelling actual speech, but instead compelling a subsidy that others will use for expression. See Brief for Eugene Volokh et al. as *Amici Curiae* (offering many examples to show that the First Amendment "simply do[es] not guarantee that one's hard-earned dollars will never be spent on speech one disapproves of"). So when a government mandates a speech subsidy from a public employee — here, we might think of it as levying a tax to support collective bargaining — it should get at least as much deference as when it restricts the employee's speech. As this case shows, the former may advance a managerial interest as well as the latter — in which case the government's "freer hand" in dealing with its employees should apply with equal (if not greater) force. *NASA.* . . .

The key point about *Abood* is that it fit naturally with this Court's consistent teaching about the permissibility of regulating public employees' speech. The

Court allows a government entity to regulate that expression in aid of managing its workforce to effectively provide public services. That is just what a government aims to do when it enforces a fair-share agreement. And so, the key point about today's decision is that it creates an unjustified hole in the law, applicable to union fees alone. This case is *sui generis* among those addressing public employee speech — and will almost surely remain so.

III

But the worst part of today's opinion is where the majority subverts all known principles of *stare decisis*. The majority makes plain, in the first 33 pages of its decision, that it believes *Abood* was wrong.[4] But even if that were true (which it is not), it is not enough. "Respecting *stare decisis* means sticking to some wrong decisions." *Kimble v. Marvel Entertainment, LLC* (2015). Any departure from settled precedent (so the Court has often stated) demands a "special justification — over and above the belief that the precedent was wrongly decided." And the majority does not have anything close. To the contrary: all that is "special" in this case — especially the massive reliance interests at stake — demands retaining *Abood,* beyond even the normal precedent.

Consider first why these principles about precedent are so important. *Stare decisis* — "the idea that today's Court should stand by yesterday's decisions" — is "a foundation stone of the rule of law." *Kimble* (quoting *Michigan v. Bay Mills Indian Community* (2014)). It "promotes the evenhanded, predictable, and consistent development" of legal doctrine. *Payne v. Tennessee* (1991). It fosters respect for and reliance on judicial decisions. And it "contributes to the actual and perceived integrity of the judicial process," by ensuring that decisions are "founded in the law rather than in the proclivities of individuals," *Vasquez v. Hillery* (1986).

And *Abood* is not just any precedent: It is embedded in the law (not to mention, as I'll later address, in the world) in a way not many decisions are. Over four decades, this Court has cited *Abood* favorably many times, and has affirmed and applied its central distinction between the costs of collective bargaining (which the government can charge to all employees) and those of political activities (which it cannot). Reviewing those decisions not a decade ago, this Court — unanimously — called the *Abood* rule "a general First Amendment principle." *Locke.* And indeed, the Court has relied on that rule when deciding cases involving compelled speech subsidies outside the labor sphere — cases today's decision does not question.

Ignoring our repeated validation of *Abood,* the majority claims it has become "an outlier among our First Amendment cases." That claim fails most spectacularly for reasons already discussed: *Abood* coheres with the *Pickering* approach

---

4. And then, after ostensibly turning to *stare decisis,* the majority spends another four pages insisting that *Abood* was "not well reasoned," which is just more of the same.

to reviewing regulation of public employees' speech. Needing to stretch further, the majority suggests that *Abood* conflicts with "our political patronage decisions." But in fact those decisions strike a balance much like *Abood*'s. On the one hand, the Court has enabled governments to compel policymakers to support a political party, because that requirement (like fees for collective bargaining) can reasonably be thought to advance the interest in workplace effectiveness. On the other hand, the Court has barred governments from extending that rule to non-policymaking employees because that application (like fees for political campaigns) can't be thought to promote that interest; the government is instead trying to "leverage the employment relationship" to achieve other goals. So all that the majority has left is *Knox* and *Harris*. Dicta in those recent decisions indeed began the assault on *Abood* that has culminated today. But neither actually addressed the extent to which a public employer may regulate its own employees' speech. Relying on them is bootstrapping — and mocking *stare decisis*. Don't like a decision? Just throw some gratuitous criticisms into a couple of opinions and a few years later point to them as "special justifications."

The majority is likewise wrong to invoke "workability" as a reason for overruling *Abood*. Does *Abood* require drawing a line? Yes, between a union's collective-bargaining activities and its political activities. Is that line perfectly and pristinely "precis[e]," as the majority demands? Well, not quite that — but as exercises of constitutional linedrawing go, *Abood* stands well above average. In the 40 years since *Abood,* this Court has had to resolve only a handful of cases raising questions about the distinction. To my knowledge, the circuit courts are not divided on any classification issue; neither are they issuing distress signals of the kind that sometimes prompt the Court to reverse a decision. And that tranquility is unsurprising: There may be some gray areas (there always are), but in the mine run of cases, everyone knows the difference between politicking and collective bargaining. The majority cites some disagreement in two of the classification cases this Court decided — as if non-unanimity among Justices were something startling. And it notes that a dissenter in one of those cases called the Court's approach "malleable" and "not principled" — as though those weren't stock terms in dissenting vocabulary. As I wrote in *Harris* a few Terms ago: "If the kind of hand-wringing about blurry lines that the majority offers were enough to justify breaking with precedent, we might have to discard whole volumes of the U.S. Reports."

And in any event, one *stare decisis* factor — reliance — dominates all others here and demands keeping *Abood*. *Stare decisis,* this Court has held, "has added force when the legislature, in the public sphere, and citizens, in the private realm, have acted in reliance on a previous decision." *Hilton v. South Carolina Public Railways Comm'n* (1991). That is because overruling a decision would then "require an extensive legislative response" or "dislodge settled rights and expectations." *Ibid.* Both will happen here: The Court today wreaks havoc on entrenched legislative and contractual arrangements.

Over 20 States have by now enacted statutes authorizing fair-share provisions. To be precise, 22 States, the District of Columbia, and Puerto Rico — plus another two States for police and firefighter unions. Many of those States have multiple statutory provisions, with variations for different categories of public employees. Every one of them will now need to come up with new ways — elaborated in new statutes — to structure relations between government employers and their workers. The majority responds, in a footnote no less, that this is of no proper concern to the Court. See *ante*. But in fact, we have weighed heavily against "abandon[ing] our settled jurisprudence" that "[s]tate legislatures have relied upon" it and would have to "reexamine [and amend] their statutes" if it were overruled. *Allied-Signal, Inc. v. Director, Div. of Taxation* (1992).

Still more, thousands of current contracts covering millions of workers provide for agency fees. Usually, this Court recognizes that "[c]onsiderations in favor of *stare decisis* are at their acme in cases involving property and contract rights." *Payne*. Not today. The majority undoes bargains reached all over the country.[5] It prevents the parties from fulfilling other commitments they have made based on those agreements. It forces the parties — immediately — to renegotiate once-settled terms and create new tradeoffs. It does so knowing that many of the parties will have to revise (or redo) multiple contracts simultaneously. (New York City, for example, has agreed to agency fees in 144 contracts with 97 public-sector unions.) It does so knowing that those renegotiations will occur in an environment of legal uncertainty, as state governments scramble to enact new labor legislation. It does so with no real clue of what will happen next — of how its action will alter public-sector labor relations. It does so even though the government services affected — policing, firefighting, teaching, transportation, sanitation (and more) — affect the quality of life of tens of millions of Americans.

The majority asserts that no one should care much because the canceled agreements are "of rather short duration" and would "expire on their own in a few years' time." But to begin with, that response ignores the substantial time and effort that state legislatures will have to devote to revamping their statutory schemes. And anyway, it misunderstands the nature of contract negotiations when the parties have a continuing relationship. The parties, in renewing an old collective-bargaining agreement, don't start on an empty page. Instead, various "long-settled" terms — like fair-share provisions — are taken as a given. So the majority's ruling does more than advance by a few years a future renegotiation (though even that would be significant). In most cases, it commands new bargaining over how to replace a term that the parties never expected to change. And not just new bargaining; given the interests at stake, complicated and possibly contentious bargaining as well.

The majority, though, offers another reason for not worrying about reliance: The parties, it says, "have been on notice for years regarding this Court's misgivings about *Abood*." Here, the majority proudly lays claim to its 6-year crusade to ban agency fees. In *Knox*, the majority relates, it described *Abood* as an

---

5. Indeed, some agency-fee provisions, if canceled, could bring down entire contracts because they lack severability clauses.

"anomaly." Then, in *Harris,* it "cataloged *Abood*'s many weaknesses." Finally, in *Friedrichs,* "we granted a petition for certiorari asking us to" reverse *Abood,* but found ourselves equally divided. "During this period of time," the majority concludes, public-sector unions "must have understood that the constitutionality of [an agency-fee] provision was uncertain." And so, says the majority, they should have structured their affairs accordingly.

But that argument reflects a radically wrong understanding of how *stare decisis* operates. Justice Scalia once confronted a similar argument for "disregard[ing] reliance interests" and showed how antithetical it was to rule-of-law principles. *Quill Corp. v. North Dakota* (1992) (concurring opinion). He noted first what we always tell lower courts: "If a precedent of this Court has direct application in a case, yet appears to rest on reasons rejected in some other line of decisions, [they] should follow the case which directly controls, leaving to this Court the prerogative of overruling its own decisions." That instruction, Justice Scalia explained, was "incompatible" with an expectation that "private parties anticipate our overrulings." He concluded: "[R]eliance upon a square, unabandoned holding of the Supreme Court is *always* justifiable reliance." *Abood*'s holding was square. It was unabandoned before today. It was, in other words, the law — however much some were working overtime to make it not. Parties, both unions and governments, were thus justified in relying on it. And they did rely, to an extent rare among our decisions. To dismiss the overthrowing of their settled expectations as entailing no more than some "adjustments" and "unpleasant transition costs," is to trivialize *stare decisis.*

IV

There is no sugarcoating today's opinion. The majority overthrows a decision entrenched in this Nation's law — and in its economic life — for over 40 years. As a result, it prevents the American people, acting through their state and local officials, from making important choices about workplace governance. And it does so by weaponizing the First Amendment, in a way that unleashes judges, now and in the future, to intervene in economic and regulatory policy.

Departures from *stare decisis* are supposed to be "exceptional action[s]" demanding "special justification" — but the majority offers nothing like that here. In contrast to the vigor of its attack on *Abood,* the majority's discussion of *stare decisis* barely limps to the finish line. And no wonder: The standard factors this Court considers when deciding to overrule a decision all cut one way. *Abood*'s legal underpinnings have not eroded over time: *Abood* is now, as it was when issued, consistent with this Court's First Amendment law. *Abood* provided a workable standard for courts to apply. And *Abood* has generated enormous reliance interests. The majority has overruled *Abood* for no exceptional or special reason, but because it never liked the decision. It has overruled *Abood* because it wanted to.

Because, that is, it wanted to pick the winning side in what should be — and until now, has been — an energetic policy debate. Some state and local governments (and the constituents they serve) think that stable unions promote healthy labor relations and thereby improve the provision of services to the public. Other state and local governments (and their constituents) think, to the contrary, that strong unions impose excessive costs and impair those services. Americans have debated the pros and cons for many decades—in large part, by deciding whether to use fair-share arrangements. Yesterday, 22 States were on one side, 28 on the other (ignoring a couple of in-betweeners). Today, that healthy—that democratic—debate ends. The majority has adjudged who should prevail. Indeed, the majority is bursting with pride over what it has accomplished: Now those 22 States, it crows, "can follow the model of the federal government and 28 other States."

And maybe most alarming, the majority has chosen the winners by turning the First Amendment into a sword, and using it against workaday economic and regulatory policy. Today is not the first time the Court has wielded the First Amendment in such an aggressive way. See, e.g., *National Institute of Family and Life Advocates v. Becerra* (invalidating a law requiring medical and counseling facilities to provide relevant information to users); *Sorrell v. IMS Health Inc.* (2011) (striking down a law that restricted pharmacies from selling various data). And it threatens not to be the last. Speech is everywhere—a part of every human activity (employment, health care, securities trading, you name it). For that reason, almost all economic and regulatory policy affects or touches speech. So the majority's road runs long. And at every stop are black-robed rulers overriding citizens' choices. The First Amendment was meant for better things. It was meant not to undermine but to protect democratic governance—including over the role of public-sector unions.

* * *

ASSIGNMENT 3

STUDY GUIDE:

- What is the "all-comers" policy?
- Does it violate the Freedom of Association to allow anyone to join a club?
- Do you think the risk is real that non-adherents will try to infiltrate the Christian Legal Society?
- What is this case really about? Free speech? Freedom of association? Or free exercise?

Christian Legal Society Chapter of the University of California, Hastings College of Law v. Martinez
130 S. Ct. 2971 (2010)

JUSTICE GINSBURG delivered the opinion of the Court.

In a series of decisions, this Court has emphasized that the First Amendment generally precludes public universities from denying student organizations access to school-sponsored forums because of the groups' viewpoints. See *Rosenberger v. Rector and Visitors of Univ. of Va.* (1995); *Widmar v. Vincent* (1981); *Healy v. James* (1972). This case concerns a novel question regarding student activities at public universities: May a public law school condition its official recognition of a student group—and the attendant use of school funds and facilities—on the organization's agreement to open eligibility for membership and leadership to all students?

In the view of petitioner Christian Legal Society (CLS), an accept-all-comers policy impairs its First Amendment rights to free speech, expressive association, and free exercise of religion by prompting it, on pain of relinquishing the advantages of recognition, to accept members who do not share the organization's core beliefs about religion and sexual orientation. From the perspective of respondent Hastings College of the Law (Hastings or the Law School), CLS seeks special dispensation from an across-the-board open-access requirement designed to further the reasonable educational purposes underpinning the school's student-organization program.

In accord with the District Court and the Court of Appeals, we reject CLS's First Amendment challenge. Compliance with Hastings' all-comers policy, we conclude, is a reasonable, viewpoint-neutral condition on access to the student-organization forum. In requiring CLS—in common with all other student organizations—to choose between welcoming all students and forgoing the benefits of official recognition, we hold, Hastings did not transgress constitutional limitations. CLS, it bears emphasis, seeks not parity with other organizations, but a preferential exemption from Hastings' policy. The First Amendment shields CLS against state prohibition of the organization's expressive activity, however exclusionary that activity may be. But CLS enjoys no constitutional right to state subvention of its selectivity.

I

Through its "Registered Student Organization" (RSO) program, Hastings extends official recognition to student groups. Several benefits attend this school-approved status. . . . In exchange for these benefits, RSOs must abide by certain conditions. . . .

The Law School's Policy on Nondiscrimination (Nondiscrimination Policy), which binds RSOs, states:

> "[Hastings] is committed to a policy against legally impermissible, arbitrary or unreasonable discriminatory practices. All groups, including administration, faculty, student governments, [Hastings]-owned student residence facilities and programs sponsored by [Hastings], are governed by this policy of nondiscrimination. [Hasting's] policy on nondiscrimination is to comply fully with applicable law.
>
> "[Hastings] shall not discriminate unlawfully on the basis of race, color, religion, national origin, ancestry, disability, age, sex or sexual orientation. This nondiscrimination policy covers admission, access and treatment in Hastings-sponsored programs and activities."

Hastings interprets the Nondiscrimination Policy, as it relates to the RSO program, to mandate acceptance of all comers: School-approved groups must "allow any student to participate, become a member, or seek leadership positions in the organization, regardless of [her] status or beliefs." From Hastings' adoption of its Nondiscrimination Policy in 1990 until the events stirring this litigation, "no student organization at Hastings . . . ever sought an exemption from the Policy."

In 2004, CLS became the first student group to do so. At the beginning of the academic year, the leaders of a predecessor Christian organization — which had been an RSO at Hastings for a decade — formed CLS by affiliating with the national Christian Legal Society (CLS-National). CLS-National, an association of Christian lawyers and law students, charters student chapters at law schools throughout the country. CLS chapters must adopt bylaws that, *inter alia,* require members and officers to sign a "Statement of Faith" and to conduct their lives in accord with prescribed principles. Among those tenets is the belief that sexual activity should not occur outside of marriage between a man and a woman; CLS thus interprets its bylaws to exclude from affiliation anyone who engages in "unrepentant homosexual conduct." CLS also excludes students who hold religious convictions different from those in the Statement of Faith. . . .

On September 17, 2004, CLS submitted to Hastings an application for RSO status, accompanied by all required documents, including the set of bylaws mandated by CLS-National. Several days later, the Law School rejected the application; CLS's bylaws, Hastings explained, did not comply with the Nondiscrimination Policy because CLS barred students based on religion and sexual orientation. . . .

On October 22, 2004, CLS filed suit against various Hastings officers and administrators under 42 U.S.C. § 1983. Its complaint alleged that Hastings' refusal to grant the organization RSO status violated CLS's First and Fourteenth Amendment rights to free speech, expressive association, and free exercise of religion. . . .

                                         III

In support of the argument that Hastings' all-comers policy treads on its First Amendment rights to free speech and expressive association, CLS draws on two lines of decisions. First, in a progression of cases, this Court has employed forum analysis to determine when a governmental entity, in regulating property in its charge, may place limitations on speech. . . .

Second, as evidenced by another set of decisions, this Court has rigorously reviewed laws and regulations that constrain associational freedom. In the context of public accommodations, we have subjected restrictions on that freedom to close scrutiny; such restrictions are permitted only if they serve "compelling state interests" that are "unrelated to the suppression of ideas" — interests that cannot be advanced "through . . . significantly less restrictive [means]." *Roberts v. United States Jaycees* (1984). See also, *e.g., Boy Scouts of America v. Dale* (2000). "Freedom of association," we have recognized, "plainly presupposes a freedom not to associate." *Roberts*. Insisting that an organization embrace unwelcome members, we have therefore concluded, "directly and immediately affects associational rights." *Dale*.

CLS would have us engage each line of cases independently, but its expressive-association and free-speech arguments merge: *Who* speaks on its behalf, CLS reasons, colors *what* concept is conveyed. See Brief for Petitioner 35 (expressive association in this case is "the functional equivalent of speech itself"). It therefore makes little sense to treat CLS's speech and association claims as discrete. . . . Instead, three observations lead us to conclude that our limited-public-forum precedents supply the appropriate framework for assessing both CLS's speech and association rights.

First, the same considerations that have led us to apply a less restrictive level of scrutiny to speech in limited public forums as compared to other environments, apply with equal force to expressive association occurring in limited public forums. As just noted, speech and expressive-association rights are closely linked. See *Roberts* (Associational freedom is "implicit in the right to engage in activities protected by the First Amendment."). When these intertwined rights arise in exactly the same context, it would be anomalous for a restriction on speech to survive constitutional review under our limited-public-forum test only to be invalidated as an impermissible infringement of expressive association. That result would be all the more anomalous in this case, for CLS suggests that its expressive-association claim plays a part auxiliary to speech's starring role.

Second, and closely related, the strict scrutiny we have applied in some settings to laws that burden expressive association would, in practical effect, invalidate a defining characteristic of limited public forums — the State may "reserv[e] [them] for certain groups." *Rosenberger*. See also *Perry Ed. Assn.* ("Implicit in the concept" of a limited public forum is the State's "right to make distinctions in access on the basis of . . . speaker identity."); *Cornelius* ("[A] speaker may be excluded from" a limited public forum "if he is not a member of the class of speakers for whose especial benefit the forum was created.").

An example sharpens the tip of this point: Schools, including Hastings, ordinarily, and without controversy, limit official student-group recognition to organizations comprising only students — even if those groups wish to associate with nonstudents. See, *e.g.,* Volokh, Freedom of Expressive Association and Government Subsidies, 58 Stan. L. Rev.1919, 1940 (2006). The same ground rules must govern both speech and association challenges in the limited-public-forum context, lest strict scrutiny trump a public university's ability to "confin[e] a [speech] forum to the limited and legitimate purposes for which it was created." *Rosenberger*. See also *Healy* ("Associational activities need not be tolerated where they infringe reasonable campus rules.").

Third, this case fits comfortably within the limited-public-forum category, for CLS, in seeking what is effectively a state subsidy, faces only indirect pressure to modify its membership policies; CLS may exclude any person for any reason if it forgoes the benefits of official recognition. The expressive-association precedents on which CLS relies, in contrast, involved regulations that *compelled* a group to include unwanted members, with no choice to opt out. See, *e.g., Dale* (regulation "forc[ed] [the Boy Scouts] to accept members it [did] not desire"; *Roberts* ("There can be no clearer example of an intrusion into the internal structure or affairs of an association than" forced inclusion of unwelcome participants.).[7]

In diverse contexts, our decisions have distinguished between policies that require action and those that withhold benefits. See, *e.g., Grove City College v. Bell* (1984); *Bob Jones Univ. v. United States* (1983). Application of the less restrictive limited-public-forum analysis better accounts for the fact that Hastings, through its RSO program, is dangling the carrot of subsidy, not wielding the stick of prohibition. Cf. *Norwood v. Harrison* (1973) ("That the Constitution may compel toleration of private discrimination in some circumstances does not mean that it requires state support for such discrimination.")

In sum, we are persuaded that our limited-public-forum precedents adequately respect both CLS's speech and expressive-association rights, and fairly balance those rights against Hastings' interests as property owner and educational institution. We turn to the merits of the instant dispute, therefore, with the limited-public-forum decisions as our guide. . . .

We first consider whether Hastings' policy is reasonable taking into account the RSO forum's function and "all the surrounding circumstances." *Cornelius.*

With appropriate regard for school administrators' judgment, we review the justifications Hastings offers in defense of its all-comers requirement. First, the open-access policy "ensures that the leadership, educational, and social opportunities afforded by [RSOs] are available to all students." . . . Just as "Hastings does not allow its professors to host classes open only to those students with a certain status or belief," so the Law School may decide, reasonably in our view, "that the . . . educational experience is best promoted when all participants in the forum must provide equal access to all students." . . .

Second, the all-comers requirement helps Hastings police the written terms of its Nondiscrimination Policy without inquiring into an RSO's motivation for membership restrictions. To bring the RSO program within CLS's view of the Constitution's limits, CLS proposes that Hastings permit exclusion because of *belief* but forbid discrimination due to *status.* . . . But that proposal would impose on Hastings a daunting labor. How should the Law School go about determining whether a student organization cloaked prohibited status exclusion in belief-based garb? If a hypothetical Male-Superiority Club barred a female student

---

7. CLS also brackets with expressive-association precedents our decision in *Hurley v. Irish-American Gay, Lesbian and Bisexual Group of Boston, Inc.* (1995). There, a veterans group sponsoring a St. Patrick's Day parade challenged a state law requiring it to allow gay individuals to march in the parade behind a banner celebrating their Irish heritage and sexual orientation. In evaluating that challenge, the *Hurley* Court focused on the veterans group's interest in controlling the message conveyed by the organization. Whether Hurley is best conceptualized as a speech or association case (or both), however, that precedent is of little help to CLS. Hurley involved the application of a statewide public-accommodations law to the most traditional of public forums: the street. That context differs markedly from the limited public forum at issue here: a university's application of an all-comers policy to its student-organization program.

from running for its presidency, for example, how could the Law School tell whether the group rejected her bid because of her sex or because, by seeking to lead the club, she manifested a lack of belief in its fundamental philosophy?

This case itself is instructive in this regard. CLS contends that it does not exclude individuals because of sexual orientation, but rather "on the basis of a conjunction of conduct and the belief that the conduct is not wrong." Our decisions have declined to distinguish between status and conduct in this context. See *Lawrence v. Texas* (2003) ("When homosexual *conduct* is made criminal by the law of the State, that declaration in and of itself is an invitation to subject homosexual *persons* to discrimination." . . .

Third, the Law School reasonably adheres to the view that an all-comers policy, to the extent it brings together individuals with diverse backgrounds and beliefs, "encourages tolerance, cooperation, and learning among students." And if the policy sometimes produces discord, Hastings can rationally rank among RSO-program goals development of conflict-resolution skills, toleration, and readiness to find common ground. . . .

In sum, the several justifications Hastings asserts in support of its all-comers requirement are surely reasonable in light of the RSO forum's purposes.

Law School's policy is all the more creditworthy in view of the "substantial alternative channels that remain open for [CLS-student] communication to take place." . . . In this case, Hastings offered CLS access to school facilities to conduct meetings and the use of chalkboards and generally available bulletin boards to advertise events. Although CLS could not take advantage of RSO-specific methods of communication, the advent of electronic media and social-networking sites reduces the importance of those channels. . . .

CLS nevertheless deems Hastings' all-comers policy "frankly absurd." . . . "There can be no diversity of viewpoints in a forum," it asserts, "if groups are not permitted to form around viewpoints." *Id.*, at 50; accord *post*, at 3013 (Alito, J., dissenting). This catchphrase confuses CLS's preferred policy with constitutional limitation — the *advisability* of Hastings' policy does not control its *permissibility*. . . . Instead, we have repeatedly stressed that a State's restriction on access to a limited public forum "need not be the most reasonable or the only reasonable limitation." *Cornelius*.

CLS also assails the reasonableness of the all-comers policy in light of the RSO forum's function by forecasting that the policy will facilitate hostile takeovers; if organizations must open their arms to all, CLS contends, saboteurs will infiltrate groups to subvert their mission and message. This supposition strikes us as more hypothetical than real. CLS points to no history or prospect of RSO-hijackings at Hastings. . . . Students tend to self-sort and presumably will not endeavor en masse to join — let alone seek leadership positions in — groups pursuing missions wholly at odds with their personal beliefs. And if a rogue student intent on sabotaging an organization's objectives nevertheless attempted a takeover, the members of that group would not likely elect her as an officer.

RSOs, moreover, in harmony with the all-comers policy, may condition eligibility for membership and leadership on attendance, the payment of dues, or other neutral requirements designed to ensure that students join because of their commitment to a group's vitality, not its demise. Several RSOs at Hastings limit their membership rolls and officer slates in just this way. . . .

Finally, CLS asserts (and the dissent repeats, *post,* at 3015-3016) that the Law School lacks any legitimate interest—let alone one reasonably related to the RSO forum's purposes—in urging "religious groups not to favor co-religionists for purposes of their religious activities." CLS's analytical error lies in focusing on the benefits it must forgo while ignoring the interests of those it seeks to fence out: Exclusion, after all, has two sides. Hastings, caught in the crossfire between a group's desire to exclude and students' demand for equal access, may reasonably draw a line in the sand permitting *all* organizations to express what they wish but *no* group to discriminate in membership.[8]

D

Although this aspect of limited-public-forum analysis has been the constitutional sticking point in our prior decisions, as earlier recounted we need not dwell on it here. It is, after all, hard to imagine a more viewpoint-neutral policy than one requiring *all* student groups to accept *all* comers. In contrast to *Healy, Widmar,* and *Rosenberger,* in which universities singled out organizations for disfavored treatment because of their points of view, Hastings' all-comers requirement draws no distinction between groups based on their message or perspective. An all- comers condition on access to RSO status, in short, is textbook viewpoint neutral.[9]

. . . Even if a regulation has a differential impact on groups wishing to enforce exclusionary membership policies, "[w]here the [State] does not target conduct on the basis of its expressive content, acts are not shielded from regulation merely because they express a discriminatory idea or philosophy." *R.A.V. v. St.*

---

8. The question here, however, is not whether Hastings *could,* consistent with the Constitution, provide religious groups dispensation from the all-comers policy by permitting them to restrict membership to those who share their faith. It is instead whether Hastings *must* grant that exemption. This Court's decision in *Employment Div., Dept. of Human Resources of Ore. v. Smith* (1990), unequivocally answers no to that latter question.

9. Relying exclusively on *Board of Regents of Univ. of Wis. System v. Southworth* (2000), the dissent "would not be so quick to jump to th[e] conclusion" that the all-comers policy is viewpoint neutral. Careful consideration of *Southworth,* however, reveals how desperate the dissent's argument is. In *Southworth,* university students challenged a mandatory student-activity fee used to fund student groups. Finding the political and ideological speech of certain groups offensive, the student-challengers argued that imposition of the fee violated their First Amendment rights. This Court upheld the university's choice to subsidize groups whose expression some students found distasteful, but we admonished that the university could not "prefer some viewpoints to others" in the distribution of funds. We cautioned that the university's referendum process, which allowed students to vote on whether a student organization would receive financial support, risked violation of this principle by allowing students to select groups to fund based on their viewpoints. In this case, in contrast, the all-comers policy governs all RSOs; Hastings does not pick and choose which organizations must comply with the policy on the basis of viewpoint. *Southworth* accordingly provides no support for the dissent's warped analysis.

Paul (1992). See also *Roberts* (State's nondiscrimination law did not "distinguish between prohibited and permitted activity on the basis of viewpoint.").

Hastings' requirement that student groups accept all comers, we are satisfied, "is justified without reference to the content [or viewpoint] of the regulated speech." . . .

Finding Hastings' open-access condition on RSO status reasonable and viewpoint neutral, we reject CLS' free-speech and expressive-association claims.

JUSTICE STEVENS, concurring.

To be sure, the policy may end up having greater consequence for religious groups — whether and to what extent it will is far from clear *ex ante* — inasmuch as they are more likely than their secular counterparts to wish to exclude students of particular faiths. But there is likewise no evidence that the policy was intended to cause harm to religious groups, or that it has in practice caused significant harm to their operations. And it is a basic tenet of First Amendment law that disparate impact does not, in itself, constitute viewpoint discrimination. . . .

JUSTICE KENNEDY, concurring.

An objection might be that the all-comers policy, even if not so designed or intended, in fact makes it difficult for certain groups to express their views in a manner essential to their message. A group that can limit membership to those who agree in full with its aims and purposes may be more effective in delivering its message or furthering its expressive objectives; and the Court has recognized that this interest can be protected against governmental interference or regulation. See *Boy Scouts of America v. Dale* (2000). By allowing like-minded students to form groups around shared identities, a school creates room for self-expression and personal development. See *Board of Regents of Univ. of Wis. System v. Southworth* (2000) ("The University's whole justification for [its student activity program] is that it springs from the initiative of the students, who alone give it purpose and content in the course of their extracurricular endeavors").

In the instant case, however, if the membership qualification were enforced, it would contradict a legitimate purpose for having created the limited forum in the first place. Many educational institutions, including respondent Hastings College of Law, have recognized that the process of learning occurs both formally in a classroom setting and informally outside of it. . . .

Law students come from many backgrounds and have but three years to meet each other and develop their skills. They do so by participating in a community that teaches them how to create arguments in a convincing, rational, and respectful manner and to express doubt and disagreement in a professional way. A law school furthers these objectives by allowing broad diversity in registered student organizations. But these objectives may be better achieved if students can act cooperatively to learn from and teach each other through interactions in social and intellectual contexts. A vibrant dialogue is not possible if students wall themselves off from opposing points of view. . . . The school's policy therefore represents a permissible effort to preserve the value of its forum.

JUSTICE ALITO, with whom THE CHIEF JUSTICE, JUSTICE SCALIA, and JUSTICE THOMAS join, dissenting.

The proudest boast of our free speech jurisprudence is that we protect the freedom to express "the thought that we hate." *United States v. Schwimmer* (1929) (Holmes, J., dissenting). Today's decision rests on a very different principle: no freedom for expression that offends prevailing standards of political correctness in our country's institutions of higher learning. . . .

The Court's treatment of this case is deeply disappointing. The Court does not address the constitutionality of the very different policy that Hastings invoked when it denied CLS's application for registration. Nor does the Court address the constitutionality of the policy that Hastings now purports to follow. And the Court ignores strong evidence that the accept-all-comers policy is not viewpoint neutral because it was announced as a pretext to justify viewpoint discrimination. Brushing aside inconvenient precedent, the Court arms public educational institutions with a handy weapon for suppressing the speech of unpopular groups — groups to which, as Hastings candidly puts it, these institutions "do not wish to . . . lend their name[s]." . . .

IV

Analyzed under this framework, Hastings' refusal to register CLS pursuant to its Nondiscrimination Policy plainly fails. . . .

Unlike the Court, Justice Stevens attempts a defense, contending that the Nondiscrimination Policy is viewpoint neutral. But his arguments are squarely contrary to established precedent.

Justice Stevens first argues that the Nondiscrimination Policy is viewpoint neutral because it "does not regulate expression or belief at all" but instead regulates conduct. . . . This Court has held, however, that the particular conduct at issue here constitutes a form of expression that is protected by the First Amendment. It is now well established that the First Amendment shields the right of a group to engage in expressive association by limiting membership to persons whose admission does not significantly interfere with the group's ability to convey its views. See *Dale*; *Roberts v. United States Jaycees* (1984); see also *New York State Club Assn., Inc. v. City of New York* (1988) (acknowledging that an "association might be able to show that it is organized for specific expressive purposes and that it will not be able to advocate its desired viewpoints nearly as effectively if it cannot confine its membership to those who share the same sex, for example, or the same religion"); *Widmar,* ("[T]he First Amendment rights of speech and association extend to the campuses of state universities"). Indeed, the opinion of the Court, which Justice Stevens joins, acknowledges this rule.

Here, the Nondiscrimination Policy permitted membership requirements that expressed a secular viewpoint. But religious groups were not permitted to express a religious viewpoint by limiting membership to students who shared their religious viewpoints. Under established precedent, this was viewpoint discrimination. . . .

It bears emphasis that permitting religious groups to limit membership to those who share the groups' beliefs would not have the effect of allowing other groups to discriminate on the basis of religion. It would not mean, for example, that fraternities or sororities could exclude students on that basis. As our cases have recognized, the right of expressive association permits a group to exclude an applicant for membership only if the admission of that person would "affec[t] in a significant way the group's ability to advocate public or private viewpoints." *Dale*. Groups that do not engage in expressive association have no such right. Similarly, groups that are dedicated to expressing a viewpoint on a secular topic (for example, a political or ideological viewpoint) would have no basis for limiting membership based on religion because the presence of members with diverse religious beliefs would have no effect on the group's ability to express its views. But for religious groups, the situation is very different. This point was put well by a coalition of Muslim, Christian, Jewish, and Sikh groups: "Of course there is a strong interest in prohibiting religious discrimination where religion is irrelevant. But it is fundamentally confused to apply a rule against religious discrimination to a religious association." . . .

In short, the RSO forum, true to its design, has allowed Hastings students to replicate on campus a broad array of private, independent, noncommercial organizations that is very similar to those that nonstudents have formed in the outside world.

The accept-all-comers policy is antithetical to the design of the RSO forum for the same reason that a state-imposed accept-all-comers policy would violate the First Amendment rights of private groups if applied off campus. As explained above, a group's First Amendment right of expressive association is burdened by the "forced inclusion" of members whose presence would "affec[t] in a significant way the group's ability to advocate public or private viewpoints." *Dale*. The Court has therefore held that the government may not compel a group that engages in "expressive association" to admit such a member unless the government has a compelling interest, " 'unrelated to the suppression of ideas, that cannot be achieved through means significantly less restrictive of associational freedoms.' " *Ibid.* (quoting *Roberts*). . . .

The Court is also wrong in holding that the accept-all-comers policy is viewpoint neutral. The Court proclaims that it would be "hard to imagine a more viewpoint-neutral policy," *ante,* at 2993, but I would not be so quick to jump to this conclusion. Even if it is assumed that the policy is viewpoint neutral on its face,[10] there is strong evidence in the record that the policy was announced as a pretext . . . for the law school's unlawful denial of CLS's registration application under the Nondiscrimination Policy.

---

10. . . . The Court attempts to distinguish *Southworth* as involving a funding mechanism for student groups that operated selectively, based on groups' viewpoints. But that mechanism—a student referendum process—placed all students at risk of "being required to pay fees which are subsidies for speech they find objectionable, even offensive," solely upon a majority vote of the student body. That is no different in principle than an accept-all-comers policy that places all student organizations at risk of takeover by a majority that is hostile to a group's viewpoint.

Justice Kennedy takes a similarly mistaken tack. He contends that CLS "would have a substantial case on the merits if it were shown that the all-comers policy was . . . used to infiltrate the group or challenge its leadership in order to stifle its views," (concurring opinion), but he does not explain on what ground such a claim could succeed. The Court holds that the accept-all-comers policy is viewpoint neutral and reasonable in light of the purposes of the RSO forum. How could those characteristics be altered by a change in the membership of one of the forum's registered groups? No explanation is apparent.

In the end, the Court refuses to acknowledge the consequences of its holding. A true accept-all-comers policy permits small unpopular groups to be taken over by students who wish to change the views that the group expresses. Rules requiring that members attend meetings, pay dues, and behave politely, would not eliminate this threat.

The possibility of such takeovers, however, is by no means the most important effect of the Court's holding. There are religious groups that cannot in good conscience agree in their bylaws that they will admit persons who do not share their faith, and for these groups, the consequence of an accept-all-comers policy is marginalization. . . . This is where the Court's decision leads.

* * *

I do not think it is an exaggeration to say that today's decision is a serious setback for freedom of expression in this country. Our First Amendment reflects a "profound national commitment to the principle that debate on public issues should be uninhibited, robust, and wide-open." *New York Times Co. v. Sullivan* (1964). Even if the United States is the only Nation that shares this commitment to the same extent, I would not change our law to conform to the international norm. I fear that the Court's decision marks a turn in that direction. Even those who find CLS's views objectionable should be concerned about the way the group has been treated — by Hastings, the Court of Appeals, and now this Court. I can only hope that this decision will turn out to be an aberration.

Chapter 18

The Free Exercise of Religion

STUDY GUIDE:

- Is baking a cake "speech" protected by the Freedom of Speech? The majority opinion ultimately does not resolve this question.
- Why did the Court find a violation of the Free Exercise Clause? Does this ruling call into question other laws that discriminate in the workplace?
- How does Justice Ginsburg's dissent distinguish this case from "*Church of Lukumi Babalu Aye, Inc. v. Hialeah* (1993), where the government action that violated a principle of religious neutrality implicated a sole decision-making body, the city council"?

Masterpiece Cakeshop, Ltd. v. Colorado Civil Rights Commission
138 S. Ct. 1719 (2018)

JUSTICE KENNEDY delivered the opinion of the Court.

In 2012 a same-sex couple visited Masterpiece Cakeshop, a bakery in Colorado, to make inquiries about ordering a cake for their wedding reception. The shop's owner told the couple that he would not create a cake for their wedding because of his religious opposition to same-sex marriages—marriages the State of Colorado itself did not recognize at that time. The couple filed a charge with the Colorado Civil Rights Commission alleging discrimination on the basis of sexual orientation in violation of the Colorado Anti-Discrimination Act.

The Commission determined that the shop's actions violated the Act and ruled in the couple's favor. The Colorado state courts affirmed the ruling and its enforcement order, and this Court now must decide whether the Commission's order violated the Constitution.

The case presents difficult questions as to the proper reconciliation of at least two principles. The first is the authority of a State and its governmental entities to protect the rights and dignity of gay persons who are, or wish to be, married but who face discrimination when they seek goods or services. The second is the right of all persons to exercise fundamental freedoms under the First Amendment, as applied to the States through the Fourteenth Amendment.

The freedoms asserted here are both the freedom of speech and the free exercise of religion. The free speech aspect of this case is difficult, for few persons who have seen a beautiful wedding cake might have thought of its creation as an exercise of protected speech. This is an instructive example, however, of the proposition that the application of constitutional freedoms in new contexts can deepen our understanding of their meaning.

One of the difficulties in this case is that the parties disagree as to the extent of the baker's refusal to provide service. If a baker refused to design a special cake with words or images celebrating the marriage—for instance, a cake showing words with religious meaning—that might be different from a refusal to sell any cake at all. In defining whether a baker's creation can be protected, these details might make a difference.

The same difficulties arise in determining whether a baker has a valid free exercise claim. A baker's refusal to attend the wedding to ensure that the cake is cut the right way, or a refusal to put certain religious words or decorations on the cake, or even a refusal to sell a cake that has been baked for the public generally but includes certain religious words or symbols on it are just three examples of possibilities that seem all but endless.

Whatever the confluence of speech and free exercise principles might be in some cases, the Colorado Civil Rights Commission's consideration of this case was inconsistent with the State's obligation of religious neutrality. The reason and motive for the baker's refusal were based on his sincere religious beliefs and convictions. The Court's precedents make clear that the baker, in his capacity as the owner of a business serving the public, might have his right to the free exercise of religion limited by generally applicable laws. Still, the delicate question of when the free exercise of his religion must yield to an otherwise valid exercise of state power needed to be determined in an adjudication in which religious hostility on the part of the State itself would not be a factor in the balance the State sought to reach. That requirement, however, was not met here. When the Colorado Civil Rights Commission considered this case, it did not do so with the religious neutrality that the Constitution requires.

Given all these considerations, it is proper to hold that whatever the outcome of some future controversy involving facts similar to these, the Commission's actions here violated the Free Exercise Clause; and its order must be set aside.

I

A

Masterpiece Cakeshop, Ltd., is a bakery in Lakewood, Colorado, a suburb of Denver. The shop offers a variety of baked goods, ranging from everyday cookies and brownies to elaborate custom-designed cakes for birthday parties, weddings, and other events.

Jack Phillips is an expert baker who has owned and operated the shop for 24 years. Phillips is a devout Christian. He has explained that his "main goal in life is to be obedient to" Jesus Christ and Christ's "teachings in all aspects of his life." And he seeks to "honor God through his work at Masterpiece Cakeshop." One of Phillips' religious beliefs is that "God's intention for marriage from the beginning of history is that it is and should be the union of one man and one woman." To Phillips, creating a wedding cake for a same-sex wedding would be equivalent to participating in a celebration that is contrary to his own most deeply held beliefs.

Phillips met Charlie Craig and Dave Mullins when they entered his shop in the summer of 2012. Craig and Mullins were planning to marry. At that time, Colorado did not recognize same-sex marriages, so the couple planned to wed legally in Massachusetts and afterwards to host a reception for their family and friends in Denver. To prepare for their celebration, Craig and Mullins visited the shop and told Phillips that they were interested in ordering a cake for "our wedding." They did not mention the design of the cake they envisioned.

Phillips informed the couple that he does not "create" wedding cakes for same-sex weddings. He explained, "I'll make your birthday cakes, shower cakes, sell you cookies and brownies, I just don't make cakes for same sex weddings." The couple left the shop without further discussion.

The following day, Craig's mother, who had accompanied the couple to the cakeshop and been present for their interaction with Phillips, telephoned to ask Phillips why he had declined to serve her son. Phillips explained that he does not create wedding cakes for same-sex weddings because of his religious opposition to same-sex marriage, and also because Colorado (at that time) did not recognize same-sex marriages. He later explained his belief that "to create a wedding cake for an event that celebrates something that directly goes against the teachings of the Bible, would have been a personal endorsement and participation in the ceremony and relationship that they were entering into."

B

For most of its history, Colorado has prohibited discrimination in places of public accommodation. . . .

Today, the Colorado Anti-Discrimination Act (CADA) carries forward the state's tradition of prohibiting discrimination in places of public accommodation. Amended in 2007 and 2008 [CADA] prohibit[s] discrimination on the basis of sexual orientation. . . .

C

Craig and Mullins filed a discrimination complaint against Masterpiece Cakeshop and Phillips in August 2012, shortly after the couple's visit to the shop. The complaint alleged that Craig and Mullins had been denied "full and equal service" at the bakery because of their sexual orientation, and that it was Phillips' "standard business practice" not to provide cakes for same-sex weddings. . . .

The [Civil Rights] Commission found it proper to conduct a formal hearing, and it sent the case to a State Administrative Law Judge (ALJ). . . . Phillips raised two constitutional claims before the ALJ. He first asserted that applying CADA in a way that would require him to create a cake for a same-sex wedding would violate his First Amendment right to free speech by compelling him to exercise his artistic talents to express a message with which he disagreed. The ALJ rejected the contention that preparing a wedding cake is a form of protected speech and did not agree that creating Craig and Mullins' cake would force Phillips to adhere to "an ideological point of view." Applying CADA to the facts at hand, in the ALJ's view, did not interfere with Phillips' freedom of speech.

Phillips also contended that requiring him to create cakes for same-sex weddings would violate his right to the free exercise of religion, also protected by the First Amendment. Citing this Court's precedent in *Employment Div., Dept. of Human Resources of Ore.* v. *Smith* (1990), the ALJ determined that CADA is a "valid and neutral law of general applicability" and therefore that applying it to Phillips in this case did not violate the Free Exercise Clause. The ALJ thus ruled against Phillips and the cakeshop and in favor of Craig and Mullins on both constitutional claims.

The Commission affirmed the ALJ's decision in full. . . . Phillips appealed to the Colorado Court of Appeals, which affirmed the Commission's legal determinations and remedial order. The court rejected the argument that the "Commission's order unconstitutionally compels" Phillips and the shop "to convey a celebratory message about same sex marriage." . . . The court concluded that requiring Phillips to comply with the statute did not violate his free exercise rights. The Colorado Supreme Court declined to hear the case.

Phillips sought review here, and this Court granted certiorari. He now renews his claims under the Free Speech and Free Exercise Clauses of the First Amendment.

II

A

Our society has come to the recognition that gay persons and gay couples cannot be treated as social outcasts or as inferior in dignity and worth. For that reason the laws and the Constitution can, and in some instances must, protect them in the exercise of their civil rights. The exercise of their freedom on terms equal to others must be given great weight and respect by the courts. At the same time, the religious and philosophical objections to gay marriage are protected views and in some instances protected forms of expression. As this Court observed in *Obergefell* v. *Hodges* (2015), "[t]he First Amendment ensures that religious organizations and persons are given proper protection as they seek to teach the principles that are so fulfilling and so central to their lives and faiths." Nevertheless, while those religious and philosophical objections are protected, it is a general rule that such objections do not allow business owners and other actors in the economy and in society to deny protected persons equal access to goods and services under a neutral and generally applicable public accommodations law. See *Newman* v. *Piggie Park Enterprises, Inc.* (1968) (*per curiam*); see also *Hurley* v. *Irish-American Gay, Lesbian and Bisexual Group of Boston, Inc.* (1995) ("Provisions like these are well within the State's usual power to enact when a legislature has reason to believe that a given group is the target of discrimination, and they do not, as a general matter, violate the First or Fourteenth Amendments").

When it comes to weddings, it can be assumed that a member of the clergy who objects to gay marriage on moral and religious grounds could not be compelled to perform the ceremony without denial of his or her right to the free exercise of religion. This refusal would be well understood in our constitutional order as an exercise of religion, an exercise that gay persons could recognize and accept without serious diminishment to their own dignity and worth. Yet if that exception were not confined, then a long list of persons who provide goods and services for marriages and weddings might refuse to do so for gay persons, thus resulting in a community-wide stigma inconsistent with the history and dynamics of civil rights laws that ensure equal access to goods, services, and public accommodations. . . .

Phillips claims, however, that a narrower issue is presented. He argues that he had to use his artistic skills to make an expressive statement, a wedding endorsement in his own voice and of his own creation. As Phillips would see the case, this contention has a significant First Amendment speech component and implicates his deep and sincere religious beliefs. In this context the baker likely found it difficult to find a line where the customers' rights to goods and services became a demand for him to exercise the right of his own personal expression for their message, a message he could not express in a way consistent with his religious beliefs.

Phillips' dilemma was particularly understandable given the background of legal principles and administration of the law in Colorado at that time. His decision and his actions leading to the refusal of service all occurred in the year 2012. At that point, Colorado did not recognize the validity of gay marriages performed in its own State. At the time of the events in question, this Court had not issued its decisions either in *United States* v. *Windsor* (2013), or *Obergefell*. . . .

At the time, state law also afforded storekeepers some latitude to decline to create specific messages the storekeeper considered offensive. Indeed, while enforcement proceedings against Phillips were ongoing, the Colorado Civil Rights Division itself endorsed this proposition in cases involving other bakers' creation of cakes, concluding on at least three occasions that a baker acted lawfully in declining to create cakes with decorations that demeaned gay persons or gay marriages.

There were, to be sure, responses to these arguments that the State could make when it contended for a different result in seeking the enforcement of its generally applicable state regulations of businesses that serve the public. And any decision in favor of the baker would have to be sufficiently constrained, lest all purveyors of goods and services who object to gay marriages for moral and religious reasons in effect be allowed to put up signs saying "no goods or services will be sold if they will be used for gay marriages," something that would impose a serious stigma on gay persons. But, nonetheless, Phillips was entitled to the neutral and respectful consideration of his claims in all the circumstances of the case.

B

The neutral and respectful consideration to which Phillips was entitled was compromised here, however. The Civil Rights Commission's treatment of his case has some elements of a clear and impermissible hostility toward the sincere religious beliefs that motivated his objection.

That hostility surfaced at the Commission's formal, public hearings, as shown by the record. On May 30, 2014, the seven-member Commission convened publicly to consider Phillips' case. At several points during its meeting, commissioners endorsed the view that religious beliefs cannot legitimately be carried into the public sphere or commercial domain, implying that religious beliefs and persons are less than fully welcome in Colorado's business community. One commissioner suggested that Phillips can believe "what he wants to believe," but cannot act on his religious beliefs "if he decides to do business in the state." A few moments later, the commissioner restated the same position: "[I]f a businessman wants to do business in the state and he's got an issue with the—the law's impacting his personal belief system, he needs to look at being able to compromise." Standing alone, these statements are susceptible of different interpretations. On the one hand, they might mean simply that a business cannot refuse to provide services based on sexual orientation, regardless of the proprietor's personal views. On the other hand, they might be seen as inappropriate and dismissive comments showing lack of due consideration for Phillips' free exercise rights and the dilemma he faced. In view of the comments that followed, the latter seems the more likely.

On July 25, 2014, the Commission met again. This meeting, too, was conducted in public and on the record. On this occasion another commissioner made specific reference to the previous meeting's discussion but said far more to disparage Phillips' beliefs. The commissioner stated:

> "I would also like to reiterate what we said in the hearing or the last meeting. Freedom of religion and religion has been used to justify all kinds of discrimination throughout history, whether it be slavery, whether it be the holocaust, whether it be—I mean, we—we can list hundreds of situations where freedom of religion has been used to justify discrimination. And to me it is one of the most despicable pieces of rhetoric that people can use to—to use their religion to hurt others."

To describe a man's faith as "one of the most despicable pieces of rhetoric that people can use" is to disparage his religion in at least two distinct ways: by describing it as despicable, and also by characterizing it as merely rhetorical—something insubstantial and even insincere. The commissioner even went so far as to compare Phillips' invocation of his sincerely held religious beliefs to defenses of slavery and the Holocaust. This sentiment is inappropriate for a Commission charged with the solemn responsibility of fair and neutral enforcement of Colorado's antidiscrimination law—a law that protects discrimination on the basis of religion as well as sexual orientation.

The record shows no objection to these comments from other commissioners. And the later state-court ruling reviewing the Commission's decision did not mention those comments, much less express concern with their content. Nor were the comments by the commissioners disavowed in the briefs filed in this Court. For these reasons, the Court cannot avoid the conclusion that these statements cast doubt on the fairness and impartiality of the Commission's adjudication of Phillips' case. Members of the Court have disagreed on the question whether statements made by lawmakers may properly be taken into account in determining whether a law intentionally discriminates on the basis of religion. See *Church of Lukumi Babalu Aye, Inc.* v. *Hialeah* (1993) (Scalia, J., concurring in part and concurring in judgment). In this case, however, the remarks were made in a very different context—by an adjudicatory body deciding a particular case.

Another indication of hostility is the difference in treatment between Phillips' case and the cases of other bakers who objected to a requested cake on the basis of conscience and prevailed before the Commission.

As noted above, on at least three other occasions the Civil Rights Division considered the refusal of bakers to create cakes with images that conveyed disapproval of same-sex marriage, along with religious text. Each time, the Division found that the baker acted lawfully in refusing service. It made these determinations because, in the words of the Division, the requested cake [for one Mr. William Jack] included "wording and images [the baker] deemed derogatory," featured "language and images [the baker] deemed hateful," or displayed a message the baker "deemed as discriminatory."

The treatment of the conscience-based objections at issue in these three cases contrasts with the Commission's treatment of Phillips' objection. The Commission ruled against Phillips in part on the theory that any message the requested wedding cake would carry would be attributed to the customer, not to the baker. Yet the Division did not address this point in any of the other cases with respect to the cakes depicting anti-gay marriage symbolism. Additionally, the Division found no violation of CADA in the other cases in part because each bakery was willing to sell other products, including those depicting Christian themes, to the prospective customers. But the Commission dismissed Phillips' willingness to sell "birthday cakes, shower cakes, [and] cookies and brownies," to gay and lesbian customers as irrelevant. The treatment of the other cases and Phillips' case could reasonably be interpreted as being inconsistent as to the question of whether speech is involved, quite apart from whether the cases should ultimately be distinguished. In short, the Commission's consideration of Phillips' religious objection did not accord with its treatment of these other objections.

Before the Colorado Court of Appeals, Phillips protested that this disparity in treatment reflected hostility on the part of the Commission toward his beliefs. He argued that the Commission had treated the other bakers' conscience-based objections as legitimate, but treated his as illegitimate—thus sitting in judgment of his religious beliefs themselves. The Court of Appeals addressed the disparity only in passing and relegated its complete analysis of the issue to a footnote. There, the court stated that "[t]his case is distinguishable from the Colorado

Civil Rights Division's recent findings that [the other bakeries] in Denver did not discriminate against a Christian patron on the basis of his creed" when they refused to create the requested cakes. In those cases, the court continued, there was no impermissible discrimination because "the Division found that the bakeries . . . refuse[d] the patron's request . . . because of the offensive nature of the requested message."

A principled rationale for the difference in treatment of these two instances cannot be based on the government's own assessment of offensiveness. Just as "no official, high or petty, can prescribe what shall be orthodox in politics, nationalism, religion, or other matters of opinion," *West Virginia Bd. of Ed.* v. *Barnette* (1943), it is not, as the Court has repeatedly held, the role of the State or its officials to prescribe what shall be offensive. See *Matal* v. *Tam* (2017) (opinion of ALITO, J.). The Colorado court's attempt to account for the difference in treatment elevates one view of what is offensive over another and itself sends a signal of official disapproval of Phillips' religious beliefs. The court's footnote does not, therefore, answer the baker's concern that the State's practice was to disfavor the religious basis of his objection.

C

For the reasons just described, the Commission's treatment of Phillips' case violated the State's duty under the First Amendment not to base laws or regulations on hostility to a religion or religious viewpoint.

In *Church of Lukumi Babalu Aye,* the Court made clear that the government, if it is to respect the Constitution's guarantee of free exercise, cannot impose regulations that are hostile to the religious beliefs of affected citizens and cannot act in a manner that passes judgment upon or presupposes the illegitimacy of religious beliefs and practices. The Free Exercise Clause bars even "subtle departures from neutrality" on matters of religion. Here, that means the Commission was obliged under the Free Exercise Clause to proceed in a manner neutral toward and tolerant of Phillips' religious beliefs. . . .

Factors relevant to the assessment of governmental neutrality include "the historical background of the decision under challenge, the specific series of events leading to the enactment or official policy in question, and the legislative or administrative history, including contemporaneous statements made by members of the decisionmaking body." In view of these factors the record here demonstrates that the Commission's consideration of Phillips' case was neither tolerant nor respectful of Phillips' religious beliefs. The Commission gave "every appearance," of adjudicating Phillips' religious objection based on a negative normative "evaluation of the particular justification" for his objection and the religious grounds for it. It hardly requires restating that government has no role in deciding or even suggesting whether the religious ground for Phillips' conscience-based objection is legitimate or illegitimate. On these facts, the Court must draw the inference that Phillips' religious objection was not considered with the neutrality that the Free Exercise Clause requires.

While the issues here are difficult to resolve, it must be concluded that the State's interest could have been weighed against Phillips' sincere religious objections in a way consistent with the requisite religious neutrality that must be strictly observed. The official expressions of hostility to religion in some of the commissioners' comments—comments that were not disavowed at the Commission or by the State at any point in the proceedings that led to affirmance of the order—were inconsistent with what the Free Exercise Clause requires. The Commission's disparate consideration of Phillips' case compared to the cases of the other bakers suggests the same. For these reasons, the order must be set aside.

III

The Commission's hostility was inconsistent with the First Amendment's guarantee that our laws be applied in a manner that is neutral toward religion. Phillips was entitled to a neutral decisionmaker who would give full and fair consideration to his religious objection as he sought to assert it in all of the circumstances in which this case was presented, considered, and decided. In this case the adjudication concerned a context that may well be different going forward in the respects noted above. However later cases raising these or similar concerns are resolved in the future, for these reasons the rulings of the Commission and of the state court that enforced the Commission's order must be invalidated.

The outcome of cases like this in other circumstances must await further elaboration in the courts, all in the context of recognizing that these disputes must be resolved with tolerance, without undue disrespect to sincere religious beliefs, and without subjecting gay persons to indignities when they seek goods and services in an open market.

The judgment of the Colorado Court of Appeals is reversed.

JUSTICE KAGAN, with whom JUSTICE BREYER joins, concurring.

"[I]t is a general rule that [religious and philosophical] objections do not allow business owners and other actors in the economy and in society to deny protected persons equal access to goods and services under a neutral and generally applicable public accommodations law." But in upholding that principle, state actors cannot show hostility to religious views; rather, they must give those views "neutral and respectful consideration." I join the Court's opinion in full because I believe the Colorado Civil Rights Commission did not satisfy that obligation. I write separately to elaborate on one of the bases for the Court's holding. . . .

As Justice Gorsuch sees it, the product that Phillips refused to sell here—and would refuse to sell to anyone—was a "cake celebrating same-sex marriage." But that is wrong. The cake requested was not a special "cake celebrating same-sex marriage." It was simply a wedding cake—one that (like other standard wedding cakes) is suitable for use at same-sex and opposite-sex weddings alike. And contrary to Justice Gorsuch's view, a wedding cake does not become something different whenever a vendor like Phillips invests its sale to particular customers with "religious significance." As this Court has long held, and reaffirms today, a vendor cannot escape a public accommodations law because his religion disapproves selling a product to a group of customers, whether defined by sexual orientation, race, sex, or other protected trait. See *Newman* v. *Piggie Park Enterprises, Inc.* (1968) (*per curiam*) (holding that a barbeque vendor must serve black customers even if he perceives such service as vindicating racial equality, in violation of his religious beliefs). A vendor can choose the products he sells, but not the customers he serves—no matter the reason. Phillips sells wedding cakes. As to that product, he unlawfully discriminates: He sells it to opposite-sex but not to same-sex couples. And on that basis—which has nothing to do with Phillips' religious beliefs—Colorado could have distinguished Phillips from the bakers in the *Jack* cases, who did not engage in any prohibited discrimination. . . .

Colorado law, the Court says, "can protect gay persons, just as it can protect other classes of individuals, in acquiring whatever products and services they choose on the same terms and conditions as are offered to other members of the public." For that reason, Colorado can treat a baker who discriminates based on sexual orientation differently from a baker who does not discriminate on that or any other prohibited ground. But only, as the Court rightly says, if the State's decisions are not infected by religious hostility or bias.

I accordingly concur.

JUSTICE GORSUCH, with whom JUSTICE ALITO joins, concurring.

In *Employment Div., Dept. of Human Resources of Ore.* v. *Smith*, this Court held that a neutral and generally applicable law will usually survive a constitutional free exercise challenge. *Smith* remains controversial in many quarters. But we know this with certainty: when the government fails to act neutrally toward the free exercise of religion, it tends to run into trouble. Then the government can prevail only if it satisfies strict scrutiny, showing that its restrictions on religion both serve a compelling interest and are narrowly tailored. *Church of Lukumi Babalu Aye, Inc.* v. *Hialeah* (1993).

Today's decision respects these principles. As the Court explains, the Colorado Civil Rights Commission failed to act neutrally toward Jack Phillips's religious faith. Maybe most notably, the Commission allowed three other bakers to refuse a customer's request that would have required them to violate their secular commitments. Yet it denied the same accommodation to Mr. Phillips when he refused a customer's request that would have required him to violate his religious beliefs. As the Court also explains, the only reason the Commission seemed to supply for its discrimination was that it found Mr. Phillips's religious beliefs "offensive." That kind of judgmental dismissal of a sincerely held religious belief is, of course, antithetical to the First Amendment and cannot begin to satisfy strict scrutiny. The Constitution protects not just popular religious exercises from the condemnation of civil authorities. It protects them all. Because the Court documents each of these points carefully and thoroughly, I am pleased to join its opinion in full.

The only wrinkle is this. In the face of so much evidence suggesting hostility toward Mr. Phillips's sincerely held religious beliefs, two of our colleagues have written separately to suggest that the Commission acted neutrally toward his faith when it treated him differently from the other bakers — or that it could have easily done so consistent with the First Amendment. But, respectfully, I do not see how we might rescue the Commission from its error. . . .

The Commission cannot have it both ways. The Commission cannot slide up and down the *mens rea* scale, picking a mental state standard to suit its tastes depending on its sympathies. Either actual proof of intent to discriminate on the basis of membership in a protected class is required (as the Commission held in Mr. Jack's case), or it is sufficient to "presume" such intent from the knowing failure to serve someone in a protected class (as the Commission held in Mr. Phillips's case). Perhaps the Commission could have chosen either course as an initial matter. But the one thing it can't do is apply a more generous legal test to secular objections than religious ones. See *Church of Lukumi Babalu Aye.* That is anything but the neutral treatment of religion.

The real explanation for the Commission's discrimination soon comes clear, too — and it does anything but help its cause. This isn't a case where the Commission self-consciously announced a change in its legal rule in all public accommodation cases. Nor is this a case where the Commission offered some persuasive reason for its discrimination that might survive strict scrutiny. Instead, as the Court explains, it appears the Commission wished to condemn Mr. Phillips for expressing just the kind of "irrational" or "offensive . . . message" that the bakers in the first case refused to endorse. Many may agree with the Commission and consider Mr. Phillips's religious beliefs irrational or offensive. Some may believe he misinterprets the teachings of his faith. And, to be sure, this Court has held same-sex marriage a matter of constitutional right and various States have enacted laws that preclude discrimination on the basis of sexual orientation. But it is also true that no bureaucratic judgment condemning a sincerely held religious belief as "irrational" or "offensive" will ever survive strict scrutiny under the First Amendment. In this country, the place of secular officials isn't to sit in judgment of religious beliefs, but only to protect their free exercise. Just as it is the "proudest boast of our free speech jurisprudence" that we protect speech that we hate, it must be the proudest boast of our free exercise jurisprudence that we protect religious beliefs that we find offensive. See *Matal* v. *Tam.* Popular religious views are easy enough to defend. It is in protecting unpopular religious beliefs that we prove this country's commitment to serving as a refuge for religious freedom. See *Church of Lukumi Babalu Aye*; *Thomas* v. *Review Bd. of Indiana Employment Security Div.* (1981); *Wisconsin* v. *Yoder* (1972); *Cantwell* v. *Connecticut* (1940). . . .

It is no answer . . . simply to slide up a level of generality to redescribe Mr. Phillips's case as involving only a wedding cake like any other, so the fact that Mr. Phillips would make one for some means he must make them for all. See *ante* (Kagan, J., concurring). . . .

Suggesting that this case is only about "wedding cakes" — and not a wedding cake celebrating a same-sex wedding — actually points up the problem. At its most general level, the cake at issue in Mr. Phillips's case was just a mixture of flour and eggs; at its most specific level, it was a cake celebrating the same-sex wedding of Mr. Craig and Mr. Mullins. We are told here, however, to apply a sort of Goldilocks rule: describing the cake by its ingredients is *too general*; understanding it as celebrating a same-sex wedding is *too specific*; but regarding it as a generic wedding cake is *just right*. The problem is, the Commission didn't play with the level of generality in Mr. Jack's case in this way. It didn't declare, for example, that because the cakes Mr. Jack requested were just cakes about weddings generally, and all such cakes were the same, the bakers had to produce them. Instead, the Commission accepted the bakers' view that the specific cakes Mr. Jack requested conveyed a message offensive to their convictions and allowed them to refuse service. Having done that there, it must do the same here.

Any other conclusion would invite civil authorities to gerrymander their inquiries based on the parties they prefer. Why calibrate the level of generality in Mr. Phillips's case at "wedding cakes" exactly—and not at, say, "cakes" more generally or "cakes that convey a message regarding same-sex marriage" more specifically? If "cakes" were the relevant level of generality, the Commission would have to order the bakers to make Mr. Jack's requested cakes just as it ordered Mr. Phillips to make the requested cake in his case. Conversely, if "cakes that convey a message regarding same-sex marriage" were the relevant level of generality, the Commission would have to respect Mr. Phillips's refusal to make the requested cake just as it respected the bakers' refusal to make the cakes Mr. Jack requested. In short, when the same level of generality is applied to both cases, it is no surprise that the bakers have to be treated the same. Only by adjusting the dials *just right*—fine-tuning the level of generality up or down for each case based solely on the identity of the parties and the substance of their views—can you engineer the Commission's outcome, handing a win to Mr. Jack's bakers but delivering a loss to Mr. Phillips. Such results-driven reasoning is improper. Neither the Commission nor this Court may apply a more specific level of generality in Mr. Jack's case (a cake that conveys a message regarding same-sex marriage) while applying a higher level of generality in Mr. Phillips's case (a cake that conveys no message regarding same-sex marriage). Of course, under *Smith* a vendor cannot escape a public accommodations law just because his religion frowns on it. But for any law to comply with the First Amendment and *Smith*, it must be applied in a manner that treats religion with neutral respect. That means the government must apply the *same* level of generality across cases—and that did not happen here.

It is no more appropriate for the United States Supreme Court to tell Mr. Phillips that a wedding cake is just like any other—without regard to the religious significance his faith may attach to it—than it would be for the Court to suggest that for all persons sacramental bread is *just* bread or a kippah is *just* a cap.

Only one way forward now remains. Having failed to afford Mr. Phillips's religious objections neutral consideration and without any compelling reason for its failure, the Commission must afford him the same result it afforded the bakers in Mr. Jack's case. . . . Mr. Phillips has conclusively proven a First Amendment violation and, after almost six years facing unlawful civil charges, he is entitled to judgment.

JUSTICE THOMAS, with whom JUSTICE GORSUCH joins, concurring in part and concurring in the judgment.

I agree that the Colorado Civil Rights Commission (Commission) violated Jack Phillips' right to freely exercise his religion. As Justice Gorsuch explains, the Commission treated Phillips' case differently from a similar case involving three other bakers, for reasons that can only be explained by hostility toward Phillips' religion. The Court agrees that the Commission treated Phillips differently, and it points out that some of the Commissioners made comments disparaging Phillips' religion. Although the Commissioners' comments are certainly disturbing, the discriminatory application of Colorado's public-accommodations law is enough on its own to violate Phillips' rights. To the extent the Court agrees, I join its opinion.

While Phillips rightly prevails on his free-exercise claim, I write separately to address his free-speech claim. . . .

In *Obergefell*, I warned that the Court's decision would "inevitabl[y] . . . come into conflict" with religious liberty, "as individuals . . . are confronted with demands to participate in and endorse civil marriages between same-sex couples." This case proves that the conflict has already emerged. Because the Court's decision vindicates Phillips' right to free exercise, it seems that religious liberty has lived to fight another day. But, in future cases, the freedom of speech could be essential to preventing *Obergefell* from being used to "stamp out every vestige of dissent" and "vilify Americans who are unwilling to assent to the new orthodoxy." If that freedom is to maintain its vitality, reasoning like the Colorado Court of Appeals' must be rejected.

Even after describing his conduct this way, the Court of Appeals concluded that Phillips' conduct was not expressive and was not protected speech. It reasoned that an outside observer would think that Phillips was merely complying with Colorado's public-accommodations law, not expressing a message, and that Phillips could post a disclaimer to that effect. This reasoning flouts bedrock principles of our free-speech jurisprudence and would justify virtually any law that compels individuals to speak. It should not pass without comment. . . .

Phillips' creation of custom wedding cakes is expressive. The use of his artistic talents to create a well-recognized symbol that celebrates the beginning of a marriage clearly communicates a message—certainly more so than nude dancing, *Barnes* v. *Glen Theatre, Inc.* (1991), or flying a plain red flag, *Stromberg* v. *California* (1931). By forcing Phillips to create custom wedding cakes for same-sex weddings, Colorado's public-accommodations law "alter[s] the expressive content" of his message. *Hurley*. The meaning of expressive conduct, this Court has explained, depends on "the context in which it occur[s]." *Johnson*. Forcing Phillips to make custom wedding cakes for same-sex marriages requires him to, at the very least, acknowledge that same-sex weddings are "weddings" and suggest that they should be celebrated—the precise message he believes his faith forbids. The First Amendment prohibits Colorado from requiring Phillips to "bear witness to [these] fact[s]," *Hurley*, or to "affir[m] . . . a belief with which [he] disagrees." . . .

The Colorado Court of Appeals also noted that Masterpiece is a "for-profit bakery" that "charges its customers." But this Court has repeatedly rejected the notion that a speaker's profit motive gives the government a freer hand in compelling speech. See *Virginia Bd. of Pharmacy v. Virginia Citizens Consumer Council, Inc.* (1976). Further, even assuming that most for-profit companies prioritize maximizing profits over communicating a message, that is not true for Masterpiece Cakeshop. Phillips routinely sacrifices profits to ensure that Masterpiece operates in a way that represents his Christian faith. He is not open on Sundays, he pays his employees a higher-than-average wage, and he loans them money in times of need. Phillips also refuses to bake cakes containing alcohol, cakes with racist or homophobic messages, cakes criticizing God, and cakes celebrating Halloween — even though Halloween is one of the most lucrative seasons for bakeries. These efforts to exercise control over the messages that Masterpiece sends are still more evidence that Phillips' conduct is expressive. See *Miami Herald Publishing Co.* v. *Tornillo* (1974); *Walker* v. *Texas Div., Sons of Confederate Veterans, Inc.* (2015). . . .

Because Phillips' conduct (as described by the Colorado Court of Appeals) was expressive, Colorado's public-accommodations law cannot penalize it unless the law withstands strict scrutiny. Although this Court sometimes reviews regulations of expressive conduct under the more lenient test articulated in *O'Brien*, that test does not apply unless the government would have punished the conduct regardless of its expressive component. . . . Here, however, Colorado would not be punishing Phillips if he refused to create any custom wedding cakes; it is punishing him because he refuses to create custom wedding cakes that express approval of same-sex marriage. In cases like this one, our precedents demand " 'the most exacting scrutiny.' " *Johnson*; accord, *Holder* v. *Humanitarian Law Project* (2010). . . .

States cannot punish protected speech because some group finds it offensive, hurtful, stigmatic, unreasonable, or undignified. "If there is a bedrock principle underlying the First Amendment, it is that the government may not prohibit the expression of an idea simply because society finds the idea itself offensive or disagreeable." *Johnson*. A contrary rule would allow the government to stamp out virtually any speech at will. . . . As the Court reiterates today, "it is not . . . the role of the State or its officials to prescribe what shall be offensive." . . . If the only reason a public-accommodations law regulates speech is "to produce a society free of . . . biases" against the protected groups, that purpose is "decidedly fatal" to the law's constitutionality, "for it amounts to nothing less than a proposal to limit speech in the service of orthodox expression." *Hurley*. "[A] speech burden based on audience reactions is simply government hostility . . . in a different guise." *Matal* v. *Tam* (2017) (Kennedy, J., concurring in part and concurring in judgment).

Consider what Phillips actually said to the individual respondents in this case. After sitting down with them for a consultation, Phillips told the couple,

" 'I'll make your birthday cakes, shower cakes, sell you cookies and brownies, I just don't make cakes for same sex weddings.' " It is hard to see how this statement stigmatizes gays and lesbians more than blocking them from marching in a city parade, dismissing them from the Boy Scouts, or subjecting them to signs that say "God Hates Fags"—all of which this Court has deemed protected by the First Amendment. See *Hurley*; *Dale*; *Snyder* v. *Phelps* (2011). Moreover, it is also hard to see how Phillips' statement is worse than the racist, demeaning, and even threatening speech toward blacks that this Court has tolerated in previous decisions. Concerns about "dignity" and "stigma" did not carry the day when this Court affirmed the right of white supremacists to burn a 25-foot cross, *Virginia* v. *Black* (2003); conduct a rally on Martin Luther King Jr.'s birthday, *Forsyth County* v. *Nationalist Movement* (1992); or circulate a film featuring hooded Klan members who were brandishing weapons and threatening to " 'Bury the niggers,' " *Brandenburg* v. *Ohio* (1969) (*per curiam*).

Nor does the fact that this Court has now decided *Obergefell* v. *Hodges* (2015), somehow diminish Phillips' right to free speech. "It is one thing . . . to conclude that the Constitution protects a right to same-sex marriage; it is something else to portray everyone who does not share [that view] as bigoted" and unentitled to express a different view. *Obergefell* (Roberts, C. J., dissenting). This Court is not an authority on matters of conscience, and its decisions can (and often should) be criticized. The First Amendment gives individuals the right to disagree about the correctness of *Obergefell* and the morality of same-sex marriage. *Obergefell* itself emphasized that the traditional understanding of marriage "long has been held—and continues to be held—in good faith by reasonable and sincere people here and throughout the world." If Phillips' continued adherence to that understanding makes him a minority after *Obergefell*, that is all the more reason to insist that his speech be protected. See *Dale* ("[T]he fact that [the social acceptance of homosexuality] may be embraced and advocated by increasing numbers of people is all the more reason to protect the First Amendment rights of those who wish to voice a different view").

* * *

Because the Court's decision vindicates Phillips' right to free exercise, it seems that religious liberty has lived to fight another day. But, in future cases, the freedom of speech could be essential to preventing *Obergefell* from being used to "stamp out every vestige of dissent" and "vilify Americans who are unwilling to assent to the new orthodoxy." *Id* (Alito, J., dissenting). If that freedom is to maintain its vitality, reasoning like the Colorado Court of Appeals' must be rejected. . . .

JUSTICE GINSBURG, with whom JUSTICE SOTOMAYOR joins, dissenting.

There is much in the Court's opinion with which I agree. "[I]t is a general rule that [religious and philosophical] objections do not allow business owners and other actors in the economy and in society to deny protected persons equal access to goods and services under a neutral and generally applicable public accommodations law." "Colorado law can protect gay persons, just as it can protect other classes of individuals, in acquiring whatever products and services they choose on the same terms and conditions as are offered to other members of the public." "[P]urveyors of goods and services who object to gay marriages for moral and religious reasons [may not] put up signs saying 'no goods or services will be sold if they will be used for gay marriages.'" Gay persons may be spared from "indignities when they seek goods and services in an open market." I strongly disagree, however, with the Court's conclusion that Craig and Mullins should lose this case. All of the above-quoted statements point in the opposite direction.

The Court concludes that "Phillips' religious objection was not considered with the neutrality that the Free Exercise Clause requires." This conclusion rests on evidence said to show the Colorado Civil Rights Commission's (Commission) hostility to religion. Hostility is discernible, the Court maintains, from the asserted "disparate consideration of Phillips' case compared to the cases of" three other bakers who refused to make cakes requested by William Jack, an *amicus* here. The Court also finds hostility in statements made at two public hearings on Phillips' appeal to the Commission. The different outcomes the Court features do not evidence hostility to religion of the kind we have previously held to signal a free-exercise violation, nor do the comments by one or two members of one of the four decisionmaking entities considering this case justify reversing the judgment below. . . .

Statements made at the Commission's public hearings on Phillips' case provide no firmer support for the Court's holding today. Whatever one may think of the statements in historical context, I see no reason why the comments of one or two Commissioners should be taken to overcome Phillips' refusal to sell a wedding cake to Craig and Mullins. The proceedings involved several layers of independent decisionmaking, of which the Commission was but one. First, the Division had to find probable cause that Phillips violated CADA. Second, the ALJ entertained the parties' cross-motions for summary judgment. Third, the Commission heard Phillips' appeal. Fourth, after the Commission's ruling, the Colorado Court of Appeals considered the case *de novo*. What prejudice infected the determinations of the adjudicators in the case before and after the Commission? The Court does not say. Phillips' case is thus far removed from the only precedent upon which the Court relies, *Church of Lukumi Babalu Aye, Inc.* v. *Hialeah* (1993), where the government action that violated a principle of religious neutrality implicated a sole decisionmaking body, the city council.

* * *

For the reasons stated, sensible application of CADA to a refusal to sell any wedding cake to a gay couple should occasion affirmance of the Colorado Court of Appeals' judgment. I would so rule.

Espinoza v. Montana Department of Revenue
591 U.S. ___ (2020)

CHIEF JUSTICE ROBERTS delivered the opinion of the Court.

The Montana Legislature established a program to provide tuition assistance to parents who send their children to private schools. The program grants a tax credit to anyone who donates to certain organizations that in turn award scholarships to selected students attending such schools. When petitioners sought to use the scholarships at a religious school, the Montana Supreme Court struck down the program. The Court relied on the "no-aid" provision of the State Constitution, which prohibits any aid to a school controlled by a "church, sect, or denomination." The question presented is whether the Free Exercise Clause of the United States Constitution barred that application of the no-aid provision.

I

A

In 2015, the Montana Legislature sought "to provide parental and student choice in education" by enacting a scholarship program for students attending private schools. The program grants a tax credit of up to $150 to any taxpayer who donates to a participating "student scholarship organization." The scholarship organizations then use the donations to award scholarships to children for tuition at a private school.

So far only one scholarship organization, Big Sky Scholarships, has participated in the program. Big Sky focuses on providing scholarships to families who face financial hardship or have children with disabilities. Scholarship organizations like Big Sky must, among other requirements, maintain an application process for awarding the scholarships; use at least 90% of all donations on scholarship awards; and comply with state reporting and monitoring requirements.

A family whose child is awarded a scholarship under the program may use it at any "qualified education provider"—that is, any private school that meets certain accreditation, testing, and safety requirements. Virtually every private school in Montana qualifies. Upon receiving a scholarship, the family designates its school of choice, and the scholarship organization sends the scholarship funds directly to the school. Neither the scholarship organization nor its donors can restrict awards to particular types of schools. . . .

The Montana Legislature also directed that the program be administered in accordance with Article X, section 6, of the Montana Constitution, which contains a "no-aid" provision barring government aid to sectarian schools. In full, that provision states:

> "**Aid prohibited to sectarian schools**. . . . The legislature, counties, cities, towns, school districts, and public corporations shall not make any direct or indirect

appropriation or payment from any public fund or monies, or any grant of lands or other property for any sectarian purpose or to aid any church, school, academy, seminary, college, university, or other literary or scientific institution, controlled in whole or in part by any church, sect, or denomination." Mont. Const., Art. X, §6(1).

Shortly after the scholarship program was created, the Montana Department of Revenue promulgated "Rule 1," over the objection of the Montana Attorney General. That administrative rule prohibited families from using scholarships at religious schools. It did so by changing the definition of "qualified education provider" to exclude any school "owned or controlled in whole or in part by any church, religious sect, or denomination." The Department explained that the Rule was needed to reconcile the scholarship program with the no-aid provision of the Montana Constitution.

The Montana Attorney General disagreed. In a letter to the Department, he advised that the Montana Constitution did not require excluding religious schools from the program, and if it did, it would "very likely" violate the United States Constitution by discriminating against the schools and their students. The Attorney General is not representing the Department in this case.

B

This suit was brought by three mothers whose children attend Stillwater Christian School in northwestern Montana. Stillwater is a private Christian school that meets the statutory criteria for "qualified education providers." It serves students in prekindergarten through 12th grade, and petitioners chose the school in large part because it "teaches the same Christian values that [they] teach at home." The child of one petitioner has already received scholarships from Big Sky, and the other petitioners' children are eligible for scholarships and planned to apply. While in effect, however, Rule 1 blocked petitioners from using scholarship funds for tuition at Stillwater. To overcome that obstacle, petitioners sued the Department of Revenue in Montana state court. Petitioners claimed that Rule 1 conflicted with the statute that created the scholarship program and could not be justified on the ground that it was compelled by the Montana Constitution's no-aid provision. Petitioners further alleged that the Rule discriminated on the basis of their religious views and the religious nature of the school they had chosen for their children.

The trial court enjoined Rule 1, holding that it was based on a mistake of law. The court explained that the Rule was not required by the no-aid provision, because that provision prohibits only "appropriations" that aid religious schools, "not tax credits." . . .

In December 2018, the Montana Supreme Court reversed the trial court. The Court first addressed the scholarship program unmodified by Rule 1, holding that the program aided religious schools in violation of the no-aid provision of the Montana Constitution. . . .

The Montana Supreme Court went on to hold that the violation of the no-aid provision required invalidating the entire scholarship program. . . . As a result, the tax credit is no longer available to support scholarships at either religious or secular private schools.

The Montana Supreme Court acknowledged that "an overly-broad" application of the no-aid provision "could implicate free exercise concerns" and that "there may be a case" where "prohibiting the aid would violate the Free Exercise Clause." But, the Court concluded, "this is not one of those cases." . . .

II

A

The Religion Clauses of the First Amendment provide that "Congress shall make no law respecting an establishment of religion, or prohibiting the free exercise thereof." We have recognized a " 'play in the joints' between what the Establishment Clause permits and the Free Exercise Clause compels." *Trinity Lutheran Church of Columbia, Inc. v. Comer* (2017) (quoting *Locke v. Davey* (2004)). Here, the parties do not dispute that the scholarship program is permissible under the Establishment Clause. Nor could they. We have repeatedly held that the Establishment Clause is not offended when religious observers and organizations benefit from neutral government programs. See, *e.g., Locke*; *Rosenberger v. Rector and Visitors of Univ. of Va.* (1995). Any Establishment Clause objection to the scholarship program here is particularly unavailing because the government support makes its way to religious schools only as a result of Montanans independently choosing to spend their scholarships at such schools. See *Locke*; *Zelman v. Simmons-Harris* (2002). The Montana Supreme Court, however, held as a matter of state law that even such indirect government support qualified as "aid" prohibited under the Montana Constitution.

The question for this Court is whether the Free Exercise Clause precluded the Montana Supreme Court from applying Montana's no-aid provision to bar religious schools from the scholarship program. For purposes of answering that question, we accept the Montana Supreme Court's interpretation of state law — including its determination that the scholarship program provided impermissible "aid" within the meaning of the Montana Constitution — and we assess whether excluding religious schools and affected families from that program was consistent with the Federal Constitution.[2]

The Free Exercise Clause, which applies to the States under the Fourteenth Amendment, "protects religious observers against unequal treatment" and against "laws that impose special disabilities on the basis of religious status."

---

2. Justice Sotomayor argues that the Montana Supreme Court "expressly declined to reach any federal issue." Not so. As noted, the Montana Supreme Court recognized that certain applications of the no-aid provision could "violate the Free Exercise Clause." But the Court expressly concluded that "this is not one of those cases."

Trinity Lutheran; see *Cantwell v. Connecticut* (1940). Those "basic principle[s]" have long guided this Court. *Trinity Lutheran*. See, *e.g.*, *Everson v. Board of Ed. of Ewing* (1947) (a State "cannot exclude individual Catholics, Lutherans, Mohammedans, Baptists, Jews, Methodists, Non-believers, Presbyterians, or the members of any other faith, *because of their faith, or lack of it*, from receiving the benefits of public welfare legislation"); *Lyng v. Northwest Indian Cemetery Protective Assn.* (1988) (the Free Exercise Clause protects against laws that "penalize religious activity by denying any person an equal share of the rights, benefits, and privileges enjoyed by other citizens").

Most recently, *Trinity Lutheran* distilled these and other decisions to the same effect into the "unremarkable" conclusion that disqualifying otherwise eligible recipients from a public benefit "solely because of their religious character" imposes "a penalty on the free exercise of religion that triggers the most exacting scrutiny." In *Trinity Lutheran*, Missouri provided grants to help non-profit organizations pay for playground resurfacing, but a state policy disqualified any organization "owned or controlled by a church, sect, or other religious entity." Because of that policy, an otherwise eligible church-owned preschool was denied a grant to resurface its playground. Missouri's policy discriminated against the Church "simply because of what it is — a church," and so the policy was subject to the "strictest scrutiny," which it failed. We acknowledged that the State had not "criminalized" the way in which the Church worshiped or "told the Church that it cannot subscribe to a certain view of the Gospel." But the State's discriminatory policy was "odious to our Constitution all the same."

Here too Montana's no-aid provision bars religious schools from public benefits solely because of the religious character of the schools. The provision also bars parents who wish to send their children to a religious school from those same benefits, again solely because of the religious character of the school. This is apparent from the plain text. The provision bars aid to any school "controlled in whole or in part by any church, sect, or denomination." Mont. Const., Art. X, §6(1). The provision's title — "Aid prohibited to sectarian schools" — confirms that the provision singles out schools based on their religious character. And the Montana Supreme Court explained that the provision forbids aid to any school that is "sectarian," "religiously affiliated," or "controlled in whole or in part by churches." The provision plainly excludes schools from government aid solely because of religious status.

The Department counters that *Trinity Lutheran* does not govern here because the no-aid provision applies not because of the religious character of the recipients, but because of how the funds would be used — for "religious education." In *Trinity Lutheran*, a majority of the Court concluded that the Missouri policy violated the Free Exercise Clause because it discriminated on the basis of religious status. A plurality declined to address discrimination with respect to "religious uses of funding or other forms of discrimination."

[* Note: Footnote 3 of *Trinity Lutheran* stated: "This case involves express discrimination based on religious identity with respect to playground resurfacing. We do not address religious uses of funding or other forms of discrimination."]

Trinity Lutheran at n. 3.* The plurality saw no need to consider such concerns because Missouri had expressly discriminated "based on religious identity," which was enough to invalidate the state policy without addressing how government funds were used.

This case also turns expressly on religious status and not religious use. The Montana Supreme Court applied the no-aid provision solely by reference to religious status. . . . The Montana Constitution discriminates based on religious status just like the Missouri policy in *Trinity Lutheran*, which excluded organizations "owned or controlled by a church, sect, or other religious entity." . . .

The Department . . . contrasts what it characterizes as the "completely non-religious" benefit of playground resurfacing in *Trinity Lutheran* with the unrestricted tuition aid at issue here. . . . Regardless, those considerations were not the Montana Supreme Court's basis for applying the no-aid provision to exclude religious schools; that hinged solely on religious status. Status-based discrimination remains status based even if one of its goals or effects is preventing religious organizations from putting aid to religious uses.

Undeterred by *Trinity Lutheran*, the Montana Supreme Court applied the no-aid provision to hold that religious schools could not benefit from the scholarship program. So applied, the provision "impose[s] special disabilities on the basis of religious status" and "condition[s] the availability of benefits upon a recipient's willingness to surrender [its] religiously impelled status." *Trinity Lutheran* (quoting *Church of Lukumi Babalu Aye, Inc. v. Hialeah* (1993)). To be eligible for government aid under the Montana Constitution, a school must divorce itself from any religious control or affiliation. Placing such a condition on benefits or privileges "inevitably deters or discourages the exercise of First Amendment rights." *Trinity Lutheran*) (quoting *Sherbert v. Verner* (1963) (alterations omitted)). The Free Exercise Clause protects against even "indirect coercion," and a State "punishe[s] the free exercise of religion" by disqualifying the religious from government aid as Montana did here. *Trinity Lutheran*. Such status-based discrimination is subject to "the strictest scrutiny."

None of this is meant to suggest that we agree with the Department, that some lesser degree of scrutiny applies to discrimination against religious uses of government aid. See *Lukumi* (striking down law designed to ban religious practice involving alleged animal cruelty, explaining that a law "target[ing] religious conduct for distinctive treatment or advanc[ing] legitimate governmental interests only against conduct with a religious motivation will survive strict scrutiny only in rare cases"). Some Members of the Court, moreover, have questioned whether there is a meaningful distinction between discrimination based on use or conduct and that based on status. See *Trinity Lutheran*, (Gorsuch, J., joined by Thomas, J., concurring in part) (citing, *e.g.*, *Lukumi* and *Thomas v. Review Bd. of Ind. Employment Security Div.* (1981)). We acknowledge the point but need not examine it here. It is enough in this case to conclude that strict scrutiny applies under *Trinity Lutheran* because Montana's no-aid provision discriminates based on religious status.

B

Seeking to avoid *Trinity Lutheran*, the Department contends that this case is instead governed by *Locke* v. *Davey* (2004). *Locke* also involved a scholarship program. The State of Washington provided scholarships paid out of the State's general fund to help students pursuing postsecondary education. The scholarships could be used at accredited religious and nonreligious schools alike, but Washington prohibited students from using the scholarships to pursue devotional theology degrees, which prepared students for a calling as clergy. This prohibition prevented Davey from using his scholarship to obtain a degree that would have enabled him to become a pastor. We held that Washington had not violated the Free Exercise Clause.

Locke differs from this case in two critical ways. First, *Locke* explained that Washington had "merely chosen not to fund a distinct category of instruction": the "essentially religious endeavor" of training a minister "to lead a congregation." Thus, Davey "was denied a scholarship because of what he proposed *to do*—use the funds to prepare for the ministry." *Trinity Lutheran*. Apart from that narrow restriction, Washington's program allowed scholarships to be used at "pervasively religious schools" that incorporated religious instruction throughout their classes. *Locke*. By contrast, Montana's Constitution does not zero in on any particular "essentially religious" course of instruction at a religious school. Rather, as we have explained, the no-aid provision bars all aid to a religious school "simply because of what it is," putting the school to a choice between being religious or receiving government benefits. *Trinity*. At the same time, the provision puts families to a choice between sending their children to a religious school or receiving such benefits.

Second, *Locke* invoked a "historic and substantial" state interest in not funding the training of clergy, explaining that "opposition to . . . funding 'to support church leaders' lay at the historic core of the Religion Clauses," *Trinity Lutheran*. As evidence of that tradition, the Court in *Locke* emphasized that the propriety of state-supported clergy was a central subject of founding-era debates, and that most state constitutions from that era prohibited the expenditure of tax dollars to support the clergy.

But no comparable "historic and substantial" tradition supports Montana's decision to disqualify religious schools from government aid. In the founding era and the early 19th century, governments provided financial support to private schools, including denominational ones. Even States with bans on government-supported clergy, such as New Jersey, Pennsylvania, and Georgia, provided various forms of aid to religious schools. Congress provided support to denominational schools in the District of Columbia until 1848, and Congress paid churches to run schools for American Indians through the end of the 19th century. After the Civil War, Congress spent large sums on education for emancipated freedmen, often by supporting denominational schools in the South through the Freedmen's Bureau. McConnell.[3]

---

3. Justice Breyer sees "no meaningful difference" between concerns animating bans on support for clergy and bans on support for religious schools. But evidently early American governments

The Department argues that a tradition *against* state support for religious schools arose in the second half of the 19th century, as more than 30 States—including Montana—adopted no-aid provisions. Such a development, of course, cannot by itself establish an early American tradition. Justice Sotomayor questions our reliance on aid provided during the same era by the Freedmen's Bureau, but we see no inconsistency in recognizing that such evidence may reinforce an early practice but cannot create one. In addition, many of the no-aid provisions belong to a more checkered tradition shared with the Blaine Amendment of the 1870s. That proposal—which Congress nearly passed—would have added to the Federal Constitution a provision similar to the state no-aid provisions, prohibiting States from aiding "sectarian" schools. See *Mitchell v. Helms* (2000). "[I]t was an open secret that 'sectarian' was code for 'Catholic.'" *Ibid.* The Blaine Amendment was "born of bigotry" and "arose at a time of pervasive hostility to the Catholic Church and to Catholics in general"; many of its state counterparts have a similarly "shameful pedigree." *Mitchell.* The no-aid provisions of the 19th century hardly evince a tradition that should inform our understanding of the Free Exercise Clause.

The Department argues that several States have rejected referendums to overturn or limit their no-aid provisions, and that Montana even re-adopted its own in the 1970s, for reasons unrelated to anti-Catholic bigotry. But, on the other side of the ledger, many States today—including those with no-aid provisions—provide support to religious schools through vouchers, scholarships, tax credits, and other measures. According to petitioners, 20 of 37 States with no-aid provisions allow religious options in publicly funded scholarship programs, and almost all allow religious options in tax credit programs.

All to say, we agree with the Department that the historical record is "complex." And it is true that governments over time have taken a variety of approaches to religious schools. But it is clear that there is no "historic and substantial" tradition against aiding such schools comparable to the tradition against state-supported clergy invoked by *Locke*.

C

Two dissenters would chart new courses. Justice Sotomayor would grant the government "some room" to "single . . . out" religious entities "for exclusion," based on what she views as "the interests embodied in the Religion Clauses." Justice Breyer, building on his solo opinion in *Trinity Lutheran*, would adopt

---

did. . . . Justice Breyer also invokes Madison's objections to the Virginia Assessment Bill, but Madison objected in part because the Bill provided special support to certain churches and clergy, thereby "violat[ing] equality by subjecting some to peculiar burdens." Memorial and Remonstrance Against Religious Assessments. It is far from clear that the same objections extend to programs that provide equal support to all private primary and secondary schools. If anything, excluding religious schools from such programs would appear to impose the "peculiar burdens" feared by Madison.

a "flexible, context-specific approach" that "may well vary" from case to case. As best we can tell, courts applying this approach would contemplate the particular benefit and restriction at issue and discern their relationship to religion and society, taking into account "context and consequences measured in light of [the] purposes" of the Religion Clauses. What is clear is that Justice Breyer would afford much freer rein to judges than our current regime, arguing that "there is 'no test-related substitute for the exercise of legal judgment.'"

The simplest response is that these dissents follow from prior separate writings, not from the Court's decision in *Trinity Lutheran* or the decades of precedent on which it relied. These precedents have "repeatedly confirmed" the straightforward rule that we apply today: When otherwise eligible recipients are disqualified from a public benefit "solely because of their religious character," we must apply strict scrutiny. *Trinity Lutheran*. This rule against express religious discrimination is no "doctrinal innovation." Far from it. As *Trinity Lutheran* explained, the rule is "unremarkable in light of our prior decisions."

For innovation, one must look to the dissents. Their "room[y]" or "flexible" approaches to discrimination against religious organizations and observers would mark a significant departure from our free exercise precedents. The protections of the Free Exercise Clause do not depend on a "judgment-by-judgment analysis" regarding whether discrimination against religious adherents would somehow serve ill-defined interests. Cf. *Medellín v. Texas* (2008).

D

Because the Montana Supreme Court applied the no-aid provision to discriminate against schools and parents based on the religious character of the school, the "strictest scrutiny" is required. That "stringent standard," is not "watered down but really means what it says," *Lukumi*. To satisfy it, government action "must advance 'interests of the highest order' and must be narrowly tailored in pursuit of those interests."

The Montana Supreme Court asserted that the no-aid provision serves Montana's interest in separating church and State "more fiercely" than the Federal Constitution. But "that interest cannot qualify as compelling" in the face of the infringement of free exercise here. *Trinity Lutheran*, 582 U.S., at ___ (slip op., at 14). A State's interest "in achieving greater separation of church and State than is already ensured under the Establishment Clause . . . is limited by the Free Exercise Clause." *Ibid.* (quoting *Widmar v. Vincent* (1981)).

The Department, for its part, asserts that the no-aid provision actually *promotes* religious freedom. In the Department's view, the no-aid provision protects the religious liberty of taxpayers by ensuring that their taxes are not directed to religious organizations, and it safeguards the freedom of religious organizations by keeping the government out of their operations. An infringement of First Amendment rights, however, cannot be justified by a State's alternative view that the infringement advances religious liberty. Our federal system prizes state experimentation, but not "state experimentation in the suppression of free speech," and the same goes for the free exercise of religion. *Boy Scouts of America v. Dale* (2000).

Furthermore, we do not see how the no-aid provision promotes religious freedom. As noted, this Court has repeatedly upheld government programs that spend taxpayer funds on equal aid to religious observers and organizations, particularly when the link between government and religion is attenuated by private choices. A school, concerned about government involvement with its religious activities, might reasonably decide for itself not to participate in a government program. But we doubt that the school's liberty is enhanced by eliminating any option to participate in the first place. . . .

the prohibition before us today burdens not only religious schools but also the families whose children attend or hope to attend them. Drawing on "enduring American tradition," we have long recognized the rights of parents to direct "the religious upbringing" of their children. *Wisconsin v. Yoder* (1972). Many parents exercise that right by sending their children to religious schools, a choice protected by the Constitution. See *Pierce v. Society of Sisters* (1925). But the no-aid provision penalizes that decision by cutting families off from otherwise available benefits if they choose a religious private school rather than a secular one, and for no other reason.

The Department also suggests that the no-aid provision advances Montana's interests in public education. According to the Department, the no-aid provision safeguards the public school system by ensuring that government support is not diverted to private schools. But, under that framing, the no-aid provision is fatally underinclusive because its "proffered objectives are not pursued with respect to analogous nonreligious conduct." *Lukumi.* . . . Montana's interest in public education cannot justify a no-aid provision that requires only religious private schools to "bear [its] weight." *Ibid.*

A State need not subsidize private education. But once a State decides to do so, it cannot disqualify some private schools solely because they are religious.

III

The Department argues that, at the end of the day, there is no free exercise violation here because the Montana Supreme Court ultimately eliminated the scholarship program altogether. According to the Department, now that there is no program, religious schools and adherents cannot complain that they are excluded from any generally available benefit.

Two dissenters agree. Justice Ginsburg reports that the State of Montana simply chose to "put all private school parents in the same boat" by invalidating the scholarship program, and Justice Sotomayor describes the decision below as resting on state law grounds having nothing to do with the federal Free Exercise Clause.

The descriptions are not accurate. The Montana Legislature created the scholarship program; the Legislature never chose to end it, for policy or other reasons. The program was eliminated by a court, and not based on some innocuous principle of state law. Rather, the Montana Supreme Court invalidated the program pursuant to a state law provision that expressly discriminates on the basis of religious status. The Court applied that provision to hold that religious schools were barred from participating in the program. Then, seeing no other "mechanism" to make absolutely sure that religious schools received no aid, the court chose to invalidate the entire program.

The final step in this line of reasoning eliminated the program, to the detriment of religious and non-religious schools alike. But the Court's error of federal law occurred at the beginning. When the Court was called upon to apply a state law no-aid provision to exclude religious schools from the program, it was obligated by the Federal Constitution to reject the invitation. Had the Court recognized that this was, indeed, "one of those cases" in which application of the no-aid provision "would violate the Free Exercise Clause," the Court would not have proceeded to find a violation of that provision. And, in the absence of such a state law violation, the Court would have had no basis for terminating the program. Because the elimination of the program flowed directly from the Montana Supreme Court's failure to follow the dictates of federal law, it cannot be defended as a neutral policy decision, or as resting on adequate and independent state law grounds.[4]

The Supremacy Clause provides that "the Judges in every State shall be bound" by the Federal Constitution, "any Thing in the Constitution or Laws of any State to the Contrary notwithstanding." Art. VI, cl. 2. "[T]his Clause creates a rule of decision" directing state courts that they "must not give effect to state laws that conflict with federal law[]." *Armstrong v. Exceptional Child Center, Inc.*, 575 U.S. 320, 324 (2015). Given the conflict between the Free Exercise Clause and the application of the no-aid provision here, the Montana Supreme Court should have "disregard[ed]" the no-aid provision and decided this case "conformably to the [C]onstitution" of the United States. *Marbury v. Madison*, 1 Cranch 137, 178 (1803). That "*supreme* law of the land" condemns discrimination against religious schools and the families whose children attend them. They are "member[s] of the community too," and their exclusion from the scholarship program here is "odious to our Constitution" and "cannot stand." *Trinity Lutheran*.[5]

* * *

The judgment of the Montana Supreme Court is reversed, and the case is remanded for further proceedings not inconsistent with this opinion.

---

4. Justice Sotomayor worries that, in light of our decision, the Montana Supreme Court must "order the State to recreate" a scholarship program that "no longer exists.". But it was the Montana Supreme Court that eliminated the program, in the decision below, which remains under review. Our reversal of that decision simply restores the status quo established by the Montana Legislature before the Court's error of federal law. We do not consider any alterations the Legislature may choose to make in the future.

5. In light of this holding, we do not address petitioners' claims that the no-aid provision, as applied, violates the Equal Protection Clause or the Establishment Clause.

JUSTICE THOMAS, with whom JUSTICE GORSUCH joins, concurring.

The Court correctly concludes that Montana's no-aid provision expressly discriminates against religion in violation of the Free Exercise Clause. And it properly provides relief to Montana religious schools and the petitioners who wish to use Montana's scholarship program to send their children to such schools. I write separately to explain how this Court's interpretation of the Establishment Clause continues to hamper free exercise rights. Until we correct course on that interpretation, individuals will continue to face needless obstacles in their attempts to vindicate their religious freedom.

I

A

This case involves the Free Exercise Clause, not the Establishment Clause. But as in all cases involving a state actor, the modern understanding of the Establishment Clause is a "brooding omnipresence," *Southern Pacific Co. v. Jensen* (1917) (Holmes, J., dissenting), ever ready to be used to justify the government's infringement on religious freedom. Under the modern, but erroneous, view of the Establishment Clause, the government must treat all religions equally and treat religion equally to nonreligion. As this Court stated in its first case applying the Establishment Clause to the States, the government cannot "pass laws which aid one religion, aid all religions, or prefer one religion over another." *Everson v. Board of Ed. of Ewing*, 330 U.S. 1, 15 (1947). This "equality principle," the theory goes, prohibits the government from expressing any preference for religion — or even permitting any signs of religion in the governmental realm. Thus, when a plaintiff brings a free exercise claim, the government may defend its law, as Montana did here, on the ground that the law's restrictions are *required* to prevent it from "establishing" religion.

This understanding of the Establishment Clause is unmoored from the original meaning of the First Amendment. As I have explained in previous cases, at the founding, the Clause served only to "protec[t] States, and by extension their citizens, from the imposition of an established religion by the *Federal* Government."

There is mixed historical evidence concerning whether the Establishment Clause was understood as an individual right at the time of the Fourteenth Amendment's ratification. Even assuming that the Clause creates a right and that such a right could be incorporated, however, it would only protect against an "establishment" of religion as understood at the founding, *i.e.*, " 'coercion of religious orthodoxy and of financial support by force of law and threat of penalty.' "[1]

---

1. A party wishing to expand the scope of the Establishment Clause beyond its meaning at the founding carries the burden of demonstrating that this broader reading is historically sound. *Town of Greece v. Galloway* (2014) (Thomas, J., concurring in part and concurring in judgment).

Thus, the modern view, which presumes that States must remain both completely separate from and virtually silent on matters of religion to comply with the Establishment Clause, is fundamentally incorrect. Properly understood, the Establishment Clause does not prohibit States from favoring religion. They can legislate as they wish, subject only to the limitations in the State and Federal Constitutions.

B

I have previously made these points in Establishment Clause cases to show that the Clause likely has no application to the States or, if it is capable of incorporation, that the Court employs a far broader test than the Clause's original meaning. But the Court's wayward approach to the Establishment Clause also impacts its free exercise jurisprudence. Specifically, its overly expansive understanding of the former Clause has led to a correspondingly cramped interpretation of the latter.

Under this Court's current approach, state and local governments may rely on the Establishment Clause to justify policies that others wish to challenge as violations of the Free Exercise Clause. Once the government demonstrates that its policy is *required* for compliance with the Constitution, any claim that the policy infringes on free exercise cannot survive. . . .

The Court has also repeatedly stated that a government has a compelling interest in avoiding an Establishment Clause violation altogether, which "may justify" abridging other First Amendment freedoms. Unsurprisingly, governmental employers have relied on these pronouncements to defeat challenges from employees who alleged violations of their First Amendment rights.

Finally, this Court's infamous test in *Lemon v. Kurtzman* (1971), has sometimes been understood to prohibit governmental practices that have the effect of endorsing religion. This, too, presupposes that the Establishment Clause prohibits the government from favoring religion or taking steps to promote it. But as described, the Establishment Clause does nothing of the sort. The concern with avoiding endorsement has nevertheless been used to prohibit voluntary practices that potentially implicate free exercise rights, with courts and governments going so far as to make the "remarkable" suggestion "that even while off duty, a teacher or coach cannot engage in any outward manifestation of religious faith."

II

The Court's current understanding of the Establishment Clause actually thwarts, rather than promotes, equal treatment of religion. Under a proper understanding of the Establishment Clause, robust and lively debate about the role of religion in government is permitted, even encouraged, at the state and local level. The Court's distorted view of the Establishment Clause, however, removes the entire subject of religion from the realm of permissible governmental activity, instead mandating strict separation.

This interpretation of the Establishment Clause operates as a type of content-based restriction on the government. The Court has interpreted the Free Speech Clause to prohibit content-based restrictions because they "value some forms of speech over others," *City of Ladue v. Gilleo* (1994) (O'Connor, J., concurring), thus tending to "tilt public debate in a preferred direction," *Sorrell v. IMS Health Inc.* (2011). The content-based restriction imposed by this Court's Establishment Clause jurisprudence operates no differently. It communicates a message that religion is dangerous and in need of policing, which in turn has the effect of tilting society in favor of devaluing religion. . . .

Historical evidence suggests that many advocates for this separationist view were originally motivated by hostility toward certain disfavored religions. . . . Although such hostility may not be overtly expressed by the Court any longer, manifestations of this "trendy disdain for deep religious conviction" assuredly live on. *Locke* (Scalia, J., dissenting). They are evident in the fact that, unlike other constitutional rights, the mere exposure to religion can render an "'offended observer'" sufficiently injured to bring suit against the government, *American Legion* (Gorsuch, J., concurring in judgment), even if he has not been coerced in any way to participate in a religious practice.[2] We also see them in the special privilege of taxpayer standing in Establishment Clause challenges, even though such suits directly contravene Article III's restrictions on standing. And they persist in the repeated denigration of those who continue to adhere to traditional moral standards, as well as laws even remotely influenced by such standards, as outmoded at best and bigoted at worst. See *Masterpiece Cakeshop, Ltd. v. Colorado Civil Rights Comm'n*, (2018) (Thomas, J., concurring in part and concurring in judgment); *Obergefell v. Hodges*, 576 U.S. 644, 712 (2015) (Roberts, C. J., dissenting). So long as this hostility remains, fostered by our distorted understanding of the Establishment Clause, free exercise rights will continue to suffer.

* * *

As I have recently explained, this Court has an unfortunate tendency to prefer certain constitutional rights over others. See *United States v. Sineneng-Smith* (Thomas, J., concurring). The Free Exercise Clause, although enshrined explicitly in the Constitution, rests on the lowest rung of the Court's ladder of rights, and precariously so at that. Returning the Establishment Clause to its proper scope will not completely rectify the Court's disparate treatment of constitutional rights, but it will go a long way toward allowing free exercise of religion to flourish as the Framers intended. I look forward to the day when the Court takes up this task in earnest.

---

2. This stands in striking contrast to the Court's view in the free speech context that "the burden normally falls upon the viewer" to avoid offense "simply by averting his eyes." *Hill v. Colorado*, (2000) (Scalia, J., dissenting).

JUSTICE ALITO, concurring.

I join the opinion of the Court in full. The basis of the decision below was a Montana constitutional provision that, according to the Montana Supreme Court, forbids parents from participating in a publicly funded scholarship program simply because they send their children to religious schools. Regardless of the motivation for this provision or its predecessor, its application here violates the Free Exercise Clause.

Nevertheless, the provision's origin is relevant under the decision we issued earlier this Term in *Ramos v. Louisiana* (2020). The question in *Ramos* was whether Louisiana and Oregon laws allowing non-unanimous jury verdicts in criminal trials violated the Sixth Amendment. The Court held that they did, emphasizing that the States originally adopted those laws for racially discriminatory reasons. The role of the Ku Klux Klan was highlighted.

I argued in dissent that this original motivation, though deplorable, had no bearing on the laws' constitutionality because such laws can be adopted for non-discriminatory reasons, and "both States readopted their rules under different circumstances in later years." But I lost, and *Ramos* is now precedent. If the original motivation for the laws mattered there, it certainly matters here.

The origin of Montana's "no-aid" provision, Mont. Const., Art. X, §6(1) (1972), is emphasized in petitioners' brief and in the briefs of numerous supporting *amici*. These briefs, most of which were not filed by organizations affiliated with the Catholic Church, point out that Montana's provision was modeled on the failed Blaine Amendment to the Constitution of the United States. Named after House Speaker James Blaine, the Congressman who introduced it in 1875, the amendment was prompted by virulent prejudice against immigrants, particularly Catholic immigrants. In effect, the amendment would have "bar[red] any aid" to Catholic and other "sectarian" schools. *Mitchell v. Helms* (2000). As noted in a publication from the United States Commission on Civil Rights, a prominent supporter of this ban was the Ku Klux Klan.

The Blaine Amendment was narrowly defeated, passing in the House but falling just short of the two-thirds majority needed in the Senate to refer the amendment to the States. Afterwards, most States adopted provisions like Montana's to achieve the same objective at the state level, often as a condition of entering the Union. Thirty-eight States still have these "little Blaine Amendments" today.

This history is well-known and has been recognized in opinions of this Court. But given respondents' and one dissent's efforts to downplay it in contravention of *Ramos*, it deserves a brief retelling. . . .

A wave of immigration in the mid-19th century, spurred in part by potato blights in Ireland and Germany, significantly increased this country's Catholic population. Nativist fears increased with it. An entire political party, the Know Nothings, formed in the 1850s "to decrease the political influence of immigrants and Catholics," gaining hundreds of seats in Federal and State Government.

Catholics were considered by such groups not as citizens of the United States, but as "soldiers of the Church of Rome," who "would attempt to subvert representative government." Catholic education was a particular concern.

The feelings of the day are perhaps best encapsulated by this famous cartoon, published in Harper's Weekly in 1871, which depicts Catholic priests as crocodiles slithering hungrily toward American children as a public school crumbles in the background:

THE AMERICAN RIVER GANGES.

The resulting wave of state laws withholding public aid from "sectarian" schools cannot be understood outside this context. Indeed, there are stronger reasons for considering original motivations here than in *Ramos* because, unlike the neutral language of Louisiana's and Oregon's nonunanimity rules, Montana's no-aid provision retains the bigoted code language used throughout state Blaine Amendments.

The failed Blaine Amendment would have prohibited any public funds or lands devoted to schooling from "ever be[ing] under the control of any religious sect." . . . Backers of the Blaine Amendment either held nativist views or capitalized on them.

Montana's no-aid provision was the result of this same prejudice. . . . Montana thereafter adopted its constitutional rule against public funding for any school "controlled" by a "sect." There appears to have been no doubt which schools that meant. As petitioners show, Montana's religious schools—and its private schools in general—were predominantly Catholic, and anti-Catholicism was alive in Montana too. . . .

Respondents and one dissent argue that Montana's no-aid provision was cleansed of its bigoted past because it was readopted for non-bigoted reasons in Montana's 1972 constitutional convention. They emphasize that the convention included Catholics, just as the constitutional convention that readopted

Louisiana's purportedly racist non-unanimous jury provision included black delegates. As noted, a virtually identical argument was rejected in *Ramos*, even though 'no mention was made of race'" during the Louisiana convention debates. Under *Ramos*, it emphatically does not matter whether Montana readopted the no-aid provision for benign reasons. The provision's "uncomfortable past" must still be "[e]xamined." And here, it is not so clear that the animus was scrubbed.

Delegates at Montana's constitutional convention in 1972 acknowledged that the no-aid provision was "a badge of bigotry," with one Catholic delegate recalling "being let out of school in the fourth grade to erase three 'Ks' on the front doors of the Catholic church in Billings." Nevertheless the convention proposed, and the State adopted, a provision with the *same* material language, prohibiting public aid "for any *sectarian* purpose or to aid any . . . school . . . controlled in whole or in part by any church, *sect*, or denomination." Mont. Const., Art. X, §6(1) (1972). . . .

Thus, the no-aid provision's terms keep it "[t]ethered" to its original "bias," and it is not clear at all that the State "actually confront[ed]" the provision's "tawdry past in reenacting it." After all, whereas the no-aid provision had originally been foisted on Montana, the State readopted it voluntarily—"sectarian" references included. . . . And even if Montana had done more to address its no-aid provision's past, that would of course do nothing to resolve the bias inherent in the Blaine Amendments among the 17 States, by respondents' count, that have not readopted or amended them since around the turn of the 20th century.

. . . The tax-credit program adopted by the Montana Legislature but overturned by the Montana Supreme Court provided necessary aid for parents who pay taxes to support the public schools but who disagree with the teaching there. The program helped parents of modest means do what more affluent parents can do: send their children to a school of their choice. The argument that the decision below treats everyone the same is reminiscent of Anatole France's sardonic remark that " '[t]he law, in its majestic equality, forbids the rich as well as the poor to sleep under bridges, to beg in the streets, and to steal bread.'" J. Cournos, A Modern Plutarch 35 (1928).

Justice Gorsuch, concurring.

. . . I write separately only to address an additional point. The Court characterizes the Montana Constitution as discriminating against parents and schools based on "religious status and not religious use." No doubt, the Court proceeds as it does to underscore how the outcome of this case follows from *Trinity Lutheran Church of Columbia, Inc.* v. *Comer* (2017), where the Court struck down a similar public benefits restriction that, it held, discriminated on the basis of religious status. No doubt, too, discrimination on the basis of religious status raises grave constitutional questions for the reasons the Court describes. But I was not sure about characterizing the State's discrimination in *Trinity Lutheran* as focused only on religious status, and I am even less sure about characterizing the State's discrimination here that way.

In the first place, discussion of religious activity, uses, and conduct—not just status—pervades this record. The Montana Constitution forbids the use of public funds "for any sectarian purpose," including to "aid" sectarian schools. Art. X, §6(1). . . . Meanwhile, Ms. Espinoza admits that she would like to use scholarship funds to enable her daughters to be taught in school the "same Christian values" they are taught at home. Finally, in its briefing before this Court, Montana has represented that its Constitution focuses on preventing the use of tax credits to subsidize religious activity.

Not only is the record replete with discussion of activities, uses, and conduct, any jurisprudence grounded on a status-use distinction seems destined to yield more questions than answers. Does Montana seek to prevent religious parents and schools from participating in a public benefits program (status)? Or does the State aim to bar public benefits from being employed to support religious education (use)? Maybe it's possible to describe what happened here as status-based discrimination. But it seems equally, and maybe more, natural to say that the State's discrimination focused on what religious parents and schools *do* — teach religion. Nor are the line-drawing challenges here unique; they have arisen before and will again.

Most importantly, though, it is not as if the First Amendment cares. The Constitution forbids laws that prohibit the free exercise of religion. That guarantee protects not just the right to *be* a religious person, holding beliefs inwardly and secretly; it also protects the right to *act* on those beliefs outwardly and publicly. . . . By speaking of a right to "free exercise," rather than a right "of conscience," an alternative the framers considered and rejected, our Constitution "extended the broader freedom of action to all believers." McConnell, The Origins and Historical Understanding of Free Exercise of Religion (1989). So whether the Montana Constitution is better described as discriminating against religious status or use makes no difference: It is a violation of the right to free exercise either way, unless the State can show its law serves some compelling and narrowly tailored governmental interest, conditions absent here for reasons the Court thoroughly explains.

Our cases have long recognized the importance of protecting religious actions, not just religious status. In its very first decision applying the Free Exercise Clause to the States, the Court explained that the First Amendment protects the "freedom to act" as well as the "freedom to believe." *Cantwell v. Connecticut* (1940). . . . In fact, this Court has already recognized that parents' decisions about the education of their children — the very conduct at issue here — can constitute protected religious activity. In *Wisconsin v. Yoder*, 406 U.S. 205 (1972), the Court held that Amish parents could not be compelled to send their children to a public high school if doing so would conflict with the dictates of their faith. . . .

Consistently, too, we have recognized the First Amendment's protection for religious conduct in public benefits cases. When the government chooses to offer scholarships, unemployment benefits, or other affirmative assistance to its citizens, those benefits necessarily affect the "baseline against which burdens on religion are measured." *Locke v. Davey* (2004) (Scalia, J., dissenting). So, as we have long explained, the government "penalize[s] religious activity" whenever it denies to religious persons an "equal share of the rights, benefits, and privileges enjoyed by other citizens." *Lyng v. Northwest Indian Cemetery Protective Assn.* (1988). What benefits the government decides to give, whether meager or munificent, it must give without discrimination against religious conduct.

Our cases illustrate the point. In *Sherbert v. Verner*, 374 U.S. 398 (1963), for example, a State denied unemployment benefits to Adell Sherbert not because she was a Seventh Day Adventist but because she had put her faith into practice by refusing to labor on the day she believed God had set aside for rest. Recognizing her right to exercise her religion freely, the Court held that Ms. Sherbert was entitled to benefits. . . .

The First Amendment protects religious uses and actions for good reason. What point is it to tell a person that he is free to *be* Muslim but he may be subject to discrimination for *doing* what his religion commands, attending Friday prayers, living his daily life in harmony with the teaching of his faith, and educating his children in its ways? What does it mean to tell an Orthodox Jew that she may have her religion but may be targeted for observing her religious calendar? Often, governments lack effective ways to control what lies in a person's heart or mind. But they can bring to bear enormous power over what people say and do. The right to *be* religious without the right to *do* religious things would hardly amount to a right at all.

If the government could intrude so much in matters of faith, too, winners and losers would soon emerge. Those apathetic about religion or passive in its practice would suffer little in a world where only inward belief or status is protected. But what about those with a deep faith that requires them to do things passing legislative majorities might find unseemly or uncouth — like knocking on doors to spread their beliefs, refusing to build tank turrets during wartime, or teaching their children at home? A right meant to protect minorities instead could become a cudgel to ensure conformity.

It doesn't take a long or searching look through history or around the world to see how this can go. . . . Even today, in fiefdoms small and large, people of faith are made to choose between receiving the protection of the State and living lives true to their religious convictions.

Of course, in public benefits cases like the one before us the stakes are not so dramatic. Individuals are forced only to choose between forgoing state aid or pursuing some aspect of their faith. The government does not put a gun to the head, only a thumb on the scale. But, as so many of our cases explain, the Free Exercise Clause doesn't easily tolerate either; any discrimination against religious exercise must meet the demands of strict scrutiny. . . .

Montana's Supreme Court disregarded these foundational principles. Effectively, the court told the state legislature and parents of Montana like Ms. Espinoza: You can have school choice, but if anyone dares to choose to send a child to an accredited religious school, the program will be shuttered. That condition on a public benefit discriminates against the free exercise of religion. Calling it discrimination on the basis of religious status or religious activity makes no difference: It is unconstitutional all the same.

JUSTICE GINSBURG, with whom JUSTICE KAGAN joins, dissenting.

. . . Because the state court's decision does not so discriminate, I would reject petitioners' free exercise claim. . . . Petitioners argue that the Montana Supreme Court's decision fails when measured against *Trinity Lutheran.* I do not see how. Past decisions in this area have entailed *differential treatment* occasioning a burden on a plaintiff's religious exercise. This case is missing that essential component. Recall that the Montana court remedied the state constitutional violation by striking the scholarship program in its entirety. Under that decree, secular and sectarian schools alike are ineligible for benefits, so the decision cannot be said to entail differential treatment based on petitioners' religion. Put somewhat differently, petitioners argue that the Free Exercise Clause requires a State to treat institutions and people neutrally when doling out a benefit—and neutrally is how Montana treats them in the wake of the state court's decision.

Accordingly, the Montana Supreme Court's decision does not place a burden on petitioners' religious exercise. Petitioners may still send their children to a religious school. And the Montana Supreme Court's decision does not pressure them to do otherwise. Unlike the law in *Trinity Lutheran,* the decision below puts petitioners to no "choice": Neither giving up their faith, nor declining to send their children to sectarian schools, would affect their entitlement to scholarship funding. There simply are no scholarship funds to be had. . . .

These considerations should be fatal to petitioners' free exercise claim, yet the Court does not confront them. Instead, the Court decides a question that, in my view, this case does not present: "[W]hether excluding religious schools and affected families from [the scholarship] program was consistent with the Federal Constitution." The Court goes on to hold that the Montana Supreme Court's application of the no-aid provision violates the Free Exercise Clause because it " 'condition[s] the availability of benefits upon a recipient's willingness to surrender [its] religiously impelled status.' " As I see it, the decision below—which maintained neutrality between sectarian and nonsectarian private schools—did no such thing.

. . . The Montana court determined that the scholarship program violated the no-aid provision because it resulted in aid to religious schools. Declining to rewrite the statute to exclude those schools, the state court struck the program in full. 393 Mont. 446, 463–468, 435 P. 3d 603, 612–614 (2018). In doing so, the court never made religious schools ineligible for an otherwise available benefit, and it never decided that the Free Exercise Clause would allow that outcome.[1]

. . . The no-aid provision can be implemented in two ways. A State may distinguish within a benefit program between secular and sectarian schools, or it may decline to fund all private schools. The Court agrees that the First Amendment

---

1. In its opinion, Montana's highest court stated without explanation that this case is not one in which application of the no-aid provision violates the Free Exercise Clause. 393 Mont., at 468, 435 P.3d, at 614. When the court made that statement, it had already invalidated the entire scholarship program. . . .

permits the latter course. Because that is the path the Montana Supreme Court took in this case, there was no reason for this Court to address the alternative.

By urging that it is impossible to apply the no-aid provision in harmony with the Free Exercise Clause, the Court seems to treat the no-aid provision itself as unconstitutional. Petitioners, however, disavowed a facial First Amendment challenge, and the state courts were never asked to address the constitutionality of the no-aid provision divorced from its application to a specific government benefit. This Court therefore had no call to reach that issue. The only question properly raised is whether application of the no-aid provision to bar all state-sponsored private-school funding violates the Free Exercise Clause. For the reasons stated, it does not.

Nearing the end of its opinion, the Court writes: "A State need not subsidize private education. But once a State decides to do so, it cannot disqualify some private schools solely because they are religious." Because Montana's Supreme Court did not make such a decision — its judgment put all private school parents in the same boat — this Court had no occasion to address the matter.[2] On that sole ground, and reaching no other issue, I dissent from the Court's judgment.

JUSTICE BREYER, with whom JUSTICE KAGAN joins as to Part I, dissenting.

The First Amendment's Free Exercise Clause guarantees the right to practice one's religion. At the same time, its Establishment Clause forbids government support for religion. Taken together, the Religion Clauses have helped our Nation avoid religiously based discord while securing liberty for those of all faiths.

This Court has long recognized that an overly rigid application of the Clauses could bring their mandates into conflict and defeat their basic purpose. See, *e.g.*, *Walz v. Tax Comm'n of City of New York* (1970). And this potential conflict is nowhere more apparent than in cases involving state aid that serves religious purposes or institutions. In such cases, the Court has said, there must be constitutional room, or " 'play in the joints,' " between "what the Establishment Clause permits and the Free Exercise Clause compels." *Trinity Lutheran Church of Columbia, Inc. v. Comer* (quoting *Locke v. Davey* (2004)). Whether a particular state program falls within that space depends upon the nature of the aid at issue, considered in light of the Clauses' objectives.

The majority barely acknowledges the play-in-the-joints doctrine here. It holds that the Free Exercise Clause forbids a State to draw any distinction between secular and religious uses of government aid to private schools that is not required by the Establishment Clause. The majority's approach and its conclusion in this case, I fear, risk the kind of entanglement and conflict that the Religion Clauses are intended to prevent. I consequently dissent.

---

2. The Montana Supreme Court's decision leaves parents where they would be had the State never enacted a scholarship program. In that event, no one would argue that Montana was obliged to provide such a program solely for parents who send their children to religious schools. But cf. *ante* (Alito, J., concurring) (inapt reference to Anatole France's remark).

I

. . . .The majority finds that the school-playground case, *Trinity Lutheran*, and not the religious-studies case, *Locke*, controls here. I disagree. In my view, the program at issue here is strikingly similar to the program we upheld in *Locke* and importantly different from the program we found unconstitutional in *Trinity Lutheran*. Like the State of Washington in *Locke*, Montana has chosen not to fund (at a distance) "an essentially religious endeavor" — an education designed to " 'induce religious faith.' " *Locke*. That kind of program simply cannot be likened to Missouri's decision to exclude a church school from applying for a grant to resurface its playground.

The Court in *Locke* recognized that the study of devotional theology can be "akin to a religious calling as well as an academic pursuit." . . . Nothing in the Constitution discourages this type of instruction. To the contrary, the Free Exercise Clause draws upon a history that places great value upon the freedom of parents to teach their children the tenets of their faith. Cf. *Wisconsin v. Yoder* (1972). . . . But the bitter lesson of religious conflict also inspired the Establishment Clause and the state-law bans on compelled support the Court cited in *Locke*. Cf., *e.g.*, J. Madison, Memorial and Remonstrance Against Religious Assessments. . . .

It is true that Montana's no-aid provision broadly bars state aid to schools based on their religious affiliation. But this case does not involve a claim of status-based discrimination. The schools do not apply or compete for scholarships, they are not parties to this litigation, and no one here purports to represent their interests. We are instead faced with a suit by *parents* who assert that *their* free exercise rights are violated by the application of the no-aid provision to prevent them from *using* taxpayer-supported scholarships to attend the schools of their choosing. In other words, the problem, as in *Locke*, is what petitioners " 'propos[e] *to do* — use the funds to' " obtain a religious education.

Even if the schools' status were relevant, I do not see what bearing the majority's distinction could have here. There is no dispute that religious schools seek generally to inspire religious faith and values in their students. How else could petitioners claim that barring them from using state aid to attend these schools violates their free exercise rights? Thus, the question in this case — unlike in *Trinity Lutheran* — boils down to what the schools would *do* with state support. And the upshot is that here, as in *Locke*, we confront a State's decision not to fund the inculcation of religious truths.

The majority next contends that there is no " 'historic and substantial' tradition against aiding" religious schools "comparable to the tradition against state-supported clergy invoked by *Locke*." But the majority ignores the reasons for the founding era bans that we relied upon in *Locke*.

"Perhaps the most famous example," is the 1786 defeat of a Virginia bill (often called the Assessment Bill) that would have levied a tax in support of "learned teachers" of "the Christian Religion." A Bill Establishing a Provision for Teachers of the Christian Religion. In his Memorial and Remonstrance against that proposal, James Madison argued that compelling state sponsorship of religion in this way was "a signal of persecution" that "degrades from the equal rank of citizens all those whose opinions in religion do not bend to those of the Legislative authority." Even among those who might benefit from such a tax, Madison warned, the bill threatened to "destroy that moderation and harmony which the forbearance of our laws to intermeddle with Religion, has produced among its several sects."

The opposition galvanized by Madison's Remonstrance not only scuttled the Assessment Bill; it spurred Virginia's Assembly to enact a very different law, the Bill for Religious Liberty drafted by Thomas Jefferson.

Like the Remonstrance, Jefferson's bill emphasized the risk to religious liberty that state-supported religious indoctrination threatened. "[T]o compel a man to furnish contributions of money for the propagation of opinions which he disbelieves," the preamble declared, "is sinful and tyrannical." . . .

I see no meaningful difference between the concerns that Madison and Jefferson raised and the concerns inevitably raised by taxpayer support for scholarships to religious schools. . . That is not to deny that the history of state support for denominational schools is " 'complex.' " But founding era attitudes toward compelled support of clergy were no less complex. Many prominent members of the founding generation, including George Washington, Patrick Henry, and John Marshall, supported Virginia's Assessment Bill. Some who supported this kind of government aid thought it posed no threat to freedom of conscience; others denied that provisions for aid to religion amounted to an "establishment" at all. Indeed, at least one historian has persuasively argued that it is next to impossible to attribute to the Founders any uniform understanding as to what constitutes, in the Constitution's phrase, "an Establishment of religion."

This diversity of opinion made no difference in *Locke* and it makes no difference here. For our purposes it is enough to say that, among those who gave shape to the young Republic were people, including Madison and Jefferson, who perceived a grave threat to individual liberty and communal harmony in tax support for the teaching of religious truths. These "historic and substantial" concerns have consistently guided the Court's application of the Religion Clauses since. The Court's special attention to these views should come as no surprise, for the risks the Founders saw have only become more apparent over time. In the years since the Civil War, the number of religions practiced in our country has grown to scores. And that has made it more difficult to avoid suspicions of favoritism — or worse — when government becomes entangled with religion. . . .

Private choice cannot help the taxpayer who does not want to finance the propagation of religious beliefs, whether his own or someone else's. It will not help religious minorities too few in number to support a school that teaches their beliefs. And it will not satisfy those whose religious beliefs preclude them from participating in a government-sponsored program. Some or many of the persons who fit these descriptions may well feel ignored — or worse — when public funds are channeled to religious schools. These feelings may, in turn, sow religiously inspired political conflict and division — a risk that is considerably greater where States are *required* to include religious schools in programs like the one before us here. And it is greater still where, as here, those programs benefit only a handful of a State's many religious denominations. . . .

If, for 250 years, we have drawn a line at forcing taxpayers to pay the salaries of those who teach their faith from the pulpit, I do not see how we can today require Montana to adopt a different view respecting those who teach it in the classroom.

II

In reaching its conclusion that the Free Exercise Clause requires Montana to allow petitioners to use taxpayer supported scholarships to pay for their children's religious education, the majority makes several doctrinal innovations that, in my view, are misguided and threaten adverse consequences.

Although the majority refers in passing to the "play in the joints" between that which the Establishment Clause forbids and that which the Free Exercise Clause requires, its holding leaves that doctrine a shadow of its former self. Having concluded that there is no obstacle to subsidizing a religious education under our Establishment Clause precedents, the majority says little more about Montana's antiestablishment interests or the reasoning that underlies them. It does not engage with the State's concern that its funds not be used to support religious teaching. Instead, the Court holds that it need not consider how Montana's funds would be used because, in its view, all distinctions on the basis of religion—whether in respect to playground grants or devotional teaching—are similarly and presumptively unconstitutional.

Setting aside the problems with the majority's characterization of this case, I think the majority is wrong to replace the flexible, context-specific approach of our precedents with a test of "strict" or "rigorous" scrutiny. And it is wrong to imply that courts should use that same heightened scrutiny whenever a government benefit is at issue. . . .

Montana's law does not punish religious exercise. And it does not require students to choose between their religious beliefs and receiving secular government aid such as unemployment benefits. The State has simply chosen not to fund programs that, in significant part, typically involve the teaching and practice of religious devotion. . . .

I disagree, then, with what I see as the majority's doctrinal omission, its misplaced application of a legal presumption, and its suggestion that this presumption is appropriate in many, if not all, cases involving government benefits. As I see the matter, our differences run deeper than a simple disagreement about the application of prior case law. . . .

Nor does the majority's approach avoid judicial entanglement in difficult and sensitive questions. To the contrary, as I have just explained, it burdens courts with the still more complex task of untangling disputes between religious organizations and state governments, instead of giving deference to state legislators' choices to avoid such issues altogether. At the same time, it puts States in a legislative dilemma, caught between the demands of the Free Exercise and Establishment Clauses, without "breathing room" to help ameliorate the problem. . . .

* * *

It is not easy to discern "the boundaries of the neutral area between" the two Religion Clauses "within which the legislature may legitimately act." *Tilton.* And it is more difficult still in cases, such as this one, where the Constitution's policy in favor of free exercise, on one hand, and against state sponsorship, on the other, are in conflict. In such cases, I believe there is "no test-related substitute for the exercise of legal judgment." *Van Orden* (opinion of BREYER, J.). That judgment "must reflect and remain faithful to the underlying purposes of the Clauses, and it must take account of context and consequences measured in light of those purposes." Here, those purposes, along with the examples set by our decisions in *Locke* and *Trinity Lutheran*, lead me to believe that Montana's differential treatment of religious schools is constitutional. "If any room exists between the two Religion Clauses, it must be here." For these reasons, I respectfully dissent from the Court's contrary conclusion.

JUSTICE SOTOMAYOR, dissenting.

. . . In *Trinity Lutheran Church of Columbia, Inc. v. Comer* (2017), this Court held, "for the first time, that the Constitution requires the government to provide public funds directly to a church." *Id.* (Sotomayor, J., dissenting). Here, the Court invokes that precedent to require a State to subsidize religious schools if it enacts an education tax credit. Because this decision further "slights both our precedents and our history" and "weakens this country's longstanding commitment to a separation of church and state beneficial to both," I respectfully dissent.

I

A

. . . Because no secondary school (secular or sectarian) is eligible for benefits, the state court's ruling neither treats petitioners differently based on religion nor burdens their religious exercise. Petitioners remain free to send their children to the religious school of their choosing and to exercise their faith. . . .

Notably, petitioners did not allege that the no-aid provision itself caused their harm or that invalidating the entire tax-credit scheme would create independent constitutional concerns. . . . Petitioners thus have no cognizable as-applied claim arising from the disparate treatment of religion, because there is no longer a program to which Montana's no-aid provision can apply. . . .[2] . . .

---

2. Petitioners here have not asserted a free exercise claim on a theory that they were victims of religious animus, either. Instead, one concurrence seeks to make the argument for them while attempting to compare the state constitutional provision here with a nonunanimous jury rule rooted in racial animus. But those questions are not before the Court. In any case, the concurrence's arguments are as misguided as they are misplaced. Citing the Court's opinion in *Ramos*, the concurrence maintains that a law's " 'uncomfortable past' must still be '[e]xamined.' " But as previously explained: "Where a law otherwise is untethered to [discriminatory] bias — and perhaps also where a legislature actually confronts a law's tawdry past in reenacting it — the new law may well be free

II

. . . The Court's analysis of Montana's defunct tax program reprises the error in *Trinity Lutheran*. Contra the Court's current approach, our free exercise precedents had long granted the government "some room to recognize the unique status of religious entities and to single them out on that basis for exclusion from otherwise generally applicable laws." *Id.* (Sotomayor, J., dissenting).

Until *Trinity Lutheran*, the right to exercise one's religion did not include a right to have the State pay for that religious practice. That is because a contrary rule risks reading the Establishment Clause out of the Constitution. . . . Thus, to determine the constitutionality of government action that draws lines based on religion, our precedents "carefully considered whether the interests embodied in the Religion Clauses justify that line." *Trinity Lutheran* (Sotomayor, J., dissenting). The relevant question had always been not whether a State singles out religious entities, but why it did so.

Here, a State may refuse to extend certain aid programs to religious entities when doing so avoids "historic and substantial" antiestablishment concerns. Properly understood, this case is no different from *Locke* because petitioners seek to procure what the plaintiffs in *Locke* could not: taxpayer funds to support religious schooling. Indeed, one of the concurrences lauds petitioners' spiritual pursuit, acknowledging that they seek state funds for manifestly religious purposes like "teach[ing] religion" so that petitioners may "outwardly and publicly" live out their religious tenets. But those deeply religious goals confirm why Montana may properly decline to subsidize religious education. Involvement in such spiritual matters implicates both the Establishment Clause, and the free exercise rights of taxpayers, "denying them the chance to decide for themselves whether and how to fund religion," *Trinity Lutheran*, (Sotomayor, J., dissenting). Previously, this Court recognized that a "prophylactic rule against the use of public funds" for "religious activities" appropriately balanced the Religion Clauses' differing but equally weighty interests. . . .

Finally, it is no answer to say that this case involves "discrimination." *Ante*, at 11–12. A "decision to treat entities differently based on distinctions that the Religion Clauses make relevant does not amount to discrimination." *Trinity Lutheran* (Sotomayor, J., dissenting). So too here.

* * *

---

of discriminatory taint." *Ramos* (Sotomayor, J., concurring in part). That could not "be said of the laws at issue" in *Ramos*. It can be here. The concurrence overlooks the starkly different histories of these state laws. Also missing from the concurrence (and the *amicus* briefs it repeats) is the stubborn fact that the constitutional provision at issue here was adopted in 1972 at a convention where it was met with overwhelming support by religious leaders (Catholic and non-Catholic), even those who examined the history of prior no-aid provisions. These supporters argued that it would be wrong to put taxpayer dollars to religious purposes and that it would invite unwelcome entanglement between church and state.

Today's ruling is perverse. Without any need or power to do so, the Court appears to require a State to reinstate a tax-credit program that the Constitution did not demand in the first place. We once recognized that "[w]hile the Free Exercise Clause clearly prohibits the use of state action to deny the rights of free exercise to anyone, it has never meant that a majority could use the machinery of the State to practice its beliefs." *Schempp.* Today's Court, by contrast, rejects the Religion Clauses' balanced values in favor of a new theory of free exercise, and it does so only by setting aside well-established judicial constraints.

I respectfully dissent.

Our Lady of Guadalupe School v. Morrisey-Berru
591 U.S. ___ (2020)

JUSTICE ALITO delivered the opinion of the Court.

These cases require us to decide whether the First Amendment permits courts to intervene in employment disputes involving teachers at religious schools who are entrusted with the responsibility of instructing their students in the faith. The First Amendment protects the right of religious institutions "to decide for themselves, free from state interference, matters of church government as well as those of faith and doctrine." *Kedroff v. Saint Nicholas Cathedral of Russian Orthodox Church in North America* (1952). Applying this principle, we held in *Hosanna-Tabor Evangelical Lutheran Church and School v. EEOC* (2012), that the First Amendment barred a court from entertaining an employment discrimination claim brought by an elementary school teacher, Cheryl Perich, against the religious school where she taught. Our decision built on a line of lower court cases adopting what was dubbed the "ministerial exception" to laws governing the employment relationship between a religious institution and certain key employees. We did not announce "a rigid formula" for determining whether an employee falls within this exception, but we identified circumstances that we found relevant in that case, including Perich's title as a "Minister of Religion, Commissioned," her educational training, and her responsibility to teach religion and participate with students in religious activities.

In the cases now before us, we consider employment discrimination claims brought by two elementary school teachers at Catholic schools whose teaching responsibilities are similar to Perich's. Although these teachers were not given the title of "minister" and have less religious training than Perich, we hold that their cases fall within the same rule that dictated our decision in *Hosanna-Tabor.* The religious education and formation of students is the very reason for the existence of most private religious schools, and therefore the selection and supervision of the teachers upon whom the schools rely to do this work lie at the core of their mission. Judicial review of the way in which religious schools discharge those responsibilities would undermine the independence of religious institutions in a way that the First Amendment does not tolerate.

I

A

The first of the two cases we now decide involves Agnes Morrissey-Berru, who was employed at Our Lady of Guadalupe School (OLG), a Roman Catholic primary school in the Archdiocese of Los Angeles. For many years, Morrissey-Berru was employed at OLG as a lay fifth or sixth grade teacher. Like most elementary school teachers, she taught all subjects, and since OLG is a Catholic school, the curriculum included religion. As a result, she was her students' religion teacher. . . .

Like all teachers in the Archdiocese of Los Angeles, Morrissey-Berru was "considered a catechist," *i.e.*, "a teacher of religio[n]." Catechists are "responsible for the faith formation of the students in their charge each day." Morrissey-Berru provided religious instruction every day using a textbook designed for use in teaching religion to young Catholic students. . . .

Morrissey-Berru also prayed with her students. Her class began or ended every day with a Hail Mary. . . . Morrissey-Berru testified that she tried to instruct her students "in a manner consistent with the teachings of the Church," and she said that she was "committed to teaching children Catholic values" and providing a "faith-based education." And the school principal confirmed that Morrissey-Berru was expected to do these things.

In 2014, OLG asked Morrissey-Berru to move from a full-time to a part-time position, and the next year, the school declined to renew her contract. She . . . filed suit under the Age Discrimination in Employment Act of 1967, claiming that the school had demoted her and had failed to renew her contract so that it could replace her with a younger teacher. . . .

Invoking the "ministerial exception" that we recognized in *Hosanna-Tabor*, OLG successfully moved for summary judgment, but the Ninth Circuit reversed in a brief opinion. The court . . . held that Morrissey-Berru did not fall within the "ministerial exception." . . .

B

The second case concerns the late Kristen Biel, who worked for about a year and a half as a lay teacher at St. James School, another Catholic primary school in Los Angeles. . . . Like Morrissey-Berru, she taught all subjects, including religion.

. . . Biel's employment agreement was in pertinent part nearly identical to Morrissey-Berru's. The agreement set out the same religious mission; required teachers to serve that mission; imposed commitments regarding religious instruction, worship, and personal modeling of the faith; and explained that teachers' performance would be reviewed on those bases. . . .

Like Morrissey-Berru, Biel instructed her students in the tenets of Catholicism. She was required to teach religion for 200 minutes each week, and administered a test on religion every week. . . .

Biel worshipped with her students. . . . Biel taught her students about "Catholic practices like the Eucharist and confession." At monthly Masses, she prayed with her students. . . .

St. James declined to renew Biel's contract after one full year at the school. She . . . alleg[ed] that she was discharged because she had requested a leave of absence to obtain treatment for breast cancer. . . .

Like OLG, St. James obtained summary judgment under the ministerial exception, but a divided panel of the Ninth Circuit reversed, reasoning that Biel lacked Perich's "credentials, training, [and] ministerial background." . . .

II

A

The First Amendment provides that "Congress shall make no law respecting an establishment of religion, or prohibiting the free exercise thereof." Among other things, the Religion Clauses protect the right of churches and other religious institutions to decide matters " 'of faith and doctrine' " without government intrusion. *Hosanna-Tabor* (quoting *Kedroff*). State interference in that sphere would obviously violate the free exercise of religion, and any attempt by government to dictate or even to influence such matters would constitute one of the central attributes of an establishment of religion. The First Amendment outlaws such intrusion.

The independence of religious institutions in matters of "faith and doctrine" is closely linked to independence in what we have termed " 'matters of church government.' " This does not mean that religious institutions enjoy a general immunity from secular laws, but it does protect their autonomy with respect to internal management decisions that are essential to the institution's central mission. And a component of this autonomy is the selection of the individuals who play certain key roles.

The "ministerial exception" was based on this insight. Under this rule, courts are bound to stay out of employment disputes involving those holding certain important positions with churches and other religious institutions. The rule appears to have acquired the label "ministerial exception" because the individuals involved in pioneering cases were described as "ministers." Not all pre-*Hosanna-Tabor* decisions applying the exception involved "ministers" or even members of the clergy. But it is instructive to consider why a church's independence on matters "of faith and doctrine" requires the authority to select, supervise, and if necessary, remove a minister without interference by secular authorities. Without that power, a wayward minister's preaching, teaching, and counseling could contradict the church's tenets and lead the congregation away from the faith. The ministerial exception was recognized to preserve a church's independent authority in such matters.

B

When the so-called ministerial exception finally reached this Court in *Hosanna-Tabor*, we unanimously recognized that the Religion Clauses foreclose certain employment discrimination claims brought against religious organizations. The constitutional foundation for our holding was the general principle of church autonomy to which we have already referred: independence in matters of faith and doctrine and in closely linked matters of internal government. . . .

C

In *Hosanna-Tabor*, Cheryl Perich, a kindergarten and fourth grade teacher at an Evangelical Lutheran school, filed suit in federal court, claiming that she had been discharged because of a disability, in violation of the Americans with Disabilities Act of 1990 (ADA). . . . We held that her suit was barred by the "ministerial exception" and noted that it "concern[ed] government interference with an internal church decision that affects the faith and mission of the church." We declined "to adopt a rigid formula for deciding when an employee qualifies as a minister," and we added that it was "enough for us to conclude, in this our first case involving the ministerial exception, that the exception covers Perich, given all the circumstances of her employment." We identified four relevant circumstances but did not highlight any as essential.

First, we noted that her church had given Perich the title of "minister, with a role distinct from that of most of its members.". Although she was not a minister in the usual sense of the term—she was not a pastor or deacon, did not lead a congregation, and did not regularly conduct religious services—she was classified as a "called" teacher . . .

Second, Perich's position "reflected a significant degree of religious training followed by a formal process of commissioning."

Third, "Perich held herself out as a minister of the Church by accepting the formal call to religious service, according to its terms," and by claiming certain tax benefits.

Fourth, "Perich's job duties reflected a role in conveying the Church's message and carrying out its mission." . . . Although Perich also provided instruction in secular subjects, she taught religion four days a week, led her students in prayer three times a day, took her students to a chapel service once a week, and participated in the liturgy twice a year. . . .

The case featured two concurrences. In the first, Justice Thomas stressed that courts should "defer to a religious organization's good-faith understanding of who qualifies as its minister." That is so, Justice Thomas explained, because "[a] religious organization's right to choose its ministers would be hollow . . . if secular courts could second-guess" the group's sincere application of its religious tenets.

The second concurrence argued that application of the "ministerial exception" should "focus on the function performed by persons who work for religious bodies" rather than labels or designations that may vary across faiths. *Id.* (opinion of Alito, J., joined by Kagan, J.). This opinion viewed the title of "minister" as "relevant" but "neither necessary nor sufficient." . . .

D

1

In determining whether a particular position falls within the *Hosanna-Tabor* exception, a variety of factors may be important.[10]

... Take the question of the title "minister." Simply giving an employee the title of "minister" is not enough to justify the exception. And by the same token, since many religious traditions do not use the title "minister," it cannot be a necessary requirement. Requiring the use of the title would constitute impermissible discrimination, and this problem cannot be solved simply by including positions that are thought to be the counterparts of a "minister," such as priests, nuns, rabbis, and imams. Nuns are not the same as Protestant ministers. A brief submitted by Jewish organizations makes the point that "Judaism has many 'ministers,'" that is, "the term 'minister' encompasses an extensive breadth of religious functionaries in Judaism." For Muslims, "an inquiry into whether imams or other leaders bear a title equivalent to 'minister' can present a troubling choice between denying a central pillar of Islam — *i.e.*, the equality of all believers — and risking loss of ministerial exception protections."

If titles were all-important, courts would have to decide which titles count and which do not, and it is hard to see how that could be done without looking behind the titles to what the positions actually entail. Moreover, attaching too much significance to titles would risk privileging religious traditions with formal organizational structures over those that are less formal. . . .

What matters, at bottom, is what an employee does. And implicit in our decision in *Hosanna-Tabor* was a recognition that educating young people in their faith, inculcating its teachings, and training them to live their faith are responsibilities that lie at the very core of the mission of a private religious school. . . .

Religious education is vital to many faiths practiced in the United States. This point is stressed by briefs filed in support of OLG and St. James by groups affiliated with a wide array of faith traditions. . . .

Religious education is a matter of central importance in Judaism. As explained in briefs submitted by Jewish organizations, the Torah is understood to require Jewish parents to ensure that their children are instructed in the faith.[17] One brief quotes Maimonides's statement that religious instruction "is an obligation of the highest order, entrusted only to a schoolteacher possessing 'fear of Heaven.'"[18] "The contemporary American Jewish community continues to place the education of children in its faith and rites at the center of its communal efforts." This

---

10. In considering the circumstances of any given case, courts must take care to avoid "resolving underlying controversies over religious doctrine." *Presbyterian Church in U. S. v. Mary Elizabeth Blue Hull Memorial Presbyterian Church* (1969).

17. See Deuteronomy 6:7, 11:19.

18. Brief amici curiae of General Conference of Seventh-day Adventists and Jewish Coalition for Religious Liberty as *Amici Curiae* 7–8 (quoting Maimonides, Mishne Torah, Hilkhot Talmud Torah 1:2; 2:1, 3). [Professor Blackman is on the Board of Directors of the Jewish Coalition for Religious Liberty — Eds.].

brief survey does not do justice to the rich diversity of religious education in this country, but it shows the close connection that religious institutions draw between their central purpose and educating the young in the faith.

2

When we apply this understanding of the Religion Clauses to the cases now before us, it is apparent that Morrissey-Berru and Biel qualify for the exemption we recognized in *Hosanna-Tabor*. There is abundant record evidence that they both performed vital religious duties. Educating and forming students in the Catholic faith lay at the core of the mission of the schools where they taught, and their employment agreements and faculty handbooks specified in no uncertain terms that they were expected to help the schools carry out this mission and that their work would be evaluated to ensure that they were fulfilling that responsibility. As elementary school teachers responsible for providing instruction in all subjects, including religion, they were the members of the school staff who were entrusted most directly with the responsibility of educating their students in the faith. And not only were they obligated to provide instruction about the Catholic faith, but they were also expected to guide their students, by word and deed, toward the goal of living their lives in accordance with the faith. They prayed with their students, attended Mass with the students, and prepared the children for their participation in other religious activities. Their positions did not have all the attributes of Perich's. Their titles did not include the term "minister," and they had less formal religious training, but their core responsibilities as teachers of religion were essentially the same. And both their schools expressly saw them as playing a vital part in carrying out the mission of the church, and the schools' definition and explanation of their roles is important. In a country with the religious diversity of the United States, judges cannot be expected to have a complete understanding and appreciation of the role played by every person who performs a particular role in every religious tradition. A religious institution's explanation of the role of such employees in the life of the religion in question is important.

III

In holding that Morrissey-Berru and Biel did not fall within the *Hosanna-Tabor* exception, the Ninth Circuit misunderstood our decision. . . .[26]

_____

26. The dissent charges that we transform the holding in *Hosanna Tabor*, but that is what the dissent does. According to the dissent: "*Hosanna-Tabor* charted a way to separate leaders who 'personify' a church's 'beliefs' [and] 'minister to the faithful' from individuals who may simply relay religious tenets." The dissent cobbles together this new test by taking phrases out of context from separate passages and inserting a proposition never suggested in *Hosanna-Tabor*, namely, that an individual cannot qualify for the exception if he or she "simply relay[s] religious tenets" without "'minister[ing] to the faithful.'" *Hosanna-Tabor* never adopted this unworkable test. It did not

The Ninth Circuit's rigid test produced a distorted analysis. First, it invested undue significance in the fact that Morrissey-Berru and Biel did not have clerical titles. . . .

Second, the Ninth Circuit assigned too much weight to the fact that Morrissey-Berru and Biel had less formal religious schooling than Perich. . . . The schools in question here thought that Morrissey-Berru and Biel had a sufficient understanding of Catholicism to teach their students, and judges have no warrant to second-guess that judgment or to impose their own credentialing requirements. . . .

In Biel's appeal, the Ninth Circuit suggested that the *Hosanna-Tabor* exception should be interpreted narrowly because the ADA and Title VII contain provisions allowing religious employers to give preference to members of a particular faith in employing individuals to do work connected with their activities. But the *Hosanna-Tabor* exception serves an entirely different purpose. Think of the quintessential case where a church wants to dismiss its minister for poor performance. The church's objection in that situation is not that the minister has gone over to some other faith but simply that the minister is failing to perform essential functions in a satisfactory manner.

While the Ninth Circuit treated the circumstances that we cited in *Hosanna-Tabor* as factors to be assessed and weighed in every case, respondents would make the governing test even more rigid. In their view, courts should begin by deciding whether the first three circumstances — a ministerial title, formal religious education, and the employee's self-description as a minister — are met and then, in order to check the conclusion suggested by those factors, ask whether the employee performed a religious function. For reasons already explained, there is no basis for treating the circumstances we found relevant in *Hosanna-Tabor* in such a rigid manner. . . .

Respondents argue that Morrissey-Berru cannot fall within the *Hosanna-Tabor* exception because she said in connection with her lawsuit that she was not "a practicing Catholic," but acceptance of that argument would require courts to delve into the sensitive question of what it means to be a "practicing" member of a faith, and religious employers would be put in an impossible position. . . .

---

suggest that the exception it recognized applied only to "leaders." The term is never used in the opinion of the Court. Insisting on leadership as a qualification would shrink the exception even more than respondents advocate. For example, they agree that it should apply to nuns, but, under the dissent's test, is every cloistered nun — or every cloistered monk — disqualified? And even if leadership were a requirement, why couldn't a religious teacher be regarded as a leader of the students in the class? Nor did our opinion in *Hosanna-Tabor* draw a critical distinction between a person who "simply relay[s] religious tenets" and one who relays such tenets while also " 'minister[ing] to the faithful.'" A teacher, such as an instructor in a class on world religions, who merely provides a description of the beliefs and practices of a religion without making any effort to inculcate those beliefs could not qualify for the exception, but otherwise the distinction makes no sense. If a member of the Christian clergy or a rabbi spends almost all of his or her time studying Scripture or theology and writing instead of ministering to a congregation, would that individual fall outside the exception as understood by the dissent?

Was OLG supposed to interrogate Morrissey-Berru to confirm that she attended Mass every Sunday?

Respondents argue that the *Hosanna-Tabor* exception is not workable unless it is given a rigid structure, but we declined to adopt a "rigid formula" in *Hosanna-Tabor*, and the lower courts have been applying the exception for many years without such a formula. Here, as in *Hosanna-Tabor*, it is sufficient to decide the cases before us. When a school with a religious mission entrusts a teacher with the responsibility of educating and forming students in the faith, judicial intervention into disputes between the school and the teacher threatens the school's independence in a way that the First Amendment does not allow.

JUSTICE THOMAS, with whom JUSTICE GORSUCH joins, concurring.

I agree with the Court that Morrissey-Berru's and Biel's positions fall within the "ministerial exception,"[1] because, as Catholic school teachers, they are charged with "carry[ing] out [the religious] mission" of the parish schools. The Court properly notes that "judges have no warrant to second-guess [the schools'] judgment" of who should hold such a position "or to impose their own credentialing requirements." Accordingly, I join the Court's opinion in full. I write separately, however, to reiterate my view that the Religion Clauses require civil courts to defer to religious organizations' good-faith claims that a certain employee's position is "ministerial." See *Hosanna-Tabor Evangelical Lutheran Church and School v. EEOC* (2012) (Thomas, J., concurring).

This deference is necessary because, as the Court rightly observes, judges lack the requisite "understanding and appreciation of the role played by every person who performs a particular role in every religious tradition." *Ante*, at 22. What qualifies as "ministerial" is an inherently theological question, and thus one that cannot be resolved by civil courts through legal analysis. See *Hosanna-Tabor* (Thomas, J., concurring); see also James Madison, Memorial and Remonstrance Against Religious Assessments (the idea that a "Civil Magistrate is a competent Judge of Religious truth" is "an arrogant pretension" that has been "falsified"). Contrary to the dissent's claim, judges do not shirk their judicial duty or provide a mere "rubber stamp" when they defer to a religious organization's sincere beliefs. *Post* (opinion of Sotomayor, J.). Rather, they heed the First Amendment, which "commands civil courts to decide [legal] disputes without resolving underlying controversies over religious doctrine." *Presbyterian Church in U. S. v. Mary Elizabeth Blue Hull Memorial Presbyterian Church* (1969). . . .

The Court's decision today is a step in the right direction. The Court properly declines to consider whether an employee shares the religious organization's beliefs when determining whether that employee's position falls within

---

1. As the Court acknowledges, the term "ministerial exception" is somewhat of a misnomer. The First Amendment's protection of religious organizations' employment decisions is not limited to members of the clergy or others holding positions akin to that of a "minister." Rather, as these cases demonstrate, such protection extends to the laity, provided they are entrusted with carrying out the religious mission of the organization.

the "ministerial exception," explaining that to "determin[e] whether a person is a 'co-religionist' . . . would risk judicial entanglement in religious issues." But the same can be said about the broader inquiry whether an employee's position is "ministerial." This Court usually goes to great lengths to avoid governmental "entanglement" with religion, particularly in its Establishment Clause cases. See, *e.g.*, *Lemon v. Kurtzman* (1971).[2] . . . But, when it comes to the autonomy of religious organizations in our ministerial-exception cases, these concerns of entanglement have not prevented the Court from weighing in on the theological questions of which positions qualify as "ministerial."

. . . The foregoing is more than enough to sustain the sincerity of petitioners' claims that Morrissey-Berru and Biel held ministerial roles in the parish schools. Their claims thus warrant this Court's deference and serve as a sufficient basis for applying the ministerial exception.

JUSTICE SOTOMAYOR, with whom JUSTICE GINSBURG joins, dissenting.

Two employers fired their employees allegedly because one had breast cancer and the other was elderly. Purporting to rely on this Court's decision in *Hosanna-Tabor Evangelical Lutheran Church and School v. EEOC* (2012), the majority shields those employers from disability and age-discrimination claims. In the Court's view, because the employees taught short religion modules at Catholic elementary schools, they were "ministers" of the Catholic faith and thus could be fired for any reason, whether religious or nonreligious, benign or bigoted, without legal recourse. The Court reaches this result even though the teachers taught primarily secular subjects, lacked substantial religious titles and training, and were not even required to be Catholic. In foreclosing the teachers' claims, the Court skews the facts, ignores the applicable standard of review, and collapses *Hosanna-Tabor*'s careful analysis into a single consideration: whether a church thinks its employees play an important religious role. Because that simplistic approach has no basis in law and strips thousands of schoolteachers of their legal protections, I respectfully dissent.

I

A

Our pluralistic society requires religious entities to abide by generally applicable laws. *E,g.*, *Employment Div., Dept. of Human Resources of Ore. v. Smith* (1990). Consistent with the First Amendment (and over sincerely held religious objections), the Government may compel religious institutions to pay Social

---

2. As I have previously explained, this Court's Establishment Clause jurisprudence "is unmoored from the original meaning of the First Amendment." *Espinoza v. Montana Dept. of Revenue* (concurring opinion). Properly understood, the Establishment Clause proscribes governmental " 'coercion of religious orthodoxy and of financial support by force of law and threat of penalty.'" *American Legion v. American Humanist Assn.* (2019) (Thomas, J., concurring in judgment) (quoting *Lee v. Weisman* (1992) (Scalia, J., dissenting)).

Security taxes for their employees, *United States v. Lee* (1982), deny nonprofit status to entities that discriminate because of race, *Bob Jones Univ. v. United States* (1983), require applicants for certain public benefits to register with Social Security numbers, *Bowen v. Roy* (1986), enforce child-labor protections, *Prince v. Massachusetts* (1944), and impose minimum-wage laws, *Tony and Susan Alamo Foundation v. Secretary of Labor* (1985).

Congress, however, has crafted exceptions to protect religious autonomy. Some antidiscrimination laws, like the Americans with Disabilities Act, permit a religious institution to consider religion when making employment decisions. Under that Act, a religious organization may also "require that all applicants and employees conform" to the entity's "religious tenets." Title VII further permits a school to prefer "hir[ing] and employ[ing]" people "of a particular religion" if its curriculum "propagat[es]" that religion. These statutory exceptions protect a religious entity's ability to make employment decisions—hiring or firing—for religious reasons.

The "ministerial exception," by contrast, is a judge-made doctrine. This Court first recognized it eight years ago in *Hosanna-Tabor*, concluding that the First Amendment categorically bars certain antidiscrimination suits by religious leaders against their religious employers. When it applies, the exception is extraordinarily potent: It gives an employer free rein to discriminate because of race, sex, pregnancy, age, disability, or other traits protected by law when selecting or firing their "ministers," even when the discrimination is wholly unrelated to the employer's religious beliefs or practices. That is, an employer need not cite or possess a religious reason at all; the ministerial exception even condones animus.

When this Court adopted the ministerial exception, it affirmed the holdings of virtually every federal appellate court that had embraced the doctrine. . . . That approach recognized that a religious entity's ability to choose its faith leaders—rabbis, priests, nuns, imams, ministers, to name a few—should be free from government interference, but that generally applicable laws still protected most employees. . . . This focus on leadership led to a consistent conclusion: Lay faculty, even those who teach religion at church-affiliated schools, are not "ministers." . . .

Hosanna-Tabor did not upset this consensus. Instead, it recognized the ministerial exception's roots in protecting religious "elections" for "ecclesiastical offices" and guarding the freedom to "select" titled "clergy" and churchwide leaders. To be sure, the Court stated that the "ministerial exception is not limited to the head of a religious congregation." Nevertheless, this Court explained that the exception applies to someone with a leadership role "distinct from that of most of [the organization's] members," someone in whom "[t]he members of a religious group put their faith," or someone who "personif[ies]" the organization's "beliefs" and "guide[s] it on its way."[1]

---

1. While jettisoning most of *Hosanna-Tabor*'s majority opinion and insisting on "implicit" rationales that featured in a two-Justice concurrence, today's Court curiously accuses this dissent of "cobb[ling] together" a standard focused on leadership. But leadership was central in *Hosanna-Tabor*, just as it was explicit in the appellate court consensus that *Hosanna-Tabor* embraced.

This analysis is context-specific. It necessarily turns on, among other things, the structure of the religious organization at issue. Put another way (and as the Court repeats throughout today's opinion), *Hosanna-Tabor* declined to adopt a "rigid formula for deciding when an employee qualifies as a minister." Rather, *Hosanna-Tabor* focused on four "circumstances" to determine whether a fourth-grade teacher, Cheryl Perich, was employed at a Lutheran school as a "minister": (1) "the formal title given [her] by the Church," (2) "the substance reflected in that title," (3) "her own use of that title," and (4) "the important religious functions she performed for the Church." Confirming that the ministerial exception applies to a circumscribed sub-category of faith leaders, the Court analyzed those four "factors," to situate Perich as a minister within the Lutheran Church's structure.

B

Those considerations showed that Perich had a unique leadership role within her church. . . . Because this inquiry is holistic, the Court warned that it is "wrong" to "say that an employee's title does not matter." The Court was careful not to give religious functions undue weight in identifying church leaders. . . .

Hosanna-Tabor's well-rounded approach ensured that a church could not categorically disregard generally applicable antidiscrimination laws for nonreligious reasons. By analyzing objective and easily discernable markers like titles, training, and public-facing conduct, *Hosanna-Tabor* charted a way to separate leaders who "personify" a church's "beliefs" or who "minister to the faithful" from individuals who may simply relay religious tenets.[2] This balanced First Amendment concerns of state-church entanglement while avoiding an

II

Until today, no court had held that the ministerial exception applies with disputed facts like these and lay teachers like respondents, let alone at the summary-judgment stage.

---

2. Today's Court resists this commonsense approach, warning that it might mean that "a member of the Christian clergy or a rabbi" who "spends almost all of his or her time studying Scripture or theology and writing" would not fall within the ministerial exception. Those examples betray the Court's holding: As the Court intuits (but does not recognize), the examples likely fall within the ministerial exception not just because of the functions involved but also because of the titles ("clergy" and "rabbi"), the training required to obtain those titles, and the time spent on religious activity ("almost all" of one's time). It should be equally obvious that someone who spends a sliver of time reading, writing, or teaching about religion does not automatically become a minister of that religion.

Only by rewriting *Hosanna-Tabor* does the Court reach a different result. . . . [T]he Court recasts *Hosanna-Tabor* itself: Apparently, the touchstone all along was a two-Justice concurrence. To that concurrence, "[w]hat matter[ed]" was "the religious function that [Perich] performed" and her "functional status." *Hosanna-Tabor* (opinion of Alito, J.). Today's Court yields to the concurrence's view with identical rhetoric. "What matters," the Court echoes, "is what an employee does."

But this vague statement is no easier to comprehend today than it was when the Court declined to adopt it eight years ago. It certainly does not sound like a legal framework. Rather, the Court insists that a "religious institution's explanation of the role of [its] employees in the life of the religion in question is important." see also *ante* (Thomas, J., concurring) (urging complete deference to a religious institution in determining which employees are exempt from antidiscrimination laws). But because the Court's new standard prizes a functional importance that it appears to deem churches in the best position to explain, one cannot help but conclude that the Court has just traded legal analysis for a rubber stamp.

Indeed, the Court reasons that "judges cannot be expected to have a complete understanding and appreciation" of the law and facts in ministerial-exception cases, and all but abandons judicial review. Although today's decision is limited to certain "teachers of religion," its reasoning risks rendering almost every Catholic parishioner and parent in the Archdiocese of Los Angeles a Catholic minister. That is, the Court's apparent deference here threatens to make nearly anyone whom the schools might hire "ministers" unprotected from discrimination in the hiring process. That cannot be right. Although certain religious functions may be important to a church, a person's performance of some of those functions does not mechanically trigger a categorical exemption from generally applicable antidiscrimination laws.

Today's decision thus invites the "potential for abuse" against which circuit courts have long warned. Nevermind that the Court renders almost all of the Court's opinion in *Hosanna-Tabor* irrelevant. It risks allowing employers to decide for themselves whether discrimination is actionable. Indeed, today's decision reframes the ministerial exception as broadly as it can, without regard to the statutory exceptions tailored to protect religious practice. As a result, the Court absolves religious institutions of any animus completely irrelevant to their religious beliefs or practices and all but forbids courts to inquire further about whether the employee is in fact a leader of the religion. Nothing in *Hosanna-Tabor* (or at least its majority opinion) condones such judicial abdication.

III

Faithfully applying *Hosanna-Tabor*'s approach and common sense confirms that the teachers here are not Catholic "ministers" as a matter of law. This is especially so because the employers seek summary judgment, meaning the Court must "view the facts and draw reasonable inferences in the light most favorable to" the teachers. . . .[5]

B

On these records, the Ninth Circuit correctly concluded that neither school had shown that the ministerial exception barred the teachers' claims for disability and age discrimination. At the very least, these cases should have proceeded to trial. Viewed in the light most favorable to the teachers, the facts do not entitle the employers to summary judgment. . . .

The Court then turns to irrelevant or disputed facts. The Court notes, for example, that a religiously significant term "rabbi" translates to "teacher," suggesting that Biel's and Morrissey-Berru's positions as lay teachers conferred religious titles after all. But that wordplay unravels when one imagines the Court's logic as applied to a math or gym or computer "teacher" at either school. The title "teacher" does not convey ministerial status. . . .

Second (and further undermining the schools' claims), neither teacher had a "significant degree of religious training" or underwent a "formal process of commissioning." *Hosanna-Tabor*. Nor did either school require such training or commissioning as a prerequisite to gaining (or keeping) employment. . . . This consideration instructs that the teachers here did not fall within the ministerial exception.

Third, neither Biel nor Morrissey-Berru held herself out as having a leadership role in the faith community. Neither claimed any benefits (tax, governmental, ceremonial, or administrative) available only to spiritual leaders. . . . The Court does not grapple with this third component of *Hosanna-Tabor*'s inquiry, which seriously undermines the schools' cases.

That leaves only the fourth consideration in *Hosanna-Tabor*: the teachers' function. To be sure, Biel and Morrissey-Berru taught religion for a part of some days in the week. But that should not transform them automatically into ministers who "guide" the faith "on its way." *Hosanna-Tabor*. Although the Court does not resolve this functional question with "a stopwatch," it still considers the "amount of time an employee spends on particular activities" in "assessing that employee's status." *Hosanna-Tabor*. Here, the time Biel and Morrissey-Berru spent on secular instruction far surpassed their time teaching religion. For the vast majority of class, they taught subjects like reading, writing, spelling, grammar, vocabulary, math, science, social studies, and geography. In so doing, both were like any public school teacher in California, subject to the same

---

5. The Court maintains that the Court of Appeals erred by "in effect" granting summary judgment to the teachers on the ministerial exception instead of "remand[ing] for a trial." Yet today's decision commits the exact error it claims to diagnose: The Court views the facts in the light most favorable to the schools and "in effect" grants summary judgment to the movants instead of remanding for a trial. As explained below, the Court is also wrong to assert that there is no material fact genuinely in dispute.

statewide curriculum guidelines. In other words, both Biel and Morrissey-Berru had almost exclusively secular duties, making it especially improper to deprive them of all legal protection when their employers have not offered any religious reason for the alleged discrimination. . . .

. . . [T]eaching religion in school alone cannot dictate ministerial status. If it did, then *Hosanna-Tabor* wasted precious pages discussing titles, training, and other objective indicia to examine whether Cheryl Perich was a minister. Not surprisingly, the Government made this same point earlier in Biel's case: "If teaching religion to elementary school students for a half-hour each day, praying with them daily, and accompanying them to weekly or monthly religious services were sufficient to establish a teacher as a minister of the church within the meaning of the ministerial exception, the Supreme Court would have had no need for most of its discussion in *Hosanna-Tabor*." Brief for EEOC as *Amicus Curiae*. Rather, "the Court made clear in *Hosanna-Tabor* that context matters." Indeed.[20]

Were there any doubt left about the proper result here, recall that neither school has shown that it required its religion teachers to be Catholic. The Court does not explain how the schools here can show, or have shown, that a non-Catholic "personif[ies]" Catholicism or leads the faith. *Hosanna-Tabor*. Instead, the Court remarks that a "rigid" coreligionist requirement might "not always be easy" to apply to faiths like Judaism or variations of Protestantism. Perhaps. But that has nothing to do with Catholicism.

Pause, for a moment, on the Court's conclusion: Even if the teachers were not Catholic, and even if they were forbidden to participate in the church's sacramental worship, they would nonetheless be "ministers" of the Catholic faith simply because of their supervisory role over students in a religious school. That stretches the law and logic past their breaking points. (Indeed, it is ironic that Our Lady of Guadalupe School seeks complete immunity for age discrimination when its teacher handbook promised not to discriminate on that basis.) As the Government once put it, even when a school has a "pervasively religious atmosphere," its faculty are unlikely ministers when "there is no requirement that its teachers even be members of [its] religious denomination." It is hard to imagine a more concrete example than these cases.

* * *

The Court's conclusion portends grave consequences. As the Government (arguing for Biel at the time) explained to the Ninth Circuit, "thousands of Catholic teachers" may lose employment-law protections because of today's outcome. Other sources tally over a hundred thousand secular teachers whose rights are at risk. And that says nothing of the rights of countless coaches, camp counselors, nurses, social-service workers, in-house lawyers, media-relations

---

20. Although the Government supported Biel below, it has since switched sides without explanation. Odder still, the Government's brief to this Court faults the Ninth Circuit for having embraced the Government's prior views. [The EEOC switched positions after the 2016 election. — Eds.]

personnel, and many others who work for religious institutions. All these employees could be subject to discrimination for reasons completely irrelevant to their employers' religious tenets.

In expanding the ministerial exception far beyond its historic narrowness, the Court overrides Congress' carefully tailored exceptions for religious employers. Little if nothing appears left of the statutory exemptions after today's constitutional broadside. So long as the employer determines that an employee's "duties" are "vital" to "carrying out the mission of the church," then today's laissez-faire analysis appears to allow that employer to make employment decisions because of a person's skin color, age, disability, sex, or any other protected trait for reasons having nothing to do with religion.

This sweeping result is profoundly unfair. The Court is not only wrong on the facts, but its error also risks upending antidiscrimination protections for many employees of religious entities. Recently, this Court has lamented a perceived "discrimination against religion." Yet here it swings the pendulum in the extreme opposite direction, permitting religious entities to discriminate widely and with impunity for reasons wholly divorced from religious beliefs. The inherent injustice in the Court's conclusion will be impossible to ignore for long, particularly in a pluralistic society like ours. One must hope that a decision deft enough to remold *Hosanna-Tabor* to fit the result reached today reflects the Court's capacity to cabin the consequences tomorrow.

I respectfully dissent.

Little Sisters of the Poor Saints Peter and Paul Home v. Pennsylvania
591 U.S. ___ (2020)

JUSTICE THOMAS delivered the opinion of the Court.

In these consolidated cases, we decide whether the Government created lawful exemptions from a regulatory requirement implementing the Patient Protection and Affordable Care Act of 2010 (ACA). The requirement at issue obligates certain employers to provide contraceptive coverage to their employees through their group health plans. Though contraceptive coverage is not required by (or even mentioned in) the ACA provision at issue, the Government mandated such coverage by promulgating interim final rules (IFRs) shortly after the ACA's passage. This requirement is known as the contraceptive mandate.

After six years of protracted litigation, the Departments of Health and Human Services, Labor, and the Treasury (Departments) — which jointly administer the relevant ACA provision — exempted certain employers who have religious and conscientious objections from this agency-created mandate. The Third Circuit concluded that the Departments lacked statutory authority to promulgate these exemptions and affirmed the District Court's nationwide preliminary injunction. This decision was erroneous. We hold that the Departments had the authority to provide exemptions from the regulatory contraceptive requirements for employers with religious and conscientious objections. We accordingly reverse the Third Circuit's judgment and remand with instructions to dissolve the nation-wide preliminary injunction.

. . .

We hold today that the Departments had the statutory authority to craft that exemption, as well as the contemporaneously issued moral exemption. We further hold that the rules promulgating these exemptions are free from procedural defects. Therefore, we reverse the judgment of the Court of Appeals and remand the cases for further proceedings consistent with this opinion.

JUSTICE ALITO, with whom JUSTICE GORSUCH joins, concurring.

. . .We now send these cases back to the lower courts, where the Commonwealth of Pennsylvania and the State of New Jersey are all but certain to pursue their argument that the current rule is flawed on yet another ground, namely, that it is arbitrary and capricious and thus violates the APA. This will prolong the legal battle in which the Little Sisters have now been engaged for seven years—even though during all this time no employee of the Little Sisters has come forward with an objection to the Little Sisters' conduct.

I understand the Court's desire to decide no more than is strictly necessary, but under the circumstances here, I would decide one additional question: whether the Court of Appeals erred in holding that the Religious Freedom Restoration Act (RFRA), does not compel the religious exemption granted by the current rule. If RFRA requires this exemption, the Departments did not act in an arbitrary and capricious manner in granting it. And in my judgment, RFRA compels an exemption for the Little Sisters and any other employer with a similar objection to what has been called the accommodation to the contraceptive mandate.

I

. . . In *Burwell v. Hobby Lobby Stores, Inc.* (2014), we held that RFRA prohibited the application of the regulation to closely held, for-profit corporations that fell into this category. The Departments responded by issuing a new regulation that attempted to codify our holding by allowing closely-held corporations to utilize the accommodation.

Although this modification solved one RFRA problem, the contraceptive mandate was still objectionable to some religious employers, including the Little Sisters. We considered those objections in *Zubik* v. *Burwell* (2016), but instead of resolving the legal dispute, we vacated the decisions below and remanded, instructing the parties to attempt to come to an agreement. Unfortunately, after strenuous efforts, the outgoing administration reported on January 9, 2017, that no reconciliation could be reached. The Little Sisters and other employers objected to engaging in any conduct that had the effect of making contraceptives available to their employees under their insurance plans, and no way of providing such coverage to their employees without using their plans could be found.

In 2017, the new administration took up the task of attempting to find a solution. After receiving more than 56,000 comments, it issued the rule now before us, which made the church exemption available to non-governmental employers who object to the provision of some or all contraceptive services based on sincerely held religious beliefs.

II

A

RFRA broadly prohibits the Federal Government from violating religious liberty. . . . Thus, unless the ACA or some other subsequently enacted statute made RFRA inapplicable to the contraceptive mandate, the Departments responsible for administering that mandate are obligated to do so in a manner that complies with RFRA.

No provision of the ACA abrogates RFRA, and our decision in *Hobby Lobby*, established that application of the contraceptive mandate must conform to RFRA's demands. Thus, it was incumbent on the Departments to ensure that the rules implementing the mandate were consistent with RFRA, as interpreted in our decision.

B

Under RFRA, the Federal Government may not "substantially burden a person's exercise of religion even if the burden results from a rule of general applicability," unless it "demonstrates that application of the burden to the person—(1) is in furtherance of a compelling governmental interest; and (2) is the least restrictive means of furthering that compelling governmental interest." Applying RFRA to the contraceptive mandate thus presents three questions. First, would the mandate substantially burden an employer's exercise of religion? Second, if the mandate would impose such a burden, would it nevertheless serve a "compelling interest"? And third, if it serves such an interest, would it represent "the least restrictive means of furthering" that interest?

Substantial burden. Under our decision in *Hobby Lobby*, requiring the Little Sisters or any other employer with a similar religious objection to comply with the mandate would impose a substantial burden. Our analysis of this question in *Hobby Lobby* can be separated into two parts. First, would non-compliance have substantial adverse practical consequences? Second, would compliance cause the objecting party to violate its religious beliefs, *as it sincerely understands them*?

The answer to the first question is indisputable. If a covered employer does not comply with the mandate (by providing contraceptive coverage or invoking the accommodation), it faces penalties of $100 per day for each of its employees. . . . In *Hobby Lobby*, we found these "severe" financial consequences sufficient to show that the practical effect of non-compliance would be "substantial."[5]

Our answer to the second question was also perfectly clear. If an employer has a religious objection to the use of a covered contraceptive, and if the employer has a sincere religious belief that compliance with the mandate makes it complicit in that conduct, then RFRA requires that the belief be honored. . . . [T]he "function" of a court is " 'narrow' ": " 'to determine' whether the line drawn reflects 'an honest conviction.' " *Id.* (quoting *Thomas v. Review Bd. of Ind. Employment Security Div.* (1981)).

Applying this holding to the Little Sisters yields an obvious answer. It is undisputed that the Little Sisters have a sincere religious objection to the use of contraceptives and that they also have a sincere religious belief that utilizing the accommodation would make them complicit in this conduct. . . .

The inescapable bottom line is that the accommodation demanded that parties like the Little Sisters engage in conduct that was a necessary cause of the ulti-mate conduct to which they had strong religious objections. Their situation was the same as that of the conscientious objector in *Thomas*, who refused to partici-pate in the manufacture of tanks but did not object to assisting in the production of steel used to make the tanks. Where to draw the line in a chain of causation that leads to objectionable conduct is a difficult moral question, and our cases have made it clear that courts cannot override the sincere religious beliefs of an objecting party on that question.

For these reasons, the contraceptive mandate imposes a substantial burden on any employer who, like the Little Sisters, has a sincere religious objection to the use of a listed contraceptive and a sincere religious belief that compliance with the mandate (through the accommodation or otherwise) makes it complicit in the provision to the employer's workers of a contraceptive to which the employer has a religious objection.

Compelling interest. In *Hobby Lobby*, the Government asserted and we assumed for the sake of argument that the Government had a compelling interest in "ensuring that all women have access to all FDA-approved contraceptives without cost sharing." Now, the Government concedes that it lacks a compelling interest in providing such access, and this time, the Government is correct.

In order to show that it has a "compelling interest" within the meaning of RFRA, the Government must clear a high bar. In *Sherbert v. Verner* (1963), the decision that provides the foundation for the rule codified in RFRA, we said that " '[o]nly the gravest abuses, endangering paramount interest' " could " 'give occasion for [a] permissible limitation' " on the free exercise of religion. Thus, in order to establish that it has a "compelling interest" in providing free

---

5. This is one of the differences between these cases and *Bowen v. Roy* (1986). See *post* (opinion of Ginsburg, J.) (relying on *Bowen* to conclude that accommodation was unnecessary). In *Bowen*, the objecting individuals were not faced with penalties or "coerced by the Governmen[t] into violating their religious beliefs." *Lyng v. Northwest Indian Cemetery Protective Assn.* (1988).

contraceptives to all women, the Government would have to show that it would commit one of "the gravest abuses" of its responsibilities if it did not furnish free contraceptives to all women.

If we were required to exercise our own judgment on the question whether the Government has an obligation to provide free contraceptives to all women, we would have to take sides in the great national debate about whether the Government should provide free and comprehensive medical care for all. Entering that policy debate would be inconsistent with our proper role, and RFRA does not call on us to express a view on that issue. We can answer the compelling interest question simply by asking whether *Congress* has treated the provision of free contraceptives to all women as a compelling interest.

. . . The ACA — which fails to ensure that millions of women have access to free contraceptives — unmistakably shows that Congress, at least to date, has not regarded this interest as compelling.

First, the ACA does not provide contraceptive coverage for women who do not work outside the home. If Congress thought that there was a compelling need to make free contraceptives available for all women, why did it make no provision for women who do not receive a paycheck? Some of these women may have a greater need for free contraceptives than do women in the work force.

Second, if Congress thought that there was a compelling need to provide cost-free contraceptives for all working women, why didn't Congress mandate that coverage in the ACA itself? Why did it leave it to HRSA to decide whether to require such coverage *at all*?

Third, the ACA's very incomplete coverage speaks volumes. The ACA "exempts a great many employers from most of its coverage requirements." *Hobby Lobby. . . .* In *Hobby Lobby*, we wrote that "the contraceptive mandate 'presently does not apply to tens of millions of people,'" and it appears that this is still true apart from the religious exemption. . . .

Fourth, the Court's recognition in today's decision that the ACA authorizes the creation of exemptions that go beyond anything required by the Constitution provides further evidence that Congress did not regard the provision of cost-free contraceptives to all women as a compelling interest.

Moreover, the regulatory exemptions created by the Departments and HRSA undermine any claim that the agencies themselves viewed the provision of contraceptive coverage as sufficiently compelling. From the outset, the church exemption has applied to churches, their integrated auxiliaries, and associations. . . .

The dissent frames the allegedly compelling interest served by the mandate in different terms — as an interest in providing "seamless" cost-free coverage, *post* (opinion of Ginsburg, J.)—but this is an even weaker argument. What "seamless" coverage apparently means is coverage under the insurance plan furnished by a woman's employer. So as applied to the Little Sisters, the dissent thinks that it would be a grave abuse if an employee wishing to obtain contraceptives had to take any step that would not be necessary if she wanted to obtain any other medical service. . . . Nothing short of capitulation on the part of the Little Sisters would suffice. . . .

In short, it is undoubtedly true that the contraceptive mandate provides a benefit that many women may find highly desirable, but Congress's enactments show that it has not regarded the provision of free contraceptives or the furnishing of "seamless" coverage as "compelling."

Least restrictive means. Even if the mandate served a compelling interest, the accommodation still would not satisfy the "exceptionally demanding" least-restrictive-means standard. *Hobby Lobby.* . . .

In *Hobby Lobby*, we observed that the Government has "other means" of providing cost-free contraceptives to women "without imposing a substantial burden on the exercise of religion by the objecting parties." "The most straightforward way," we noted, "would be for the Government to assume the cost of providing the . . . contraceptives . . . to any women who are unable to obtain them under their health-insurance policies." . . .

As the Government now points out, Congress has taken steps in this direction. . . . And many women who work for employers who have religious objections to the contraceptive mandate may be able to receive contraceptive coverage through a family member's health insurance plan.

In sum, the Departments were right to conclude that applying the accommodation to sincere religious objectors violates RFRA. All three prongs of the RFRA analysis—substantial burden, compelling interest, and least restrictive means—necessitate this answer.

III

Once it was apparent that the accommodation ran afoul of RFRA, the Government was required to eliminate the violation. RFRA does not specify the precise manner in which a violation must be remedied; it simply instructs the Government to avoid "substantially burden[ing]" the "exercise of religion"—*i.e.,* to eliminate the violation. Thus, in *Hobby Lobby*, once we held that application of the mandate to the objecting parties violated RFRA, we left it to the Departments to decide how best to rectify this problem. . . .

The same principle applies here. Once it is recognized that the prior accommodation violated RFRA in some of its applications, it was incumbent on the Departments to eliminate those violations, and they had discretion in crafting what they regarded as the best solution.

The solution they devised cures the problem, and it is not clear that any narrower exemption would have been sufficient with respect to parties with religious objections to the accommodation. . . .

In any event, while RFRA requires the Government to employ the least restrictive means of furthering a compelling interest that burdens religious belief, it does not require the converse—that an accommodation of religious belief be narrowly tailored to further a compelling interest. The latter approach, which is advocated by the States, gets RFRA entirely backwards. Nothing in RFRA requires that a violation be remedied by the narrowest permissible corrective.

Needless to say, the remedy for a RFRA problem cannot violate the Constitution, but the new rule does not have that effect. The Court has held that there is a constitutional right to purchase and use contraceptives. *Griswold v. Connecticut* (1965); *Carey v. Population Services Int'l* (1977). But the Court has never held that there is a constitutional right to free contraceptives.

The dissent and the court below suggest that the new rule is improper because it imposes burdens on the employees of entities that the rule exempts,[13] but the rule imposes no such burden. A woman who does not have the benefit of contraceptive coverage under her employer's plan is not the victim of a burden imposed by the rule or her employer. She is simply not the beneficiary of something that federal law does not provide. She is in the same position as a woman who does not work outside the home or a woman whose health insurance is provided by a grandfathered plan that does not pay for contraceptives or a woman who works for a small business that may not provide any health insurance at all.

* * *

I would hold not only that it was appropriate for the Departments to consider RFRA, but also that the Departments were required by RFRA to create the religious exemption (or something very close to it). I would bring the Little Sisters' legal odyssey to an end.

JUSTICE GINSBURG, with whom JUSTICE SOTOMAYOR joins, dissenting.

In accommodating claims of religious freedom, this Court has taken a balanced approach, one that does not allow the religious beliefs of some to overwhelm the rights and interests of others who do not share those beliefs. See, *e.g.*, *Estate of Thornton v. Caldor, Inc.* (1985); *United States v. Lee* (1982). Today, for the first time, the Court casts totally aside countervailing rights and interests in its zeal to secure religious rights to the *n*th degree. Specifically, in the Women's Health Amendment to the Patient Protection and Affordable Care Act (ACA), Congress undertook to afford gainfully employed women comprehensive, seamless, no-cost insurance coverage for preventive care protective of their health and well-being. Congress delegated to a particular agency, the Health Resources and Services Administration (HRSA), authority to designate the preventive care insurance should cover. HRSA included in its designation all contraceptives approved by the Food and Drug Administration (FDA).

Destructive of the Women's Health Amendment, this Court leaves women workers to fend for themselves, to seek contraceptive coverage from sources other

---

13. Both the dissent and the court below refer to the statement in *Cutter v. Wilkinson* (2005), that "courts must take adequate account of the burdens a requested accommodation may impose on nonbeneficiaries," but that statement was made in response to the argument that RFRA's twin, the Religious Land Use and Institutionalized Persons Act, violated the Establishment Clause. The only case cited by *Cutter* in connection with this statement, Estate of Thornton v. Caldor, Inc., involved a religious accommodation that the Court held violated the Establishment Clause. Before this Court, the States do not argue—and there is no basis for an argument—that the new rule violates that Clause.

than their employer's insurer, and, absent another available source of funding, to pay for contraceptive services out of their own pockets. The Constitution's Free Exercise Clause, all agree, does not call for that imbalanced result.[1] Nor does the Religious Freedom Restoration Act of 1993 (RFRA) condone harm to third parties occasioned by entire disregard of their needs. I therefore dissent from the Court's judgment, under which, as the Government estimates, between 70,500 and 126,400 women would immediately lose access to no-cost contraceptive services. On the merits, I would affirm the judgment of the U. S. Court of Appeals for the Third Circuit. . . .

III

Because I conclude that the blanket exemption gains no aid from the ACA, I turn to the Government's alternative argument. The *religious* exemption, if not the moral exemption, the Government urges, is necessary to protect religious freedom. The Government does not press a free exercise argument, instead invoking RFRA.

A

The parties here agree that federal agencies may craft accommodations and exemptions to cure violations of RFRA. See, *e.g.*, Brief for Respondents 36.[17] But that authority is not unbounded. *Cutter* v. *Wilkinson* (2005) (construing Religious Land Use and Institutionalized Persons Act of 2000, the Court cautioned that "adequate account" must be taken of "the burdens a requested accommodation may impose on nonbeneficiaries" of the Act); *Caldor* (invalidating state statute requiring employers to accommodate an employee's religious observance for failure to take into account the burden such an accommodation would impose on the employer and other employees). "[O]ne person's right to free exercise must be kept in harmony with the rights of her fellow citizens." *Hobby Lobby,* (GINSBURG, J., dissenting).

In this light, the Court has repeatedly assumed that any religious accommodation to the contraceptive-coverage requirement would preserve women's continued access to seamless, no-cost contraceptive coverage.

---

1. In *Employment Div., Dept. of Human Resources of Ore. v. Smith* (1990), the Court explained that "the right of free exercise does not relieve an individual of the obligation to comply with a valid and neutral law of general applicability on the ground that the law proscribes (or prescribes) conduct that his religion prescribes (or proscribes)." The requirement that insurers cover FDA-approved methods of contraception "applies generally, . . . trains on women's well-being, not on the exercise of religion, and any effect it has on such exercise is incidental." *Burwell v. Hobby Lobby Stores, Inc.,* (2014) (GINSBURG, J., dissenting). *Smith* forecloses "[a]ny First Amendment Free Exercise Clause claim [one] might assert" in opposition to that requirement.

17. No party argues that agencies can act to cure violations of RFRA only after a court has found a RFRA violation, and this opinion does not adopt any such view.

The assumption made in the above-cited cases rests on the basic principle just stated, one on which this dissent relies: While the Government may "accommodate religion beyond free exercise requirements," *Cutter*, 544 U.S., at 713, when it does so, it may not benefit religious adherents at the expense of the rights of third parties. . . . Holding otherwise would endorse "the regulatory equivalent of taxing non-adherents to support the faithful."

2

Lacking any alternative insurance coverage mechanism the exemption leaves women two options, neither satisfactory.

The first option — the one suggested by the Government in its most recent rulemaking — is for women to seek contraceptive care from existing government-funded programs. . . . [A]s the Government has acknowledged, requiring women "to take steps to learn about, and to sign up for, a new health benefit" imposes "additional barriers," "mak[ing] that coverage accessible to fewer women."

The second option for women losing insurance coverage for contraceptives is to pay for contraceptive counseling and devices out of their own pockets. . . . Faced with high out-of-pocket costs, many women will forgo contraception, or resort to less effective contraceptive methods.

"No tradition, and no prior decision under RFRA, allows a religion-based exemption when [it] would be harmful to others — here, the very persons the contraceptive coverage requirement was designed to protect." *Hobby Lobby* (GINSBURG, J., dissenting).[20] I would therefore hold the religious exemption neither required nor permitted by RFRA.[21]

B

Pennsylvania and New Jersey advance an additional argument: The exemption is not authorized by RFRA, they maintain, because the self-certification accommodation it replaced was sufficient to alleviate any substantial burden on religious exercise. That accommodation, I agree, further indicates the religious exemption's flaws.

---

20. Remarkably, JUSTICE ALITO maintains that stripping women of insurance coverage for contraceptive services imposes no burden. He reaches this conclusion because, in his view, federal law does not require the contraceptive coverage denied to women under the exemption.Congress, however, called upon HRSA to specify contraceptive and other preventive services for women in order to ensure equality in women employees' access to healthcare, thus safeguarding their health and well-being.

21. As above stated, the Government does not defend the moral exemption under RFRA.

1

For years, religious organizations have challenged the self-certification accommodation as insufficiently protective of their religious rights. While I do not doubt the sincerity of these organizations' opposition to that accommodation, I agree with Pennsylvania and New Jersey that the accommodation does not substantially burden objectors' religious exercise.

As Senator Hatch observed, "[RFRA] does not require the Government to justify every action that has some effect on religious exercise." *Bowen v. Roy* (1986), is instructive in this regard. There, a Native American father asserted a sincere religious belief that his daughter's spirit would be harmed by the Government's use of her social security number. The Court, while casting no doubt on the sincerity of this religious belief, explained:

> "Never to our knowledge has the Court interpreted the First Amendment to require the Government *itself* to behave in ways that the individual believes will further his or her spiritual development or that of his or her family. The Free Exercise Clause simply cannot be understood to require the Government to conduct its own internal affairs in ways that comport with the religious beliefs of particular citizens."[22]

Roy signals a critical distinction in the Court's religious exercise jurisprudence: A religious adherent may be entitled to religious accommodation with regard to her own conduct, but she is not entitled to "insist that . . . *others* must conform *their* conduct to [her] own religious necessities.'" *Caldor* (quoting *Otten v. Baltimore & Ohio R. Co.* (2nd Cir. 1953) (Hand, J.).[23] . . . .[24]

. . . . Under the self-certification accommodation, then, the objecting employer is absolved of any obligation to provide the contraceptive coverage to which it objects; that obligation is transferred to the insurer. This arrangement "furthers the Government's interest [in women's health] but does not impinge on the [employer's] religious beliefs."

2

The Little Sisters, adopting the arguments made by religious organizations in *Zubik*, resist this conclusion in two ways. . . .

---

22. JUSTICE ALITO disputes the relevance of *Roy*, asserting that the religious adherent in that case faced no penalty for noncompliance with the legal requirement under consideration. As JUSTICE ALITO acknowledges, however, the critical inquiry has two parts. It is not enough to ask whether noncompliance entails "substantial adverse practical consequences." One must also ask whether compliance substantially burdens religious exercise. Like *Roy*, my dissent homes in on the latter question.

23 Even if RFRA sweeps more broadly than the Court's pre-*Smith* jurisprudence in some respects, there is no cause to believe that Congress jettisoned this fundamental distinction.

24. JUSTICE ALITO ignores the distinction between (1) a request for an accommodation with regard to one's own conduct, and (2) an attempt to require others to conform their conduct to one's own religious beliefs. This distinction is fatal to JUSTICE ALITO's argument that the self-certification accommodation violates RFRA.

Second, the Little Sisters assert that "tak[ing] affirmative steps to execute paperwork . . . necessary for the provision of 'seamless' contraceptive coverage to their employees" implicates them in providing contraceptive services to women in violation of their religious beliefs. At the same time, however, they have been adamant that they do not oppose merely "register[ing] their objections" to the contraceptive-coverage requirement. These statements, taken together, reveal that the Little Sisters do not object to what the self-certification accommodation asks of *them*, namely, attesting to their religious objection to contraception. They object, instead, to the particular use insurance issuers make of that attestation.[26] But that use originated from the ACA and its once-implementing regulation, not from religious employers' self-certification or alternative notice.

* * *

The blanket exemption for religious and moral objectors to contraception formulated by the IRS, EBSA, and CMS is inconsistent with the text of, and Congress' intent for, both the ACA and RFRA. Neither law authorizes it.[27] The original administrative regulation accommodating religious objections to contraception appropriately implemented the ACA and RFRA consistent with Congress' staunch determination to afford women employees equal access to preventive services, thereby advancing public health and welfare and women's well-being. I would therefore affirm the judgment of the Court of Appeals.[28]

---

26. JUSTICE ALITO asserts that the Little Sisters' "situation [is] the same as that of the conscientious objector in *Thomas* [v. *Review Bd. of Ind. Employment Security Div.*, (1981)]." I disagree. In *Thomas*, a Jehovah's Witness objected to "work[ing] on weapons," which is what his employer required of him. As above stated, however, the Little Sisters have no objection to objecting, the only other action the self-certification accommodation requires of them.

27. Given this conclusion, I need not address whether the exemption is procedurally invalid.

28. Although the Court does not reach the issue, the District Court did not abuse its discretion in issuing a nationwide injunction. The Administrative Procedure Act contemplates nationwide relief from invalid agency action. See 5 U.S.C. §706(2) (empowering courts to "hold unlawful and set aside agency action"). Moreover, the nationwide reach of the injunction "was 'necessary to provide complete relief to the plaintiffs.'" *Trump* v. *Hawaii* (2018) (SOTOMAYOR, J., dissenting). Harm to Pennsylvania and New Jersey, the Court of Appeals explained, occurs because women who lose benefits under the exemption "will turn to state-funded services for their contraceptive needs and for the unintended pregnancies that may result from the loss of coverage." This harm is not bounded by state lines. The Court of Appeals noted, for example, that some 800,000 residents of Pennsylvania and New Jersey work — and thus receive their health insurance — out of State. Similarly, many students who attend colleges and universities in Pennsylvania and New Jersey receive their health insurance from their parents' out-of-state health plans.

Chapter 19

No Law Respecting an Establishment of Religion

STUDY GUIDE:

- Why is the Bladensburg Peace Cross constitutional? What test does the Court apply?
- What is the relevance of the age of the monument? Could Bladensburg erect a new, identical peace cross today?
- Does *American Legion* develop any new Establishment Clause doctrine beyond that articulated in Justice Breyer's concurrence in *Van Orden v. Perry*?
- In what contexts should the *Lemon* test still be applied after *American Legion*? Or, should the courts treat *Lemon* as basically overruled?
- Justice Thomas maintains that the Establishment Clause does not limit the state's police power. Why does he reach this conclusion?

American Legion v. American Humanist Association
588 U.S. ___ (2019)

JUSTICE ALITO announced the judgment of the Court and delivered the opinion of the Court with respect to Parts I, II-B, II-C, III, and IV, and an opinion with respect to Parts II-A and II-D, in which THE CHIEF JUSTICE, JUSTICE BREYER, and JUSTICE KAVANAUGH join.

Since 1925, the Bladensburg Peace Cross (Cross) has stood as a tribute to 49 area soldiers who gave their lives in the First World War. Eighty-nine years after the dedication of the Cross, respondents filed this lawsuit, claiming that they are offended by the sight of the memorial on public land and that its presence there and the expenditure of public funds to maintain it violate the Establishment Clause of the First Amendment. To remedy this violation, they asked a federal court to order the relocation or demolition of the Cross or at least the removal of its arms. The Court of Appeals for the Fourth Circuit agreed that the memorial is unconstitutional and remanded for a determination of the proper remedy. We now reverse. . . .

For nearly a century, the Bladensburg Cross has expressed the community's grief at the loss of the young men who perished, its thanks for their sacrifice, and its dedication to the ideals for which they fought. It has become a prominent community landmark, and its removal or radical alteration at this date would be seen by many not as a neutral act but as the manifestation of "a hostility toward religion that has no place in our Establishment Clause traditions." *Van Orden v. Perry*, (2005) (Breyer, J., concurring in judgment). . . . The Religion Clauses of the Constitution aim to foster a society in which people of all beliefs can live together harmoniously, and the presence of the Bladensburg Cross on the land where it has stood for so many years is fully consistent with that aim.

I

A

The cross came into widespread use as a symbol of Christianity by the fourth century, and it retains that meaning today. But there are many contexts in which the symbol has also taken on a secular meaning. Indeed, there are instances in which its message is now almost entirely secular. . . . The image used in the Bladensburg memorial — a plain Latin cross[6] — . . . took on new meaning after World War I. "During and immediately after the war, the army marked soldiers' graves with temporary wooden crosses or Stars of David" — a departure from the prior practice of marking graves in American military cemeteries with uniform rectangular slabs. The vast majority of these grave markers consisted of crosses,[7] and thus when Americans saw photographs of these cemeteries, what struck them were rows and rows of plain white crosses. As a result, the image of a simple white cross "developed into a 'central symbol'" of the conflict.

B

Recognition of the cross's symbolism extended to local communities across the country. In late 1918, residents of Prince George's County, Maryland, formed a committee for the purpose of erecting a memorial for the county's fallen soldiers. Among the committee's members were the mothers of 10 deceased soldiers. The committee decided that the memorial should be a cross and hired sculptor and architect John Joseph Earley to design it. Although we do not know precisely why the committee chose the cross, it is unsurprising that the committee — and many others commemorating World War I — adopted a symbol so widely associated with that wrenching event. . . .

---

6. The Latin form of the cross "has a longer upright than crossbar. The intersection of the two is usually such that the upper and the two horizontal arms are all of about equal length, but the lower arm is conspicuously longer."

7. Of the roughly 116,000 casualties the United States suffered in World War I, some 3,500 were Jewish soldiers. In the congressional hearings involving the appropriate grave markers for those buried abroad, one Representative stated that approximately 1,600 of these Jewish soldiers were buried in overseas graves marked by Stars of David.

The completed monument is a 32-foot tall Latin cross that sits on a large pedestal. The American Legion's emblem is displayed at its center, and the words
"Valor," "Endurance," "Courage," and "Devotion" are inscribed at its base, one
on each of the four faces. The pedestal also features a 9- by 2.5-foot bronze
plaque explaining that the monument is "Dedicated to the heroes of Prince
George's County, Maryland who lost their lives in the Great War for the liberty
of the world." The plaque lists the names of 49 local men, both Black and White,
who died in the war. It identifies the dates of American involvement, and quotes
President Woodrow Wilson's request for a declaration of war: "The right is more
precious than peace. We shall fight for the things we have always carried nearest
our hearts. To such a task we dedicate our lives."

At the dedication ceremony, a local Catholic priest offered an invocation. . . .
The ceremony closed with a benediction offered by a Baptist pastor. Since its
dedication, the Cross has served as the site of patriotic events honoring veterans, including gatherings on Veterans Day, Memorial Day, and Independence
Day. . . .

As the area around the Cross developed, the monument came to be at the
center of a busy intersection. In 1961, the Maryland-National Capital Park and
Planning Commission (Commission) acquired the Cross and the land on which
it sits in order to preserve the monument and address traffic-safety concerns.

C

In 2012, nearly 90 years after the Cross was dedicated and more than 50 years
after the Commission acquired it, the American Humanist Association (AHA)
lodged a complaint with the Commission. The complaint alleged that the Cross's
presence on public land and the Commission's maintenance of the memorial
violate the Establishment Clause of the First Amendment. The AHA, along with
three residents of Washington, D.C., and Maryland, also sued the Commission
in the District Court for the District of Maryland, making the same claim. The
AHA sought declaratory and injunctive relief requiring "removal or demolition
of the Cross, or removal of the arms from the Cross to form a non-religious slab
or obelisk." The American Legion intervened to defend the Cross.

The District Court granted summary judgment for the Commission and the
American Legion. The Cross, the District Court held, satisfies both the three-
pronged test announced in *Lemon v. Kurtzman* (1971), and the analysis applied
by Justice Breyer in upholding the Ten Commandments monument at issue in
Van Orden v. Perry. Under the *Lemon* test, a court must ask whether a challenged
government action (1) has a secular purpose; (2) has a "principal or primary
effect" that "neither advances nor inhibits religion"; and (3) does not foster "an
excessive government entanglement with religion," . . . .

A divided panel of the Court of Appeals for the Fourth Circuit reversed. The
majority relied primarily on the *Lemon* test but also took cognizance of Justice
Breyer's *Van Orden* concurrence. While recognizing that the Commission acted
for a secular purpose, the court held that the Bladensburg Cross failed *Lemon*'s

"effects" prong because a reasonable observer would view the Commission's ownership and maintenance of the monument as an endorsement of Christianity. The court emphasized the cross's "inherent religious meaning" as the " 'pre-eminent symbol of Christianity.' " . . . In the alternative, the court concluded, the Commission had become excessively entangled with religion by keeping a display that "aggrandizes the Latin cross" and by spending more than *de minimis* public funds to maintain it.

II

A

The Establishment Clause of the First Amendment provides that "Congress shall make no law respecting an establishment of religion." While the concept of a formally established church is straightforward, pinning down the meaning of a "law respecting an establishment of religion" has proved to be a vexing problem. Prior to the Court's decision in *Everson v. Board of Ed. of Ewing* (1947), the Establishment Clause was applied only to the Federal Government, and few cases involving this provision came before the Court. After *Everson* recognized the incorporation of the Clause, however, the Court faced a steady stream of difficult and controversial Establishment Clause issues, ranging from Bible reading and prayer in the public schools, to Sunday closing laws, to state subsidies for church-related schools or the parents of students attending those schools.

After grappling with such cases for more than 20 years, *Lemon* ambitiously attempted to distill from the Court's existing case law a test that would bring order and predictability to Establishment Clause decisionmaking. That test, as noted, called on courts to examine the purposes and effects of a challenged government action, as well as any entanglement with religion that it might entail. Court later elaborated that the "effect[s]" of a challenged action should be assessed by asking whether a "reasonable observer" would conclude that the action constituted an "endorsement" of religion. *County of Allegheny v. American Civil Liberties Union, Greater Pittsburgh Chapter* (1989).

If the *Lemon* Court thought that its test would provide a framework for all future Establishment Clause decisions, its expectation has not been met. In many cases, this Court has either expressly declined to apply the test or has simply ignored it. *Van Orden*; *Town of Greece v. Galloway* (2014); *Trump v. Hawaii* (2018).

This pattern is a testament to the *Lemon* test's shortcomings. As Establishment Clause cases involving a great array of laws and practices came to the Court, it became more and more apparent that the *Lemon* test could not resolve them. It could not "explain the Establishment Clause's tolerance, for example, of the prayers that open legislative meetings, . . . certain references to, and invocations of, the Deity in the public words of public officials; the public references to God on coins, decrees, and buildings; or the attention paid to the religious objectives of certain holidays, including Thanksgiving." *Van Orden* (opinion of Breyer, J.). The test has been harshly criticized by Members of this Court, lamented by lower court judges, and questioned by a diverse roster of scholars.

For at least four reasons, the *Lemon* test presents particularly daunting problems in cases, including the one now before us, that involve the use, for ceremonial, celebratory, or commemorative purposes, of words or symbols with religious associations.[16] Together, these considerations counsel against efforts to evaluate such cases under *Lemon* and toward application of a presumption of constitutionality for longstanding monuments, symbols, and practices.

B

First, these cases often concern monuments, symbols, or practices that were first established long ago, and in such cases, identifying their original purpose or purposes may be especially difficult. . . . The truth is that 70 years after the fact, there was no way to be certain about the motivations of the men who were responsible for the creation of the monument. And this is often the case with old monuments, symbols, and practices. Yet it would be inappropriate for courts to compel their removal or termination based on supposition.

Second, as time goes by, the purposes associated with an established monument, symbol, or practice often multiply. Take the example of Ten Commandments monuments, the subject we addressed in *Van Orden* and *McCreary County v. American Civil Liberties Union of Ky.* (2005). For believing Jews and Christians, the Ten Commandments are the word of God handed down to Moses on Mount Sinai, but the image of the Ten Commandments has also been used to convey other meanings. They have historical significance as one of the foundations of our legal system, and for largely that reason, they are depicted in the marble frieze in our courtroom and in other prominent public buildings in our Nation's capital. In *Van Orden* and *McCreary*, no Member of the Court thought that these depictions are unconstitutional. . . .

The existence of multiple purposes is not exclusive to longstanding monuments, symbols, or practices, but this phenomenon is more likely to occur in such cases. Even if the original purpose of a monument was infused with religion, the passage of time may obscure that sentiment. As our society becomes more and more religiously diverse, a community may preserve such monuments, symbols, and practices for the sake of their historical significance or their place in a common cultural heritage.

---

16. While we do not attempt to provide an authoritative taxonomy of the dozens of Establishment Clause cases that the Court has decided since *Everson v. Board of Ed. of Ewing* (1947), most can be divided into six rough categories: (1) religious references or imagery in public monuments, symbols, mottos, displays, and ceremonies, (2) religious accommodations and exemptions from generally applicable laws, (3) subsidies and tax exemptions, (4) religious expression in public schools, (5) regulation of private religious speech, and (6) state interference with internal church affairs. A final, miscellaneous category, including cases involving such issues as Sunday closing laws, and church involvement in governmental decisionmaking, might be added. We deal here with an issue that falls into the first category.

Third, just as the purpose for maintaining a monument, symbol, or practice may evolve, "[t]he 'message' conveyed . . . may change over time." *Pleasant Grove City v. Summum,* (2009). . . .

Fourth, when time's passage imbues a religiously expressive monument, symbol, or practice with this kind of familiarity and historical significance, removing it may no longer appear neutral, especially to the local community for which it has taken on particular meaning. A government that roams the land, tearing down monuments with religious symbolism and scrubbing away any reference to the divine will strike many as aggressively hostile to religion. Militantly secular regimes have carried out such projects in the past, and for those with a knowledge of history, the image of monuments being taken down will be evocative, disturbing, and divisive. Cf. *Van Orden* (opinion of Breyer, J.) ("[D]isputes concerning the removal of longstanding depictions of the Ten Commandments from public buildings across the Nation . . . could thereby create the very kind of religiously based divisiveness that the Establishment Clause seeks to avoid").

These four considerations show that retaining established, religiously expressive monuments, symbols, and practices is quite different from erecting or adopting new ones. The passage of time gives rise to a strong presumption of constitutionality.

C

The role of the cross in World War I memorials is illustrative of each of the four preceding considerations. . . . The solemn image of endless rows of white crosses became inextricably linked with and symbolic of the ultimate price paid by 116,000 soldiers. And this relationship between the cross and the war undoubtedly influenced the design of the many war memorials that sprang up across the Nation.

This is not to say that the cross's association with the war was the sole or dominant motivation for the inclusion of the symbol in every World War I memorial that features it. But today, it is all but impossible to tell whether that was so. The passage of time means that testimony from those actually involved in the decisionmaking process is generally unavailable, and attempting to uncover their motivations invites rampant speculation. And no matter what the original purposes for the erection of a monument, a community may wish to preserve it for very different reasons, such as the historic preservation and traffic-safety concerns the Commission has pressed here. . . . Whether in a cemetery or a city park, a World War I cross remains a memorial to the fallen.

Finally, as World War I monuments have endured through the years and become a familiar part of the physical and cultural landscape, requiring their removal would not be viewed by many as a neutral act. And an alteration like the one entertained by the Fourth Circuit — amputating the arms of the Cross — would be seen by many as profoundly disrespectful. One member of the majority below viewed this objection as inconsistent with the claim that the Bladensburg Cross serves secular purposes, but this argument misunderstands the complexity of monuments. A monument may express many purposes and convey many different messages, both secular and religious. Thus, a campaign to obliterate items with religious associations may evidence hostility to religion even if those religious associations are no longer in the forefront. . . .

D

While the *Lemon* Court ambitiously attempted to find a grand unified theory of the Establishment Clause, in later cases, we have taken a more modest approach that focuses on the particular issue at hand and looks to history for guidance. Our cases involving prayer before a legislative session are an example.

In *Marsh v. Chambers* (1983), the Court upheld the Nebraska Legislature's practice of beginning each session with a prayer by an official chaplain, and in so holding, the Court conspicuously ignored *Lemon* and did not respond to Justice Brennan's argument in dissent that the legislature's practice could not satisfy the *Lemon* test. Instead, the Court found it highly persuasive that Congress for more than 200 years had opened its sessions with a prayer and that many state legislatures had followed suit. We took a similar approach more recently in *Town of Greece.*

We reached these results even though it was clear, as stressed by the *Marsh* dissent, that prayer is by definition religious. The prevalence of this philosophy at the time of the founding is reflected in other prominent actions taken by the First Congress. It requested — and President Washington proclaimed — a national day of prayer, and it reenacted the Northwest Territory Ordinance, which provided that "[r]eligion, morality, and knowledge, being necessary to good government and the happiness of mankind, schools and the means of education shall forever be encouraged." President Washington echoed this sentiment in his Farewell Address, calling religion and morality "indispensable supports" to "political prosperity." The First Congress looked to these "supports" when it chose to begin its sessions with a prayer. This practice was designed to solemnize congressional meetings, unifying those in attendance as they pursued a common goal of good governance. . . .

In *Town of Greece,* which concerned prayer before a town council meeting, there was disagreement about the inclusiveness of the town's practice. . . . But there was no disagreement that the Establishment Clause permits a nondiscriminatory practice of prayer at the beginning of a town council session. Of course, the specific practice challenged in *Town of Greece* lacked the very direct connection, via the First Congress, to the thinking of those who were responsible for framing the First Amendment. But what mattered was that the town's practice "fi[t] within the tradition long followed in Congress and the state legislatures."

The practice begun by the First Congress stands out as an example of respect and tolerance for differing views, an honest endeavor to achieve inclusivity and nondiscrimination, and a recognition of the important role that religion plays in the lives of many Americans. Where categories of monuments, symbols, and practices with a longstanding history follow in that tradition, they are likewise constitutional.

III

Applying these principles, we conclude that the Bladensburg Cross does not violate the Establishment Clause.

As we have explained, the Bladensburg Cross carries special significance in commemorating World War I. Due in large part to the image of the simple wooden crosses that originally marked the graves of American soldiers killed in the war, the cross became a symbol of their sacrifice, and the design of the Bladensburg Cross must be understood in light of that background. That the cross originated as a Christian symbol and retains that meaning in many contexts does not change the fact that the symbol took on an added secular meaning when used in World War I memorials.

Not only did the Bladensburg Cross begin with this meaning, but with the passage of time, it has acquired historical importance. It reminds the people of Bladensburg and surrounding areas of the deeds of their predecessors and of the sacrifices they made in a war fought in the name of democracy. As long as it is retained in its original place and form, it speaks as well of the community that erected the monument nearly a century ago and has maintained it ever since. . . .

The monument would not serve that role if its design had deliberately disrespected area soldiers who perished in World War I. More than 3,500 Jewish soldiers gave their lives for the United States in that conflict, and some have wondered whether the names of any Jewish soldiers from the area were deliberately left off the list on the memorial or whether the names of any Jewish soldiers were included on the Cross against the wishes of their families. There is no evidence that either thing was done, and we do know that one of the local American Legion leaders responsible for the Cross's construction was a Jewish veteran. . . .

We can never know for certain what was in the minds of those responsible for the memorial, but in light of what we know about this ceremony, we can perhaps make out a picture of a community that, at least for the moment, was united by grief and patriotism and rose above the divisions of the day. . . .

IV

The cross is undoubtedly a Christian symbol, but that fact should not blind us to everything else that the Bladensburg Cross has come to represent. For some, that monument is a symbolic resting place for ancestors who never returned home. For others, it is a place for the community to gather and honor all veterans and their sacrifices for our Nation. For others still, it is a historical landmark. For many of these people, destroying or defacing the Cross that has stood undisturbed for nearly a century would not be neutral and would not further the ideals of respect and tolerance embodied in the First Amendment. For all these reasons, the Cross does not offend the Constitution.

JUSTICE BREYER, with whom JUSTICE KAGAN joins, concurring.

I have long maintained that there is no single formula for resolving Establishment Clause challenges. See *Van Orden v. Perry* (2005) (opinion concurring in judgment). The Court must instead consider each case in light of the basic purposes that the Religion Clauses were meant to serve: assuring religious liberty and tolerance for all, avoiding religiously based social conflict, and maintaining that separation of church and state that allows each to flourish in its "separate spher[e]." *Ibid.*

I agree with the Court that allowing the State of Maryland to display and maintain the Peace Cross poses no threat to those ends. . . . The case would be different, in my view, if there were evidence that the organizers had "deliberately disrespected" members of minority faiths or if the Cross had been erected only recently, rather than in the aftermath of World War I. . . . But those are not the circumstances presented to us here, and I see no reason to order *this* cross torn down simply because *other* crosses would raise constitutional concerns.

Nor do I understand the Court's opinion today to adopt a "history and tradition test" that would permit any newly constructed religious memorial on public land. The Court appropriately "looks to history for guidance," but it upholds the constitutionality of the Peace Cross only after considering its particular historical context and its long-held place in the community. A newer memorial, erected under different circumstances, would not necessarily be permissible under this approach. . . .

JUSTICE KAVANAUGH, concurring. . . .

Consistent with the Court's case law, the Court today applies a history and tradition test in examining and upholding the constitutionality of the Bladensburg Cross. . . . The opinion identifies five relevant categories of Establishment Clause cases: (1) religious symbols on government property and religious speech at government events; (2) religious accommodations and exemptions from generally applicable laws; (3) government benefits and tax exemptions for religious organizations; (4) religious expression in public schools; and (5) regulation of private religious speech in public forums. The *Lemon* test does not explain the Court's decisions in any of those five categories. . . .

Today, the Court declines to apply *Lemon* in a case in the religious symbols and religious speech category, just as the Court declined to apply *Lemon* in *Town of Greece v. Galloway*, *Van Orden v. Perry*, and *Marsh v. Chambers*. The Court's decision in this case again makes clear that the *Lemon* test does not apply to Establishment Clause cases in that category. And the Court's decisions over the span of several decades demonstrate that the *Lemon* test is not good law and does not apply to Establishment Clause cases in any of the five categories.

On the contrary, each category of Establishment Clause cases has its own principles based on history, tradition, and precedent. And the cases together lead to an overarching set of principles: If the challenged government practice is not coercive *and* if it (i) is rooted in history and tradition; or (ii) treats religious people, organizations, speech, or activity equally to comparable secular people, organizations, speech, or activity; or (iii) represents a permissible legislative accommodation or exemption from a generally applicable law, then there ordinarily is no Establishment Clause violation.*

The practice of displaying religious memorials, particularly religious war memorials, on public land is not coercive and is rooted in history and tradition. The Bladensburg Cross does not violate the Establishment Clause. . . . I fully agree with the Court's reasons for allowing the Bladensburg Peace Cross to remain as it is, and so join Parts I, II-B, II-C, III, and IV of its opinion, as well as Justice Breyer's concurrence.

Although I agree that rigid application of the *Lemon* test does not solve every Establishment Clause problem, I think that test's focus on purposes and effects is crucial in evaluating government action in this sphere—as this very suit shows. I therefore do not join Part II-A. I do not join Part II-D out of perhaps an excess of caution. Although I too "look[] to history for guidance," I prefer at least for now to do so case-by-case, rather than to sign on to any broader statements about history's role in Establishment Clause analysis. But I find much to admire in this section of the opinion—particularly, its emphasis on whether longstanding monuments, symbols, and practices reflect "respect and tolerance for differing views, an honest endeavor to achieve inclusivity and nondiscrimination, and a recognition of the important role that religion plays in the lives of many Americans." Here, as elsewhere, the opinion shows sensitivity to and respect for this Nation's pluralism, and the values of neutrality and inclusion that the First Amendment demands.

JUSTICE THOMAS, concurring in the judgment.

The Establishment Clause states that "Congress shall make no law respecting an establishment of religion." U.S. Const., Amdt. 1. The text and history of this Clause suggest that it should not be incorporated against the States. Even if the Clause expresses an individual right enforceable against the States, it is limited by its text to "law[s]" enacted by a legislature, so it is unclear whether the Bladensburg Cross would implicate any incorporated right. And even if it did, this religious display does not involve the type of actual legal coercion that was a hallmark of historical establishments of religion. Therefore, the Cross is clearly constitutional. . . .

[T]he First Amendment by its terms applies only to "law[s]" enacted by "Congress." Obviously, a memorial is not a law. And respondents have not identified any specific law they challenge as unconstitutional, either on its face or as applied. Thus, respondents could prevail on their establishment claim only if the prohibition embodied in the Establishment Clause was understood to be an individual right of citizenship that applied to more than just "law[s]" "ma[de]" by "Congress."

---

* That is not to say that challenged government actions outside that safe harbor are unconstitutional. Any such cases must be analyzed under the relevant Establishment Clause principles and precedents.

Even if the Clause applied to state and local governments in some fashion, "[t]he mere presence of the monument along [respondents'] path involves no coercion and thus does not violate the Establishment Clause." *Van Orden* (Thomas, J., concurring). The *sine qua non* of an establishment of religion is "'actual legal coercion.'" At the founding, "[t]he coercion that was a hallmark of historical establishments of religion was coercion of religious orthodoxy and of financial support by force of law and threat of penalty." *Lee v. Weisman* (1992) (Scalia, J., dissenting). . . . In an action claiming an unconstitutional establishment of religion, the plaintiff must demonstrate that he was actually coerced by government conduct that shares the characteristics of an establishment as understood at the founding.[2] . . . As to the long-discredited test set forth in *Lemon v. Kurtzman* (1971), . . . I would take the logical next step and overrule the *Lemon* test in all contexts. First, that test has no basis in the original meaning of the Constitution. Second, "since its inception," it has "been manipulated to fit whatever result the Court aimed to achieve." *McCreary County v. American Civil Liberties Union of Ky.* (2005) (Scalia, J., dissenting). Third, it continues to cause enormous confusion in the States and the lower courts. In recent decades, the Court has tellingly refused to apply *Lemon* in the very cases where it purports to be most useful. The obvious explanation is that *Lemon* does not provide a sound basis for judging Establishment Clause claims. However, the court below "s[aw] fit to apply *Lemon*." It is our job to say what the law is, and because the *Lemon* test is not good law, we ought to say so.

* * *

Regrettably, I cannot join the Court's opinion because it does not adequately clarify the appropriate standard for Establishment Clause cases. Therefore, I concur only in the judgment.

JUSTICE GORSUCH, with whom JUSTICE THOMAS joins, concurring in the judgment. . . .

In my judgment, . . . it follows from the Court's analysis that suits like this one should be dismissed for lack of standing. Accordingly, while I concur in the judgment to reverse and remand the court of appeals' decision, I would do so with additional instructions to dismiss the case. The Association claims that its members "regularly" come into "unwelcome direct contact" with a World War I memorial cross in Bladensburg, Maryland "while driving in the area." (C.A.4 2017). And this, the Association suggests, is enough to allow it to insist on a federal judicial decree ordering the memorial's removal. . . .

This "offended observer" theory of standing has no basis in law. Federal courts may decide only those cases and controversies that the Constitution and

---

2. Of course, cases involving state or local action are not strictly speaking Establishment Clause cases, but instead Fourteenth Amendment cases about a privilege or immunity of citizenship. It is conceivable that the salient characteristics of an establishment changed by the time of the Fourteenth Amendment, see *Town of Greece v. Galloway* (2014) (Thomas, J., concurring in part and concurring in judgment), but respondents have presented no evidence suggesting so.

Congress have authorized them to hear. And to establish standing to sue consistent with the Constitution, a plaintiff must show: (1) injury-in-fact, (2) causation, and (3) redressability. The injury-in-fact test requires a plaintiff to prove "an invasion of a legally protected interest which is (a) concrete and particularized . . . and (b) actual or imminent, not conjectural or hypothetical." *Lujan v. Defenders of Wildlife* (1992). . . .

If individuals and groups could invoke the authority of a federal court to forbid what they dislike for no more reason than they dislike it, we would risk exceeding the judiciary's limited constitutional mandate and infringing on powers committed to other branches of government. Courts would start to look more like legislatures, responding to social pressures rather than remedying concrete harms, in the process supplanting the right of the people and their elected representatives to govern themselves. . . .

Lower courts invented offended observer standing for Establishment Clause cases in the 1970s in response to this Court's decision in *Lemon v. Kurtzman* (1971). Here alone, lower courts concluded, though never with this Court's approval, an observer's offense must "suffice to make an Establishment Clause claim justiciable." *Suhre v. Haywood Cty.* (C.A.4 1997).

. . . *Lemon* was a misadventure. It sought a "grand unified theory" of the Establishment Clause but left us only a mess. How much "purpose" to promote religion is too much (are Sunday closing laws that bear multiple purposes, religious and secular, problematic)? How much "effect" of advancing religion is tolerable (are even incidental effects disallowed)? What does the "entanglement" test add to these inquiries? Even beyond all that, how "reasonable" must our "reasonable observer" be, and what exactly qualifies as impermissible "endorsement" of religion in a country where "In God We Trust" appears on the coinage, the eye of God appears in its Great Seal, and we celebrate Thanksgiving as a national holiday ("to Whom are thanks being given")? Nearly half a century after *Lemon* and, the truth is, no one has any idea about the answers to these questions. . . . Scores of judges have pleaded with us to retire *Lemon*, scholars of all stripes have criticized the doctrine, and a majority of this Court has long done the same. Today, not a single Member of the Court even tries to defend *Lemon* against these criticisms — and they don't because they can't. As Justice Kennedy explained, *Lemon* is "flawed in its fundamentals," has proved "unworkable in practice," and is "inconsistent with our history and our precedents." *County of Allegheny.*

In place of *Lemon*, Part II-D of the plurality opinion relies on a more modest, historically sensitive approach, recognizing that "the Establishment Clause must be interpreted by reference to historical practices and understandings." . . . The constitutionality of a practice doesn't depend on some artificial and indeterminate three-part test; what matters, the plurality reminds us, is whether the challenged practice fits " 'within the tradition' " of this country.

I agree with all this and don't doubt that the monument before us is constitutional in light of the nation's traditions. But then the plurality continues on to suggest that "longstanding monuments, symbols, and practices" are "presumpt[ively]" constitutional. And about that, it's hard not to wonder: How old must a monument, symbol, or practice be to qualify for this new presumption? It seems 94 years is enough, but what about the Star of David monument erected in South Carolina in 2001 to commemorate victims of the Holocaust, or the cross that marines in California placed in 2004 to honor their comrades who fell during the War on Terror? And where exactly in the Constitution does this presumption come from? The plurality does not say, nor does it even explain what work its presumption does. To the contrary, the plurality proceeds to analyze the "presumptively" constitutional memorial in this case for its consistency with "'historical practices and understandings'" under *Marsh* and *Town of Greece* — exactly the same approach that the plurality, quoting *Town of Greece*, recognizes "'must be'" used *whenever* we interpret the Establishment Clause.

Though the plurality does not say so in as many words, the message for our lower court colleagues seems unmistakable: Whether a monument, symbol, or practice is old or new, apply *Town of Greece*, not *Lemon*. . . . But if that's the real message of the plurality's opinion, it seems to me exactly right — because what matters when it comes to assessing a monument, symbol, or practice isn't its age but its compliance with ageless principles. The Constitution's meaning is fixed, not some good-for-this-day-only coupon, and a practice consistent with our nation's traditions is just as permissible whether undertaken today or 94 years ago.

With *Lemon* now shelved, little excuse will remain for the anomaly of offended observer standing, and the gaping hole it tore in standing doctrine in the courts of appeals should now begin to close. Nor does this development mean colorable Establishment Clause violations will lack for proper plaintiffs. By way of example only, a public school student compelled to recite a prayer will still have standing to sue. . . .

Abandoning offended observer standing will mean only a return to the usual demands of Article III, requiring a real controversy with real impact on real persons to make a federal case out of it. Along the way, this will bring with it the welcome side effect of rescuing the federal judiciary from the sordid business of having to pass aesthetic judgment, one by one, on every public display in this country for its perceived capacity to give offense. It's a business that has consumed volumes of the federal reports, invited erratic results, frustrated generations of judges, and fomented "the very kind of religiously based divisiveness that the Establishment Clause seeks to avoid." *Van Orden v. Perry* (2005) (Breyer, J., concurring in judgment). . . . No one can predict the rulings — but one thing is certain: Between the challenged practices and the judicial decisions, just about everyone will wind up offended. . . .

In a large and diverse country, offense can be easily found. Really, most every governmental action probably offends *somebody*. No doubt, too, that offense can be sincere, sometimes well taken, even wise. But recourse for disagreement and offense does not lie in federal litigation. . . . Today's decision represents a welcome step toward restoring this Court's recognition of these truths, and I respectfully concur in the judgment.

JUSTICE GINSBURG, with whom JUSTICE SOTOMAYOR joins, dissenting.

. . . Decades ago, this Court recognized that the Establishment Clause of the First Amendment to the Constitution demands governmental neutrality among religious faiths, and between religion and nonreligion. See *Everson v. Board of Ed. of Ewing* (1947). Numerous times since, the Court has reaffirmed the Constitution's commitment to neutrality. Today the Court erodes that neutrality commitment, diminishing precedent designed to preserve individual liberty and civic harmony in favor of a "presumption of constitutionality for longstanding monuments, symbols, and practices."[2]

The Latin cross is the foremost symbol of the Christian faith, embodying the "central theological claim of Christianity: that the son of God died on the cross, that he rose from the dead, and that his death and resurrection offer the possibility of eternal life." Precisely because the cross symbolizes these sectarian beliefs, it is a common marker for the graves of Christian soldiers. For the same reason, using the cross as a war memorial does not transform it into a secular symbol, as the Courts of Appeals have uniformly recognized. as a Star of David is not suitable to honor Christians who died serving their country, so a cross is not suitable to honor those of other faiths who died defending their nation. Soldiers of all faiths "are united by their love of country, but they are not united by the cross."

By maintaining the Peace Cross on a public highway, the Commission elevates Christianity over other faiths, and religion over nonreligion. Memorializing the service of American soldiers is an "admirable and unquestionably secular" objective. *Van Orden v. Perry* (2005) (Stevens, J., dissenting). But the Commission does not serve that objective by displaying a symbol that bears "a starkly sectarian message." *Salazar v. Buono* (Stevens, J., dissenting).

As I see it, when a cross is displayed on public property, the government may be presumed to endorse its religious content. The venue is surely associated with the State; the symbol and its meaning are just as surely associated exclusively with Christianity. . . . To non-Christians, nearly 30% of the population of the United States, the State's choice to display the cross on public buildings or spaces conveys a message of exclusion: It tells them they "are outsiders, not full members of the political community," *County of Allegheny* (O'Connor, J., concurring in part and concurring in judgment). . . .

The Commission nonetheless urges that the Latin cross is a "well-established" secular symbol commemorating, in particular, "military valor and sacrifice [in] World War I." Calling up images of United States cemeteries overseas showing row upon row of cross-shaped gravemarkers, the Commission overlooks this reality: The cross was never perceived as an appropriate headstone or memorial for Jewish soldiers and others who did not adhere to Christianity. . . .

---

2. Some of my colleagues suggest that the Court's new presumption extends to all governmental displays and practices, regardless of their age. I read the Court's opinion to mean what it says: "[R]etaining established, religiously expressive monuments, symbols, and practices is quite different from erecting or adopting new ones," and, consequently, only "longstanding monuments, symbols, and practices" enjoy "a presumption of constitutionality."

Holding the Commission's display of the Peace Cross unconstitutional would not, as the Commission fears, "inevitably require the destruction of other cross-shaped memorials throughout the country." When a religious symbol appears in a public cemetery — on a headstone, or as the headstone itself, or perhaps integrated into a larger memorial — the setting counters the inference that the government seeks "either to adopt the religious message or to urge its acceptance by others." *Van Orden* (Souter, J., dissenting). In a cemetery, the "privately selected religious symbols on individual graves are best understood as the private speech of each veteran." Such displays are "linked to, and sho[w] respect for, the individual honoree's faith and beliefs." *Buono* (Stevens, J., dissenting). They do not suggest governmental endorsement of those faith and beliefs. Recognizing that a Latin cross does not belong on a public highway or building does not mean the monument must be "torn down."[17] In some instances, the violation may be cured by relocating the monument to private land or by transferring ownership of the land and monument to a private party.

* * *

In 1790, President Washington visited Newport, Rhode Island, "a longtime bastion of religious liberty and the home of one of the first communities of American Jews." *Town of Greece v. Galloway* (2014) (Kagan, J., dissenting). In a letter thanking the congregation for its warm welcome, Washington praised "[t]he citizens of the United States of America" for "giv[ing] to mankind . . . a policy worthy of imitation": "All possess alike liberty of conscience and immunities of citizenship." As Washington and his contemporaries were aware, "some of them from bitter personal experience," *Engel*, religion is "too personal, too sacred, too holy, to permit its 'unhallowed perversion' by a civil magistrate," quoting [Madison's] Memorial and Remonstrance. The Establishment Clause, which preserves the integrity of both church and state, guarantees that "however . . . individuals worship, they will count as full and equal American citizens." *Town of Greece*, 572 U.S. at 615, 134 S.Ct. 1811. "If the aim of the Establishment Clause is genuinely to uncouple government from church," the Clause does "not permit . . . a display of th[e] character" of Bladensburg's Peace Cross. *Capitol Square Review and Advisory Bd. v. Pinette* (1995) (Ginsburg, J., dissenting).

---

17. The Court asserts that the Court of Appeals "entertained" the possibility of "amputating the arms of the cross." The appeals court, however, merely reported Plaintiffs' "desired injunctive relief," namely, "removal or demolition of the Cross, or removal of the arms from the Cross 'to form a non-religious slab or obelisk.'"

Chapter 20

The Right to Keep and Bear Arms

ASSIGNMENT 3

STUDY GUIDE:

- In the next case, decided after *Ezell*, writing for the Court of Appeals for the Ninth Circuit, Judge O'Scannlain now employs a First Amendment-type approach, rather than the abortion regulation approach he previously used in *Nordyke*.
- Should courts take cognizance of the hostility to the constitutional right to keep and bear arms that motivated the County's decision in the case, as they have with other constitutional rights, for example, to restrictions on the First Amendment right to the free exercise of religion invalidated in *Church of the Lukumi Babalu Aye, Inc. v. Hialeah* (Chapter 18)?

Teixeira v. County of Alameda
822 F. 3d 1047 (9th Cir. 2016)[1]

O'SCANNLAIN, Circuit Judge:

We must decide whether the right to keep and to bear arms, as recognized by the Second Amendment, necessarily includes the right of law-abiding Americans to purchase and to sell firearms. In other words, we must determine whether the Second Amendment places any limits on regulating the commercial sale of firearms.

I

A

In the fall of 2010, John Teixeira, Steve Nobriga, and Gary Gamaza decided to open a retail business that would offer firearm training, provide gun-smith services, and sell firearms, ammunition, and gun-related equipment. . . . All that

---

1. In December 2016, the 9th Circuit Court of Appeals voted to rehear *Teixiera* en banc, so the panel opinion is no longer of precedential value.

remained was to ensure that Valley Guns & Ammo would be in compliance with the Alameda County code.

[Under the zoning laws in Alameda County, "firearms sales business[es]" cannot be located "within five hundred feet of a "[r]esidentially zoned district; elementary, middle or high school; pre-school or day care center; other firearms sales business; or liquor stores or establishments in which liquor is served." — EDS.]

The Alameda County Planning Department informed Teixeira, Nobriga, and Gamaza (collectively "Teixeira") that the 500-foot zoning requirement was to be measured from the closest door of the proposed business location to the front door of any disqualifying property. . . .

The West County Board of Zoning Adjustment. . . . concluded that a zoning variance would be required because the proposed site, contrary to the survey Teixeira had commissioned, was in fact within 500 feet of a residential property and therefore failed to qualify for a permit. . . . Despite the report, at a public hearing on December 14, 2011, the West County Board of Zoning Adjustments voted to grant a variance and approved the issuance of a permit. . . . The San Lorenzo Village Homes Association, some of whose members "are opposed to guns and their ready availability and therefore believe that gun shops should not be located within [their] community," challenged the Board's decision. On February 28, 2012, the Alameda County Board of Supervisors voted to sustain the appeal, thus revoking Teixeira's Conditional Use Permit and variance.

B

Teixeira challenged the County's decision in the United States District Court for the Northern District of California, arguing that it violated his right to due process and denied him equal protection of the law, and that the Ordinance was impermissible under the Second Amendment both facially and as applied. In preparation for the suit, Teixeira commissioned a study, which determined that, as a result of the 500-foot rule, "there are no parcels in the unincorporated areas of Alameda County which would be available for firearm retail sales." He argued that the zoning ordinance "is not reasonably related to any possible public safety concerns" and effectively "redlin[es] . . . gun stores out of existence." . . .

III

. . . The Second Amendment states that "[a] well regulated Militia, being necessary to the security of a free State, the right of the people to keep and bear arms, shall not be infringed." In *District of Columbia v. Heller* (2008), the Supreme Court held that the Amendment guarantees an individual right to possess firearms for traditionally lawful purposes, such as self-defense. The Court subsequently applied the right against the States via the Fourteenth Amendment in (2010) Though the Supreme Court has yet to "clarify the entire field" of Second Amendment jurisprudence, *Heller,* it has established a broad framework for addressing challenges such as the one at hand. In reviewing Alameda County's ordinance, we employ a two-step inquiry, which begins by asking whether a challenged law burdens conduct protected by the Second Amendment; if the answer is in the affirmative, we apply the appropriate level of scrutiny.

A

Turning to the inquiry's first step, we must determine whether the commercial sale of firearms implicates the Second Amendment right to keep and to bear arms by reviewing the "historical understanding of the scope of the right."

1

Teixeira ultimately bases his Second Amendment challenge on a purported right to purchase firearms — that is, a right to *acquire* weapons for self-defense. Though *Heller* did not recognize explicitly a right to purchase or to sell weapons, the Court's opinion was not intended to serve as "an exhaustive historical analysis . . . of the full scope of the Second Amendment." *Heller*. Therefore it is incumbent upon us to take a fresh look at the historical record to determine whether the right to keep and to bear arms, as understood at the time it was enshrined in the Constitution, embraced a right to acquire firearms.

Our forefathers recognized that the prohibition of commerce in firearms worked to undermine the right to keep and to bear arms. . . . The right of citizens to possess firearms was a proposition that necessarily extended from the fundamental tenet of natural law that a man had a right to defend himself. . . .

As British subjects, colonial Americans believed that they shared equally in the enjoyment of this guarantee, and that the right necessarily extended to commerce in firearms. Colonial law reflected such an understanding. . . .

In ratifying the Second Amendment, the States sought to codify the English right to keep and to bear arms. The historical record indicates that Americans continued to believe that such right included the freedom to purchase and to sell weapons. In 1793, Thomas Jefferson noted that "[o]ur citizens have always been free to make, vend, and export arms. It is the constant occupation and livelihood of some of them." Thomas Jefferson, 3 *Writings* 558 (H.A. Washington ed., 1853). . . . At the time the Fourteenth Amendment was ratified, which *McDonald* held applied the Second Amendment against the States, at least some American jurists simply assumed that the "right to keep arms, necessarily involve[d] the right to purchase them." *Andrews v. State,* 50 Tenn. 165, 178 (1871).

As our predecessors recognized, logic compels such an inference. If "the right of the people to keep and bear arms" is to have any force, the people must have a right to acquire the very firearms they are entitled to keep and to bear. Indeed, where a right depends on subsidiary activity, it would make little sense if the right did not extend, at least partly, to such activity as well. The Supreme Court recognized this principle in very different contexts when it held that "[l]imiting the distribution of nonprescription contraceptives to licensed pharmacists clearly imposes a significant burden on the right of the individuals to use contraceptives," *Carey v. Population Servs., Int'l* (1977), and when it held that a tax on paper and ink products used by newspapers violated the First Amendment because it impermissibly burdened freedom of the press, *see Minneapolis Star & Tribune Co. v. Minn. Comm'r of Revenue* (1983). . . . *Cf. Ezell v. City of Chicago* (7th Cir.2011) ("The right to possess firearms for protection implies a corresponding right to . . . maintain proficiency in their use; the core right wouldn't mean much without the training and practice that make it effective."). Thus, the Second Amendment "right must also include the right to *acquire* a firearm." *Illinois Ass'n of Firearms Retailers v. City of Chicago* (N.D. Ill. 2014). . . .

Alameda County has offered nothing to undermine our conclusion that the right to purchase and to sell firearms is part and parcel of the historically recognized right to keep and to bear arms. . . .

B

Having determined that, contrary to the district court's ruling, the Alameda County ordinance burdens conduct protected by the Second Amendment, the next step in the inquiry is to identify the proper standard of review.

1

Though we typically subject a regulation interfering with a constitutionally protected right to some form of heightened scrutiny and require the Government to justify the burden it has placed on such right, the *Heller* court made clear that certain regulations enjoy more deferential treatment:

> [N]othing in our opinion should be taken to cast doubt on longstanding prohibitions on the possession of firearms by felons and the mentally ill, or laws forbidding the carrying of firearms in sensitive places such as schools and government buildings, or laws imposing conditions and qualifications on the commercial sale of arms.

Heller. The Court went on to explain in a footnote that this list of "presumptively lawful regulatory measures" was not intended to be exhaustive. *McDonald v. City of Chicago,* which incorporated the Second Amendment against the States, made similar assurances regarding such "longstanding regulatory measures."

Teixeira argues that the passage in *Heller* is merely a prediction by the Court that such regulations would likely survive if subjected to some form of heightened scrutiny—it did not exempt listed activities from the analysis altogether. A dismissal of the language as dicta, however, is something we have considered previously and rejected. We instead treat *Heller*'s "presumptively lawful regulatory measures" as examples of prohibitions that simply "fall outside the historical scope of the Second Amendment." *Jackson v. City & County of San Francisco* (9th Cir.2014). Given their longstanding acceptance, such measures are not subjected to the more exacting scrutiny normally applied when reviewing a regulation that burdens a fundamental right.

But an exemption for certain "laws imposing conditions and qualifications on the commercial sale of arms," *Heller*, does not mean that there is a categorical exception from Second Amendment scrutiny for the regulation of gun stores. If such were the case, the County could enact a total prohibition on the commercial sale of firearms. There is no question that "[s]uch a result would be untenable under *Heller*." *United States v. Marzzarella* (3d Cir. 2010). Indeed, if all regulations relating to the commercial sale of firearms were exempt from heightened scrutiny, there would have been no need to specify that certain "conditions and qualifications on the commercial sale of arms" were "presumptively lawful." *Heller*. As discussed, *supra*, we are satisfied that the historical right that the Second Amendment enshrined embraces the purchase and sale of firearms. The proper question, therefore, is whether Alameda County's ordinance is the type of longstanding "condition[]" or "qualification[]" on the commercial sale of arms," *Heller* whose interference with the right to keep and to bear arms historically would have been tolerated. . . .

Here . . . the County has failed to demonstrate that the Ordinance is the type of longstanding regulation that our predecessors considered an acceptable intrusion into the Second Amendment right. Such burden was the County's to carry.

But such reasoning does not signify that the Ordinance violates the Second Amendment. It does mean, however, that the Ordinance must be subjected to heightened scrutiny — something beyond mere rational basis review, for, as the *Heller* Court noted, "If all that was required to overcome the right to keep and bear arms was a rational basis, the Second Amendment would be redundant with the separate constitutional prohibitions on irrational laws, and would have no effect." *Heller.*

2

Though neither *Heller* nor *McDonald* dictates a specific standard of scrutiny for Second Amendment challenges, "[b]oth *Heller* and *McDonald* suggest that First Amendment analogues are more appropriate," *Ezel*, as does our own jurisprudence, *see Jackson*. "When ascertaining the appropriate level of scrutiny, 'just as in the First Amendment context,' we consider: '(1) how close the law comes to the core of the Second Amendment right and (2) the severity of the law's burden on the right.'" *Id.*

a

[In] *Ezell,* the Seventh Circuit held that a regulation prohibiting most firearm ranges within the city limits of Chicago constituted a "serious encroachment on the right to maintain proficiency in firearm use, an important corollary to the meaningful exercise of the core right to possess firearms for self-defense."

Here, there is no question that an ordinance restricting the commercial sale of firearms would burden 'the right of a lawabiding, responsible citizen to possess and carry a weapon," *Chovan*, because it would inhibit his ability to acquire weapons. We are therefore satisfied that such a regulation comes close to the core of the Second Amendment right.

b

Having determined that a law such as Alameda County's ordinance burdens protected conduct, we must next determine the severity of such burden.

The County argues that the Ordinance "simply restricts the location of gun stores." If such is the case, the Ordinance "does not impose the sort of severe burden imposed by the handgun ban at issue in *Heller* that rendered it unconstitutional" because the Ordinance "does not substantially prevent law-abiding citizens from using firearms to defend themselves in the home." *Jackson*. If the district court's assumption is indeed correct—that the Ordinance merely regulates where gun stores can be located rather than banning them—it burdens only the "*manner* in which persons may exercise their Second Amendment rights." *Chovan*. It is thus analogous to "a content-neutral speech restriction that regulates only the time, place, or manner of speech." *Jackson*. To put it another way, the Ordinance would be a regulation rather than a prohibition. Though the Ordinance might implicate "the core of the Second Amendment right, [if] it does not impose a substantial burden on conduct protected by the Second Amendment," intermediate scrutiny would be appropriate. *Id.*

Teixeira . . . , however, alleges that Alameda County has enacted something beyond a mere regulation—Teixeira alleges that the Conditional Use Permit's 500-foot rule, as applied, amounts to a complete ban on gun stores: "according to the plaintiffs' research, which is based primarily on government agency data, there are no parcels in the unincorporated areas of Alameda County which would be available for firearm retail sales." . . . Though such an assertion may yet prove false, there is no way to tell that from the face of the complaint. And if Teixeira had been given a chance to demonstrate that the Ordinance was "not merely regulatory," but rather functioned as a total ban on all new gun retailers, "a more rigorous showing" than even intermediate scrutiny, "if not quite 'strict scrutiny,'" would have been warranted. *Ezell*.

c

Having determined that the Second Amendment compels us to apply some form of heightened scrutiny to a regulation that would significantly burden the commercial sale of firearms, we must finally examine the district court's disposition of Teixeira's claims.

1

Because Teixeira alleges here that the Ordinance's 500-foot requirement is unconstitutional on its face, we assume that the Ordinance merely regulates the location of gun stores and thus intermediate scrutiny applies. "Although courts have used various terminology to describe the intermediate scrutiny standard, all forms of the standard require (1) the government's stated objective to be significant, substantial, or important; and (2) a reasonable fit between the challenged regulation and the asserted objective." *Chovan*. . . .

Under heightened scrutiny, the County "bears the burden of justifying its action." *Ezell*. The County failed to satisfy its burden because it never justified the assertion that gun stores act as magnets for crime. Indeed, Teixeira took pains to remind the court that "all employees working at a gun store, and all clients/customers are required to be law-abiding citizens."

In upholding other gun regulations, we have not simply accepted government assertions at face value. In *Chovan*, we reviewed evidence presented by the Government in support of a statute forbidding domestic violence misdemeanants from owning firearms—specifically, a series of studies relied upon previously by the Seventh Circuit supporting the Government's assertion that "a high rate of domestic violence recidivism exists." Likewise in *Jackson*, we required that San Francisco provide evidence to demonstrate that requiring handguns to be stored in locked containers was reasonably related to the objective of reducing handgun-related deaths. . . . And in *Fyock v. Sunnyvale* (9th Cir. 2015), we affirmed a denial of a preliminary injunction against a city's ban on large-capacity magazines because we were satisfied with the district court's determination that "pages of credible evidence, from study data to expert testimony to the opinions of Sunnyvale public officials, indicat[ed] that the Sunnyvale ordinance is substantially related to the compelling government interest in public safety."

The district court should have followed our approach in *Jackson, Chovan,* and *Fyock* and required at least some evidentiary showing that gun stores increase crime around their locations. Likewise, the record lacks any explanation as to how a gun store might negatively impact the aesthetics of a neighborhood. The district court simply did not bother to address how the Ordinance was related to such an interest. Although under intermediate scrutiny the district court was not required to "impose 'an unnecessarily rigid burden of proof,'" the court should have at least required the County to demonstrate that it "reasonably believed [the evidence upon which it relied was] relevant to the problem that the [Ordinance] addresses." The burden was on the County to demonstrate that there was "a reasonable fit between the challenged regulation and the asserted objective." *Chovan*. The County failed to carry such burden. . . .

IV

. . . We reiterate *Heller* and *McDonald's* assurances that government enjoys substantial leeway under the Second Amendment to regulate the commercial sale of firearms. Alameda County's Ordinance may very well be permissible. Thus far, however, the County has failed to justify the burden it has placed on the right of law-abiding citizens to purchase guns. The Second Amendment requires something more rigorous than the unsubstantiated assertions offered to the district court. Consequently, we reverse the dismissal of Teixeira's well-pled Second Amendment claims and remand for the district court to subject Alameda County's 500-foot rule to the proper level of scrutiny.

ASSIGNMENT 4

Since the Supreme Court's 2010 decision in *McDonald v. City of Chicago*, the Supreme Court has denied review in every single Second Amendment case affecting gun rights.[2] On three occasions, Justice Thomas has dissented from the denial of certiorari, explaining why the Court should have heard the cases. In this section, we provide a sampling of those dissents to illustrate the current state of Second Amendment jurisprudence at the Supreme Court.

1.   Safe Storage Laws

The Supreme Court denied review of a decision upholding a San Francisco law that required firearms to be stored at all times in a locked container, even if a person lived alone. Justice Thomas, joined by Justice Scalia, dissented from the denial of certiorari.

Espanola Jackson v. City of San Francisco
135 S. Ct. 2799 (2015)

Petition for writ of certiorari to the United States Court of Appeals for the Ninth Circuit denied.

JUSTICE THOMAS, with whom JUSTICE SCALIA joins, dissenting from the denial of certiorari.

"Self-defense is a basic right" and "the central component" of the Second Amendment's guarantee of an individual's right to keep and bear arms. *McDonald v. Chicago*, (2010). Less than a decade ago, we explained that an ordinance requiring firearms in the home to be kept inoperable, without an exception for self-defense, conflicted with the Second Amendment because it "ma [de] it impossible for citizens to use [their firearms] for the core lawful purpose of self-defense." *District of Columbia v. Heller* (2008). Despite the clarity with which we described the Second Amendment's core protection for the right

---

2. In *Caetano v. Massachusetts*, the Justices issued a brief, 460-word summary reversal of a decision concerning a ban on stun guns. 136 S. Ct. 1027 (2016) ("*Heller* rejected the proposition "that only those weapons useful in warfare are protected.").

of self-defense, lower courts, including the ones here, have failed to protect it. Because Second Amendment rights are no less protected by our Constitution than other rights enumerated in that document, I would have granted this petition.

I

Section 4512 of the San Francisco Police Code provides that "[n]o person shall keep a handgun within a residence owned or controlled by that person unless" (1) "the handgun is stored in a locked container or disabled with a trigger lock that has been approved by the California Department of Justice" or (2) "[t]he handgun is carried on the person of an individual over the age of 18" or "under the control of a person who is a peace officer under [California law]." The law applies across the board, regardless of whether children are present in the home.

According to petitioners, the law impermissibly rendered their handguns "[in] operable for the purpose of immediate self-defense" in the home. Because it is impossible to "carry" a firearm on one's person while sleeping, for example, petitioners contended that the law effectively denies them their right to self-defense at times when their potential need for that defense is most acute. . . .

Applying intermediate scrutiny, the court [of appeals] evaluated San Francisco's proffered "evidence that guns kept in the home are most often used in suicides and against family and friends rather than in self-defense and that children are particularly at risk of injury and death." The court concluded that the law served "a significant government interest by reducing the number of gun-related injuries and deaths from having an unlocked handgun in the home" and was "substantially related" to that interest.

II

San Francisco's law allows residents to *use* their handguns for the purpose of self-defense, but it prohibits them from *keeping* those handguns "operable for the purpose of *immediate* self-defense" when not carried on their person. The law thus burdens their right to self-defense at the times they are most vulnerable—when they are sleeping, bathing, changing clothes, or otherwise indisposed. There is consequently no question that San Francisco's law burdens the core of the Second Amendment right.

That burden is significant. One petitioner, an elderly woman who lives alone, explained that she is currently forced to store her handgun in a lock box and that if an intruder broke into her home at night, she would need to "turn on the light, find [her] glasses, find the key to the lockbox, insert the key in the lock and unlock the box (under the stress of the emergency), and then get [her] gun before being in position to defend [herself]." . . . And that delay could easily be the difference between life and death.

Since our decision in *Heller*, members of the Courts of Appeals have disagreed about whether and to what extent the tiers-of-scrutiny analysis should apply to burdens on Second Amendment rights. . . . One need not resolve that dispute to know that something was seriously amiss in the decision below. . . . But nothing in our decision in *Heller* suggested that a law must rise to the level of the absolute prohibition at issue in that case to constitute a "substantial burden" on the core of the Second Amendment right. And when a law burdens a constitutionally protected right, we have generally required a higher showing than the Court of Appeals demanded here. . . .

The Court should have granted a writ of certiorari to review this questionable decision and to reiterate that courts may not engage in this sort of judicial assessment as to the severity of a burden imposed on core Second Amendment rights.

The Court's refusal to review this decision is difficult to account for in light of its repeated willingness to review splitless decisions involving alleged violations of other constitutional rights. . . . I see no reason that challenges based on Second Amendment rights should be treated differently. . . .

2.   "Assault Weapons"

In 2005, the Supreme Court denied review of an "assault weapons" ban imposed by the City of Highland Park in Illinois. The term "assault weapon" refers to a semi-automatic rifle—that is, a rifle in which one bullet is fired each time the trigger is pulled. These are not automatic, or "machine" guns. Moreover, the adjective "assault" does not refer to a firearm's power, but instead reflects certain cosmetic features, such as whether the rifle has a detachable magazine or a pistol grip.

Friedman v. City of Highland Park
136 S. Ct. 447 (2015)

The petition for a writ of certiorari is denied.

JUSTICE THOMAS, with whom JUSTICE SCALIA joins, dissenting from the denial of certiorari.

"[O]ur central holding in" *District of Columbia v. Heller* (2008), was "that the Second Amendment protects a personal right to keep and bear arms for lawful purposes, most notably for self-defense within the home." *McDonald v. Chicago* (2010) (plurality opinion). And in *McDonald,* we recognized that the Second Amendment applies fully against the States as well as the Federal Government.

Despite these holdings, several Courts of Appeals—including the Court of Appeals for the Seventh Circuit in the decision below—have upheld categorical bans on firearms that millions of Americans commonly own for lawful purposes. Because noncompliance with our Second Amendment precedents warrants this Court's attention as much as any of our precedents, I would grant certiorari in this case.

I

The City of Highland Park, Illinois, bans manufacturing, selling, giving, lending, acquiring, or possessing many of the most commonly owned semiautomatic firearms, which the City branded "Assault Weapons." For instance, the ordinance criminalizes modern sporting rifles (*e.g.,* AR-style semiautomatic rifles), which many Americans own for lawful purposes like self-defense, hunting, and target shooting. The City also prohibited "Large Capacity Magazines," a term the City used to refer to nearly all ammunition feeding devices that "accept more than ten rounds." . . .

Petitioners—a Highland Park resident who sought to keep now-prohibited firearms and magazines to defend his home, and an advocacy organization—brought a suit to enjoin the ordinance on the ground that it violates the Second Amendment. . . . The [Seventh Circuit] majority . . . found no constitutional problem with the ordinance. It recognized that *Heller* "holds that a law banning the possession of handguns in the home . . . violates" the Second Amendment. But beyond *Heller*'s rejection of banning handguns in the home, the majority believed, *Heller* and *McDonald* "leave matters open" on the scope of the Second Amendment. . . .

II

. . . We explained in *Heller* and *McDonald* that the Second Amendment "guarantee[s] the individual right to possess and carry weapons in case of confrontation." *Heller*. We excluded from protection only "those weapons not typically possessed by law-abiding citizens for lawful purposes." *Heller*. And we stressed that "[t]he very enumeration of the right takes out of the hands of government—even the Third Branch of Government—the power to decide on a case-by-case basis whether the right is really worth insisting upon."

Instead of adhering to our reasoning in *Heller,* the Seventh Circuit limited *Heller* to its facts, and read *Heller* to forbid only total bans on handguns used for self-defense in the home. All other questions about the Second Amendment, the Seventh Circuit concluded, should be defined by "the political process and scholarly debate." But *Heller* repudiates that approach. We explained in *Heller* that "since th[e] case represent[ed] this Court's first in-depth examination of the Second Amendment, one should not expect it to clarify the entire field." We cautioned courts against leaving the rest of the field to the legislative process: "Constitutional rights are enshrined with the scope they were understood to have when the people adopted them, whether or not future legislatures or (yes) even future judges think that scope too broad."

Based on its crabbed reading of *Heller,* the Seventh Circuit felt free to adopt a test for assessing firearm bans that eviscerates many of the protections recognized in *Heller* and *McDonald*. The court asked in the first instance whether the banned firearms "were common at the time of ratification" in 1791. 784 F.3d, at 410. But we said in *Heller* that "the Second Amendment extends, prima facie, to all instruments that constitute bearable arms, even those that were not in existence at the time of the founding." 554 U.S., at 582, 128 S. Ct. 2783.

The Seventh Circuit alternatively asked whether the banned firearms relate "to the preservation or efficiency of a well regulated militia." . . . Because the Second Amendment confers rights upon individual citizens — not state governments — it was doubly wrong for the Seventh Circuit to delegate to States and localities the power to decide which firearms people may possess.

Lastly, the Seventh Circuit considered "whether law-abiding citizens retain adequate means of self-defense," and reasoned that the City's ban was permissible because "[i]f criminals can find substitutes for banned assault weapons, then so can law-abiding homeowners." . . .

That analysis misreads *Heller*. The question under *Heller* is not whether citizens have adequate alternatives available for self-defense. Rather, *Heller* asks whether the law bans types of firearms commonly used for a lawful purpose — regardless of whether alternatives exist. And *Heller* draws a distinction between such firearms and weapons specially adapted to unlawful uses and not in common use, such as sawed-off shotguns. The City's ban is thus highly suspect because it broadly prohibits common semiautomatic firearms used for lawful purposes. Roughly five million Americans own AR-style semiautomatic rifles. The overwhelming majority of citizens who own and use such rifles do so for lawful purposes, including self-defense and target shooting. Under our precedents, that is all that is needed for citizens to have a right under the Second Amendment to keep such weapons.

. . . This case illustrates why. If a broad ban on firearms can be upheld based on conjecture that the public might *feel* safer (while being no safer at all), then the Second Amendment guarantees nothing.

III

The Court's refusal to review a decision that flouts two of our Second Amendment precedents stands in marked contrast to the Court's willingness to summarily reverse courts that disregard our other constitutional decisions. . . . There is no basis for a different result when our Second Amendment precedents are at stake. I would grant certiorari to prevent the Seventh Circuit from relegating the Second Amendment to a second-class right.

3.   The Right to Bear Arms Outside the Home

Both *Heller* and *McDonald* concerned the right to keep a handgun in the home. Does the Second Amendment extend to the right to carry in public places? Several courts of appeals held that it does not. In *Peruta v. California*, the Supreme Court declined to review a law that requires applicants to demonstrate "good cause" before receiving a concealed-carry permit. Justice Thomas, now joined by Justice Gorsuch, dissented from denial of certiorari.

STUDY GUIDE:

1. Why do you think the Supreme Court had not heard oral arguments in any Second Amendment cases since *McDonald v. Chicago* (2010), but routinely considers First and Fourth Amendment cases?
2. Justice Thomas wrote that "[t]his Court has already suggested that the Second Amendment protects the right to carry firearms in public in some fashion." Did the Court in *Heller* so hold?
3. Justice Thomas noted that the Second Amendment's "core purpose further supports the conclusion that the right to bear arms extends to public carry." What is the "core purpose" of the Second Amendment?
4. Why does Justice Thomas suggest that the majority views the Second Amendment as "antiquated and superfluous" and a "disfavored right"?

Peruta v. California
137 S. Ct. 1995 (2017)

The petition for a writ of certiorari is denied.

JUSTICE THOMAS, with whom JUSTICE GORSUCH joins, dissenting from the denial of certiorari.

. . . At issue in this case is whether that guarantee protects the right to carry firearms in public for self-defense. Neither party disputes that the issue is one of national importance or that the courts of appeals have already weighed in extensively. I would therefore grant the petition for a writ of certiorari.

I

California generally prohibits the average citizen from carrying a firearm in public spaces, either openly or concealed. With a few limited exceptions, the State prohibits open carry altogether. It proscribes concealed carry unless a resident obtains a license by showing "good cause," among other criteria, and it authorizes counties to set rules for when an applicant has shown good cause.

In the county where petitioners reside, the sheriff has interpreted "good cause" to require an applicant to show that he has a particularized need, substantiated by documentary evidence, to carry a firearm for self-defense. The sheriff's policy specifies that "concern for one's personal safety" does not "alone" satisfy this requirement. . . . As a result, ordinary, "law-abiding, responsible citizens," *District of Columbia v. Heller* (2008), may not obtain a permit for concealed carry of a firearm in public spaces.

Petitioners are residents of San Diego County . . . who are unable to obtain a license for concealed carry due to the county's policy and, because the State generally bans open carry, are thus unable to bear firearms in public in any manner. They sued . . . alleging that this near-total prohibition on public carry violates their Second Amendment right to bear arms. . . . The District Court granted respondents' motion for summary judgment, and petitioners appealed to the Ninth Circuit.

In a thorough opinion, a panel of the Ninth Circuit reversed. . . . .Based on these sources, the court concluded that "the carrying of an operable handgun outside the home for the lawful purpose of self-defense . . . constitutes 'bear[ing] Arms' within the meaning of the Second Amendment." . . .

The Ninth Circuit *sua sponte* granted rehearing en banc and, by a divided court, reversed the panel decision. . . . [The en banc court] held only that "the Second Amendment does not preserve or protect a right of a member of the general public to carry *concealed* firearms in public."

II

The en banc court's decision to limit its review to whether the Second Amendment protects the right to concealed carry — as opposed to the more general right to public carry — was untenable. . . .

This Court has already suggested that the Second Amendment protects the right to carry firearms in public in some fashion. As we explained in *Heller*, to "bear arms" means to " 'wear, bear, or carry upon the person or in the clothing or in a pocket, for the purpose of being armed and ready for offensive or defensive action in a case of conflict with another person.'" Heller (quoting *Muscarello v. United States* (1998) (Ginsburg, J., dissenting)). The most natural reading of this definition encompasses public carry. I find it extremely improbable that the Framers understood the Second Amendment to protect little more than carrying a gun from the bedroom to the kitchen.

The relevant history appears to support this understanding. The panel opinion below pointed to a wealth of cases and secondary sources from England, the founding era, the antebellum period, and Reconstruction, which together strongly suggest that the right to bear arms includes the right to bear arms in public in some manner. For example, in *Nunn v. State* — a decision the *Heller* Court discussed extensively as illustrative of the proper understanding of the right — the Georgia Supreme Court struck down a ban on open carry although it upheld a ban on concealed carry. Other cases similarly suggest that, although some regulation of public carry is permissible, an effective ban on all forms of public carry is not.

Finally, the Second Amendment's core purpose further supports the conclusion that the right to bear arms extends to public carry. The Court in *Heller* emphasized that "self-defense" is "the *central component* of the [Second Amendment] right itself." This purpose is not limited only to the home, even though the need for self-defense may be "most acute" there. "Self-defense has to take place wherever the person happens to be," and in some circumstances a person may be more vulnerable in a public place than in his own house. . . .

Even if other Members of the Court do not agree that the Second Amendment likely protects a right to public carry, the time has come for the Court to answer this important question definitively. Twenty-six States have asked us to resolve the question presented, and the lower courts have fully vetted the issue. At least four other Courts of Appeals and three state courts of last resort have decided cases regarding the ability of States to regulate the public carry of firearms. Those decisions (plus the one below) have produced thorough opinions on both sides of the issue. Hence, I do not see much value in waiting for additional courts to weigh in, especially when constitutional rights are at stake.

The Court's decision to deny certiorari in this case reflects a distressing trend: the treatment of the Second Amendment as a disfavored right. See *Friedman v. Highland Park* (2015) (Thomas, J., dissenting from denial of certiorari); *Jackson v. City and County of San Francisco* (2015). The Constitution does not rank certain rights above others, and I do not think this Court should impose such a hierarchy by selectively enforcing its preferred rights. The Court has not heard argument in a Second Amendment case in over seven years — since March 2, 2010, in *McDonald v. Chicago*. Since that time, we have heard argument in, for example, roughly 35 cases where the question presented turned on the meaning of the First Amendment and 25 cases that turned on the meaning of the Fourth Amendment. This discrepancy is inexcusable, especially given how much less developed our jurisprudence is with respect to the Second Amendment as compared to the First and Fourth Amendments.

* * *

For those of us who work in marbled halls, guarded constantly by a vigilant and dedicated police force, the guarantees of the Second Amendment might seem antiquated and superfluous. But the Framers made a clear choice: They reserved to all Americans the right to bear arms for self-defense. I do not think we should stand by idly while a State denies its citizens that right, particularly when their very lives may depend on it. I respectfully dissent.

STUDY GUIDE:

- Why does the majority find the controversy is moot?
- Justice Alito dissented. Why does he find the controversy is not moot? Does the majority engage any of the dissent's arguments?
- What standard of scrutiny does the dissent use? Why does Justice Alito think New York's justifications were pretextual?
- Justice Thomas joined all of Justice Alito's dissent, except for Part IV-B. Why do you think he did not join this portion of the dissent?

NY State Rifle & Pistol Association, Inc. v. City of New York, NY, et al.
590 U.S. __ (2020)

PER CURIAM.

In the District Court, petitioners challenged a New York City rule regarding the transport of firearms. Petitioners claimed that the rule violated the Second Amendment. Petitioners sought declaratory and injunctive relief against enforcement of the rule insofar as the rule prevented their transport of firearms to a second home or shooting range outside of the city. The District Court and the Court of Appeals rejected petitioners' claim. After we granted certiorari, the State of New York amended its firearm licensing statute, and the City amended the rule so that petitioners may now transport firearms to a second home or shooting range outside of the city, which is the precise relief that petitioners requested in the prayer for relief in their complaint. Petitioners' claim for declaratory and injunctive relief with respect to the City's old rule is therefore moot. Petitioners now argue, however, that the new rule may still infringe their rights. In particular, petitioners claim that they may not be allowed to stop for coffee, gas, food, or restroom breaks on the way to their second homes or shooting ranges outside of the city. The City responds that those routine stops are entirely permissible under the new rule. We do not here decide that dispute about the new rule; as we stated in *Lewis v. Continental Bank Corp.* (1990):

> "Our ordinary practice in disposing of a case that has become moot on appeal is to vacate the judgment with directions to dismiss. See, *e.g., Deakins v. Monaghan* (1988); *United States v. Munsingwear, Inc.* (1950). However, in instances where the mootness is attributable to a change in the legal framework governing the case, and where the plaintiff may have some residual claim under the new framework that was understandably not asserted previously, our practice is to vacate the judgment and remand for further proceedings in which the parties may, if necessary, amend their pleadings or develop the record more fully. See *Diffenderfer v. Central Baptist Church of Miami, Inc.* (1972)."

Petitioners also argue that, even though they have not previously asked for damages with respect to the City's old rule, they still could do so in this lawsuit. Petitioners did not seek damages in their complaint; indeed, the possibility of a damages claim was not raised until well into the litigation in this Court. The City argues that it is too late for petitioners to now add a claim for damages. On remand, the Court of Appeals and the District Court may consider whether petitioners may still add a claim for damages in this lawsuit with respect to New York City's old rule. The judgment of the Court of Appeals is vacated, and the case is remanded for such proceedings as are appropriate.

It is so ordered.

JUSTICE KAVANAUGH, concurring.

I agree with the *per curiam* opinion's resolution of the procedural issues before us — namely, that petitioners' claim for injunctive relief against New York City's old rule is moot and that petitioners' new claims should be addressed as appropriate in the first instance by the Court of Appeals and the District Court on remand.

I also agree with Justice Alito's general analysis of *Heller* and *McDonald*. *District of Columbia v. Heller* (2008); *McDonald v. Chicago* (2010); *Heller v. District of Columbia* (C.A.D.C. 2011) (KAVANAUGH, J., dissenting). And I share Justice ALITO's concern that some federal and state courts may not be properly applying *Heller* and *McDonald*. The Court should address that issue soon, perhaps in one of the several Second Amendment cases with petitions for certiorari now pending before the Court.

JUSTICE ALITO, with whom JUSTICE GORSUCH joins, and with whom JUSTICE THOMAS joins except for Part IV–B, dissenting.

By incorrectly dismissing this case as moot, the Court permits our docket to be manipulated in a way that should not be countenanced. Twelve years ago in *District of Columbia v. Heller* (2008), we held that the Second Amendment protects the right of ordinary Americans to keep and bear arms. Two years later, our decision in *McDonald v. Chicago* (2010), established that this right is fully applicable to the States. Since then, the lower courts have decided numerous cases involving Second Amendment challenges to a variety of federal, state, and local laws. Most have failed. We have been asked to review many of these decisions, but until this case, we denied all such requests.

On January 22, 2019, we granted review to consider the constitutionality of a New York City ordinance that burdened the right recognized in *Heller*. Among other things, the ordinance prohibited law-abiding New Yorkers with a license to keep a handgun in the home (a "premises license") from taking that weapon to a firing range outside the City. Instead, premises licensees wishing to gain or maintain the ability to use their weapons safely were limited to the seven firing ranges in the City, all but one of which were largely restricted to members and their guests.

In the District Court and the Court of Appeals, the City vigorously and successfully defended the constitutionality of its ordinance, and the law was upheld based on what we are told is the framework for reviewing Second Amendment claims that has been uniformly adopted by the Courts of Appeals.[1] One might have thought that the City, having convinced the lower courts that its law was consistent with *Heller*, would have been willing to defend its victory in this Court. But once we granted certiorari, both the City and the State of New York sprang into action to prevent us from deciding this case. Although the City had previously insisted that its ordinance served important public safety purposes, our grant of review apparently led to an epiphany of sorts, and the City quickly changed its ordinance. And for good measure the State enacted a law making the old New York City ordinance illegal.

Thereafter, the City and *amici* supporting its position strove to have this case thrown out without briefing or argument. The City moved for dismissal "as soon as is reasonably practicable" on the ground that it had "no legal reason to file a brief." When we refused to jettison the case at that early stage, the City submitted a brief but "stress[ed] that [its] true position [was] that it ha[d] no view at all regarding the constitutional questions presented" and that it was "offer[ing]

---

1. See Brief for Second Amendment Law Professors [Joseph Blocher, Darrell Miller, and Eric Ruben] as *Amici Curiae* [, https://bit.ly/3eTFtJ3 ("Amici urge the Court to hold that the two-part frame-work that the courts of appeals are using to adjudicate Second Amendment claims is the proper doctrinal analysis.")—Eds.]

a defense of the . . . former rul[e] in the spirit of something a Court-appointed *amicus curiae* might do."

A prominent brief supporting the City went further. Five United States Senators, four of whom are members of the bar of this Court, filed a brief insisting that the case be dismissed. If the Court did not do so, they intimated, the public would realize that the Court is "motivated mainly by politics, rather than by adherence to the law," and the Court would face the possibility of legislative reprisal. Brief for Sen. Sheldon Whitehouse et al. as *Amici Curiae* 2–3, 18 [https://bit.ly/3bJFld9].

Regrettably, the Court now dismisses the case as moot. If the Court were right on the law, I would of course approve that disposition. Under the Constitution, our authority is limited to deciding actual cases or controversies, and if this were no longer a live controversy — that is, if it were now moot — we would be compelled to dismiss. But if a case is on our docket and we have jurisdiction, we have an obligation to decide it. As Chief Justice Marshall wrote for the Court in *Cohens v. Virginia* (1821), "[w]e have no more right to decline the exercise of jurisdiction which is given, than to usurp that which is not given."

Thus, in this case, we must apply the well-established standards for determining whether a case is moot, and under those standards, we still have a live case before us. It is certainly true that the new City ordinance and the new State law give petitioners *most of* what they sought, but that is not the test for mootness. Instead, "a case 'becomes moot only when it is *impossible* for a court to grant *any effectual relief whatever* to the prevailing party.'" *Chafin v. Chafin* (2013). "'As long as the parties have a concrete interest, *however small*, in the outcome of the litigation, the case is not moot.'" *Ibid.* (emphasis added).

Respondents have failed to meet this "heavy burden." *Adarand Constructors, Inc. v. Slater* (2000). This is so for two reasons. First, the changes in City and State law do not provide petitioners with all the injunctive relief they sought. Second, if we reversed on the merits, the District Court on remand could award damages to remedy the constitutional violation that petitioners suffered.

I

A

. . . New York State law contemplates two primary forms of handgun license — a premises license, which allows the licensee to keep the registered handgun at a home or business, and a carry license, which permits the licensee to carry a concealed handgun outside the home. In this case, only premises licenses are at issue. . . .

The ordinance that petitioners challenged in this case was adopted in 2001. Before then, the NYPD issued both premises licenses and so-called "target licenses," which allowed licensees to transport their handguns to specified, pre-approved ranges outside of the City. Target licenses were eliminated in 2001, and from that time until the City's post-certiorari change of heart, premises licensees could practice with their guns only if: they traveled "directly to and from an *authorized* small arms range/shooting club"; their guns were unloaded and secured in a locked container; and any ammunition was "carried separately.". And—what is most important for present purposes—the only "authorized" ranges or clubs were ones "located in New York City." At the relevant time, there were only seven such ranges in the entire City: two in Staten Island, two in Queens, one in Brooklyn, one in Manhattan, and one in the Bronx. All but one generally admitted only members and their guests, and the only range open to the public was closed for a time during the pendency of the case below.

B

1

In 2013, three individuals and one organization representing New York gun owners brought suit . . . against the City and the NYPD License Division, contending that the restrictive premises license scheme violated their rights under the Second Amendment and other provisions of the Constitution. . . .

Petitioners' amended complaint maintained that the Second Amendment requires "*unrestricted* access to gun ranges and shooting events in order to practice and perfect safe gun handling skills." The complaint asserts that practice is necessary for "the safe and responsible use of firearms for . . . self-defense, and the defense of one's home." . . . According to the complaint, the City, by limiting licensees like petitioners to the seven ranges in the City, imposed a serious burden on the exercise of their Second Amendment right.

The amended complaint's prayer for relief sought an injunction against enforcement of the travel restriction, as well as attorney's fees, costs of suit, declaratory relief . . . and "[a]ny such further relief as the [c]ourt deems just and proper."

2

The City vigorously defended its law. The ordinance did not impinge on petitioners' Second Amendment right, the City told the lower courts, and even if it did, the law survived heightened scrutiny. That was so, the City maintained, because the travel restrictions were "necessary to protect the public safety insofar as the transport of firearms outside the home potentially endangers the public." . . .

To support this assertion, the City relied on the declaration of Inspector Lunetta, which attempted to explain why the restrictions were "necessary to address . . . public safety concerns." . . .

The District Court deemed any burden on petitioners' Second Amendment right "minimal or, at most, modest." And the court credited the City's public safety rationale, citing the Lunetta declaration approvingly and discussing the importance of the travel restrictions in limiting the movement of licensees with their handguns.

The Second Circuit affirmed. The panel derided the ordinance's burdens on petitioners' Second Amendment right as "trivial" and expressly credited Lunetta's explanation of the public safety purposes served by the travel restriction.

When petitioners filed a petition for certiorari, the City opposed review, contending, among other things, that the travel restriction promoted public safety, as demonstrated by Lunetta's declaration (which the City cited six times). We nevertheless granted review on January 22, 2019, and this, as noted, apparently led the City to reconsider whether the travel restriction was actually needed for public safety purposes.

C

On April 12, the NYPD published a proposed amendment to the travel restriction that was admittedly spurred at least in part by our grant of review. Under this amendment, holders of premises licenses would be allowed to take their guns to ranges, competitions, and second homes outside the City provided that the licensees traveled "directly" between their residences and the permitted destinations. After a period of notice and comment, the proposed amendment was adopted on June 21 and took effect on July 21.

Our grant of certiorari also prompted action by New York State. With the support of the City, the Legislature enacted a new law abrogating any local law, rule, or regulation that prevented the holder of a premises license from transporting a licensed handgun "directly to or from" an authorized range, competition, or second home.

Shortly after the new State law took effect, the City filed a Suggestion of Mootness, asking us to vacate the decision below and to remand with instructions to dismiss. The City urged us to rule on this matter expeditiously so that it would not be required to file a brief defending its prior law. When we refused to vacate at that stage, the City protested that briefing the merits "require[d] the City to do what Article III's case-or-controversy requirement is designed to avoid: engage in litigation regarding the constitutionality of a law that no longer exists" and that the City would not reenact. When the case was argued, counsel for the City was asked whether the repeal of the travel restriction had made the City any less safe, and his unequivocal answer was no.

II

The Court vacates the judgment of the Court of Appeals, *apparently* on the ground that this case is now moot. (Other than mootness, no other basis for vacating comes to mind, and therefore I proceed on that assumption.) And if that is the reason for what the Court has done, the Court is wrong. This case is not moot.

Article III, § 2 of the Constitution limits the jurisdiction of the federal courts to "Cases" and "Controversies," and as a result, we may not " 'decide questions that cannot affect the rights of litigants in the case before [us].'" *Chafin*. Nor may we advise "'what the law would be upon a hypothetical state of facts.'" This means that the dispute between the parties in a case must remain alive until its ultimate disposition. If a live controversy ceases to exist — *i.e.*, if a case becomes moot — then we have no jurisdiction to proceed. But in order for this to happen, a case must really be dead, and as noted, that occurs only "'when it is impossible for a court to grant any effectual relief whatever to the prevailing party.'" Thus, to establish mootness, a "demanding standard" must be met. *Mission Product Holdings, Inc.* (2019).

We have been particularly wary of attempts by parties to manufacture mootness in order to evade review. And it is black-letter law that we have a "virtually unflagging" obligation to exercise our jurisdiction. *Colorado River Water Conservation Dist. v. United States* (1976).

In this case, the amended City ordinance and the new State law gave petitioners most of what they sought in their complaint, but the new laws did not give them complete relief. It is entirely possible for them to obtain more relief, and therefore this case is not moot. This is so for the following reasons.

A

First, this case is not moot because the amended City ordinance and new State law do not give petitioners all the *prospective relief* they seek. Petitioners asserted in their complaint that the Second Amendment guarantees them, as holders of premises licenses, "unrestricted access" to ranges, competitions, and second homes outside of New York City, and the new laws do not give them that.

The new City ordinance has limitations that petitioners claim are unconstitutional, namely, that a trip outside the City must be "direc[t]" and travel within the City must be "continuous and uninterrupted." Exactly what these restrictions mean is not clear from the face of the rule, and the City has done little to clarify their reach. At argument, counsel told us that the new rule allows "bathroom breaks," "coffee stops," and any other "reasonably necessary stops in the course of travel." But the meaning of a "reasonably necessary" stop is hardly clear. What about a stop to buy groceries just before coming home? Or a stop to pick up a friend who also wants to practice at a range outside the City? Or a quick visit to a sick relative or friend who lives near a range? The City does not know the answer to such questions . . . The bottom line is that petitioners, who sought "unrestricted access" to out-of-city ranges and competitions, are still subject to restrictions of undetermined meaning. . . .

Petitioners got most, but not all, of the prospective relief they wanted, and that means that the case is not dead.

B

The case is not moot for a separate and independent reason: If this Court were to hold, as petitioners request and as I believe we should, that violated petitioners' Second Amendment right, the District Court on remand could (and probably should) award damages. Petitioners brought their claims under 42 U.S.C. § 1983, which permits the recovery of damages. And while the amended complaint does not expressly seek damages, it is enough that it requests "[a]ny other such further relief as the [c]ourt deems just and proper." Under modern pleading standards, that suffices. . . .

With this is mind, the possibility of actual damages cannot be ruled out. One or more of the petitioners could seek compensation for out-of-pocket expenses, such as membership fees at in-city ranges. The current record shows that at least one of the petitioners is a member of a range in the City. In addition, a petitioner may be entitled to compensation for expenses incurred in registering for out-of-city competitions from which he was compelled to withdraw. The record shows that one petitioner signed up for such a competition but had to pull out as a result of the City ordinance . . . Among other things, depriving a licensee of the opportunity to obtain the benefits of competing and perhaps obtaining recognition at a well-known competition may cause a real loss. Lower courts have affirmed awards of compensatory damages for similar kinds of injuries resulting from constitutional violations. Petitioners could introduce evidence on remand to show such loss . . .

For purposes of determining whether this case is moot, the question is not whether petitioners would actually succeed in obtaining such damages or whether their loss was substantial. If there is a possibility of obtaining damages in any amount, the case is not moot. . . .

C

Relief would be particularly appropriate here because the City's litigation strategy caused petitioners to incur what are surely very substantial attorney's fees in challenging the constitutionality of a City ordinance that the City went to great lengths to defend. Of course, a claim for attorney's fees is not alone sufficient to preserve a live controversy. *Lewis v. Continental Bank Corp.* (1990). But where a live controversy remains, a defendant who would otherwise be liable for attorney's fees should not be able to wiggle out on the basis of a spurious claim of mootness. . . .

Here, the City fought petitioners tooth and nail in the District Court and the Court of Appeals, insisting that its old ordinance served important public safety purposes. When petitioners sought review in this Court, the City opposed certiorari on the same ground. But once we granted review, the City essentially attempted to impose a unilateral settlement that deprived petitioners of attorney's fees. And those fees would likely be substantial. They would reflect five years of intensive litigation — everything from the drafting of the complaint, through multiple rounds of District Court motion practice, to appellate review, and proceedings in this Court.

III

The *per curiam* provides no sound reason for holding that this case is moot. The *per curiam* states that the City's current rule gave petitioners "the precise relief [they] requested" in their prayer for relief, but that is not so. Petitioners' prayer for relief asks the court to enjoin 38 N.Y.C.R.R. § 5–23 insofar as it "prohibit[s]" travel outside the City to ranges, competitions, and second homes. The new rule's conditions unmistakably continue to prohibit some travel outside the City to those destinations. For this reason, petitioners have not obtained the "unrestricted access" that, they have always maintained, the Second Amendment guarantees. The *per curiam* implies that the current rule, as interpreted at oral argument by counsel for the City, gives petitioners everything that they now seek, but that also is not true. Petitioners still claim the right to "unrestricted access" and counsel's off-the-cuff concessions do not give them that.[11] The *per curiam*'s main argument appears to go as follows: Petitioners' original claim was a challenge to New York's old rule; this claim is now moot due to the repeal of that rule; and what the petitioners are now asserting is a new claim, namely, that New York's current rule is also unconstitutional.

This argument also misrepresents the nature of the claim asserted in petitioners' complaint. What petitioners claimed in their complaint and still claim is that they are entitled to "unrestricted access" to out-of-city ranges and competitions. The City's replacement of one law denying unrestricted access with another that also denies that access did not change the nature of petitioners' claim or render it moot.

Consider where acceptance of the argument adopted by the *per curiam* leads. . . . A State enacts a law providing that any woman wishing to obtain an abortion must submit certification from five doctors that the procedure is medically necessary. After a woman sues, claiming that any requirement of physician certification is unconstitutional, the State replaces its old law with a new one requiring certification by three physicians. Would the court be required to dismiss the woman's suit? Suppose the court, following the precedent set by today's decision, holds that the case is moot, and suppose that the woman brings a second case challenging the new law on the same ground. If the State repeals that law and replaces it with one requiring certification by two doctors, would the second suit be moot? And what if the State responds to a third suit by enacting replacement legislation demanding certification by one doctor?

Mootness doctrine does not require such results. A challenge to an allegedly unconstitutional law does not become moot with the enactment of new legislation that reduces but does not eliminate the injury originally alleged. And that is the situation here.

[The Plaintiffs] are not asserting a new claim. Their original claim—that they have the right under the Second Amendment to unrestricted access to out-of-city ranges and competitions—is unchanged, and this claim does not require

---

11. The City's enforcement position as to "coffee, gas, food, or restroom breaks" by no means resolves the meaning of § 5–23. The City's counsel informed the Court that those stops are permissible because they are "reasonably necessary" under the new rule. But what that means is far from clear, and, at any rate, coffee breaks and the like are just illustrative examples of potential ways in which the new rule affords something less than unfettered access to gun ranges, competitions, and second homes outside the City.

an amendment of the complaint or any supplementation of the record to support their allegations of injury.

For these reasons, there is no justification for holding that this case is moot.

IV

A

Having shown that this case is not moot, I proceed to the merits of plaintiffs' claim that the City ordinance violated the Second Amendment. This is not a close question. The answer follows directly from *Heller*.

In *Heller*, we held that a District of Columbia rule that effectively prevented a law-abiding citizen from keeping a handgun in the home for purposes of self-defense constituted a core violation of the Second Amendment. We based this decision on the scope of the right to keep and bear arms as it was understood at the time of the adoption of the Second Amendment. We recognized that history supported the constitutionality of some laws limiting the right to possess a firearm, such as laws banning firearms from certain sensitive locations and prohibiting possession by felons and other dangerous individuals. But history provided no support for laws like the District's.

For a similar reason, 38 N.Y.C.R.R. § 5–23 also violated the Second Amendment. We deal here with the same core Second Amendment right, the right to keep a handgun in the home for self-defense. As the Second Circuit "assume[d]," a necessary concomitant of this right is the right to take a gun outside the home for certain purposes. One of these is to take a gun for maintenance or repair, which City law allows. Another is to take a gun outside the home in order to transfer ownership lawfully, which the City also allows. And still another is to take a gun to a range in order to gain and maintain the skill necessary to use it responsibly. As we said in *Heller*, " 'to bear arms implies something more than the mere keeping [of arms]; it implies the learning to handle and use them in a way that makes those who keep them ready for their efficient use.' " *Heller* (quoting T. Cooley, Constitutional Law (1880)); see also *Luis* v. *United States* (2016) (THOMAS, J., concurring in judgment) ("The right to keep and bear arms . . . 'implies a corresponding right . . . to acquire and maintain proficiency in their use' "); *Ezell v. Chicago* (7th Cir. 2011) (Sykes, J.) ("[T]he core right wouldn't mean much without the training and practice that make it effective").

It is true that a lawful gun owner can sometimes practice at a range using a gun that is owned by and rented at the range. But the same model gun that the person owns may not be available at a range, and in any event each individual gun may have its own characteristics. Once it is recognized that the right at issue is a concomitant of the same right recognized in *Heller*, it became incumbent on the City to justify the restrictions its rule imposes, but the City has not done so. It points to no evidence of laws in force around the time of the adoption of the Second Amendment that prevented gun owners from practicing outside city limits. The City argues that municipalities restricted the places within their jurisdiction where a gun could be fired, and it observes that the Second Amendment surely does not mean that a New York City resident with a premises license can practice in Central Park or Times Square. That is certainly true, but that is not the question. Petitioners do not claim the right to fire weapons in public places *within the City*. Instead, they claim they have a right to practice at ranges and competitions *outside the City*, and neither the City, the courts below, nor any of the many *amici* supporting the City have shown that municipalities during the founding era prevented gun owners from taking their guns outside city limits for practice.

B

If history is not sufficient to show that the New York City ordinance is unconstitutional, any doubt is dispelled by the weakness of the City's showing that its travel restriction significantly promoted public safety. Although the courts below claimed to apply heightened scrutiny, there was nothing heightened about what they did. . . .

First, Inspector Lunetta asserted that the travel restrictions discouraged licensees from taking their guns outside the home, but this is a strange argument for several reasons. It would make sense only if it is less convenient or more expensive to practice at a range in the City, but that contradicts the City's argument that the seven ranges in the City provide ample opportunity for practice. And discouraging trips to a range contradicts the City's own rule recommending that licensees practice. Once it is recognized that a reasonable opportunity to practice is part of the very right recognized in *Heller*, what this justification amounts to is a repudiation of part of what we held in that decision.

Second, Inspector Lunetta claimed that prohibiting trips to out-of-city ranges helps prevent a person who is taking a gun to a range from using it in a fit of rage after an auto accident or some other altercation that occurs along the way . . . [T]his argument does not explain why a person headed for a range outside the City is any more likely to engage in such conduct than a person whose destination is a range in the City. . . .

Inspector Lunetta's final justification for the travel restrictions was only marginally stronger. It goes like this. Suppose that a patrol officer stops a premises licensee and finds that this individual is carrying a gun, and suppose that that the licensee says he is taking the gun to a range to practice or is returning from a range. If the range in question is one in the City, the officer will be better able to check the story than if the range is outside the officer's jurisdiction.

How strong is this argument? The City presumably has access to records of cases in which licensees were cited for unauthorized possession of guns outside the home, and it failed to provide any evidence that holders of target licenses had used their right to practice at out-of-city ranges as a pretext. And it is dubious that it would be much harder for an officer to check whether a licensee was really headed for an out-of-city range as opposed to one in the City. If a licensee claims to be headed for a range in the City, the officer can check whether the range is open and whether the individual appears to be on a route that plausibly leads to that range. But how much more difficult would it be to do the same thing if the range is in one of the counties that border New York City or across the Hudson River in New Jersey? A phone call would be enough to determine the range's operating hours, and the route would still be easy to determine: There are only a few bridges and tunnels to New Jersey and just a few main thoroughfares to the neighboring New York counties. A court conducting any form of serious scrutiny would have demanded that the City provide some substantiation for this claim, but nothing like that was provided or demanded. . . .

In sum, the City's travel restriction burdened the very right recognized in *Heller*. History provides no support for a restriction of this type. The City's public safety arguments were weak on their face, were not substantiated in any way, and were accepted below with no serious probing. And once we granted review in this case, the City's public safety concerns evaporated.

We are told that the mode of review in this case is representative of the way *Heller* has been treated in the lower courts. If that is true, there is cause for concern.

* * *

This case is not moot. The City violated petitioners' Second Amendment right, and we should so hold. I would reverse the judgment of the Court of Appeals and remand the case to the District Court to provide appropriate relief. I therefore respectfully dissent.

Rogers v. Grewal
590 U.S. __ (2020)

The petition for a writ of certiorari is denied.

JUSTICE THOMAS, with whom JUSTICE KAVANAUGH joins as to all but Part II, dissenting from the denial of certiorari.

The text of the Second Amendment protects "the right of the people to keep and bear Arms." We have stated that this "fundamental righ[t]" is "necessary to our system of ordered liberty." *McDonald v. Chicago* (2010). Yet, in several jurisdictions throughout the country, law-abiding citizens have been barred from exercising the fundamental right to bear arms because they cannot show that they have a "justifiable need" or "good reason" for doing so. One would think that such an onerous burden on a fundamental right would warrant this Court's review. This Court would almost certainly review the constitutionality of a law requiring citizens to establish a justifiable need before exercising their free speech rights. And it seems highly unlikely that the Court would allow a State to enforce a law requiring a woman to provide a justifiable need before seeking an abortion. But today, faced with a petition challenging just such a restriction on citizens' Second Amendment rights, the Court simply looks the other way.

Petitioner Rogers is a law-abiding citizen who runs a business that requires him to service automated teller machines in high-crime areas. He applied for a permit to carry his handgun for self-defense. But, to obtain a carry permit in New Jersey, an applicant must, among other things, demonstrate "that he has a justifiable need to carry a handgun." For a "private citizen" to satisfy this "justifiable need" requirement, he must "specify in detail the urgent necessity for self-protection, as evidenced by specific threats or previous attacks which demonstrate a special danger to the applicant's life that cannot be avoided by means other than by issuance of a permit to carry a handgun." "Generalized fears for personal safety are inadequate." Petitioner could not satisfy this standard and, as a result, his permit application was denied. With no ability to obtain a permit, petitioner is forced to operate his business in high-risk neighborhoods with no firearm for self-defense.

Petitioner asks this Court to grant certiorari to determine whether New Jersey's near-total prohibition on carrying a firearm in public violates his Second Amendment right to bear arms, made applicable to the States through the Fourteenth Amendment. See *McDonald* (THOMAS, J., concurring in part and concurring in judgment). This case gives us the opportunity to provide guidance on the proper approach for evaluating Second Amendment claims; acknowledge that the Second Amendment protects the right to carry in public; and resolve a square Circuit split on the constitutionality of justifiable-need restrictions on that right. I would grant the petition for a writ of certiorari.

I

It has been more than a decade since this Court's decisions in *McDonald* v. *Chicago* and *District of Columbia v. Heller* (2008). In the years since those decisions, lower courts have struggled to determine the proper approach for analyzing Second Amendment challenges.

Although our decision in *Heller* did not provide a precise standard for evaluating all Second Amendment claims, it did provide a general framework to guide lower courts. In *Heller*, we recognized that "the Second Amendment . . . codified a *pre-existing* right." This right was "enshrined with the scope [it was] understood to have when the people adopted" it. To determine that scope, we analyzed the original meaning of the Second Amendment's text as well as the historical understanding of the right. We noted that "limitation[s]" on the right may be supported by "historical tradition," but we declined to "undertake an exhaustive historical analysis . . . of the full scope of the Second Amendment." Instead, we indicated that courts could conduct historical analyses for restrictions in the future as challenges arose.

Consistent with this guidance, many jurists have concluded that text, history, and tradition are dispositive in determining whether a challenged law violates the right to keep and bear arms. See, *e.g.*, *Mance v. Sessions* (5th Cir. 2018) (Elrod, J., joined by Jones, Smith, Willett, Ho, Duncan, and Engelhardt, JJ., dissenting from denial of reh'g en banc); *Tyler v. Hillsdale Cty. Sheriff's Dept.* (6th Cir. 2016) (Batchelder, J., concurring in most of judgment); *Gowder v. Chicago* (ND Ill. 2012); *Heller v. District of Columbia*, (D.C. Cir. 2011) (*Heller II*) (Kavanaugh, J., dissenting).

But, as I have noted before, many courts have resisted our decisions in *Heller* and *McDonald*. See *Silvester v. Becerra* (2018) (opinion dissenting from denial of certiorari). Instead of following the guidance provided in *Heller*, these courts minimized that decision's framework. See, *e.g.*, *Gould v. Morgan* (1st Cir. 2018) (concluding that our decisions "did not provide much clarity as to how Second Amendment claims should be analyzed in future cases"). They then "filled" the self-created "analytical vacuum" with a "two-step inquiry" that incorporates tiers of scrutiny on a sliding scale. *National Rifle Assn. of Am., Inc. v. Bureau of Alcohol, Tobacco, Firearms, and Explosives*, (5th Cir. 2012); *Powell v. Tompkins* (1st Cir. 2015) (compiling Circuit opinions adopting some form of the sliding-scale framework).

Under this test, courts first ask "whether the challenged law burdens conduct protected by the Second Amendment." *United States v. Chovan* (9th Cir. 2013). If so, courts proceed to the second step—determining the appropriate level of scrutiny. To do so, courts generally consider "how close the law comes to the core of the Second Amendment right" and "the severity of the law's burden on the right." Depending on their analysis of those two factors, courts then apply what purports to be either intermediate or strict scrutiny—at least recognizing that *Heller* barred the application of rational basis review.

This approach raises numerous concerns. For one, the courts of appeals' test appears to be entirely made up. The Second Amendment provides no hierarchy of "core" and peripheral rights. And "[t]he Constitution does not prescribe tiers of scrutiny." *Whole Woman's Health v. Hellerstedt* (2016) (THOMAS, J., dissenting); see also *Heller II* (Kavanaugh, J., dissenting) (listing constitutional rights that are not subject to means-ends scrutiny). Moreover, there is nothing in our Second Amendment precedents that supports the application of what has been described as "a tripartite binary test with a sliding scale and a reasonable fit." *Duncan v. Becerra* (S.D. Cal. 2017).

Even accepting this test on its terms, its application has yielded analyses that are entirely inconsistent with *Heller*. There, we cautioned that "[a] constitutional guarantee subject to future judges' assessments of its usefulness is no constitutional guarantee at all," stating that our constitutional rights must be protected "whether or not future legislatures or (yes) even future judges think that scope too broad." On that basis, we explicitly rejected the invitation to evaluate Second Amendment challenges under an "interest-balancing inquiry, with the interests protected by the Second Amendment on one side and the governmental public-safety concerns on the other." *Id.* (BREYER, J., dissenting). But the application of the test adopted by the courts of appeals has devolved into just that.[1] In

---

1. See, e.g., *Kachalsky v. County of Westchester*, (2d Cir. 2012) (deferring to the legislature's conclusion that "public safety . . . outweighs the need to have a handgun for an unexpected confrontation"); New York State Rifle & Pistol Assn., Inc. v. New York (2d Cir. 2018) (stating that a "review of state and local gun control" involves a "balancing of the individual's constitutional right to keep and bear arms against the states' obligation to 'prevent armed mayhem'"); Gould v. Morgan (1st Cir. 2018) (stating that "courts must defer to a legislature's choices among reasonable alternatives" when the legislature has "take[n] account of the heightened needs of some individuals to carry firearms for

fact, at least one scholar has contended that this interest-balancing approach has ultimately carried the day, as the lower courts systematically ignore the Court's actual holding in *Heller*. See Rostron, Justice Breyer's Triumph in the Third Battle Over the Second Amendment, 80 Geo. Wash. L. Rev. 703 (2012). With what other constitutional right would this Court allow such blatant defiance of its precedent?

Whatever one may think about the proper approach to analyzing Second Amendment challenges, it is clearly time for us to resolve the issue.

II

This case also presents the Court with an opportunity to clarify that the Second Amendment protects a right to public carry. While some Circuits have recognized that the Second Amendment extends outside the home, see *Wrenn v. District of Columbia* (D.C. Cir. 2017); *Moore v. Madigan* (7th Cir. 2012), many have declined to define the scope of the right, simply assuming that the right to public carry exists for purposes of applying a scrutiny-based analysis, see *Woollard v. Gallagher* (4th Cir. 2013); *Drake v. Filko* (3d Cir. 2013); *Kachalsky v. County of Westchester* (2d Cir. 2012).[2] Other courts have specifically indicated that they would not interpret the Second Amendment to apply outside the home without further instruction from this Court. *United States v. Masciandaro*, 638 F.3d 458, 475 (CA4 2011) ("On the question of *Heller*'s applicability outside the home environment, we think it prudent to await direction from the Court itself"); *Williams v. State*, 417 Md. 479, 496, 10 A.3d 1167, 1177 (2011) ("If the Supreme Court . . . meant its holding [in *Heller*] to extend beyond home possession, it will need to say so more plainly"). We should provide the requested instruction.

A

The text of the Second Amendment guarantees that "the right of the people to keep and bear Arms, shall not be infringed." As this Court explained in *Heller*, "[a]t the time of the founding, as now, to 'bear' meant to 'carry.'" "When used with 'arms,' . . . the term has a meaning that refers to carrying for a particular purpose—confrontation." *Ibid.* Thus, the right to "bear arms" refers to the right to "'wear, bear, or carry upon the person or in the clothing or in a pocket, for the

---

self-defense and balance[d] those needs against the demands of public safety"); Drake v. Filko (CA3 2013) ("refus[ing] . . . to intrude upon the sound judgment and discretion of the State of New Jersey" that only "those citizens who can demonstrate a 'justifiable need' to do so" may carry handguns outside the home).

2. It is not clear how these courts can apply the made-up sliding scale test without determining the scope of the right. See Peruta v. County of San Diego (CA9 2014) (noting that courts "must fully understand the historical scope of the right before [they] can determine whether and to what extent the [challenged law] burdens the right or whether it goes even further and amounts to a destruction of the right altogether.")

purpose of being armed and ready for offensive or defensive action in a case of conflict with another person.'"

"The most natural reading of this definition encompasses public carry." *Peruta* v. *California* (2017) (THOMAS, J., dissenting from denial of certiorari). Confrontations, of course, often occur outside the home. See, *e.g.*, *Moore* (noting that "most murders occur outside the home" in Chicago). Thus, the right to carry arms for self-defense inherently includes the right to carry in public. This conclusion not only flows from the definition of "bear Arms" but also from the natural use of the language in the text. As I have stated before, it is "extremely improbable that the Framers understood the Second Amendment to protect little more than carrying a gun from the bedroom to the kitchen."

The meaning of the term "bear Arms" is even more evident when read in the context of the phrase "right . . . to keep and bear Arms." U. S. Const., Amdt. 2. "To speak of 'bearing' arms solely within one's home . . . would conflate 'bearing' with 'keeping,' in derogation of [*Heller*'s] holding that the verbs codified distinct rights." *Drake* (Hardiman, J., dissenting). In short, it would take serious linguistic gymnastics—and a repudiation of this Court's decision in *Heller*—to claim that the phrase "bear Arms" does not extend the Second Amendment beyond the home.

B

Cases and treatises from England, the founding era, and the antebellum period confirm that the right to bear arms includes the right to carry in public.

1

"[T]he Second Amendment . . . codified a *pre-existing* right." *Heller*, *supra*, at 592, 128 S. Ct. 2783. So, as in *Heller*, my analysis of the scope of that right begins with our country's English roots.

In 1328, during a time of political transition, the English Parliament enacted the Statute of Northampton. The Statute provided that no man was permitted to "bring . . . force in affray of the peace, nor to go nor ride armed by night nor by day, in Fairs, Markets, nor in the presence of the Justices or other Ministers, nor in no part elsewhere." Statute of Northampton 1328. On its face, the statute could be read as a sweeping ban on the carrying of arms. However, both the history and enforcement of the statute reveal that it created a far more limited restriction.

From the beginning, the scope of the Statute of Northampton was unclear. Some officers were ordered to arrest all persons that "go armed," regardless of whether the bearer was carrying arms peacefully. See Letter to Mayor and Bailiffs of York (Jan. 30, 1334). Other officers, however, were ordered to arrest only "persons riding or going armed *to disturb the peace*." Letter to Keeper and Justices of Northumberland (Oct. 28, 1332).

Whatever the initial breadth of the statute, it is clear that it was not strictly enforced in the ensuing centuries. To the contrary, "[d]uring most of England's history, maintenance of an armed citizenry was neither merely permissive nor cosmetic but essential" because "[u]ntil late in the seventeenth century England had no standing army, and until the nineteenth century no regular police force." Malcom, The Right of the People To Keep and Bear Arms: The Common Law Tradition (1983). Citizens were not only expected to possess arms, they were encouraged to maintain skills in the use of those arms, which, of course, required carrying arms in public. See, e.g., id. (describing King Henry VIII's order requiring villages to maintain targets at which local men were to practice shooting).

The religious and political turmoil in England during the 17th century thrust the scope of the Statute of Northampton to the forefront. See J. Malcom, To Keep and Bear Arms (1994) (hereinafter Malcom). King James II, a Catholic monarch, sought to revive the Statute of Northampton as a weapon to disarm his Protestant opponents. Id., at 104. To this point, "[a]lthough men were occasionally indicted for carrying arms to terrorize their neighbours, the strict prohibition [of the Statute of Northampton] had never been enforced." Ibid. But, in November 1686, the Attorney General brought Sir John Knight—an opponent of James II—to trial before the King's Bench. The information alleged that Knight violated the Statute of Northampton by "walk[ing] about the streets armed with guns, and [entering] into the church of St. Michael, in Bristol, in the time of divine service, with a gun, to terrify the King's subjects." At trial, the Chief Justice of the King's Bench stated that the Statute of Northampton only "punish[ed] people who go armed to terrify the King's subjects." He explained that the Statute of Northampton was "almost gone in desuetudinem" for "now there be a general connivance to gentlemen to ride armed for their security." The Chief Justice also noted that only "where the crime shall appear to be malo animo [i.e., with a wrongful intent,] it will come within the Act." Ibid. In other words, the Statute of Northampton was almost obsolete from disuse and prohibited only the carrying arms to terrify. Knight was ultimately acquitted.[3]

James II's attempts to disarm his opponents continued. Only two weeks after Knight's acquittal, James II ordered general disarmaments of regions inhabited by his Protestant enemies under the auspices of the Game Act of 1671. As we explained in Heller, "[t]hese experiences caused Englishmen to be extremely wary of concentrated military forces run by the state and to be jealous of their arms."

In 1688, James II was deposed in an uprising which came to be known as The Glorious Revolution. Soon thereafter, the English compiled the Declaration of Rights, which contained a list of grievances against James II and sought assurances from William and Mary that Protestants would not be disarmed. William and Mary accepted the Declaration of Rights, which was later codified as the

---

3. At least one scholar has asserted that Sir John Knight was acquitted because he fell within the Statute of Northampton's exception for the "King's Officers and Ministers." Charles, The Faces of the Second Amendment Outside the Home: History Versus Ahistorical Standards of Review (2012). This assertion has been repudiated by subsequent scholarship. See Kopel, The First Century of Right to Arms Litigation (2016); see also Young v. Hawaii, 896 F.3d 1044, 1064, n. 17 (CA9 2018). Moreover, regardless of the ground for acquittal, the Chief Justice's pronouncement of law remains.

English Bill of Rights, agreeing that "the Subjects which are Protestants may have Arms for their Defence suitable to their Conditions, and as allowed by Law."

The Statute of Northampton remained in force following the codification of the English Bill of Rights, but the narrow interpretation of the statute adopted in *Sir John Knight's Case* became blackletter law in England. Writing in 1716, Serjeant William Hawkins, author of an influential English treatise, explained that "no wearing of Arms is within the meaning of [the Statute of Northampton], unless it be accompanied with such Circumstances as are apt to terrify the People; from whence it seems clearly to follow, That Persons of Quality are in no Danger of Offending against this Statute by wearing common Weapons." Theodore Barlow, another legal commentator, also explained that "Wearing Arms, if not accompanied with Circumstances of Terror, is not within this Statute; therefore People of Rank and Distinction do not offend by wearing common Weapons." Sir William Blackstone concluded the Statute of Northampton banned only the carrying of "dangerous and unusual weapons." *Heller.* He explained that the right to arms protected by the 1689 English Bill of Rights preserved "the natural right of resistance and self-preservation" and "the right of having and using arms for self-preservation and defence." 1 Commentaries on the Laws of England (1765); see also ("[E]veryone is at liberty to keep or carry a gun, if he does not use it for the [illegal] destruction of game" (editor's note)).

In short, although England may have limited the right to carry in the 14th century, by the time of the founding, the English right was "an individual right protecting against both *public* and private violence." *Heller.* And for purposes of discerning the original meaning of the Second Amendment, it is this founding era understanding that is most pertinent.

2

Founding era legal commentators in America also understood the Second Amendment right to "bear Arms" to encompass the right to carry in public.

St. George Tucker, in his 1803 American edition of Blackstone's Commentaries, explained that the right to armed self-defense is the "first law of nature." He described "the right of the people to keep and bear arms" as "the true palladium of liberty." Tucker makes clear that bearing arms in public was common practice at the founding: "In many parts of the United States, a man no more thinks, of going out of his house on any occasion, without his rifle or musket in his hand, than a European fine gentleman without his sword by his side."

Similarly, William Rawle, a member of the Pennsylvania Assembly that ratified the Bill of Rights, acknowledged the right to carry arms in public. Rawle noted that the right should not "be abused to the disturbance of the public peace" and explained that if a man carried arms "attended with circumstances giving just reason to fear that he purposes to make an unlawful use of them," he may be required "to give surety of the peace."[4] But his general understanding appeared to mirror Hawkins' articulation of the English right—public carry was permitted so long as it was not done to terrify.

Other commentators took a similar view. James Wilson, a prominent Framer and one of the six original Justices of the Supreme Court, understood founding era law to prohibit only the carrying of "dangerous and unusual weapons, in such a manner, as will naturally diffuse a terrour among the people." Charles Humphreys, a law professor, reiterated "that in this country the constitution guarranties to all persons the right to bear arms" and that "it can only be a crime to exercise this right in such a manner, as to terrify the people unnecessarily."

3

This view persisted in the early years of the Republic. The majority of the relevant cases during the antebellum period—many of which *Heller* relied on—support the understanding that the phrase "bear Arms" includes the right to carry in public.

In *Bliss v. Commonwealth* (1822), the Kentucky Court of Appeals held that its state constitutional right to "bear arms" invalidated a concealed carry restriction. The court stated that "whatever restrains the full and complete exercise of [the right to bear arms], though not an entire destruction of it, is forbidden by the explicit language of the constitution."

Eleven years after *Bliss*, Tennessee's highest court interpreted its State Second Amendment analog in a similar manner in *Simpson v. State* (1833). In that case, a jury convicted Simpson of carrying arms "in a warlike manner . . . and to the great terror and disturbance of . . . good citizens." Simpson challenged the conviction, arguing that the State merely proved that he carried arms, not that he did so in a manner to provoke violence. The State asserted that violence was not "essential" to support the conviction, pointing to a statement of Serjeant Hawkins regarding the English Statute of Northampton. The court rejected the State's argument. First, it noted that the State had selectively quoted Hawkins' statement about "'dangerous and unusual weapons,'" and that Hawkins actually explained that "persons of quality are in no danger of offending [the Statute of Northampton] by wearing their common weapons . . . in such places and upon occasions in which it is the common fashion to make use of them without causing the least suspicion of an intention to commit any act of violence or disturbance of the peace." Second, the court held that even assuming "that our ancestors adopted and brought over with them [the Statute of Northampton], or [a] portion of the common law," the state-law "right to keep and to bear arms" "completely abrogated it."

---

4. Lower courts looking to historical practice have concluded that, even in these circumstances, if a surety was provided or the accused was exempt from providing a surety, he could continue to bear arms in public. *Wrenn v. District of Columbia*, 864 F.3d 650, 661 (D.C. Cir. 2017) (explaining the application of surety laws); *Young*, 896 F.3d at 1061–1062.

In 1840, the Supreme Court of Alabama concluded that, while the legislature could impose limitations on "the manner in which arms shall be borne," it could not bar the right to bear arms in public for self-defense. *State v. Reid.* The court upheld a prohibition on the "practice of carrying weapons secretly." In doing so, however, the court recognized that there were limits to the State's ability to restrict the right to carry in public: "A statute which, under the pretence of regulating, amounts to a destruction of the right [to bear arms], or which requires arms to be so borne as to render them wholly useless for the purpose of defence, would be clearly unconstitutional." In the court's view, "it is only when carried openly, that [arms] can be efficiently used for defence." Thus, the court allowed some regulation of the form of carrying arms in public, but it firmly concluded that the right to carry in public for self-defense could not be eliminated altogether.

Other state courts adopted a similar view. In *Nunn v. State* (1846), the Supreme Court of Georgia held that "seek[ing] to suppress the practice of carrying certain weapons *secretly* . . . is valid" but that "a prohibition against bearing arms *openly* is in conflict with the Constitution, and void." And, in *State* v. *Chandler* (1850), the Supreme Court of Louisiana held that the State could ban concealed carry but that the "right to carry arms . . . in full open view" was "guaranteed by the Constitution of the United States."

These cases show that, with few exceptions,[5] courts in the antebellum period understood the right to bear arms as including the right to carry in public for self-defense.

C

Finally, in the wake of the Civil War, "there was an outpouring of discussion of the Second Amendment in Congress and in public discourse, as people debated whether and how to secure constitutional rights for newly free slaves." *Heller.* These discussions confirm that the Second Amendment right to bear arms was understood to protect public carry at the time the Fourteenth Amendment was ratified.[6]

As I have previously explained, "Southern anxiety about an uprising among the newly freed slaves peaked" after the Civil War. *McDonald* (opinion concurring in part and concurring in judgment). Acting on this fear, States of the "old Confederacy" engaged in "systematic efforts" to disarm recently freed slaves and many of the 180,000 blacks who served in the Union Army. "Throughout the

---

5. In *State v. Buzzard*, 4 Ark. 18 (1842), the Supreme Court of Arkansas upheld a law that prohibited concealed carry. *Id.,* at 27 (opinion of Ringo, C. J.); *id.,* at 32 (opinion of Dickinson, J.); but see *id.,* at 34–35 (Lacy, J., dissenting).

6. Although these discussions occurred well after the ratification of the Bill of Rights, *Heller* treated them as "instructive" in determining the meaning of the Second Amendment. The discussions also inform our understanding of the right to keep and bear arms guaranteed by the Fourteenth Amendment as a privilege of American citizenship. See *McDonald v. Chicago* (2010) (THOMAS, J., concurring in part and concurring in judgment).

South, armed parties, often consisting of ex-Confederate soldiers serving in the state militias, forcibly took firearms from newly freed slaves." In addition, some States passed laws that explicitly prohibited blacks from carrying arms without a license (a requirement not imposed on white citizens) or barred blacks from possessing arms altogether. See Cottrol & Diamond, The Second Amendment: Toward an Afro–Americanist Reconsideration (1991) (compiling laws from Alabama, Louisiana, and Mississippi).

The Federal Government acknowledged that these abuses violated blacks' fundamental right to carry arms in public. In 1866, a report of the Commissioner of the Freedmen's Bureau recognized that "[t]he civil law [of Kentucky] prohibits the colored man from bearing arms" and concluded that such a restriction infringed "the right of the people to keep and bear arms as provided in the Constitution." Similarly, a circular in a congressional Report acknowledged that "in some parts of [South Carolina,] armed parties are, without proper authority, engaged in seizing all fire-arms found in the hands of the freedmen . . . in plain and direct violation of their personal rights [to keep and bear arms] as guaranteed by the Constitution of the United States." The circular noted the "peaceful and orderly conduct" of freed slaves when carrying arms, as well as their need "to kill game for subsistence, and to protect their crops from destruction by birds and animals," clearly indicating that the bearing of arms occurs in public. Finally, numerous Congressmen expressed dismay at the denial of blacks' rights to bear arms when discussing the Civil Rights Act of 1866, the Freedmen's Bureau Act of 1866, and the Fourteenth Amendment. See Halbrook, The Jurisprudence of the Second and Fourteenth Amendments (1981).

The importance of the right to carry arms in public during Reconstruction and thereafter cannot be overstated. "The use of firearms for self-defense was often the only way black citizens could protect themselves from mob violence." *McDonald* (opinion of THOMAS, J.). And, unfortunately, "[w]ithout federal enforcement of the inalienable right to keep and bear arms, . . . militias and mobs were tragically successful in waging a campaign of terror" against Southern blacks. On this record, it is clear that "the Framers of the Privileges or Immunities Clause and the ratifying-era public understood — just as the Framers of the Second Amendment did — that the right to keep and bear arms" encompassed the right to carry arms in public for self-defense.

In short, the text of the Second Amendment and the history from England, the founding era, the antebellum period, and Reconstruction leave no doubt that the right to "bear Arms" includes the individual right to carry in public in some manner.

III

Recognizing that the Constitution protects the right to carry arms in public does not mean that there is a "right to . . . carry any weapon whatsoever in any manner whatsoever and for whatever purpose." *Heller.* "The protections enumerated in the Second Amendment . . . are not absolute prohibitions against government regulation." *Voisine* v. *United States* (2016) (THOMAS, J., dissenting). States can impose restrictions on an individual's right to bear arms that are consistent with historical limitations. "Some laws, however, broadly divest an individual of his Second Amendment rights" altogether. This case gives us the ideal opportunity to at least begin analyzing which restrictions are consistent with the historical scope of the right to bear arms.

It appears that a handful of States throughout the country prohibit citizens from carrying arms in public unless they can establish "good cause" or a "justifiable need" for doing so. The majority of States, while regulating the carrying of arms to varying degrees, have not imposed such a restriction, which amounts to a "[b]a[n] on the ability of most citizens to exercise an enumerated right." *Wrenn.* The Courts of Appeals are squarely divided on the constitutionality of these onerous "justifiable need" or "good cause" restrictions. The D. C. Circuit has held that a law limiting public carry to those with a "good reason to fear injury to [their] person or property" violates the Second Amendment. *Wrenn.*[7] By contrast, the First, Second, Third, and Fourth Circuits have upheld the constitutionality of licensing schemes with "justifiable need" or "good reason" requirements, applying what purported to be an intermediate scrutiny standard.

"One of this Court's primary functions is to resolve 'important matter[s]' on which the courts of appeals are 'in conflict.'" *Gee v. Planned Parenthood of Gulf Coast, Inc.* (2018) (THOMAS, J., dissenting from denial of certiorari) (quoting this Court's Rule 10(a)). The question whether a State can effectively ban most citizens from exercising their fundamental right to bear arms surely qualifies as such a matter. We should settle the conflict among the lower courts so that the fundamental protections set forth in our Constitution are applied equally to all citizens.

* * *

This case gives us an opportunity to provide lower courts with much-needed guidance, ensure adherence to our precedents, and resolve a Circuit split. Each of these reasons is independently sufficient to grant certiorari. In combination, they unequivocally demonstrate that this case warrants our review. Rather than prolonging our decade-long failure to protect the Second Amendment, I would grant this petition.

---

7. A panel of the Ninth Circuit, in an exhaustive and scholarly opinion, also held that a law violated the Second Amendment by limiting public carry to those with "urgency," "need," or a "reason to fear injury." *Young.* That decision, however, was vacated when a majority of the active judges on the Ninth Circuit voted to grant en banc review.

Chapter 21

Taking Private Property for Public Use

STUDY GUIDE:

- The Takings Clause provides that "private property [shall not] be taken for public use, without just compensation." At what point does the government violate the Constitution? When it "take[s]" property? Or when it fails to provide "just compensation"? The majority and the dissent vigorously disagree about this question.
- Justice Kagan writes in her dissent: "Now, when a government undertakes land use regulation (and what government doesn't?), the responsible employees will almost inescapably become constitutional malefactors. That is not a fair position in which to place persons carrying out their governmental duties." How does the majority respond to this argument? How does Justice Thomas respond in his concurrence?

Knick v. Township of Scott, Pennsylvania
588 U.S. ___ (2019)

CHIEF JUSTICE ROBERTS delivered the opinion of the Court.

The Takings Clause of the Fifth Amendment states that "private property [shall not] be taken for public use, without just compensation." In *Williamson County Regional Planning Comm'n v. Hamilton Bank of Johnson City* (1985), we held that a property owner whose property has been taken by a local government has not suffered a violation of his Fifth Amendment rights — and thus cannot bring a federal takings claim in federal court — until a state court has denied his claim for just compensation under state law.

The *Williamson County* Court anticipated that if the property owner failed to secure just compensation under state law in state court, he would be able to bring a "ripe" federal takings claim in federal court. But as we later held in *San Remo Hotel, L. P. v. City and County of San Francisco* (2005), a state court's resolution of a claim for just compensation under state law generally has preclusive effect in any subsequent federal suit. The takings plaintiff thus finds himself in a Catch-22: He cannot go to federal court without going to state court first; but if he goes to state court and loses, his claim will be barred in federal court. The federal claim dies aborning.

The *San Remo* preclusion trap should tip us off that the state-litigation requirement rests on a mistaken view of the Fifth Amendment. The Civil Rights Act of 1871, after all, guarantees "a federal forum for claims of unconstitutional treatment at the hands of state officials," and the settled rule is that "exhaustion of state remedies is *not* a prerequisite to an action under [42 U.S.C.] § 1983." *Heck v. Humphrey* (1994). But the guarantee of a federal forum rings hollow for takings plaintiffs, who are forced to litigate their claims in state court.

We now conclude that the state-litigation requirement imposes an unjustifiable burden on takings plaintiffs, conflicts with the rest of our takings jurisprudence, and must be overruled. A property owner has an actionable Fifth Amendment takings claim when the government takes his property without paying for it. That does not mean that the government must provide compensation in advance of a taking or risk having its action invalidated: So long as the property owner has some way to obtain compensation after the fact, governments need not fear that courts will enjoin their activities. But it does mean that the property owner has suffered a violation of his Fifth Amendment rights when the government takes his property without just compensation, and therefore may bring his claim in federal court under § 1983 at that time.

I

Petitioner Rose Mary Knick owns 90 acres of land in Scott Township, Pennsylvania, a small community just north of Scranton. Knick lives in a single-family home on the property and uses the rest of the land as a grazing area for horses and other farm animals. The property includes a small graveyard where the ancestors of Knick's neighbors are allegedly buried. Such family cemeteries are fairly common in Pennsylvania, where "backyard burials" have long been permitted.

In December 2012, the Township passed an ordinance requiring that "[a]ll cemeteries . . . be kept open and accessible to the general public during daylight hours." . . . In 2013, a Township officer found several grave markers on Knick's property and notified her that she was violating the ordinance by failing to open the cemetery to the public during the day. Knick responded by seeking declaratory and injunctive relief in state court on the ground that the ordinance effected a taking of her property. Knick did not seek compensation for the taking by bringing an "inverse condemnation" action under state law. Inverse condemnation is "a cause of action against a governmental defendant to recover the value of property which has been taken in fact by the governmental defendant." *United States v. Clarke* (1980). Inverse condemnation stands in contrast to direct condemnation, in which the government initiates proceedings to acquire title under its eminent domain authority. Pennsylvania, like every other State besides Ohio, provides a state inverse condemnation action.

In response to Knick's suit, the Township withdrew the violation notice and agreed to stay enforcement of the ordinance during the state court proceedings. The court, however, declined to rule on Knick's request for declaratory and injunctive relief because, without an ongoing enforcement action, she could not demonstrate the irreparable harm necessary for equitable relief.

Knick then filed an action in Federal District Court under 42 U.S.C. §1983, alleging that the ordinance violated the Takings Clause of the Fifth Amendment.[2] The District Court dismissed Knick's takings claim under *Williamson County* because she had not pursued an inverse condemnation action in state court. On appeal, the Third Circuit noted that the ordinance was "extraordinary and constitutionally suspect," but affirmed the District Court in light of *Williamson County*.

We granted certiorari to reconsider the holding of *Williamson County* that property owners must seek just compensation under state law in state court before bringing a federal takings claim under §1983.

In *Williamson County*, a property developer brought a takings claim under §1983 against a zoning board that had rejected the developer's proposal for a new subdivision. *Williamson County* held that the developer's Fifth Amendment claim was not "ripe" for two reasons. First, the developer still had an opportunity to seek a variance from the appeals board, so any taking was therefore not yet final. Knick does not question the validity of this finality requirement, which is not at issue here.

The second holding of *Williamson County* is that the developer had no federal takings claim because he had not sought compensation "through the procedures the State ha[d] provided for doing so." That is the holding Knick asks us to overrule. According to the Court, "if a State provides an adequate procedure for seeking just compensation, the property owner cannot claim a violation of the [Takings] Clause until it has used the procedure and been denied just compensation." The Court concluded that the developer's federal takings claim was "premature" because he had not sought compensation through the State's inverse condemnation procedure.

The unanticipated consequences of this ruling were not clear until 20 years later, when this Court decided *San Remo*. In that case, the takings plaintiffs complied with *Williamson County* and brought a claim for compensation in state court. The complaint made clear that the plaintiffs sought relief only under the takings clause of the State Constitution, intending to reserve their Fifth Amendment claim for a later federal suit if the state suit proved unsuccessful. When that happened, however, and the plaintiffs proceeded to federal court, they found that their federal claim was barred. This Court held that the full faith and credit statute, 28 U.S.C. §1738, required the federal court to give preclusive effect to the state court's decision, blocking any subsequent consideration of whether the plaintiff had suffered a taking within the meaning of the Fifth Amendment. The adverse state court decision that, according to *Williamson County*, gave rise

---

2. Section 1983 provides: "Every person who, under color of any statute, ordinance, regulation, custom, or usage, of any State or Territory or the District of Columbia, subjects, or causes to be subjected, any citizen of the United States or other person within the jurisdiction thereof to the deprivation of any rights, privileges, or immunities secured by the Constitution and laws, shall be liable to the party injured in an action at law . . . ."

to a ripe federal takings claim, simultaneously barred that claim, preventing the federal court from ever considering it.

The state-litigation requirement relegates the Takings Clause "to the status of a poor relation" among the provisions of the Bill of Rights. *Dolan v. City of Tigard* (1994). Plaintiffs asserting any other constitutional claim are guaranteed a federal forum under §1983, but the state-litigation requirement "hand[s] authority over federal takings claims to state courts." *San Remo* (Rehnquist, C.J., concurring in judgment). Fidelity to the Takings Clause and our cases construing it requires overruling *Williamson County* and restoring takings claims to the full-fledged constitutional status the Framers envisioned when they included the Clause among the other protections in the Bill of Rights.

III

A

Contrary to *Williamson County*, a property owner has a claim for a violation of the Takings Clause as soon as a government takes his property for public use without paying for it. The Clause provides: "[N]or shall private property be taken for public use, without just compensation." It does not say: "Nor shall private property be taken for public use, without an available procedure that will result in compensation." If a local government takes private property without paying for it, that government has violated the Fifth Amendment—just as the Takings Clause says—without regard to subsequent state court proceedings. And the property owner may sue the government at that time in federal court for the "deprivation" of a right "secured by the Constitution."

We have long recognized that property owners may bring Fifth Amendment claims against the Federal Government as soon as their property has been taken. The Tucker Act, which provides the standard procedure for bringing such claims, gives the Court of Federal Claims jurisdiction to "render judgment upon any claim against the United States founded either upon the Constitution" or any federal law or contract for damages "in cases not sounding in tort." We have held that "[i]f there is a taking, the claim is 'founded upon the Constitution' and within the jurisdiction of the Court of Claims to hear and determine." *United States v. Causby* (1946). And we have explained that "the act of taking" is the "event which gives rise to the claim for compensation." *United States v. Dow* (1958).

The Fifth Amendment right to full compensation arises at the time of the taking, regardless of post-taking remedies that may be available to the property owner. That principle was confirmed in *Jacobs v. United States* (1933), where we held that a property owner found to have a valid takings claim is entitled to compensation as if it had been "paid contemporaneously with the taking"—that is, the compensation must generally consist of the total value of the property when taken, plus interest from that time. We rejected the view of the lower court that a property owner is entitled to interest only when the government provides a particular remedy—direct condemnation proceedings—and not when the owner brings a takings suit under the Tucker Act. "The form of the remedy d[oes] not qualify the right. It rest[s] upon the Fifth Amendment."

Jacobs made clear that, no matter what sort of procedures the government puts in place to remedy a taking, a property owner has a Fifth Amendment entitlement to compensation as soon as the government takes his property without paying for it. Whether the government does nothing, forcing the owner to bring a takings suit under the Tucker Act, or whether it provides the owner with a statutory compensation remedy by initiating direct condemnation proceedings, the owner's claim for compensation "rest[s] upon the Fifth Amendment."

Although *Jacobs* concerned a taking by the Federal Government, the same reasoning applies to takings by the States. The availability of any particular compensation remedy, such as an inverse condemnation claim under state law, cannot infringe or restrict the property owner's federal constitutional claim—just as the existence of a state action for battery does not bar a Fourth Amendment claim of excessive force. The fact that the State has provided a property owner with a procedure that may subsequently result in just compensation cannot deprive the owner of his Fifth Amendment right to compensation under the Constitution, leaving only the state law right. And that is key because it is the existence of the Fifth Amendment right that allows the owner to proceed directly to federal court under §1983. . . .

A later payment of compensation may remedy the constitutional violation that occurred at the time of the taking, but that does not mean the violation never took place. The violation is the only reason compensation was owed in the first place. A bank robber might give the loot back, but he still robbed the bank. The availability of a subsequent compensation remedy for a taking without compensation no more means there never was a constitutional violation in the first place than the availability of a damages action renders negligent conduct compliant with the duty of care.

In sum, because a taking without compensation violates the self-executing Fifth Amendment at the time of the taking, the property owner can bring a federal suit at that time. Just as someone whose property has been taken by the Federal Government has a claim "founded . . . upon the Constitution" that he may bring under the Tucker Act, someone whose property has been taken by a local government has a claim under §1983 for a "deprivation of [a] right[ ] . . . secured by the Constitution" that he may bring upon the taking in federal court. The "general rule" is that plaintiffs may bring constitutional claims under §1983 "without first bringing any sort of state lawsuit, even when state court actions addressing the underlying behavior are available." This is as true for takings claims as for any other claim grounded in the Bill of Rights.

B

. . . The dissent, doing what respondents do not even dare to attempt, defends the original rationale of *Williamson County*—that there is no Fifth Amendment violation, and thus no Fifth Amendment claim, until the government denies the property owner compensation in a subsequent proceeding. But although the dissent makes a more thoughtful and considered argument than *Williamson County*, it cannot reconcile its view with our repeated holdings that a property owner acquires a constitutional right to compensation at the time of the taking. The only reason that a taking would automatically entitle a property owner to the remedy of compensation is that, as Justice Brennan explained, with the uncompensated taking "the landowner has *already* suffered a constitutional violation." *San Diego Gas & Elec. Co.* (dissenting opinion). The dissent here provides no more reason to resist that conclusion than did *Williamson County*. . . .

* * *

We conclude that a government violates the Takings Clause when it takes property without compensation, and that a property owner may bring a Fifth Amendment claim under §1983 at that time. That does not as a practical matter mean that government action or regulation may not proceed in the absence of contemporaneous compensation. Given the availability of post-taking compensation, barring the government from acting will ordinarily not be appropriate. But because the violation is complete at the time of the taking, pursuit of a remedy in federal court need not await any subsequent state action. Takings claims against local governments should be handled the same as other claims under the Bill of Rights. *Williamson County* erred in holding otherwise.

IV

The next question is whether we should overrule *Williamson County*, or whether *stare decisis* counsels in favor of adhering to the decision, despite its error. The doctrine of *stare decisis* reflects a judgment "that 'in most matters it is more important that the applicable rule of law be settled than that it be settled right.'" *Agostini v. Felton* (1997). The doctrine "is at its weakest when we interpret the Constitution," as we did in *Williamson County*, because only this Court or a constitutional amendment can alter our holdings.

We have identified several factors to consider in deciding whether to overrule a past decision, including "the quality of [its] reasoning, the workability of the rule it established, its consistency with other related decisions, . . . and reliance on the decision." *Janus v. State, County, and Municipal Employees* (2018). All of these factors counsel in favor of overruling *Williamson County*.

Williamson County was not just wrong. Its reasoning was exceptionally ill founded and conflicted with much of our takings jurisprudence. . . . The decision has come in for repeated criticism over the years from Justices of this Court and many respected commentators. Even the academic defenders of the state-litigation requirement base it on federalism concerns (although they do not reconcile those concerns with the settled construction of §1983) rather than the reasoning of the opinion itself. . . .

The state-litigation requirement has also proved to be unworkable in practice. . . . [M]any takings plaintiffs never have the opportunity to litigate in a federal forum that §1983 by its terms seems to provide. . . . Finally, there are no reliance interests on the state-litigation requirement. We have recognized that the force of *stare decisis* is "reduced" when rules that do not "serve as a guide to lawful behavior" are at issue. Our holding that uncompensated takings violate the Fifth Amendment will not expose governments to new liability; it will simply allow into federal court takings claims that otherwise would have been brought as inverse condemnation suits in state court.

Governments need not fear that our holding will lead federal courts to invalidate their regulations as unconstitutional. As long as just compensation remedies are available—as they have been for nearly 150 years—injunctive relief will be foreclosed. . . .

In light of all the foregoing, the dissent cannot, with respect, fairly maintain its extreme assertions regarding our application of the principle of *stare decisis*.

* * *

The state-litigation requirement of *Williamson County* is overruled. A property owner may bring a takings claim under §1983 upon the taking of his property without just compensation by a local government. The judgment of the United States Court of Appeals for the Third Circuit is vacated, and the case is remanded for further proceedings consistent with this opinion.

It is so ordered.

JUSTICE THOMAS, concurring.

The Fifth Amendment's Takings Clause prohibits the government from "tak[ing]" private property "without just compensation." The Court correctly interprets this text by holding that a violation of this Clause occurs as soon as the government takes property without paying for it.

The United States, by contrast, urges us not to enforce the Takings Clause as written. It worries that requiring payment to accompany a taking would allow courts to enjoin or invalidate broad regulatory programs "merely" because the program takes property without paying for it. . . . Government officials, the United States contends, should be able to implement regulatory programs "without fear" of injunction or invalidation under the Takings Clause, "even when" the program is so far reaching that the officials "cannot determine whether a taking will occur."

This "sue me" approach to the Takings Clause is untenable. The Fifth Amendment does not merely provide a damages remedy to a property owner willing to "shoulder the burden of securing compensation" after the government takes property without paying for it. Instead, it makes just compensation a "prerequisite" to the government's authority to "tak[e] property for public use." A "purported exercise of the eminent-domain power" is therefore "invalid" unless the government "pays just compensation before or at the time of its taking." If this requirement makes some regulatory programs "unworkable in practice," so be it—our role is to enforce the Takings Clause as written. . . .

JUSTICE KAGAN, with whom JUSTICE GINSBURG, JUSTICE BREYER, and JUSTICE SOTOMAYOR join, dissenting.

Today, the Court formally overrules *Williamson County Regional Planning Comm'n v. Hamilton Bank of Johnson City* (1985). But its decision rejects far more than that single case. *Williamson County* was rooted in an understanding of the Fifth Amendment's Takings Clause stretching back to the late 1800s. On that view, a government could take property so long as it provided a reliable mechanism to pay just compensation, even if the payment came after the fact. No longer. The majority today holds, in conflict with precedent after precedent, that a government violates the Constitution whenever it takes property without advance compensation—no matter how good its commitment to pay. That conclusion has no basis in the Takings Clause. Its consequence is to channel a mass of quintessentially local cases involving complex state-law issues into federal courts. And it transgresses all usual principles of *stare decisis.* I respectfully dissent.

I

Begin with the basics—the meaning of the Takings Clause. The right that Clause confers is not to be free from government takings of property for public purposes. Instead, the right is to be free from those takings when the government fails to provide "just compensation." In other words, the government *can* take private property for public purposes, so long as it fairly pays the property owner. That precept, which the majority does not contest, comes straight out of the constitutional text: "[P]rivate property [shall not] be taken for public use, without just compensation." Amdt. 5. "As its language indicates, [the Takings Clause] does not prohibit the taking of private property, but instead places a condition on the exercise of that power." *First English Evangelical Lutheran Church of Glendale v. County of Los Angeles* (1987). And that constitutional choice accords with ancient principles about what governments do. The eminent domain power—the capacity to "take private property for public uses"—is an integral "attribute of sovereignty." Small surprise, then, that the Constitution does not prohibit takings for public purposes, but only requires the government to pay fair value.

In that way, the Takings Clause is unique among the Bill of Rights' guarantees. It is, for example, unlike the Fourth Amendment's protection against excessive force—which the majority mistakenly proposes as an analogy. Suppose a law enforcement officer uses excessive force and the victim recovers damages for his injuries. Did a constitutional violation occur? Of course. The Constitution prohibits what the officer did; the payment of damages merely remedied the constitutional wrong. But the Takings Clause is different because it does not prohibit takings; to the contrary, it permits them provided the government gives just compensation. So when the government "takes and pays," it is not violating the Constitution at all. Put another way, a Takings Clause violation has two necessary elements. First, the government must take the property. Second, it must deny the property owner just compensation. If the government has not done both, no constitutional violation has happened. All this is well-trod ground. Even the majority (despite its faulty analogy) does not contest it.

Similarly well-settled—until the majority's opinion today—was the answer to a follow-on question: At what point has the government denied a property owner just compensation, so as to complete a Fifth Amendment violation? For over a hundred years, this Court held that advance or contemporaneous payment was not required, so long as the government had established reliable procedures for an owner to later obtain just compensation (including interest for any time elapsed). . . .

Today's decision thus overthrows the Court's long-settled view of the Takings Clause. The majority declares, as against a mountain of precedent, that a government taking private property for public purposes must pay compensation at that moment or in advance. If the government fails to do so, a constitutional violation has occurred, regardless of whether "reasonable, certain and adequate" compensatory mechanisms exist. And regardless of how many times this Court has said the opposite before. Under cover of overruling "only" a single decision, today's opinion smashes a hundred-plus years of legal rulings to smithereens.

II

. . . [T]he majority contends that its rule follows from the constitutional text, because the Takings Clause does not say "[n]or shall private property be taken for public use, without an available procedure that will result in compensation." There is a reason the majority devotes only a few sentences to that argument. Because here's another thing the text does not say: "Nor shall private property be taken for public use, without advance or contemporaneous payment of just compensation, notwithstanding ordinary procedures." In other words, the text no more states the majority's rule than it does *Williamson County's* (and its precursors'). As constitutional text often is, the Takings Clause is spare. It says that a government taking property must pay just compensation—but does not say through exactly what mechanism or at exactly what time. That was left to be worked out, consistent with the Clause's (minimal) text and purpose. And from 1890 until today, this Court worked it out *Williamson County's* way, rather than the majority's. Under our caselaw, a government could use reliable post-taking compensatory mechanisms (with payment calculated from the taking) without violating the Takings Clause. . . .

To the extent it deals with these cases (mostly, it just ignores them), the majority says only that they (like *Williamson County*) were "confused" or wrong. But maybe the majority should take the hint: When a theory requires declaring precedent after precedent after precedent wrong, that's a sign the theory itself may be wrong. The majority's theory is just that.

And not only wrong on prior law. The majority's overruling of *Williamson County* will have two damaging consequences. It will inevitably turn even well-meaning government officials into lawbreakers. And it will subvert important principles of judicial federalism.

To begin with, today's decision means that government regulators will often have no way to avoid violating the Constitution. There are a "nearly infinite variety of ways" for regulations to "affect property interests." *Arkansas Game and Fish Comm'n v. United States* (2012). And under modern takings law, there is "no magic formula" to determine "whether a given government interference with property is a taking." For that reason, a government actor usually cannot know in advance whether implementing a regulatory program will effect a taking, much less of whose property. Until today, such an official could do his work without fear of wrongdoing, in any jurisdiction that had set up a reliable means for property owners to obtain compensation. Even if some regulatory action turned out to take someone's property, the official would not have violated the Constitution. But no longer. Now, when a government undertakes land-use regulation (and what government doesn't?), the responsible employees will almost inescapably become constitutional malefactors. That is not a fair position in which to place persons carrying out their governmental duties. . . .

This case highlights the difficulty. The ultimate constitutional question here is: Did Scott Township's cemetery ordinance "go[] too far" (in Justice Holmes's phrase), so as to effect a taking of Rose Mary Knick's property? *Pennsylvania Coal Co. v. Mahon* (1922). But to answer that question, it is first necessary to address an issue about background state law. In the Township's view, the ordinance did little more than codify Pennsylvania common law, which (the Township says) has long required property owners to make land containing human remains open to the public. If the Township is right on that state-law question, Knick's constitutional claim will fail: The ordinance, on that account, didn't go far at all. But Knick contends that no common law rule of that kind exists in Pennsylvania. And if she is right, her takings claim may yet have legs. But is she? Or is the Township? I confess: I don't know. Nor, I would venture, do my colleagues on the federal bench. But under today's decision, it will be the Federal District Court for the Middle District of Pennsylvania that will have to resolve this question of local cemetery law.

And if the majority thinks this case is an outlier, it's dead wrong; indeed, this case will be easier than many. Take *Lucas v. South Carolina Coastal Council* (1992). There, this Court held that a South Carolina ban on development of beachfront property worked a taking of the plaintiff's land—unless the State's nuisance law already prohibited such development. The Court then—quite sensibly—remanded the case to the South Carolina Supreme Court to resolve that question. . . .

Today's decision sends a flood of complex state-law issues to federal courts. It makes federal courts a principal player in local and state land-use disputes. It betrays judicial federalism.

IV

Everything said above aside, *Williamson County* should stay on the books because of *stare decisis*. Adherence to precedent is "a foundation stone of the rule of law." *Michigan v. Bay Mills Indian Community* (2014). "[I]t promotes the evenhanded, predictable, and consistent development of legal principles, fosters reliance on judicial decisions, and contributes to the actual and perceived integrity of the judicial process." *Payne v. Tennessee* (1991). *Stare decisis*, of course, is "not an inexorable command." But it is not enough that five Justices believe a precedent wrong. Reversing course demands a "special justification—over and above the belief that the precedent was wrongly decided." *Kimble v. Marvel Entertainment, LLC* (2015). The majority offers no reason that qualifies.

In its only real stab at a special justification, the majority focuses on what it calls the "*San Remo* preclusion trap." As the majority notes, this Court held in a post-*Williamson County* decision interpreting the full faith and credit statute, that a state court's resolution of an inverse condemnation proceeding has preclusive effect in a later federal suit. The interaction between *San Remo* and *Williamson County* means that "many takings plaintiffs never have the opportunity to litigate in a federal forum."

But . . . [w]hen "correction can be had by legislation," Justice Brandeis once stated, the Court should let stand even "error[s on] matter[s] of serious concern." Or otherwise said, *stare decisis* then "carries enhanced force." Here, Congress can reverse the *San Remo* preclusion rule any time it wants, and thus give property owners an opportunity—*after* a state-court proceeding—to litigate in federal court. The *San Remo* decision, as noted above, interpreted the federal full faith and credit statute; Congress need only add a provision to that law to flip the Court's result. . . .

And the majority has no other special justification. It says *Williamson County* did not create "reliance interests." But even if so, those interests are a *plus-factor* in the doctrine; when they exist, *stare decisis* becomes "superpowered." . . . Here, the majority's only citation is to last Term's decision overruling a 40-year-old precedent. *Janus v. State, County, and Municipal Employees* (2018). If that is the way the majority means to proceed—relying on one subversion of *stare decisis* to support another—we may as well not have principles about precedents at all.

What is left is simply the majority's view that *Williamson County* was wrong. The majority repurposes all its merits arguments—all its claims that *Williamson County* was "ill founded"—to justify its overruling. But the entire idea of *stare decisis* is that judges do not get to reverse a decision just because they never liked it in the first instance. Once again, they need a reason *other than* the idea "that the precedent was wrongly decided." *Halliburton Co. v. Erica P. John Fund, Inc.* (2014); for it is hard to overstate the value, in a country like ours, of stability in the law.

Just last month, when the Court overturned another longstanding precedent, Justice Breyer penned a dissent. See *Franchise Tax Bd. of Cal. v. Hyatt* (2019). He wrote of the dangers of reversing legal course "only because five Members of a later Court" decide that an earlier ruling was incorrect. He concluded: "Today's decision can only cause one to wonder which cases the Court will overrule next." Well, that didn't take long. Now one may wonder yet again.